Writing for the Academic Disciplines

A Rhetoric, Reader, and Handbook

Sally Hayward

OXFORD
UNIVERSITY PRESS

OXFORD
UNIVERSITY PRESS

Oxford University Press is a department of the University of Oxford.
It furthers the University's objective of excellence in research, scholarship,
and education by publishing worldwide. Oxford is a registered trade mark of
Oxford University Press in the UK and in certain other countries.

Published in Canada by
Oxford University Press
8 Sampson Mews, Suite 204,
Don Mills, Ontario M3C 0H5 Canada

www.oupcanada.com

Library and Archives Canada Cataloguing in Publication

Hayward, Sally Kerry, 1957–, author
Writing for the academic disciplines : a rhetoric,
reader, and handbook / Sally Hayward.

Includes bibliographical references and index.

ISBN 978–0–19–900237–5 (pbk.)

1. English language—Rhetoric—Textbooks. 2. Academic
writing—Textbooks. 3. Academic writing—Problems, exercises,
etc. 4. College readers. I. Title.

PE1408.H3779 2014   808'.042   C2014-905894-2

Cover image: artant/iStockphoto

Oxford University Press is committed to our environment.
Wherever possible, our books are printed on paper
which comes from responsible sources.

MIX
Paper from
responsible sources
FSC® C103567

Printed and bound in Canada

1 2 3 4 — 18 17 16 15

CONTENTS

8   Academic Persuasion   167

PART III ◆ THE READER

FROM THE PUBLISHER

Oxford University Press is delighted to introduce *Writing for the Academic Disciplines*, a new rhetoric, reader, and handbook that uses an interdisciplinary approach to immerse students in academic reading and writing.

This three-in-one text demystifies academic writing by focusing on genre—the conventions and forms particular to specific types of writing—so that students understand what is expected of them when reading and writing for academic purposes. Chapters on essay writing, structure and rhetorical techniques, research and documentation, and grammar and style provide a basis for analyzing professional readings and samples of student writing. Students will learn to write academic essays, summaries, reports, and literature reviews, increasing their confidence in their ability to write well.

Key Features

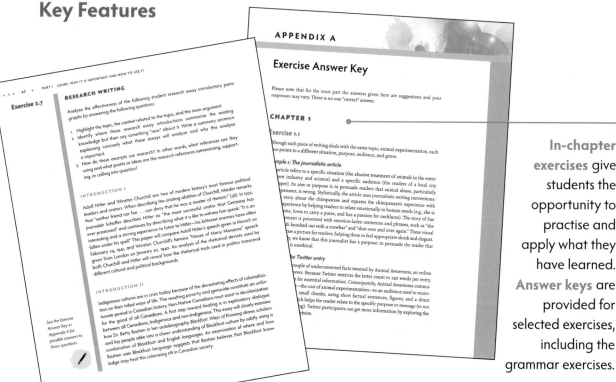

In-chapter exercises give students the opportunity to practise and apply what they have learned. **Answer keys** are provided for selected exercises, including the grammar exercises.

Professional readings from the humanities, sciences, and social sciences demonstrate discipline-specific writing conventions and provide students with models of effective writing. Each reading is introduced with a biographical note on the author and is followed by critical thinking and discussion questions.

IDENTITY AND DIFFERENCE ◆ 399

Coming Home. DVD. Directed by Hal Ashby. Hollywood: MGM/UA, 1978.
Davis, Lennard J. Enforcing Normalcy: Disability, Deafness, and the Body. New York: Verso, 1995.
Garland-Thomson, Rosemarie. Extraordinary Bodies: Figuring Physical Disability in American Culture and Literature. New York: Columbia Univ. Press, 1997.
Gerbart, Ann. "Paralyzed Into Action: The Men Of 'Murderball.'" Washington Post. July 24, 2005.
Hacking, Ian. The Taming of Chance. Cambridge: Cambridge Univ. Press, 1990.
Halberstam, Judith. Female Masculinity. Durham: Duke Univ. Press, 1998.
Linton, Simi. My Body Politic: A Memoir. Ann Arbor, MI: Univ. of Michigan Press, 2005.
Press, 2006.
McRuer, Robert. Crip Theory: Cultural Signs of Queerness and Disability. New York: New York Univ. Press, 2005.
Murderball. DVD. Directed by Dana Adam Shapiro and Henry-Alex Rubin. New York: Think Film Co., 2005.
Sea Inside. DVD. Directed by Alejandro Amenábar. Hollywood: Fine Line Features, 2004.
Cheryl Marie. "A Woman with Juice." http://www.brava.org/Pages/Archives/Juice.html. Accessed 27 July 2006.
Michael. The Trouble with Normal: Sex, Politics, and the Ethics of Queer Life. Cambridge: Harvard Univ. Press, 2000.

Garland-Thomson, Rosemarie. "Shape Structures Story: Fresh and Feisty Stories about Disability" 35.1 (Jan 2007) pp. 113–23. Print.

QUESTIONS FOR DISCUSSION

...a dictionary to look up any terms from the reading that you don't understand... or use the surrounding context to understand them. Is the meaning clear now?

...Garland-Thomson's argument toward "making the world a more inclusive and equitable place for people with disabilities?" Provide reasons for your opinion.

...storytelling challenge and possibly revise how we see those who are different...provide evidence.

...section does the detailed description of the SDS dance play in this piece? How is this primary text different from the other primary texts Garland-...analyzes?

...TO WRITING

...way Garland-Thomson has logically organized the main points...in her essay. Does this outline help you to better understand...

...Garland-Thomson use endnotes? What information does she convey...to these endnotes inform her argument? Write a paragraph out...of endnotes; discuss with your classmates.

◆ ◆ ◆ ◆ Identity and Difference ◆ ◆ ◆ ◆ ◆ ◆ ◆ ◆ ◆

Shape Structures Story: Fresh and Feisty Stories about Disability[1]
BY ROSEMARIE GARLAND-THOMSON

INTRODUCTION

Rosemarie Garland-Thomson is a professor of women's studies at Emory University in Atlanta, Georgia. She specializes in feminist theory, American literature, and disability studies. In "Shape Structures Story," Garland-Thomson engages with and departs from the work of Caroline Walker Bynum to argue that stories about people with disabilities revise and challenge normative stories or narratives. She goes on to provide and analyze four diverse examples of how this revision happens.
The theory in this essay can be used, similar to the way Garland-Thomson uses it herself, to frame an argument about other stories or situations. For example, you might use it to make an argument about Raymond Carver's "Cathedral" or Susan Musgrave's "Arctic Poppies," pointing out that the blind man or the hunchback revise how we see and think about "normal" people and situations.

1   In her deeply wise meditation on the question of continuity in human identity, the medieval historian Caroline Walker Bynum offers us the elegant concept that "shape carries story."[2] Her inquiry arose from her own personal experience of observing her father's shift in identity over 10 years of living with progressive dementia. Bynum acknowledges three aspects of identity: individual personality, ascribed or achieved group affiliation, and spatio-temporal integrity, which is the sense of identity upon which she focuses. Her fundamental question is, "How can I be the same person I was a moment ago?" In other words, she asks how we can maintain a continuous sense of self as our bodies change over time. Being an historian, Bynum frames this issue as a historical one; being a literary critic, I am going to frame this question as a narrative one. That different framing leads me to adapt Bynum's phrase and refer to shape "structuring" rather than "carrying" story. Narrative is a way of constructing continuity over time; it is a coherent knitting of one moment to the next. Bynum's wisdom is to understand the narrative link between time and space, more precisely perhaps, between time and human materiality.
A clunkier explication of this formulation is that the configuration and function of our human body determines our narrative identity, the sense of who we are to ourselves and others. In Bynum's words, "Story spreads out through time the behaviors or bodies—the

◆ ◆ ◆ ◆ 36   PART I   GENRE: WHY IT IS IMPORTANT AND HOW TO USE IT

The Unethical Use and Legalization of Aspartame: Poisoning the People
BY DELANEY BLEWETT

[Very good opening sentence: Delaney introduces aspartame.]

1   In 1965, James Schlatter, a Searle ch... dentally when he was investigating a poten... Searle began the necessary testing of asp... calorie sweetener for dry goods by the FD... approval of aspartame in 1973, but was den... by the FDA). Researcher Ann Reynolds, w...

[Good context: background history on aspartame.]

...safety of aspartame, and neuroscientist Dr. ... acid (a component of aspartame) causes h... recommended that more testing should be ... approval for use in foods and beverages. T... the FDA Division of Metabolic and Endoc... ded that "until safety is proven, aspartam...

[Good introduction to health hazards of aspartame.]

[Thesis statement. In true expository form, Delaney highlights the main arguments around the issue.]

(Gold n.pag). Although aspartame has no... has not been scrutinized by the researchers' con...

2   Regardless of the researchers' con... was approved for use in 1974, with the ... dry goods only (Gold n.pag). In 1975, the...

[Summary of conflict over the legalization of aspartame.]

approval raised by Dr. Olney, the FDA ... entists to review Searle's "mis... Brodsky, said he "had never seen anything... results had been "manipulated" (Gold n...

[Background information on FDA investigation]

3   At the discovery of Searle's "mis... material facts and making false statement... n.pag) and its manipulation of results, ... investigation of a manufacturer" (Mur... US Attorney-General's office to start Gr... "knowingly misrepresenting findings a... ing false statements in aspartame safe... ation of aspartame, the Bressler Repo... directed by Jerome Bressler and asses...

[Good use of a long quote: note how it is indented and does not have quotation marks around it. A sentence or two after the quote would help contextualize it in the larger argument.]

98 of the 196 animals died duri... autopsied until later dates, in s... Many other errors and inconsis... was reported alive, then dead, ... uterine polyp, and ovarian neo... reported or diagnosed in Searl...

10   RESEARCH WRITING   ◆ 275   ◆ ◆ ◆ ◆

Read Sheridan's paper, then read the student paper below. Pay attention to how it engages with Sheridan's paper, presenting an original argument and successfully using secondary sources.

(Mis)Understanding Literate Culture: An Analysis of Joe Sheridan's "The Silence before Drowning in Alphabet Soup"
BY TYRELL DASILVA

[Good title: goes from general to specific.]

1   In Joe Sheridan's work "The Silence before Drowning in Alphabet Soup," a metaphor of silence is used to describe the way in which oral and literate cultures understand nature, and thus reality (Sheridan 24). For Sheridan, both literate and oral culture understands nature and reality through a default to their respective literate or oral definition and interpretation of silence or sound. Sheridan believes that alphabetization (literate definition) cannot truly interpret nature because it is unable to represent silence or the unsayable (24). In stating this, Sheridan negates the literate definition of reality and describes the affects of literacy on orality as negative (31) without fully considering the role that orality and silence play in today's culture. It is not the case that silence is the key to understanding nature or saving oral tradition, but that sound-based literate invention (secondary orality) is an innovation with the same final cause, a cause aimed at developing characteristic understandings of nature and sensual experience, which is esteemed within oral culture (25).

[Good opening sentence: focused summary of Sheridan's essay.]

[Concise summary of the essay.]

2   The concepts of oral practice (speech), and oral values (sensation), are still regarded highly in contemporary literate culture[1] and are practiced in a number of mediums. Within these mediums, all of which have roots in radio broadcasting, silence/sound can be reconciled with contemporary literate values, and still impose the contemplative, qualitative moods that Sheridan believes literate culture is lacking (30).

[Tyrell takes issue with Sheridan's argument and presents his own thesis.]

[Tyrell's thesis: radio broadcasting can create silence and contemplation.]

3   Walter J. Ong recognized that oral practice and values have not been abandoned by literal culture but have been incorporated into it and still exist today. Sound, or an absence of it for that matter, is still representable through electronic media and has given way to a new form of orality, "which Ong has styled the world of 'Secondary Orality'" (Ong qtd in: Weeks and Hoogestratt 14). Secondary orality is the development and incorporation of oral values like sound sensation within literate culture. This incorporation was arguably made most easily with the invention of the broadcast radio and advanced later with personal music players and other devices. These devices allowed oral

[Good evidence and support for his argument (Walter Ong).]

[Definition of Ong's concept of secondary orality, a key term for Tyrell's proper.]

1   Contemporary literate culture refers to technology based, or electronic media culture (i.e. television, radio, internet.)

Annotated student essays help students to explore the distinctions among the different writing genres while drawing inspiration for their own writing. Many of the student essays have been written in response to the professional readings featured in this volume.

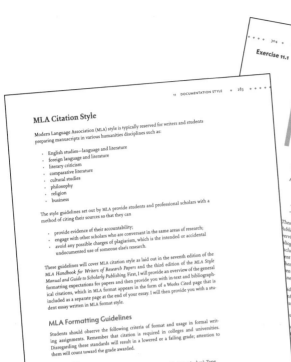

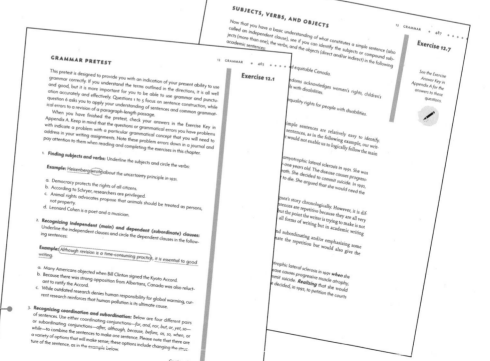

Thorough coverage of documentation styles provides students with a valuable resource on MLA and APA citation and manuscript-preparation methods.

A **grammar pretest** and **post-test** offer students a chance to assess their grammar knowledge before and after working through the grammar chapter. Grammar examples include sample sentences and paragraphs from academic writing.

Supportive pedagogy in each chapter includes learning objectives, "Academic Focus" boxes, boldfaced key terms defined in the glossary, chapter summaries, and questions to consider.

Online Resources

For Instructors

An **instructor's manual** offers chapter overviews, suggested in-class assignments and group activities, discussion questions, suggested lecture topics, and annotated further resources.

A **test bank** provides questions in multiple-choice, true-or-false, short-answer, and essay format to assess students' understanding of the chapters.

For Students

Online student resources include **grammar quizzes** and a **full-length chapter on business and technical writing** that provides instruction on the writing conventions in the business and technology fields.

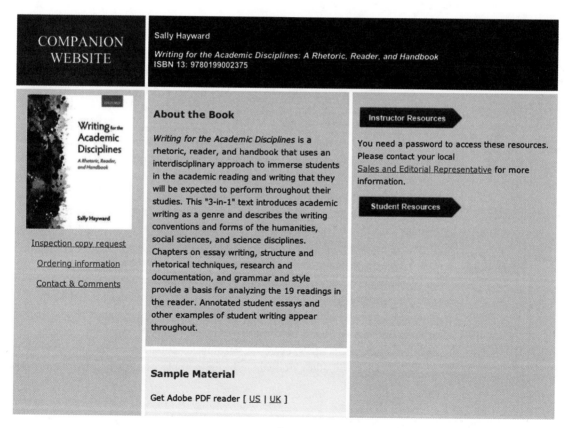

COMPANION WEBSITE

Sally Hayward
Writing for the Academic Disciplines: A Rhetoric, Reader, and Handbook
ISBN 13: 9780199002375

Inspection copy request

Ordering information

Contact & Comments

About the Book

Writing for the Academic Disciplines is a rhetoric, reader, and handbook that uses an interdisciplinary approach to immerse students in the academic reading and writing that they will be expected to perform throughout their studies. This "3-in-1" text introduces academic writing as a genre and describes the writing conventions and forms of the humanities, social sciences, and science disciplines. Chapters on essay writing, structure and rhetorical techniques, research and documentation, and grammar and style provide a basis for analyzing the 19 readings in the reader. Annotated student essays and other examples of student writing appear throughout.

Sample Material

Get Adobe PDF reader [US | UK]

Instructor Resources

You need a password to access these resources. Please contact your local Sales and Editorial Representative for more information.

Student Resources

www.oupcanada.com/Hayward

PREFACE

Writing in the Academic Disciplines is designed to empower the student writer while providing the instructor with a framework of readings, assignments, and lessons that he or she can adapt to classroom teaching. One way in which this book differs from many other books that teach academic reading and writing is that it attempts to demystify academic writing with a focus on genre. The general premise is that an understanding of genre—the conventions and forms particular to a specific type of writing—will help students more easily understand what is expected of them when reading and writing for academic purposes.

Ultimately, the focus is on how academic writing differs from other forms and styles of writing. For example, a written news report requires a different writing style and structure from a written advertisement or an academic essay. To help students understand these distinctions, I have provided numerous exercises, model essays, excerpts of student writing, readings, and examples that illustrate different writing styles.

Part III of this volume is a reader, designed to immerse the student in a formal engagement with academic writing. Although many of the readings are academic, those that are not still demand a formal, objective academic response. Additionally, the handbook of grammar and style, found in Part IV, is unique in that it features examples and exercises that are largely academic. This exposure to academic writing will help students become familiar with academic prose and proficient at writing in this style.

To develop this proficiency more specifically, I have emphasized academic writing in different disciplines. Particular chapters pertain to writing for the arts and social sciences and writing for the sciences. By paying attention to the conventions and expectations of a particular discipline, students will be better able to write for their area of study. More generally, throughout this book, students will learn how to write summaries, reports, literature reviews, and academic essays, with a focus on the research essay. The skills students will learn from this book are supported by chapter objectives, academic focus boxes, examples, exercises, readings, chapter summaries, and questions to consider, which will allow students to begin to apply what they have learned with practiced confidence.

To the Student

Many student writers enter university with the belief that writing is an unpleasant and difficult experience. Often, this belief is a result of the misconception that writing at the university level is either an extension of high school literature classes, and creative writing in general, or that it is "something academics do" to make themselves sound authoritative and knowledgeable. These misconceptions not only reinforce the belief that academic writing is difficult but also contribute to a lack of understanding about what academic writing is and why and how it differs, in terms of its conventions and techniques, from other forms of writing.

This book will alleviate any concerns you, as students, might have about academic reading and writing by clearly outlining how it works as a genre distinct from other kinds of writing and by providing you with a process for being able to read, think, and write as academics. Central to this transformation is the ability to understand and to communicate effectively about issues and topics of interest, as they relate to a respective discipline (for example, philosophy, history, science) and/or to the larger culture in which you live.

As students new to academic writing, you will first need to learn the basic conventions common to all academic writing (commonly called "writing across the disciplines," or WAC), but then, second, you will need to learn the ways of communicating knowledge within your chosen area of study (commonly called "writing in the disciplines," or WID). For example, you might learn how to write a summary of an academic essay, which will teach you how to accurately read and convey that knowledge in writing, but you might then write a critique of the essay that will allow you to think about how it conforms to the conventions and requirements of a specific discipline. We will discuss this process in greater detail throughout the book, but for now, it is important to understand that being able to write well is crucial to your all-round academic success. When you learn the conventions, processes, and strategies associated with all forms of academic writing, you will gain confidence in your ability to write well.

Benefits of Academic Writing

Your engagement with academic writing, both as a reader and as a writer, can provide you, as a student, with some distinct advantages relevant to both academia and the larger cultural context. To begin with, you will, if you read and internalize the processes and skills in this book, make easier the often difficult transition from high school to college- or university-level reading and writing. In terms of developing a clear knowledge of and practice in academic reading and writing skills, you will be able to develop the ability to read, to accurately understand, and to critically engage with academic and real-world texts and contexts and clearly convey that understanding in writing. In doing this, you will learn the importance of audience, context, and purpose within your writing, as well as learning how to revise your work for an effective logical structure and effective use of language, grammar, and tone. Additionally, you will learn how to conduct research and write a research essay that speaks to your own interests and perceptions, as they relate to an academic discipline that uses correct citation and referencing standards.

While these benefits might seem quite abstract, especially if you are a first-year student, we can assure you that there is great satisfaction and benefit to be had from communicating your ideas and arguments clearly and accurately. Not only will these skills enable you to be successful in the academic context, but also you will find that these skills are transferable to the larger culture or workplace.

According to a study conducted at North Carolina State University to ascertain the importance of writing in the workplace (engineers, programmers, management, marketing, sales, accounting, and banking were some of the professions surveyed), Carolyn R. Miller, Jamie Larsen, and Judi Gaitens found that "[a]cross all professions, workers spend nearly one third of their time writing" (10). Moreover, when asked "how important the quality of their writing is for the performance of their jobs, 90% of the respondents said it was either essential (50%) or very important (40%). None said it was irrelevant. When asked how important the quality of their writing is for their own career advancement, 82% said essential (45%) or very important (37%), and only a few people (2%) in marketing and management said it was irrelevant" (12). Writing, therefore, is not simply an academic hurdle that must be overcome to earn credit; it has direct and practical applications that will benefit you in both the academic and non-academic workplace.

Below are some testimonials from former students that speak to the value of academic writing:

I.   "Taking a course in academic writing has benefited me a thousand times over. Not only did it allow me to hone my writing skills to the level demanded by university instructors, but it also taught me how to interpret difficult academic [texts], work comfortably with APA and MLA, and become a confident and efficient researcher. Although academic writing might sound intimidating, learning these essential skills at the beginning of my degree has been an advantage in every course I have taken since and will undoubtedly continue to serve me throughout the rest of my post-secondary career."

—Jacqueline Burt

II.   "[Academic writing] brought out the best in my linguistic abilities [and enabled me to bridge] the gap between high school writing and the university standard. Without the work ethic that this course helped to instill, I would not have been able to achieve the goal of being on the Dean's Honour List, and I have [a course in academic writing] to thank, for setting the tone for the rest of my academic career."

—Savannah Simpson

III. "I learned a lot in academic writing. I feel like I made it over a big writing-style/technique hurdle. My writing will be forever changed for the better."

—Ann Goble

IV. "I'm a bachelor of arts and science student majoring in English and psychology and I took Writing 1000 as a GLER in the first semester of my first year. I found this course to be both interesting and extremely useful for my other courses as it helped me to make the transition from high school writing to university writing. It further enhanced my essay writing skills and especially helped me to master the art of citation, something that was previously unknown to me."

—Jordan Bartlett

My hope is that you will also see the benefits of taking a course in academic writing and, concomitantly, see the benefits of engaging seriously and rigorously with the information in this book. In doing this, you will learn to enjoy thinking critically about the world in which you live and, as academics are trained to do, convey that understanding in your writing.

To the Instructor

The discipline-specific academic approach adopted in this book will be useful to you if you are an instructor of academic writing. The book begins with an introduction to academic writing as a genre; subsequent chapters dedicated to essay writing, structure and rhetorical techniques, and grammar and style are meant to provide a basis for understanding and relating to a variety of discipline-specific readings. Because there is a consistent focus on academic reading and writing and because the readings, the grammar, and the rhetoric are cross-referenced in terms of themes and concepts, you will be able to use the information either in the order presented or according to your own course design. Perhaps more importantly, your students will learn both the processes and the conventions of academic reading and writing as they read, relate to, and respond to clear examples of academic writing.

While the interdisciplinary approach presented in this book conforms to a "writing across the disciplines" (WAC) focus, considering the conventions common to all academic disciplines, it also includes a focus on "writing in the disciplines" (WID). I believe that both approaches are essential for students who are attempting to learn how to position themselves successfully in academia. Consequently, the rhetoric, the reader, and the handbook focus not only on English as a discipline, following an approach typical of many writing courses taught in post-secondary English departments, but also on approaches and conventions specific to other academic disciplines. Sections on writing in the sciences and in the social sciences provide information on the discipline-specific style conventions and the forms of writing common to each discipline. An online chapter addressing writing for business and technology is found at the companion site for this book, located at www.oupcanada.com/Hayward.

To make the material more accessible and more useful in terms of its teachable content, I have created an instructor's manual, which offers additional resources, lesson plans, handouts, and supplementary material that will help you to put together a complete introductory course or to extend a basic introductory-level academic writing course to a more advanced upper-level course. The instructor's manual also features grammar quizzes.

For the grammar and style handbook, found in Part IV, I have found that many students new to academic writing are frustrated with texts that fail to provide full answer keys to grammar exercises; their concern is that if they are unable to confirm their answers, they cannot be sure they are mastering the concepts. In response to this concern, I have provided, in Appendix A, answer keys to selected exercises throughout the book, and to all the grammar exercises in Chapter 12. An additional concern that students and many instructors have is that the quotidian examples in most grammar texts do not translate to the students' ability to understand grammar and punctuation in an academic context. With this in mind, I have provided clearly explicated academic examples within the text to define and reinforce concepts. Appendix A also provides sample academic answers for many of the exercises throughout the book.

It is my goal to ensure that while the rhetoric, reader, and handbook will be accessible—providing a logical and general guide to the world of academic writing for students—they will also be informative and comprehensive in their arrangement and coverage so that instructors will be able to use them to teach focused, discipline-specific, and interdisciplinary writing courses.

Acknowledgements

This book was conceived when I was working at the University of Lethbridge teaching academic writing. It was born out of my desire to have a book that would encompass a focus on academic writing across the disciplines, a grammar book that would include academic examples and contain an answer key for students, and readings that would directly relate to the concepts being taught in the rhetoric. I was thrilled when Oxford University Press also thought the book was a good idea, so I must first thank them and, in particular, Mark Thompson, Leah-Ann Lymer, and Gillian Scobie for their support, encouragement, and amazing editing skills.

My thanks must also go to my colleagues at the University of Lethbridge, especially Cliff Lobe and Ann Braybrooks, who believed their students would profit from a genre-based approach to academic writing and helped me to formulate my own approach to this instruction. Thanks particularly go to Ann Braybrooks, who wrote the first draft of Chapter 4: Writing in the Sciences. Her expertise in this area was invaluable.

I would also like to acknowledge the following individuals who gave me help and direction with their reviews of the book: Laura K. Davis (Red Deer College); Suzanne James (University of British Columbia); Christine Kirchner (Camosun College); Melanie Murray (Okanagan College); Marissa Reaume (University of Windsor); and Beth Ann Wiersma (Lambton College). Your advice and suggestions were much appreciated. I trust you will be able to recognize your influence in this book.

On a personal note, I am very thankful for the love and support of my late husband, Nigel Fox, who encouraged me and provided the space and time for me to write, and his sister, Jackie, whose endless patience, meals on wheels, and dog-walking skills will not be forgotten.

Sally Hayward
July 2014

PART I

GENRE: WHY IT IS IMPORTANT AND HOW TO USE IT

The general premise of this section is that an understanding of genre can help you become a better reader and writer. When you are able to identify the language use, conventions, and structures that inform a piece of academic writing, not only will you become a better reader of academic texts, but you will also be better able to participate in the community of writers who write them.

Chapter 1 refines this intention with a focus on general misconceptions of academic writing as a genre (what academic writing is *not*), and chapter 2 explores how genre informs academic writing in particular. In chapter 2, you will also be introduced to academic writing in the various academic disciplines. An introduction to and examination of the conventions for writing in the humanities and social sciences (chapter 3), and in the sciences (chapter 4) will help you refine your academic writing skills in your specific subject and discipline.

1

Genre: "Real-World" and Academic Contexts

LEARNING OBJECTIVES

In this chapter, you will learn:

- What genre is and how and why the definition of genre has changed over time.

- Why an awareness of genre is important to an understanding of how language is used in "real-world" writing contexts to persuade a particular audience.

- How academic writing, as a genre, is often misconceived as creative or convoluted writing and/or conflated with other writing genres (advertising, journalism, or high school writing).

- How academic writing might be defined in general terms as a genre that differs from other forms of writing.

Genre: Defined

The word **genre** comes from the Latin term *genus* = kind. Genres are thus "kinds" of writing or speech or kinds of film or music. In education, genre is used to categorize music (classical, hip hop, rap), movies (horror, psychological thrillers, comedy), and literary forms (poems, novels, plays, essays). Genre has traditionally been defined by its ability to categorize similar types, strategies, or techniques of writing. It has thus enabled the different educational subject areas or disciplines to organize their curricula according to specific courses.

More recently, however, genre theorists have argued that this definition of genre is reductionist because it relies too heavily on rules, formal patterns of writing, and restrictive classifications (Miller 151). For these critics (John H. Patton, Thomas M. Conley, and Kathleen Hall Jamieson, for example), genre must be considered not only in terms of categorizations and classifications but also in terms of the social, historical, cultural, and political contexts to which it speaks. As genre theorist Caroline Miller emphasizes, genre must be considered in relation to the *substance* (the medium through which we experience the form: aural, written language, music, etc.), *form* (the primary object that is used to communicate the language (letter, essay, postcard, film, etc.), and *situation* (the larger communicative context in which the writing appears) (151). In this new definition, **substance**, which refers to how language is used to create meaning (**semantics**), and **form**, which refers indirectly to the rules of grammatical writing (**syntax**), are intrinsically connected to situation, which involves the larger social, political, or historical context. Situation also involves the writer's motive for writing, the **rhetorical action** or purpose that the writer hopes to achieve, and his or her awareness of **audience** (152).

For the purposes of this text, I am going to simplify this linguistic definition of genre to the following pattern: genre = situation + form + content. This simplified definition parallels Miller's linguistic definition of **situation**, the entire communicative context, including the writer's purpose and his or her awareness of audience. In my definition, form is both the primary object of communication (letter, legal document, etc.) and

---

ACADEMIC FOCUS

DEFINITIONS OF GENRE

Traditional definition:
Genre = organizational categorization of types of writing, film, music, etc.

The focus is entirely on the traditional rules of classifying and categorizing different types of texts.

vs

Linguistic definition:
Genre = substance + form + situation

Substance and form are always considered in the larger context, which includes a focus on the social, historical, and political contexts, the writer's awareness of audience, as well as the writer's motive and expected rhetorical action or purpose.

My definition:
Genre = situation + form + content

Situation stands for the entire communicative context, including the writer's purpose and his or her awareness of audience. *Form* is the primary object of communication (letter, legal document, etc.), and the organization of the piece at both the sentence and paragraph levels. This organization reflects both the meaning of a piece (semantics) and its syntax, or rules of language. *Content* refers to what is being said and argued. It includes a focus on language and cannot easily be separated from how it is structured (form) or from the situation or context of the entire piece.

the structure of the piece at both the sentence and paragraph levels. The content refers to the actual message or argument communicated in the piece, which includes how language is used to create meaning (semantics), using standard English rules of grammar (syntax). In practice, form and content work together to communicate a message or an argument.

This new understanding of genre tells us something about the way in which genre is connected to the situations people find themselves in and how they respond to these situations. In other words, it is possible to see that genre is intricately connected to what people do in a particular situation: people write advertisements to sell a product or find a partner, write postcards to friends when on holiday, and write letters to local politicians or newspapers. These situations indicate the purpose or motive for writing and the content. For example, if you are upset about what someone writes in your local paper, you might write a letter to the editor. That, in turn, dictates the form. If you wanted to sell a house, you would write an advertisement and put it in the local paper; you would not try to sell it by writing about it in a letter to your best friend. That purpose also dictates the language you use.

It is important to realize, however, that while the purpose of the writer dictates the genre, the genre itself dictates and shapes the spoken and written language use of individuals and groups (what they say and how they say it). This means that as a student writer, you need to be aware of the genre required from your specific context (academic essays that your university or college requires you to write). Being aware of the related context or situation and the required content and form of the writing is the first step toward making your writing successful within the university or college context. To write effectively, then, a writer must have a considered and valid argument (content) about a specific subject and an awareness of the conventions and forms of academic writing.

In other "real-world" contexts, the writer must, similarly, think about how his or her specific piece of writing conforms to the language and form of a specific genre. For example, the writer contemplating writing a speech, a letter, or an advertisement would examine how established writers use language conventions and particular structures that are in keeping with the style requirements of their specific genre. Once again, this larger situation includes the writer's purpose or reason for writing, which involves an awareness of when, where, and how (for example, under what social, political, historical, or psychological circumstances) this writing normally occurs, as well as the writer's awareness of his or her audience.

An examination of a specific genre might be useful at this point. Consider how the writer uses content, situation, and form in the following example, taken from Harriet Jacobs's *Incidents in the Life of a Slave Girl*, published in 1861:

> Could you have seen that mother clinging to her child, when they fastened the irons upon his wrists; could you have heard her heart-rending groans, and seen her bloodshot eyes wander wildly from face to face, vainly pleading for mercy; could you have witnessed that scene as I saw it, you would exclaim, Slavery is damnable!
>
> — Harriet Jacobs, *Incidents in the Life of a Slave Girl*

In terms of *content*, Harriet Jacobs presents us with a violent scene of abuse against a slave mother and her child. Her argument is that slavery, and the ensuing violence, is wrong (*damnable!*). The larger context or *situation* here is the Southern United States and the slave trade in the mid-nineteenth century. Jacobs shows an awareness of the conflicted emotions of her mainly women abolitionist readers by attempting to elicit their sympathy about the plight of those who are destined for slavery (audience awareness). To do this, she uses the diary *form* of autobiographical writing, a slave narrative, that depends on sensationalized language, in-depth description, the emotional use of adverbs (wander *wildly*; *vainly* pleading) and the use of direct address (you), which demands a response from the reader. This language, although it seems a little sentimental and coercive to a modern reader, could be said to parallel the severity of the situation Jacobs is writing about. We might argue that in this way Jacobs's content matches her form. Her use of language illustrates that she has a very good sense not only of her situation but also of her nineteenth-century audience. Going even further, we might argue that, given Jacobs's reasons for writing, this slave narrative functions as a kind of emancipation: it shows and legitimizes her truth as a slave girl and allows her to find some agency in writing to and finding common community with her imagined audience (purpose).

Now consider the following excerpt from the blog *Diary of a Mad Woman*, written on 25 January 2013.

> I'm so thankful for you crazy muthas. Yesterday I blogged about how I thought I had some sort of mental disturbance because I've been secretly freaked out about my kids dying. I really didn't even let on to the true nature of my frightfulness because I didn't want anyone to call the muscled guys at the mental institution and tell them to trick me into the van. Your responses have changed my life. I'm not kidding.

This anonymous blog (*form*), written in the same diary form and therapeutic vein as Jacobs's, relies less on sensationalistic description than humour to elicit sympathy. Although the sentiment behind the story is depressing at best, the blog author uses **hyperbole** to imagine not a horrific scene where her children might be dying, but rather a scene that allows the reader to laugh at her imagined abduction to a mental institution (*content*). To help lighten the tone of this piece, she uses colloquialisms (everyday expressions), such as *freaked out,* and *I'm not kidding* (form). These colloquialisms, along with her direct address to the reader—*I'm so thankful for you crazy muthas* and *Your responses have changed my life*—work to affirm her truth-telling authority. It is as though she is personally telling the story to the reader over a morning coffee in the kitchen. Like Jacobs, then, this writer has a good understanding of her twenty-first-century audience (*situation*): she not only emulates the way her largely female readers might speak, because she is, after all, just like them (*crazy muthas*), but she appeals to their desire to be entertained, rather than troubled, by what she writes. Ultimately, her *purpose* for writing is to help her deal emotionally with her husband's suicide and her struggle to raise her children as a single parent after her husband's death.

These examples also illustrate that genre, like language itself, is never static. Through a consideration of genre, it is possible to see that texts, such as the diary form, represented in both Jacobs's and the "mad" woman's diaries, function according to language *and* the writing/speaking conventions that change through time and in relation to a changing situational context. For example, whereas Jacobs's diary was first published in print, serialized in a newspaper, the *New York Tribune*, the Mad Woman's diary is published electronically, as a blog.

You might also consider the letter in this respect: the situational context of letter writing has changed the way letters are formed and transmitted. Letters used to be written formally, often by hand, over several pages, following a fairly strict format. However, nowadays people are more likely to email each other, rather than send a letter. Emails have a much more informal structure and liberties with formal grammar are almost to be expected. Taking this development one step further, text messages not only refuse a strict format, using a continuous conversational note-form style, but have changed

ACADEMIC FOCUS

GENRE AND ACADEMIC FORMS OF WRITING

Listed below are three traditional academic forms, or primary objects of communication, that you might be asked to write within in a specific academic discipline. Using my concept of genre, I have illustrated how situation, form, and content might apply to these specific sub-genres or forms of writing.

Genre = situation + form + content

Literature review: Overview and analysis (analyses different arguments and theoretical approaches) of existing literature (*content*) related to subject of interest and written for other academics who work in the same discipline (psychology, sociology, education etc.) and who are interested in the same or related subject matter (*situation*). The review should follow a logical structure (*form*) related to your own research interests (*form + content*).

English essay: Analytical examination of a text—this could be literature or simply anything that can be analyzed (a play, a film, a government paper, a legal trial, a shopping centre etc.)—(*content*) written for other academics in the discipline of English (*situation*) using formal English and a deductive structure (one that rarely uses subheadings) (*form*). An essay must always provide evidence of a larger cultural context related to the writer's argument (*situation*).

Technical/scientific report: Detailed report about a problem, an issue, or a process (*content*) to specific person(s) (other scientists, engineers, business people, government officials) (*situation*) using specific language and stylistic conventions (detailed logical structure, formal English, some jargon, subheadings) (*form*). The subject of the report is related to the writer's purpose and communicative or cultural context (*situation*).

the language itself (refusal of punctuation or proper sentences, use of abbreviations, phonetic use of language, such as u for you, etc.). Similarly, letters used to be delivered either by hand or by a letter carrier, which took time, but emails and text messaging are transmitted instantly and stored electronically.

A Special Note about Situation

As noted earlier, *situation* is taken to mean the entire communicative context, including the writer's purpose and his or her awareness of audience. For example, you probably noticed when you read the two diaries above that *situation* refers to both the larger cultural context or situation (United States slave trade and suicide and single parenthood) *and* the contextualized interaction between the writer and reader. In other words, both of these writers, as part of their situation for writing, imagine and speak to a specific audience for a specific purpose (to elicit sympathy, to raise consciousness, as a cathartic exercise). This interaction or *communicative context* can then be broken up into the larger cultural *situation,* the writer's awareness of *audience,* and the writer's intentions or *purpose* in writing. Here are some definitions of these terms so that you can recognize them in your reading and writing, and be able to recognize them in an academic context:

Situation

- The relationship between the event(s) that gives rise to the writing and the *situation* or *context* (cultural, social, psychological, physical) in which the writing will be read.
- *Academic* writing is shaped by the academic context, which is driven by a need to create, test, and communicate rigorously and precisely certain kinds of knowledge (research) valued within academic communities.

Audience

- The individual or group to whom the writer addresses the writing.
- Many documents have primary and secondary audiences, intended and unintended audiences.
- Specific audiences have particular kinds of knowledge, values and beliefs, interests, attitudes, and motives. These features influence their ways of using language and their expectations of language use.
- Academic writing presupposes an academic audience, which might include tenured scholars and graduate or undergraduate students. However, academic writing also addresses professionals in other fields, who are required to stay up to date on research, new or modified theories, innovative procedures, etc. Therefore, a more general definition might be that the intended audience for academic writing is professionals in the same field who can be presumed to share specific concepts, background knowledge, and methodological practices.

Purpose

- The writer's *reason* for writing is related not only to *what* the writer wants to say but also to what the writer wants his or her writing to *do* as a reader engages with (understands, develops, and critiques) it.
- The primary purpose of *academic writing* is to communicate specific kinds of scholarly *knowledge* (*research*) valued within academic communities. Purpose is thus closely connected to the writer's *argument* (*content*). The reader of academic writing is expected to engage with the concepts and knowledge presented.

Because the communicative context (situation, audience, purpose) shapes decisions about how we effectively organize or shape the content and style of a speech or piece of writing, we need to consider it carefully when speaking or listening or when reading or writing. This consideration does not suggest that we must strictly adhere to a set of rules when addressing a particular community. It means, rather, that we must gain a *sense* of the way in which a particular community or group of people use language, style, and organization to create a sense of shared meaning. Understanding this will allow you to participate in and contribute to the ongoing conversations of a particular community of speakers or writers.

Exercise 1.1

READING AND COMPARING GENRES

Read the following three passages, follow the directions below, and answer the following questions related to situation, content, and form:

Situation

- Where might you find these written or visual excerpts (i.e., on a post board or website, in a local newspaper, etc.)? What larger situation or context do they imply?
- What *audience* are the writers targeting?
- What *purpose* might the writers have for writing?

Content

- How does the content indicate a specific genre?
- What is the specific message or argument?

Form

- Identify three or four examples of how the writer's use of language reflects the specific genre. For example, a text message uses abbreviations, shorter sentences, and unconventional spelling and grammar whereas a newspaper article might use biased storytelling, short paragraphs, sentence fragments, and emotion-laden adjectives (describing words) to persuade the reader.
- How does the larger organizational structure enhance both the content and the genre?

EXAMPLE 1: JOURNALISTIC ARTICLE

Sue Ellen, a.k.a. Susie Goose, loves to carry a purse with lollipops in it and has a fondness for necklaces.

A little background: Sue Ellen is a 43-year-old chimpanzee who survived 15 years in the entertainment business, during which time she had her teeth knocked out with a crowbar so that she couldn't bite her trainer.

When the biz tired of her, she was sold to a biomedical facility, where she was repeatedly infected with HIV and endured dozens of invasive surgeries. Before chimps are operated on, by the way, they are shot with a tranquillizer gun. If the lab technician is a bad shot, the chimpanzee is shot over and over again, with no concern for tender body parts, until the animal collapses.

Sue Ellen has a hard time trusting humans.

Source: Excerpt taken from Greenaway, Kathryn. "Cruelty Dealt Out in the Name of Science: Profiles of Chimps Rescued from Research are Heart-Wrenching." *Edmonton Journal.* 26 June 2011. Postmedia News, a division of Postmedia Network Inc.

EXAMPLE 2: TWITTER ENTRY

"Animal testing costs the public over $136 bill. Animal testing costs your family over $300 dollars a year. Alternatives cost way less."

Source: No Animal Testing, 27 Jul 2009.

EXAMPLE 3: ADVERTISEMENT

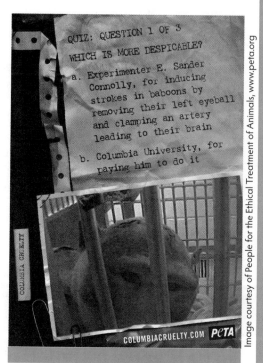

Image courtesy of People for the Ethical Treatment of Animals, www.peta.org

Photo 1.1

See the Exercise Answer Key in Appendix A for a sample analysis of these texts.

After reading the excerpts in Exercise 1.1 and completing the assigned questions, you should be starting to see that although each piece of writing deals with the same topic, each has a different content and approach to the subject matter. In other words, while the examples above share many characteristics—they all target an audience (the general public) concerned with the ethics of animal testing, they all document a specific situation, and they all communicate a specific purpose (to expose the unethical use of animal experimentation)—they also all use different forms or genres to communicate their purpose. These different genres (a journalistic article, a tweet, and an advertisement) require the use of different language conventions and stylistic choices.

As you have probably noted, however, the examples above are not academic but would serve as the **primary texts** for your analysis, in other words as objects of critique for the analysis that you will write in your academic paper. Because you will be expected to present that critique in an academic essay, this is the genre you will mainly be concerned with in this book. Once you are able to identify how academic writing works as a genre that is different from other real-world genres, you will become a more informed, better-equipped, and thus a more empowered and successful academic writer.

However, because students come to university from an immersion in the "real world" and, at best, an immersion in high school essay writing, they often confuse the genre of academic writing with other forms of writing. Extending the above examination of genre to a consideration of the way in which academic writing is often misperceived or confused with other genres will help you understand more fully what academic writing is *not* as well as what academic writing *is*.

Academic Writing: Common Misconceptions

This section will provide you with a basic introduction to academic writing as a genre by first making you aware of what academic writing is *not*. By dispelling some of the conventions and practices that are commonly mistaken as being typical of academic writing, you will begin to feel more comfortable with the genre (and the sub-genres of your particular discipline). As you gain a basic and more accurate understanding of some of the academic techniques and conventions, writing in an academic context will seem less abstract and intimidating and more accessible and manageable. Below are four basic misconceptions that obscure students' understanding of academic writing:

- Academic writing is convoluted and inaccessible.
- Academic writing is creative writing.
- Academic writing is high school writing.
- Academic writing is journalistic writing.

Misconception 1: Academic Writing Is Convoluted and Inaccessible

The Calvin and Hobbes cartoon (see Photo 1.2) is amusing precisely because it speaks to the fears that a student might experience when thinking about writing at the university

CALVIN AND HOBBES © 1993 by Watterson. Reprinted with permission of UNIVERSAL UCLICK. All rights reserved.

Photo 1.2

level. When you encounter an academic text for the first time, you may, like Calvin, feel overwhelmed and intimidated. You know there must be some important meaning buried in the complicated and unfamiliar language, but why, you wonder, does the text have to be so difficult—perhaps even impossible at your current academic level—to access? You may even feel, as Calvin and many students do, that academic writing is an "impenetrable and intimidating fog" and that mastering writing at this level demands that you think and write in as convoluted a way as possible.

As Calvin recognizes, this misconception is, ironically, the very thing that causes you as a student to "inflate weak ideas, obscure poor reasoning, and inhibit clarity." The reason you find academic writing so difficult is that you have not yet been initiated into the academic community and its use of language and form conventions. While academic writing might feel inaccessible and daunting to you—the uninitiated—the more you interact with academic texts, the less foreign they will seem, and you will begin to recognize some of the common terms, strategies, and conventions that academics in your discipline use to communicate knowledge.

Central to academic writing, as stressed earlier, is an awareness of situation, which includes an awareness of audience and purpose. In this respect, you might also note that Calvin is guilty of not understanding his situation, his audience, or his purpose, aspects that are crucial to any writing assignment. Ironically, Calvin misses the point that academic writing has, as its main purpose, absolute clarity. If you write with Calvin's attitude and approach in mind, you will tend to skim the surface, alluding to ideas by using big words and sentence structures that emulate academic prose, but fail to present any clear argument.

Misconception 2: Academic Writing Is Creative Writing

This misconception causes students to falsely believe that academic writing is similar to the creative writing taught in high school English classes. As such, you might believe that all writing should be descriptive, personal, and opinionated. Consider the following excerpt of student writing:

> I loved reading Edith Wharton's *The House of Mirth* because it made me feel sad for all the bad things that happened to Lily Bart. It's not fair that women are treated badly by men who take advantage of a vulnerable woman's situation. This happened to my mom when dad left. She had a very difficult life because of it.

In the above excerpt, the writer's main purpose is to let us know how he or she feels, thus generalizing Lily Bart's fictional experiences in 1905 to her own experiences. In academic terms, this form of writing is known as **expressivist writing**. As implied, its purpose is to encourage you to write about your personal experiences, reactions, feelings, and opinions.

This method of teaching writing has gained much popularity in writing programs in recent years because, in Peter Elbow's words, "it help[s] writers take more authority over their writing: not to feel so intimidated by it and not to write so much tangled or uninvested prose or mechanical or empty thinking" (17). To imply that if students attempt to write academically, they will engage in uninvested, mechanical, or empty prose is to underestimate their ability to learn this new genre. Although expressivist writing does have a place in helping first-year or inexperienced writers gain confidence (Villanueva, Berlin, Elbow), it is not academic writing, and treating it as such is, in my opinion, confusing to undergraduate students. It is possible to learn how to write academically and it is possible to learn how to write well.

Academic writing differs most fundamentally from expressivist writing in that the focus is on the impersonal or objective point of view and the knowledge. Here is an example of academic writing. Compare it with the example above:

> In *The House of Mirth*, Edith Wharton represents Lily Bart as a victim of her time and the circumstances she finds herself in. Unable to conform to tradition and conventions that demand she marry for social standing and wealth, Lily wants to marry for love. As a consequence, she becomes socially unacceptable and is abandoned to a life of increasing poverty. Unfortunately, it is precisely Lily Bart's strong moral standards that cause her downfall.

In the above academic example, the evidence presented is not from personal experience but from the novel itself, and while the focus is still on the victimization of women, there is now only one time frame and an objective argument about Bart's experiences.

Exercise 1.2

FREEWRITING

Read David Bartholomae's essay "Writing with Teachers: A Conversation with Peter Elbow" (see page 330 in the Reader) and employ Peter Elbow's informal process-orientated strategy of freewriting to articulate your opinions about the text.

1. Using a sentence starter, such as "I think Bartholomae is . . ." or "Expressivism is . . . ," write without stopping for five minutes. Do not worry if you go off-topic or write ungrammatical or personal sentences.
2. Review your freewrite: Highlight the important points. Do you agree or disagree with Bartholomae? Why?

Keep in mind that you will become a more confident and authoritative writer when you learn the conventions of academic writing and when you objectively engage with the knowledge and issues at hand.

Misconception 3: Academic Writing Is High School Writing

As a first-year university or college student, you might be surprised to learn that high school writing is not appropriate for the university environment and that you will have to adapt or discard altogether much of what you have learned. This awareness often elevates the anxiety that you, along with many students, have about your writing ability. It is important, therefore, to understand how the goals of high school writing and university writing differ.

The goals of high school involve teaching students how to express their personal experiences, beliefs, and feelings in an atmosphere of respect, support, and collaboration. Communication in a high school English classroom involves *describing* events, characters, and their motives, retelling the plot, exploring themes, and identifying the author's tone (Alberta Curriculum: English, Grade 12).

In an academic-writing class, respect and collaboration are expected. You will also need to go beyond the goals of a high school English class to develop an informed and knowledgeable perspective based on an objective evaluation of facts, a clear understanding of the essay as a form, and a self-reflective awareness of grammar and style. As an academic writer, you are moving beyond the narrow scope of your personal experiences and finding meaning at a broader societal or cultural level. The expectations, quite simply, are a lot higher.

However, it is important to know that the differences between a high school education and a university or college education do not indicate a hierarchical relationship. Rather, the education you receive in a high school English class and the education you receive in a university class reflect the fact that they are two different institutions with different goals and demands and with different language and situational expectations. In other words, they constitute two different genres. While high school education requires that a student demonstrate behavioural, social, creative, and academic skills suitable to the formation of good citizens, a university education requires students to demonstrate the research skills suitable to their discipline and the demands of a research institution.

Misconception 4: Academic Writing Is Journalistic Writing

This misconception, although not as common as the other errors, occurs when the conventions of academic writing are conflated with those of journalism or even advertising copy. Often seen in the writing of students who have an interest in business or journalism, this misconception manifests in their attempt to emulate the work of professionals who function successfully in media-related fields.

This kind of writing, which "sells" a product, is an appropriate style for writers who write advertising copy or journalistic articles where the goal is to persuade the audience to buy a product, a service, or an idea, or to entertain an audience. It is not appropriate for an academic writer, whose goal is to generate and contribute to the existing knowledge about a topic.

If you write from a journalistic or marketing perspective, you probably won't include your own experience, but you will attempt to narrate a story that might sell your ideas or opinions about the topic. You will also tend to use descriptive **adjectives** and sensational biased **verbs** and opinions to persuade the reader that they must not only "buy" your perspective but also literally "buy" the product, service, belief, or ideology. Academic writers, conversely, are more concerned with the knowledge than the "story," truth as opposed to **bias**, an objective analysis that has depth rather than superficial description, and neutral and informed verbs (analyze, inform, examine) as opposed to more sensational verbs.

ACADEMIC FOCUS

COMPARING GENRES: HIGH SCHOOL, JOURNALISTIC, ACADEMIC

Below is a comparison of the central tenets of
- high school writing, where students get the idea that academic writing is creative writing;
- journalistic writing or writing for the general public;
- academic writing.

Keep in mind that these different forms of writing reflect different genres of writing.

HIGH SCHOOL WRITING

Encourages students to
- Explore thoughts, ideas, feeling, experiences;
- Use personal expression and personal opinion, rather than objective analysis or research;
- Use third-person **point of view**;
- Use language in a generalizing, universalizing form;
- Respond critically and creatively, with clarity and artistry;
- Focus on **summary** and description. Usually not persuasive;
- Use the five-paragraph essay;
- Envision a high school teacher as an audience.

WRITING FOR THE GENERAL PUBLIC (JOURNALISM, ADVERTISING, ETC.).

Focuses on

* Exploring ideas and issues that refer to public opinion;
* Personal experience and opinion rather than objective analysis;
* Tendency to not use research appropriately. Research is not documented;
* First- and second-person point of view. First-person perspective is often presented as the "truth;"
* Simple, direct, informal language. Uses colloquialisms, slang, clichés;
* Emotion (**pathos**) rather than reason or logic (**logos**);
* Writer credibility (**ethos**), which is sometimes suspect;
* The use of description, narration, and summary in the service of persuasion;
* Strategies that attract and keep the reader's interest (the "hook," sensationalism, etc.);
* Short paragraphs;
* An audience that is the general public. Often geared to the specific market that the work speaks to;
* Low reading level (approximately grade 6).

ACADEMIC WRITING

Stresses

* Writing that is knowledge- and idea-driven and discipline-specific;
* Persuasive and analytical, sometimes expository essays;
* Use of first or third person. Second person (you) is never used;
* Objective writing that presents a balanced, analytical perspective;
* Simple, direct, and concise language. Uses formal diction and correct grammar; may use some jargon, but avoids slang, contractions, or clichés;
* Use of logic/reason (logos) and ethos (authorial trust);
* Use of definition, cause-effect, classification, and division;
* Thorough research: the sources of all ideas are cited in the body of the text and works are documented in a reference page at the end of the document;
* Longer paragraphs because the content has depth. Facts and figures are accessible, accurate, and complete;
* The imagined audience as an intelligent person who is immersed in similar academic studies.

IDENTIFYING STUDENT MISCONCEPTIONS

Exercise 1.3

Below are five examples of academic writing typically written by first-year students. Using the chart above and the descriptions of the common misconceptions, read the examples and answer the following questions:

1. Identify which of the following examples could serve as a model for each of the four common misconceptions:
   * academic writing as convoluted and inaccessible
   * academic writing as creative
   * academic writing as high school based
   * academic writing as journalism

   Which example is a model of good clear academic writing?

Continued

2. Identify
   - two or three typical characteristics of the writing that indicate one of these common student misconceptions; or
   - some characteristics that indicate that the writing is an example of good academic writing.

PASSAGE 1

Different people in the world have grown up in many different "soundscapes" that remind them of different moments in their past that were happy, sad, exciting or boring. An ordinary sound can bring a memory of the past but because over time "materials change, sounds change, social customs change (Schafer 211) the meaning of the "soundscape" can change and sometimes make a person feel negative. I recently walked past a pet store and heard a dog barking and it reminded me of how much fun I had with my nanny's dog, rufus. Whenever I walked into her house, Rufus would jump up and down excitedly. But then came the beginning of the end. Rufus got old and sick and I no longer heard his feet tapping on the tile or hear him barking as he came to the door. My "soundscape" was changed and I was very sad.

PASSAGE 2

John Milton's fascination with chastity persuaded him of the need to both live and write virtuously. Expressing what seems to be a genuine concern with morals, Milton spent a vast amount of time composing controversial works on education, monarchy, religion, and divorce. In *The Doctrine and Discipline of Divorce*, Milton's conception of conjugal love insists that a blissful union lies not in "the satisfaction of the flesh," but in a spiritual meeting of true minds in "cheerful and agreeable conversation" (188). He writes, in short, that if there is no love and peace in marriage, there is, in God's eyes, no marriage. This essay will examine Milton's views on marriage, as illustrated in *The Doctrine and Discipline of Divorce*, and compare them to the dominant religious views of his time. Ultimately, I will attempt to argue that Milton's views were not only moral but liberal.

PASSAGE 3

Anne Fadiman's non-fiction book *The Spirit Catches You and You Fall Down* is a sensational book that tells the story of a Hmong refugee family living in the United States. It documents the moving and disturbing story of the daughter who has epilepsy and is treated extremely badly by the American medical system. It is a fantastic read and should not be missed.

PASSAGE 4

Findley establishes a bureaucratic patriarchal power structure characterized by gender roles and authoritarianism. He bases these structures on binary constructs, which deal with the deconstruction of traditional gender roles, authoritarianism, and militarism. In doing this, you can see that Findley is able to de-emphasize authoritarianist attitudes against women in favor of group unity, strength, intelligence and feminism as a means of achieving social freedom.

PASSAGE 5

In Lewis Carroll's *The Adventures of Alice in Wonderland,* Alice is a pretty great girl who is incredibly tired and bored and falls down, down and down a deep well after she had followed a curious white rabbit down his large rabbit hole. She was "not a bit hurt" when she eventually stopped falling and found herself in a strange land that was full of strange things, such as three-legged tables, talking rabbits, magical potions, and lovely, beautiful gardens and pools full of speaking animals.

See the Exercise Answer Key in Appendix A for an analysis of these passages.

Imitation: A Writing Technique

Now that you have a "feel" for what it means to write in the different genres and for to write as a student new to academia, you will need to begin practising writing in these genres. One way of doing this is to use the practice of **imitation**. Imitation has been used since ancient Greece, when Aristotle considered how imitation enables the speaker or writer to not only make something new but to, potentially, make something better than the original. Many famous writers, including John Milton and Malcolm X, used imitation, copying exemplary texts while paying attention to the stylistic arrangement of the words and sentences to learn their craft.

The practice of imitation requires a conscious awareness of how words and sentences can be put together to create an effect, making you aware of how issues of arrangement and **style** can alter your own writing and make it more powerful. Imitation also helps you go beyond an intellectual understanding of different forms and genres of writing to one that is immersed in the actual practices of writing in these different forms and genres. Imitation builds a bridge between your reading and writing. Instead of simply writing from what you think you know and have read about what constitutes good writing, with imitation you are able to practise writing by emulating exemplary models.

You can use this technique to learn how to write in any genre, including creative writing, short-story writing, poetry, advertising copy, and, of course, academic writing. Take, for example, the following creative writing passage written by Ernest Hemingway, and the student imitation of it that follows:

The hills across the valley of the Ebro were long and white. On this side there was no shade and no trees and the station was between two lines of rails in the sun. Close against the side of the station there was the warm shadow of the building and a curtain, made of strings of bamboo beads, hung across the open door into the bar, to keep out flies. The American and the girl with him sat at a table in the shade outside the building. It was very hot and the express from Barcelona would come in forty minutes. It stopped at this junction for two minutes and went on to Madrid.
—Ernest Hemingway, "Hills Like White Elephants."

Student imitation:

The waves against the horizon in the west were dark and blue. On the water there was no wind and no sound and the boat was making two lines of waves in its wake. Far along the edge of the coast there was the cold silhouette of the lighthouse and a pier, made of pillars of Douglas fir, stretching far into the open ocean, for catching crab. The fisherman and the boy with him sat in the rocking boat in the setting sun. It was very warm and the ferry from Vancouver would come in thirty minutes. It would stop at this port for five minutes and go on to Pender.

The student imitation of Hemingway's passage is very good. The student has successfully used her own content while capturing Hemingway's sense of landscape, which moves from a distant to a close-up scene. Using Hemingway's technique of repetition and combining compound sentences without the use of commas—"there was no shade and no trees and the station"—the writer encourages us to read quickly, as if we too are surveying the horizon. Like Hemingway's own writing, however, this flow stops as soon as we get to the interaction between the people. Here, short, direct, and factual sentences, along with a focus on nouns and verbs, slow the action down and help us to focus on the close-up scene.

The following imitation example is academic. You might note that while Hemingway's passage creates a scene, using description, this passage is more intellectually rigorous. It will probably feel quite dense and demand that you read slowly and carefully. This is because the ideas are more complex, requiring sentences that are often quite long, using compound and even **compound-complex sentences**. Unlike Hemingway, who omits commas in his compound sentences, academic punctuation follows formal grammatical rules. The focus is not on setting a scene but on objectively examining an issue or a problem. In other words, the focus is on knowledge. After you have read this example, read the student imitation of the passage. How successful is the student imitation? Provide reasons for your answer.

There is something rather religious about Oprah Winfrey. Recent episodes of *The Oprah Winfrey Show* advertise ways to "awake Spirit;" headlines in *O, The Oprah Magazine* advocate methods of meditation and prayer, and in her treatment of books from "The Oprah Book Club," Winfrey frequently encourages her reading audience to "find truths for your revolution." Every product of Winfrey's empire combines spiritual counsel with practical encouragement, inner awakening with capitalist pragmatism. . . . An analysis of Winfrey's world necessarily begs fundamental questions about the study of market culture: how should scholars interpret the practices of capitalism that are inflected with spirituality?

—Kathryn Lofton, "Practicing Oprah; or the Prescriptive Compulsion of a Spiritual Capitalism."

Student imitation:

There is something fantastic about Fairy Tales. Recent productions of Fairy Tales try to highlight their "practicality;" stories in *Tales, The Fantasy Magazine* highlight how magic speaks to reality, and stories in "The Grimm Story Club" focus on Fairy Tale characters who often implore the real-world audience to "look for truths for your world." Every element of the Fantasy World combines enchanting adventures with real-world lessons, spellbinding stories with fantastic factualism. . . . An analysis of the Fairy Tale World certainly asks rudimentary questions about the study of Fairy Tale culture: How should people interpret the rituals of enchantment that are inflected with actuality.

Although this student successfully emulates the sentence structure and punctuation of the original, the imitation is not as successful when it comes to content or, more specifically, when it comes to creating clear meaning and a clear logical argument. The first sentence uses the word "fantastic" but the reader is unclear what the writer means. Abstract words like fantastic, beautiful, and amazing have different meanings for different people, so they are not the best words to use when you want to make a specific statement. What is fantastic about fairy tales becomes increasingly unclear as we begin to see that the passage is about how fairy tales speak to reality, expressing "truths for your world."

The last sentence needs some work too. The writer switches focus to make an argument, not about the "real world" but about "fairy tale culture" and references "rituals" and "enchantment," which are not synonymous with fairy tales. More important, the reader becomes confused as to whether the argument purports to be examining fairy tales or the larger culture. This imitation, while promising, would be strengthened if the writer had a clearer argument and paid more careful attention to her choice of words. Another problem is that the writer uses capital letters inconsistently. These simple mistakes, along with spelling errors, should be avoided at all costs.

The following exercises will not only help you to *understand* the differences between genres but will also help you gain some practical *experience* writing them.

IMITATION

Read the following passages.

1. Find one that appeals to you as an exemplary or interesting model.
2. Imitate it by using the same form, but change the content.
3. Review your writing and think about how you might want to consciously work with the sentence structure and some of the stylistic choices in your own compositions.

Exercise 1.4

Continued

4. Discuss your passages with your classmates. If possible, edit the passages for each other. Is there any way you could make them stronger, either in terms of their content or in terms of their sentence structure and language use?

PASSAGE 1 (JOURNALISTIC)

If anyone needed to learn how to settle an over-taxed brain, it would be me. Even as I wait for the plane in Vancouver International Airport, I am aware of the network of knots in my back. Not that long ago, just after my 40th birthday, I left a demanding executive job with its packed agenda and ball-and-chain Blackberry to spend more time with family, get healthy, and find a new career. After years of multitasking, I'm training to focus on just one thing at a time. . . . I take a deep breath and imagine a sign with the word "de-stress" written on it.

—Susan Rybar, "Take Five." *British Columbia Magazine*. 30 May 2013.

PASSAGE 2 (FICTION)

Some hours before dawn Henry Perowne, a neurosurgeon, wakes to find himself already in motion, pushing back the covers from a sitting position, and then rising to his feet. It's not clear to him when exactly he became conscious, nor does it seem relevant. He's never done such a thing before, but he isn't alarmed or even faintly surprised, for the movement is easy, and pleasurable in his limbs, and his back and legs feel unusually strong. He stands there, naked by the bed—he always sleeps naked—feeling his full height, aware of his wife's patient breathing and of the wintry bedroom air on his skin.

—Ian McEwan, *Saturday*

PASSAGE 3 (NON-FICTION)

And so we detour from the routine of the feeding tube to the routine of the diaper. . . . The trick is to pin his arms to keep him from whacking himself. But how do you change a 45 pound boy's brimming diaper while immobilizing both his hands so he doesn't bang his head or (even worse) reach down to scratch his tiny, plum-like but suddenly liberated backside, thereby smearing excrement everywhere? While at the same time immobilizing his feet because ditto? You can't let your attention wander for a second.

—Ian Brown, *The Boy in the Moon*

PASSAGE 4 (ACADEMIC)

Is it possible that ethical action might depend less on analytical reasoning than on responding to a dilemma as we might respond to a story? "Thinking with stories" is a concept I borrow from sociologist Arthur W. Frank in *The Wounded Storyteller*. By thinking Frank means and I mean a process very different from the exclusive operation of reason. Thought clearly involves reasoning, in addition to various forms of cognitive activity from memory to meditation, but I want to emphasize that thinking also involves a crucial collaboration with feeling.

—David B. Morris, *Illness and Culture in the Postmodern Age*

EXEMPLARY WRITING

Exercise 1.5

If you don't have one already, start keeping a journal of examples of exemplary writing. Make sure that this journal is unique to who you are. Decorate it, cover it, or do what you need to do so that you want to write in it. Keep it with you at all times, and when you find a passage of writing that appeals to you, that contains some noteworthy content or form, write it down carefully, word for word, punctuation-mark-perfect, in your journal.

Make sure you record the author's name so you can become aware of your tastes and preferences, but don't prejudge your choices. My daughter keeps a journal of song verses and philosophical quotes that appeal to her, and that is fine. She says she has discovered that the song verses and philosophical quotes complement each other because, in finding a sense of her preferences, she is also finding a sense of her own voice, which is edgy, poetic, and imbued with a reflective depth of thought. You might choose at some point to practise rewriting these passages, imitating their form but replacing the content with your own words and ideas.

WHO ARE YOU AS A WRITER?

Exercise 1.6

1. Find a piece of writing that you completed at some time in the past (e.g., in high school or in the workplace). See if you can identify who you have been as a writer. Does your writing show that you subscribed to the idea that writing should be convoluted (i.e., using big words and convoluted ideas), creative (i.e., using a lot of adjectives and personal opinion), or journalistic (i.e., using description, sensational verbs, and bias)? Does your writing reflect a high school education or a university education?

2. Use the rhetorical exercise of imitation and rewrite one paragraph of your former writing using an academic style. How does it feel to take out your personal experience and focus only on the knowledge or ideas (even if you use first person)? How does it feel to take out the sensational verbs and bias, replacing them with simple straightforward verbs and objective impersonal writing? How does it feel to make a clear argument about some issue you care about? Recognizing that your writing style is a matter of habit, how does it feel to change the way you write and think?

Now that you have a feeling for your own writing style and have compared your style with what academic writing *is not*, as well as getting a feel for what academic writing *is* by using the rhetorical strategy of imitation, you should be starting to get a feel for the gap that exists between your current writing style and an academic writing style. At this point, you might be thinking that although you have an idea about what academic writing is *not*—expressing personal opinions, trying to sell a product or idea, or appearing to be intelligent by using convoluted language and ideas—you still feel unsure about what academic writing really *is*. And more important, you might be wondering how you, as a first-year student, are expected to learn how to write for academia.

Academic Writing: A Brief Definition

Academic writing is text that is written *by* members of the academic community *for* other academics in the same scholarly areas who create new knowledge and expand on existing knowledge. At an undergraduate level, this writing might include lab reports, book reviews, summaries, case studies, critical essays, and research assignments. The basic premise of all academic writing is clarity and a sustained thoughtful engagement with the material or ideas that the writer is working with. It uses logical, reasoned responses and it aims to make connections with the ideas and research of other academics by recognizing, building on, and expanding these ideas so that a communal interactive body of knowledge about a certain topic grows and develops.

CHAPTER SUMMARY

In this chapter, you have gained an understanding of what academic writing is by learning what academic writing, as a genre, is not. In doing the exercises, you might also have become aware of how you, as a writer, might have had misconceptions about writing in an academic context. You should have learned that academic writing is not similar to the genre-specific writing performed in high school, in journalism, or in advertising. You should also have learned that academic writing is not personal, emotional, convoluted, or creative, but, rather, clear, concise, and logical.

In the next chapter, you will formulate a clearer idea of what academic writing is, as a discipline-specific genre, by being introduced to and by practising some of the conventions and particularities of academic writing. Once you become aware of those, you will become a more successful university student and writer. Eventually, you will become well-versed and knowledgeable in your discipline and subject area, and you will feel empowered to act, write, and participate successfully as a member of the academic community. As an added bonus, learning will become more meaningful and, I hope, more enjoyable.

QUESTIONS FOR CONSIDERATION

1. Why is the new understanding of genre, and its attempt to include situation or context, important?
2. How does an emphasis on situation (including purpose and audience), content, and form (structure, grammar, or style) help you to understand what you need to do to become a successful academic writer?
3. How do you think an understanding of different real-world genres will help you to understand what academic writing is?
4. Does your writing conform to the common misconceptions about academic writing: Is it convoluted, creative, or based on high school or journalistic ideas about writing?
5. What is academic writing? In other words, can you list some of the conventions an academic writer might use?
6. What do you need to do to make your writing more academic?

2

Academic Writing as a Genre

LEARNING OBJECTIVES

In this chapter, you will learn:

◆ The importance of situation or context, content, organization, and grammar or style.

◆ What academic writing *is* by understanding some of the common conventions academics use when writing to other members of the academic community.

◆ What academic writing *is* by considering how these conventions and analytical frameworks differ across academic disciplines.

◆ To identify the common forms of essay writing: the expository essay, the persuasive essay, and the persuasive research essay.

According to Derek Soles in *The Essentials of Academic Writing*, an "academic essay is a written text, rarely fewer than 500 words or more than 5000 words in length, on a topic related to a course that is taught at school, college, or university" (6). It uses formal **standard English** and projects a logical reflective engagement with the issues at hand. While some essays you will write in academia are informative expository essays that are designed to teach the reader, most essays will be the critical persuasive kind. In these essays, you will be expected to make an argument about a topic that will change or deepen the reader's understanding of the topic or, possibly, encourage a course of action.

Although Soles's explanation is concise and useful, this chapter aims to provide you with more detail and information about what essay writing is in a general sense and in the academic disciplines in particular. Using common academic conventions and your understanding of situation, content, and form, introduced in chapter 1, I will first outline a list of rules and expectations for engaging in the genre of academic writing. Second, I will consider the common academic writing forms. Third, I will do a brief overview of writing in the academic disciplines.

Academic Writing: Rules, Expectations, Conventions

Like any genre, academic writing is informed by a number of rules, expectations, and conventions to which successful academic writers conform. Once you understand what these conventions are and are able to use them in your own writing, the process will become easier, and with time and practice you will become a more proficient and successful academic writer.

Academic Writing as a Knowledge-Making Activity

The first rule that the genre of academic writing demands is a focus on knowledge. As Janet Giltrow argues, academics are concerned with the "state of knowledge: its limits, the conditions under which it was produced, the positions from which statements issue" (197). By engaging with this knowledge, academic writers can establish a position of their own and in doing so contribute and add to the existing knowledge. Importantly, this knowledge must be contextualized in a formal objective exploration of a topic pertinent to the concerns of a specific academic discipline and its related methodologies—quantitative or qualitative research—forms—inductive or deductive structures—and conventions.

The Knowledge Gap

Regardless of discipline, in developing an analysis, academic writers' most important task is to expose the gaps and errors in existing knowledge and make an argument for what needs to be added. This new or revised knowledge is usually small and specific. For example, you might take issue with Joe Sheridan's privileging of oral culture, as Tyrell DaSilva did in his research essay (see chapter 10: Research Essay Writing), and find, as DaSilva did with his analysis of radio broadcasting, a technology or philosophy that challenges Sheridan's ideas. In doing this, you could focus on information that has been omitted or on the presentation of the argument (as Brook Biesenthal does in his critique of Catherine Schryer's essay (see chapter 7), or find information that might add to or deepen the argument, thus contributing to the existing knowledge (see Schryer's essay in the Reader to see how she contributes to Schön's argument). This knowledge gap can be found in the thesis statement, as an argument that will be proven, or in the hypothesis, as a suggested plausible argument that must be tested.

Situation or Context

Engaging with this knowledge demands that the writer develop a considered contextualized argument. This should take the following elements into consideration: the specific event(s) or situation(s) and the larger social, academic, historical, and cultural contexts that speak to a clearly defined time period and audience central to the specific argument. An awareness of situation means that the academic writer is aware of his or her own purpose for writing, the specific occasion or event and its relevance to the writing, and the audience to which the writing speaks. Established academics writing and working at an accredited university tend to write for colleagues who are in their specific discipline or who are already concerned with the issues presented. A first-year student should assume an intelligent or academic audience that has not read the works or issues being discussed.

Content

What academics mean when they talk about **content** is not only context but the knowledge they are engaging with or, more specifically, their topic or what they are discussing or analyzing. Central to content, then, is the establishment of a position, main argument, or **thesis statement** about the topic (why it is important to make the argument). This argument should articulate a considered, and contextualized opinion about a text. This opinion, however, must be fully and objectively contextualized in the knowledge about the topic. This means that you will be concerned not only with your own viewpoint or position but also with the clearly summarized and evaluated viewpoint or position of the writer or text you are engaging with.

That is why having a thesis statement or hypothesis is not enough on its own. To fully engage with the knowledge and opinions of other writers working on the same topic, you must support your analytical argument with **evidence**. This evidence might be taken directly from the primary text you are analyzing or from research material. Either way, it consists of facts, examples, and expert opinions that can support your assertions. When using evidence, there must be a clear logical relationship between your assertion and the supporting evidence. A knowledge of logical structure can be helpful in this respect. The use of a logically constructed argument and supporting evidence will help make your argument persuasive.

Form or Structure

In one sense, form refers to the genre you are working with, which in this case is the academic essay; in another sense, form refers to your ability to structure and organize your work effectively. Organization is essential to a clear articulation of your content: if you don't present your argument logically, in an organized fashion, your argument, quite simply, will not be clear.

On a basic level, you will need to consciously and carefully employ either a general **inductive** (specific statement to general **hypothesis**, usually seen in the sciences) or

ACADEMIC FOCUS

INDUCTION AND DEDUCTION

Induction: Mostly used in the social sciences and sciences.
reasoning from the specific to the general
specific hypothesis → larger implications

Example: As predicted, between June and August of 2007, real estate prices in Calgary and Edmonton dropped by 13 per cent. This collapse has preceded a general collapse in the real estate market.

Deduction: Mostly used in the humanities.
reasoning from the general to the specific.
general thesis statement → specific conclusions

Example: The Canada-wide real estate market collapse was preceded by specific global and provincial events.

deductive (general statement to specific thesis, usually used in the humanities) structure and reasoning. See chapter 3 for more detail on these methods.

Knowing how to use summary (see chapter 6), definition, and other **analytical patterns**, such as compare–contrast and classification and division, will help you develop your argument. These patterns, used to *analyze* and *organize* a work, help writers structure and organize their ideas to support and help develop their argument. Below is a description of **definition**, an analytical pattern that is crucial to all academic writing. See chapter 5 for a detailed description of more analytical patterns.

Definition

Definition is essential to academic writing in all disciplines and at all levels of writing. It allows writers to make their position clear by highlighting certain terms and bringing them into focus. This intent can be seen in the *Oxford English Dictionary* (OED), where the word is defined:

> The word define comes from the Latin *finire*, to limit or end, which itself comes from *finis*, boundary. To define something, then, is to establish limits, to make distinctions, to draw out-lines, to articulate boundaries. The function of a definition is to allow someone to distinguish the defined concept from all else. (317)

Definitions matter because they describe and identify concepts, which influence our perceptions and interpretations. As Janet Giltrow argues, "definition confirms common ground" between scholars who are writing on a particular subject (71). Consequently, definitions must support your precise use of the word in the context of your own argument. Because of this need for precision, dictionary definitions are often inadequate.

WAYS TO INCORPORATE SHORT DEFINITIONS INTO YOUR WORK

There are several ways you can include short definitions in your text. For example, you might use a sentence or two to define a particular concept or you might use a quotation, parenthesis, dashes, or non-restrictive clauses. Consider the following examples:

Quotation: As Mencken argues, "Democracy is the theory that the common people know what they want and deserve to get it good and hard" (qtd in Daziger 155).

Dashes: Democratic rule—a form of government that privileges equality and fraternity—does not in practice always address the needs of those in need.

Parenthesis: Democracy (government by the people for the people) is the dominant form of western government.

Commas: Democratic power, which is based on the division of interest and competition, has become increasingly complicit with consumerism.

As you might have noted, these examples illustrate different aspects of democratic rule, which is why it is crucial to find a definition that suits your purpose.

For example, you might need to find an expert in the area that you are studying and use the definition that he or she uses to support your argument. It is important to note therefore that within the academic community, definitions are always in process, being defined and redefined, as scholars find common ground or expand or diverge from definitions, according to their own particular arguments.

There are three different types of definitions:

- formal: stating a class to which the term belongs and then showing how it is distinct from all other members of that class (a chair is a piece of furniture (class) that seats one person (distinction))
- essential: defining something in terms of its essence
- operational: defining the use or function of the object or thing

You might need to use a more complete extended definition, containing both a precise formal definition and an extended version that gives a fuller sense of the concept. Definitions can be extended with the use of etymology, synonyms, examples, analogies, compare and contrast, process analysis, classification, and division. By defining and refining your definitions, you will be able to arrive at the definition that best suits your topic and argument. Consider the following example of an extended definition ("issues management") and how it has been defined and refined so that the writers of the article can eventually define the term as they wish to use it:

The process of addressing such issues has been labeled "issues management." . . . This process is conceptualized as a firm's identifying, analyzing, and responding to social and political concerns that can significantly affect it. . . . Ideally, issues management acts as an early warning system (Ansoff, 1980) through which firms anticipate the demands of or constraints imposed by various actors in their external environment, including legislators, regulatory agencies, public interest groups, and the media. In practice, however, issues management comprises both anticipatory responses and responses to crises when firms have been unable to anticipate and avert them.

We distinguish issues management from the broader "strategic issues management" referred to by Dutton and her colleagues (Dutton & Duncan, 1987; Dutton & Jackson, 1988). Those authors defined strategic issues as those perceived as having an effect on organizational objectives. We focused on corporate responses to social and political issues.

—Greening, D., and Gray, B., 467–98.

UNDERSTANDING DEFINITION

Exercise 2.1

1. Compare and contrast Carl L. Becker's and E.B. White's definitions of democracy (see pages 456 and 458 in the Reader). Can you identify the implied audience and the context (time, place etc.)?
2. Which definition, in your opinion, is more effective? Why?
3. Discuss your thoughts and analysis with your classmates.

WRITING DEFINITION

Exercise 2.2

1. Write a formal extended definition of a term that appeals to you or that you might be interested in using in a future essay. It should be a key term that not everyone is familiar with or that is used in a specialized way. Remember, an extended definition will use the formal definition, then employ any of the following: operational definition, etymology, description, a comparison with a similar term, examples, and discussions of context.
2. Begin by looking up the formal definition of the word you choose in a good dictionary (the *Oxford English Dictionary* is preferable), then develop the contextual aspect by searching an appropriate library database for essays that use the word in context.

Suggestions: You may wish to define "brand," "brand management," "brand identity," or "commodity" if you are writing a business paper; "First- or Third-Wave Feminism," in a paper on feminism; or "passive" or "active" euthanasia in a paper on euthanasia. Feel free to choose your own term, but ensure that it is a term worth defining.

More generally, you will need to make sure that your ideas are organized logically at both the sentence level and the paragraph level. That means organizing your words into clear grammatical sentences that move your argument forward by developing it point by point and making clear, logical connections between paragraphs (see chapter 6).

Grammar or Style

With respect to the last point about logical organization, you need to be particularly aware of the importance of grammar and style, especially on a last edit. When academics talk about grammar, they are talking about your ability to write grammatically correct sentences, using punctuation and language choices that convey clearly and logically what you want to communicate. When academics talk about style, they are referring to your ability to write sentences and use words that effectively express your ideas. For the experienced writer, style can thus imply exercising a certain latitude with grammatical rules.

However, there are some basic academic rules that should be adhered to:

- Use the first- and third-person point of view, but never use the second-person point of view (you, your).
- Use active voice, unless asked specifically to use the passive voice.
- Establish grammatically sound varied sentence structures.
- Use appropriate diction, avoiding jargon wherever possible and slang always unless you are quoting someone else. In other words, use formal standard English.

Formal Standard English

With the exception of some creative writing classes, academic writing uses formal standard English. That means that you must conform to the rules of correct English usage: you will need to use grammatically correct sentence structure, punctuation, and formal diction or language choices that convey clearly and logically what you want to communicate. Informal language, the type you might see in an advertisement, a journalistic piece (to varying degrees), or in a conversation with a friend, tends to use an informal and grammatically incorrect sentence structure (fragments are common), informal and often grammatically incorrect punctuation choices (exclamation marks, use of dashes and semicolons), colloquial or slang language, and a personal or subjective perspective.

Consider the following two sentences: one written using everyday language and one written using academic language.

You know Suzy needs her head examined, spending all night on that citation crap.

Smith disagrees with Suzy Marshall, who insists that citation is important.

The first informal sentence is not persuasive because it is too personal, using the personal pronoun "you," a clichéd metaphor ("needs her head examined"), and the slang and somewhat offensive colloquialism "crap." Its tone, resulting from its use of these offensive phrases, could be taken as a personal and direct attack on Suzy. The second sentence, however, does not use sensational words and clichéd phrases and remains objective and impartial. There are no offensive words and the verbs—"disagrees" and "insists"—are carefully chosen to accurately and impartially reflect the situation.

ACADEMIC SENTENCES

Use the sentence examples above as models of non-academic and academic writing and see if you can change the following colloquial and personal sentences into academic, objective, and authoritative sentences. Pay attention to your use of verbs, making sure that they are, if possible, academic.

> When I went to the doctor he told me that vitamin B12 is essential to good health.

> I heard that global warming is supposed to make the weather get warmer everywhere.

> So this lawyer that my mom went to said that child support is a right and she should apply for it.

Exercise 2.3

See the Exercise Answer Key in Appendix A for some possible answers to these questions.

Style

Taking this awareness of grammar further, you will need to be aware of the following stylistic conventions, familiar to academic writers.

Limiting Expressions

Academics use expressions, such as *seems, could, might, most, some, usually, generally, evidently* to indicate the limitations of their knowledge and to acknowledge the possibility of other interpretations. This convention prevents generalizations and respectfully opens up the subject to other academics who might agree or disagree with the statement.

Analytical Verbs

Academic writers do not use verbs that are sensationalistic or descriptive; their verbs tend to be informative and analytical, in keeping with the focus in the rest of their writing. Examples of these verbs include *analyses, posits, describes, suggests,* and *examines.*

Words such as *believes* and *thinks* are not as acceptable, since they imply a personal rather than an objective perspective. For a more complete listing, see analytical verbs in the focus box on academic reporting verbs on page 33.

Citation

Citation is "the attributing of a statement to another speaker" or writer (Giltrow 14).

By using citation, the writer can

- Take a position in relation to the ideas of other scholars, dialoguing with them about a specific topic.

- Identify him- or herself with other scholars who make similar arguments.
- Expose a gap or deficit in the knowledge.
- Construct new knowledge on the topic.

Citation methods vary according to discipline and will be further explained in chapter 11, "Documentation Style." For now, however, it is important to know that citations appear in the body of the text in parentheses and at the end of the text in a bibliography that documents the sources you have used in the essay.

Reporting Expressions or Signal Phrases

Academic writers use reporting expressions, also called signal phrases, to introduce (to signal) the words or quotations of others. Reporting expressions introduce the ideas of others by citing the quoted author and using an academic verb, such as *analyzes, discusses, describes, refers to, contends,* and *examines*, to introduce the quotation. For example, a writer might state:

> **Susan Smith discusses** Victorian rationality, and explains that . . .

> In *The History of Sexuality*, **Michel Foucault examines** how the confession has been used to oppress and repress human sexuality.

These expressions accurately summarize the document or idea, and point to studies or theories related to this knowledge, as well as larger contexts or issues.

Exercise 2.4

See the Exercise Answer Key in Appendix A for a sample revision. Compare your paragraph with this sample paragraph revision.

USING ACADEMIC STANDARDS AND CONVENTIONS

- Read the following excerpt of student writing.
- Rewrite it to conform to the academic standards of writing listed above. You can cut, add, replace, or move words around; however, when revising, it is best to keep your revisions as simple as possible.
- When you have finished your rewrite, compare your paragraph with those of your classmates. Can you help each other improve your paragraphs so that they more successfully appropriate an academic style?
- Observe whether the paragraphs get longer or shorter. Why do you think this is?

When entering the teaching profession, student teachers have to learn to be professional. There are standards you have to uphold because the children you'll be teaching are very impressionable. Some of these standards involve discipline in the classroom, including respect for the teacher and the other students in the class. There are also standards that can't be ignored, such as maintaining a high standard of work. When I was a student teacher, I told the children that they should be proud of themselves and their work. Being proud of the work you do is important.

ACADEMIC FOCUS

ACADEMIC REPORTING VERBS

Because it is repetitive and tedious to write (and read) "Johnston writes" or "Johnston says" over and over again, you will need to vary your use of academic verbs. The verbs you choose to use depend on the context you are using them in. You will need to make sure that they accurately reflect your intent and your reaction to the ideas of others. The chart below provides you with a list of common academic verbs and their possible contexts.

Table 2.1 ◆ Reporting Verbs

Context for using verbs	List of verbs that can be used in a specific context
Thesis/argument	posit, hypothesize, speculate, predict, argue, advocate
Analysis	analyze, examine, investigate, justify, measure, appraise, assess, calculate, debate, discuss, criticize
Acknowledgement of and/ or agreement with ideas/ statements (yours & others)	Acknowledge, attribute, observe, induce, state, attribute, explain, admit, concede, summarize, survey, assert, insist, concur, validate, agree
Describing/defining evidence and/or data	Describe, define, demonstrate, indicate, reflect, articulate, clarify, show, comprise, constitute
Expanding on ideas/ statements	Expand, elaborate, interpret, suggest, revise, propose, posit, predict, speculate, relate, infer
Emphasizing important points	Emphasize, stress, insist
Disagreeing with or questioning evidence	Disagree, question, criticize, disregard, negate, refute, measure, assess, calculate, appraise, classify, test, verify, reject, deny, dispute, challenge
Conclusions	Conclude, discover, infer, find, determine, propose, justify

Also, please note that verbs can be followed by prepositions, nouns, or the relative pronoun "that." Below is a short example of how this might look in an academic paper.

Verbs followed by prepositions: Smith defines X *as* Y; Smith compares X *to* Y; Smith critiques X *for* Y; Smith concurs *with* X; Smith accuses X *of* Y.

Verbs followed by nouns: Smith analyses *Weston's work*; Smith investigates *legal issues*; Smith validates *the study*.

Verbs followed by "that": Smith accepts *that*; Smith advocates *that*; Smith recognizes *that*.

Exercise 2.5

Check the conventions you have identified with my analysis of the passage in the Exercise Answer Key in Appendix A.

IDENTIFYING ACADEMIC CONVENTIONS

Identify the implied audience, any definitions, and academic writing conventions—academic verbs, reporting expression, limiting expressions, citation—in the following excerpt:

> Orientalism is never far from what Denys Hay has called the idea of Europe, a collective notion identifying "us" Europeans as against all "those" non-Europeans, and indeed it can be argued that the major component in European culture is precisely what made that culture hegemonic both in and outside Europe: the idea of European identity as a superior one in comparison with all the non-European peoples and cultures. There is in addition the **hegemony** of European ideas about the Orient, themselves reiterating European superiority over Oriental backwardness, usually overriding the possibility that a more independent, or more skeptical, thinker might have had different views on the matter.
>
> —Edward Said, *Orientalism* (7).

Introduction to Some Basic Academic-Writing Forms

Although, as the above example shows, clear concise writing and a thorough engagement with the existing knowledge is common to all academic disciplines, a shared understanding of the major academic essay forms is also common. These essays include the expository essay, the persuasive essay, and the research essay.

Expository Essay

The **expository essay** does not present readers with an argument or a personal opinion but objectively relays information to the reader. Its goal is to teach the reader. It contains a thesis or controlling idea, but the thesis is usually a matter of fact rather than a central argument about the topic or issue. An expository essay might, for example, explain how to do something, describe a process, or relay a series of significant facts as related to an autobiographical account or historical event. Usually, students are given a general topic, often called a prompt. A sample essay topic or prompt might ask students to explain a technical process. For example, a student might explain the process by which SAGD (steam-assisted gravity drainage), or fracking, is used in the Alberta oil sands to extract oil from the ground. Although research is usually required, expository essays differ from persuasive research essays in that they focus on the facts without

ACADEMIC FOCUS

EXPOSITORY ESSAY WRITING PROMPTS

- Explain the events leading up to the US Civil War.
- Research the life of a person you admire and outline the key points of his or her life.
- Explain how any engine or piece of machinery works.
- Describe the composition, function, and/or history of aspartame.
- Explain how to ride a horse or train any animal of your choice.
- Describe the development of feminism since the nineteenth century.

- Describe a major environmental problem and the efforts that have been made to address it.
- Discuss the causes of and problems resulting from teenage marijuana smoking.
- Explain the meaning of tolerance.
- Describe how you might go about recording your family's history and outline some of the questions you could ask of a significant older relative.
- Write an essay explaining the main issues about some aspect of global warming.

questioning their validity. In this way, the expository essay is closer to the summary or report than an essay that articulates a persuasive argument designed to change the reader's opinion.

Expository essays follow the same format as deductive essays: there is an introduction; a summary of the topic, text, event, action, or concept being examined; body paragraphs outlining one particular aspect of the topic; and a conclusion that summarizes the main points of the essay without repeating them, while pointing to the larger discussion of the topic.

What follows is a sample expository essay that has been written in response to the prompt "Describe the composition, function, and/or history of aspartame." The essay is a good example of writing executed by a student early in his or her academic career. You will note, however, that while this essay meets the summarizing requirements of an expository essay (summarizing the information about a topic and relaying it clearly and effectively to the reader), it does not meet the requirements of a persuasive essay, which demands an "original" argument, that is, an argument that attempts to persuade the reader to consider a certain perspective. The essay is annotated, which means that it includes critical comments designed to help you understand how an expository essay is developed and organized.

The Unethical Use and Legalization of Aspartame: Poisoning the People

BY DELANEY BLEWETT

Very good opening sentence: Delaney introduces aspartame.	**1** In 1965, James Schlatter, a Searle chemist, discovered aspartame accidentally when he was investigating a potential anti-ulcer drug (Murray n.pag). Searle began the necessary testing of aspartame to get approved as a zero calorie sweetener for dry goods by the FDA in 1967. Searle first applied for approval of aspartame in 1973, but was denied. (Aspartame was denied 8 times by the FDA). Researcher Ann Reynolds, who was hired by Searle to test the safety of aspartame, and neuroscientist Dr. John Olney, discovered that aspartic acid (a component of aspartame) causes holes in the brains of infant mice and recommended that more testing should be done before the FDA gave aspartame approval for use in foods and beverages. Dr. Martha Freeman, a scientist from the FDA Division of Metabolic and Endocrine Drug Products, also recommended that "until safety is proven, aspartame should be taken off the market" (Gold n.pag). Although aspartame has now been approved for consumption, it has not been scrutinized or thoroughly tested enough to guarantee its safety.

Good context: background history on aspartame.

Good introduction to health hazards of aspartame.

Thesis statement. In true expository form, Delaney highlights the main arguments around the issue.

2   Regardless of the researchers' concern about the safety of aspartame, it was approved for use in 1974, with the restriction that it be limited to use in dry goods only (Gold n.pag). In 1975, however, because of objections to the approval raised by Dr. Olney, the FDA created a task force of respected scientists to review Searle's testing methods. The leader of the task force, Philip Brodsky, said he "had never seen anything as bad as Searle's testing" and said results had been "manipulated" (Gold n.pag).

Summary of conflict over the legalization of aspartame.

Background information on FDA investigation

3   At the discovery of Searle's "misrepresenting findings and 'concealing material facts and making false statements' in aspartame safety tests" (Murray n.pag) and its manipulation of results, the FDA began its first ever "criminal investigation of a manufacturer" (Murray n.pag). In 1977, the FDA asked the US Attorney-General's office to start Grand Jury proceedings against Searle for "knowingly misrepresenting findings and concealing material facts and making false statements in aspartame safety" (Murray n.pag). During the investigation of aspartame, the Bressler Report was released. The report, which was directed by Jerome Bressler and assembled by FDA investigators, noted that

Good use of a long quote: note how it is indented and does not have quotation marks around it. A sentence or two after the quote would help contextualize it in the larger argument.

> 98 of the 196 animals died during one of Searle's studies and weren't autopsied until later dates, in some cases over one year after death. Many other errors and inconsistencies are noted. For example, a rat was reported alive, then dead, then alive, then dead again; a mass, a uterine polyp, and ovarian neoplasms were found in animals but not reported or diagnosed in Searle's reports. (Murray n.pag)

4   However, later in the year, the US attorney leading the investigation against Searle, Samuel Skinner, resigned from his position and withdrew from the case. His resignation delayed the investigation and caused the charges to run out, resulting in the investigation being dropped. A few months later, Samuel Skinner began working for Sidley & Austin, the firm that was representing Searle (Murray n.pag). Three years later, a review by the Public Board of Inquiry determined aspartame should not have been approved. The Public Board of Inquiry said it had "not been presented with proof of reasonable certainty that aspartame is safe for use as a food additive" (Murray n.pag). Although the FDA attempted to criminally investigate the testing of aspartame, aspartame remained legal for use in dry foods because the investigation was dropped and never re-opened, even though the Public Board of Inquiry had evidence that the investigation should continue.

> This paragraph highlights Searle's corruption in trying to get aspartame approved.

5   During the investigation in 1977, Searle hired a new CEO—Donald Rumsfeld, a "prominent Washington insider" (Murray n.pag), former Secretary of Defense under US President Gerald Ford, and later Secretary of Defense under President George W. Bush. Rumsfeld was able to bring in several of his associates from Washington to accompany him in top managerial positions. In 1981, during a sales meeting, Rumsfeld stated that "he was going to make a big push to get aspartame approved for all foods and beverages within the year" and that "he would use his political pull in Washington, rather than scientific means, to make sure it got approved" (Murray n.pag). In an attempt to maximize profit, Rumsfeld was not only an accomplice to illegally altering test lab results, but also promised to use his political power to persuade the FDA to approve aspartame, furthering the unethical actions taken by Searle.

> Good chronological development throughout this essay. This paragraph focuses on Rumsfeld's role in attempting to get aspartame approved.

6   Rumsfeld fulfilled this promise of using political muscle to get aspartame approved by the FDA (Hasselberger n.pag) when, later in the year, as a member of Ronald Regan's transition team, he handpicked the new FDA Commissioner, Arthur Hull Hayes. Hayes proved to be just as corrupt as Rumsfeld when he single-handedly approved aspartame for use in food and carbonated beverages. In a review of the issues raised by the Board of Public Inquiry during the investigation, three of six FDA scientists voted against the approval of aspartame on the grounds that "Searle tests are unreliable and not adequate to determine the safety of aspartame" (Murray n.pag). The National Soft Drink Association urged the FDA and Commissioner Hayes to delay the approval of aspartame in carbonated beverages until further testing on the safety of aspartame was completed. However, Hayes chose to disregard this advice, "overrule the Public Board of Inquiry, ignore the recommendations of his own internal FDA team" (Hasselberger n.pag), and approve aspartame for use in limited food and carbonated beverages.

> Once again, good evidence and development in this paragraph, which ends with the legalization of aspartame.

7   In 1983, Hayes left the FDA amid charges of impropriety; the Internal Department of Health and Human Services investigated him for accepting

gratuities from FDA-regulated companies (Murray n.pag). After he lost his job he went to work as a consultant for Searle's public relations firm. The FDA finally urged congress to prosecute Searle for giving the government false and incomplete test results (Gold n.pag), but the two government attorneys assigned to the case decided not to prosecute. Later, they went to work for the law firm that represented Searle. Despite ninety-two different recorded symptoms resulting from ingestion of aspartame, the FDA approved it for use without restriction in 1996 (Gold n.pag).

> Good paragraph transition to medical reasons and evidence as to why aspartame should not have been approved for public consumption.

8   Although legally aspartame is considered safe, the chemical constituents of aspartame have extremely negative effects on the neurological development of infants, and can cause severe damage and contribute to chronic illnesses in adults through long-time use. "Aspartame or its component parts . . . produce deleterious effects in sensitive animal species" (Simintzki et al. 2399). Phenylalanine, for example, may "play a role in the occurrence of developmental disorders" (Naudé 458) and has been shown to cause memory loss by deteriorating neurons in the brain (Mehl-Madrona n.pag). Clearly, aspartame is a "product with immense public health implications" (Santoro 4), and, as such, it should never have been approved for use in foods and beverages.

> Call for further testing, which is a very good, traditional academic strategy.

9   Aspartame should be put through scrutinized testing and "it is suggested that serious further testing and research be undertaken to eliminate any and all controversies surrounding this product" (Naudé 461). However, even though independent scientists have proved that aspartame is harmful, Searle has chosen to continue sales and distribution of aspartame, which is cleverly marketed as a zero calorie sweetener.

> Good conclusion: holds Searle ethically responsible for its practices and extends the argument to a consideration of other pharmaceutical companies and business in general.

10   Searle manipulated and dishonourably persuaded the FDA to approve aspartame through false test results and political persuasion that produced "conflicts . . . between the profit maximization objectives of pharmaceutical companies and the ethical requirements of scientific research and medicine, particularly in regard to safety concerns and the diseases that are targeted" (Santoro 3). Selling a product that causes such damage is immoral, and is evidence that companies such as Searle focus on "enormous industry profits" (Santoro 2) at the expense of the wellbeing of the public. In a world that is increasingly focused on economic advancement, ethical behavior has lost its value as the importance of profit has skyrocketed. Searle's company embraced these new business values of profit over ethical behavior when they chose to sell a product that causes such damage, ultimately choosing to poison people for profit.

WORKS CITED

Gold, Mark. "Scientific Abuse in Methanol/Formaldehyde Research Related to Aspartame." Web. 7 Apr. 2009.

Hasselberger, Sepp. "Aspartame: RICO Complaint Filed Against Nutrasweet, ADA, Monsanto." 17 Sep. 2004. Web. 12 Apr. 2009.

Mehl-Madrona, Lewis. "Autism: An overview and theories on its causes." 2005. Web. Apr. 2009.

Murray, Rich. "How Aspartame Became Legal—The Timeline." Dec. 2002. Web. 5 Apr. 2009.

Santoro, Michael A., Thomas M. Gorrie. "Ethics and the Pharmaceutical Industry." 28 Feb. 2006. Web. 7 Apr. 2009.

Simintzi, Irene, Kleopatara Schulpis, Panagoula Angelogianni, Charis Liapi. "The Effect of Aspartame Metabolites on the Suckling Rat Frontal Cortex Acetylcholinesterase: An In Vitro Study." *Food and Chemical Toxicity*. 45.12 (2007): 2397–401. Web. 15 Apr. 2009.

General comment about this essay: This is a very good expository essay. Delaney, the student writer, uses a very logical, chronological structure and does a good job of balancing history with an analysis of the harmful effects of the drug. Although Delaney uses a fair amount of research, her paper would be strengthened by using more academic research (as opposed to Web-based information and facts). Delaney's writing is clear, concise, grammatically correct, and logical.

Persuasive Essay

The persuasive essay is also known as an argumentative or critical essay. The thesis outlines a debatable main argument designed to alter the opinion of the reader and possibly encourage a change of view and/or course of action. A persuasive essay engages with a primary text that allows you, the writer, to use analysis and evidence to support the central argument and convince the reader that your argument is a valid one.

Analysis is a fundamental reasoning process in academic writing. When analyzing a subject, you generate knowledge about it through patterns of decomposition (breaking down the topic into its components) and re-composition (reassembling your ideas about the topic into a new argument or form of discussion). Persuasion organizes the information generated through analysis to convince your reader of your academic position.

The critical persuasive essay differs from the expository essay in that it does more than summarize the existing information about the topic. It considers a primary text that presents a particular perspective and then makes an argument in relation to that perspective. For example, an expository essay focusing on the general topic of the oil industry's technology SAGD (steam-assisted gravity drainage) and its relationship to the environment would summarize all of the existing arguments about the topic to try to represent the central argument to the reader. A critical persuasive essay, engaging with the same topic, might find a newspaper article on the issue and critique the way in

ACADEMIC FOCUS

SAMPLE PERSUASIVE ESSAY TOPICS

Please note that these topics are quite broad. You will need to refine and focus them to make them manageable.

- Analyze the objectivity of a newspaper or magazine article. Since even respected journalists have personal opinions, analyze how they offer personal opinions and/or reflect public opinion to shape the way they report the facts. This means you will have to read between the lines to determine the author's personal biases or opinions, and how these opinions affect the ways the article presents the facts.
- Analyze a speech given by a Canadian prime minister, a US president, or a presidential candidate. Is it or is it not effective and why?
- Analyze two contradictory interpretations of a historical event and make an argument for which interpretation is the more valid.
- A symbol is a word or an object that stands for another word or object. Authors use symbols to suggest hidden or deeper meanings that are not immediately evident to the reader. Look at how symbols are used in Joy Kogawa's *Obasan*. How are these symbols used repeatedly throughout the work to indicate a deeper or more complex meaning than is evident at first? How do these layers of meaning add to our understanding of the novel's major themes?

which the writer of the article represents the relationship between SAGD or the oil companies and the environment. In this way, the writer would find a space (a knowledge gap) within the argument made by the newspaper article writer to find and articulate his or her own argument.

Critical Persuasive Essay: Writing Process

When asked to write a critical persuasive essay, students often struggle precisely because they have to make an argument of their own. It is important that you read the work (the **primary text**, which is the work you are studying and writing about) closely and critically, and out of this reading develop a clear thesis statement or main argument that will structure your entire essay. A clear process for doing this work is essential to your essay-writing success. What follows is a step-by-step process for writing a critical persuasive essay:

1. Do a close reading of the text's thesis, concepts, and themes so that you can understand the argument and how it is constructed. Summarizing the gist, or

main points, or ideas that logically develop the argument, can be useful. You will need to look for repeated patterns, themes, or emphasized points as you make this gist outline. Think about what the writer is attempting to argue in establishing these repeated points or patterns.

2. Once you feel you have a good understanding of the text under consideration, the next step is to come up with a research question: a question about the text that intrigues you. You should state your research question explicitly. It might, for example, take the question above about Joy Kogawa's *Obasan* and ask the question about one repeated symbol or concept. The question might, at this stage, be as simple as, "What work does 'silence' achieve in this novel?" Develop this question by trying to answer it.

3. You will therefore need to analyze your primary text (*Obasan*, in this case), going through your work a second time to find and list all of the examples of evidence related to your research question (all the places where silence appears in the novel). This process helps you define and redefine the manageability and focus of your research question. You might see a pattern or central concern emerging in relation to this symbol or concept. This analysis should help you realize how and why the author is using this symbol or concept— to what end?—and enable you to come up with an argument of your own about it.

4. Rewrite this question so that you have a specific thesis statement or main argument. In the case above, you might write something like, "In *Obasan*, Joy Kogawa uses silence to emphasize the silence surrounding the treatment of the Japanese Canadians in World War II." You will then organize the information generated through your analysis by structuring the points and evidence (taken directly from *Obasan* in this case) in a way that best develops and supports your argument/thesis statement. Your structure will have an introduction, clearly defined body paragraphs, and a conclusion.

What follows is an example of a short persuasive essay. Note that the essay is focused less on summarizing the research on a particular topic (such as in an expository essay topic) than on performing a close critical reading of a text to persuade the reader to agree with the writer's perspective. This particular sample essay engages critically with the film *Evolution*, which is part of the Dove Real Beauty Campaign.

Before you read the student essay, it would be helpful to find the video on the Internet and watch it. However, you should not have to watch or read the primary text to understand the argument that is being made. As you are reading the student essay, try to decide if you agree or disagree with the main argument. Make sure you think about why you agree or disagree. The essay is annotated, which means that it includes critical comments designed to help you understand how a persuasive essay is developed and organized.

The Role of the Media in Defining Beauty: An Analysis of the Dove Film *Evolution*

BY DIANA LIM

"Beauty is bought by judgement of the eye"
—*Love's Labours Lost*, Act II, Sc 1.

Although this opening sentence is vague, it works because the following sentences define the term in more precise terms.

1   Beauty can be defined in many ways. It is a subjective quality "of excellence" that, as Shakespeare implies, depends on who is doing the judging. The definition of a beautiful person varies from society to society and changes over time. Nevertheless, because of the widespread influence of the media, North American society seems to have a specific notion about what it means for a woman to be beautiful. The media constantly bombards women with advertisements about what is beautiful and how to achieve it; fashion magazines, health magazines, and even celebrity gossip magazines are filled with stereotypical skinny, blonde, busty, "beautiful" models. As a result, women of all ages strive to reach this ideal by going on diets, colouring their hair, and constantly critiquing their own appearance. This intense self-criticism leads to severe issues with body image and self-esteem in women of all ages, especially young girls.

In a short essay the thesis statement is normally at the end of the first paragraph. However, Lim uses this paragraph to introduce the media's role in defining beauty.

Lim introduces her topic and primary text—the Dove film *Evolution* and summarizes the campaign and the film and then presents her thesis.

2   A recent film advertisement by Dove© Beauty Products strives to abolish this ideal and show that media advertising has distorted our perception of beauty. The film, called *Evolution*, is part of the Dove self-esteem fund called "Campaign for Real Beauty." This campaign is for women of all ages, but is specifically aimed at young girls. By showing that the current definition of beauty is based on an illusion designed to profit cosmetic companies, Dove hopes to end the stereotypes we have about beauty. The goal is to encourage women of all ages to redefine beauty and embrace their own natural beauty. The Dove film *Evolution*, uses classic methods of persuasion—ethos (credibility), pathos (emotion), and logo (reason)—to convince the audience that the media is responsible for distorting our perception of beauty and affecting women's mental health; however, a close analysis of the film reveals an element of self-interest that undermines Dove's argument.

This paragraph chronologically describes the film.

3   The film begins with a woman walking onto set and sitting in front of the camera. She faces the camera head-on with only her head and shoulders visible. She is a modest-looking woman, with no makeup and dishevelled hair. The lights switch on, and the film speeds up; soon her makeup is being applied, her hair is being styled, and a wind machine blows her hair. The photo is then edited extensively: her neck is elongated, her eyes and lips are enlarged, and her face is thinned. The edited image is translated on to a billboard advertisement on the street, and two young girls look at the advertisement as they walk by. This is followed by a line of text that states, "No wonder our perception of beauty is distorted."

4   Ethos is a form of persuasion that emphasizes the character or authority of the speaker. By establishing a good, or moral, character, the speaker becomes more credible to the audience and this lends support to the argument. In this case, Dove exerts itself as an expert on beauty even though this "Dove" film never explicitly states that Dove sells beauty products. It is assumed that Dove is an expert on beauty and so the message that they are trying to relay about beauty must be true. Although this appeal to authority could be used to lend support to the argument, it is also somewhat contradictory; Dove, as a beauty product company, clearly has a vested interest in how beauty is defined.

> The transition is abrupt, but this paragraph deals with the first point in Lim's thesis (ethos) and the appeal to authority. Note how the sentences in Lim's work build logically one after the other to develop her argument.

5   Pathos is an appeal to emotion. Pathos is used in many forms of expression (such as literature and music) to arouse emotion and persuade the audience. The emotion in this advertisement is created by the juxtaposition of the film and written narrative. There is very little written narrative, except for the title of the film at the beginning, and two lines of text at the end stating, "No wonder our perception of beauty is distorted" and "Take part in the Dove Real Beauty Workshops for Girls." The text itself presents a simple message; that beauty is stereotyped and distorted, and that Dove is trying to counter this through their workshops and, indirectly, their products. Both of these messages, though strong, are problematic because the references to "our" and "Real" are too general. While "our" is an indirect appeal to community, and a community of women in particular, the word "Real" is too vague to carry much weight.

> The next paragraph picks up Lim's second point (pathos). The analysis needs more development.

6   Another way that emotion is created in this film is through the use of music. There is a piano tune that plays throughout the clip. The base melody repeats the same rhythm throughout and has a steady tempo, but as the "evolution" of the model begins (as they begin to apply her makeup and style her hair) a beat with an increased tempo is introduced. As the transformation continues a complex melody overlays the beat and the base melody. The music is a hidden metaphor for the distortion. This is a clever way of invoking emotion because it is discreet and adds layers of emotions to the film.

> Second paragraph on pathos. This is a well-written, innovative argument.

7   Finally, the clip uses logos, an appeal to logic, in order to persuade the audience. The idea behind the film is to show viewers the truth about advertising; that is, to show them the process of making an advertisement, from start to finish. Although the film does appear to portray the bare truth, it is an overgeneralization. It would be incorrect to assume that because the advertisement shown in this film was modified, all advertisements are similarly modified. This film never reports any statistics or facts so there is virtually no concrete evidence presented in the film. What appears to be logos is, in fact, pathos. The technique of masquerading pathos as logos and making sweeping generalizations is utilized in advertising and presented as the truth.

> This paragraph addresses logos. Lim's point that logos needs evidence and facts is a good one.

8   Additionally, this film uses logic to imply that companies profit from the manipulation of beauty because we correlate beauty with success and happiness; companies take advantage of this by showing artificially beautiful people using their products. Moreover, the film implies that this type of advertising

> This paragraph on logos argues Lim's point about self-interest again, from the perspective of Dove's concern for vulnerable adolescent girls.

has a strong influence on adolescent girls who are particularly vulnerable to media advertisements (Clay, Vignoles, and Dittmar, 2005). This vulnerability is reflected at the very end of the clip when two young girls walk by the billboard advertisement and look at it. The film suggests that young girls are impressionable and will continue to strive for this ideal, without realizing that it is impossible to reach. While this logic is effective, it hides the fact that Dove is not only likely to edit their own advertisements, but also has motive to sell its own beauty products to women of all ages, including impressionable adolescents. These problems are easy to overlook because the film suggests Dove is working to change the definition of beauty.

> Lim's conclusion successfully sums up the entire argument without feeling like it is repeating the points. At the same time, it leaves us with something to think about (Dove's ethics).

9   This Dove film reveals that beauty shown in advertisements is an illusion. This film is powerful and persuasive because it contains the classic methods of persuasion. It has many elements of pathos in it, which make us want to believe it. However, it is not a very logically sound argument because the authority of the company is never directly established and there are no facts or evidence presented to bolster the argument. Nonetheless, the film does a good job of encouraging the audience to evaluate our current definition of beauty and its effects on women's self-esteem. Although there are some problems with how Dove is trying to change the perception of beauty, it seems to be a genuine attempt at eliminating false ideals and promoting positive body-image and self-esteem.

REFERENCES

Clay, D., Vignoles, V.L., & Dittmar, H. (2005). Body Image and Self-esteem Among Adolescent Girls: Testing the Influence of Sociocultural Factors. *Journal of Research on Adolescence, 15* (4), 451–77. Print.

Unilever. Dove Evolution of Beauty (2006). Video. Retrieved 10 January 2008 from http://www.campaignforrealbeauty.ca/dsef07/t5.aspx?id=7985.

General comment: This essay is a well-written and thoughtful exploration of Dove's film Evolution. *Lim successfully uses description and analysis, along with enough evidence from the film itself, to present a well-constructed and balanced essay.*

Exercise 2.6

EXPOSITORY VERSUS CRITICAL-PERSUASIVE ESSAY WRITING

- Reread the two annotated student essays (expository and critical-persuasive) in this chapter. Keep in mind that the expository essay and the critical persuasive essay serve different purposes.

- Answer the following questions (you might want to refer back to the list of academic conventions at the beginning of the chapter):
  1. Which essay do you think would be easier to write and why?
  2. While each essay engages in the state of knowledge on a specific topic, which essay is more in keeping with the demands of academic writing, in that it adds new knowledge to the topic? Provide evidence of this new knowledge.
  3. Compare the organizational structure of both essays: How do they use evidence differently in relation to the student's attempt to support their thesis statements?
  4. Find examples of first- and third-person point of view and compare this use with my use of second person (you) in the instructional parts and explanations in this text. Why do you think the second person might be acceptable in my writing and not acceptable in an academic essay?

See also chapter 8 for a more complete introduction to persuasive essay writing.

Research Essay

The persuasive research essay, often simply called the research essay, is an extension of the persuasive essay. It is based on an argument you have about a primary text, but it uses research from other researchers to support, refute, and elucidate your argument. Including research from other academics constitutes an acknowledgement that the topic under discussion speaks to a community of researchers interested in the same topic. The goal is not consensus—indeed, there is often significant disagreement among experts within a discipline—but rather the advancement of knowledge about the subject.

As an undergraduate student, your research will be qualitative or soft self-reflexive research. This means that rather than using a broad-based statistical study, you will be examining a few representative examples, looking for what Janet Giltrow calls "patterns and regularities" in the research to find your own position and specific argument in relation to the research topic examples (201).

Using the sample argument topic of SAGD from the persuasive essay, the research you would be involved in would be qualitative in that you would be looking at one instance of a much broader situation and using an analytical framework to interpret the information you have at hand. You might use research from environmentalists to support your argument or you might use research that focuses on the SAGD process itself. By refuting parts of opposing arguments and adopting other parts that support your original and contextualized thesis, you establish your position and take your place as a contributor to the academic conversation.

See chapter 3 for a more extensive comparison of qualitative and quantitative research.

An example of a persuasive research essay can be found in chapter 10, "Research Writing." Below, I have included two research essay introductory paragraphs and an exercise that will help you to analyze how the writers use persuasion and research.

Exercise 2.7

RESEARCH WRITING

Analyze the effectiveness of the following student research essay introductory paragraphs by answering the following questions:

1. Highlight the topic, the context related to the topic, and the main argument.
2. Identify where these research essay introductions summarize the existing knowledge but then say something "new" about it. Write a summary sentence explaining concisely what these essays will analyze and why this analysis is important.
3. How do these excerpts use research? In other words, what references are they using and what points or ideas are the research references summarizing, supporting, or calling into question?

INTRODUCTION I

Adolf Hitler and Winston Churchill are two of modern history's most famous political leaders and orators. When describing the orating abilities of Churchill, Mieder remarks that "neither friend nor foe . . . can deny that he was a master of rhetoric" (58). In 1932, journalist Scheffer describes Hitler as "the most successful orator that Germany has ever possessed" and continues by describing what it is like to witness him speak: "It is an interesting and a stirring experience to listen to Hitler—his bitterest enemies have often fallen under his spell." This paper will compare Adolf Hitler's speech given in Munich on February 24, 1941, and Winston Churchill's famous "House of Many Mansions" speech given from London on January 20, 1940. An analysis of the rhetorical devices used by both Churchill and Hitler will reveal how the rhetorical tools used in politics transcend different cultural and political backgrounds.

INTRODUCTION II

See the Exercise Answer Key in Appendix A for possible answers to these questions.

Indigenous cultures are in crisis today because of the devastating effects of colonialization on their tribal ways of life. The resulting poverty and genocide constitute an unfortunate period in Canadian history. Non-Native Canadians must assist in decolonization for the good of all Canadians. A first step toward healing is in exploratory dialogue between all Canadians, Indigenous and non-Indigenous. This essay will closely examine how Dr. Betty Bastien in her autobiography *Blackfoot: Ways of Knowing* draws scholars and lay people alike into a closer understanding of Blackfoot culture by subtly using a combination of Blackfoot and English languages. An examination of where and how Bastien uses Blackfoot language suggests that Bastien believes that Blackfoot knowledge may heal this colonizing rift in Canadian society.

EXPOSITORY AND PERSUASIVE RESEARCH ESSAYS

Exercise 2.8

Expository essays are often confused with persuasive research essays. An expository essay summarizes material that is already known. A persuasive research essay presents a new argument related to the existing research: it might add to the existing knowledge or call the existing knowledge into question.

Below are two introductory paragraphs, one taken from a student research essay and one from a student expository research essay.

- Can you identify which essay is an argumentative research essay and which essay, although it uses research, is an expository essay?
- In a short paragraph, provide reasons for your answers, then compare your paragraph with that of your classmates. Be prepared to defend your reasons.

INTRODUCTION I

The youth "Fit for Life Protocol," documented by Annesi, Tennant, Westcott, Faigenbaum, and Smith (2009), was an after-school program conducted at a YMCA in Calgary, Alberta. The purpose of the program was to see if an education and training in nutrition and physical fitness would be effective in changing behavior, habits and physiology. The study successfully showed significant improvement in each area. Information of the benefits received from proper exercise and nutrition is widely available. However, youth are not educated properly in these areas. The Fit for Life Protocol has been used to educate children about correct health habits and has had successful results. This paper will examine the importance of proper exercise and diet in maintaining health and preventing obesity in youth and adolescents and show how The Fit for Life Protocol in schools could be a solution to the rising health problems in youth.

INTRODUCTION II

The word "freak" has become a common word in the language of the twenty-first century. This word is commonly applied to individuals who possess uncommon characteristics that negatively set the individual apart from society (Garland-Thompson, 2008). In the movie *Spider-Man*, the main character, Peter Parker, who is a scientifically inclined, awkward high-school student, is considered a "freak," which is made worse when Peter suffers a bite from a genetically modified "super spider" (Raimi, Bryce & Ziskin, 2002). Throughout the movie, it is possible to see how language is able to create a "freak" form of life, and how this "freak" is perceived by other characters, and society as a whole. Indeed Peter Parker's self-perceptions, along with the perceptions of others, exemplify how language works with the imagination to create, in Wittgenstein's terms, socially constructed meanings and norms that, in turn, negatively label individuals as social Others.

See the Exercise Answer Key in Appendix A for a summary of this comparison.

It is important to remember that the forms above, in the persuasive research essay in particular, require that writers acknowledge the source of any information they are using both in the body of the essay and again at the end. The most typical document-ation styles used include the Modern Language Association (MLA) and the American Psychological Association (APA), although there are many others. Check with your pro-fessor to ensure you are using the required standard. See chapter 11 for more specific information on citation.

Writing in the Academic Disciplines

Sometimes, what makes academic writing difficult is that while it can be taught as a genre that includes conventions shared among all academic disciplines (commonly called writing across the curriculum or WAC), it is also a genre that addresses the differ-ences between academic disciplines (writing in the disciplines or WID). In other words, whereas many of the conventions and forms of writing specific to academia apply to all of the disciplines, each discipline—for example, psychology, biological science, English, history, social work, or education—takes different approaches to topics and uses differ-ent conventions and forms of writing to reflect this.

Each of these differing approaches includes **commonplaces** that are recognizable and familiar to the *insiders*—those familiar with the writing conventions specific to their discipline—of each academic community. If you are going to be successful in your dis-cipline and in courses that you take in other disciplines, it is important to develop an awareness not only of the shared academic conventions but also of the conventions that are specific to your discipline. An understanding of these discipline-specific conven-tions will alleviate any concerns you might have about correct form, terminology, and stylistic conventions and help you to adapt to the demands of your particular university so you can communicate effectively within your discipline.

Discipline-Specific Frameworks or Approaches to the Material

To understand the discipline-specific nature of academic writing, it is important to first understand that different academic disciplines take different approaches to topics and establish different analytical frameworks. For example, disability as a broad topic is addressed differently by the different disciplines: political science might look at policy issues; economics might look at income distribution for people with disabilities; history might consider the contributions of major historical figures who lived with physical disabilities; English might examine writing by authors who have cognitive disabilities, asking how this writing reflects their self-identity; and philosophy might consider the ethics of institutionalizing people with disabilities by considering philosophical theor-ies, such as contractarianism or utilitarianism.

Discipline-Specific Writing Conventions

As previously stated, when approaching a topic, each of the disciplines, such as the social sciences, the sciences, the humanities, and business, use different conventions and forms of writing. Below, I have provided a brief introduction to the types, conventions, and forms of writing you might find in the following broadly categorized disciplines.

Social Sciences

This category includes sociology, education, anthropology, cultural studies, economics, political science, and psychology. You might write in the third person, but as a result of the current call for "responsibility" and "accountability" about controversial issues such as global warming, there is a growing tendency to use the first person. A social sciences writer might use jargon specific to his or her discipline, headings and subheadings, graphs, charts, and illustrations.

In terms of form, the social sciences writer typically uses an **abstract**—a one-paragraph summary presented at the beginning of the essay—an American Psychological Association (APA) citation, a literature review, a case study, an expository essay, and a persuasive research essay.

A **literature review**, which is often required in science courses as well, is a summary of the current state of knowledge on a topic. You might be asked to write a literature review that functions as a stand-alone assignment for a course, or you might write a review that is part of a larger assignment, such as a thesis or dissertation. When writing a review, your perspective will be determined by the focus of your research.

A **case study** is a form of qualitative research that involves a close examination of an individual or a small group of people according to pre-established criteria, a research question, and a specific context. It often includes accounts of the subjects themselves, which are carefully described and analyzed.

Humanities

This category includes the fine arts, history, languages, literature, philosophy, and religion. Because the writing is more idea-based (as opposed to fact-based), the sentences tend to be more complex, using a variety of sentence lengths and forms that reflect the complexity of the ideas presented. There may or may not be headings or subheadings. The most common documentation style is MLA, but history usually uses the *Chicago Manual of Style* (CMS). If you are studying courses in the humanities, you might be asked to write summary, expository, persuasive, and research essays. If you are taking a creative-writing course in an English class, you might also be required to write creative non-fiction essays, short stories, poems, or plays.

Please see chapter 3 for a full development of humanities writing practices.

Sciences

This category includes astronomy, biology, chemistry, computer science, geography, and physics, among others. Because the writing is fact-based (rather than idea-based), the sentences are typically short and to the point. Headings and subheadings are also often used for clarity. Third-person point of view is often used in the sciences, although, once again, there is a move toward the use of the first person. People working in the sciences use a variety of citation systems, such as the Council of Science Editors (CSE), formerly the Council of Biology Editors, so check with your professor to ensure you are writing to his/her specifications.

The most common sub-genre in science is the academic journal article, which includes an *introduction* to the topic, the experimental *methodology*, the *results*, and the *discussion* (IMRAD). Most typically, an abstract will precede the body of the article, highlighting the study's purpose, methodology, major findings, and future implications. Other science genres include the book chapter, the literature review, and the critique (10).

Lab reports are assignments common to all laboratory courses. They involve documenting the methodological parameters of your experiment, explaining what you learned from the experiment, and discussing the larger significance of the results. The format for a lab report often involves the following sections: introduction/hypothesis, materials, methods, data, results, analysis, and conclusions.

Please see chapter 4 for a full development of writing in the sciences.

Business

This category includes accounting, finance, human resources, management, and marketing. This style of writing is influenced by both the academic context and a larger, more general, audience or context. Business writing geared to the general public might thus be less formal than business writing for an expert in the field. As an example, an essay on advertising for a university class might demand formal language and conventional academic structures, while advertising copy written for a general audience might apply different conventions more suitable to the genre by using more emphatic language, fragments, and exclamation marks. If you are in business, you might use MLA or APA documentation and use the following forms: essays, prospectuses, business letters, and annual reports.

Go to www.oupcanada.com/Hayward to view the online chapter on business and technical writing.

Exercise 2.9

ACADEMIC WRITING

Freewriting, a writing technique established by Peter Elbow, is a low-stakes prewriting exercise that allows you to use stream of consciousness writing to tap into what you know or don't know about a topic. When freewriting, it is important to forget about the rules and conventions of writing and simply write continuously, without stopping to think about what you should write next or wondering how to spell something.

- Take two minutes and freewrite about what you know and still need to know about academic writing as a genre.

- If it helps, you can use the following sentence starters: "What I know for sure about academic writing is . . ." and / or "What I still don't understand about academic writing is . . ."
- When you have finished this exercise, compare your notes with the material you have studied in this chapter or discuss your responses with your instructor and with members of your class in a large- or small-group setting.

CHAPTER SUMMARY

After reading this chapter, you should be developing a clearer idea of what academic writing is. You should also be starting to understand that academic writing, as opposed to, say, journalistic writing or high school writing, is something you *can* learn. By learning some of the conventions, you will be better able to participate in a community of scholars who are communicating about similar ideas and concepts. Rest assured, however, that as a first-year undergraduate student, you will not be expected to write to the same level as a fourth-year university student, a graduate student, or a tenure-track professor; you will, however, be expected to be able to write as a first-year undergraduate student who understands the forms and conventions of academic writing. In other words, the expectations for each level of writing are contingent upon your knowledge base and your understanding of the conventions that academic writing typically employs.

It is important to remember, then, that learning how to write in academia is a process. The first time you rode a bicycle or tried skiing, you didn't do it well; it took a lot of patience and practice. You will make many mistakes, but if you learn the conventions and expectations demanded of you as an academic writer, as outlined in this book, your writing will improve and with it your confidence and competency as an initiate of the academic community.

QUESTIONS FOR CONSIDERATION

1. Why is it important to understand some broad definitions of academic writing conventions?
2. How does an understanding of situation or context, content, and form (organization and grammar) help you to understand how you might use and apply these conventions?
3. What are the main differences between expository and persuasive writing? Why is it important to understand what these differences are?
4. Why is it important to consider how these common academic conventions might or might not apply to a discipline-specific writing assignment?
5. How might you go about making sure that you use these academic conventions in your own academic writing assignments?

3

Writing for the Humanities and Social Sciences

LEARNING OBJECTIVES

In this chapter, you will learn:

◆ The discipline-specific subjects and courses related to the humanities and social sciences.

◆ A brief history of the social sciences and humanities with a specific focus on English.

◆ How to design and write a social sciences essay, which will include an overview of some basic design systems and instructions for writing a report.

◆ The difference between qualitative and quantitative research.

◆ How to write a humanities essay with a specific focus on the conventions, style, and different forms related to literary essay writing.

The social sciences and the humanities study the human condition in all of its cultural and communicative practices, and, according to Canada's Social Sciences and Humanities Research Council, "raise profound questions about who we are as human beings," at the same time as they "enhance our understanding of modern social, cultural, technological, environmental, economic and wellness issues" (n.pag.). Where these disciplines differ is in the methods they use: humanities-based methodologies are primarily **qualitative** and speculative; that is, the method used involves analyzing in depth a subjective and descriptive fictional or self-report, such as diaries, interviews, case studies, literature, and art. Traditionally, a social sciences methodology would use objective observation, experimentation, and fact-based or **quantitative** approaches to analysis and research.

However, according to Patricia Leavy and many other scholars, this divide is artificial (2). Artistic (qualitative) and scientific (quantitative) theory have many points of connection, and in practice they are not exclusive. Social science researchers are increasingly challenging traditional methods, which are grounded in "hard science," with qualitative arts-based projects, to establish what Leavy calls a "holistic, integrated perspective" (2). In her book *Method Meets Art: Arts-Based Research Practice*, Leavy states that art, and by extension literature, works to provide a critique of these contexts by "promoting reflection, building empathetic connections, forming coalitions, challenging stereotypes, and fostering social action" (255). In this way, a researcher in the social sciences might use the "resistive potential of art" to enhance a quantitative study, bringing depth and context to it (256).

Similarly, researchers in the humanities, whose focus is primarily qualitative, have struggled to find ways to quantify the work they do. For example, in "The Function of Criticism at the Present Time," Northrop Frye stresses the importance of ordering and documenting literary works, which often appear "as a huge aggregate or miscellaneous pile of creative efforts," with no organizing principle and no clearly defined relationship to the culture that gives rise to them (44). For Frye, "it should be possible to get a clearer and more systematic comprehension of what [criticism] is doing" (39) by using a more quantitative approach. Frye argues that if humanities scholars were to adopt the methods used by social science scholars, they would be able to routinely classify and organize their material into objective "disinterested" categories that would enable literary works to be better understood and, maybe more important, better valued (35).

Although what follows might be taken as an attempt to outline some of the key features of social science– and humanities-based writing, it must be kept in mind that, in some ways, it might be more useful to consider the points of connection between these disciplines.

The Social Sciences

The social sciences are concerned with the relationship between individuals and society, and include sociology, anthropology, economics, political science, education, psychology, geography, and communication studies. Often the research is cross-disciplinary, involving collaboration between different disciplines. Similarly, social scientists will often use a combination of both positivist empirical research and interpretive critical studies. Methods include case studies, interviews, participant observation, surveys, and interviews.

A Brief History of the Development of the Social Sciences

Although the social sciences have a long and often contentious history, dating back to before the Renaissance and its privileging of scientific thought, it was first conceived as a discipline in the nineteenth century by William Thompson, who coined the term "social science" in 1824. At first associated primarily with sociology, in the nineteenth and twentieth centuries social sciences became an umbrella term for disciplines such as sociology, social work, psychology, law, and economics. The purpose of these disciplines was the objective and standardized analysis of human nature as it appears in relation to society and culture. Key figures include Émile Durkheim, Karl Marx, Max Weber, and, more recently, Karl Popper and Talcott Parsons. Today the social sciences value a quantitative methodology and a focus on empirical data and statistical evidence and analysis; however, as previously stated, these boundaries are being blurred by interdisciplinary projects that often involve qualitative research.

Writing for the Social Sciences

Although the social sciences include a variety of disciplines, all of which take an individual approach to research methodology and language use, this section will provide a general introduction to the traditional methodologies, practices, and research basic to good social science writing.

General Expectations

In a university or college setting, your writing will, necessarily, be assignment-driven and thus require that you meet a set of standards and expectations. Do not risk losing marks by not accurately reading the assignment requirements or by simply meeting the minimum requirements. Also, do not assume that your instructor has read the text that you are engaging with. You will need to provide, simply and clearly, the necessary context, summaries, descriptions, and detail to make the text clear to an intelligent reader who has not read the material at hand.

To write a good social science essay, you will also need to think about your purpose, which is always about the knowledge and your considered hypothesis about it (content). Moreover, you need to remember when writing for any course in the social sciences that your audience is an academic reader, who is informed in and conversant with the discipline of the social sciences.

Language Use

As in any discipline, writing in the social sciences requires you to write logically and clearly, keeping your writing concise and objective.

As a result, your sentences will probably be shorter, more direct, and more factually driven than an essay you might write for the humanities, but keep in mind that you will still need some sentence variety. Consider the following comparison of a sentence written for a humanities discipline and a sentence written for the social sciences.

Humanities sentence:

The conclusion to be drawn, however, is not that focusing on forms is irrelevant to the act of composing, but that the focus one finds in the grammar books is on the worn forms, on forms detached from the underlying form that must be in place before any technical terms can be meaningful or alive. (Fish 15)

As you have probably noted, this sentence is quite long. This is because the writer is engaged with concepts rather than facts. At issue here is the representation and teaching of forms. Because Stanley Fish, the author, is trying to get his reader to think about these questions of form, he uses a compound–complex sentence with independent and dependent clauses, and a "not this, but this" structure that encourages the reader to develop his or her own reflective opinion.

Social science sentences:

This manual is written for the individual responsible for choosing the passing score on an educational or occupational test. It concentrates on practical advice to help select and apply a method for choosing the passing score. Decisions, standards, and judgments are defined and discussed in terms of considerations in choosing a passing score method. Three how-to-do-it sections discuss methods based on judgments about (1) test questions, (2) individual test-takers, and (3) groups of test-takers. (Livingston and Zeiky, 1982)

As you can see, there are four sentences here, all of which are simple (subject–verb–object) sentences. They are taken from the abstract of an educational manual titled *Passing Scores: A Manual for Setting Standards of Performance on Educational and Occupational Tests*. The simple sentences focus the reader's attention not on arriving at his or her own conclusions or engaging with the conclusions of the author, but on understanding the facts, which are directly, clearly, and simply laid out.

Your choice of language for the social sciences will need to be precise, informative, and formal. You should avoid slang words and colloquialisms and focus on clearly articulating what you need to impress upon the reader. Never use contractions (can't for cannot), abbreviations (ad for advertisement), or exclamation marks, and avoid the use of adjectives and adverbs unless the reader absolutely needs to know the detail referenced by them. For example, do not tell the reader that the *car is yellow* (adjective) or that the *boy ran quickly* (adverb), unless it is essential that your reader know this detail.

Point of View

One question that students always seem to ask is whether or not they should use first or third person. It is probably wise to ask your instructor. Whereas the third person tends to be more neutral than the first person, there is a general move to using the first-person point of view across all the disciplines. However, if you use first person, you need to use it consistently and avoid falling into the trap of getting too personal. To say, *I think* or *I believe* is ineffective. You need to continue to use academic verbs, such as *I examine* or *I posit*, and to support your point with evidence and analysis.

Passive or Active Voice?

One of the dangers of using third person is that you will use passive voice. While there are sometimes uses for passive voice, most of the time you will need to keep the voice active (active voice). This means that you need to use the subject–verb–object sentence construction. For example, using active voice, you might write *theorists analyze genre-theory research*. This sentence highlights exactly *who* is performing the research. When you are using passive voice, the sentence structure hides the subject performing the action and takes the object as the subject of the sentence, as in the following revision of the above example: *genre theory research is analyzed by theorists*. In this sentence, *genre theory* becomes the subject of the sentence, and *theorists*, the people responsible for the research, are secondary. See more on active and passive voice in chapter 4.

Citation

Citation, as previously stated, is essential to academic writing. The social sciences usually use APA (American Psychological Association) citation methods. This is because APA citation conforms to the factual and informative emphasis expected of a social science discipline. APA provides this information in the body of the text and at the end of the essay in a reference page. See chapter 11, "Documentation Style," for more information.

Design

Good design, a term that can be related to form or organization, is fundamental to good research. Because your aim in writing a social science essay is to persuade, good design involves planning a project in advance so that your paper will be a well-argued, clear analysis of a question you want answered. Consequently, you will need to make sure that the problem or question you want answered is worth answering and specific enough in focus to be manageable.

Inductive reasoning is the structure used in the social sciences. That means that the material is organized from a specific hypothesis, which makes a claim about a specific issue or case, to a general statement or conclusion about the research at hand. Valid inductive reasoning must be based on the inclusion of reliable evidence and an accurate representation of the larger situation and cultural context. The general format for an inductive essay is as follows:

- introduction (including hypothesis)
- discussion
- conclusion
- recommendations

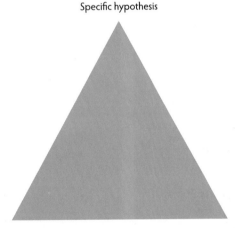

Specific hypothesis

General conclusion

Figure 3.1 ◆ General Format for Inductive Essays

When planning and writing, you will also need to keep in mind that good research is **well-triangulated**, in an inductive sense, throughout your entire essay. That is, you will need to ensure that your use of evidence, assertions, and interpretations follows an inductive structure, working from the specifics of an argument to a general conclusion.

To support this structure, your paragraphs need to logically develop your hypothesis by presenting your discussion, evidence, and conclusions in a logical, ordered fashion. The general rule is one topic or one element of a topic per paragraph. The social sciences use headings and subheadings to make the logic clearer and easier to read.

Quantitative versus Qualitative Research

A basic understanding of quantitative and qualitative research will help you to understand how academics engage with the knowledge of their particular discipline and, indirectly, with other members of the academic community. Although much of your research as an undergraduate student will be qualitative, you will spend a significant part of your time learning established methods and techniques for quantitative study. What follows is an overview of these basic academic methods.

Qualitative Research

Qualitative research is characterized by human perception and understanding, as well as interpretation and skepticism. It is also empirical or experiential; it relies on the observations of participants, and is situational, organized around a specific event, context, place, and time. While qualitative research can stand on its own as a research method, it is also interwoven in quantitative research as well. In many ways, all scientific thinking involves both quantitative and qualitative thinking.

However, qualitative research from a social sciences perspective specifically analyzes real-life situations, compares them, or reads them in relation to other situations, relationships, contexts, or theories and then reconceives them in relation to the argument that has been made and the support garnered for the argument. These cases are usually single-case studies (or case studies that involve only a few people) that are descriptive and inductive.

It is important to remember, then, that as a qualitative researcher, you will always have to make well-informed strategic choices about what argument you are going to make and what evidence and theory you will use to support that argument. In making these choices, you will be contributing to the knowledge on the topic.

There are many types of qualitative research: ethnographic, naturalistic, phenomenological, hermeneutic, and holistic. When performing either a microanalysis (situational or personal interpretation) or a macroanalysis (large studies that make interpretations at the cultural, national, or even global level), it is important to have an ethical awareness of real-life people and situations, and empathetic research and handling of a subject can help this particular problem. An awareness of individual experience (when you are concerned with the particulars of a particular person or experience) versus collective knowledge can also help you avoid making generalizing assumptions.

The main weakness of qualitative research is that it is subjective. This might open up the researcher to certain biases. If the researcher is unable to render an objective assessment, the validity of the project might be jeopardized.

Quantitative Research

Science explains how things work, across a broad range of systems, such as solar, biological, and cultural systems. As a result, a great deal of social science research is of the survey variety, where you will be quantitatively examining the relationship between measurable variables, using questionnaire or interview data, linear attributes, measurements, and statistical analysis. Quantitative researchers use a variety of methods that vary according to discipline and the specific requirements of the experiment. In general, quantitative researchers perform comparison and correlational studies, combining experimentation with an analysis of the contributing conditions and the changes involved in these conditions.

Quantitative research attempts to analyze a broad range of samples objectively by setting aside biases caused by the researcher's beliefs and background and by controlling the conditions under which the studies or experiments are performed. For example, researchers might compare the results of and conditions around standardized tests in mathematics across a number of different countries. To control the study, they might limit it to a specific grade level and to a comparison of teaching systems, content, skill levels, and concepts. In narrowing the study in this way, the researchers might hope to provide an objective account of the current national standards and, at the same time, suggest some solutions for how these standards might be improved.

The data in an experiment such as this might, at first, appear overwhelming. However, if you read a research report or article based on quantitative data, it is important not to be intimidated by the charts, graphs, tables, and measurements because the information is usually broken down and analyzed for you in the accompanying report. These measurements simply provide you with a condensed picture of the data. As a new researcher to your field, it would be wise to try to consider these data as a researcher would, through objective eyes. Below is an example of a questionnaire, which is one of the techniques for garnering quantitative data.

Quantitative research, while thorough, is often accused of being too objective, verification-oriented, and reductionist, avoiding the complexities of real life and real people in preference to a required outcome and reliable, "hard," and replicable data (see Table 3.1).

Reading Survey

Please complete the following questionnaire by circling the appropriate responses. This research is conducted on an anonymous basis, so please do not include your name or any identifying information. Thank you for your assistance.

1.	What gender are you?	Male		Female	
2.	What age category do you fall into?	Under 25	26–35	36–45	46–66	56–65
3.	Do you have post-secondary education?	None	University: undergraduate	University: graduate	College diploma	
4.	How many books do you read a month on average?	0	1–2	3–6	7–10	10+
5.	What genre do you mostly read?	Romance	Drama	Poetry	Science fiction	
		Autobiography	Horror	Short story	Historical fiction	
		Fantasy	Crime	Children's literature	Other	
6.	How often do you challenge yourself to read outside of your comfort zone?	Never		Occasionally	Often	
7.	Do you prefer to read one book at a time or several at once?	One			Several at once	
8.	Approximately how many books do you have on your shelf at home?	0–20	21–40	41–60	61–80	81–100
9.	Do you use a library?	Yes			No	
10.	Do you belong to a book club?	Yes			No	
11.	Do you use an e-reader?	Yes, all the time		Yes, sometimes	No	
12.	Does your job involve reading?	Yes, a small amount		Yes, extensively	No	

Figure 3.2 ◆ Reading Survey

Table 3.1 ◆ Qualitative versus Quantitative Evaluation

Qualitative Evaluation	Quantitative Evaluation
Inductive approach to gathering data, interpreting, and organizing report.	Inductive approach to researching hypotheses that are tested in the evaluation.
The researcher measures and evaluates the lived experience of research subjects.	Emphasis on measurement process and procedures that lend themselves to numerical representations of variables.
Use of case studies, autobiographies, poetry, and other forms of literature.	Finding patterns in data that either corroborate or disconfirm the original hypotheses.
	Representative samples of involved parties are large enough to wield sufficient statistical power and, thereby, make the experiment reliable and valid.
Holistic naturalist approach (does not manipulate the setting).	Evaluator control and ability to manipulate the setting.

Variables

One term you will need to understand when working with quantitative data and writing in the social sciences is a **variable**, a characteristic or condition that can change from one person or situation to another. There are several kinds of variables. An independent variable is a variable that is not dependent on the variation or change in another variable. A dependent variable is a variable that is altered by changes made to another variable. An intervening variable is a causal variable that explains the changes in a dependent variable. A conditioning variable is a variable that determines the conditions, positive or negative, that an independent variable might have on a dependent variable. Independent variables can be considered *causes* whereas dependent variables refer to *effects*.

For example, if asked to write an essay analyzing consumerism as a morally suspect force in Canada today, you might decide that one independent variable or cause might be the extensive television, newspaper, and Internet advertising methods that encourage us to consume a plethora of products. A dependent variable might look closely at who is consuming (age group, gender, location) as a way of looking at how a certain group is affected by this advertising.

Exercise 3.1

QUESTIONNAIRES

Explore your family history in depth by completing the following exercise:

1. Write 10 to 20 survey questions that will help you understand your family history. Think carefully about what you want to explore in your history and focus the questions around this exploration.
2. Using the questionnaire, interview at least *five* family members, going back as many generations as possible.

3. Collect and analyze the data, then interpret the data by identifying some independent and dependent variables and considering patterns that emerge and re-emerge across time and location. Consider how social and historical factors speak to individual differences, particularly as these differences relate to gender and age. If there are differences, why do you think this is?

4. Write an essay considering the societal, psychological, and/or historical influences on your family history. How has this history influenced your own identity?

Study Systems

Here are four study designs that can help you understand some of the information you might see and work with in both qualitative and quantitative research.

Relational Studies

Relational studies are comparative studies that examine one cause and one effect, and the conditions that make them strong or weak, positive or negative. In this type of study, the dependent variables are examined for the way in which they suppress or magnify the independent variable. Context is important to a relational study, and within this context, it is important to take into account *deviant cases* that do not conform to the norm.

Predictive Studies

Predictive studies speculate about one cause and two or more effects. Some of these studies can be identified by their attempt to apply a theory to a combination of real and imagined data. Plato's *Republic*, which imagines an ideal society, would be an example of predictive or speculative research. Here, one independent variable is used to predict or speculate about the likely effects. Experiments, a form of quantitative research, test predictions. This research generally requires a controlled study, including laboratory work, data collection, and analysis.

Explanatory Studies

This type of study attempts to explain why something happens or does not happen. Here the dependent variable (the effect) is explained by relating it to two or more independent variables (or causes). Student papers are often of this type. You might, for example, be asked to explain poverty in one part of a city by examining the employment ratio, the standard of living, and the familial situation. Please note, however, that because there are significant institutional, ethical, and evaluative requirements demanded of a quantitative study, most of your research will either be mainly qualitative in nature or gleaned from studies that have already been performed by scholars working in your particular area of interest.

Systemic Studies

Systemic studies explain how two or more causes are created by two or more effects. The researcher's goal, as the title implies, is to try to find systemic links between the causes and effects. For example, explaining the causes of 9/11 would require a systematic study in that it had many causes related to complex situational contexts.

Exercise 3.2

EXPLANATORY STUDIES

Using an explanatory study methodology, make up some preliminary design questions in response to the following question: What social values are important in developing children who grow up to be good citizens? When you have done this, answer the following questions:

1. Reword the question to clearly identify the causes and effects.
2. Propose several answers to this question.
3. Identify how the factors above are related to each other. In other words, identify some of the connections between the causes and effects you have identified and see if you can rework them to develop a coherent argument that answers the question. This could be the beginning of a paper or report that you will need to support with established research written by scholars working at a university.

Exercise 3.3

CULTURAL DIFFERENCES

This exercise will help you understand culture and the different perspectives within a culture. Read the excerpt documented below that outlines Stephen Harper's apology to First Nations peoples for the residential school system on behalf of Canadians and then complete the next steps:

1. Read Drew Hayden Taylor's and Richard Wagamese's essays (see pages 422 and 427 in the Reader), both of which are responses to Harper's apology speech.
2. When reading, consider how and why Harper, Taylor, and Wagamese come from different social locations and different perspectives. What are some of the assumptions each writer is making based on what each knows as a norm or a truth about their experience?
3. Now ask which perspective, for you, seems to be the most rational perspective. Why do you think you are swayed by this particular perspective? In other words, how does it reflect your own social location and cultural perspective? Discuss and compare notes with your classmates.

EXCERPTS FROM HARPER'S SPEECH

The treatment of children in Indian Residential Schools is a sad chapter in our history. Today, we recognize this policy of assimilation was wrong, has caused great harm, and has no place in our country. The Government of Canada sincerely apologizes and asks the forgiveness of the Aboriginal peoples of this country for failing them so profoundly. . . . The Government recognizes that the absence of an apology has been an impediment to healing and reconciliation. . . . Years of work by survivors, communities and Aboriginal organizations culminated in an Indian Residential Schools Settlement Agreement and the Truth and Reconciliation Commission. These are the foundations of a new relationship between Aboriginal people and other Canadians, a relationship based on knowledge of our shared history, a respect for each other and a desire to move forward together with a renewed understanding that strong families, strong communities and vibrant cultures and traditions will contribute to a stronger Canada for all of us.

—Harper, Stephen. "Statement of Apology on Behalf of Canadians for the Indian Residential School System." Source: Office of the Prime Minister of Canada © Her Majesty the Queen in Right of Canada, 2014.

Writing a Research Report

Research reports are similar to reports you will see in the sciences. The report follows an inductive outline that mirrors the research project itself: the abstract, research problem, literature review, methodology, argument, and conclusion.

The Abstract

The abstract provides a short summary of your entire report. Approximately one paragraph long (about half a page), it provides the reader with an invaluable introduction to your hypotheses, your argument, and your major points.

The Research Problem

The research problem, which is the first part of the research report, provides an overview of the structure of the research project you are working with. It provides context (time, place, situation) and states the topic to be discussed and the question to be answered. It should also indicate the projected practical or theoretical value of the research by showing its contribution to the scholarly debate. For example, you might make an argument for the need to revise child-care laws and government guidelines that would indicate the practical application to and the value of the project for the parents of these children and for those involved in child care.

The Literature Review

The literature review indicates the extent of your immersion in and analysis of research that has been published on the topic. It might also be called *background* or *previous research*, but what is important here is a clear articulation of work that has been done in the area in which you are working as well as any areas that might apply to your area of study. For example, in the above child-care topic, you would need to research work that has been done in the area of child-care management, but you might also research work that has been done on the rhetoric of government or legal language, either generally or more specifically in the area of child care (child laws, child rights, and child-care responsibilities might also work as synonymous library search terms). The goal here is to use the literature review to deepen your own thinking about your research problem, enabling you to hypothesize or predict how your data might be interpreted.

Methodology

This section of your paper is sometimes called *Measures*, *Sampling*, or *Data Collection*. It is the place where you explain the processes and theory that you used to obtain your results, by outlining the methods and measures (data or theory) you used to answer the question you asked in your research problem section at the beginning of the essay.

Argument

The purpose of this section, sometimes called *Results, Findings, Data Analysis, Discussion*, or *Conclusion*, is to interpret the data collected while at the same time analyzing whether or not it supports the hypotheses at the beginning of the essay. This is where you draw conclusions about your hypotheses, either confirming or modifying them, and making suggestions for further research that will further test or expand your argument.

Remember that a good research report reaches backwards and forwards: backwards, by situating itself in the existing literature about the topic, and forwards, by contributing new information, revised theories, and questions for further research that will refine your reader's understanding of the topic. As student research, your report does not have to be groundbreaking, significantly reinterpreting or calling into question the existing literature on the topic, but it does have to engage closely with one small, manageable aspect of a larger issue and arrive at a conclusion by using the above process.

Exercise 3.4

ANALYZING A SOCIAL SCIENCE ESSAY

Read Catherine Schryer's essay "The Lab vs. the Clinic" (see page 350 in the Reader), which is taken from the discipline of sociology, and examine the conceptual structure of the essay by answering the following questions:

1. Does Schryer use quantitative or qualitative research?
2. Use the headings and subheadings to make an outline of her essay to determine if the structure Schryer uses conforms to the report methodology outlined above.
3. Is Schryer's argument inductive (specific to general conclusions) or deductive (general to specific conclusions)?
4. What is her hypothesis/thesis statement? What conclusions does she arrive at in relation to this statement?
5. One of the tools of social science scholars is theory. Reread Schryer's essay and name the theorists she uses to support her argument. Name the dominant and supporting theories.

Writing for the Arts and Humanities

Although writing for the arts and humanities includes a broad range of disciplines—fine arts, history, languages, linguistics, English literature, drama, cultural studies, classics, philosophy, law, women's studies, music, film studies, and religion—this chapter will focus on the discipline of English, which includes English literature, English language, rhetoric, composition, and cultural studies. This study, however, applies to the other humanities disciplines, and comparisons to them, where applicable, will be made. In truth, the "common and 'recurrent' element of traditional humanistic study, [is that] all the humanities deal in the study of language and discourse." All of the disciplines, including English, are concerned with critical approaches that take into consideration cultural factors, practices, and events where important social, psychological, historical, and rhetorical forces combine and contend (Con, Davis, and Schleifer 3).

Brief History of the Development of English as a Discipline

Although the value of literature has been debated since ancient Greek times, when Plato considered poetry dangerous, it only became a popular area of academic study in the nineteenth century. In the face of the advance of scientific thought and declining religious values, literature was considered useful for retaining and advancing normative cultural and political values.

These normative values are maybe best exemplified in Mathew Arnold's *Culture and Anarchy,* which was first published in 1867 under the more telling title *Culture and its Enemies.* Arnold, who was fearful of the way in which the developing broad-based democracy could instigate an uprising of the masses, saw the dissemination of literature and the arts as a way of controlling the working classes. If the masses were provided with a taste of "the best that has been thought and said in the world," then the best would prevail and the established class hierarchy would be secured.

However, as F.R. Leavis argues, literature both manages culture and "grows out" of it (41), so, maybe not surprisingly, there have been artistic and literary intellectual movements that have responded to and challenged the culture in which they are situated.

Literary Movements

These literary movements, which include classicism, neoclassicism, romanticism, realism, naturalism, modernism, postmodernism, and now post-postmodernism, are not only reflections of major shifts in culture, in the way we think and act, but also catalysts for how art, music, and literature, in turn, respond to and influence that culture. Here are three of the dominant literary movements, which, as you will see, constitute specific responses to a specific time and culture.

Realism (High Period, 1830–90)

The term **realism** is often defined in its literary usage as a method or form in fiction that provides a "slice of life," an "accurate representation of reality" ("life as it really is"). Although most commonly applied to an analysis of nineteenth-century novels, this term is still the dominant form today. Unless a work is situated in a specific genre, such as fantasy, science fiction, or horror, we expect the novel or short story to be situated in our own reality, with recognizable characters and actions. A realist work tends to focus on ordinary characters and the day-to-day events of those characters' lives. Although realistic fiction attempts an accurate representation of concrete reality, it nevertheless calls into question the "extent to which language, and thus fiction, actually constitute our perception of 'reality'" (Childers, Joseph, and Hentzi).

Modernism (1890–1945)

Modernism began as a reaction to realism's stringent aesthetic formulas and to the morals of the Victorian period. Believing that the old ways of explaining, portraying, and understanding the world were no longer appropriate, **modernism** attempted to expose the morals and false structures of society. However, although modernism used experimental forms to break with tradition and convention, it was ultimately criticized for its tendency to reinscribe traditional and elitist attitudes under the guise of those experimental forms (imagism, avante garde, Dadism, etc.).

Postmodernism (1945–)

Postmodernism can be seen as a reaction to modernism and as an attempt to understand the world in the latter half of the twentieth century. In a world threatened by nuclear war, the environmental destruction of the planet, rampant capitalism, and the rapid development of technology, postmodernism can be seen as a continuation of the experimental nature of modernist art and literature and as a refusal of the modernist attempt to fashion a unified coherent worldview. Here are some of the major tenets of postmodernism:

- Meaning is indeterminate; there are no universal truths.
- There is no authenticity (think Madonna). Everything is a fiction because everything is imbued with personal meaning and perspective.
- It is concerned with multiplicity, fragmentation, alienation, and isolation.
- Identity is socially constructed.

- The human condition is one of anxiety and absurdity.
- It focuses on difference and marginality.
- It is no longer concerned with the "original" work of art but with reproduction and regeneration.
- It is interested in questioning received systems of information and studying the often contentious relationship between these systems.

Critical Approaches

These intellectual movements, in turn, spawned different art forms and theoretical approaches to literature, otherwise known as schools of criticism. Some of these approaches include formalism, structuralism, reader-response criticism, new historicism, post-colonial criticism, psychoanalytic criticism, Marxist criticism, feminist criticism, eco-criticism, and cultural studies. This list is by no means complete; you might want to find a book on literary theory and look up more critical approaches, but here is a summary of three dominant critical approaches.

New Criticism

New Criticism refers to a primarily American critical method that became popular from the 1930s to the 1960s. This criticism attempted to treat works of literature objectively. Works were seen as self-contained and autonomous texts whose intrinsic qualities were privileged over biographical, historical, or cultural factors. This is probably the type of criticism you are most familiar with; it demands a close reading, taking into account the language, form, and content of any given text. Most of your instructors, if not all, will encourage proficiency in this type of reading because it functions as a base for all other readings.

Post-Colonial Criticism

This critical method functions as a critique of first-world imperialism. It is concerned with critiquing the oppression of third-world countries and examining the sometimes problematic restoration of their pre-colonial culture after the empires were dismantled in the early to mid-twentieth century. An analysis of the literature specific to a particular time and a particular country can reveal cultural tensions and specifics related to both third-world people's oppression and liberation.

Psychoanalytical Criticism

This form of criticism began with Sigmund Freud and his practice of applying his psychoanalytical theories to culture, interpreting literature from a psychoanalytical perspective. A critical psychoanalytical reading might consider how, for example, wish fulfillment, repression, the Oedipus complex, or the uncanny function in a piece of literature.

A branch of psychoanalytical criticism that was very popular in the 1950s and 1960s was Jungian criticism, after Carl Gustav Jung's psychoanalytical theories. Jung theorized how archetypes, that is, recurring patterns, ideas, or thoughts, are embedded in the collective unconscious and appear as recurring motifs or symbols in literature, art, and mythology. This criticism is rarely used today because it has been heavily criticized for its omission of historical or cultural factors.

More popular is another revision of Freud's theories, called Lacanian criticism. This form of criticism came about when Jacques Lacan applied structural linguistics to Freud's theories. Lacanian criticism considers the relationship between language and the psyche, arguing that although reality cannot be captured in language, language, because it reveals the unconscious, always mediates the external world.

Exercise 3.5

APPLYING CRITICAL THEORY

1. Read Raymond Carver's "Cathedral" (see page 400 in the Reader). Using one of the methods of psychoanalytical criticism outlined above, see if you can use the theory to make some notes on this short story. For example, you might note that the characters function as archetypes for a certain type of person, that one or more of the characters struggle with repression, or that the language reveals this repression.
2. Now read Rosemarie Garland-Thomson's essay "Shape Structures Story" (see page 389 in the Reader), and see if you can deepen your own initial analysis of the story. Can you come up with a working thesis statement for an argument you would like to make about the story? Can Rosemarie Garland-Thomson's analysis support your thesis?

Literary Forms

When writing in the arts and humanities, you will be required to engage qualitatively with several essay forms or patterns. Below I have included a description of the three basic essay forms: summary, critique, and research.

Summary

Summary involves effectively and accurately condensing the information and main arguments of other writers who are writing on the same topic of interest. When writing a summary you are showing your reader that you understand the key claims of the text. A summary might constitute an entire essay or a few sentences that summarize only a small part of the text you are engaging with. In this latter sense, you might use a quotation to summarize an idea or a concept. Summaries are often used in the arts and humanities disciplines to test your knowledge about a certain topic. For example, you might be asked to summarize a certain Second World War battle for a history class or a certain concept or theory for a philosophy class. See chapter 6 for more information on writing a summary.

Critique

To write a successful critique, first you need to understand that critique does not necessarily mean that you must be negative. Critical thinking might involve finding what is ineffective in a **text**—understood in the larger sense of the term as any work (an essay, a short story, a film, an event) that can be read and interpreted—but it might also involve pointing out what is effective in terms of the text's purpose and ability to persuade an audience. Second, it is essential to understand that a critique involves the use of evidence, analysis, and persuasion. The strength of your argument or, in other words, its ability to persuade the reader, depends on how you use evidence and analysis to support an argument or a thesis.

SUMMARY AND CRITIQUE

Exercise 3.6

1. Write a one-paragraph summary of Sherman Alexie's poem "How to Write the Great American Indian Novel" (see page 420 in the Reader).
2. Use your analytical skills to see if you can find some points that either confirm or call into question the poem's effectiveness.
3. Find the best three points and then see if you can arrive at a one-sentence working thesis statement or argument.
4. Compare and discuss with your classmates.

Research

Academic inquiry begins with a contextualized observation, an observation made about the subject and its context, and moves to reflective critique, asking questions and examining alternatives and possibilities. This critique seeks and values complexity while refusing binary (black or white) thinking. Academics tend to see writing as a conversation they have with other scholars: as they demonstrate their knowledge and their sense of shared values, they are also open to changing their position. They understand that their perceptions might be flawed and limited and are willing to revise them when new perspectives are introduced. This does not mean that they do not take a strong scholarly position, but that this position is based on their ability to persuade others who might also have given the subject considerable thought.

The research essay asks you to dialogue with a **primary text** (the text you are analyzing and making an argument about) and **secondary sources** (the academic texts that you are using to either support or refute your argument), keeping this awareness of scholarly engagement in mind. You will need to selectively integrate these secondary texts into your thinking and your work. The research paper should show your ability to

(a) analyze the facts, opinions, values, etc., of other scholars;
(b) construct a clear, "original" argument;
(c) write clearly, concisely, and effectively; and
(d) locate, evaluate, summarize, and cite key academic sources.

You can find more information on research writing in chapter 10.

ACADEMIC FOCUS

QUESTIONS FOR RESPONSIBLE READING (DOCUMENTING INCREASING COMPLEXITY)

Ask:

WHAT? ⟶ WHY? ⟶ HOW?

What is this text about?   *Why* write it?   *How* is it written?

Reader responsibility:

- understanding
- content reading
- summary writing

- discernment, analysis, judgment (merits and flaws) of content
- critical reading/writing
- research writing

- discernment, analysis, judgment (merits and flaws) of language and/or structure
- rhetorical reading/writing
- research writing

Writing Conventions

When writing a literary essay, certain academic conventions need to be followed. A list of these conventions follows.

Structure

Similar to most humanities-based disciplines, English essays are deductive, meaning that they begin with a general statement and work toward a specific thesis statement or main argument that is laid out for the reader at the end of the introductory paragraph or paragraphs. Paragraphs are logically connected and developed, usually without subheadings. Instead of subheadings, an English essay uses clear and logical transitions between the introduction, body, and conclusion, and clear and logical transitions between sentences and between high-level arguments or abstractions and the evidence that supports them.

Sentence length tends to be longer, with attached dependent clauses and phrases, because the ideas are often complex and using more compound-complex sentence structures enables the writer to make these connections clear.

Language

English, as a humanities-based course, uses active voice (subject–verb–object) and first- or third-person point of view, which calls attention to the writer's role or position (subject position) in relation to the knowledge: "I take a feminist standpoint to articulate ..." As an aside, unless you are quoting someone, never use second person (*you, your*), and avoid the use of adjectives and adverbs, unless they are absolutely essential to the reader's understanding of the material. You will need to make sure that your use of verbs, in the immediate simple present form, is academic: "Rowlings *argues* that…" or "Smith *analyzes* video games…," for example.

Another technique is the use of **limiting expressions** (*seems, could, might,* etc.) to indicate that the writer's perspective on the knowledge being discussed is limited. Expressions such as "it might be possible to conclude" leave open the possibility that other researchers "might" arrive at a different conclusion, opening up a space for other scholars to refute the claim. They balance and provide support for statements of fact, which on their own do not include any limiting information or words.

General statement

Specific thesis statement

Figure 3.3 ◆ General Format for Deductive Essays

Citation

Scholars use citation to repeat the ideas of other scholars, using them as a "shortcut to authority, … a way to support an argument" (Giltrow 14). This might involve identifying with, expanding on, or refuting the current knowledge. It might also expose a **knowledge gap**: something that has been missed or not accounted for in the current knowledge.

In citing the reported speech of other researchers, scholars use what Giltrow calls **"reporting expressions"** (also called **signal phrases** because they signal or alert the reader to another scholar's research). *"Peter Smith posited"* and *"Foucault argues that"* are two examples of reporting expressions. English, along with other humanities disciplines, uses MLA (Modern Language Association) citation methods. History uses the CMS (*Chicago Manual of Style*).

See chapter 2 for a more in-depth analysis of academic conventions and chapter 11 for more information on citation.

IDENTIFYING CONVENTIONS

Exercise 3.7

Identify at least *four* academic writing conventions—limiting expressions, point of view, verb use, reporting expressions, the knowledge gap—in the following essay excerpt. Discuss your choices with your classmates.

EXCERPT

For many African Americans, including those who do not particularly like [Michael] Jackson's music, his achievement retains a special significance. While Jackson was preceded by many vastly talented African-American musicians and entertainers, his achievement in shattering the sales records for an album in any music category was a

Continued

See the Exercise Answer Key in Appendix A for possible answers to these questions.

long-awaited moment for African Americans. Jackson was told that there was a ceiling for black stars in America—the biggest black star still could not surpass the biggest white star. When Jackson, irked by the fact that "They call Elvis [Presley] the King, "asked "Why don't they call me that" he was advised to curb his ambition because "the white man will never let you be bigger than Elvis" (445). When Jackson actually surpassed Presley in record sales, it was a signal event in American cultural history.

—Yuan, David D. "The Celebrity Freak: Michael Jackson's 'Grotesque Glory.'"

Exercise 3.8

FREEWRITING

- Complete the following freewriting exercise, and write without stopping for three minutes.
- Use the following sentence starter: "What I still don't understand about writing an essay for a humanities course or, specifically, for an English course is . . . ."
- Discuss your responses to this exercise with your classmates in a small-group setting and/or with your instructor.

CHAPTER SUMMARY

This chapter has introduced you briefly to some of the historical development and main features of writing in the arts/humanities and social science disciplines. While it has been impossible to cover all of the disciplines in these areas, this exploration should enable you to have a general understanding of what might be expected should you take courses in these disciplines or adopt one of them as your major.

QUESTIONS FOR CONSIDERATION

1. Identify three social science disciplines and three arts or humanities disciplines.
2. What are the main differences between the social sciences and the arts and humanities disciplines?
3. Identify three writing conventions related to both the social sciences and arts and humanities disciplines.
4. What is the difference between inductive and deductive essays?
5. What is the difference between qualitative and quantitative research?
6. What is a variable and why is it important to understand how variables can be used in social science research?
7. Can you outline the main sections of a social science essay?
8. Why might it be important to have an understanding of different schools of literary criticism? How might this understanding help you approach an essay assignment?
9. What are some of the main forms (organizational structures) of writing used in the arts and humanities, and in English in particular?

Writing for the Sciences

LEARNING OBJECTIVES

In this chapter, you will learn:

◆ The basic conventions that apply to writing for the sciences.

◆ A brief history of science writing.

◆ The importance of audience and voice (passive and active), as they contribute to clarity, focus, and conciseness.

◆ The appropriate use of metaphor in science writing.

◆ How to write a science essay: IMRAD (Introduction, Methods, Results, and Discussion).

Science has a reputation for being highly technical, challenging, and out of reach of the layperson. Flipping through a scientific publication, you will typically encounter many tables, charts, graphs, and formulae, which you might find confusing, especially if you don't have a background in the natural sciences. To compound the confusion, each of the main branches of the natural sciences, which include chemistry, physics, math, biology, geography, and astronomy, has a sub-discipline, such as biochemistry, quantum physics, or microbiology. Many of them have even more specific sub-disciplines. However, an understanding of some fundamental conventions for writing in the sciences will help you to understand how to read and write effectively in the scientific disciplines.

An imperative in writing about scientific research is that it must be reproducible; that is, it must be described in enough detail and with enough accuracy for someone to be able to reproduce the experiment or study, and test their results against yours, and, in doing so, add to the body of knowledge about the subject. To do this, scientific papers must be written clearly and effectively. This means recognizing the standard conventions of scientific writing.

The style of writing in the sciences is largely **pragmatic**, based on fact and statistical information that is clearly, concisely, and directly conveyed. That is not to say that there is no place for **rhetorical tropes**, such as metaphor, in science—in fact, they have a long and continuing history—but if used carelessly, the consequences can be dire.

A Brief History of Writing in the Sciences

The role of scientist has undergone significant changes over the last century. This history can be traced through an analysis of the structure and style of science writing. Up until the eighteenth century, European society felt an awed respect for the mysteries of science. It recognized that science's contributions significantly improved the quality of their lives, but felt distanced from knowledge that was largely inaccessible. However, in modern times, science, which can be defined as "the study of nature and the practice of making knowledge about nature," has become increasingly accessible. This is due in part to a public awareness of the rhetoric of science, that is, an awareness of how science has been used to persuade and dissuade the general population about facts in nature.

Thomas Kuhn (1922–1996) was the first to suggest a relationship between rhetoric and science. Kuhn claimed that all science is rhetorical and that persuasion plays a key role in advancing scientific knowledge. That is, the way language is used to communicate scientific knowledge determines how and what we believe to be true. Like other writers, scientists use rhetorical constructions and appeals—logical, ethical, and emotional—that they believe their audience will respond to favourably.

In this respect, it is possible to see, as Kuhn argues, that science is not fixed and immutable but is constructed in fits and starts, with one established "truth," or paradigm, replacing another at key junctions. The paradigm that "wins" (i.e., that is accepted as the truth) is not necessarily objectively truer (though often it is), but it *is* necessarily more persuasive.

Exercise 4.1

DEBATE

Academic analysis requires that your opinion be considered and reflective rather than dogmatic and uncompromising. Can you think of some opposing viewpoints related to a "hot" issue in science? You might, for example, debate global warming, genetically modified foods, or genetic engineering.

- Make a list of points for both sides of an argument.
- Pick one side of the argument and develop it by refuting the opposing arguments.
- Use this process to debate these issues with your classmates.

This emphasis on persuasion is in part the result of public awareness and a desire for scientific solutions to integral problems, such as finding cures for diseases, maximizing crop yields, mitigating the effects of global climate change, etc. Scientists increasingly rely on the public, who often heavily influence the decisions of funding bodies that have the power to initiate, increase, or discontinue research funding. In recent decades, the scientific community has attempted to establish a sense of trust with the public. This has resulted in a co-operative, interdependent, and at times somewhat uneasy relationship. The public is asking more questions and demanding more answers, and the scientific community is bridging the gap between its fading traditional, obscure, even mystical role and its emerging transparent modern one.

SUMMARY

Exercise 4.2

It's time to practise your summary skills.

* Write a short one-paragraph summary of the preceding section, "A Brief History of Writing in the Sciences." Make sure you have not included your own opinions or ideas (see the Academic Focus box below) and that your information is accurate.
* Discuss your summary with your classmates. Did writing this summary help you understand and remember the main points? Did you focus on the same points or were there slight differences in emphasis? Why might this discrepancy in detail occur?

ACADEMIC FOCUS

USING VERBS TO ESTABLISH AN OBJECTIVE TONE

An awareness of how you contextualize your ideas and the ideas of others will help you to recognize when you slide from an objective neutral position concerned with conveying the information at hand to a subjective personal perspective that is more interested in conveying what you personally believe to be true. Often, a personal perspective will include the use of emotional verbs, such as *believe, think,* and *feel,* whereas an objective perspective will use more neutral academic verbs, such as *argue, analyze, examine, contend,* etc.

The following are examples of these two kinds of verbs:

1. Introductory words and verbs grounded in personal opinion:

   I believe . . .   I feel . . .
   In my opinion . . .   I think . . .

2. Introductory words and verbs grounded in an objective, neutral position that is concerned only with the knowledge at hand.

This must include an acknowledgement of the context and source of the information:

In *Origin*, Charles Darwin argues that . . .
While Watson and Crick posit that . . . ,
Oswald suggests that. . .
Because Campbell contends that . . .

Exercise 4.3

FACT OR OPINION?

You have probably read this brief history of science as fact. You assume that I have done my research and, since I am an authority on the subject, that my research is accurate. As Jean Fahnestock informs us, though, "A fact is a statement that can be verified" (12).

- Skim over the previous section on the history of science, carefully distinguishing between statements of fact and statements that might indicate a personal opinion. Remember that statements of fact or conviction must be supported by evidence, which might consist of support from other scholars and/or grounds and reasons that support the argument.
- Share your observations with your classmates.

The Importance of Audience

Although language within the scientific community is still largely jargon-laden and inaccessible to the general public, scientists are increasingly redesigning their rhetoric to engage the public by using a common language. The scientific community, in other words, has come to recognize the importance of audience.

Watson and Crick: A Case Study

A key text in any consideration of audience is James Watson and Francis Crick's seminal paper "Molecular Structure of Nucleic Acids: A Structure for Deoxyribose Nucleic Acid" which they wrote in 1953 (see page 452 in the Reader). This paper boldly and assertively introduced Watson and Crick's model of the double-helix DNA molecule and in doing so caused what Thomas Kuhn would have called a "scientific revolution." Because the language used was jargon-free, simple, and accessible, both the scientific community and the public were able to read Watson and Crick's paper. Both communities were astounded by this breakthrough, the discovery of a structure that could open the door to understanding the genetic basis of all life.

Interestingly, Oswald Avery and two colleagues had identified DNA as the structure that transfers genetic information nearly nine years earlier, but the publication of their paper created barely a ripple of interest in either the scientific community or the public. Although DNA was recognized at this point, it was thought to be biologically irrelevant; it wasn't until Watson and Crick's paper that its biological significance was brought to light.

The difference between the reception of the Avery paper and the Watson and Crick paper, argues S. Michael Halloran, came down to the authors' handling of their audience, and, more specifically, the relationship **ethos** they established with their audiences. The language used by Watson and Crick was designed to engage the general reader; it was free of perplexing jargon and highly technical computations and formulae, and the tone was relaxed and informal, even boldly poking fun at their competitors.

They also wrote much of the paper in the active voice rather than the traditional—and often somewhat stuffy—passive voice. And the length of the paper—under one thousand words—did not intimidate readers; those who wanted more technical details were promised that "full details of the structure . . . will be published elsewhere" (737). These were bold and somewhat daring deviations from the conventions that defined scientific writing at the time, but it was a well-calculated gamble, one that firmly established Watson and Crick at the forefront of molecular science.

The Avery paper, by comparison, was much longer, much more technical, and written in the passive voice, and the authors didn't make any strong proprietary claims about the importance of their findings. Compare this with Watson and Crick who boldly assert ownership of their findings: "We wish to suggest," "in our opinion," "we wish to put forward." In doing this, they redefined the public role of the scientist, one that the public could relate to. It could be argued that this was the turning point in the relationship between the scientific community and the public. Watson and Crick, in effect, broke the stereotype of the inaccessible scientist and redefined him or her as a recognizable figure. Although studies have not been done to confirm this, there is evidence that in the fields of molecular biology and genetics, an ethos of bold assertive authority has emerged that did not exist before Watson and Crick's paper. What is important to note here is that language, and the way it is used, can have a profound effect on the persuasive success of writing in the sciences—or any discipline.

Few of us write words as influential as Watson and Crick's, but what is important to aspire to is an awareness of audience. Implicit in that is establishing an ethos (a sense of credibility and trust) with your readers. Always consider who you are addressing, what they need to know and what they already know, and how best to make a connection with them. Know what might offend your readers so you can prepare to navigate successfully around problematic areas without risking losing your audience. Failure to lay this critical groundwork will make your audience's acceptance of your position a challenging—if not impossible—task.

AUDIENCE

Exercise 4.4

Read either Watson and Crick's essay "Molecular Structure of Nucleic Acids" or Werner Heisenberg's "What Is an Elementary Particle?" (see pages 452 and 442 in the Reader). Highlight some of the strategies that were used to make the paper accessible to a particular audience.

- Define the audience.
- Define the strategies used to establish an ethos for the work. These strategies might include the use of accessible (or non-accessible) language, diagrams, active or passive voice, a clear concise structure, etc.
- Discuss these strategies with your classmates.

Voice: Active or Passive?

A major concern related to questions of audience is voice. The question of whether to use the active or passive voice in science writing often confuses students. The active voice—the use of first-person pronouns (*I, we*) and a focus on the doer of the action—is increasingly the favoured form, though this was not always so. The passive voice—a focus on the receiver of the action—was, up until several decades ago, the favoured form. A quick look at the submission guidelines of many scientific publications quickly reveals that the active voice is becoming more widely preferred in the sciences. One of the main criticisms of the passive voice is that it allows for a lack of accountability or responsibility on the part of the writer, a disengagement that tends to exclude the public reader. Over the past few decades, due in part to the public's demand for greater accountability from the scientific community, the use of the active voice, because it allows for greater clarity and directness, has become more common.

Consider the following two sentences: the first, written in the active voice, is taken directly from a paper written by Brian Van Hezewijk and Robert S. Bourchier. The second sentence is the same sentence rewritten in the passive voice. What do you notice about the clarity of each sentence?

Example of active voice:

We found that over the 10-fold range in release beetle density, the emigration rate from patches was relatively constant and approximately 27% per day. (Van Hezewijk and Bourchier 17)

Example of passive voice:

It was found that over the 10-fold range in release beetle density, the emigration rate from patches was relatively constant and approximately 27% per day.

The first sentence clearly establishes who (the writers) made the observation, whereas the second sentence leaves us unsure of who made the observation—the writers themselves, or previous researchers, or someone else altogether?

Passive voice has the effect of hiding the person who is performing the action (the scientist in this case) and, at the same time, distancing the writers from their research findings. Rather than appearing to be in control of the research, they appear to be passively observing it happen. This leads to a perception of a lack of accountability that has, in recent years, been a major critique of scientists and scientific research. Ironically, it can also have a distancing effect on readers, who may interpret the passive voice as stuffy and pretentious. Compare the tone of the claim "It has been observed that" with "We observed." The passive voice gives the impression of elitism and pomposity; the active voice is direct and unassuming.

You may have noticed that in their seminal essay, Watson and Crick do sometimes use the passive voice in their paper ("if it is assumed that;" "it has been found experimentally") but it only appears when the doer of the action is not directly relevant or when they want to downplay the contributions of others. When acknowledging the work of Chagall, for example, they write "it has been found experimentally," to avoid having to directly credit a research competitor. When they state their research findings, however, they do so very clearly using the active voice. Not only is this clearer for the reader, it also establishes ownership of the research results. Watson and Crick clearly stake their claim on the research and their place in the field of genetics.

Despite the varied reasons for this shift in style, many high school students are still taught to write in the passive voice, and many continue to do so once they write in university. They do so out of familiarity, but also because the passive sounds, at first blush, more "academic." However, its use is often at the sacrifice of clarity or precision. Please note though that there are still some journals, though fewer all the time, as well as some university professors, that prefer the passive voice, so be sure to confirm what your professors' preferences are with respect to voice.

ACTIVE AND PASSIVE VOICE

Change the following passive sentences into active sentences:

The experiment was designed by the researcher.

Difficulty was experienced when attempting to separate the fluids.

It was agreed that the experiment should be supervised.

Evidence of global warming was examined by researchers working in the North Pole.

ANALYZING VOICE

- Go through Werner Heisenberg's paper "What Is an Elementary Particle" (see page 442 in the Reader).
- Note all the instances where he has used the active voice and where he has used the passive voice. Can you determine why he chose the voice he did in each instance? What happens when you transform each sentence from one voice to the other? What happens to the clarity, length, and tone of the paper?
- Play around with this and then compare notes with your classmates.

Exercise 4.5

See the Exercise Answer Key in Appendix A for possible answers to these questions.

Exercise 4.6

Metaphor

Traditionally, metaphors were primarily literary figures of speech, but over the past several decades, literary linguists and theorists have begun to recognize their practical value in science. An effective way to understand something we don't know is to put it in terms of something we do know, something familiar. A metaphor is a figure of speech in which an implicit comparison is made between two things that are unalike in all but one salient way by creating an image of something familiar in the mind of the audience. Metaphors are used to bring difficult concepts into clearer focus by eliminating extraneous factors that are not directly relevant to focus on the essence of the concept.

For example, we might describe political debate as a mud-slinging match; clearly, there is no actual mud being flung, but the metaphor clearly creates an image of the aggression and hostility that would be expected at a mud-slinging match, and we immediately understand the tone of the debate. We use metaphors all the time in daily speech, so much so that we often don't even notice that we are doing it:

Traffic was a nightmare.

My boss is an ogre.

Today's meeting opened a Pandora's box.

The price of gas is through the roof.

In each of these instances, what the subject is being compared with bears no likeness to it in any way but one. It is that one salient characteristic that conveys our meaning.

To a greater extent than in the social sciences or humanities, metaphor is used in the sciences to increase understanding of complex or complicated processes. Metaphor has always had a place in science and not just in communicating with the outside world; even among scientists invisible processes are difficult to conceptualize without such a tool. Consider Watson and Crick's model of the DNA molecule. To understand the complicated processes involved in the base pairings of the proteins would have been very challenging—especially in the early 1950s when public science was in its infancy—without the use of metaphor. However, the authors' inclusion of a sketch of the double-helix DNA "ladder" made it much easier for a general audience to visualize. Another more current example is the "greenhouse effect," which clearly illustrates the trapping of heat by gases in the earth's atmosphere in much the same way that heat is trapped by glass in a greenhouse, something that we are all familiar with. Despite its usefulness in science, however, metaphor can have detrimental effects on the understanding of science.

Dangers of Metaphor

Although metaphor is an important device in communicating the often baffling patterns of nature, it is not without dangers. Chew and Laubichler (2003) explain that despite metaphor's obvious usefulness, its interpretation is dependent on cultural influences, and this can lead to complications. For example, the rhetoric that resulted in the practice of eugenics in Germany and North America up until the 1960s persuaded the public that eugenics was a legitimate and necessary practice; it relieved society of its moral obligation to care for people who were portrayed as *burdens*, who were likened to *deadly diseases*, and who were a *threat* to "normal" society, resulting in disastrous consequences for entire segments of the population.

Such culturally specific language can also influence our understanding of science in detrimental ways. Chew and Laubichler argue that metaphors can mislead scientific investigation because they are not precise enough. The term "natural enemies," for example, is a metaphor common in ecology, one that Chew and Laubichler find problematic. The danger, they argue, is that the term immediately identifies a species as a non-desirable "enemy" to the human race. Using metaphor to apply human characteristics to non-human species means that we inevitably judge the behaviour of those species as we would judge and condemn our own.

Consider metaphors that are common in everyday parlance, and think about how they affect our perceptions. For example, consider metaphors, such as "frankenfoods" (genetically modified foods), "dirty oil" (crude oils and residual fuels such as heavy fuel oils), and "tree huggers" (environmental activists). Each term evokes a judgment-laden value; the overt message is that these are things to be wary of. The subconscious effect is a categorical rejection of these things based on fear generated by the rhetoric. This can result in an emotional response, which is often void of reason or critical thought. This is where the danger of metaphor lies.

Metaphor can remove objectivity from the realm of science, particularly when targeted to a general audience who will likely interpret metaphors in terms of what is familiar and/or important to them. This may very well result in misinterpretation, which can have devastating results. If you use metaphor in your science writing, think very carefully about whether you have applied a metaphor that accurately describes your subject. Does it evoke any social or cultural biases? Can you explain your subject without using metaphor? Does your use of metaphor remove the objectivity of your writing?

METAPHORS

Exercise 4.7

- Consider other "real-life" metaphors (those related to illness are especially informative) in the media.
  or
- Take one science essay from the Reader and find several metaphors you can analyze. How does the writer use metaphors to create meaning? How might the use of metaphors be dangerous? Why might they be dangerous? Discuss with your classmates.

By now, you should be starting to develop a sense of what scientific writing is, though it will take time before you feel comfortable with it. Remember that, despite recent

ACADEMIC FOCUS

DEAD AND MIXED METAPHORS

When writing, be particularly careful to avoid dead metaphors—metaphors that have lost their original meaning through overuse—and mixed metaphors, which confuse the meaning by making several different and incongruous comparisons.

Example: Metaphors get *under your skin* and *flood* your senses with *devilish* desires.

attempts to accommodate a general audience, academic writing is mainly written *by* academics *for* academics. As an undergraduate student, you will not be expected to understand a paper entitled "Antifungal activity of volatile metabolites emitted by mycelial cultures of saprophytic fungi" because you are not a member of the scientific community to whom that paper is addressed. You will, however, be expected to grapple with the readings and the language, and you will be expected to write clear, concise papers that critically engage scientific forms and scientific ideas.

Remember that the more your scientific knowledge and understanding of scientific rhetoric grows (that is, the more you become a part of the scientific community), the easier you will find it to work with scientific texts. Follow these strategies for understanding difficult texts:

1. Read the abstract, the introduction, and the conclusion: all of these provide a summary of the paper.
2. Reword sentences or points that you don't understand in your own words.
3. Outline the major points paragraph by paragraph as they appear in the paper so you can begin to understand the general argument.
4. Read the beginning and end of the paragraph where the main information is.
5. Summarize sections of the paper that you do not understand until you have a general idea of the argument.

Exercise 4.8

READING DIFFICULT PAPERS

- Read the Heisenberg paper (see page 442 in the Reader). Bear in mind that you are not the target audience, so you may find it more difficult than your other reading.
- Outline the main points, the gist, of the paper, paragraph by paragraph, highlighting any specialized language. It is not important for you to understand

every word, but to understand the basic argument and development of the paper.

- If you complete this exercise in class, compare your reading—your understanding and lack of understanding—with the readings done by your classmates.

Science Genres

One of the key distinctions between writing in the sciences and writing in the humanities is that science writing focuses more on fact than on argumentation. While most of the scientific writing you will be required to do will be expository, there is plenty of room for argumentation in the sciences. Scientific argumentation goes beyond the field or laboratory where the research is conducted, and where most scientific knowledge is initiated, and extends that knowledge to include new parameters and new knowledge. Lab reports, literature reviews (see below), and technical reports are important sub-genres.

Organization in Science Writing

Typically, scientists want to describe an experiment or a controlled investigation in an empirically designed way that is more structured and rule-driven than that of other disciplines. Therefore, as writers of science, it is important to be familiar with how science writing is typically organized. Before 1600, scientific investigation was conducted using the *deductive* method of research (general claims to specific conclusion). Scientists started with simple axioms or accepted truths, and built scientific knowledge that accommodated these truths. However, some of the leading scientific minds of the day, among them Galileo and Francis Bacon, recognized that it was very difficult to determine the simple truths that were the starting points of research; as a result, much of the scientific truth that was generated was actually false. Around 1600, scientific inquiry began to adopt the *inductive* method of research (specific observation(s) to general conclusion or discussion). This came to be known as the scientific method.

The inductive method is the reverse of the deductive method. It involves exploring one or several observations about a specific subject and from those, arriving at an accepted truth about how nature works. This has become extremely successful in the pursuit of scientific knowledge, and it is how almost all scientific research is conducted today. The most common organizational method for inductive research is known as IMRAD (Introduction, Methods, Results, and Discussion).

IMRAD

Research papers or journal articles are typically written using the basic IMRAD structure, which, once again, clearly outlines the inductive research process. A lab report that you might be assigned at university follows the IMRAD structure although it is less involved, since you are simply reporting your observations, and less detailed than an article written for journal publication, which reports and makes a tentative argument about a particular observation. What follows are the essential components of IMRAD, along with a brief description of how they might be used in your own science writing.

The Abstract

The abstract serves as a synopsis or summary of each section of the article and is placed after the title and before the introduction of the article. It briefly (rarely more than 250 words) describes the purpose of the study, the experimental methods used, the overall results, and the conclusions. The abstract is a useful tool for readers and other researchers because it provides them with a very brief overview of the article from which they can quickly determine whether the paper is relevant to them. This can save a lot of reading time, especially as many journal articles can run to 20 or 30 pages or more.

Typically in an abstract, the methods are written in the past tense ("plots were monitored") because the study was conducted in the past, but the results are written in the present tense ("These results suggest") because the relevance of the results persists. A list of key words relevant to the study is placed directly following the abstract. This is another way readers can determine the usefulness of the paper at a glance. Key words can also provide helpful search terms for locating other relevant sources.

The Introduction

The introduction sets up the topic and indicates what is to come. It clearly defines the problem and explains why it is important; it provides context by means of a literature review, and it provides justification for the study. It also shows how the current study contributes to a solution to the problem. The introduction must be objective; at this stage the author's goal is to establish context, not to persuade.

The literature review is a comprehensive review of the existing relevant literature; it includes the opposing viewpoints and research findings of similar studies, and an exhaustive catalogue of all the past and current research. It thus provides the background information and context necessary for your readers to effectively evaluate the findings and conclusions that you present later in the paper. Writing a paper without a literature review is akin to building a house without a foundation; it cannot be done if the integrity of the structure is to hold. The literature review relies heavily on reported speech, typically citing numerous authorities and sources; often these sources will express contrasting views, but this contrast is important in providing the reader with a well-rounded, objective, and balanced account of the many voices contributing to the academic discussion.

Importantly, a literature review will often address a *knowledge deficit*, sometimes called a *knowledge gap*. This is a metaphorical gap in the existing knowledge, a space on the map, as discourse analyst Janet Giltrow explains, where no one has settled; that is, no one has established a claim of knowledge. The knowledge gap is identified in the literature review in the introduction and serves several purposes:

1. It identifies where knowledge in the current information base is lacking (that is, what is *not* known or what is not well understood).
2. It prepares the current researcher to step into the breach and fill the gap (by presenting new knowledge and increasing understanding).
3. It justifies the current academic research by demonstrating its scientific value.

Scientists may spend a considerable amount of time and space identifying the knowledge deficit, or they may get directly to it. Let's look again at the Watson and Crick paper. The authors waste no time in stating the weaknesses of the current research: "[t]his structure [proposed by contemporary researchers] is unsatisfactory for two reasons"; similarly, when writing about another researcher's findings, they comment that "this structure is ill defined." The authors are, in effect, rather unceremoniously discrediting the work of their competition—wiping them off the map—to position themselves to step in and fill the newly vacated spot. They are replacing the existing knowledge, which they claim is "unsatisfactory," with their own.

The purpose is often stated as a **hypothesis**, a premise that will be tested; it is roughly equivalent to the thesis statement in a humanities or social science paper. It is from the hypothesis that the study methodology is developed. This is key in the inductive approach to science; rather than beginning with a claim and then attempting to prove it, a probable assumption is presented that is then tested. If the same results are repeated, they will usually be accepted and will then become knowledge. Another approach is to present a **null hypothesis**, a rejection of the expected results in which scientists present the opposite of what they think will happen. A null hypothesis, rather than a hypothesis, is presented to avoid premature assumptions. It is a rhetorical device that forces an alternative perspective of a scientific question.

After you have

- introduced the study problem;
- provided necessary context and a review of the existing knowledge;
- identified and positioned yourself to address identified knowledge gaps;
- presented a hypothesis; and
- announced the objectives of your study;

you are now ready to explain your methodology.

Methods (sometimes called Materials and Methods)

The Methods section outlines the methods of the experiment clearly and with great attention to accuracy. The Methods section is often divided into subheadings for greater clarity; these subheadings are often ordered by physical features (site description, sample design, equipment used), and non-physical (statistical analysis), but there can be many different subheadings to reflect the nature of the study. The most distinctive feature of this section is its adherence to objectivity; the steps of the experiment are presented in the order in which they were performed, with no reference to results or attempts to persuade the audience. The purpose of the Methods section is to provide enough detail—with respect to design, equipment, measurements, timelines, and procedure—for successful replication of the study by another party.

The Methods section is often the least carefully written part of a paper. Great patience and attention to detail are required to include all the necessary steps of a study or experiment because often there are many factors that can influence the results. Some of these are seemingly insignificant but may ultimately prove to be significant. Often the level of detail in the description is insufficient to accurately replicate the experiment. Readers and researchers who attempt to replicate the study conditions may then make assumptions, leading to misinterpretation. As you write this important section, always keep in mind the reason that it is so important; put yourself in the shoes of someone who would want to test the validity of your claims by repeating your study.

Results

The Results section is the culmination of the study and the most important part of a paper. It provides the data from which the conclusions are drawn. The conclusions are presented objectively, in the past tense, and without any attempt to interpret the results or draw any conclusions. That is, the data, measurements, and observations are presented clearly and directly, but because many studies generate vast amounts of data, they are often condensed and presented in the form of tables, charts, and graphs, which provide visual trends in the results. It is important that the results reflect what was *not* found (particularly if this goes against the hypothesis), as well as what was found. This may be helpful information for those who replicate your study, whether under the same or different conditions.

What comes before (Introduction and Methods) explains why and how the results were obtained; what comes after (Discussion) interprets the results and explains what they mean. The importance of clarity in this section is another reason why brevity is key; it is critically important that the results not be misunderstood, a greater risk if they are buried in verbiage.

Discussion

In the Discussion section, the author interprets the results of the study and defends how they support the hypothesis or explains how they do not. This is often the most difficult, but also the most interesting, section to write. It is not a simple statement of results, as in the previous section. It is an analysis and interpretation of what the results mean and how and why they may be influenced by other factors. It requires a great deal of critical thought as researchers relate their results to existing knowledge, either contributing to it or arguing that the results alter or negate existing knowledge. Sometimes, during the course of study or experimentation, new knowledge gaps are identified and discussed in this section. This may lead to suggestions for areas of subsequent research. The study may have brought to light some inadequacies in the design of the experiment, which may lead to suggestions for improvements in subsequent studies. It is appropriate here to elevate the results of the study to a higher level, to look for relevance in other areas, and to put the study into a broader context.

Some journals require a Conclusions section following the Discussion, but increasingly the conclusion is tied into the Discussion section, providing the reader with the most salient findings of the study.

Acknowledgements

It is good scientific, and indeed academic, etiquette to include a short paragraph at the end of a research paper acknowledging the assistance the author has received from other researchers, funding bodies, educational and governmental institutions, and individuals. This section comes directly before the References section.

References

The References section contains a complete list of all the sources cited in the text. These are most commonly listed alphabetically by authors' last names, chronologically by publication date, or in the order in which they appear in the paper. Science papers that you will write in university will typically be formatted using APA or the Council of Science Editors (CSE) format, but those written for journal publication must adopt the in-house style of the journal to which they are submitted. The differences between formatting styles range from slight to significant, but all require attention to detail. Do not underestimate the importance of accuracy—sloppy attention to detail may prejudice a reviewer against your paper, despite the value of the new knowledge that it may contain. A common mistake that many scientists make is neglecting to take due care for correct formatting, despite having gone to great lengths to meticulously design and conduct their research.

ANALYZING FORM AND CONTENT

Exercise 4.9

- Take a quick look at Watson and Crick's or Heisenberg's paper (see pages 452 and 442 in the Reader).
- Find the literature review or at least the place where the authors engage with other scientists familiar with their area of research. How many sources do they reference?
- Look at each of the citations and find the related research in the body of the paper. How is this research used? Does it confirm, expand, or refute the information to which it refers?
- Find the knowledge gap and the hypothesis. How do they relate to or build on each other?

CHAPTER SUMMARY

In this chapter, you have been provided with a brief history of writing in the sciences and you have been made aware of its present accessible public image. You have also learned some of the common writing conventions for writing in the sciences. Although scientific writing might use metaphor and passive voice at times, good science writing is, like all academic writing, clear and concise. An awareness of audience will help you establish clarity, as will an awareness of the appropriate use of active and passive voice and the use of metaphor. You have also been given an outline of one of the main inductive forms used in science writing, which will help you structure your scientific essays: IMRAD (Introduction, Methods, Results, and Discussion).

QUESTIONS FOR CONSIDERATION

1. Name some of the disciplines and sub-disciplines related to a study of science.
2. What aspect of the history of science writing do you find most interesting and why?
3. What role does public funding play in the development of scientific ideas and in how scientific writing is presented?
4. Why would Watson and Crick choose to make their paper on the double-helix DNA molecule more accessible to the general public? Name at least three of the strategies they used to do this.
5. What is the significance of Thomas Kuhn's ideas to the way in which science writing has developed and is perceived?
6. Name some of the writing conventions common to writing in the sciences.
7. Why is an awareness of audience and voice important to writers of science?
8. When is it appropriate to use passive voice in science writing?
9. What are some of the dangers of using metaphors in science writing?
10. What do you still need to know about IMRAD?

PART II

THE RHETORIC

Rhetoric, classically defined, is the art of effective persuasion. However, other, more contemporary definitions include the notion that rhetoric is the art of effective communication or the art of using language to persuade a particular audience. Part Two, The Rhetoric, is designed to provide you with the skills for effectively communicating with or persuading an academic audience. It takes you through a step-by-step process and teaches you strategies and techniques for accurately reading, critically analyzing, and then persuasively writing and revising an academic essay.

To begin this process, chapter 5, "Academic Reading," teaches you how to accurately read a text, and an academic essay in particular, for relevance and meaning. Chapter 6, "Summary Writing," extends these skills by providing you with a specific technique and process for reading and understanding a text accurately. Chapter 7, "Academic Analysis," provides you with some basic techniques for interpreting and analyzing a text. Chapter 8, "Academic Persuasion," asks you to take your ability to analyze a text and apply it to the process of writing an academic essay.

Chapter 9, "Drafting and Revision," teaches you strategies for both drafting and revising your essay while keeping your focus on the meaning you want to convey. Chapter 10, "Research Writing," takes all the skills you have learned in the previous chapters and asks you to apply them to writing a research essay. Plagiarism will also be covered in detail, as will the differences between quantitative and qualitative research.

Finally, chapter 11, "Documentation Style," will provide you with everything you need to know about documenting your research, both in the body of your essay and in a bibliographical reference page at the end. In that chapter, the two most often used documentation styles, the American Psychological Association (APA) style and the Modern Language Association (MLA) style, are covered in depth.

Academic Reading

LEARNING OBJECTIVES

In this chapter, you will learn:

- The importance of reading for relevance and meaning. Strategies for note-taking and reading difficult texts are highlighted.

- The difference between reading passively and reading actively.

- That in order to write well, you have to be able to read accurately and carefully.

- How an understanding of some common reading strategies and techniques will help you to become a better reader.

- How academics use structure and theory to frame their analysis.

- Reading strategies for students who have learning disabilities or for whom English is a second language.

While the reading you do in academia will involve reading a variety of real-world and academic texts, such as journal articles, literature reviews, novels, poems, short stories, business reports, science experiments, advertisements, films, etc., the reading students find most difficult is the academic essay. This is because it is the medium most foreign to first-year students. However, it is important to know that any fears you have can be alleviated by being aware of some of the strategies and techniques used by academic writers.

Keep in mind, too, that the skills you learn in the process of becoming an academic writer will help you in your life outside the university to become more literate, informed, and empowered citizens. As Janet Giltrow argues, academic skills and "scholarly concerns" are not divorced from real-world issues and concerns (10).

This chapter will thus focus on reading to understand, relate, and respond with the focus on reading for meaning. With this in mind, some useful techniques and common approaches to reading will be outlined that should help you become an accomplished academic reader.

Reading to Understand, Relate, and Respond

Using language to meet our personal, social, creative, and intellectual needs is something we learn from birth. In the context of speaking, listening, reading, and writing, we use language to learn and expand our knowledge of the world. Learning how to be literate in a university or college setting and speaking and using the language that is familiar to those who work in this setting means that you must learn how to use reading and writing to explore, construct, and extend meaning as accomplished academics do. This requires you to familiarize yourself, first, with the genre, learning how academics read, understand, and respond to texts, and, second, with the way academics write these texts.

Active and Passive Reading

Reading to understand, relate, and respond might also be called the **active reading** process. This engaged, reflective reading method can be defined in relation to its opposite: **passive reading**.

Passive Reading

When you are reading passively, you are reading for content, and you absorb that content, more or less, without question. This form of reading is often the reading you do for pleasure and might be considered a form of escapism or reading for information or facts. For example, you might read a popular science magazine that has interesting and accessible articles on black holes or dark matter, a manual on how to repair the electrics in your car, or a novel that provides insight into the life of a courtesan in nineteenth-century China. Because the writer is an expert who is an authority in his or her field and can impart useful and interesting information, the reader suspends his or her disbelief and generally believes the information is accurate and indisputable.

Active Reading

Active reading, on the other hand, is involved and engaged reading and demands that the reader dialogue with what the writer has to say. Active reading will help you to understand what is being communicated so that there are no inaccuracies or misperceptions. Using a real-world analogy here, you might have an interest in planes, but while it is possible to buy a remote-control airplane and have fun flying it by following some simple directions, you will not be able to take one apart or build one on your own unless you fully understand the complexities of model airplane construction. If your construction is inaccurate and you try to fly this airplane, you will most likely crash and break it. In an academic assignment or course, crashing means failing to pass the essay assignments with respectable marks or, worse still, failing to pass the course.

Therefore, it is important to recognize that while your prior knowledge and experience can help you passively understand most material you read, it will not be enough for articles or books that go beyond what you already know. High-context- and discipline-specific texts will be largely inaccessible, even with an active reading; however, you can alleviate your frustration when reading texts such as this by learning some strategies for understanding and working with this material. First, then, reading to understand demands that you relate actively to the text. Although it might feel too simple to ask yourself how you *feel* about the assigned reading, it is a good place to start. Your ability to recognize your feelings about the reading is the first step in becoming a self-reflective reader (and writer) in that it will help you to understand the beliefs and opinions about the reading, and maybe academic reading in general, that interfere with your comprehension. Reflecting on these initial responses, moreover, will provide you with the insight you need to begin to engage productively with the text.

For example, negative feelings about a reading, such as a belief that the reading is boring, will create a resistance that may prevent you from reading it at all. Unfortunately, if you want to do well in university or college, you will sometimes have to read and respond to material that does *not* interest you. In that case, then, the secret is to find a way of making the reading interesting and meaningful for yourself. This might involve the following strategies:

1. Relate the reading to your prior knowledge or experience. Ask, what can I infer from this context? Is there anything here I can relate to?
2. When possible, choose courses that relate to your discipline and area of interest, and then find a way of relating the readings, if only peripherally, to those discipline-specific interests. Synthesizing your reading with the overall course content or work you have done in other courses is essential to develop- ing a depth of understanding.
3. Sometimes, however, it is not always possible to take a course you are inter- ested in, especially if it is a required course. In that case, you still need to find a point of interest, however small, that enables you to engage with the ideas in the text. For example, Joe Sheridan's essay "The Silence before Drowning in Alphabet Soup," would appeal mostly to students in education or Native stud- ies because it is concerned with how we learn and relate to the world. If you are not interested in that, though, you might find his other points interesting: about photography, how we live in an overstimulated culture, or even how he has structured the essay.
4. This last point speaks to the *usability* of the text. Asking yourself how you can *use* this text to expand your awareness of the topic, argument, or the skills you will need to acquire to become a more accomplished academic reader or writer is an important strategy for making the text meaningful.

5. However, if your resistance to the reading is because of an inability to understand the material, stopping to identify what you know and don't know about the subject matter will help. In this respect, the following strategies might be useful:

   • Identify and look up words or concepts you are unsure of, using a dictionary or encyclopedia.
   • If the argument is difficult to understand, go through the reading to find one point that you understand, and then find another point, and another. This will help you begin to piece together the writer's argument. It will also help you realize that you *don't* have to understand everything about a text to understand the main argument and why it is important.
   • Form small reading groups in and out of class. This can also help you comprehend difficult texts. It will also give you confidence when you understand that you are not the only student who is having difficulty.

Note-Taking

Although you don't have to understand everything, you do have to make sure that your reading and understanding is as accurate as possible. One essential strategy for helping create an accurate, relevant, and meaningful engagement with the text is note-taking. This informal writing activity is essential to your success in academia; it helps you to understand and relate to what you know and don't know in a text, and it provides you with a context and record of your engagement with the text.

Reviewing your notes when you write essays or prepare for exams can prove invaluable. However, the need to make this engagement as meaningful as possible cannot be stressed enough. Clarity is also key. Write enough so that you remember your points when you go back and review your notes; however, do not worry about writing grammatically or correctly when taking notes. Unless told otherwise, they are for your eyes only.

As you read, take notes, either in the margins of your book or in a notebook. A useful notebook strategy is to either split the page into two sections—content and my connections/ideas—or use different-coloured pens: one for writing down the important key points and one for your response to them. Also, implement critical reading and writing techniques: freewriting, clustering, close-reading guidelines, summary writing, and critical response writing. All of these techniques will help you engage with and understand the text you are reading. Find out what works for you. See the three-reading strategy below for instructions on how to take notes when reading.

What to Pay Attention to in Class

You will also need to take notes in class: Write key points in your note book related to the main ideas as emphasized by your instructor and as you see them. If your instructor writes a main point or concept on the black- or whiteboard in the class, you will be expected to remember and think about its relevance. Write your ideas or responses to the material in the margins of the book or in a different-coloured pen. Also, pay attention to the following points:

- information, especially grammar errors, etc., that you struggle with. You might make a note to look something up if it is unclear;
- strategies, terminology, instructions, directions, processes, dates, etc. highlighted by your instructor;
- topics, issues, processes, etc., that interest you: anything that you like or find disturbing; anything you want to know more about. These notes will increase your interest in the course and provide you with class discussion or essay ideas.

Strategies for Reading Actively and Accurately

Current theories of reading comprehension recognize the importance of actively engaging in the creation of meaning. On one level, you need to be aware of your prior or existing knowledge. Prior knowledge, formulated in the brain according to schemata, or ways of knowing, refining, and restructuring this information, enhances and enables your understanding of a text. On another level, you need to formulate new knowledge by considering contexts and reading carefully and critically, making sense of the work while making sure that you are not reading too much into it or missing the main argument. Expanding and applying your knowledge of writing strategies and techniques will not only help demystify academic writing, as a discipline-specific genre, it will help you organize, categorize, and expand your schemata so that reading, thinking, and, ultimately, writing become easier and, more important, accomplished.

What follows are some active reading strategies that you might apply when reading texts for your courses. You will need to experiment with them to decide which strategy works best for you. As a general rule, though, you will need to read the text at least twice and engage actively with it, using one or a combination of any of the following strategies.

Three-Reading Strategy

This strategy involves in-depth note-taking and reflection. Breaking it up into three readings allows you to engage with the reading in increasing complexity and depth.

First Reading (or Pre-Reading)

1. Ask yourself what genre and/or what discipline this piece of writing might emerge from. For example, is it taken from a newspaper, a grammar book, a novel, a speech, or an academic journal? Who is the intended audience? One useful technique for determining the discipline is to take a look at the citation for the essay. The essay title and the name of the scholarly journal in which the essay is published should give you a good idea of the discipline.

2. At this stage, you simply scan the text, asking yourself what you already know about the topic (prior knowledge). Are there any readings, television shows, or related background information that will help you make sense of the work? One important strategy is to begin to synthesize the information you are learning in different courses. For example, you might be studying brain functions and their relationship to behaviour in both a psychology class and a philosophy class. The information you receive in one class can enhance, add to, or call into question the information you receive in another class.

3. You will also need to scan the text to get an overview of the content. Take into consideration the article's title, author (academic? journalistic? gender?), bolded headings, and italicized words. Then pay attention to the introduction, conclusion, and the beginnings and endings of paragraphs where the main ideas might be. Look for the central argument (thesis statement) and the main points that support the argument. Remember, every text has an argument.

4. Ask questions: Highlight what you don't know by asking questions. Be aware of **jargon** and be specific.

Second Reading

Read the article through quickly, using the following strategies:

1. Highlight the main points of the article. You might also write an outline of the article, using two- or three-word summaries, down the side of the page. This strategy helps you to understand both the main argument and how the argument is developed.

2. Highlight points, arguments, concepts, and/or words you don't understand by putting a question mark and/or a comment in the margin. You can come back to these problematic areas on a third reading.

3. In the margins, make comments that outline your personal response to the work. Do not be afraid to write that you don't understand or you dislike something. That will provide you with a base for examining a specific point more carefully. You might also synthesize this work with other similar works or contexts that you are aware of here.

Third Reading

1. Read through the article a third time; this time, read slowly, stopping and trying to understand parts of the essay you don't understand. Sometimes, you might have to look up a word, concept, or notion that is unclear to you in the dictionary; however, you can often understand a certain concept or idea by understanding how it relates to the larger context of the writing. Don't be afraid, in the personal response section, to make comments that might seem negative. Writing "I find this frustrating" or "I hate this essay" can often help you to move beyond your frustration to a greater understanding.

ACADEMIC FOCUS

TECHNIQUES FOR GENERATING AND ORGANIZING INFORMATION

Clustering: As a technique, clustering can help you not only develop and deepen your ideas but can also enable you to understand the relationship between your ideas. Look at the example below to see how clustering can be used in this way. Think about how you might organize these ideas if you wanted to write an essay on the dangers of children watching too much television.

Brainstorming: This technique involves spontaneously generating ideas on a particular topic. You can do this on your own or with classmates. It is important, however, not to judge the ideas you come up with. When you have enough ideas, you can put them into categories and check to see how useful they are for your purpose.

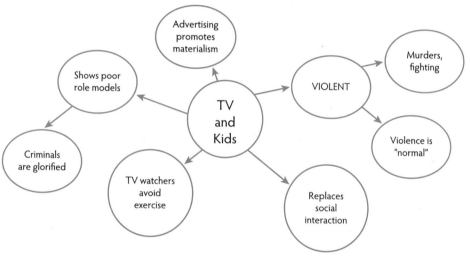

Figure 5.1   ◆   Example of Clustering

2. Besides note-form responses, use **paraphrasing**, **summary**, or **précis-writing** to help you develop a good understanding of the article (see chapter 6).
3. Consider how the content of the article is developed throughout the essay. The structure or logical development of the essay should support the content. Make an outline of the main essay points. If the writer diverges at any point, can you understand why?
4. Consider how the author uses context (an analysis of the situation, time, place, event, etc.) to support his or her main argument. Why and how is context important?

5. Consider the author's tone (indicating genre, author's intent, projected audience, etc.). Look at how the author uses words to persuade the reader (verbs, adjectives, nouns, etc.). Is the author biased?

6. Ask questions: Is the author presenting mostly facts or opinions? Is this argument valid? Do I "buy" it? Who is the intended audience? What tone is the author using? What is not being said here? What is missing or implied in the work? Is there a knowledge gap?

7. Implement critical reading and writing techniques: freewriting, **clustering**, **brainstorming**, close-reading guidelines, summary writing, critical-response writing. Find out what works for you!

In responding to a text in this way, you can begin imagining yourself as a scholar and take a scholarly position; in this way, you will be participating in the knowledge-making activities of the university. Just as important, make sure you use these strategies to understand and edit your own writing.

Exercise 5.1

ACTIVE/PASSIVE READING

- Read the following two passages, both of which deal with brain research: the first was published in *Discovery* magazine in 2009, the second in the academic online journal *Philosophical Transactions of the Royal Society*. The first passage is in a journalistic genre designed to make difficult concepts accessible to the general public. The second paragraph is designed for academics working in the same area of research.
- Follow the three-readings rule.
- As you do so, answer the following questions:
  1. When reading, do I feel inclined to ask questions? What are they?
  2. Are there any places in the text where I become lost or confused?
  3. Which paragraph demands a greater knowledge base? Do I feel the need to use a dictionary?
  4. Do I believe or trust this writer?
  5. Am I aware of any omissions or gaps in the argument?
  6. Having answered the above questions, which excerpt, in my opinion, is easier to read passively? Which excerpt demands an active response, because it demands a careful and reflective reading?

PASSAGE 1

The nature of wisdom has long been the domain of philosophers, but . . . neuroscientists Thomas Meeks and Dilip Jeste have thrown their hats into the ring with the likes of Plato and Kant. They analyzed decades of research and found that the multitude of characteristics associated with wisdom—including social decision making and control of emotions—may be accounted for by a surprisingly small number of brain regions: a putative wisdom network. One brain area, the anterior cingulate cortex, detects conflicts and makes decisions. . . . A recent study . . . found that damage to this area made people less susceptible to guilt and could lead to poorer social decision making. As Meeks and Jeste continue developing their model of wisdom in the brain, they plan to study the distribution of wisdom in the general population and examine brain-damaged individuals to confirm the region involved. *(Labrecque)*

PASSAGE 2

The lateral frontal cortex appears to be functionally organized along both a rostral-caudal axis and a dorsal-ventral axis. The most caudal frontal region, the motor region on the precentral gyrus, is involved in fine motor control and direct sensorimotor mappings, whereas the caudal lateral prefrontal region is involved in higher order control processes that regulate the selection among multiple competing responses and stimuli based on conditional operations. Further rostrally, the mid-lateral prefrontal region plays an even more abstract role in cognitive control. The mid-lateral prefrontal region is itself organized along a dorsal-ventral axis of organization, with the mid-dorsolateral prefrontal cortex being involved in the monitoring of information in working memory and the mid-ventrolateral prefrontal region being involved in active judgments on information held in posterior cortical association regions that are necessary for active retrieval and encoding of information. *(Petrides 1456)*

See the Exercise Answer Key in Appendix A for my comments on these excerpts.

Close Reading

When actively reading an academic text, it is crucial to consider not only *what* is presented (the topic of the writing and the argument the writer is making) but also what the inferred context is (which situation—personal, geographic, political, social context does the writing speak to? Which conventions show that the writer is working within a specific genre? *Where* and *when* is the writing situated?) and in what way the information is presented (*how* is the argument organized and *why*?). This strategy is often called a close reading. Following the general guidelines for a close reading can be a useful tool for helping you understand a dense and difficult academic essay. What follows are some questions you can ask when doing a close reading:

1. What is the significance of the title?
2. What do I need to know about genre, audience, purpose, etc., to enhance my understanding of the text?
3. What is the thesis statement or main argument of the text? Summarize it in one or two sentences.
4. How is the thesis developed logically? You might want to outline the structure of the piece here.
5. Interpretation: Do I like the piece? What points interest me? Why?

6. Insights: What points or sentences do I feel are particularly useful to my under-standing of the work and its ideas?
7. What points do I disagree with or feel need more development? What has been left out?
8. What terms do I need to understand or know?

The Think-Aloud Protocol

Another reading strategy, a particularly good one for reading difficult texts, is outlined by Beth Davey in her 1983 essay "Think Aloud: Modeling the Cognitive Processes of Reading Comprehension." This strategy allows you to make your thinking explicit by verbalizing or writing down your thoughts as you read. By reading the passage either out loud or silently to yourself, you are listening and responding to parts of the text that you find dif-ficult. You can also read the text out loud to a partner, taking turns to read and comment on the text, and either stopping the reader to share your thoughts about any relevant or difficult points or taking notes and then discussing the points at the end of the reading.

If you adopt this strategy you will, as Giltrow states, need to "simply report what is going through [your head]" (126). Do not make any judgments when using this method. As you read, you will

(a) comment on things you understand and like and things you don't understand and/or dislike;
(b) report on "the gist [main ideas] of what you are reading;" and
(c) add ideas of your own (130).

These reports will provide you with a record of and context for understanding your personal response to the text as well as synthesizing the ideas with other similar works or ideas that you are already familiar with.

As Davey stresses, this strategy helps you understand the text by enabling you to see and understand the logical connections between the main and supporting ideas. However, taking notes, using a first-person ("I") detailed response, is crucial. Sentences, such as "I'm confused about what utilitarianism means" followed possibly by what you do know or come to realize: "Oh, okay I sort of get it now: while everyone's interests count, they only count as long as everyone has the same interests," will enable you to engage with and understand the logic of the argument. It does this by assisting you in keeping a record of your thinking process, a skill that is important for learning how to read a difficult text.

Exercise 5.2

THINK-ALOUD

Use Davey's reading method to perform an active reading of the following excerpt. As you read:
• Stop and outline the gist of the argument.

- Report in the margins moments when you have trouble following the argument or, alternatively, are stimulated either to synthesize the argument with the ideas of others or record ideas of your own.
- Make sure you use "I" sentences. For example, *I am having trouble understanding this concept*; *This word feels out of place to me*; or *I get this point*.

Also answer the following questions:

1. *What* genre is this piece of writing taken from? Is it a fictional novel or short story excerpt, an advertisement, a play, or an academic essay? If it is an academic essay, can you make any assumptions about the discipline from which it might derive?
2. *What* immediate situation does this piece of writing suggest? Is there a larger social, cultural, or political context to which this writing speaks?
3. *How* is the writer using language and stylistic conventions (i.e., point of view, quotations, reporting expressions, definition, compare-contrast, citation, etc.) to convey information?
4. *What* argument might the writer be making here and *how* is it structured?

EXCERPT

Buddhists and psychologists alike believe that emotions strongly influence people's thoughts, words, and actions. . . . From a Buddhist perspective, however, some emotions are conducive to genuine and enduring happiness, and others are not. A Buddhist term for such happiness is *sukha*, which may be defined in this context as a state of flourishing that arises from mental balance and insight into the nature of reality. . . .

Two Research Directions

We have begun to examine highly experienced Buddhist practitioners, who presumably have achieved *sukha*, to determine whether that trait manifests itself in their biological activity during emotional episodes (Lutz, Greischar, Rawlings, Ricard, & Davidson, 2009) or increases their sensitivity to the emotions of other people and to see how their interactive style may transform the nature of conflictual interactions. . . . Another possible area of research concerns the reliability of self-report about mental states.

—from Paul Ekman et al., "Buddhist and Psychological Perspectives on Emotions and Well-Being."

See the Exercise Answer Key in Appendix A for an analysis of this excerpt.

You may or may not have been convinced that the Buddhist study in Exercise 5.2 was an interesting or valid one. This skepticism might well have been because you didn't trust the authoritative claims presented in the text. If you were able to identify the context or some of the stylistic conventions in the text, if you had any questions or doubts about the text, or if you were able to extend the arguments in the text with other reading you have done, then you were engaging actively or critically with the text. You might also have noted that when reading actively, you go beyond the denotative or literal meaning of words and begin to think about the connotative meaning of words, making associative inferences about the way the words are used. For example, when reading Ekman's excerpt, you might have begun to think about the word "experience" and realized that it can be interpreted in many different ways. When reading actively, you might also begin to think about questions related to audience, context, bias, validity, etc.

Exercise 5.3

FREEWRITING

- Read the following passage.
- Respond to it by choosing one of the freewriting sentence starters below.
- Use that sentence to write non-stop for ten minutes.

> In the argument culture, criticism, attack, or opposition are the predominant if not the only ways of responding to people or ideas. . . . What I question is the ubiquity, the knee-jerk nature, of approaching almost any issue, problem, or public person in an adversarial way. One of the dangers of the habitual use of adversarial rhetoric is a kind of verbal inflation. . . . the legitimate, necessary denunciation is muted, even lost, in the general cacophony of oppositional shouting. What I question is using opposition to accomplish *every* goal, even those that do not require fighting but might also . . . be accomplished by other means, such as exploring, expanding, discussing, investigating, and the exchanging of ideas suggested by the word "dialogue." I am questioning the assumption that *everything* is a matter of polarized opposites, the proverbial "two sides to every question." (Tannen 7–8)

Freewriting prompt: "I like/dislike this passage because . . ."
Once you have written your freewrite, go through it and highlight what you consider to be important points.

- Does your freewrite demonstrate a clear understanding of the passage?
- Are there any clear points that demonstrate either an agreement or a disagreement with the ideas in the passage?
- Could you work this into a tentative argument about the text?
- If you go off topic, are there any interesting ideas in this passage that you might use in another assignment?
- Remember not to judge your grammar in this exercise. You are writing to find out what you know, what you don't know, and what interests you. Did you surprise yourself?

The K-W-L Strategy

K-W-L stands for What do I <u>k</u>now? What do I <u>w</u>ant to know? What did I <u>l</u>earn? This strategy asks you to

1. Begin with what you already know about a subject or topic.
2. Find out what you need to know. As you do so, reflect on your current knowledge, then generate and attempt to answer questions about what you don't

ACADEMIC FOCUS

FREEWRITING

This technique was designed by Peter Elbow, whose academic work focuses on writing and the writing process. Elbow claims that freewriting can help you discover what you know while also enabling you to write without fear or judgment. It involves writing non-stop for five to ten minutes on a topic of interest. You may go off topic and you may end up writing about something else entirely, but the key is to keep writing. Elbow suggests writing "I have nothing to write" or something similar if you find yourself lost for words (12), but you must keep your pen or pencil moving on the page. Do not worry about grammar when completing this exercise. As Elbow states, you might surprise yourself with the quality of writing you produce when using this exercise.

know about the topic. When answering this question, keep your focus on the text and the ideas in the text. Be careful not to go off topic.

3. Identify what you learned. This strategy can provide the basis for understanding the text and can lead to further discussion and exploration to clarify, internalize, and expand on what you have learned.

Structural Frameworks

When writing lengthy essays, academics need to be aware not only of their ideas but also of how they are going to present their ideas. To do this, they establish analytical frameworks with different structures. Structural organization means that you will need to think about how a text is organized according to a major pattern or organizational method, such as compare–contrast, cause–effect, classification and division, etc.

Once you become aware of the importance of text organization and learn how to search for the relationship between concepts and developing ideas, you are in a better position to comprehend the argument and its development. As Coe argues, these patterns of development, which occur at the sentence and paragraph level, allow you to generate and deepen your insight into a particular topic (302). All of the following patterns require the reader or writer to become aware of how the development of meaning is constructed. Here are some of the major analytical patterns that you will see regularly in a text.

Compare–Contrast

Comparing and contrasting two texts, events, things, or ideas requires that you be aware of how these two properties are the same in some ways and different in other ways. These might be obvious likenesses and differences, for example, a simple descriptive juxtaposition of two or more things, but there might also be so-called ironic differences, that speak to the gap between what is actually said or observed and what is hidden, consciously or unconsciously, below the surface. For example, when comparing and contrasting the ethical and social responsibilities of two major oil companies, you might highlight what is not said and maybe should be said in their statements of environmental concern.

Exercise 5.4

COMPARE–CONTRAST

- Read Bartholomae's "Writing with Teachers" (see page 330 in the Reader).
- Outline both Bartholomae's and Elbow's perspectives.
- Use a compare–contrast method to identify the similarities and differences in their perspectives. Which perspective do you identify with and why?

Cause–Effect

Cause and effect analysis presupposes a logical relationship between a cause and its effect. More specifically, when academics posit a relationship between one fact and another, they are concerned about analyzing *why* something happens (the cause) and *what* happens as a result (the effect). This type of pattern is often seen in science and social science disciplines because they work from an inductive perspective, examining and discussing the larger implications of a specific argument to draw broad conclusions.

Typical sentence patterns associated with cause and effect are as follows:

The polar ice caps are melting and decreasing *because* the rate of global warming has increased over the last 20 years.

The polar ice caps are *affected by* the rate of global warming, which has increased over the last 20 years.

Global warming *causes* [*produces/results in*] the melting of the ice caps.

When global warming increases as it has over the last 20 years, the polar ice caps melt correspondingly.

Keep in mind that at this point these statements are broad generalizations. You will be required to support these generalizations with clear, documented, and valid evidence so you can make reasonable and logical connections between causes and their effects.

Classification and Division

As Coe explains, "to classify is to put your subject into a larger category or class. To divide (sometimes called analysis) is to break your subject down into smaller parts or aspects" (310). You might, for example, use this process to write an essay on how gender (a larger category or class) is divided into male/female distinctions and maybe even further into distinctions involving social practices that blur the boundaries between these distinctions. Remember, however, that when using this process these distinctions carry hidden assumptions or biases that have implications for your analysis. Your own subject position and your argument might influence where you place your emphasis, but you will always need to consider any possible refutations or objections to the way in which you choose to classify and divide your argument. Classification and division can provide an easy way of arranging your paper into logical sections.

Description

Descriptive writing appeals to a reader's senses (sight, sound, smell, taste, and touch). It communicates the writer's perceptions of a person, a place, or an object, and may locate them within a certain perspective or argument. Description is used sparingly, on a need-to-know basis, in academic writing. The general rule is that if your reader does not need the description to understand all the complexities of the argument, then it shouldn't be used.

Analogy

An analogy is an extended comparison between two things, objects or ideas, that are unalike. It is most effective when the unfamiliar terms are explained in terms of the familiar ones. An analogy can help the reader understand a complicated subject or concept in a new way precisely because he or she is able to relate to it through a common experience. Please note that metaphor is different from analogy: whereas metaphor is the comparison of two unlike things, describing something as if it *is* something else, an analogy extends the comparison into a logical argument.

For example, the metaphor *rhetoric is war* compares a combative rhetorical style to the actual act of war. An example of metaphor can be found in E.B. White's "Democracy" (see page 458 in the Reader), when he compares democracy to a number of metaphors: the line that forms on the right. . . . It is the hole in the stuffed shirt . . . [and] the dent in the high hat." An example of analogy can be found in Wayne Booth's introductory paragraph in "The Rhetorical Stance," where he explains his interaction with a student and uses it as to introduce the basic problem students have when writing. Another example can be found in Tom Regan's "The Case for Animal Rights" (see page 378 in the Reader) when Regan uses an analogy of a person who kicks his or her dog to explain the difficult concept of "indirect duty views."

ANALOGY

Exercise 5.5

1. What other analogies can you find in Tom Regan's essay (see page 378 in the Reader)?
2. How do these analogies work to support and make clear his argument?
3. Are these analogies persuasive? If so, why? If not, why not? Discuss with your classmates.

Narration

Narration is concerned with *what* happened. It tells the narrative or story of what happened and is usually written in chronological sequence. In academic writing, narration is used mostly in the social sciences. It takes the form of qualitative analysis, using stories as its data to describe and analyze human actions and events. Narration might also be used in the arts and humanities disciplines to analyze an autobiographical account or a memoir.

Exercise 5.6

NARRATION

1. Drew Hayden Taylor, Richard Wagamese, and Joe Sheridan all use narration. Can you identify the places where this happens?
2. How do their methods differ?
3. In your opinion, which style of incorporating narration works best? Discuss with your classmates.

Examples

An essay or a paragraph developed by example uses illustrations to provide evidence that supports the main idea. Examples are highly effective; they provide a reader with concrete specific information or evidence and thus help to make the concept clearer. Consider the following example, which is taken from Werner Heisenberg's "What Is an Elementary Particle?" (see page 442 in the Reader).

> In the experiments of the fifties and sixties, this new situation was repeatedly confirmed: many new particles were discovered, with long and short lives, and no unambiguous answer could be given any longer to the question about what these particles consisted of, since this question no longer has a rational meaning. A proton, for example, could be made up of neutron and pion, or A-hyperon and kaon, or out of two nucleons and matter, and all these statements are equally correct or equally false.

As you have probably noted, the example of the proton provides evidence for the fact that it is almost impossible to identify conclusively what particles, such as the proton, consist of, thus making an abstract point easy to understand.

Process Analysis

Process analysis is concerned with how a particular process happens. It can take the form of instructions (as in a recipe or in instructions on how to quit smoking, which often describe a linear process), or it can involve more complex processes that address the simultaneity and depth of the subject being analyzed. Process analysis is often found in informative expository essays.

Definition

The function of a definition is "to allow someone to distinguish the defined concept from all else" (Coe 317). Definitions matter because they describe and identify concepts, which influence our perceptions and interpretations. See chapter 2 for more on definition.

Theoretical Frameworks

In academia, theory is important because it helps develop and support or refute any common understanding of a subject. Theory might explain or predict an outcome or draw comparisons to other work, but inevitably it does the work of contributing to knowledge about a subject by framing the knowledge within a larger theoretical context. These theories, because they are based on cognitive abstractions rather than concrete social responses, can be difficult to relate to. As you continue with your studies, you will become more familiar with these knowledge-making theories, and, as they do for other scholars, they will begin to inform your own academic reading and writing practice. Understanding how these theories work to support or refute an argument in a text can help your overall understanding of the logic of the main argument.

Note, for example, in the Reader how Tom Regan draws on the theories of utilitarianism, contractarianism, and the cruelty–kindness view. Similarly, Carl Cohen draws heavily on the speciesist theories of Peter Singer, Catherine Schryer draws on D.A. Schön's theory of "Technical Rationality," and Rosemarie Garland-Thomson draws on the work of Caroline Walker Bynum. It is important to know, however, that the writer will summarize concisely the theory he or she is using, explaining how it is useful for his or her own study or diverging from that theory, as Regan and Schryer do, to come up with a theory of their own. Looking for definitions, summaries, or statements of agreement or divergence from these theories can help you understand what they are and how they are used.

THEORETICAL FRAMEWORKS

Exercise 5.7

Although the theoretical engagement that Regan makes with contractarianism, utilitarianism, and the cruelty–kindness view is difficult to read and understand, it is not insurmountable. Follow the following process and see if your understanding of these theories improves:

- Identify places where Regan defines or summarizes these theories for his reader.
- Outline Regan's engagement with these theories, looking for places where he agrees or disagrees with them. Can you identify the theory that Regan finally arrives at as being the best theory for proving his argument that animals should have rights comparable to humans?
- Discuss with your classmates.

Relevance Theory

Understanding how scholars engage with theoretical frameworks is useful, but, as is the case with Tom Regan, the complexity and density of the writing can still make for difficult reading. Students find it difficult to read academic essays in part because of the syntactic (language-driven) and semantic (knowledge- or meaning-driven) density of the argument; in part because scholars, especially when engaging with theory, use

abstractions—mental concepts or ideas that have little or no grounding in concrete reality—to relate to difficult cognitive ideas and concepts. Take, for example, the following sentence, taken from Martin Heidegger's *On Time and Being*, "Not only in the Greek determination of Being, but, for example, also in the Kantian 'position' and in the Hegelian dialectic as the movement of thesis, antithesis and synthesis (here again a being-posited) the present speaks" (34). Most people would have trouble understanding this sentence if they were not grounded in the knowledge of the discipline of philosophy. Because, as undergraduate students, you don't have that knowledge, I have included a strategy for coping with the dense abstract passages you might read in the academic environment, called relevance theory.

Giltrow outlines this approach in *Academic Writing*. According to Giltrow, "[a] statement is relevant in indirect relation to the effort it takes to find the context in which it is meaningful" (145). In other words, in an academic context, abstractions work as long as they build logical contexts, connections, or transitions between things or ideas for the reader.

Drawing from psychology, Giltrow advises students to use the mental desktop, a management device for sorting through relevant or non-relevant material (149). Using this device, a journal or notebook, students are encouraged to make decisions about the relevance of statements as they read any given text. They can decide to

(a) completely discard certain information;
(b) put the information aside for possible future use or relevance;
(c) combine or synthesize information with prior information; or
(d) put the information into long-term memory (149).

This device is useful because students are often not aware that not all information carries equal weight and relevance. In other words, you don't have to remember everything, but you do have to remember and possibly use the information that is relevant to your thinking at the time. Understanding the material's relevance also helps you to build on the information. For example, when reading Heidegger's sentence above, you might choose to remember simply that in all these theories "the present speaks" or makes itself known. If you choose to look up the individual theories, all well and good, but my point is that often you don't have to understand the meaning.

Specific Reading Problems

This chapter has focused predominantly on active reading strategies, which will provide you with specific frameworks for understanding and constructing meaning. However, it is important to recognize that students who have reading problems often find the shift from reading passively to reading actively to learn and construct meaning, interacting with the author as they do so, difficult.

These problems might involve difficulty grasping a concept, a word, or an important idea in the text. Becoming conscious of why this difficulty is occurring is the first step in coming up with a strategy for dealing with it. As Richard and Jo Anne Vacca point out in *Content Area Reading*, students have to learn to be aware of "text, task and self," learning how they interact with the text and how they perceive themselves as readers (49). Developing a **metacognitive** understanding of why you have difficulty reading and understanding a text can significantly help you overcome any difficulties you might have.

In this respect, using the following metacognitive problem-solving processes should help: "(1) recognizing *when* problem situations occur, (2) identifying *what* is wrong, (3) recognizing *why* the problem situation is occurring, (4) identifying *what* strategies might be used to deal with the problem, (5) selecting a strategy that gets at *what* is wrong, (6) knowing *how* to apply the strategy, and (7) *deciding* whether or not using the strategy has solved the problem and if the problem-solving process should continue" (49). What follows are some strategies related to specific learning difficulties that can help you ask these questions.

Learning Disabilities: Dyslexia, ADHD

If you have been diagnosed with specific learning disabilities, such as dyslexia or ADHD, that affect reading comprehension, employing some of the strategies mentioned in this chapter can be helpful. Understanding *what* the task is, *why* you are being asked to perform a specific task related to the reading (i.e., Do you understand the assignment?), and *why* the task is difficult for you can help you to figure out strategies that will work for you.

In your attempt to understand why the text is difficult for you, it is important to know that comprehension problems occur when words, phrases, sentences, and paragraphs, and how they relate to one another, are misunderstood. Having a repertoire of strategies to help you when you misunderstand or become confused can help you.

Some strategies include:

1. Ignoring the word or phrase where you read or stumble and reading on until the meaning becomes clear;
2. Thinking of an example or, alternatively, an image that will help you understand the meaning or concept;
3. Rereading to make connections and meaning;
4. Recognizing the text patterns, such as compare–contrast, to help you understand.

Recognizing signal words, such as "for example," or "because," will help you understand these patterns. To understand the material, asking questions, such as "What is important?," "What are the key concepts or terms?," or "What can I ignore or put to the side?" will help, as will monitoring your comprehension of difficult concepts with other students or your teacher.

The reading strategy called **PQ4R**, an acronym for Preview, Question, Read, Reflect, Recite, and Review can also help because of its focus on repetition and review. The recite section might include discussing the material with another person or using graphic organizers, such as mapping or clustering, to aid memory skills.

Students with ADHD might, in addition to difficulties with comprehension, have particular difficulties with attention, especially when reading academic essays because they are lengthy and the content is not always compelling or stimulating. These students would do well to adopt the active reading strategies already mentioned, but using notes, highlighting with different-coloured pens, and reading the material out loud might also help. Students with ADHD also often work better if they read for short periods of time, minimizing outside distractions. Alternatively, they might work better if they use white noise or music to help increase their understanding of difficult concepts.

Any of these strategies can help students who have difficulty reading or retaining information. In this respect, the strategic reading practices outlined earlier in the chapter should also be taken in to consideration, as well as finding out how you process information.

If you are a more visual learner, you might need to take notes and even ask your instructor for more handouts, but if you are a mostly auditory learner, you might ask if you can take a recorder into the lecture. It is important to remember that there is no one strategy that works for everyone. Finding out what works for you is essential to your success.

English for Academic Purposes

Students whose first language is not primarily English have particular difficulties with English reading comprehension, and, in particular, with translating reading into writing. Culturally different schemata (or background knowledge) vocabulary, and grammar problems can frustrate these students, who have often been taught a bottom-up approach in university-readiness programs, focusing on, grammatical structure: words, phrases, and sentences. Once in university, however, students need to read and write from a top-down approach, contextualizing the individual focus on the word and sentence in the meaning and message contained within the whole text.

Because the schemata are different for foreign-language students, these students will usually be more successful if they can read and write about topics that help them integrate their prior knowledge. If this strategy is not possible, they will do better working with a top-down approach, attempting to understand the central message and overall meaning of a text. For many students, essay organization is also a problem. Whereas English texts tend to have a highly structured logical organization, many European and Asian texts tend to be more theoretical and abstract.

Vocabulary problems can be addressed by using a dictionary, but the tendency in English to use words that have more than one meaning can be confusing (i.e., breakfast table versus a table of contents). As previously mentioned, the use of articles, verb construction, agreement, and tense can be confusing for foreign-language students. If the student knows and understands English grammatical rules, most of these problems can be fixed at the editing stage of the revision process. When revising, however, it is important to keep the whole meaning of the text, the central message, in mind. The danger in extensive editing is that the meaning gets lost. The think-aloud protocol can work well to enable English as a second language students to become aware of their own particular errors.

REVIEW

Exercise 5.8

- Use any *one* of the processes explained in this chapter and apply it to a reading of any *one* of the readings in the Reader.
- Make notes as you develop your understanding of the text. Ask, how is this text relevant? A self-reflective awareness of what you don't know, as well as what you think you know, will help you avoid misreading or misinterpreting the material.
- Share your insights with your classmates. Find out what works for you.

CHAPTER SUMMARY

In this chapter you have considered the differences between passive and active reading, and developed an understanding of some of the conventions deployed by academic writers. To be able to write well, you must be able to understand and read a text accurately. This chapter has provided you with some practical strategies for reading and responding to a text and some theoretical approaches to reading that can give you deeper insight into your own reading methods and provide you with alternative approaches.

In the next chapter, I will show you how summary can be used both as a strategy for understanding a text and as an essential tool for developing your ideas. Summary will continue the emphasis on note-taking in this chapter and extend it to writing. It is important to know that reading, thinking, and writing are not separate activities but are intertwined, each component an essential part of the academic process.

QUESTIONS FOR CONSIDERATION

1. Do you think there is any place for passive reading in any of your university classes?
2. What strategies can you use to develop your skills in active reading? How will these strategies deepen your understanding of a text?
3. Why is it important to be aware of how a text is structured? How might this help you understand it?
4. How do you think an awareness of theoretical approaches will help you when reading?
5. What strategies might you use if you have learning or second-language difficulties?

6

Summary Writing

LEARNING OBJECTIVES

In this chapter, you will learn:

◆ How and why summary writing is important to academic reading and writing.

◆ How to recognize and use summary in others' writing assignments and your own.

◆ How to use summary as a strategy for understanding a text.

◆ A process for reading for summary and writing summaries.

◆ How to write a summary essay.

◆ How to structure/organize an essay.

◆ The difference between summary, paraphrasing, the formal précis, and the **abstract**.

This chapter takes us from reading to writing: you will consider not only how summary appears in the texts you read but also how you might use summary in your own writing. In this respect, Peter Elbow argues that the reading-thinking-writing process implies a fixed and linear order, reflecting "the implicit assumption that reading comes first and that writing must follow." However, the process is, in fact, recursive, causing you to circle unavoidably backwards and forwards, repeating the steps as you refine and redefine what you find to be true (8). As a result, you will make a substantial shift to writing in this chapter although you will cover summary as a reading strategy.

Within the academic reading-thinking-writing process, summary writing is crucial. In learning how to write the summary, you will be establishing yourself as someone who is familiar with the knowledge-making practices and the reading and writing skills required in academia. Throughout your academic writing career, you might be asked to summarize the content of an academic article, a chapter in a book, or, for example, a film. Your accuracy in summarizing a text like this will not only prove you are a good reader, it will also prove that you can use analytical processes to identify the main points of a text.

However, since academics do not simply repeat the ideas of others but add to these ideas, you will also be expected to understand how summary works in critical research papers written by other academics to establish a basis of understanding, and then to extend the argument beyond that understanding.

Summary: A Definition

A summary is a condensed and accurate restatement of a text, rarely more than one-quarter as long as the original text, written in your own words. It uses a neutral tone and avoids judgment or interpretation. The main purpose of the summary is to highlight the *main* points of a text. This enables your reader to clearly understand the text without having to read the original work.

What Summary Is Not: Summary versus Paraphrase

Often students become confused about the difference between summary and **paraphrase**. Both techniques ask students to restate the meaning of the text in their own words, but a summary significantly shortens the text (usually so it is about one-quarter of the original length) and a paraphrase includes *all* of the main information. As a result, paraphrasing works better for reports, where all the detail needs to be accounted for, or for shorter pieces of work where all of the main points can be restated. Consider the following example comparing a paraphrase and a summary:

Original passage:

In *Wuthering Heights*, Emily Bronte reveals a number of characters who are confined by their desire to conform to the conventional norms of society. Truth, to them is contained in tried and true notions of reality. The Socratic conception of truth, however, tells us that truth is revealed, not in any official claim to a ready-made conception, but from an intelligent questioning of our reality.

Paraphrase:

In her novel *Wuthering Heights*, Emily Bronte's characters conform to conventional societal norms. Their reality is based upon what everyone in society knows to be true. This belief is complicated by Socrates' argument that truth is a result of a serious and intelligent examination of everything we know.

Summary:

In *Wuthering Heights*, the tendency of Emily Bronte's characters to conform to societal norms is complicated by Socrates' concept of truth.

Table 6.1 ◆ Summary versus Paraphrase

Summarizing is the process by which a writer identifies and extracts the *main* points from a work and rearranges them in his or her own words to accurately reflect the main idea or argument. A summary is considerably shorter than the original work, often as much as one-quarter as long.	**Paraphrasing** is the process by which a writer puts someone else's ideas into his or her own words. The emphasis here is on accounting for everything the writer has written. This means that the paraphrase is usually around the same length as the original work.

As you can see, both the paraphrase and the summary are accurate interpretations of the material, but whereas the paraphrase simply restates the original passage using approximately the same number of words, the summary condenses and focuses the information and, in doing so, is far shorter than the original passage. As a result, the summary, in terms of academic writing, is effective precisely because it is in keeping with an academic style that demands a concise and focused form of writing.

How Summary Appears in Different Genres

Sometimes, it is easier to understand how summary works by considering and comparing how it appears in both academic and non-academic texts. Complete the following exercise so you can see how summary appears in a variety of genres and contexts.

Exercise 6.1

SUMMARY IN DIFFERENT GENRES

Compare how summary works in different genres in the following short summary passages.

- See if you can identify *what* is being summarized and the genre of the piece. Is the information an *accurate* and *condensed* restatement of the original material?
- Consider *how* the information is being summarized. How are these writers engaging with other sources, writers, and/or studies?
- In your opinion, which excerpt has the most credibility? Which excerpt carries the most authority? Which excerpt do you trust the most?

PASSAGE 1

"I heard on the television that they have come up with a cure for skin cancer. Statistics show that it's really working."

PASSAGE 2

Back in the 80s, one of the most-used products by guitarists of a certain style was the A/DA MP-1, a 128-patch, programmable 19-inch rack preamp that was the first to combine value with what was, at the time, a mind-boggling level of MIDI-driven versatility. It offered a modest number of voicings, plus an onboard chorus that caused players of the time, still reeling at the demise of the original Van Halen line-up, to scrabble for their piggy banks. What's more, in those halcyon pre-Nevermind days, it sounded fantastic. (Bradley 125)

PASSAGE 3

Scholars have suggested that women caught up to men in college graduation rates as a result of declining discrimination, occupational restructuring, changing norms, patters of family formation, and increasing returns to college degrees for women, all of which encouraged increased educational attainment for women relative to men (DiPrete & Bachman, 2006, Goldin et al., 2006). Although such processes may help to explain why women caught up to men in college graduation rates, these explanations cannot fully account for why women *surpassed* men. That is, why are women currently *more* likely than men to graduate? In order to shed light on this puzzling female advantage in college graduation, this study examines contemporary gender disparities in higher education. (Ewert 824–50)

See the Exercise Answer Key in Appendix A for an analysis of the examples.

Summary Writing and Its Place in University and College Writing

In the academic context, summary, which provides a condensed understanding of a text, allows academics to summarize concepts, movements, specific moments in history, etc., or their own work. Perhaps more important, summary allows academics to position their research in relation to a community of scholars concerned with the same knowledge or subject matter. In summarizing another scholar's engagement with a specific knowledge base (cancer research, poverty in cities, third-world literature, etc.), a researcher can, in turn, take a position him- or herself. Scholars can thus construct new knowledge that will add to the knowledge that is already out there. Summary thus provides a way for researchers to share and build on the knowledge that is specific to their particular discipline and community.

For students new to academia, summary is an essential first phase in the reading and writing process. Your ability to use summary will be directly correlated to your success as a student.

Summary as a Strategy for Reading and Understanding a Text

Summary writing will teach you to

- Accurately read and write someone else's words in your own words.
- Become a close reader.

- Become an accurate and focused writer.
- Distinguish between summarizing someone else's ideas and your interpretation or analysis of someone else's ideas, one of the most common mistakes made by undergraduate students.
- Identify and attribute someone else's ideas while recognizing and owning the ideas that are your own.

ACADEMIC FOCUS

SUMMARY WRITING: BENEFITS FOR STUDENTS

Beyond its status in academia, summary has a diverse array of benefits for student writers, which I have listed below.

As a skill, summary writing

- Helps students to identify the thesis statement (central message), topic sentences, supporting ideas, and evidence.
- Helps with comprehension problems.
- Teaches students to express the ideas of other writers in their own words, without altering the original meaning, helping students to translate their academic reading into academic writing.
- Helps students to appreciate and emulate concise logical writing.
- Enables students to recognize the difference between summarizing and interpretation.

Exercise 6.2

SUMMARY VERSUS INTERPRETATION

- Analyze the following student passage.
- Highlight the points where the student summarizes Keats.
- Highlight the points where the student uses her own analysis or interpretation of Keats's work.

In the second stanza of "Ode on Melancholy," Keats goes on to explore the melancholic state by stating it is the "weeping cloud / that fosters the droop-headed flowers all" (12–13). Stressing the extreme and self-perpetuating force of the melancholic state, Keats argues that it is the veil that hides "the green hill" (14) and prevents us from discriminating between Spring, which implies life, and the shroud, which implies death. For Keats, then, life is over laden with a cover of melancholy from which it is hard to escape.

Besides being able to distinguish between your ideas and someone else's, summary writing is quite simply an excellent strategy for reading and understanding texts. It works well for difficult academic texts that are hard to understand and follow. Remember that when you summarize, you are simply accurately restating the most important original ideas in your own words in a more manageable, concise form. Keep in mind, however, that while you want your summary to be accurate, other students doing the same exercise might highlight or emphasize certain points more than others. One writer might even omit a point, if he or she does not consider it essential to an understanding of the text, whereas another writer might decide that it is important enough to include.

How to Use Summary

In scholarly texts, you will see summary being used in two main ways: There might be a summary essay; a longer summary, comprising a paragraph or even a few paragraphs; or a very short summary only one or two sentences long. Consider how this student is using summary to introduce her essay topic and argument:

> In *Oedipus the King*, Oedipus possesses his mother and takes her to his bed as his wife, but the whole plot revolves around the fact that this is unconscious. He is characterized by non-knowing. He "knows nothing" about his origins, his parentage, or his present circumstances (474). As Teiresias informs him, "even [his] own words / miss the mark" (348–9). In not knowing who he is, Oedipus is a curse to both himself and his kin (460). He destroys his family and ends up as a blind outcast himself. This focus in the play is consistent historically with, as R. W. Connell states, the belief that men's knowledge hinges not on familial relations, but on an identification with a "fixed, true masculinity" that remains unquestioned (45).

In this paragraph, the writer uses summary in several ways:

1. To provide a summary of the story and background information; and
2. To reveal her point of view and her position or main argument.

In the first sentence, the writer provides a plot summary: Oedipus possesses his mother and takes her to his bed as his wife. The summary is not complete, but it serves the writer's purpose here, to explore Oedipus's unconscious behaviour. In the rest of the paragraph, the writer uses summary to highlight the sections of the play that support her argument that Oedipus's lack of consciousness is a result of his identification with a normative masculinity. To do this, she cites small excerpts from the play. Giltrow calls this use of citation "tiny summaries," summaries that provide the gist of a certain pertinent section of a work. As you might have observed, the writer summarizes R.W. Connell's idea about masculinity, while using his authority in a citation to support her position.

You might also note that the writer of this excerpt uses another academic convention that we covered in chapter 2, reporting expressions (also called signal phrases because they signal the inclusion of a quote or summary), which include the use of academic verbs: Teiresias *informs* him; as R.W. Connell *states*. See chapter 2 for an extensive list of academic verbs (page 33).

RULES FOR USING SUMMARY

When writing a summary, you must

- Identify the author and the title, and summarize the author's main argument—the thesis or the main message of the essay— the main ideas (generalizing abstractions), and the supporting ideas (concrete detail or examples).
- Be concise. A summary is rarely longer than one-quarter the length of the original, often much briefer.
- Sum up the work in your own words, providing an accurate and concise summary of the main points of the original, but not necessarily in the same order.
- Not attempt to judge or interpret the text.
- Include *significant* quotations to capture the tone of the work. Be careful, however, about overusing quotations. They should be used only to support your points. Quotations must be contained within quotation marks, employ varied and appropriate reporting expressions, and be cited both in the body of the text and in the works cited page.
- Write your summary in the present tense.

Exercise 6.3

SUMMARY VERSUS INTERPRETATION II

Highlight all the places in the Oedipus introduction above where summary and interpretation are highlighted.

Writing the Summary Essay

While summary, as in the example above, is used throughout your work to provide a concise and brief summary of someone else's work, to present necessary background information, such as when you include a historical, psychological, or biographical context for your main argument, or, indeed, to summarize your own previous argument, it can also be used in essay form to summarize a theory, a concept, or an entire article. For example, academics write summary essays on feminist movements, philosophical theories, or historical events. Learning how to write a summary essay will teach you to become an accurate reader, but it will also teach you how to identify the main points of a text, and then organize these points into a clear logical structure.

Summary Writing Process

Here is a process for writing a summary essay.

1. Read the article at least twice: the first time, read it quickly to get the gist of the article's main points. Pay attention to the title, headings, bolded words, and the thesis statement or main argument, etc.

2. The second time, read the article slowly and carefully. Identify the main argument or thesis statement. In a short essay, this will usually be at the end of the first paragraph or first section of the paper. If you cannot find it in the introduction (which should introduce all the main points of the essay and the main argument), you will find it, restated for emphasis, in the conclusion. In your summary, you must clearly articulate the author's thesis in your own words

3. Make a **gist outline** of the main points either down the side of the page or in a notebook. At this stage, this outline should be in point form, but remember that unlike a paraphrase that requires you to write down *all* the points, a summary requires only that you write down the most important points. You should be able to find the main points in the **topic sentences** of each paragraph. However, keep in mind that one topic might extend over several paragraphs, extending and developing the particular point and/or providing evidence to support the point, so you might not need to write down the main points in every paragraph. The best way is to keep the article's thesis statement in mind and then identify which of the gist outline points most clearly relate to it.

4. Follow this up with an outline of the large **abstractions** and **concrete reference points**. You will need to keep your essay structure in mind at this point. Picking one abstraction and one or two supporting points will enable you to distinguish between evidence you can use as examples and evidence you can discard as being peripheral to your summary (see example later in this chapter).

5. Translate your reading into writing. After identifying the main points of the article, and checking to make sure you haven't missed anything or misread anything, concisely restate, in your own words, the main points of the article. Although your gist outline will, at this point, be listed chronologically as it follows the logic of the article you are summarizing, you can move the gist points around, shaping them to reflect the logical development of your summary.

6. You might include brief but significant quotations to capture the tone of the piece and to emphasize the main points. Make sure that you cite these points. The length of your summary will depend on your assignment: You might be asked to write a few sentences, a paragraph, a page, or an entire essay.

7. Most important, do *not* write about your reaction to the text. You are simply restating the article in your own words.

Modelling the Summary Process

Writing the summary essay is a good exercise in accurate reading and essay structure because essay writing teaches you how to organize your information logically and clearly. In this section, I will do a sample reading of Wayne Booth's "The Rhetorical

Stance" (see page 335 in the Reader) for you, which will include a gist outline, a map showing of the large abstractions or ideas and concrete reference points or evidence, and an annotated sample student essay.

Step 1. Read the Essay

First, read Wayne Booth's essay "The Rhetorical Stance" (see page 335 in the Reader). You might have noted that Booth's essay is relatively informal. This is because it was originally written as a conference paper, which is another academic genre altogether. These papers are meant for an audience, so the tone tends to be more informal and to contain, as Booth illustrates in this paper, some personal examples. The paper is also usually shorter than a published academic paper (approximately 8 pages rather than 25 pages).

Because these papers are often later developed into longer academic papers, you will often find that the structure is not as tight as it could be. You might have noted, for example, that Booth includes far more examples for the Pedant's stance than he does for the Advertiser's or Entertainer's stances. You might also have noticed that the thesis is not completely clear at the beginning of the essay but that it gets reiterated later in the essay.

The main challenge in summarizing Booth's essay will be to pick examples—concrete evidence (in this case, the three stances)—that accurately speak to the larger abstraction articulated in his thesis.

Exercise 6.4

WAYNE BOOTH'S "THE RHETORICAL STANCE"

Read Wayne Booth's essay "The Rhetorical Stance" (see page 335 in the Reader) and answer the following questions.

1. Is there a clear introductory paragraph?
2. Can you identify the thesis statement?
3. Are the body paragraphs easy to follow?

Make notes in the margins about anything that interests or disturbs you about the essay.
- What is clear and/or unclear?
- How does the essay conform to academic writing standards as you understand them at this time?

Compare your analysis with that of your classmates.

Step 2. Make a Gist Outline of the Essay

Most students will find Booth's essay hard to follow and understand. This difficulty stems from the fact that the thesis statement is not clearly or completely articulated at the end of the first paragraph. Also, the evidence and examples are not equally balanced in relation to Booth's three stances, so it is hard to identify the logical development of the essay. To thoroughly understand the main points, you will need to make a gist outline of Booth's essay. To begin with, this gist outline will, as my sample gist outline does, include all the main points of the essay, similar to a point-form paraphrase. Once you have this gist outline, though, you will then need to go through it and highlight the most important points for communicating Booth's main argument. Do not attempt to use all of Booth's points: Be selective and omit the points that are less important.

GIST OUTLINE

Exercise 6.5

1. Write a gist outline for Booth's essay and compare it with the one I have provided in the academic focus box. Did you write down the same points? If not, how is your gist outline different? Did you omit some information? If so, was it essential or non-essential information?

2. Now go through my gist outline and highlight the relevant information. Compare it with your outline and discuss with your classmates which important points you have highlighted.

ACADEMIC FOCUS

GIST OUTLINE: WAYNE BOOTH'S "A RHETORICAL STANCE"

Please note that I have bolded Booth's several articulations of his thesis. Keep in mind that you will not use all of Booth's examples or evidence but you can pick the example you consider most useful for each stance.

Introduction/ Paragraph 1. (thesis, loosely *defined*) Students have a "rhetorical problem": They struggle to write a "stimulating, organized, convincing" argument (3). **To do this, they have to pay attention to audience, argument, and "tone of voice" (3)**

Paragraph 2. Rhetoric *defined* loosely.

Paragraph 3. *Booth's definition*: "Rhetoric is the art of finding and employing the most effective means of persuasion on any subject, considered independently of intellectual mastery of that subject" (3). The problem is can and should we teach it to students: "should it be taught? If it should, how do we go about it, head on or obliquely?" (4).

Paragraph 4. It is important to teach rhetoric in all disciplines/subjects (structural linguistics).

Paragraph 5. Rhetoric is hidden and refused in favour of discussions about a topic.

Paragraph 6. Misconceptions about natural ability vs learning rhetoric.

Paragraph 7. Responsibility/need to teach rhetoric or the "art of persuasion." *Examples* of Booth's own struggles with rhetoric (pretentious tone, transitions, evidence, structure, generalizations).

Paragraph 8. Returns to controversy here. Need to teach rhetoric. Good strategy when teaching rhetoric is to look for what is common to "both

Continued

of good writing and good writing instruction" (5). Leads to his thesis (par 9/10).

Paragraph 9. Common ingredient in good writing/persuasion is **"the rhetorical stance, a stance which depends on discovering and maintaining in any writing situation a proper balance among the three elements that are at work in any communicative effort: the available arguments about the subject itself, the interests and peculiarities of the audience and the voice, the implied character of the speaker"** (re-articulation and re-specification of first general thesis).

Paragraph 10. The "true rhetorician's stance can best be seen by contrasting it" with *corruptions* of this balance. The main idea here is that **when** students or writers become aware of the corruptions, they will be better able to achieve a rhetorical balance and their writing will become more effective.

Paragraph 11. "The pedant's stance": "ignoring or underplaying the personal relationship of speaker and audience and depending entirely on statements about a subject" (6).

Paragraph 12. *Solution:* Teaching students that they don't have to pay attention to "what their expositions are for" results in "meaningless paper[s]" (6). Must have a "question . . . worth answering" and an audience in mind.

Paragraph 13. *Example/evidence* of freshman texts and his assignment.

Paragraph 14. *Example/evidence:* ETS.

Paragraph 15. Analysis of these results: students and judges of essays "given no purpose and no audience."

Paragraph 16. *Solution:* workshops: "arrange for weekly confrontations of groups of students over their own papers."

Paragraph 17. Summary of first stance and introduction to second stance, which is the **"advertiser's stance"**: the "undervaluing of the subject and overvaluing of pure effect: how to win friends and influence people" (8).

Paragraph 18. *Solution:* Avoid writing in a "controversial or argumentative" way that "stir[s] up the audience" as "an end in itself" (8). Remember that "good persuasion is honest persuasion" and a "good rhetorician must be master of his subject" (8). Accommodating the audience in an honest way is often different from accommodating them in terms of "what will sell" (8).

Paragraphs 19, 20. *Example/evidence* of advertiser's stance: author's strategy of polling audience.

Paragraph 21. "Desire to persuade" not as important as clear purpose: Burke/Churchill.

Paragraph 22. "The entertainer's stance": the "willingness to sacrifice substance to personality and charm" (9). *Examples/evidence:* Walker Gibson and James Thurber.

Paragraph 23. *Examples/evidence* of balanced rhetorical stances: Milton, Churchill, and Burke are writers who have thought "an important question through, in the company of an audience" (9).

Paragraphs 24, 25. Conclusion: Teaching/ importance of balance (Churchill). Important to "our" reputation as a nation.

Step 3. Outline the Large Abstractions and Concrete Detail or Evidence

Once you have your gist outline, you will need to decide which of the points are most useful to your summary. You must also keep in mind the need to balance your main points with an equal amount of supporting evidence. A useful strategy is to map out the relationship between the large abstractions and specific concrete detail. This outline is also useful for students who work better with visual references. What follows is an outline of the Oedipus paragraph (see "How to Use a Summary" above). Note how the abstract statements are supported by concrete detail or evidence, which leads to another abstraction and more detail.

Oedipus: unconscious (overriding abstraction)

|

Knows nothing of origins (concrete detail 1)

|

Tiresias: quote. (concrete detail 2)

|

Curse to himself and his kin (abstraction)

|

Destroys family and blind outcast himself (concrete detail)

|

Oedipus—product of men's fixed knowledge: unconscious (large abstraction)

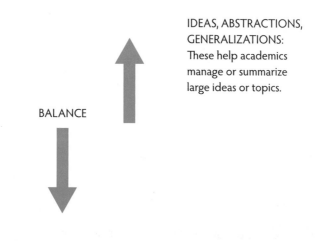

IDEAS, ABSTRACTIONS, GENERALIZATIONS: These help academics manage or summarize large ideas or topics.

BALANCE

EVIDENCE: Specific information or references that ground larger ideas in specific reference points. Helps reader to understand larger ideas by providing concrete reference points.

Figure 6.1 ◆ **Relationship between Abstractions and Evidence (Concrete Reference Points)**

Exercise 6.6

DIAGRAM OF ABSTRACTIONS AND CONCRETE EVIDENCE

- As explained in Step 3 above, remember that you need to make a clear and balanced distinction between main statements or abstractions and supporting detail or concrete evidence.
- Take the *main* points from the gist outline and create a diagram illustrating how they work in the essay. Begin by identifying Booth's thesis statement. This will force you to think not only about the main points or the large abstractions but also about the concrete evidence or examples that will support those points.
- Compare your diagram with the diagram below.
- Work on this with your classmates, so you can compare readings.

ACADEMIC FOCUS

SAMPLE DIAGRAM OF ABSTRACTIONS AND CONCRETE DETAIL

Wayne Booth, "The Rhetorical Stance"

Thesis, part A: The common ingredient in good writing/persuasion is "the rhetorical stance, a stance which depends on discovering and maintaining in any writing situation a proper balance among the three elements that are at work in any communicative effort: the available **arguments** about the subject itself, the interests and peculiarities of the **audience**, and the **voice**, the implied character of the speaker."

Thesis, part B: An awareness of the corruptions of this balance will enable more effective/persuasive writing

"Pedant's stance"	"Advertiser's stance"	"Entertainer's stance"
Definitions:		
Ignoring audience; depending on subject	Overvaluing of "pure effect"	Sacrifice substance to charm
e.g.: student assignment	**e.g.:** novelist polling audience	**e.g.:** Walker Gibson
Solutions:		
Must have a "question . . . worth answering" and a clear audience	Avoid writing in a "controversial or argumentative" way; be honest	Think "an important question through," in the company of clear audience; be objective
Know audience: workshops can help	Master subject while keeping audience in mind	Balance needed: Milton, etc., as examples of people who do it well

Conclusion: An awareness of the Pedant's, Advertiser's, and Entertainer's stances will make for more effective persuasive writing. Becoming a more accomplished writer is important not only to students but also, as Booth argues, to the development of the nation.

Note that in outlining the essay in this diagram a lot of the original information from the gist outline has been omitted, for example, the extensive discussion of teaching rhetoric and a number of the examples. Instead, this diagram focuses on the essential information—the thesis, the stances, the examples to support them, and the solutions—pertinent to Booth's argument. Moreover, not all of the supporting examples are included in the diagram. Instead, only relevant examples have been chosen to balance the three stances.

This diagram, as you might have already noted, will provide you with a base outline for writing a summary essay. You now have a clear outline for organizing your essay into an introduction, concluding with Booth's thesis, body paragraphs—one for each of the stances and their corresponding evidence and solution—and a conclusion. What follows is a basic introduction to essay organization. Going beyond the five-paragraph essay, it includes a description of the information each part of your essay should contain. Can you see how the above process for outlining an essay into large abstractions and concrete detail or evidence can help you achieve a clear, logical structure?

Essay Organization: Paragraph and Sentence Structure

When organizing your ideas and writing, it is important to make sure that you structure your ideas logically in a basic academic essay format. To introduce you to essay writing, I will use, as an example, a deductive essay, which works logically from general to specific premises, in other words, from a general statement to concrete specifics. All essays must include

- an introductory paragraph that indicates the main idea of the essay;
- body paragraphs that develop the main idea; and
- a conclusion that summarizes the main ideas and points to a larger consideration (in a summary essay, this will be a larger consideration raised by the author in the essay).

Introductions

- The introductory paragraph needs to arouse the reader's interest, but, more important, it should clearly show what the essay is about, offer some background information, and get straight to the point. Make sure that you mention the author and the name of the work you are summarizing or analyzing.
- Body sentences should provide an introduction to or *summary* of your essay, mentioning briefly all of your main essay points. Think of the summary as a contract with your reader. It tells your reader exactly what you are agreeing to write about in the body of your essay.
- Sentences should flow logically from point to point, allowing readers to easily follow the main points of your argument, to move your argument forward.

Your introduction must contain your thesis statement or main argument, showing the direction the essay will take. In a deductive essay, this comes at the end of your introductory paragraph (or section). In a summary essay, this thesis statement will be the thesis given by the writer you are summarizing.

Body Paragraphs

- Each paragraph should articulate and develop *one* topic or aspect of your overall larger argument. Always keep your larger or main argument in mind. Remember that this main argument is what you are proving with *each* and *every* body paragraph.
- Good paragraphs have unity, coherence, and logical development. All the sentences should support and clarify the main idea of the paragraph.
- Here is an outline of basic paragraph structure:

  Topic sentence: main idea of paragraph; clarifies the thesis statement or a subtopic of the thesis statement.

  Second sentence: limits and clarifies the main idea.

  Body sentences: support the main idea. All sentences should be logically connected; all sentences should move the idea(s) forward by adding depth to your argument in the form of significant and relevant detail. You can achieve paragraph coherence by organizing your ideas, by being specific, and by using transitional devices.

  Concluding sentence: reinforces the main idea of the paragraph, without repeating or summarizing, and points forward to the next paragraph.

Conclusion

- Rounds out the previous discussion.
- Briefly summarizes the main points of the essay (without being repetitive, and without stating the obvious, "to summarize, to conclude," etc.).
- Points to a larger consideration of the topic under discussion. Answers the question *why* you wrote this, and *why* your reader should read it.

Sentence Transitions

As previously stated, sentences should logically and clearly develop your argument point by point. Keep in mind that transitional words or phrases help bring coherence to a paragraph by signalling relationships between sentences and paragraphs.

Example: Consider the following passage: Is it clear and easy to understand?

> In "The Rhetorical Stance," Wayne C. Booth describes rhetoric as "the art of finding and employing the most effective means of persuasion on any subject" (3). Many students do not write effectively. Booth suggests teaching students how to find a rhetorical balance in their writing. There are three elements that work together to create balance: "the available arguments about the subject itself, the interests and peculiarities of the audience, and the voice, the implied character, of the speaker" (5). Booth highlights the errors that are commonly made when rhetoric becomes unbalanced.

You might have noted that the meaning embedded in these sentences was hard to follow because it appears to jump from rhetoric to elements to errors. Providing sentence transitions in the form of words or phrases can help clarify meaning for your reader. Consider the following passage with these transitions (italicized) in place: Is the meaning clearer now? Does the inclusion of the transitional words and phrases help develop the writer's ideas logically?

> In "The Rhetorical Stance," Wayne C. Booth describes rhetoric as "the art of finding and employing the most effective means of persuasion on any subject" (3). *However,* many students do not write effectively. *Consequently,* Booth suggests teaching students how to find a rhetorical balance in their writing. *According to Booth,* there are three elements that work together to create balance: "the available arguments about the subject itself, the interests and peculiarities of the audience, and the voice, the implied character, of the speaker" (5). *In order to better teach this rhetorical balance,* Booth highlights the errors that are commonly made when rhetoric becomes unbalanced.

Can you see how these transitional devices help the reader follow the logic of the writer's argument? When writing, it is important to realize that the reader cannot understand what you are thinking if you don't make it absolutely clear on paper. Transitional devices can help to create a logical relationship between ideas and, perhaps more important, clarity.

Organizing Evidence

Organizing or structuring your evidence, as you did in Exercise 6.6: "Diagram of Abstractions and Concrete Evidence," is another crucial aspect of essay writing. When writing a summary, as when writing a critical or research essay, keep in mind that academics always support their statements with evidence. This might include any of the following: authorities cited or quoted; research findings, evidence, data; examples, whether brief or extended (including anecdotes); logical illustrations, such as analogies; literary devices, such as metaphors, imagery, etc.

Another way of considering this relationship between general statements and concrete evidence is to recognize that academics work from abstract generalizations

ACADEMIC FOCUS

TRANSITIONAL DEVICES

Refer to these commonly used transitions when trying to make your sentences flow logically and accurately.

1. To show time, use:

presently	before	meanwhile	at length
immediately	next	while	from then on
thereupon	thereafter	afterward	beforehand
when	then	soon	

2. To contrast, use:

but	though	nevertheless	yet
on the one hand	conversely	in contrast	surely
on the other hand	although	notwithstanding	
on the contrary	however	still	

3. To compare, use:

Likewise	similarly	at the same time	in like manner
once more	once again	In much the same way	

4. To summarize or conclude, use:

as a result	therefore	hence	so
as a consequence	consequently	for this reason	and so
in other words	finally	because	accordingly
first, second, third, etc.			

5. To add, use:

furthermore	moreover	first, second, etc.	in addition
and	in fact	besides	indeed
again	also		

6. To give an example, use:

for example	likewise	frequently	similarly
that is	whenever	in general	generally
for instance	specifically	in particular	to illustrate
occasionally			

7. To repeat, use:

in other words	to repeat	indeed	in fact
in any case	besides	to put it another way	

8. To prove, use:

because	besides	evidently	for
in any case	furthermore	indeed	in addition
in fact	that is	moreover	obviously
since	for the same reason		

or statements to specific concrete detail to provide increasing depth and detail. For instance, take the following example of student writing:

> Booth criticizes the way educators teach students how to write. In order to correct this problem, he creates a guideline, which encourages educators to focus on teaching students to maintain a balance between their argument, audience, and voice.

Here, the student begins with a large abstraction: Booth criticizes educators about their ability to teach students how to write, but we don't know why or how. The next sentence gets more concrete, or specific. It lets the reader know how Booth attempts to correct the problem by making a guideline for educators and that this guideline, even more specifically, focuses on teaching students how to balance argument, audience, and voice.

Before you go on and read the annotated student essay that has gone through the above process, review the diagram of abstractions and concrete evidence (Figure 6.1) outlined earlier in relation to Booth's essay. Can you predict this essay's paragraph construction and use of evidence?

Wayne Booth's "The Rhetorical Stance": A Summary

BY SAVANNAH SIMPSON

1   In Wayne C. Booth's "The Rhetorical Stance," rhetoric is defined as "the art of finding and employing the most effective means of persuasion on any subject, considered independently of intellectual mastery of that subject" (3). In order to write both successfully and persuasively, Booth stresses the importance of "the rhetorical stance, a stance which depends on discovering and maintaining in any writing situation a proper balance among the three elements that are at work in any communicative effort: the available arguments about the subject itself, the interest and peculiarities of the audience, and the voice, the implied character, of the speaker" (5). To effectively demonstrate "the true rhetorician's stance" (6), he uses "corruptions" (6) to contrast the proper balance. These corruptions include "the pedant's stance" (ignoring his or her audience), "the advertiser's stance" (overlooking the subject), and "the entertainer's stance" (losing the implied character) (6). Booth emphasizes that rhetoric and balance will result when a writer identifies his or her audience, has a strong argument and exercises the "proper tone of voice" (3).

2   The first corruption Booth explains is "the pedant's stance" (6). This corruption incorporates "ignoring or underplaying the personal relationship of the speaker and audience and depending entirely on statements about a subject" (6). To demonstrate how important it is for writers to determine who his or

Annotations:

Good opening sentence: Savannah mentions Booth and his essay, and defines rhetoric. Good sentence transition to Booth's "rhetorical stance" definition. Note that the first time Booth is mentioned, he is referred to by his full name but in subsequent references he is referred to as "Booth."

Good shift to the unbalanced or "corrupt" stances. Note the short summary definition in parenthesis.

Booth's thesis or main argument.

Pedant's stance: Paragraph structure: first, second, third, etc.

First thesis point and definition.

Example/evidence.

Summary of Booth's analysis.

Booth's solution to the problem.

Advertiser's stance: Second thesis point and definition.

Supporting example/evidence and solution.

Entertainer's stance: Third thesis point and definition.

Supporting example/evidence and solution.

Conclusion reiterates, without repeating, Booth's thesis, while also extending it, as Booth does, to a consideration of the nation.

her audience is, Booth discusses a paper he assigned to students where he did not clearly state "what their expositions were for" (6). Because the students did not have a clear purpose or audience, they wrote very weak and pointless papers. Booth uses this example to stress the need to discover "a desire to say something to somebody" and learn "to control his [or her] diction for a purpose" (6). A way to effectively overcome the "pedantic stance is to arrange for weekly confrontations of groupings of students over their own papers" (8). Students need to have a purpose and clear audience in order to overcome the pedant's stance.

3   The second corruption is "the advertiser's stance," which "comes from undervaluing the subject and overvaluing pure effect: how to win friends and influence people" (8). Booth recalls a novelist who polled an audience about his book title to see what would sell the best. When Booth asked if the title chosen was accurate, the novelist replied, "not quite as well as the others, but that doesn't matter" (9) This novelist was not following "the old Platonic truth that good persuasion is honest persuasion" (8). The solution Booth provides to this unbalanced stance is for writers to be honest and a "master of [their] subject[s]" (8) while staying true to the audience.

4   The last corruption Booth mentions is the "entertainer's stance," which is "the willingness to sacrifice substance to personality and charm" (9). The example Booth provides is of Walker Gibson; as Walker tries to "startle us out of dry pedantry, his exhortations to find and develop the speaker's voice can lead to empty colorfulness" (9). In trying to make his material entertaining, Gibson is not being true to his own voice or subject matter. In order to correct this unbalance, Booth suggests that writers "think through the important questions in the company of an audience," and show readers, through their writing, that what they have to say is important (9).

5   Booth has given these three corruptions and possible solutions to help communicate effective balance. Booth claims that "as a nation . . . we are more inclined to the perversions of rhetoric than to the rhetorical balance (10). Proper balance can only be mastered when a writer knows "more about the subject then we do, and if he [or she] then engages us in the process of thinking . . . it through" (9). By identifying his or her audience, having a strong argument, and exercising the "proper tone of voice" (3), a writer can succeed in "the true arts of persuasion" (10).

General comment: This is a good summary essay: the student has demonstrated a clear understanding of Booth's essay without inserting her own opinion. In doing so, she highlights Booth's important points, making the reading accessible to someone who has not actually read Booth's essay.

As you can see, this essay covers the main points of Booth's essay; it does not, however, focus on teaching. Although teaching is a major focus of Booth's essay, it is not essential to an understanding of the main points, which focus on what writers need to do to write persuasively. The choice to include teaching here would be an individual one; however, if the writer had included a focus on teaching, it would need to inform the introduction, all the body paragraphs, and the conclusion. Booth's debate about whether rhetoric should or should not be taught in higher education is peripheral to the main argument, since he concludes, and his entire essay supports, that it should be taught. Keep in mind that you can use this process to understand a difficult essay as well as to organize your points for writing an essay.

The following exercise will help you review how summary is used to support and develop an argument.

SUMMARY AND ACADEMIC WRITING

Exercise 6.7

This exercise is designed to help you review the many ways that summary might be used in an academic essay.

- Choose an academic essay from the Reader. Highlight the summary sections of the essay. Remember that this might include a summary of the main text, a summary of another writer's ideas, or a summary of the writer's own points. You might want to use different-coloured highlighters to note the different ways summary is used.
- Discuss with your classmates how summary enables the writer to establish background information or to position himself or herself in relation to current studies in order to make an argument of his or her own.

Specialized Summaries: The Formal Précis, the Executive Summary, and the Abstract

Summaries take different forms in different contexts and disciplinary expectations. Here are three summary models, varieties of a general summary, that you might encounter in different disciplinary contexts.

1. The **formal précis** and the executive summary are more often seen in business contexts. The formal précis is similar to the summary, but the précis tends to be shorter and more focused than the summary.
2. The **executive summary** summarizes the main idea of a business proposal (sales proposal, bid, grant, etc.). Rather than focusing on accuracy, however, the executive proposal attempts to persuade the audience (customers, consumers,

corporate managers) of the validity of the proposition. It often focuses on a particular problem, for which it offers a solution. It attempts to "sell" this solution by stating the outcomes and benefits for a particular audience.

3. An **abstract** might appear sometimes at the beginning of a government report, a legal document, or a patent, but most often it is used at the beginning of an academic essay. Used primarily by academics working in the social sciences, the sciences, engineering, and business, it functions as a condensed summary of the essay, thus providing an overview or preview. In keeping with the writing conventions and style expected in these disciplines, the abstract includes a presentation of the problem (the general hypothesis), a methodology section, and a report on the writer's observations, results, conclusions, and recommendations. Although the abstract appears at the beginning of the essay, the writer may well choose to write it after he or she has fully formulated and written the essay.

Exercise 6.8

SUMMARY REVISION

- Choose any academic essay in the Reader and write your own summary of that essay.
- Use the essay writing process outlined in this chapter: a gist outline and an outline of the main and supporting points in the essay.
- Use a formal essay structure for this exercise (introduction (thesis), body paragraphs, conclusion), but do not write more than two pages. Writing a short essay will force you to be concise as you choose and focus the material you want to use.

CHAPTER SUMMARY

In this chapter, I considered the role that summary plays in academic writing. Summary takes different forms; however, a basic understanding of how summary is used in academia will help you become a better reader and writer. Summary writing will develop and reinforce your reading, analytical, organizational, and writing skills as you learn the process of taking a text apart to find the main points and then organizing it into the clear logical order. In the next chapter, I will develop a focus on analysis. This focus will help you make the transition from summary writing, where you reiterate someone else's points, to critical persuasive writing, where you can articulate your own thoughts and ideas on a topic.

QUESTIONS FOR CONSIDERATION

1. What are some of the main benefits of summary writing?
2. Why is summary writing important to academic reading and writing?
3. Can you outline the process for summarizing a text?
4. What role does evidence play in supporting large summary statements?
5. Can you summarize the main organizational structure of a deductive academic essay?
6. Why are sentence and paragraph transitions important?
7. Can you summarize some of the main features of summary writing in academia?
8. How does summary writing work to support and develop analytical persuasive writing?
9. What do I still need to know about Booth's essay to fully understand it?

7

Academic Analysis

LEARNING OBJECTIVES

In this chapter, you will learn:

- What analysis is and why it is an essential academic reasoning skill.

- Some key definitions for criticism, analysis, and argument.

- How to think critically.

- Some basic analytical strategies for performing a critical analysis of a text.

- A fundamental understanding of logic: ethos (ethics), pathos (emotion), logos (logic), syllogisms, and logical fallacies.

- How to write a preliminary or working thesis statement.

- The difference between discipline-specific types of critical analysis, including philosophy, literary, and scientific analysis.

- How and why a theoretical framework works.

Analysis is a fundamental reasoning process in academic reading. The depth of your analytical reading skills is directly correlated with, and precedes, your academic writing skills. When analyzing a subject, you generate knowledge about it through patterns of decomposition (breaking down the topic into its components) and re-composition (reassembling your ideas about the topic into a new argument or form of discussion). This is, essentially, what you learned to do in chapter 6, "Summary Writing," when you learned how to break down and discriminate between the lesser and the main points in Booth's essay "The Rhetorical Stance." In this chapter, however, you will go beyond summarizing the reading to developing your own analytical reading skills. You will be engaging with the text not simply to understand (although this is the first part of the process) but also to participate in critically analyzing the subject. As you begin to engage in the scholarly conversation about a text, you will find that you not only become a better, more informed, reader, but also a more successful academic writer.

Some Important Definitions

Once again, reading and writing are rarely linear processes. Reading, summarizing, and analyzing are rarely experienced in isolation. Indeed, many of you, as you read Booth's essay, probably found yourself engaging in a critique of it. You might, for example, have thought, "I don't understand what he is doing here" or "I don't know why he provides so much evidence for the Pedant's stance and next to no evidence for the Entertainer's stance." Questions like this are the starting place for an analytical critique.

Before we go any further, though, let's look at some definitions for criticism, analysis, and argument. Definitions are essential to academic writing and, specifically, to academic analysis. The general rule is that all ambiguous terms *must* be defined. By looking at these particular definitions, you will get a clearer idea of what is expected of you when you perform a critical analysis.

Here are some definitions of key words that will help you understand what is meant by critical analysis:

> **criticism:** (1) The action of criticizing, or passing judgment upon, the qualities or merits of anything; *especially* the passing of unfavourable judgment; fault-finding, censure; (2) The art of estimating the qualities and character of literary or artistic work; the function or work of a critic; (3) An act of criticizing; a critical remark, comment; a critical essay, critique; (4) A nice point or distinction, a minute particular, a nicety, a subtlety; in bad sense, a quibble. (*OED* Online)

> **analysis:** (1) The resolution or breaking up of anything complex into its various simple elements, the opposite process to *synthesis*; the exact determination of the elements or components of anything complex. . . . all things duly considered and weighed. (*OED* Online)

We might see that these definitions of analysis and criticism, both taken from the online version of *The Oxford English Dictionary* (*OED*), are useful because they help us to obtain a clearer understanding of the relationship between the two terms. Analysis, in breaking something up into its elements, involves judgment. However, while all things should be "duly considered and weighed," and while, in this process, "passing judgment" is inevitable, a critical analysis does not necessarily imply a "negative" judgment. You might choose to look favourably or unfavourably on the qualities or merits of a given work.

As we can see in both definitions, a critical analysis is always concerned with closely examining "the elements or components" of a given work, looking for "nice point[s] or distinction, . . . minute particular[s], [niceties and subtleties]." Most important, a critical analysis should have depth: It should never be reduced to a "quibble," but, rather, reflect a sustained engagement with some aspect of the text under consideration.

Ultimately, a critical analysis must, in an academic sense, develop a clear sustainable argument about a topic or an issue. If you consider the following OED definition for argument, you will get a good idea of what your critical analysis should work toward.

> **argument:** (1) Proof, evidence, manifestation, token; (2) *Astronomy* and *Mathematics*. The angle, arc, or other mathematical quantity, from which another required quantity may be deduced, or on which its calculation depends; (3) A statement or fact advanced for the purpose of influencing the mind; a reason urged in support of a proposition; *specifically* in *logic*, the middle term in a syllogism. Also *figuratively*; (4) A connected series of statements or reasons intended to establish a position (and, *hence*, to refute the opposite); a process of reasoning; argumentation; (5) **a.** Statement of the reasons for and against a proposition; discussion of a question; debate. **b.** Subject of contention, or debate.

In performing a critical analysis of a text, therefore, you will be looking to make an argument about that text, either verbally or, most often in a university assignment, in a written essay format. The argument you make will establish a position, a certain "angle," that calls into question some aspect of the text. You might argue "for or against a proposition" or, alternatively, simply add to the debate. Understanding that the given aim is to "influence the mind" of your readers, your concern will be to provide "proof" or evidence for the argument you are making.

In this chapter, then, we will focus on the "process of reasoning," finding reasons and evidence for a specific argument or critique (a necessary precursor to persuasive

Photo 7.1

writing, covered in the following chapter). First, however, let's take a moment to review the difference between summary and analysis or interpretation in the exercise below.

SUMMARY VERSUS INTERPRETATION OR CRITICAL ANALYSIS

Exercise 7.1

- Read the following student passage.
- Highlight the places where summary and interpretation or critical analysis appear.
- Can you see the difference? While summary is relating *what happened in a text*, critical analysis or interpretation is making an argument *about a text*.

There are a number of laws/bills that appear to criminalize animal activists, perhaps most notably the Animal Enterprise Terrorism Act (AETA), which states that it is a crime to not only threaten/harass employees of an animal enterprise and their families, but "to cause economic disruption to an animal enterprise or those who do business with animal enterprises" as well (Bills 22). The written rhetoric (persuasiveness) of the bill privileges the enterprise over protesting animal activists who are indirectly labeled in this bill detrimentally as criminals. The name "Animal Enterprise Terrorism Act" seems to imply that the activities undertaken by animal activists are comparable to those undertaken by groups such as Al-Qaeda, a Muslim-extremist group. This implied comparison seems to indicate that the U.S. House and Senate views animal activists as terrorists and consequently labels them as criminals and/or social deviants.

Critical Thinking

Interpretation or critical analysis, then, goes beyond summary to make a statement or pose questions about either the content or structure of the text. In the above exercise, the student takes issue with how the AETA discriminates against animal activists. In making this argument, this student is demonstrating excellent critical thinking skills. While there are many debated definitions of critical thinking, the definition I have picked best parallels the work that you will be doing in your academic studies. From this perspective, critical thinking (CT) strives to emulate "[r]easonable reflective thinking" that attempts

to seek a clear statement of the thesis or question; to seek reasons; to try to be well informed; to use credible sources and mention them; to take into account the total situation; to try to remain relevant to the main point; to keep in mind the original or basic concern; to look for alternatives; to be open-minded; to take a position when the evidence and reasons are sufficient to do so; to seek as much precision as the subject permits; to deal in an orderly manner with the parts of a complex whole; to *use* one's CT abilities; to be sensitive to feelings, level of knowledge, and degree of sophistication of others. (Ennis 5–15)

This means that the reader engages actively with the text, generating critical questions and synthesizing prior knowledge in an attempt to consider the weight and validity of the argument and to evaluate how the rhetorical techniques and language used contribute to the effectiveness of the argument. The reader might thus address the writer's claims to logic, and use of evidence, organization, and tone of voice (technique). In performing this analysis, the reader, moreover, would attempt to remain objective and open-minded, acknowledging that these issues are complicated by such things as author bias and historical perspectives. The reader should always be aware of his or her own complicity in reading any text critically.

Reading critically demands, of course, that the first thing you must do is read the text in question. Remember that a text is anything you can "read." You might, for example, analyze a novel, a short story, a poem, an event, an academic essay, a film, an advertisement, or even a government bill. Second, you will then need to find a way to engage with it critically. This critique *must* offer new insight into the topic or issue. You will no longer be reading simply for content and understanding (as in summary reading) but, rather, to understand and respond to the content with a critical analytical response. This means that you have to read carefully and selectively, paying attention to the argument and the way the work is structured and presented in context. You will be looking for patterns to emerge that will help you make a persuasive argument *about* a text, so you will need to keep notes on both the text itself and your response to the text. What follows are some specific analytical techniques to help you with this process.

The Critical Reasoning Process: Analytical Techniques

Ask Questions

Questions provide you with a lens for highlighting some features and not others. In attempting to answer the question, you will not only reveal a problem with the text, but also come up with reasons and evidence for your analysis. Moreover, the questions you choose to ask will point to an argument or a framework that you might be able to develop into an essay at a later point.

You might begin by asking some *entry-point questions*. These questions indicate a first personal response to the text and suggest questions such as the following: What do I like/dislike about this text? What bothers me about the argument/structure/voice, etc.? In answering these questions, you will be trying to find a focus for an argument. Your job, then, is to read the rest of the text carefully, looking for similar troubling sections in the text or similar patterns. What you find will form the basis of your essay's argument.

Here is a list of preliminary questions to ask when analyzing a text:

- What are the main issues or concerns here? What larger disciplinary or real-world concerns do they speak to? Do I think they are valid?

- Who is the intended audience? (A senior scholar, the general public, educators, your professor, fellow students?) Is the appeal to audience clear and consistent?
- What are the contexts/circumstances/parameters of the argument (time period, nation, community)? Are they clearly and sufficiently conveyed? Does the context support the argument being made?
- Is the writer's purpose clear? Does he or she communicate effectively and clearly to others? Does he or she present a convincing position, given the projected audience?
- Does the writer seem authoritative and trustworthy? Is his or her tone formal and objective?
- What technique is the author using to persuade the reader (consider here the use of personal evidence, anecdotes, factual evidence, specific description, definition, metaphor, lists, graphs and statistics, etc.)? Are these techniques effective?
- How is the writer framing the issue (i.e., using a lens to structure her point)? Why is this particular frame important to her argument?
- Is there a knowledge gap or deficit, something the writer may have overlooked or ignored when discussing a given issue?

When you are reading, look for repetition or patterns that indicate an area of concern. Remember too that you will need to focus your argument. You cannot answer all of these questions in one essay, so you will need to focus your questions around a specific question or area. You might, for example, find one knowledge gap or focus instead on bias or structure, but you will not be able to cover all three in one essay. If you do, your argument will be too general and superficial, and will not demonstrate detail and depth.

Remember that the *evidence* you find to support your close critical reading will determine the viability of your argument. As previously stated, you want depth rather than coverage, so while any one of those questions could form the basis of your essay's argument, you must have enough evidence or examples from the text to sustain a thorough examination. Also, while you might begin with a personal response, you will need to move to an impartial judgment that will allow you to focus not on your own personal opinion but *on the text itself* and the *knowledge* it presents.

Interpretation, Synthesis, and Evaluation

Another way of approaching an analysis is to think of it as a three-step process, using interpretation, synthesis, and evaluation. While you will still ask questions of the text you are reading, how you interpret the text, synthesize this knowledge with the reading and other forms of knowledge, and evaluate this knowledge will form the basis of your analysis. Although I have presented these three processes in a chronological order below, in practice they are more often used simultaneously. Remember, you need to use this information in a way that works for you as you read and analyze a text.

Interpretation

To interpret means to bring clarity and an understanding of a text to your readers. This means that you will need to examine and re-examine your perspective, clarifying, refining, and refocusing your interpretation until you can be sure of its credibility. You may well use a questioning process to initiate this examination, but you will need to make sure your questions do not take you off-topic. You will thus need to focus on *one* interpretation of the text you are reading, not many. This interpretation might focus on the text's content, context, organization, evidence, rhetorical techniques, use of logic or emotion, etc., but unless you can combine some of these elements under one focus, you should restrict your interpretation to only one of these areas. When interpreting the text, don't take the text at face value, but also don't read too much into it. Your inferences need to fit the evidence found in the text.

Synthesis

You will need to synthesize the parts of a text or parts of your reading (your interpretation and analysis of the patterns, etc.) to arrive at an analytical vision of the whole. This vision should tell us something new about the text. However, synthesizing a text also demands that you make connections between your own personal responses or reactions to the text. This is your knowledge base, which could include the reading you have done in other courses, and the evidence found within the text. You need to take into account, then, other knowledge that might inform your specific reading of the text. Making these connections can help you develop depth to your analysis, assisting you in determining different aspects related to your topic of interest, so that you are able to broaden and deepen your understanding of your specific focus.

Evaluation

Evaluating or assessing the text, whether it is the structure, the logic, or the content of the text, is essential to the academic reasoning process. Evaluation asks you to determine whether or not the assumptions you make when reading and interpreting the text are sound. The strength of your evaluation of a text will be based on the strength and validity of the *evidence* you cite and the logical connections you are able to make to support your assertions. Keep your focus on a logical, impartial exploration of the knowledge presented within the text. Refuse to be tempted into a personal response, a forceful insistent tone, or emotional appeal. You will then be better able to evaluate the text according to academic standards.

Knowledge Gap or Deficit

This technique relates to an evaluation of the content of a particular text. As Giltrow argues, a writer approaches the state of knowledge on a specific topic to show a concern with "the limits of knowledge, the conditions under which it was produced, and positions from which statements issue" (270). When a writer does not fully address these concerns, a knowledge gap or deficit is created. Finding a knowledge gap in a text—discovering "what hasn't been said, [or] what needs to be said" (270)—can provide you with the material for your own analysis. This type of analysis demands an examination of the places in the text where you feel as though something is missing, left out, or not covered in sufficient depth. Here are some questions you might ask to find a possible knowledge gap:

- Which aspects of the text are emphasized, left out, or de-emphasized? How does this emphasis or lack of emphasis influence the reader?
- Does what is left out of the text tell us something about the author's agenda or bias?

In identifying a knowledge gap, you will be exposing a point, a fact, or an opinion that was presented as truth and that you have now called into question. This is a common academic practice that involves either (a) adding to the existing knowledge by adding new information, data, or reasoning to a tentative argument or claim, or (b) attempting to prove that previously established arguments are faulty or incomplete. While exposing the knowledge gap is often a research activity, it is also possible to find logical gaps or inconsistencies in a close analytical reading of a text.

Remember, however, that the knowledge deficit has to relate directly to the knowledge provided by the author of the text you are analyzing. For instance, arguing that Drew Hayden Taylor's essay does not adequately address the dominant perspective might constitute a knowledge gap; however, arguing that he does not provide us with Stephen Harper's political history would not constitute a knowledge gap because Harper's political history is irrelevant to Taylor's essay.

FINDING A KNOWLEDGE GAP

Exercise 7.2

- Consider either David Bartholomae's essay "Writing with Teachers," or Richard Wagamese's "Returning to Harmony" (see pages 330 and 427 in the Reader) and see if you can find one knowledge gap.
- Be prepared to provide reasons for the particular knowledge gap you have identified and share your observations with your classmates. Do you think there is enough evidence to support your point so that you could develop this specific point into a fully developed essay?

Style and Structure

Whereas the knowledge gap is focused on the content of the work you are studying, a focus on the writer's style or logical organization considers how the content is supported by language and essay organization. A focus on style—the way that language is used persuasively—or structure—the way that the larger organization supports the content—can help you understand at a deeper level how the content is supported by *how* the writer makes his or her argument. You will thus be analyzing and reflecting on the processes and strategies the writer uses when he or she considers how best to present and support an argument.

Style

When you focus on style, you consider how the tone, vocabulary, grammar, and sentence structure support the writer's content or meaning. You must also take into account the genre of the piece. A journalistic tone and grammar usage, for example, is very different from an academic tone. If the work you are analyzing is academic, you will also need to consider the academic discipline involved. Bear in mind, however, that all academic writing uses common conventions, a clear and concise sentence structure, and a formal use of language. Review chapter 2 for a list of academic conventions. Chapter 13 will provide you with more specific information on style. For now, though, keep in mind the following preliminary questions you might ask about style:

- Does the style—the effective use of grammar, vocabulary, and sentence structure—successfully appropriate the meaning and expectations of the given genre? For example, if you are analyzing an academic essay, does it successfully appropriate an academic style (clear, concise, formal language) and grammar (complete grammatically correct sentences)?
- Does the style conform to the conventions of its genre?
- Is the language and grammar used an adequate vehicle for the form or content of the work?

Structure or Logical Organization

This technique evaluates how the content of a particular text is supported by a clear analytical and logical organization at both the sentence and the paragraph level. You will be considering the overall inherent structure, which includes the use of analytical patterns, and logical structure both at the sentence and the paragraph level. See chapter 5 for more information on how academic writers use structure or organization to frame their argument.

Here are some preliminary questions you might ask about a text's use of structure:

- Is there a clear argument or focus that is developed throughout the work?
- Is there a predominant analytical pattern (compare–contrast, for example)? See chapter 5 for more information on analytical patterns.
- Does the work provide the reader with signposts that signal the clear and logical development of ideas and argument?
- Does each paragraph only contain one focused topic?
- Are there clear, logical transitions between each paragraph and sentence so that the reader is able to easily follow the logic of the argument without having to look back in the text to reorient him- or herself?
- Does the writer smoothly and logically include secondary sources and evidence to support the argument?
- Is the structure of the text shaped by the content?

Analytical Patterns

Related to the issue of structure is an awareness of analytical patterns, which refer to the way you structure your main overall argument or parts of your argument. Being aware of some basic patterns of arrangement in a text you are reading can help you understand (a) how writers organize their written communication logically, and (b) how you might use patterns to structure your own writing. Typical patterns of arrangement that can be used to *analyze* and *organize* material include compare–contrast, cause and effect, classification and division, definition, narration, process analysis, and analogy. As Coe argues, however, these patterns go beyond simply being technical strategies for structuring information and organizing your material into identifiable "patterns of arrangement" (302). They should enable you to see how they help to communicate meaning effectively, in your own writing and in the writing of others.

Please see chapter 5 for a review of specific patterns of analysis.

STYLE AND STRUCTURAL ANALYSIS

Exercise 7.3

Consider the inductive structure of either Werner Heisenberg's "What Is an Elementary Particle?" (see page 442 in the Reader) or Catherine Schryer's "The Lab vs. the Clinic: Sites of Competing Genres" (see page 350 in the Reader).

- Find Heisenberg's or Schryer's hypothesis.
- Outline the essay. Note how the authors follow the inductive method to arrive at their conclusions at the end of the essay.
- What points would you focus on if you were going to write an essay analyzing the effective use of structure to support either Heisenberg's or Schryer's argument?
- Write a tentative thesis statement making an argument about either Heisenberg's or Schryer's structure.
- Compare your outline and tentative thesis statement with those of your classmates. Did you all focus on the same points?
- Now consider the authors' use of style (language, grammar, academic conventions): How does Heisenberg's or Schryer's use of style support both the structure and the content? Is it appropriate for the projected audience (Review academic conventions in chapter 2)?
- Compare your analysis with those of your classmates.

The Importance of Logic

Central to a focus on structure is a focus on logic. Academic texts are highly logical, so an understanding of logic will help you to interpret a text with the use of logic to persuade has a long history. For example, the Greek philosopher Aristotle (384–322 BCE) emphasized the importance of logic as a means of persuasion. Reasoning, Aristotle stated, is persuasive when it involves the use of three types of appeal—logos (**logical appeal**), **ethos** (ethical appeal), and **pathos** (emotional appeal)—and when it avoids **logical fallacies**, or mistakes in logic.

Ultimately, you will need to understand logical structure, mistakes in logic, and logical appeals (logos, pathos, and ethos). These will enable you not only to analyze and weigh the evidence about your beliefs and values in the world outside academia, but also, and most important, to analyze, weigh, and use evidence in your university writing.

Logical Appeals

In the writing of all genres, the tone, or the attention to subject and audience, is central. In academic writing, tone is primarily conveyed through establishing an objective academic voice that is aware of the requirements of an academic audience, mostly your professors and your academic peers. Different genres—such as journalism, letter writing, texting, or academic writing—require conforming to a set of conventions, formal or informal diction, and an awareness of how the use of language creates meaning. In this respect, an introduction to rhetorical appeals—logos, ethos, and pathos—can be informative.

The use of logos, ethos, and pathos reflect your style and the tone you establish in your writing. Although pathos is primarily used in informal writing, it is sometimes used in academic writing (see Regan and Cohen's essays in the Reader: pages 378 and 369). However, logos and ethos, the "ethical judgment readers make about the character of the writer" (Coe 382), are, as previously mentioned, more commonly associated with academic writing. What follows is a brief description of these rhetorical appeals, with some examples.

Pathos

Pathos is an appeal to the reader's emotions. Its success is based on the writer's ability to move the feelings and desires of the reader. Pathos is not usually used in academic writing because it is considered to be manipulative, subjective, and untrustworthy. You will, however, find it in newspapers, magazines, and personal correspondence where the writer is attempting to quickly and easily persuade the reader to agree with a point of view.

Exercise 7.4

PATHOS

Below are three examples of writing, all of them focused on the general topic of trees. See if you can identify the genre implied by the writing and then see how these examples conform, more or less, to the logical and objective style expected of academic writing.

> Trees and forests are immeasurably precious. Healthy, abundant forests don't just enhance lives, they save lives. (International Tree Federation Website)

*

From the first growth of the tree, many a limb and branch has decayed and dropped off; and all these fallen branches of various sizes may represent those whole orders, families, and genera which have now no living representatives, and which are known to us only in a fossil state. . . . As buds give rise by growth to fresh buds, and these, if vigorous, branch out and overtop on all sides many a feebler branch, so by generation I believe it has been with the great Tree of Life, which fills with its dead and broken branches the crust of the earth, and covers the surface with its ever-branching and beautiful ramifications. (Darwin)

*

Increased atmospheric CO_2 is attributable mostly to fossil fuel combustion (about 80% to 85%) and deforestation (Hamburger 1977; Schneider 1989). Atmospheric carbon is estimated to be increasing by approximately 2.6 billion metric tons (2.9 billion tons) annually (Sedjo 1989). By storing carbon through their growth process, trees act as a sink for CO_2. Increasing the number of trees can potentially slow the accumulation of atmospheric carbon (e.g., Moulton and Richards 1990). (Nowak et al. 113)

See the Exercise Answer Key in Appendix A for an analysis of these passages.

Discuss with your classmates.

Ethos

All persuasive argumentation demands the use of ethos. Ethos or ethical appeal is based on a writer's ability to present him- or herself as trustworthy and knowledgeable. In academic terms, this appeal assumes that the writer has a thorough awareness of a larger context and up-to-date research related to the argument being made. It is important for the writer to use evidence and examples to support his or her claims, demonstrating that he or she is a part of the knowledge community writing on this topic. Ethical appeal also always uses an objective, moderate, formal tone: the writer engages with and rebuts other views, but does so respectfully and ethically. When you write your essays, you will need to make sure you use ethical appeal; however, for now, you will need to be able to recognize and understand how it is used in the writing of others.

ETHOS

Exercise 7.5

Here are two examples of ethical appeal, taken from student writing examples. Which piece of writing more successfully approaches an academic style, and why?

Metaphors are used in the media all the time. Newspapers, television news programs, and soap operas use metaphors constantly. These metaphors can upset you if you let them because they are offensive to many people.

Continued

See the Exercise Answer Key in Appendix A for an analysis of these passages.

*

It is not difficult to find evidence of metaphor use in medical language. In her article "Making it Literal," Susan Sontag, supporting this claim, describes how military metaphors are used in medicine. For example, the disease is made out to be the enemy, "bacteria 'invade,'" and the body "fights against cancer" (375).

Discuss with your classmates.

Logos

Logical appeal, or logos, is based on a writer's ability to present his or her arguments in a logical reasoned way. It demands that the writer uses evidence and examples to support his or her claim and that he or she present them in a logical order that makes sense to the reader.

Exercise 7.6

LOGOS

Read the following two student-writing excerpts. In your opinion, which excerpt is the most logical?

The author states that there is a problem with education in literate cultures, but he does not supply appropriate solutions to the problems. He develops a good idea of how teachers can improve the learning experience although it would be better if the author gave strategies for the teacher to put it into action. The essay uses many examples of how oral culture teaches the act of self-reflection and how it is thought to enhance the student's development.

See the Exercise Answer Key in Appendix A for an analysis of these passages.

*

Teachers must consider that incorporating self-reflection into their teaching practices is challenging. Several problems can arise from the choice to develop a self-reflective teaching style: it requires teachers to consistently update and change their teaching methods and plans, and it demands that teachers adapt their methods to accommodate the needs of their students. This latter point has specific relevance for children who have learning disabilities.

Exercise 7.7

LOGICAL APPEALS

What follows are several passages, written by established writers, each of which demonstrates an example of pathos, ethos, or logos.

- Identify the primary orientation of each passage (pathos, logos, and/or ethos).
- Identify the audience (academic? general public?), the genre (academic, journalistic, etc.), and the possible reasons for using pathos, logos, and/or ethos for this particular audience.

- Ask, how is the passage persuasive for the projected audience?
- Be prepared to defend your arguments as you discuss them with your classmates.

PASSAGE 1

The term "disabled" is often used to obscure or repress the fact that disability is not a static category but one which expands and contracts to include "normal" people as well. In addition, while many people have rallied around the term "disability," much as African-Americans did around "Black" power, the term is at base one that has been used to create rigid categories of existence: either one is disabled, or one is not.

—Lennard Davis

PASSAGE 2

To all the men and women of the United States Armed Forces now in the Middle East, the peace of a troubled world and the hopes of an oppressed people now depend on you. That trust is well placed.

—George Bush

PASSAGE 3

Which words epitomize spring to you? For me, there are plenty—green, fresh, rebirth, rush, push, zoom, explode! There's been activity all winter—roots growing, buds forming—but it's been out of sight. Then all that stored energy, all that vitality, manifests itself, pouring out in an unstoppable stream.

—Carol Klein

Logical Argumentation

Once again, an understanding of how logical structure and argumentation work in a text will help you to be able to read and write clearly, logically, and effectively.

Good analytical argumentation uses formal logical reasoning called syllogisms. A **syllogism** consists of major and minor propositions, assertions, or statements about a problem. These provide the **premises** that support a conclusion or main argument.

ACADEMIC FOCUS

LOGICAL ARGUMENTATION

Logical Argument Uses
Syllogisms:
a series of major and minor propositions/assertions/statements,
each of which develop logically
to a conclusion.

The classic format of a deductive (general to specific) syllogism or argument is as follows:

> All humans are mortal.
> Socrates is human.
> Therefore, Socrates is mortal.

As you can see, this argument moves from a general or universal proposition or major premise (all humans are mortal) to a particular conclusion. If the premises are true or valid, then the conclusion is also valid. Here we can see that in this "if–then" structure (*if* all humans are mortal, and *if* Socrates is human, *then* he is also mortal), the universal proposition, or premise, "all humans are mortal" leads logically to the next more specific premise that "Socrates is human" and then, therefore, to the conclusion, that Socrates, by dint of being human, must also be mortal.

Unlike deductive arguments, scientific inductive arguments (specific hypotheses to a general conclusion) cannot be judged solely on whether or not they are valid. In an inductive argument, the premises provide support for the conclusion, but the support does not have to be conclusive. However, the validity of the premises does indicate the overall validity of the argument. Using the previous syllogism then, an inductive argument might go something like this:

> Socrates is mortal.
> Socrates is human.
> Therefore, all humans are mortal.

Here it is possible to see that, as in the first example, the relationship between the premises and the predicted conclusion is clear. However, it is not as conclusive as the deductive method, because it leaves open the possibility that some humans might not be mortal (just because Socrates is mortal and human does not necessarily indicate that all humans are mortal). When the relationship between the premises and the conclusion is unclear, a logical fallacy results. Consider the argument made in the penguin cartoon (Photo 7.2) and see if you can identify the major and minor premises and conclusion. Does this syllogism make a valid argument? If not, why not?

If you pointed out that the cartoon illustrates an invalid argument, you were correct. The first premise, "Penguins are black and white," and the second premise, "Some old TV shows are black and white," are not logically related (penguins and TV shows have nothing in common) and do not lead the reader logically to the conclusion that "Penguins are old TV shows," simply because they are black and white. It is reasonable to assume, however, that, given the logic in the cartoon, penguins are not good at logic.

© 1996 Randy Glasbergen, www.glasbergen.com

Photo 7.2

Now consider the logical syllogism, presented by Carl Cohen in his essay "The Case for the Use of Animals in Biomedical Research" (see page 369 in the Reader):

Animals (that is, nonhuman animals, . . .) lack the capacity for free moral judgment.

|

They are not beings capable of exercising or responding to moral claims.

|

Animals, therefore, have no rights, and they can have none.

Of course, the assumption here is that humans are capable of free moral judgment. That argument is valid, given that the first premise is true and that, by implication, human animals (as opposed to nonhuman animals) can be said to have free moral judgment. They are therefore capable of having rights and comprehending moral rules of duty.

SYLLOGISMS

Complete the middle premise in the following syllogism, based on Tom Regan's essay, "The Case for Animal Rights" (see page 378 in the Reader):

Humans, as "experiencing subjects of life," have rights.

?

Therefore, animals have rights.

Discuss your answers with your classmates. Are your arguments valid?

An awareness of the way in which arguments are constructed logically will help you analyze the structure of other writers' essays and your own. Always ask: Are the major tenets of my argument logically valid?

Exercise 7.8

See the Exercise Answer Key in Appendix A for a sample syllogism.

Logical Fallacies

While a writer or speaker might use an invalid line of argument simply out of ignorance and a lack of experience, it is important to recognize that, all too often, writers and speakers use fallacies of argument entirely by design, from a conscious intent to create humour (as in the penguin cartoon) and/or to manipulate their audience. This is particularly true in advertising and in politics. Learning to detect such fallacies can make us more aware consumers of products and ideas, and, ultimately, better readers and more ethically aware communicators.

According to Andrea Lunsford, John Ruszkiewicz, and Keith Walters in their book *Everything's An Argument*, there are three main types of fallacies:

1. **Logical fallacies** (fallacies of logos) depend upon faulty logic.
2. **Emotional fallacies** (fallacies of pathos) unfairly appeal to the audience's emotions.
3. **Ethical fallacies** (fallacies of ethos) unreasonably advance the writer's own authority or character.

Below is an abridged and adapted list of some types of logical, emotional, and ethical fallacies (re: Lunsford et al.).

Logical Fallacies

1. **Hasty generalization:** A conclusion drawn from insufficient evidence.

   Example: The conclusion drawn from the twenty-six respondents to the study would indicate that Albertans do not want to amend gun control laws.

2. **Faulty causality:** The assumption that just because one event follows another, it was *caused* by the previous event.

   Example: The university banned public demonstrations and student attendance at lectures went down.

3. **Begging the question:** Any claim made on questionable grounds. Occurs when a writer simply restates the claim in a different way; also called *circular argument.*

   Example: His lies are evident from the untruthful nature of his statements.

4. **Equivocation:** A half-truth; a lie that is given an honest appearance so it will be accepted.

   Example: Scientists argue that global warming is a natural phenomenon that has been greatly exaggerated.

5. **Non sequitur:** A breakdown in logical connection from point to point; one point does not follow logically from another.

   Example: Global warming is caused by human activity. Some scientists are corrupt.

6. **Ignoring the question:** Simply avoiding answering questions for which one has no good response.

   Example: It is not a question of whether the US should or should not increase the number of troops in Afghanistan: it is a question of debatable morals.

7. **Faulty analogy:** An illogical comparison that is taken too far.

   Example: Government is like business: financial gain is always the bottom line.

8. **Straw man:** Twisting or misrepresenting the view of the opposing side.

   Example: The problem isn't that Robert Latimer killed his disabled daughter; the problem is that social services weren't there for him.

9. **Stacked evidence:** Distorting an issue by representing only one side.

   Example: Cats are superior to dogs because they are cleaner, cuter, and more independent.

Emotional Fallacies

1. **Scare tactics:** Exaggerating possible dangers well beyond their statistical likelihood.

   Example: The polar vortex that hit the east coast of Canada in 2014 is a sign of the extreme weather conditions we will face in the future if we don't stop global warming.

2. **Red herring:** Avoiding the issue or a tough question by introducing a distraction.

   Example: We shouldn't be thinking about global warming; we should be thinking about more serious issues, such as what's happening in the Middle East.

3. **Slippery slope:** An argument that portrays today's seemingly small concession as tomorrow's catastrophe.

   Example: If Canada legalizes abortion, women will use it as a form of birth control and human life will cease to have any value.

4. **Sentimental:** Arguments that deliberately appeal to emotions to distract the audience from the facts.

   Example: "The forlornness of the veal calf is pathetic, heart-wrenching; the pulsing pain of the chimp with electrodes planted deep in her brain is repulsive" (Regan).

5. **Either/or choices:** Reducing complicated issues to only two possible courses of action.

   Example: It is important to take a stand on animal experimentation: either it is completely wrong or completely acceptable.

6. **Bandwagon:** Urging a course of action simply because the majority of people are doing so.

   Example: Most Christians are against abortion, but not all Christians are willing to take the stand they must make against it.

Ethical Fallacies

1. **False authority:** Persuading the audience by using the testimony of an unqualified, biased, or suspicious source. Also called *Ipse dixit* (Latin: "He himself said it.").

   Example: In the Superman advertisement, Brandon Routh says that milk is good for you; therefore, it is important to drink more milk.

2. **Dogmatism:** The claim that the issue at hand is beyond argument, that the solution is self-evident.

   Example: Everyone knows that abortion is murder.

3. **Moral equivalence:** Argues that because some people act a certain way, then others have a right to do so. Suggests that serious moral wrongs are minor offences.

   Example: If Robert Latimer killed his disabled daughter because he loved her, all fathers who love their disabled daughters should be able to kill them.

4. **Ad hominem:** A counter-argument that attacks the opponent's character, rather than arguing against his/her position on the issue at hand.

   Example: How can you argue your case for vegetarianism when you are enjoying your steak?

As previously stated, becoming aware of these fallacies in other people's writing can help you not only to become more aware of what constitutes a good argument but also to become a better writer and reviser of your own arguments.

Here are several examples of logical fallacies as they appear in student writing examples:

I know this is true because a lawyer, who was a friend of my father's, once told my father it was so. (fallacy of false authority)

The media's bias in its coverage of the Middle East conflict is obvious and must be addressed immediately by those in power. (hasty generalization/dogmatism)

Permitting experimentation on animals will lead inevitably to experimentation on people with disabilities, as they are also vulnerable. (slippery slope)

The world is running out of oil. People should only have one car per family. (non sequitur)

LOGICAL FALLACIES

Exercise 7.9

Using the list of common fallacies above, see if you can
- Identify the fallacies in the following student writing examples, and
- Revise the fallacies to improve the overall clarity by eliminating the fallacy and rewriting the sentence.

All people should spend time each day meditating to help improve sleep, studying, or just overall relaxing.

This greater feeling of the environment helps give the oral speaker a greater sense of the feeling of the overall environment.

Sheridan states that "Literate cultures could not accept the idea that the sacred was allied with and manifested in the natural environment" (26). This point reinforces that the use of the alphabet impacts different aspects of life.

I found that adding the "United Colors of Benetton" logo at the bottom of the information blurb was a cheap, tacky, distasteful method of including the company name in a worthy cause; a way to bask in the selfless limelight offered by a charitable cause.

See the Exercise Answer Key in Appendix A for some potential solutions to these sentence problems.

Discuss your answers with your classmates. Are you aware of making any of these fallacies in your own writing? If so, which ones? How might you avoid making them in the future?

Logic, defined as the "study of the methods and principles used to distinguish good (correct) from bad (incorrect) reasoning" (Copi and Cohen 3), can help you recognize places in a text where the reasoning is possibly irrelevant, ambiguous, or seemingly confused. In learning first how to recognize this unclear reasoning in other people's writing, you will become more conscious of the principles of reasoning and better able to recognize and use them in your own work. As Copi and Cohen argue, "the study of logic will give students techniques and methods for testing the correctness of many different kinds of reasoning, including their own; and when errors are easily detected, they are less likely to be allowed to stand" (4).

Exercise 7.10

REASONING IN REGAN AND COHEN

Carl Cohen's and Tom Regan's essays (see pages 369 and 378 in the Reader) are good examples of philosophical essays. As philosophers, Cohen and Regan deliberately use logos, ethos, and pathos, as well as logical fallacies. Read each essay and complete the following exercise:

1. Identify where and how the authors use ethos, pathos, and logos. In your opinion, which essay is more effective? Why? Provide reasons for your answer.
2. Find some specific examples of the deliberate use of logical fallacies. Which argument is, in your opinion, more valid, and why?
3. Pick two or three of these points and see if you can come up with a working thesis statement that contains within it the points you identify as important.

See the student essay "Persuasion" at the end of chapter 8 for a sample analysis of logical argumentation at work in Regan's and Cohen's essays (pages 378 and 369 in the Reader).

As you can see, the previous exercise takes you from being a reader who is attempting to understand and analyze the text, to being a writer who is attempting to write about the text. This is part of the work that academics do: respond in formal written essays to the ideas, knowledge, and arguments of other academics. While the next chapter, "Academic Persuasion," will deal directly with how to turn your analysis of a text into a written essay of your own, you need to begin thinking about your writing as you analyze the text you are reading. One way to do that is to come up with a working thesis statement. Keeping this statement in mind as you read and analyze your text will help you to focus your argument and find evidence for your points, and, ultimately, to formulate and structure a well-written analytical essay.

Thesis Statements

Once you have a perspective or an angle for reading a text (whether it is to expose some logical fallacies, for example, or highlight a knowledge gap) and are ready to move on

THESIS STATEMENTS VERSUS HYPOTHESES

The thesis statement is used primarily in the humanities disciplines where the essay follows a deductive format, working from general premises to a specific provable conclusion or argument. If you are working in the social sciences or sciences, the thesis is called a hypothesis, which can be defined as a proposed explanation for a particular phenomenon. In the sciences or social sciences, the structure of the essay is inductive, moving from the specific case or phenomenon to a general explanation. In the inductive form, the hypothesis has to be testable. The testing that you do to prove your explanation might involve statistics and quantifiable data; however, if you are in the social sciences, it is more likely to explore a concept in relationship to an issue or a problem.

For example, in Schryer's essay, "The Lab vs. the Clinic" (see page 350 in the Reader), Schryer suggests in her hypothesis that veterinary programs in universities privilege academic knowledge over practical clinical knowledge. In the body of the essay, Schryer explains how and why this is problematic by testing how different documentation forms are used in veterinary institutions. She then suggests a possible solution. Her working hypothesis outlines a problem and a statement of expectations, that is, a statement that presupposes a causality or an explanation.

Regardless of whether you are working in the humanities, the social sciences, or the sciences, your main thesis statement, or hypothesis, must be supported by evidence and logic and/or by the tests performed and the predicted results.

and write about the text, it is a good idea to establish a **working thesis statement**, also called a tentative main argument or statement of position. You might arrive at this statement early in your reading of a text, but you need to remember that this statement will change as you refine and redefine your analysis. Being too rigid with a statement at an early stage will restrict your ability to add depth and focus to your argument. Remember, too, that in a critical analysis, you will need to do more than repeat the argument that is already there: you will need to tell us something *new* about the topic.

Establishing a Working Thesis Statement

Although a thesis can be defined briefly as the main idea or the central argument of a piece of writing, it is important to remember that it functions as a promise to readers, letting them know what will be *analyzed* and *argued*. When writing a thesis statement, then, it is useful to keep in mind that a good thesis has five qualities:

1. It must argue an *original* opinion, something that someone could disagree with.
2. It introduces key terms, concepts, and the major divisions of the paper.
3. It uses a specific vocabulary.

4. It is manageable.

5. It can be supported by evidence.

Keeping these points in mind will help you manage and focus your argument. This argument should be *based solely on your engagement with and analysis of your text,* so that when you come to write your essay, you will already have a clear outline of your main analytical points.

Process

Following a specific process can help you write an effective working thesis statement. First make sure you have a focused topic: a topic you want to explore that is directly connected to the text you are analyzing. Remember that one paper cannot discuss everything. Next, formulate a working thesis statement: a preliminary argument that you will present to your reader to try to convince him or her about some aspect of the text. Your thesis is more than a topic: It is a specific argument you want to make about your topic. What follows is a process for helping you to focus and add depth to your thesis statement:

1. Articulate a *working* thesis statement early on in the writing process by articulating the *general topic* and a *specific focus.*

   Theories about global warming [general topic] are being used by environmentalists to analyze the melting of the polar ice caps in the Arctic [specific focus].

2. Develop your thesis statement by making it even more specific. Make sure you articulate all your major lines of argument. These major lines of argument should indicate the relevance or importance of the topic under consideration.

   Theories about global warming [general topic], particularly those that deny the argument of natural causes [specific focus/major line of argument] are being used by environmentalists to analyze the melting of the polar ice caps in the Artic [specific topic/major line of argument].

3. This thesis, as you can see, is still quite general. Remember that your thesis should be a complex, insightful argument that someone else might want to disagree with. The more possible contradictions or opposing points that you can think of, the stronger your thesis will be.

   Theories about global warming [general topic], particularly those that deny the argument of natural causes [specific focus/major line of argument], are being used by environmentalists in their attempt to show how journalists, working in service of corporate or political ventures [specific focus/major line of argument], ignore or deny that human pollution is the cause [specific focus/major line of argument] of the melting of the polar ice caps in the Artic.

Although this thesis has depth of analysis, its validity will depend upon finding and analyzing a theory about global warming and synthesizing the main points of this theory with your analysis of a primary text (the text/article written by a journalist that denies "human pollution is the cause" of global warming in the Arctic). Keep in mind that you will need a specific debatable argument that tells your reader something new about the topic or issue. What is important at the preliminary stage, however, is that you make the major lines of argument clear. That will give you a structure and a framework for analyzing your primary text.

DEVELOPING A THESIS (RE: SCHRYER)

Exercise 7.11

1. Brainstorm some possible thesis statements for Catherine Schryer's essay "The Lab vs The Clinic," (see page 350 in the Reader).
2. Use the technique above for establishing a working thesis statement and come up with three arguments (working thesis statements). With evidence taken directly from Schryer's essay, which argument could you most effectively support?
3. Now take a look at Brook Biesenthal's critical analysis titled, "Catherine Schryer's 'The Lab vs. The Clinic:' An Example of Bias?" at the end of this chapter and compare your thesis with the argument established and developed in this essay. Could you turn your thesis into a workable essay? If not, why not?
4. Is Brook's argument valid? Is it supported by evidence? Provide evidence for your answers. Discuss with your classmates.

ACADEMIC FOCUS

A NOTE ON PRIMARY TEXTS

Once again, a primary text—a text that you use to perform a close analysis (one specific instance of a larger general class) of your topic—might be a piece of literature, an experiment, a current or historical event, a philosophical theory, or a visual text, such as a film or an advertisement. You will be expected to observe and document your facts or insights, weighing and considering all the elements, sometimes using an additional process, framework, or theory to help you, then pulling your observations together into some kind of logical position or argument. Visual texts, such as films or advertisements, require a slightly different observational process. I have therefore included below a process for analyzing a primary text that is a film or an advertisement.

Evidence

As stated in chapter 6, effective evidence should include one or more of the following: facts or statistics (verifiable statements or numbers); examples or specifics about the issue in question; quotes from the primary text in question; expert opinions or the judgments of authorities on the topic; sound reasoning, meaning that the relationship of the evidence to the thesis is clearly stated; deductive or inductive reasoning, analytical patterns, and appeals to logos (reason) and ethos (the writer's ability to present himself or herself as knowledgeable, trustworthy, and reliable). Pathos (emotion) should be used sparingly, if at all.

Exercise 7.12

ANALYZING EVIDENCE (RE: SCHRYER)

Analyze Catherine Schryer's essay "The Lab vs. the Clinic" (see page 350 in the Reader) in terms of the evidence she uses.

1. Identify her argument.
2. Identify Schryer's primary texts, and see how she uses them to provide evidence for her argument.
3. Using the list above, analyze what other forms of evidence she uses. Does Schryer present herself as trustworthy and reliable (ethos)?
4. Now analyze the use of evidence in Brook Biesenthal's essay at the end of this chapter. Ask the same questions. How and why does Brook's essay constitute a reliable and trustworthy argument? Discuss with your classmates.

Discipline-Specific Analysis

It is important to keep in mind that the academic discipline and subject matter of study might privilege certain methods and types of knowledge, which will require you to perform different types of analysis. Understanding the types of analysis, which include the required methodologies, structures, and arguments, can help you become a more competent academic writer. Here are three discipline-specific approaches to analysis.

Philosophical Analysis

Analysis is at the centre of the philosophical method. In the process of philosophical analysis, a given concept, idea, or statement of belief or truth is explained, deconstructed (taken apart), and reconstructed or reinterpreted from the given or unquestioned meaning. Philosophical essays might be inductive or deductive, or more or less qualitative or quantitative, but the focus will be on creating a logically valid argument. In this respect, philosophical essays often engage openly with **categorical syllogisms, probability,** and rhetorical fallacies and appeals, including pathos, using them to expose and call into question a given assumption or belief. The essays by Carl Cohen and Tom Regan in the Reader are good examples of philosophical essays.

Literary Analysis

In a literature class, you might study novels, poems, plays, autobiography, biography, memoir, diaries, music, documentary, and film. You might also, however, use literary analysis in the social sciences, which is increasingly using literature as a valid form of knowledge.

In analyzing a literary text, you will either be focusing on the content of the work; performing a close analytical reading of some of the themes, representations, or strategies contained within the work; or examining the larger context, for example, taking a close look at the biographical, ideological, cultural, psychological, or feminist contexts of the work. A literary analysis always takes a deductive approach to writing, working from general premises to a specific argument about a text. The work of the writer is to prove, with the use of evidence from the primary text, and possibly research or secondary sources and logical development, that the argument they are making is valid. The tone the writer uses is always objective and neutral. One example of literary analysis is Rosemarie Garland-Thomson's essay "Shape Structures Story" (see page 389 in the Reader).

While it is important to understand literary terminology—the definitions for novel, plot, setting, irony, etc.—an understanding of the historical development of literature, along with the associated literary movements and theoretical approaches to reading literature, will help you to orient yourself historically in this discipline. For example, you might be interested in exploring literary movements such as romanticism or modernism. In critical theory, you might want to explore a rhetorical, feminist, masculine, Marxist, cultural, or psychological approach to your study of a particular text. A good book of literary theory will help you in this respect, but you might want to go one step further and look in more detail, for example, at the theories of Marx or Freud.

Scientific Analysis

Scientific theory has only been in existence for a few hundred years, but it has profoundly affected the way we see and know the world. Scientific knowledge has been at the forefront of advances made in every field of human endeavour and the resources of the natural world have been harnessed to serve our needs. As a result, we have benefited from better living standards, health, mobility, communication, and leisure. These advances have been achieved through the scientific method, which values objective direct observation (empirical method), data, and facts.

Many students study science because they are drawn either to the powerful effects science can have on humanity and the world and/or to the factual nature of science. However, scientific knowledge seeks not simply to know the factual details but also to understand them. The scientist is always seeking out more abstract or general truths to illustrate the particular instance or facts for which they serve as evidence. These abstract or general truths form patterns and general or natural laws and theories that help scientists better understand and explain our world.

Scientific explanations for natural phenomena begin with a problem. That leads to an argument or a hypothesis that is judged worthy only to the extent that there is valid evidence for it. This evidence is valid only to the extent that it is observable and makes sense, given other patterns, laws, and theories that affect its validity. A hypothesis has to be relevant, be testable, demonstrate a compatibility with other established hypotheses, and contain an element of predictability.

In this respect, the inductive method—working from a specific hypothesis to a general conclusion—is more suitable for scientific writing because it does not, as in a deductive essay, seek to establish valid or true conclusions from its premises, but, rather, attempts to point to a probable or likely true conclusion. Inductive arguments thus engage in the scholarly conversation in a way that keeps the information always in play, as probabilities rather than finalities. The format for an inductive scientific essay is as follows: an introduction, which includes a consideration of a problem and a preliminary hypotheses, an exploration of methods, results, and a discussion. Catherine Schryer's, Watson and Crick's, and Werner Heisenberg's essays (see pages 350, 452, and 442 in the Reader) all use this formula.

In relation to the other main reason that students often choose to study science—the desire to participate in science as a progressive discipline that is able to effect positive change in the world—it is important to note that the scientific desire to understand has sometimes been used unethically, in ways that do not benefit but threaten us. Nuclear weapons, weather control, and industrial and automotive pollution are all examples of scientific achievements that have been appropriated for business or political ends to challenge our simple notions of progress. As a result, in recent years there has been a call for ethics in science. Also, increasingly, scientists, who traditionally wrote from an objective and agentless or neutral perspective, are now embodying a first-person perspective, which holds them accountable and responsible for the conclusions they draw. See chapter 4, "Writing for the Sciences," for more information. Watson and Crick's "Molecular Structure of Nucleic Acids" and Werner Heisenberg's "What Is an Elementary Particle?" (pages 452 and 442 in the Reader) are good examples of science writing.

Finding a Theoretical Framework

Theoretical approaches can help you frame your argument by establishing a credible frame or context of analysis. The more you are able to use theoretical support that directly speaks to your argument, the more credible and trustworthy your argument will be. It is important, therefore, to continually develop and stretch your theoretical and analytical background. You will then build a sophisticated and knowledgeable store of perspectives and theories that you can use to frame your analysis. What follows are two theoretical audience-oriented (as opposed to reader-oriented) frameworks that you might use to frame your analysis.

The Structuralist or Semiotic Approach

One form of audience-oriented reading practice is **structuralist** and **semiotic**. Structuralists and semioticians are concerned less with the need to assign the text a meaning and more with how meaning itself is made possible in the text and "at what price and along what tracks" (Genette, quoted in Suleiman 11). As a result, the questions they ask extend from the conventions, techniques, **codes**, and **signs** present in the text to an analysis of the larger context.

According to Susan Suleiman, some typical questions asked by structuralists include the following:

- "How (by what codes) is the audience inscribed within the system of a work?" (12).
- What other aspects of the work, whether formal or thematic, determine readability or intelligibility?
- What are the signs, codes, and conventions—whether aesthetic or cultural—that allow readers to make sense of a text? How does the author facilitate or complicate this understanding? (12)

Well-known structuralists include Gerard Genette, Roland Barthes, Mikhail Bakhtin, Stanley Fish, Umberto Eco, and Jonathan Culler.

The Rhetorical Approach

Another form of audience-oriented reading is the rhetorical approach. Using and studying rhetoric, defined by Aristotle as "the faculty of observing in any given case the available means of persuasion" (1359), will improve your ability to inform, persuade, and/or motivate your readers to follow a course of action. With this end in mind, rhetorical criticism, similar to the semiotic and structuralist approach, sees the text as a form of communication between the author and reader.

Rhetorical criticism involves the author's close analysis of a topic, or **rhetorical artifact**, as it relates to the reader and the larger context. A particular topic or rhetorical artifact serves as an example of a particular social, political, philosophical, or ideological problem or issue, revealing something about a particular time, place, or issue. For example, you might examine the rhetoric in a PETA campaign to consider how women are represented in relation to animals. This analysis will go beyond the specific campaign to an analysis of the values that a particular society or culture holds. While a close reading of the artifact (in this case, several advertisements taken from the PETA campaign) is essential, theory, articulated by other researchers who have written on similar topics, might be used to build and generate further ideas.

According to Sonja K. Foss, "As a result of our study of these [rhetorical] models, we should be more skilled, discriminating, and sophisticated in our efforts to communicate—in talk with our friends and family, in the design of persuasive messages for political and advertising campaigns, in the decoration of our homes, and in our responses to television programs and films. In short, we study [and write] rhetorical criticism for a very practical purpose: to become more effective communicators" (7–8).

Exercise 7.13

See the Exercise Answer Key in Appendix A for an analysis of Schryer's theoretical framework.

THEORETICAL FRAMEWORKS IN SCHRYER

Catherine Schryer engages with a specific theoretical framework in her essay, "Lab vs. the Clinic" (see page 350 in the Reader). Can you find the section in her essay where she engages with this framework?

1. Identify the framework and explain how Schryer uses it to frame and support her essay.
2. What theorists, experts in the specific theory she uses, does she use to support her analysis?
3. How does *she* argue that this theoretical framework helps support her argument?

Read the following annotated student essay and consider how Brook Biesenthal engages with his primary text, which is written by Catherine Schryer (see page 350 in the Reader), by using a combination of summary and analysis. How would you evaluate this essay for its ability to present a strong argument and supporting evidence? Can you name the knowledge gap that the writer has identified?

Catherine Schryer's "The Lab vs. The Clinic: Sites of Competing Genres": An Example of Bias?

BY BROOK BIESENTHAL

Good introductory sentence: Brook introduces and summarizes his primary text (Schryer).

1   In "The Lab vs. the Clinic: Sites of Competing Genres," (1994) Catherine F. Schryer indicates that there are two competing genres in the veterinary sphere, specifically the research oriented IMRDS (Introduction, Methods, Results, Discussion, and Summary) and the clinically oriented POVMR (Problem Oriented Medical Record). The competition between these two genres demonstrates an intrinsic and underlying problem. The hierarchical structure of researchers, practitioners, and students is conducive to poor relations among these groups, which leads to poor cooperation. In essence, the divide between the veterinary genres symbolizes the growing turbulence between researchers and clinicians in multiple fields. Schryer suggests the adversarial

competition between the genres is a phenomenon dating back to the 1800s; "[t]he battle between research and practice was fought out in the research and practice journals, the *Revue Scientific* and the *Concours Médical* (Schryer, 1994, p. 17). Although Schryer raises some important points, it is evident that as a researcher herself any research on the division and hierarchical structure of the veterinary profession could be partial towards researchers. Schryer demonstrates her bias towards the research genre throughout her article, which calls into question her neutrality, and ultimately, her ability to objectively study the issue. In this paper, I intend to consider the bias Schryer demonstrates toward the research genre and how this bias has been reflected from the beginning of her essay in her title and abstract, structure, and prescriptions outlined in her chapter. Further, I intend to discuss the presence of students within the hierarchy and how to prevent the adversarial relationship from proliferating.

2   Schryer begins by highlighting the competitive controversy between researchers and practitioners in her title, explicitly placing the two genres and groups at odds with each other in the "The Lab vs. The Clinic" and the subheading "IMRDS vs. POVMR" (p. 26). Presenting them as competitive, but by privileging the research genre by putting it first only serves to affirm the hierarchy that she purports to critique and wants to resolve. Additionally, she begins her essay with a creative summary or abstract, which she refers to as "voices" (p. 1). These voices are taken from a 1989 literacy study, intriguingly conducted by her in 1989. Three of the statements from the literacy study are made by researchers, but only one is made by a practitioner, and only one is made by a student. The information Schryer has provided as evidence of the adversarial relationship between researchers and practitioners seems to be overly representative of the researcher's perspective.

3   Ironically, by writing in the research essay genre, Schryer has implied her audience is composed of researchers. Even though she expressed the necessity for practitioners to read journal articles to be competitive in their fields, these practitioners (and student practitioners) are, as Schryer explains, "taught to be consumers of research" (p. 21). Significantly, they are not expected to participate in the research, but rather they are "referred to as 'data-banks'," directed not to add to the research, but only "to file information in their data banks" (p. 21). As Schryer stresses, "Clinicians and practitioners who speak and write only the POVMR will not be able to compete as effectively as those socialized into IMRDS" (p. 30).

4   While Schryer admits that this privileging is a problem that is already there in veterinary institutions, she adds to this privileging when she posits that only "researchers in professional writing and writing instructors associated with professional programs, such as applied health, engineering or computer science, need be aware of the complex, competing values associated with different writing practices—especially those related to competing genres"

Annotations (right margin):

Good summary. The historical information could be omitted as it is not essential to the main argument.

Brook moves from summary to critical analysis here.

Thesis statement: the focus is on Schryer's perceived bias.

Summary of controversy, with a focus on Schryer's creative abstract: "Voices."

Analysis here: overrepresentation of research genres

Focus on audience, which indicates a further privileging.

Summary of Schryer's observation that clinicians and students are not considered equal.

(p. 14). Moreover, by requesting researcher mobilisation to prevent division between researchers and practitioners from proliferating, while denying practitioner and student input, Schryer is encouraging the hierarchy to continue with researchers at the apex. By suggesting that researchers are the only people capable of addressing the issue, Schryer demonstrates her limited capacity to transcend the hierarchical structure of the competing genres.

5   To remedy the researcher-practitioner hierarchy, Schryer proposes two changes. First, Schryer recommends that instructors teaching the first and second year students be familiar with the POVMR genre to allow the instructors to introduce basic case studies to complement their lesson, thereby familiarizing the students with this genre. Unfortunately, this solution may serve to appease the students' desire for a diverse lesson plan, but it may not resolve the basic hierarchical problem. While instructors may present basic guidance on the use of the POVMR, they will likely find the research method to be superior because it is the researcher's area of expertise. Their preference for the IMRDS would likely be apparent to the students. This negativity towards the POVMR could proliferate from the instructor to the students through socialization, and cause further strain on the researcher-practitioner relationship. Ultimately, the first proposition is focussed on the desire of the researches rather than balancing the interests of the two parties.

6   Second, Schryer recommended "that all students should be exposed to both kinds of genres and traditions" (p. 29). As an example, Schryer described a consultant program where students would solve individual cases while preventing problems at the group level, thereby eliciting both a practitioner's ability to diagnose and a researcher's ability to collect and test data. In addition to exercises that require students to act as both the researcher and the practitioner, they must also engage in cooperative activities, which would facilitate future researchers and future practitioners to view each other's activities as equal contributions. In suggesting this, Schryer assumes that knowledge of the competing genres is necessary to prevent hostility between them; however, exposure would not necessarily result in cooperation and equality among researchers and practitioners.

7   Moreover, a problem Schryer neglected to remediate or offer solutions for was not only the future but also the current hierarchy between researchers and practitioners, which could be moderated by enlisting the help of organizational psychologists to encourage solidarity. Social functions could be held, such as barbeques, holiday theme parties, or even internet blogs, to bring the two groups together in order to prevent the proliferation of the researcher-practitioner hierarchical structure by encouraging social interaction, and eventually mutual efficacy. Commonalities among researchers and practitioners should be stressed, such as providing an efficient and effective service. Finally, although genres provide an illustration of the underlying problem, the hierarchical perception of researchers and practitioners is caused by people's perceptions, which should be explored in greater depth in later studies.

Margin annotations:

Analysis of the way in which Schryer unconsciously privileges researchers.

Summary of Schryer's solution to the researcher-practitioner heirarchy.

Again, a very good analysis of the potential for bias.

Summary of Schryer's argument.

Shift to analysis.

Brook offers hypothetical solutions that he can't, within the scope of this essay, support with research.

Call for future research, indicating the writer's participation in a community of scholars.

8   Significantly, students also suffer from the subordination practitioners cope with, but likely to a greater degree. Unfortunately, students' perspectives were not as widely expressed in Schryer's chapter, and when the students' attitudes were articulated they were generally in the form of an anecdote. Veterinary students use the IMRDS predominantly during their first two years, and the POVMR predominantly during their last two years, but if students gain knowledge of the two genres simultaneously at the beginning of the degree some subordination could be avoided. In this way, Schryer did propose a very valid solution by suggesting the two genres be used in the same consultation service. If students gain an understanding of both genres then it is possible that the relationship may become less adversarial. This method has the possibility to prevent future division.

Switch to focus on students.

Analysis of Schryer's points about students: Brook concedes that she might have a point.

9   Schryer's "The Lab vs. the Clinic: Sites of Competing Genres" raises some very important concerns regarding the divide between researchers and practitioners of many fields, including applied health, engineering, and computer science. However, as a researcher in the veterinary field, Schryer has demonstrated bias through over-representing and over-privileging the research perspective and through her lack of consideration for practitioners and students. Her bias is also evident in the researcher-centric solutions she has proposed. As Schryer's paper indicates, studying the divisive nature of researchers and practitioners while being a researcher in the same field could limit the scope of one's findings and possibly even worsen the problem. More research needs to be conducted in order to establish how widespread this phenomenon is. It might be the case that the hierarchical structure of the researcher-practitioner relationship and the resulting competition are necessary, and indeed could be used for positive results. However, given Schryer's thesis that this division needs to be overcome, it is important that simultaneous knowledge of both genres is disseminated and acceptance and cooperation are promoted in order to create a productive relationship. This cooperation will likely best be achieved through current researchers, practitioners, and their students, all of whom could reconcile their division through understanding, and teambuilding exercises.

Conclusion: brief generalization of Schryer's argument.

Switch to Brook's engagement with Schryer and a summary of his own argument.

Brook uses Schryer to support his own analysis.

The conclusion ends with an emphasis on the need for further research.

REFERENCES

Schryer, C.F. (1994). The lab vs. the clinic: Sites of competing genres. In A. Freedman & P. Medway (Eds.), *Genre and the new rhetoric* (pp. 105–124). London: Taylor & Francis.

This text is a good model of APA citation style.

General comments: This essay is an excellent example of student writing. Brook spotted a knowledge gap in Schryer's work—something she herself had not considered (her own bias)—and successfully provides evidence to support this argument. The weakest part of the essay is when Brook attempts to offer solutions that cannot be supported with research. In general, though, he keeps an objective tone and successfully contextualizes his analysis in the current research on this topic.

CHAPTER SUMMARY

This chapter has provided you with a broad definition of analysis and presented you with skills for analyzing a text and refining that analysis with the ultimate end of using analysis to write an essay of your own. You have learned some strategies for analysis, including asking questions, interpreting, synthesizing, and evaluating, and finding a knowledge gap. You should now realize the importance of logic for academic reading and writing, after being provided with an awareness of basic logical argumentation (syllogisms), the use of ethos, pathos, and logos, and logical fallacies, as well as an annotated student essay on Catherine Schryer's essay "The Lab vs. the Clinic" as an example of excellent analytical writing and logical structure. Essential to your success in academia is your ability to reflect on your own work, analyzing, and thereby improving, your own writing.

You might already have noticed that your academic reading is beginning to translate into academic writing in that, as you read, you are beginning to think about topics and formulate ideas for potential arguments you might make in your own essays. In the next chapter, you will engage more consciously with this transition when you take your knowledge of analysis and turn it into a persuasive essay.

QUESTIONS FOR CONSIDERATION

1. What do I still need to know about analysis?
2. What is the difference between summary and analysis?
3. What do I need to do to translate analysis into an argument?
4. Why is logic important?
5. Why is an awareness of syllogisms and logical fallacies important?
6. Which logical fallacy do I think I am most likely to make in my own writing?
7. Which logical fallacies do I think I need to keep in mind when reading and writing; that is, which fallacies do I think would be most common?
8. What more do I need to know about discipline-specific forms of analysis or theoretical frameworks?

Academic Persuasion

LEARNING OBJECTIVES

In this chapter, you will learn:

- What persuasion is and what role it plays in academic writing.

- How the persuasive techniques of academic writing differ from other "real-world" genres and forms of writing.

- How to take your academic reading and turn it into academic writing using a persuasive written essay form and objective analysis.

- The importance of balanced evidence: types of evidence defined, including sound reasoning.

- Why structure is important to persuasion.

- How to write a good introduction, body paragraphs, and conclusion.

- How to persuade an audience by using a verbal presentation.

As we saw in chapter 7, analysis is a fundamental reasoning process that is essential to all of your academic subjects. When analyzing a subject, you generate knowledge about it through patterns of decomposition (breaking down the topic into its components) and re-composition (reassembling your ideas about the topic into a new argument or form of discussion). **Persuasion** organizes the information generated through analysis to convince your audience of your position or opinion on a specific topic and related intellectual problem or issue. Writing is the main medium you will use to persuade your audience, although you could also present your writing verbally in a presentation to your audience.

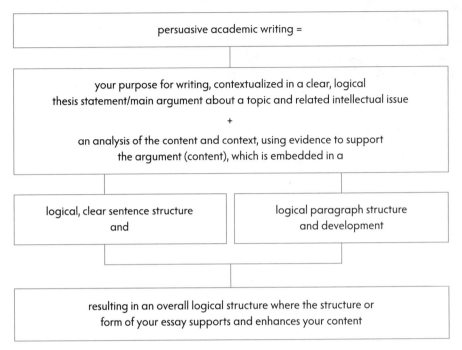

Figure 8.1 ◆ Persuasive Academic Writing

Exercise 8.1

READING PERSUASIVELY

- Go back to chapter 7 and review Brook Biesenthal's essay "'The Lab vs. The Clinic: Sites of Competing Genres': An Example of Bias?"
- How effective is the analysis in this essay? How persuasive is it? Is the organization of the analysis logical? Does it move the argument forward? Can you see how analysis (the way Brook takes apart Schryer's argument) and persuasion (his ability to synthesize his analysis with his overall argument about bias) work together to strengthen his argument? Is his thesis developed throughout the entire paper with the use of evidence, directly taken from his primary text: Schryer's essay? Are there places in this essay where you could insert additional evidence to strengthen the argument? How persuasive is Brook's essay?
- Take notes and discuss your ideas with your classmates.

Later in this chapter, I will present some strategies for helping you learn how to write persuasively for an academic audience. For now, however, it is useful to return to a focus on genre. Learning the difference between how persuasion is used in academic writing as a genre and other real-world genres, such as newspaper reporting and advertising, will help you internalize what will be expected of you in your own persuasive academic writing.

Persuasion in "Real-World" Genres and Academia: A Comparison

Writing is persuasive when it successfully communicates information, ideas, and arguments, that is, your **purpose** for writing, to other readers (audience). This implies that you have not only a clear intent for writing but also a clear argument directed at a specific audience. As we have seen, however, not all writing is directed toward an academic audience. To write persuasively in a variety of genres, you need to be aware of

1. The way in which these genres demand an awareness of different *forms* (structures, medium for conveying information to an audience).
2. How contents and situations (cultural, institutional, and social) can help you provide appropriate and necessary background information.
3. The particular conventions or general expectations for writing and using language in this particular genre.

For example, advertising as a genre uses a combination of forms (print, web, video) and specific language conventions—the use of verbs, adjectives, nouns, sentence fragments, exclamation marks—and visuals (capital letters, font size, pictures) to persuade sections of the general public to buy a product.

Moreover, writing intended to persuade the general public will often attempt to persuade through manipulative tactics, deliberately using logical fallacies (see chapter 7), such as

- stacked evidence (presenting only one side of an argument);
- scare tactics (an exaggeration of the facts);
- false authority (testimony of an unqualified expert); and
- bandwagon appeal (majority appeal).

These forms of persuasion are biased because they attempt to persuade the reader by using emotional language, by emphasizing one point, or by ignoring certain facts and opinions.

Academic writing, however, is concerned with the written academic essay as a form and assumes an intelligent reader or audience who will not be persuaded by manipulative tactics. As such, it demands the use of clear concise writing, formal language, focused sentences and paragraphs, and correct grammar (i.e., no fragments, exclamation marks, or incorrect capitalization). Most important, the writer must be able to demonstrate an understanding of the subject and the larger context related to the subject and be able to make a clear valid argument about it.

Here is a comparison of some of the writing conventions used to target the general public and academics.

Writing for the General Public and Academia: A Comparison

Writing for the General Public

- Explores ideas and issues that speak to public opinion.
- Uses personal experience and opinion rather than objective analysis.
- Tends not to document research.
- Uses first- and second-person point of view. First-person perspective presented as "truth."
- Uses language that is simple, direct, informal. Uses colloquialisms, slang, clichés.
- Uses emotion (pathos).
- Uses description, narration, and summary.
- Uses strategies that attract and keep the reader's interest (the "hook," sensationalism, etc.).
- Uses paragraphs that are short and often undeveloped.
- Speaks to the general public. Geared to an audience that has a specific political orientation or to a specific market that the writing and visuals speak to (*Cosmopolitan* magazine, for example).
- Often geared toward a low reading level.

Writing for Academia

- Writing is knowledge-/ideas-driven and discipline-specific.
- Essays are persuasive and analytical; sometimes uses expository essays.
- First or third person is used.
- Writing is objective and presents a balanced, analytical perspective.
- Language is direct and concise. Uses formal diction and correct grammar; may use some jargon but avoids slang, contractions, or clichés.
- Logic/reason (logos) and ethos (authorial trust) are used.
- Analytical patterns, such as definition or cause–effect, are used.
- Research is thorough and documented.
- Paragraphs tend to be longer because the content has depth.
- Facts and figures are accessible, accurate, and complete.
- Audience: other academics; an intelligent person who is immersed in similar academic studies or interests.
- Reading level is high.

Exercise 8.2

WRITING FOR THE GENERAL PUBLIC AND ACADEMIA

1. Consider the "Writing for the General Public and Academia" list above and see if you can identify the genre and writing style of the following texts (all related to the topic of disability).

2. Name at least five writing conventions from the lists above.

3. Provide a short paragraph-length analysis of how successfully each text meets the criteria for a text aimed either at the general public or academia. Remember to think about what purpose the writing serves: is it effective, given the audience?

TEXT A

Having a child with DS has changed my life... my life is brighter my life is more wonderful my life is filled with love

—*Lorene Kay*

Photo 8.1

Photo © iStock/alvar

TEXT B

Among his friends and neighbors in Wilkie, Sask., 41-year-old Robert Latimer was considered a typical Prairie farmer. Hard-working, clean-living and self-reliant, he would repair his vehicles or replace the barn roof himself rather than hire someone. At the local grain elevators, where he sold the wheat grown on his 1,000-acre farm 170 km west of Saskatoon, he was known as "Laddie" and viewed more as a friend than a customer. (Jenish and Fennell qtd in Janz 68)

TEXT C

Thus, the question arises again: would there be such a great outpouring of public sympathy for Robert Latimer if he had killed an able-bodied child who was in pain? This question was addressed by Dr. Margaret Somerville of the Centre of Medicine, Ethics, and Law at McGill University, in an interview with CBC's *National Magazine*, "Just think how Canada would have reacted if this little girl hadn't been handicapped and Robert Latimer had killed his twelve-year-old daughter. We would have been outraged." After pointing out that there are many, many Canadians suffering from "chronic pain of non-malignant origin," whose murder would not be widely viewed as a justifiable means of alleviating their pain, Dr. Somerville concludes, ". . . we think it's o.k. to kill her . . . because she's disabled." (Janz 70)

See the Exercise Answer Key in Appendix A for a sample analysis of these texts.

In the examples in Exercise 8.2, we can see that the debate about the value of people with disabilities is addressed in many media (advertising, news media, and academia); while all of these texts are persuasive to one degree or another, it is only the academic debate that is truly unbiased, objective, and substantive.

Thus, while it is important to be able to recognize and analyze the persuasive strategies used in advertising and in corporate, government, and legal documents, etc., when writing an academic essay, you must avoid using similar emotional manipulative tactics. In the writing examples above, the writing you should aim to emulate is Janz's article (Text C).

It is important to realize that the academic writing you do throughout your undergraduate or graduate years will deal with specific intellectual problems or issues of importance, like Janz's argument. Your arguments won't insist on a truth or correct solution, because all truths are relative and open to question, but they will *suggest* a certain problem, a truth, or a solution that might help to establish the facts in a problematic situation. Or they might *suggest* a new way of looking at a specific issue that will contribute to the already debated knowledge about the topic or issue (see Garth Forsyth's essay at the end of this chapter).

Persuasive Academic Writing

Now that we have emphasized that your concern is to learn how to write persuasively, using the genre of academic writing, here is a simple step-by-step process for writing a persuasive academic essay.

Process for Writing an Academic Essay

Step 1

Choose a primary text, ask a research question, and, if possible, identify a knowledge gap. A primary text could be an academic essay or a newspaper or magazine article or anything you can read and analyze that is suitably related to your topic.

At this stage, you might have received a primary text and an essay topic from your instructor, but you will probably need to refine it. When identifying a research question, remember that it is a question about the text that intrigues you and that you think you can analyze and make an argument about. You will need to read the primary text several times so that you thoroughly understand the argument and so you can finalize your research question.

This question might involve finding a **knowledge gap**, something that is omitted or overlooked in the text you are analyzing. For example, in the student essay at the end of this chapter, Garth Forsyth exposes the fallacies that might be overlooked in Regan's and Cohen's texts (see pages 378 and 369 in the Reader). In chapter 7, Brook Biesenthal exposes Schryer's unconscious bias and, in chapter 10, Tyrell DaSilva highlights a knowledge gap in his argument about Joe Sheridan's failure (see "The Silence before Drowning in Alphabet Soup," page 432 in the Reader) to consider radio broadcasting.

You might expose a knowledge gap by asking, for example, "Does the author's use of pathos (emotion) weaken the argument when taking into consideration the author's intended audience?" Alternatively, you might ask how the use of logic, for example, in Schryer's essay (see page 350 in the Reader) strengthens and supports the main argument. In this case, you might also ask, "How does the author develop his or her ethos or reader credibility?"

Step 2

Develop your argument by answering the question, finding evidence to prove your argument that something is missing or overlooked in the argument. For example, if you choose to write on how the writer develops his or her ethos, you will need to try to find all the places where the writer seems most credible and then make an argument about the writer's credibility.

To do this, you will need to analyze the work, going through it to find and highlight all the examples (words, sentences, and/or passages) where your focus appears. As you do this exercise, note any insights you might have on the topic or argument you are developing. Synthesize what you find, looking for recurring patterns while attempting to use these patterns to point to an emerging argument you might make about the text, and then attempting to organize these examples in a logical order.

Take Garth's student essay at the end of this chapter as an example. It is possible to see that he was interested first in examining the arguments made by both Cohen and Regan. He may well have already had an interest in how logical fallacies appear in a text and decided to see if Regan and Cohen had committed any. As he went through the article, he discovered that there were indeed several logical fallacies, so he gathered them and made the argument that they weakened the arguments of both of these writers.

Step 3

Come up with a working thesis statement. Remember from chapter 7 that your thesis must offer an "original" opinion, indicate all the major topic divisions of your paper, and be supported by evidence. Moreover, it must be specific enough to focus your argument on one particular aspect of the text and be manageable. The focus should not be too broad or so specific or unrelated to the actual text that you don't have enough evidence to work with.

In chapter 7, you were introduced to a basic method of arriving at a working thesis statement, which involved narrowing your focus and making it more specific. Another way of developing a strong thesis requires taking your tentative working thesis statement and asking:

- *What*, as in what is the essay about?
- *How* are you going to prove your argument?
- *Why* is your argument important?

This process will be discussed later in this chapter, but for now keep in mind that your thesis statement must argue a debatable opinion, which will change and need revising as you write your essay.

Step 4

Make a working outline of your essay. This outline should develop your working thesis statement by outlining the major divisions of your argument. You might choose to use a scratch outline (your main points) or one that also includes the evidence for these points.

Step 5

Write a first draft of your essay. It is a good idea to write this without editing your grammar or sentence structure. Focus on getting down all of your ideas/arguments related to your thesis statement, along with the appropriate evidence.

Step 6

Complete a second revised draft of your essay. This draft should be focused more on structure and evidence. Go through your essay slowly this time, making sure that you have the following points:

- A clear, concise, and well-defined thesis statement that makes a clear argument about your primary text (in a short paper, this will appear at the end of your introductory (outline) paragraph);
- Clear and logical transitions between the introduction, body paragraphs, and conclusion;
- Topic sentences that are adequately developed with specific and logically appropriate **evidence** for your points; and
- A conclusion that does not simply restate your thesis but restates it from a new perspective.

Do not introduce any *new* information into the conclusion; rather, synthesize the information presented in the body of the essay, and restate why the topic is important.

Step 7

Revise your essay for the third time. This revision will be focused on editing your essay so you will need to pay attention to grammar errors (focusing on your most common grammar errors), the logical development of sentences, spelling, diction, typos, formatting, quotation, and documentation style. Make sure all of your sentences are clear, focused, and concise. Take out all unnecessary words.

Step 8

Reread your essay critically and objectively. It is a good idea to set your essay aside for a day or so, and then go back and reread it slowly out loud. The places where you stumble will indicate where your argument, logic, or grammar is not clear. Reading it out loud to another person and asking him or her to tell you in one sentence what your paragraph, thesis, or essay is about is another good strategy. If they can't summarize your essay easily and clearly, then you need to revise it. Most important, make sure that you make an outline of your finished paper. This will allow you to make sure that your thesis is still clear and logically connected to your topic sentences and that your topic sentences logically develop your thesis statement. For further revision strategies see chapter 9.

I will now consider the main points of this process by exploring thesis statements, evidence, and organization in more detail. These three elements are at the centre of all academic persuasive writing.

Thesis Statements

As mentioned in chapter 7, the first step in turning your analytical reading into persuasive writing involves making an argument about the text (remember that this might be a book, poem, etc., but could also be an event, a building, an experiment, etc.). You will do this by first coming up with a tentative argument—what is called a working thesis statement—that accurately outlines the main points of your argument. Because your thesis statement will function as an agreement about what you are going to argue, coming up with a working thesis statement early in the writing process will allow you to find your perspective and find and organize your evidence to support your thesis.

Remember that a thesis statement offers a solution to the issue being addressed. It is highly persuasive, functioning as a promise to readers, letting them know what will be *analyzed* and *argued*.

Your working thesis statement should be *specific, interesting,* and *manageable*. What follows is a process for arriving at your thesis statement, which takes these three points into account.

Specific?

First make sure you have a topic: one paper cannot discuss everything. Next, formulate a thesis statement. Remember, a thesis statement is an argument you present to your reader to try to convince him or her about some aspect of the text. It is more than a topic: it is a specific argument that you want to make about your topic.

When you reflect on the specificity of your argument, you are asking if your argument is focused and clear. Your argument must let your reader know *what* you are arguing, *when* or *where* it takes place (questions of context), *how* you are going to make your argument (are you mostly concerned with statistics or interpretation, which will speak to the actual text you are analyzing), and *why* this argument is important.

Interesting

Your argument cannot meet everyone's needs and interests. As noted in the Margaret Atwood sample thesis statements (see Academic Focus box below), your argument will have specific interest for you (or why write about it?) and for a particular audience. The audience in the Atwood example would probably be predominantly female, but it might also include men who are interested in this topic. Indeed, they might be interested in how the argument shows women's objectification and commodification, and they might

ACADEMIC FOCUS

PROCESS FOR ASKING THE WHAT, WHO, HOW, AND WHY

A good thesis should answer questions like *how* or *why*, as well as *what* or *who*.

Example: using *how* and *why* to develop your thesis from a non-specific statement to a specific thesis statement.

Non-specific thesis:
Margaret Atwood's essay "The Female Body" illustrates some contemporary opinions about femininity.

This thesis illustrates *who* (Atwood's essay, females, and the female body) and *what* (contemporary opinions about femininity), but it does not adequately address the *how* or *why*. As this thesis stands now, it is simply descriptive.

More specific thesis:
In "The Female Body," Margaret Atwood uses irony and humour to expose the ways in which women are objectified and commodified in contemporary society.

This thesis still illustrates the *what* and the *who*, but it now also addresses the *how* (her use of irony and humour) and the *why* (to expose the ways in which women are objectified and commodified in contemporary society).

An even more specific thesis statement:
In "The Female Body," Margaret Atwood's attempt, through her use of irony and humour, to expose the ways in which women are objectified and commodified, succeeds only in perpetuating commonly held stereotypical gender definitions.

This thesis statement provides another layer of analysis that is going to broaden and deepen the analysis. This argument is important because it is concerned not only with the objectification and commodification of women but also with how this objectification and commodification perpetuates stereotypes about women. Implied here, then, is also the notion that the argument is speaking to a specific audience: one that would find this particular essay interesting.

relate this to their own experience by objectively analyzing what the argument means for women or, indeed, men. Alternatively, readers might be interested in the political uses of irony and humour, and/or Margaret Atwood's writing style.

What these potential readers all share, however, is an intellectual interest in the topic. They are concerned not simply with reading for pleasure but with reading to reflect upon what the text itself and your analysis of the knowledge contained within the text can tell us about the related real-world situation: in this case, the objectification and commodification of women in contemporary society.

It is important for you to imagine an audience that is not your professor, as this will lead, Wayne Booth argues, to obedient students who have no investment or interest in the subject matter about which they are writing. It is also important to not imagine an audience that knows less than you do because, in Bartholomae's terms, this will lead to "teacherly" writing that instead establishes a tone of superiority rather than a tone of equality. This type of writing works against the notion that you are writing to a like-minded community of intelligent colleagues who are concerned about the same issues.

As an undergraduate student, it is wise to imagine your essay's ideal audience member as a thoughtful, educated person, who is likely to be interested in the subject and/or issues under consideration. However, this audience is *not* familiar with the texts and the contexts you are analyzing. Thus, part of your job is to provide a context, using summary, description, definition, and specific examples or quotations where appropriate, to orient your reader. These will provide him or her with a framework for clearly understanding the text(s) you are analyzing and for understanding and being persuaded of the credibility of your argument.

Manageable

The manageability of an essay or a presentation will be determined in part by the assignment. If it is a research essay, you will be expected to write a longer paper that incorporates a number of different perspectives pertaining to your subject and issue. If your assignment involves a close analysis of a text, you will need to keep your analysis focused on the text and not on outside sources. It is important to know that it is the specifics of an argument that provide you with the means to argue, but first you need to make sure you have an argument of your own. Ask, then, if your argument is focused enough. Add, refute, qualify, or expose a gap in an existing argument. You might also use an additional text to compare one text with another one, as Garth Forsyth did in his essay at the end of this chapter.

When making your argument, it is important for you to make sure that you don't simply summarize material that is already known. You will need to make sure that you are either adding something to the argument or calling into question any easy reading of the information and knowledge that is already known. Taking the earlier Atwood thesis statement—"Margaret Atwood's essay 'The Female Body' illustrates some contemporary opinions about femininity"—it will feel as though you are stating the obvious because Atwood herself points out these "contemporary opinions." The thesis is too general as is, but adding the "how"—irony and humour—enables you to make an argument *about* the text.

To make your essay manageable, you will also need to focus it. Arguments that are too large are hard to control and students who make them tend to continue in the same generalizing vein without really saying anything that matters.

A common generalization students make is one that makes assumptions about "how people feel" about a certain issue or topic. For example, a common variant of the Atwood essay topic might go something like this: "Margaret Atwood's essay 'The Female Body' shows how many women are upset about how they are treated." To assume that "many women" feel a certain way without including statistical evidence to support this claim is a gross generalization.

Another version of this type of generalization is one that attempts to make an argument about a topic that has already been fully debated. For example, to argue that

ACADEMIC FOCUS

THESIS TEMPLATES

Although templates for effective thesis statements can restrict your thinking about the topic, they can be a useful guideline for students who are not familiar with academic writing conventions, specifically with the need to engage with either your source (the text you are reading) or with the theories put forward by another academic. Here are several templates that might help you become more proficient in writing thesis statements:

Exposing a gap in an existing argument (re: Atwood argument):

X argues that women are objectified; however, X succeeds only in perpetuating stereotypes about women.

Adding to an existing argument:

X's interpretation of string theory, although important, would be enhanced by a consideration of X.

Qualifying an existing argument:

Although X has made significant contributions to the study of X, I disagree with his interpretation of X, which demands an examination of X.

Disagreeing with an existing argument:

According to X, humanism is a liberating practice; however, an examination of three twenty-first-century human rights cases indicates that humanism is the tool of an oppressive culture.

A comparison of two different texts:

In this essay, I compare X and Y, arguing that while X has achieved more public acclaim, Y has more substantive insight into the situation than X.

abortion is wrong would demand far more than one essay could manage. The topic would need to be specifically focused, maybe by studying the legal implications of considering one specific case (primary text), before it would be manageable. You should therefore avoid these generalizing statements.

Exercise 8.3

THESIS STATEMENTS

Evaluate and discuss the following thesis statements.

- Are they specific, interesting, and manageable?
- Do they indicate not only *who* or *what* the subject is but also *how* the writer is going to approach the subject?
- Do they indicate *why* this argument is important?

Suggest ways in which you might make these arguments more specific, interesting, and manageable.

In recent years, Facebook has become a site where bullies can victimize insecure and vulnerable classmates.

From a Christian perspective, humans have the right to kill and eat animals.

Quantum physicists suggest that string theory indicates the presence of different dimensions.

I think that *The Hurt Locker* is a better Iraq war film than *Stop-Loss*.

The 1973 United States Roe vs Wade abortion case ruled that women had a constitutional right to abortion.

An examination of two US legal cases illustrates how the courts privilege the rights of able-bodied fetuses over disabled fetuses.

See the Exercise Answer Key in Appendix A for an analysis and some potential revisions of these statements.

Evidence

As briefly stated in chapter 7, your thesis statement must be supported with effective evidence. This evidence should include one or more of the following:

- facts or statistics (verifiable statements or numbers);
- examples or specifics about the issue in question;
- quotes from the primary text in question;
- expert opinions or the judgments of authorities on the topic;
- refutations or disagreements;
- sound reasoning, which means that the relationship of the evidence to the thesis is clearly stated;
- deductive or inductive reasoning, analytical patterns, and appeals to logos (reason) and ethos (the writer's ability to present him or herself as knowledgeable, trustworthy, and reliable). Pathos (emotion), if used at all, should be used sparingly.

Here is a more detailed breakdown of these different types of evidence.

Facts and Statistics

Facts and statistics are a reliable source of information: they can provide you with authoritative information to support your argument. However, it is important to remember that facts and statistics, like all other sources of information, can be biased and manipulated to meet the needs of a particular argument. Don't take facts and statistics at face value. Ask if they are verifiable and if they come from reliable sources; also, pay attention to the context related to the claims of fact. For example, the 1930s advertisement in Photo 8.2, depicting a doctor offering someone a packet of Lucky Strike

Image Courtesy of The Advertising Archives

Photo 8.2

cigarettes, makes a claim that would seem to point to a scientific study where 20,679 physicians have become convinced that the toasted "Luckies" are healthier. When we consider the context though, it is possible to see that these statements serve the purpose of the advertisement, which is to sell cigarettes and to use emotion to persuade an unsuspecting and, in the 1930s, largely unaware public to buy them.

Moreover, these "facts" are too vague to be verifiable, coming as they do from an unnamed consulting organization, study, and medical specialist(s). Similarly, the statement by the medical specialists does not quote any statistics. Clearly, this advertisement uses spin and manipulation to persuade a general audience that "science" shows that cigarette smoking does not damage your health. It is opinion posing as scientific fact.

Compare the above statement with a current claim made on the Health Canada website (www.hc-sc.gc.ca):

A wide variety of chemicals such as nicotine, sugars, minerals and proteins, are naturally-occurring in tobacco leaves. During the burning of a cigarette (combustion), both the chemicals which exist naturally in the tobacco and the new chemicals which are formed during the combustion are released into the tobacco smoke. To date, over 4,000 chemicals, comprising a combination of gases, liquids and breathable particles, have been identified in tobacco smoke. Of the 4,000 chemicals, more than 70 chemicals are known to cause, initiate or promote cancer.

This objective claim is not trying to sell anything; rather, its purpose is to warn the public of the dangers of cigarette smoking. In doing this, it documents research (a Report of the Surgeon General) outlining the composition of tobacco and its implications for initiating and promoting cancer and provides verifiable facts and statistics that can be checked and confirmed.

It is this latter use of facts and statistics that you should aim to use in your work. Make sure your facts are verifiable and are not statements of opinion designed to use emotion to persuade rather than provide objective evidence.

Exercise 8.4

ADVERTISEMENTS AND PERSUASION

- Find two advertisements that appear factual but contain factual inaccuracies or inferences. Can you see how these facts were manipulated to persuade an audience to believe the claim made in the advertisement? Can you identify an actual or implied judgment?
- Discuss with your classmates.

FACTUAL/INFERENTIAL STATEMENTS AND JUDGMENTS

Factual statements are statements that can be observed and proven as objectively true.

Example:

> Stephen Harper was elected prime minister of Canada in 2004.

Inferential statements are statements that can be inferred. Inferential statements go beyond the facts to show a degree of probability or, in other words, a careful consideration of what the facts imply. Inferential statements often follow facts and form the basis of judgment.

Example:

> Since being elected, Harper has taken a conservative stance, advocating many policies that the Canadian public does not support.

Be careful about leaping from facts to inferences to judgments. The basic rule is that if you can't support a fact or an inference with evidence, do not use it.

Consider, too, that the facts and figures in surveys, in particular, can be manipulated, so make sure you understand the parameters of the survey: who conducted it, the size of the survey, who was surveyed, and under what conditions. Also, make sure you check that the survey is current: a survey that documents poverty in Toronto in 1976, for example, would not be relevant to an argument about poverty in 2014.

Similarly, be careful how you use facts and statistics in your own writing. One common mistake students make is to fail to adequately connect the fact or statistic to their own particular argument. This logical fallacy is a result of students believing that facts, any facts, will strengthen their argument.

Consider the following sentence, which is taken from the Lucky Strike smoking advertisement above:

> 20,679 physicians point out that toasted cigarettes are healthier which means that they might resist cancer.

Given the context already examined above, you can see that the first part of this sentence is not reliable because the original source is not reliable. The second half of the sentence makes an inference that is also not accurate: toasted cigarettes, in this context, have no connection to resisting cancer or to cancer in any sense. If this statement had any chance of being true (which is doubtful), you would need to support it with additional reliable evidence, probably a government survey or a research-based industry calculation.

Examples and Authorities

These might include examples or specifics about the issue in question, quotes from the primary or **secondary text**, expert opinions, or the judgments of authorities on the topic. Quoting a text or verifiable source is a useful method of providing both context and evidence. It is important, however, not to take the quote out of context and to develop your analysis of the quote. Quotes are much stronger if the writer does not simply take the claim as fact but supports it with other facts or, alternatively, calls it into question by examining its validity. Other examples might include illustrations, case studies, or related texts and/or theories about your subject matter.

Exercise 8.5

USING EXAMPLES AND AUTHORITIES

Consider how Catherine Schryer in her essay, "The Lab vs. the Clinic" (see page 350 in the Reader) uses theory and examples or evidence to support her argument.

1. Who are the major theorists and theories that she uses?
2. How does she use them to support her argument?
3. How does she use examples to support her argument? Provide some examples and discuss your awareness with your classmates.

Expert or authoritative opinions should have some verifiable credibility and quotes pertaining to them should relate specifically to your subject of interest. For example, a statement, such as "My friend, who works in an advertising company, told me that cigarette companies manipulate facts and figures to promote their product" would not be as strong as a statement by a published doctor working at a credible university. Your evidence should be directly related to your argument or sub-argument. Evidence that is only indirectly related to your argument might also prove useful, but it is not as effective. Evidence that is only vaguely related to your argument should be omitted completely.

Refutations (Disagreements)

Because scholars communicate with each other about issues, events, theories, methods, etc., it makes sense that they would often have different perspectives. Indeed, academic debate is prefaced upon an awareness of these contentious points of view. As a result, when writing an academic essay, it is important to not simply give your own opinion, but to contextualize your opinion within the opinions of others. Some of these opinions might support your argument, providing evidence that supports your point, but some might run counter to your argument. It is important to acknowledge these counter-arguments and summarize them while possibly agreeing with a part of the opposing argument and refuting the part that you disagree with. Once again, a couple of templates can help you understand how academics formulate these arguments:

> Although I agree with X that students have to learn academic conventions, I think it is important that they do not lose their own voice.

While it is true that X is a problem, it is not insurmountable.

This research challenges X's theory, which argues that . . . ; however, on reflection . . .

On the one hand, I agree with X's formulation; however, on the other hand, I maintain that . . .

REFUTATIONS

Exercise 8.6

Reread Schryer's argument in "The Lab vs. the Clinic" (see page 350 in the Reader) and note how she engages with Schön at the beginning of her essay.

1. How does she agree and disagree with him? In other words, how does she use her summary of Schön's analysis of "technical rationality" to contextualize her own argument?
2. How does she use her basic refutation of Schön's argument to make an argument of her own?
3. What is the nature of her tone: Does she remain objective?

Discuss with your classmates.

PERSUASION: FINDING A THESIS AND EVIDENCE

Exercise 8.7

Examine the following advertisement taken from the "Got Milk" campaign: Can you come up with a working thesis statement?

- Make a list of points that you might use as evidence to support your argument.
- Check to make sure that your evidence is directly related to the text under consideration (the advertisement).
- Share your thesis statement and evidence with your classmates. Have you provided enough concrete evidence taken directly from the advertisement to make your thesis statement workable? Is the evidence concrete and verifiable when

Photo 8.3

considering the actual advertisement?

As implied in Exercise 8.7, it is important that your thesis statement be supported by evidence that is directly related to the text you are analyzing. If your thesis statement takes you "outside" the text to debate related issues, then you need to reconsider it; similarly, if your thesis statement is only marginally supported by evidence in the text, you might want to revise your thesis so that you have enough material to work with.

ACADEMIC FOCUS

ANALYZING ADVERTISEMENTS, PICTURES, OR PHOTOGRAPHS

Advertisements, photographs, and pictures also make arguments. They thus have the potential to engage readers/viewers in the basic elements of rhetoric: critical thinking about contexts, claims, assumptions, counter-arguments, persuasive manipulations, types of appeals, logical fallacies, and audience.

When analyzing a visual text—a photograph, a picture, an advertisement, etc.—you need to remember that you will, first, analyze the text (breaking up anything complex into its various simple elements: taking apart, examining, investigating, duly considering, and weighing up a statement or proposition) and then, second, synthesize your points to make a persuasive argument *about* the text (putting your analysis back together again from a new perspective).

When viewing an advertisement, for example, you will need to take into account the following aspects:

1. The rhetorical situation (context: projected intent, audience, situation, argument);
2. The persuasive tools used in the text (key points, issues, evidence, as seen in the actual advertisement), which may or may not make the intended argument effective;
3. The argument you wish to make; and
4. The evidence you might use to support and

persuade your reader of your argument's validity.

Below are some questions for analysis, related to the above points.

QUESTIONS FOR ANALYSIS

Context:

- Where does the text originate (magazine, newspaper)?
- Who created it (a company? a person?) and why?
- Who is the text directed at: how and why?
- Who or what is in the advertisement and why?
- Does it convey an ideal or a value?
- What is its purpose?
- What information/message/argument does it convey and to whom?
- What situation or context informs how the text should be read (time, place, circumstance or social, psychological, physical). ?

Analysis of visual tools:

- What is highlighted?
- What is your eye drawn to and why?
- What is in the foreground? What is in the background?
- What is in/out of focus? Why?
- What is placed high in the image? What

is placed low or to the left or right (less emphasis)?

- How is light or colour used?
- What details are emphasized or omitted? Why?
- Is the reader required to fill in some knowledge gaps?
- What is the role of the printed text that accompanies the image?
- How is logos, ethos, or pathos used?

Synthesis or pulling it all together to make your argument:

- How effective or persuasive is the advertisement, given its intended audience?
- Does it create, enforce, or challenge stereotypes?
- Does it clarify an important issue?
- Does it sacrifice/maintain its integrity?
- Is the message appropriate, given the audience, time, place of publication?

PERSUASION AND EVIDENCE

Exercise 8.8

Consider the following two student paragraphs, which are written in response to the "Got Milk" advertisement in Exercise 8.7.

1. Which paragraph provides a good working thesis statement that can be supported with evidence from the text? In other words, which paragraph is more persuasive?
2. Which paragraph ignores the advertisement to take us outside the text to an analysis of something completely unrelated?
3. Which one is more appropriate to academic writing?
4. Now compare these paragraphs with your own notes on this advertisement: which paragraph does your writing most consistently conform to?

EXCERPT 1

In the Superman "Got Milk" advertisement, Brandon Routh, who plays Superman in *Superman Returns*, stands arms crossed, cape flying out behind him, as he stares into the camera. He has the white milk moustache that is associated with the "Got Milk" campaign and as he flexes his muscles, seems to be showing viewers how strong milk has made him. In the text to the left of Superman, viewers are told that milk can make their bones strong. The text, accompanied by the picture of Superman, uses manipulative tactics to make an invalid generalization about the benefits of drinking milk.

EXCERPT 2

In the centre of the "Got Milk" advertisement, a strong Superman figure endorses drinking milk, which has made him feel "Super." It is clear from the advertisement, which is one

See the Exercise Answer Key in Appendix A for an analysis of this exercise.

Continued

of the advertisements in the very successful milk campaign, that milk does make you strong. Even if you are not from Krypton, you too can have "bones of steel." This advertisement shows the importance of including milk in your diet because it is very good for your bones and truly does make you strong.

Sound Reasoning

Sound or logical reasoning (see chapter 7), which means that the relationship of the evidence to the thesis is clearly stated, is often not thought of as evidence. However, if your reasoning is not clear and logical, your evidence, and hence your credibility, will be weak. First of all, your argument and evidence need to be logical. When your argument is logical, your credibility (ethos) as a writer will be affirmed. Pathos or emotion should be avoided because it is manipulative and subjective.

An exception to this general rule of academic study is the philosophy essay. Philosophers often deliberately use pathos and logical fallacies to make their arguments. Used in this way, however, philosophical arguments are far from superficial. They often involve complex logical constructs that demand very careful reading practices. Consider the following example, taken from Tom Regan's essay "The Case for Animal Rights" (see page 378 in the Reader):

> Animals, it is true, lack many of the abilities humans possess. They can't read, do higher mathematics, build a bookcase or make *baba ghanoush*. Neither can many human beings, however, and yet we don't (and shouldn't) say that they (these humans) therefore have less inherent value.

The fallacy of comparison (humans and animals) is, of course, an outright appeal to emotion. It asks us to acknowledge that because we don't judge humans who cannot read, do math, build, or cook as having "less inherent value," then we should not treat animals, who can also not do these things, as having "less inherent value." We are asked to judge animals and humans as equals. This point is an invitation to other scholars working in the same discipline to respond with similar rhetorical arguments. In the Reader, you will be able to read Cohen's response to Regan (see page 369).

Exercise 8.9

PATHOS AND PERSUASION

Both Cohen and Regan respond to each other in an attempt to negate their colleague's argument and reinforce their own (see pages 369 and 378 in the Reader). Take a look at these essays.

1. See if you can identify the author's use of pathos. How do they use pathos, and how does this use speak to ethos, or your sense of their credibility?
2. Write a paragraph arguing which argument (Regan's or Cohen's) is, in your opinion, the most credible argument. Make sure you provide evidence for your answer. Share your arguments with your classmates.

Remember from chapter 7 that logical analysis is a fundamental reasoning process in academic writing. When analyzing a subject, you generate knowledge about it through patterns of decomposition (breaking down the topic into its component parts) and re-composition (reassembling your ideas about the topic into a new argument or form of discussion). Persuasion logically organizes the information generated through analysis to convince your reader of your academic position.

The normal pattern is as follows:

- Present your point.
- Expand on your point by using an example (quote, fact, etc.) or two to support your point.
- Analyze the example(s) (quote, fact, etc.) by outlining in depth why and how your example supports or refutes your point.
- Elaborate: implications and reflections.

In other words, it is not enough to simply use evidence: an essay is persuasive when you reflect on the evidence you have used and elaborate on it, drawing and deepening the logical connections to your argument. Examine the following paragraph using the above structure to see if you can tell how the evidence is structured:

> Dron contended that enforced leaves were in the best interests of the mother, the child, and the nation. Mothers would benefit from better health; babies would be breast-fed and avoid gastroenteritis, the major cause of infant mortality; lower infant mortality would halt the natural decrease in population revealed in the last census and insure "the future and even the very existence of the race." (McDougall 87)

As you might have noted, the first sentence presents the point that enforced maternity leaves are desirable. The writer uses an authority (Dron) to support this point and then provides the reader with specific examples in the form of a list of these benefits: better health and lower infant mortality. The last sentence shows the desirability of maternity leaves not only for the mother and child but also for the nation by highlighting how this policy could help increase the population. The writer uses another authoritative quote to support this point, stressing, at the same time, *why* this policy is important, thus developing the author's argument and moving it forward: in this case from a general statement of desirability to a specific point about how enforced maternity leaves would help the nation.

Another way of looking at how you might structure your evidence is to consider how large abstractions and concrete evidence work together (see chapter 6) to construct what Janet Giltrow calls "levels of generality." Scholars tend to use large ideas or abstractions, but they always qualify or balance them with specific concrete details or information that grounds the large ideas in specific reference points, enabling readers to understand the larger abstractions.

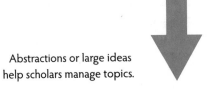

Abstractions or large ideas
help scholars manage topics.

Concrete details provide specific
information or reference points

Figure 8.2 ◆ Balancing Large Abstractions and Concrete Evidence

It might be useful to think of a teeter-totter model here: the large abstractions are on the upper end of the teeter-totter and point to the more concrete detail; the concrete detail, while being pointed to, refers to the large abstractions. One essay will contain many examples of this pattern, but what you need to know is that your writing requires a balance of both. An essay full of abstractions or large generalizations would fail to ground the essay in concrete information that the reader could understand. On the other hand, if it was full of concrete details, it would have no larger focus point to help make sense of the details.

Take the McDougall paragraph, analyzed earlier for its use of sound reasoning, and consider how abstractions and concrete evidence are used in the paragraph to make an argument. What is the relationship of concrete details to abstractions? See the example below (analysis in square brackets):

> Dron contended that enforced leaves were in the best interests of the mother, the child, and the nation. [general abstraction] Mothers would benefit from better health; [first concrete point] babies would be breast-fed and avoid gastro-enteritis, the major cause of infant mortality [second concrete point]; lower infant mortality [general abstraction] would halt the natural decrease in population revealed in the last census [concrete evidence] and insure "the future and even the very existence of the race" [general abstraction, which logically follows from her point about lower infant mortality].

The relationship between the large abstractions and the concrete evidence that follows could also be described in a diagram (see chapter 6 for further examples):

Abstraction: "enforced leaves were in the best interests
of the mother, the child, and the nation"

|

Concrete evidence: mothers and babies would benefit from better health

|

Abstraction: infant mortality as a problem

|

Concrete evidence: lower infant mortality would help population decrease,
as seen in last census.

|

Abstraction: lower infant mortality would ensure the existence of the race.

What you *really* need to know here is that evidence always needs an organizing rationale.
You could use either of the strategies above (often *after* you have written the paragraph to ensure that your writing has relevant and significant engagement with the main ideas) or you could simply arrange your evidence in order of increasing strength. For example, the sentence "Studies on the connection between asthma, allergies, cancer, and environmental pollution suggest that chemical pollution plays a major role" lists asthma, allergies, and cancer according to the severity of the illness and takes us from the more general "studies" to a specific study about chemical pollution.

PERSUADING THROUGH SOUND REASONING

Exercise 8.10

Complete the following three-step exercise. Remember that persuasive writing not only balances abstractions with concrete evidence but also takes apart and reassembles the knowledge into a new argument or perspective.

1. Consider the examples below, and see if you can identify the places where the writer has used a large abstraction and supported that abstraction with concrete evidence. Are there any gaps in these paragraphs: places where the argument becomes illogical or where the ideas are not supported and/or developed?

2. Ask if the writer is able to analyze the ideas in these essays and then reassemble these ideas into a new argument or perspective that constitutes a critical analysis of the work. Is there enough depth? Are you persuaded about the validity of the argument? Why or why not?

3. When you have analyzed these two paragraphs, take a paragraph from your own writing and see if you can outline it in the same way. Once again, look for the gaps where you have not supported or developed your own ideas. Do you have a valid argument?

The following excerpts are based on a comparison of Regan's and Cohen's essays in the Reader, pages 378 and 369.

Continued

EXCERPT 1

Regan uses various ways, mostly through emotion, to persuade the reader into believing that animals have rights. His use of emotion has a great impact on readers, which allows them to sympathize with animals. Regan uses numerous verbs to help create graphic or crude images for the audience. Regan tells us that he had attempted to create a vision about what needs to be done, not how, but why.

EXCERPT 2

Both writers' use of logos, or logic, is what really makes their arguments believable. The evidence they use is straightforward and strong. Both of their analyses are well thought out, making for a more persuasive argument that the reader can accept.

EXCERPT 3

According to these activists for, and critics of, animal rights, it is either morally wrong on every level or completely proper to experiment upon animals. This is a fallacy of false dilemma. Each side of the argument states that there are two distinct alternatives, while in reality there are more possible outcomes. Perhaps there are some occasions when it is morally right to hunt, or to test farm animals, and other instances or scenarios where the obligations that we have toward animals are violated.

See the Exercise Answer Key in Appendix A for an analysis of these excerpts.

Essay Structure

Although an awareness of how you might structure your evidence is crucial to a good essay, just as crucial is the use of effective paragraph structure.

First, you will need to think about your larger essay structure, deciding whether you are going to use an inductive or a deductive essay structure. As explained in chapter 3, this choice will depend largely on whether you are writing an essay for the humanities or arts-based courses, or for the sciences or social sciences. Writing for any of the humanities courses requires a deductive approach to essay writing, which means writing from a general statement to a specific thesis statement. If you are writing an essay for a social sciences or science course, you will use the inductive approach, beginning with a specific hypothesis and moving to a more general articulation and application of the hypothesis.

If you are writing for the social sciences or sciences, you might want to use IMRAD (see chapter 4) as a general guideline for structuring your essay. If you are writing for the humanities, you will need to expand on a specific thesis, developing each of your points in detail to prove that your argument is valid.

INDUCTIVE ARGUMENT FORM

Introduction: The introduction introduces the topic or problem to be addressed and establishes the context for the research. It will most likely include Literature Review as a subheading (though it is sometimes positioned after the introduction and before the methods section). This outlines the current literature on your topic and shows how your work contributes to the literature that has already been produced on your topic (i.e., how it exposes and addresses a knowledge gap in the current literature). The introduction then presents the writer's hypothesis, a general argument that will be tested in the essay.

While the deductive method begins with a claim or thesis statement and attempts to prove it, the inductive essay states a problem, and a possible outcome, and tests it to see if that outcome is more or less probable.

Methods: This section outlines the methods used to test your hypothesis. This section will most likely be broken up into various sections, including site description or design, theory or methods used, equipment used, statistical analysis, etc. The focus is on a detailed objective presentation and analysis of the material.

Results: The results section of your paper provides the conclusions drawn from your study. The data and observations are objective presentations of what you discovered in your experiment. It is important in this section to also present what didn't work. This helps establish the direction of future research in your topic area.

Discussion or Conclusion: This section interprets the results and explains their relevance to your hypothesis. It might include a specific direction or conclusion or it might suggest the direction for future research in your topic.

DEDUCTIVE ARGUMENT FORM

Introduction: In this section, you make contact with readers, introduce the subject and key issues, and describe the context of the debate. The "facts are set forth," and terms are defined (Coe 388).

Thesis statement: This is the main proposition or central argument. It outlines the main argument and the "parts of the argument" that you are going to develop (388) and uses ethos or ethical appeal. In short deductive arguments (under 15 pages), this usually comes at the end of the introduction. This is where you need to persuade your reader that your argument is worth reading.

Body paragraphs: This section offers arguments to support your thesis statement. Your first body paragraph might extend the facts that you gestured toward in your introduction. It includes use of evidence and anticipation of objections. Refutations are analyzed, and the disadvantages of the argument exposed.

Conclusion: This is the summary of the argument. Emphasize what you want your audience or reader to remember, while also attempting to motivate them to take a certain course of action.

Analytical Patterns

The patterns you analyzed in chapter 7 in relation to the work of other writers can be used to *analyze* and *organize* your own material. Structuring your essay's main points and internal ideas clearly and concisely is essential to all successful academic writing. As stated previously, these patterns are not simply technical strategies for organizing your material into identifiable patterns, they are also a strategy for organizing your thoughts on a certain topic. In doing this, you will be able to generate and deepen your insight into a topic or concept at the same time as you are able to structure your information in a way that is ultimately more persuasive.

To review, some of the main analytical patterns used to structure parts of the essay and the whole essay include compare–contrast, cause–effect, classification and division, and process analysis. Patterns used to support an argument and provide context include description, definition, analogy, and example. Narration might be used to support or provide the main structure of an essay, as in an essay written for the social sciences. See Garth Forsyth's essay at the end of this chapter for an example of a compare–contrast essay format.

As you are probably aware by now, in your academic writing, you will need to avoid the use of the five-paragraph essay that you learned to write in high school. While the use of analytical patterns and structure can help you focus and arrange your argument logically, keep in mind that the knowledge, rather than the form, *must* drive your essay. Outlines can be a useful tool in this respect, especially if you remember to keep your focus on the knowledge and the argument about the knowledge that you are attempting to construct.

Outlines

Because thesis statements, or, alternatively, hypotheses, do the work of structuring your ideas for the entire essay, once you have gathered all of your ideas it helps to transfer your main points into a workable essay outline. This outline might take the form of notes or a more formal structure.

There are three kinds of outlines: formal, scratch, and graphic outlines.

Formal Outlines

The formal outline includes sub-points as well as main points so you are able to show more of your essay's organization. This way, you can see at a glance how the parts interrelate. This is especially useful in longer essays. Most formal outlines use coordinated and subordinated clauses to reveal the relationship among the different elements.

Formal outline:

A Comparison of Tom Regan's and Carl Cohen's Arguments

Opening sentence: Introduction to the Animal Rights Debate

Definition of rights—"a claim, or potential claim, that one party may exercise against another" (Cohen 633). *Present the polarized sides*—"abolition of animal use" (Regan 621) vs "Why animals have no rights" (Cohen 633). *Thesis statement.*

Working thesis statement: Although the animal rights debate is a valid and important issue in North America today, faulty reasoning and rhetorical unbalance invalidate many of the animal-rights arguments. This essay will consider how both Regan's and Cohen's arguments are weakened by weak and irrelevant evidence, illogical development, and emotion.

Paragraph 1: Introduce Regan and Cohen and their basic arguments.

Paragraph 2: First point of thesis: Regan and irrelevant evidence
• use of description as evidence.

Paragraph 3: Cohen and irrelevant evidence.
• use of examples.

Paragraph 4: Regan and illogical development:
• fallacies of emotion and bias

Paragraph 5: Cohen and illogical development:
• fallacies of division and generalization

Paragraph 6: Regan and use of emotion: language

Paragraph 7: Cohen and use of emotion: language

Paragraph 8: Regan and Cohen compared; the animal rights movement calls for logical evidence and good reasoning.

Conclusion: Reiterate thesis but stress the importance of logic in the animal rights debate.

FORMAL OUTLINES

Exercise 8.11

The above outline makes a similar argument to the one made by Garth Forsyth at the end of this chapter.

• Outline Garth Forsyth's student essay at the end of this chapter and compare the two outlines. In your opinion, is there any essential information that needs to be

Continued

in the above outline? For you, as a writer, would it work better to keep the outline simple and concise or to expand it with more detail? The key is to find out what works for you.

- See if you can combine the two outlines to better reflect your own processes.
- Discuss the logical organization of these outlines with your classmates.

Scratch Outlines

A scratch outline represents only your main points, usually just by using a word or phrase. Scratch outlines help you to develop a working thesis statement to provide a rough guideline and to give you flexibility in developing your points. You can take a well-developed thesis statement, as in the one below (two sentences), and develop it into an outline for an essay.

Thesis statement:

In *An Inconvenient Truth*, Al Gore suggests that the "truth" about global warming has been concealed by scientists working in collusion with the media and big business. While there might be some truth to this claim, Gore's tendency to present only one side of the argument and to use emotional strategies, such as scare tactics, to persuade his audience ultimately weaken his argument and detract from the debate.

Scratch outline:

- Al Gore suggests that the "truth" about global warming has been concealed by scientists working in collusion with the media and big business. [summary of his argument here]
- Some truth to this claim [taken from his documentary or this point might involve some preliminary research]
- Gore's tendency to present only one side of the argument [an analysis of his biased argument? Focus on what he does not consider: research?]
- Gore's use of emotional strategies, such as scare tactics [maybe add another strategy here: pathos?]

As you can see, this point form outline provides a rough guideline for the essay. What is important at this point, however, is that you use the outline to structure, revise, or add to your ideas (as noted in my comments in square brackets). These points might represent one or more paragraphs, but you should note that the bulk of your analysis will focus on the last two points. These will form the basis of your argument. Please note also that the focus on research above could be a problem if the assignment does not allow for a research focus. You must always meet the requirements of your assignment and, in this case, a revision of your original thesis statement might be required. Remember, too, that these points must always be able to be supported by sufficient evidence from the primary text (*An Inconvenient Truth* in this instance).

Graphic Outlines

A graphic outline (see Figure 8.3) uses diagrams or pictures to organize material into a workable argument and works best for students whose learning style is highly visual.

Other Outline Models

Other effective outline models that can help you organize and rework your ideas into a manageable focus include the following formats. Please note, however, that these outlines should always be driven by a concise and clear thesis statement, as noted above.

THE COMPARE–CONTRAST OUTLINE

Use this outline when you are considering and comparing two texts. There are two possible formats for a comparison–contrast outline. Each of them must be driven by a clear thesis statement expressing your considered opinion about the texts:

Gore: Global warming truth concealed, but resorting to scare tactics does not make his argument credible.

Figure 8.3 ◆ Sample Graphic Outline

Example A:

- Introduction
- Text A is examined: points a, b, c (at least a paragraph for each sub-point)
- Text B is examined: points a, b, c (at least a paragraph for each sub-point)
- Paragraphs to sum up your perspective on the two texts
- Conclusion

Example B:

- Introduction
- First point is examined: text A
- First point is examined: text B
- Second point is examined: text A
- Second point is examined: text B
- Third point is examined: text A
- Third point is examined: text B
- Paragraph(s) to sum up your perspective on the two texts
- Conclusion

The For/Against Essay Outline

Often seen in philosophy courses, the for-or-against essay outline is sometimes misinterpreted as making a right or wrong ethical argument. You might, for example, make an argument for animal rights based on an argument for the right ethical choices. Although the structure must suit your particular argument, here is a typical format:

Introduction: Introduce both sides of the topic.

Part A: Arguments in favour of a certain perspective or issue: animal rights, for example.

Part B: Arguments against a certain perspective or issue: opposing arguments concerning animal rights, for example.

Part C: Where you stand on the issue, while maintaining an objective neutral stance.

Conclusion.

PROBLEM–SOLUTION ESSAY OUTLINES

This type of outline (often used in social sciences, business, and engineering) is a less scientific form of the IMRAD method.

Here is the general format:

Situation: Describe the situation and the larger context.

Problem: Describe the problem that needs to be solved.

Solution: Describe the solution to the problem.

Evaluation: Discuss the validity of the potential solutions.

SCIENCE ESSAY OUTLINES

This outline, commonly known by the acronym IMRAD, is most often found in science courses and can be used in social sciences, engineering, and business. Catherine Schryer's essay along with Werner Heisenberg's and Watson and Crick's essays (see pages 350, 442, and 452 in the Reader), constitute different examples of how this form is used in the social sciences and sciences. Here is the typical organization:

Abstract: Summary of paper: The main reason for the study, the hypothesis, the primary results, the main conclusions.

Introduction: What the study is and why the study was undertaken: Why is this study important? The *Literature review* and your *hypothesis* are here.

Methods and Materials: *How* the study was undertaken: Outline the parameters of the study, the methods used, etc.

Results: *What* was found.

Discussion or conclusion: *Why* these results could be significant to the issue at hand and possibly the larger context.

Organizing Paragraphs

Obviously it is not enough to simply have an outline; you will need to be able to take the points from your outline and turn them into a developed essay that contains clearly developed paragraphs that lead to a discussion or conclusion. In a deductive essay, you will need an introduction, a thesis statement, body paragraphs containing evidence to support your thesis, and a conclusion that emphasizes the validity of your argument. Your paragraphs must follow each other, logically connecting your larger points so that the reader can easily follow your argument. Your sentences within the paragraphs must do the same. See chapter 6 for a breakdown of deductive essay structure, including introduction, body paragraphs, and conclusions. You will also find directions there for using logical transitions at both the sentence and the paragraph level, along with a list of transitional words to help make your transitions smooth.

As a review, please note that a deductive essay should have the following paragraph structure:

Introductory Paragraphs

An introductory paragraph includes a clear, concise, and well-defined thesis statement.

The introductory paragraph should provide a context for your essay by introducing the topic or main text and summarizing the main points that relate to your intended argument. Your opening sentence should provide a general but informative introduction to the main focus of your essay. The rest of the introductory paragraph should provide a context by summarizing the main points of your primary text (text you are engaging with and analyzing), as they relate to your argument. In other words, you don't have to account for everything, but you do have to provide a context that demonstrates your argument. Last, you should present the thesis statement. It is essential that this thesis statement be narrowed so that it follows the guidelines outlined in the assignment. If you do not have a strong detailed thesis statement, you will not be able to write a logical, effective, or persuasive essay.

Body Paragraphs

Each paragraph should be limited to the discussion of *one* general topic that develops one aspect of your thesis statement. This focus enables you to establish clarity and direction throughout your essay. Remember that your reader is not a mind reader; what is obvious to you will not be obvious to your reader, so do not assume that your reader has any knowledge of your topic or the issues that you are engaged with. You must spell it out for your reader.

Moreover, your reader should never have to look back to a previous paragraph or point. The reader should be able to easily follow your argument as you develop it. In each paragraph, you should include appropriate and logical evidence to support your larger statements or abstract generalizations. This might also include a discussion of conflicting opinions on your topic. Rather than simply stating that these opinions are wrong, you will need to provide evidence and an analysis for why they are not appropriate to your particular argument. Your concluding sentence should not simply restate the focus of your essay but summarize it anew as it relates to your larger argument or thesis statement and as it relates to the topics and ideas that you are going to develop in your next paragraph.

Conclusions

A conclusion does not simply restate the thesis but readdresses it in an attempt to point out why your argument is important. The conclusion is the part of the essay that will most effectively persuade your reader that your thesis is valid and persuasive. As a result, your conclusion must help the reader reflect back on your argument in a new way that convinces him or her that your argument is effective and logical. However, do not introduce any new information in the conclusion. Your final sentence must affirm why your argument is important: you might want to allude to the cultural, social, and disciplinary significance of your argument or you might want to point your reader to the need for a deeper analysis of your topic that might be articulated by other academics working in this area.

Transitions

Clear and logical transitions between the introduction, body, and conclusion of the essay, between sentences, and between the high-level arguments and the concrete

---

ACADEMIC FOCUS

INTRODUCTIONS AND CONCLUSIONS

Sample student introduction and conclusion: The conclusion rounds out the previous discussion by returning to a key point and expanding on it.

Introduction: In *Oedipus the King*, Sophocles explores the concept of masculinity by examining Oedipus and Creon in terms of how their strengths and vulnerabilities manifest in their role as leaders.

Conclusion: Ultimately, Sophocles reveals that masculinity is not a single innate fixed or immutable concept, but a complex construction susceptible to life experiences and changes, and

vulnerable to what is or cannot be known: fate's unpredictable fortunes and misfortunes.

As you can probably see, the writer of this essay has expanded on "the concept of masculinity" in the introduction, using the play to draw larger conclusions.

Knowing how to write a clear argument that is developed in coherent, unified paragraphs, however, does not, on its own, make an essay persuasive. You will also need to make sure that your ideas are supported by effective paragraph and sentence transitions.

evidence that supports them, are essential. On the sentence level, transitions help the reader to follow your points as you develop them. Your reader should never have to ponder how you are connecting your ideas: the logical connection between your ideas must be clearly laid out.

On the paragraph level, transitions help your reader to follow your argument by sign-posting where you are in relation to your thesis and where you are taking your argument. Paragraph transitions should lead logically from one point to the next, wrapping up the main argument or idea from the previous paragraph and hinting at how it might be developed in the next paragraph.

At the beginning of your paragraph, your topic sentence should allude to your analysis in the previous paragraph and indicate the development of a new but related point. All of your paragraphs should develop some aspect of your thesis; keeping in mind why your thesis is important will help you to develop and focus your transitions. Last, it is essential that your evidence be thorough and directly and logically connected to your argument.

One of the easiest ways of making a paragraph transition is to use the standard first, second, third structure. However, this structure only really works for short essays. The following is an example of student writing showing one paragraph and the beginning of the following paragraph. As you will see, these paragraphs are connected by the "first–second" structure.

In the first quatrain of the Petrarchian sonnet, Helene Johnson utilizes rhythm and sound to emphasize the man's pride. The meter (iambic pentameter) is perfectly in rhythm in the first two lines, just as the man has a "perfect body and a pompous gait." Her use of alliteration of the "p's" also emphasizes the man's intimidating image. In the third line, the image of the man's "dark eyes flashing solemnly with hate" is accentuated through the consonances used, "dark, hate," allowing the reader to slow down as he or she reads. The form of the poem is strictly Petrarchian (abba abba cde cde), also reflecting the content: the "perfectibility" of man.

In the second quatrain of the octet, Johnson changes the idea as the rhyme scheme also changes.

Another way of making smooth transitions is to pick up on the ideas from the conclusion of the previous paragraph and develop them logically in the next one. Your paragraphs should lead the reader logically forward through the essay without causing the reader to stop and look back to check that he or she is able to follow your ideas correctly.

Both revelations contribute to Norman's journey of self-discovery, as he learns exactly what he may be capable of, in both the positive and the negative sense. This awareness helps Norman to discover his identity, while also relating to and understanding the position of his mother.

Like Norman, Jackson is able to establish his identity. He learns from the mistakes of others, and he incorporates this knowledge into his own self-awareness.

Each sentence of the paragraph should contribute to the main idea. These sentences should logically develop your argument in a way that the reader can easily follow as it moves forward to your conclusion. You can achieve paragraph coherence by organizing your ideas, by being specific, and by using transitional devices (words or phrases that help bring coherence to a paragraph by signalling relationships between and among sentences). One way of achieving sentence coherence is to pick up and develop the ideas in the sentence that come before it. When you don't develop the ideas in your sentences coherently, a gap in your thinking becomes visible to the reader. This is known as the fallacy of non sequitur (Latin for "it does not follow"). The following is an example of two sentences that illustrate this fallacy.

> His words clearly resonate with what he is feeling. Therefore, the attitude of the people is one of revolution.

As you probably noticed, the second sentence does not clearly or logically follow the first one. The reader is not clear how the "attitude of the people" follows from "his" feelings or even how "he" is connected to the people in general or to their attitude of revolution. It becomes clear to the reader that there are gaps in this person's thinking.

This problem is not usually the result of unclear thinking but of a failure to clearly communicate thinking. Students often assume that *what* they write is clear because it is clear to them as they are thinking about it. However, this clear thinking has to translate into clear writing. This problem can be fixed by making your points specific and crystal clear. You must assume that your reader does not know the workings of your mind, so you must pay attention to detail and carefully make sure you convey your points as accurately as possible. As an aside, be careful about using words, such as *clearly*, *obviously*, etc., and abstract words, such as *beautiful*. Words like this often substitute for specific clear information. When you see them in your own writing, substitute more accurate words in their place. See chapter 6 for more examples of logical development at the sentence and paragraph level.

Presentations: How to Persuade an Audience

In many of your university classes, you will be asked to perform oral presentations, either alone or with one or more classmates. When scholars read their work at conferences, they often simply read their papers to an audience that consists of other scholars (see Wayne Booth's essay in the Reader, page 335). You might be asked to do this, but you also might be asked to present a topic that actively engages an audience.

Presentation Structure

Regardless of whether or not you read an actual paper out loud, in many ways your presentation will be similar to a written paper: you will still need a well-planned introduction, a clear argument or thesis, body paragraphs, and a conclusion. The language you use will depend on your audience: if, for example, your presentation is intended for a business, education, or nursing class that might be more connected to situations in the non-academic sector, you could use more informal or conversational language. However, if your presentation is academic, then your language will need to remain formal.

Preparation

If you don't read from your paper, then it is a good idea to use cue cards highlighting the key points or words to remind you if you lose your focus. Practising your presentation ahead of time is crucial; you will need to make sure that you stay within the time limits set by your instructor. You need to appear relaxed and confident, so take the time to organize your material carefully before you go to your presentation, and also make sure you allow time to centre and ground yourself before you go to the presentation room. Breathing, stretching, and relaxation exercises will help as will visualizing a calm successful presentation. Also, arriving a good ten minutes before your presentation will allow you the time to set up your computer, if you are using one, and help you feel more comfortable at the front of the room.

The Presentation

Your best strategy for success is being fully prepared for your presentation, but you will still need to present your material to your audience. Calming yourself before you go up to make your presentation can help: breathe deeply, and trust that your preparation will help you once you stand in front of your class. Here are some additional tips.

Body Language

Become aware of your body language. Eye contact, body posture, and gestures are important. If you are really nervous, you can stand behind the podium, but encourage yourself to venture out if possible by arranging for some movement during your presentation, even if it is only to move to the blackboard to write something on it. Your hands give your nervousness away immediately. If they are shaking, try and steady them by holding the podium or the edge of a table. Again, move slowly and breathe. Eye contact is important because your audience will want to feel that you are paying as much attention to them as they are to you. As a result, your audience will want you to acknowledge them. One trick is to pick four or five different people in various parts of the room and make sure that you look at them during your presentation. If you are really nervous, you can look just above their heads so that they are in your peripheral rather than your direct vision.

Voice

When speaking, take your time, pause at commas, periods, or key points, and, most important, take time to breathe. Do not rush your presentation; if you find you don't have time to get through it easily without rushing, then cut some material. When practising, become aware of the times when you stumble: uumms and repetitive phrases, such as "you know" can be distracting and will need to be eliminated from your speech. You will need to make sure you speak up and project your voice to the back of the room. If you are worried about this, ask your audience if they can hear you at the back of the room. Immediately engaging with them will help you, and them, to feel more comfortable. You might also engage the audience by asking them to respond to certain parts of the presentation. Asking your audience questions or inviting their questions at the end of the presentation is also a useful strategy.

Visual Aids

Using visuals can help. I like to illustrate my points on the blackboard or computer, using a PowerPoint presentation. If you decide to use these visual aids, make sure that you keep your points focused and short. Bulleted points that you can expand on are a good strategy.

Above all, know that presentations get easier with time, so relax and have fun with them.

An Example of Critical Persuasive Writing

The following annotated student essay, written by Garth Forsyth is an excellent example of critical persuasive writing

An Examination of Tom Regan's "The Case for Animal Rights" and Carl Cohen's "The Case for the Use of Animals in Biomedical Research": Fallacious Arguments?

BY GARTH FORSYTH

> Good opening sentence. Introduces us to the overall debate.

> Well-organized summary: First Regan; Second, Cohen. The comparison of mentally incapable humans and animals is pertinent here.

1   The rights of animals, specifically whether or not animals have equal rights to humans, have been a point of argument primarily between two polarized parties. The first group are those that believe and purport that animals share and have the same rights as humans. In this respect, Tom Regan, an animal rights theorist, presents a strong argument that animals have inherent value. In light of this value, Regan calls for a complete abolition of the use of animals in science, calling the pain, suffering and loneliness (Regan 632) of animals "fundamentally wrong" (622). As part of the second group, Carl Cohen, a critic of the animal rights movement, asserts that while we do have an obligation to "act humanely" toward animals (635), rights, for animals, are not a result of that obligation. Due to the conclusion that animals are without

rights, Cohen suggests replacing human test subjects with an increased number of animals for biomedical research. While Cohen's argument for the use of animals in testing is strong, his generalization of all humans whether mentally capable to make moral claims or not, leaves some questions unanswered about his separation of obligation and rights. In evaluating these two sides of the animal rights debate, I argue that the insistence that there are only two alternatives, either it is totally and morally wrong or completely and ethically sound to allow the interests of the human species to override the interests of other species, is a result of faulty reasoning.

> Garth's thesis: the black-and-white reasoning that separates the debate is a result of faulty reasoning.

2   The view that all animals have rights equal to humans is supported by Regan's assertion that animals have an inherent value. This is in clear opposition to some critics of animal rights who affirm that animals have less value than humans and thus can morally be used as a beneficial resource. To these claims Regan responds as follows:

> Garth follows the logical order presented in his introduction by summarizing Regan's arguments first. Issue of "inherent value of animals and humans" is developed.

> What could be the basis of our having more inherent value than animals? Their lack of reason, or autonomy, or intellect? Only if we are willing to make the same judgement in the case of humans who are similarly deficient. But it is not true that such humans—the retarded child, for example, or the mentally deranged—have less inherent value than you or I. Neither, then, can we rationally sustain the view that animals like them in being the experiencing subjects of life have less inherent value. All who have inherent value have it equally, whether they be human animals or not. (Regan 630)

> Indented quote provides direct evidence for Garth's summary of Regan's position.

When recognizing the equal inherent value of animals and humans, Regan claims that reason, not emotion or sentiment, requires that animals have "their equal right to be treated with respect" and, consequently, advocates for the total abolition of the use of animals in science, agriculture and sport hunting (631).

3   In opposition to Regan, Cohen makes a strong case for the use of animals in biomedical research. In making this argument, Cohen focuses on the concept of obligation vs. rights and argues that just because we have a sense of obligation to treat animals with respect and care, animals do not have rights as a result of that obligation. Refuting Regan's argument that all animals, like all humans, have inherent value, Cohen argues that "Animals are of such a kind that it is impossible for them, in principle, to give or withhold voluntary consent or to make a moral choice. What humans retain when disabled, animals never had" (635). From Cohen's perspective, then, the "elimination of horrible disease, the increase of longevity . . . the saving of lives" (638) are results that are far too beneficial to stop testing on animal subjects. In fact, he claims that refraining "from using animals in biomedical research is, on utilitarian grounds, morally wrong" (639).

> Garth summarizes Cohen's argument (the 2nd point in his introduction).

Garth now makes the transition to his own analysis: faulty reasoning, using the fallacy of "false dilemma."

4   In summary, while each side of the debate on the rights of animals makes valid points, both sides claim that "you are either for us or against us," which detracts from the argument. According to these activists for and critics of animal rights either it is morally wrong on every level or completely proper to experiment upon animals. This is a fallacy of false dilemma. Each side of the argument states that there are two distinct black-and-white alternatives, while in reality, there are more possible outcomes. Perhaps there are some occasions when it is morally right to hunt, or to test farm animals, and other instances or scenarios where it violates the obligations that we have toward animals.

Good transitional sentence: his point is summarized briefly and developed to include a focus on Regan's fallacious use of emotion.

5   Not only is the black or white mentality of the animal rights debate fallacious, but many of the specific arguments for or against the use of animals as a resource for our benefit are also a result of faulty reasoning. Regan uses an appeal to emotion to arouse the feelings of the reader to take pity on the animals and support the animal rights movement instead of using a strictly logical deduction to persuade the reader to the same end. For example, when Regan argues that "The forlornness of the veal calf is pathetic, heart-wrenching; the pulsing pain of the chimp with electrodes planted deep in her brain is repulsive; the slow, tortuous death of the racoon caught in the leg-hold trap is agonizing" (622), he compromises his argument that "animal rights has reason...on its side" (623).

Good evidence and analysis.

Shift to Cohen: introduction to his fallacious argument: the use of generalizations and the fallacy of division.

6   Similarly, Cohen's grouping of all humans, including the mentally deficient, in the same classification in order to prove a point at first seems logically correct, but on a second look, it simply generalizes, which is not a valid form of argument. To argue in a generalizing sense that what is true of the whole must be true of all of its parts is a fallacy of division. To say that because the majority of humans have the ability to make moral decisions, all humans are equal in that respect is paralleled only by his similar fallacious argument about animals: because animals do not have the ability to understand abstract moral rights or have the capability to "give or withhold voluntary consent," all animals are inferior to humans and, therefore, have no rights (635). What is true of the whole is not necessarily true of its parts and many animals, even if they can't speak, will be able to register their resistance to humans who "justify imposing agonies" on them (636).

Second paragraph on Cohen: critiquing his concept of obligation.

7   Moreover, these arguments cannot be solved, as Cohen argues, by a generalizing argument that states we have an obligation to "the brain-damaged, the comatose, the senile" (635) and to animals alike. Cohen's speciest argument that when we choose to break that obligation to animals, as when we choose to use them in biomedical research, is a moral choice that ought to be performed compromises his concept of obligation in that the means is justified solely by the desire for human superiority, which would seem the means and the end of Cohen's argument.

Conclusion: summary of the two opposing debates and his position in relation to them.

8   It would seem, given these typical arguments, that each side of the animal-rights debate turns to irrelevant or unacceptable premises to strengthen their extreme views. These extreme views—those who feel it is always wrong to use animals as a resource for our benefit and those that believe there are no

moral implications for participating in such practices—are fallacious in their unwillingness to see any value in the other side of the debate. With incomplete evidence it is impossible to fully support either of these claims. There is a need to continue study and research into the moral capabilities and rights of all animals but at this time the advantages to human health that come from animal testing are so great that even with the possibility that we are violating the animate species' rights, that may or may not exist, our obligations possibly lie first with our own species and its progression and then comes our duty to animals.

> More research is needed.

> Garth leaves his readers with something to think about, forcing them to go back and evaluate how they feel about the issue.

General comments: This is an excellent essay: having found a knowledge gap in both Regan's and Cohen's arguments (fallacious reasoning), Garth uses a neutral objective tone and evidence and analysis to organize his essay according to a standard compare–contrast arrangement, using (a) a summary of Regan and Cohen; and then (b) an analysis of Regan and Cohen. The conclusion is good in that Garth leaves the reader with something to think about, but his argument—that considering the need for medical research, Cohen's argument might be more relevant—would have been stronger if it had been pointed to in the introduction and developed as necessary throughout the body of the essay.

CHAPTER SUMMARY

This chapter is one of the most important chapters in the book because it helps you make the transition from reading and analyzing to writing persuasively. In comparing academic writing with other forms of writing and, at the same time, considering some essential academic conventions, this chapter should give you an understanding of *how* academics make their writing persuasive. This chapter stresses the importance of a strong thesis or argument and the need for supporting analysis and relevant evidence that is contained within a logical and tight essay structure.

QUESTIONS FOR CONSIDERATION

1. How does persuasive writing appear in advertising and other popular genres? Can you provide examples?
2. Can you outline the relationship between abstractions and concrete evidence? Why is this important?
3. How and why is logical development important at both the sentence and the paragraph level?
4. Why are outlines a useful tool? Which type of outline do you think you might use?
5. What is the relationship between essay content and form (structure)? Why is it important?
6. Can I outline what needs to be focused on in an academic presentation?
7. What do I still need to know about writing a persuasive essay?

9

Drafting and Revision

LEARNING OBJECTIVES

In this chapter, you will learn:

- The difference between how inexperienced and experienced writers draft and revise.

- An understanding of the recursive nature of all writing forms.

- The importance of purpose, focus, and depth in academic writing.

- Strategies for drafting and revising your paper.

- Features of successful and unsuccessful essays.

- The necessity of revising at all three levels: content, logic and organization, and grammar/style.

- How to revise collaboratively using peer review.

- How to use a checklist for revising.

Most instructors of English are aware that first-year students have not only had very little training in how to write an essay beyond the five-paragraph essay model that they learned in high school, but that they have also had next to no training in how to revise their work. This does not mean that high school English teachers don't have standards or that they don't care about preparing their students for a college or university education, but that the secondary-level and university- or college-level education systems have entirely different aims for their students.

Unfortunately, because high school instruction has to meet many educational requirements—academic and trade-orientated education, behaviour management, citizenship aims—it is often unable to fully prepare students for the higher standards demanded by a college or university education: standards that involve preparation, sincere reflection, and revision when it comes to essay writing. While university instructors often interpret this lack of preparation as an aversion to revision, and even an aversion to thinking, in my opinion it is the result of a confusion about what constitutes essay writing at the university level.

This chapter thus attempts, step by step, to bridge the gap between high school and university writing by making the standards and the process involved in writing for academia clear. In this chapter, you will come to understand the different attitudes held by "basic" or inexperienced writers and experienced writers, and learn a process for drafting and focusing an essay for an academic reader. A central focus will, of course, be on the revision process, which will teach you how to revise first for content, focus, and depth, second for logic and organization, and last for grammar and style.

Inexperienced and Experienced Writers

Over the years, scholars working in rhetoric and composition have speculated on the different understandings experienced and inexperienced writers have of the writing process. This sentiment is encapsulated by Donald Murray (see page 343 in the Reader) when he writes, "When students complete a first draft, they consider the job of writing done…When professional writers complete a first draft, they usually feel that they are at the start of the writing process" (120). Experienced writers know that writing is as much about revision as it is about writing the first draft. Moreover, experienced writers know that writing is recursive.

Academic Writing Is Recursive Writing

Recursive writing involves repeatedly returning to the different writing steps as you work to refine your work. To say that writing is recursive, then, is to argue that it is a process that refuses any linear development. Although this process appears to involve moving through clear beginning (prewriting), middle (writing), and end (revising) stages, in practice it actually requires writers to constantly move backwards and forwards between those steps. This process might involve reading, discovering, discriminating between, selecting, generating, and synthesizing critical ideas, outlining, drafting, revising, reading, discovering, selecting, and so on.

Prewriting strategies, which refer to the steps writers typically engage in before drafting a paper, include brainstorming, freewriting, mapping or clustering, analyzing, researching, data analysis, outlining, etc. Revision strategies refer to the steps writers take to rework or reorganize their work so that it becomes clearer and, by implication, more logical and focused. Revision might include outlining, rewriting sections of the paper, reorganizing, and rethinking your paper.

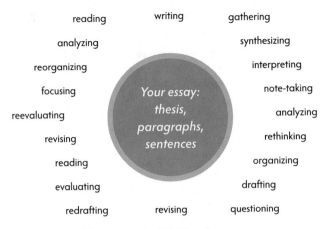

reading   writing   gathering

analyzing   synthesizing

reorganizing   interpreting

focusing   note-taking

Your essay: thesis, paragraphs, sentences

reevaluating   analyzing

revising   rethinking

reading   organizing

evaluating   drafting

redrafting   revising   questioning

Figure 9.1 ◆ The Recursive Writing Process

ACADEMIC FOCUS

PREWRITING STRATEGIES

Brainstorming: Once you have a topic, you can begin to understand it in more depth by quickly making a list of key words and phrases related to your topic.

Freewriting: Keeping your topic in mind, write as quickly as possible for a certain amount of time. Do NOT worry about grammatical correctness or perfecting your ideas: let your ideas flow. You can edit them for relevance afterwards.

Discussion: Discuss your ideas with your professor or with your peers and listen to their feedback.

Questioning: Ask yourself questions about your topic and your ideas about your topic.

Mapping or clustering: This technique is similar to brainstorming, except that it uses the form of a map or cluster to list key ideas related to your topic. When you use this strategy, write your topic in the centre of a piece of paper and draw a circle around it. Add new words or phrases related to your topic around that and draw lines to connect them. Not all of these points will have equal value: you might choose to ignore some of your points and focus on others. What you choose will depend on the argument you intend to make. Please see the example of clustering in chapter 5.

This recursive process might feel somewhat daunting, especially if you have not been used to revising your work. You might resist the entire process or parts of the process, feeling that the requirement to conform to the standards and conventions of academic writing suppresses your own creativity and ideas in some ways. This resistance reflects a central concern, articulated by scholars, that while we don't want students to reproduce the demands of academic writing by rote, preferring instead to teach students to think for themselves, we also recognize that if students don't learn the conventions of academic discourse, they will not be successful. In other words, students have to learn to reproduce the "acceptable truths, imitating the gestures and rituals of the academy" (Sommers "Between the Drafts" 283) before they are able to successfully "bring a voice of [their] own" to the scholarly conversation (284). As a result, it is important to keep in mind that as an inexperienced academic writer, you will need to learn the conventions that experienced academic writers use to be successful.

Understanding Academic Discourse

Another basic distinction between inexperienced and experienced writers is highlighted by David Bartholomae who, in "Inventing the University," argues that the "basic" or inexperienced writer's focus on word- and sentence-level errors, might, at least in part, be the result of a failure to understand the **discourse** or the language conventions of the community of writers that they are writing to. As Bartholomae argues, "the student has to learn to speak our language, to speak as we do, to try on the peculiar ways of knowing, selecting, evaluating, reporting, concluding, and arguing that define the discourse of our community" (589). His essential argument is that before a student can feel comfortable writing in an academic environment, he or she must "appropriate (or be appropriated by) a specialized discourse" (590). This appropriation demands an awareness of a specialized vocabulary and an understanding of a specialized audience: "one that already includes and excludes groups of readers" (594).

Understanding the **commonplace** conventions common to this audience will help students avoid the mistakes that Bartholomae has identified as being problematic for basic writers. What follows is a list of academic commonplace conventions, adapted from Bartholomae's essay "Inventing the University." Rather than focusing on the mistakes students make, it focuses on what students need to do to learn how to read and write well.

Academic Conventions

Here is a list of what student readers and writers need to know about academic conventions:

- When reading, make sure that you pay attention to the writer's projected audience, any hints of bias, use of citation, techniques, and the structure that the writer is working with.
- When reading, never take anything at face value: read between the lines and look for "points of discord" (Bartholomae 598).
- Use analysis to break apart complex ideas into their parts and put them back together into general conclusions.

- When engaging with other writers, make sure that you are clear about which ideas belong to you and which ideas belong to someone else. Identify other people's ideas by using reporting expressions.
- Make sure that your points (at the sentence and the paragraph level) are logical (i.e., that they follow each other in a way that develops the main points you are arguing).
- Use an appropriate tone by engaging with your ideas in a specific and clear way. Present your opinions in a considered reflective way rather than a domineering or teacherly way, offering "lessons on life," (592), "advice or homilies rather than 'academic' conclusions" (591).
- Make sure that your point of view is consistent, and never use second person (you, your).
- Build bridges between your point of view and the reader's (594).
- Build bridges for your reader by supporting general statements with specific examples.
- Build bridges for your reader and establish the direction of argument by using signposts that clearly lay out where your argument is going.
- Build bridges by locating the context of your writing.
- Never use large sweeping generalizations: since the beginning of time; women like cleaning, etc.
- Stay objective by focusing on the knowledge (avoid personal references and anecdotes).
- Define your terms.
- Avoid clichés, jargon, slang, and contractions.
- Revise your work for content and organization, not simply "sentence-level error" (612).
- Learn the style documentation conventions and use grammar in a way that is not simply utilitarian but emphasizes your meaning or content.

As Bartholomae points out,

> What our beginning students need to learn is to extend themselves, by successive approximations, into the commonplaces, set phrases, rituals and gestures, habits of mind, tricks of persuasion, obligatory conclusions and necessary connections that determine the "what might be said" and constitute knowledge within the various branches of the academic community. (600)

Clearly, as Bartholomae acknowledges, this immersion into an academic discourse will not happen overnight. However, with perseverance, you *can* learn these conventions and by being prepared to take a risk and "try on" or "appropriate" a "specialized [academic] discourse," you *can* learn to write well and appropriately for an academic context (590).

Table 9.1 ◆ Basic versus Inexperienced Writers

"Basic" or inexperienced writers tend to	Experienced writers always
• View the first draft as the final draft.	• Know that revision involves major changes to their work.
• Tend to revise just before the assignment is due to be handed in.	• Constantly revise throughout the planning, drafting, and final writing stages.
• Focus their attention on sentence-level editing errors: spelling, typos, and grammar mistakes.	• Revise at the sentence level and at the larger content and organizational levels, reorganizing, expanding, adding, or cutting concepts and ideas.
• Do not understand the discourse of the community of writers that they are writing to.	• Understand the discourse of the community of writers that they are writing to.

ACADEMIC CONVENTIONS

Exercise 9.1

- Review David Bartholomae's commonplace conventions above and highlight the points that you think might be most relevant to you as a writer. You might want to consider these points by analyzing an old essay you have written for either high school or university.
- When you have your list, put it on the wall by your computer so that you are reminded of what you need to do as you write and revise your essay.

Drafting an Essay

In academia, scholars have written a lot about the revision process; however, not as much has been written about the drafting process, mainly because the two cannot easily be separated: drafting necessarily involves revision and revision demands that you continually draft and redraft your work. As Peter Elbow stresses in *A Community of Writers,* drafting is about choosing, discarding, shaping, and rewriting your work (149). Ultimately, it is about discovering what you want to say and finding a way to say it well.

Many students, when they first come to university or college, are not familiar with the drafting process. Like many people, they often believe that good writers are simply gifted and don't need to draft or revise. As Donald Murray points out, however, "[g]ood writing is essentially rewriting," and professional writers, without exception, know this to be true (Dahl qtd in Murray 121). As Murray states, Anthony Burgess claimed he might well revise a page "twenty times" while Roald Dahl often revised one of his children's stories as much as "150 times" (121). Although this amount of revision might be shocking for first-year students who often don't revise at all, it is not unusual. Ernest Hemingway claimed that he wrote the last page of *Farewell to Arms* 39 times (*Paris Review*) before he was satisfied. Reflecting the ethos behind this tendency to rewrite, Michael Crichton wrote that "Books aren't written—they're rewritten. It is one of the hardest things to accept, especially after the seventh rewrite hasn't quite done it."

Table 9.2 ◆ Essay Types

Five-Paragraph Essay Formula	versus	Academic Essay Writing
Introductory paragraph with 3-point thesis		**Introductory paragraph:** Introduce topic, providing relevant context. Include thesis, which might use three points (explicit) or imply several points (implicit).
1st body paragraph: take first thesis point and write 3 points about it.		**Body paragraphs:** Use as many as you need to explicate the points contained in your thesis. Body paragraphs should logically develop your points so that the reader trusts and agrees with your logical conclusion.
2nd body paragraph: take second thesis point and write 3 points about it.		
3rd body paragraph: take third thesis point and write 3 points about it.		
Conclusion: expand on original 3 points.		**Conclusion:** Summarizes argument and expands on it to address the larger significance of your argument.

Unfortunately, the five-paragraph essay structure does not encourage significant revision because it provides students with a balanced fill-in-the-blank formula for essay writing. Its strength (the fact that it does provide an easy-to-follow formula) thus becomes a weakness in academia because it fosters superficial thinking, rather than the in-depth, reflective thinking required at the university level. This lack of depth becomes obvious in the formula, which requires that your thesis contain three main points that are each elaborated on in three subsequent paragraphs that each contain three points about the main paragraph point or topic. University writing resists formulas like this because they limit your thinking about the topic. When writing in a university context, it is the topic itself, and your argument about the topic, that determines which points you focus and elaborate on.

As you can see from the comparison above, the academic version is knowledge-driven instead of formula-driven. Keeping your focus on the knowledge—what argument and how you want to make it, about a text or topic—will prevent you sliding into "formula mode," which will provide only a superficial and often predictable commentary on your topic.

What follows is a process for asking and answering research questions that can and should be used instead of the five-paragraph formula. This process, a more focused version of the process outlined in chapter 8, is similarly designed to take you from the initial stages of reading a text and thinking about a topic or argument to actually beginning the first draft of your essay.

From Research Question to Essay Draft

1. Before you can even think about choosing a research question, you will need to choose a primary text: a text you are going to analyze to make an argument about it. Here are some examples of primary texts:

- The Conservative political party campaign, as laid out on the Conservatives' website.
- Carl Becker's and E. B. White's essays on democracy.
- Alice Munro's story "Voices."

2. Once you have your primary text, you can think about choosing a research question: a question about the text that intrigues you enough to want to examine or "research" it in detail. Your research question should be stated explicitly. Here are some sample research questions:
   - Considering the Conservative political campaign, how does Stephen Harper use pathos and ethical appeal to convince his audience that his values are superior to those of his opponent?
   - How does Alice Munro, in her story "Voices," challenge traditional female stereotypes?
   - What exactly does E.B. White mean by democracy? How is he using metaphor to define and use this term in the particular wartime context?

3. Next, you will need to develop this question by trying to answer it. This is where a lot of students go astray. They try to answer the question by drawing on their own knowledge or knowledge that lies outside of the primary text. Do not do this. Answer your research question by engaging with and analyzing your primary text. Reread your primary text, using a close, focused, and active reading to find and list all examples directly related to your question. This process helps you define and redefine the manageability and focus of your research question. For example, you might look at every place in the text where E.B. White uses a metaphor to define democracy and consider if any of these definitions have commonalities. This should enable you to come up with and focus an argument about the way White uses metaphor to make an argument about how democracy was enacted in 1943.

4. Rewrite the research question, taking into account your attempt to answer it, so that you have a working thesis statement or main argument. When writing your thesis statement, make sure that you explain *what* or *who* the argument is about, *how* you are going to argue it (the major lines of your argument), and *why* it is important to make this argument. Here are some sample thesis statements in relation to the above topics:

> While Stephen Harper claims to stand for trustworthy and dependable policies that emphasize criminal justice and traditional family values, this agenda, and his use of emotion or pathos in relation to it, is compromised by his determination to secure and solidify the religious right for his party's own political ends.

> In "Voices," Alice Munro uses the experiences of the young girl to challenge female stereotypes associated with the figure of the "harlot." Pointing out

that there is a continuum that extends from the experiences of the mother to the experiences of the harlot, Munro uses the young girl's experiences to argue that being female is far more complex than we would sometimes like to believe.

E.B. White uses a list of metaphors to argue that democracy is not a term that can be easily or clearly defined. Critiquing the way it is defined by bureaucratic practice, he points out that democracy should ideally be an inclusive term for all classes of people, who, even in war, must be allowed choice.

5. Organize the points and evidence that you generate through your analysis in a way that best develops and supports your argument/thesis statement. Instead of relying on the five-paragraph essay here, you will need to make an outline that is knowledge-, instead of formula-driven (see chapter 8 for more information on outlines).

> **Sample scratch outline:** Alice Munro's "Voices"
>
> - **Thesis statement:** In "Voices," Alice Munro uses the experiences of the young girl to challenge female stereotypes associated with the figure of the prostitute. Pointing out that there is a continuum that extends from the experiences of the mother to the young girl to the prostitute, Munro would seem to argue that being female is far more complex than we would sometimes like to believe.
>
> - Focus on the prostitute and how she is represented and stereotyped (define term)
>
> - Focus on the mother's fears about the daughter being in the company of the prostitute. How is the mother stereotyped?
>
> - Focus on the young girl's more complex experience of the prostitute. How is the girl stereotyped and how does meeting the prostitute call this stereotyping into question?
>
> - Show how the three different types of women can be more productively seen, not as stereotypes but as female human beings who exist on a continuum (define) between these different models.
>
> - Conclude by stressing how Munro shows that female experience is far more complicated than implied by our stereotypes.

6. Using all the information you have generated, sit down and write your essay. Everyone works differently here, and you will need to find out a system that allows you to write to the best of your ability. I prefer to write a good introduction before I go on and write the rest of the essay, but many people work from

an outline or write the entire essay in a freewriting or free-form basis and then structure it later. Remember that this is the first draft of your essay, not the finished product. Just knowing this can prevent writer's block, the fear that the essay has to be perfect the first time you write it. See chapters 6 and 8 for more information on organizing your paper.

ACADEMIC FOCUS

TIPS FOR HANDLING THE WRITING PROCESS

- Set deadlines and stick to them as much as possible: you will not be able to write a good essay the night before it is due. Make sure you allow time to write and revise several drafts well before the due date. If possible, allow yourself time to put the essay aside for at least a day before completing your final revision. This allows you to "re-vise" or "re-vision" your paper with new eyes.
- Be objective: imagine you are writing for an audience of peers who will be critical of your work.
- When writing, find a comfortable place where you will not be distracted. Write

regularly: instead of feeling compelled to write everything in one or two sittings, start in advance and try to write every day. This can make the process less stressful and more enjoyable.

- Save your work often: students often lose work because their hard drive crashes. Print off hard copies so you can show your professor drafts of your work if required.
- Get feedback: class peers or the university or college writing centre will give you useful feedback on your essay. Believe them when they say they don't understand what you are trying to say and rewrite for better quality.

EVALUATING YOUR ESSAY SKILLS

Exercise 9.2

1. Write a short one or two page essay summarizing and making an argument *about* Bartholomae's perspective in "Writing with Teachers" (see page 330 in the Reader).
2. Follow the process in the Academic Focus box above to write this essay.
3. Come up with a research question and answer it in a clearly articulated thesis statement before you go on to the next steps.
4. When you have finished writing your essay, read "Features of successful and unsuccessful essays" (see Academic Focus box below) and check off the points related to your own essay. Do you think your essay was successful or unsuccessful? What mark would you assign it if you were the instructor?

ACADEMIC FOCUS

FEATURES OF SUCCESSFUL AND UNSUCCESSFUL ESSAYS

Successful essays include the following elements:

- A clearly stated, provocative, and original insight into the object of your analysis. This does not mean that your insight has to be profound, but it does mean that you have to find a gap in the text you are reading—something that is not said or needs to be said—that will allow you to engage with the writer's argument. This might involve taking Bartholomae's response to Peter Elbow in Exercise 9.2 into consideration.
- A thesis or persuasive argument that guides and motivates the entire essay.
- Organized and flowing paragraphs that dig progressively deeper into the central insight under analysis.
- Appeals to sound logic, a critical close reading, and defensible judgment.
- Original and insightful commentary that defends your position while respecting its complexity.
- Careful selection of specific moments or elements of your object of analysis, so that you make an effective case for your central insight without deliberately ignoring or eliding aspects of the text under study.
- Contains a summary of specific contextual information that helps strengthen your argument.
- Clear, concise, accurate, and grammatically correct prose.
- Proper formatting and professional presentation; the essay should be free from typos, spelling mistakes, and all grammatical errors.

Features of unsuccessful essays include the following elements:

- Unclear, inaccurate, wordy, repetitive, and/or incorrect prose.
- Dogmatic claims that are not critically examined.
- A central insight that is not especially insightful.
- Arguments that may be logical but that do not seem intuitively plausible or ethically conscionable.
- Choppy, haphazard organization, no organization, or paragraphs that constitute a list of claims without a clear focus or sense of progression.
- An essay that is too general or superficial, lacking sophistication of thought or language.
- Grammar problems, spelling mistakes, and typographical errors.

Revision

Now that you have a feeling for what you need to do when you write your paper and what you need to focus on when you critically evaluate the potential success of your paper, it might be useful to focus more intently on the revising process.

As Nancy Sommers recognizes in her study of experienced and inexperienced writers, the most problematic area for inexperienced student writers is revision or rewriting. For these inexperienced writers, revision means revising for vocabulary errors, at the level of words and rules of grammar, rather than for meaning, at the level of concepts and ideas. As Sommers writes, "[at] best the students see their writing altogether passively through the eyes of former teachers or their surrogates, the textbooks, and are bound to the rules which they have been taught" ("Revision: Strategies for Student Writers" 379).

As Sommers notes though, experienced writers see revision as "part of the process of discovering meaning" (381). They work to develop, modify, and enhance *what* they are trying to say by revising *how* they say it. When they revise, experienced writers do make changes at the sentence level, as inexperienced writers do, but their focus is on the "whole of the composition" (382), revising content and form so that it conveys their argument more effectively. For inexperienced writers to do this, they must learn to see the "big picture," and give priority to finding the "truth" of what they are trying to convey by detaching and giving themselves critical feedback on their drafts.

What is important to remember here, however, is that while all experienced writers revise extensively, this should not be taken as a rule but as a necessary recognition of what needs to be done to turn poor or average writing into good or excellent writing. To do this, experienced writers take control of their work, and the meaning contained within their work. They all, without exception, develop a process that works for them. If you want to be successful, you *must* do this, remembering that no *one* process suits everyone. You might find that extensive detailed outlines work for you or you might prefer to free-write your first draft and outline the logic of your argument afterwards. Once you find the process that works for you, take the time to use it, knowing that revision does take time.

IDENTIFYING YOUR REVISION PROCESS

Exercise 9.3

Before we progress to strategies for revising your first draft, take a moment to think about your own revision process by reflecting and making notes on the following questions. You might want to use the passage you just wrote on Bartholomae (if you revised it) or you might pick another essay you have written so you can examine your revision process.

- What kind of reviser are you? Do you think you revise more like an inexperienced or an experienced writer?
- What revision practices do you do well? Which revision practices could you begin using that you are not using already?
- What do you think the relation is between revision and **editing** or **proofreading**? Are they essentially the same process or do they differ? If so, how? Are they both equally important at all stages of the writing process?
- Write down three ways you can be a better reviser on your next writing project. When you have read the revision section of this chapter, go back and look at your list. Is there anything you could add to this initial list? When you have revised this initial list, put it on the wall or desk close to your computer. Make sure that you leave yourself enough time for revising and use this list when you write your next academic essay.

Exercise 9.4

THE IMPORTANCE OF REVISION

1. Find Donald M. Murray's "The Maker's Eye: Revising Your Own Manuscripts" (see page 343 in the Reader) and see if you can identify why, according to Murray, revision is important and, also, what it might involve.
2. Write down his main points and then think about how they conform to or challenge your own revising process.
3. Compare them with the list you have just written about your own process. Could you add any of Murray's suggestions for revision to your own list?

As you have probably noted, Donald Murray outlines a detailed and logical process for revision.

- First, the writer must have enough information on which to base his or her argument, and this information must be formulated as a specific argument about the topic of interest.
- Second, the writer must be aware of audience and form or genre. The writer who is writing for a newspaper column would have quite a different audience and therefore quite a different form than someone who is writing for an academic audience and writing an academic essay.
- Third, writers must look at structure or organization and logical development at both the larger global level and the level of the sentence.
- Last, writers must focus at the level of the word, which involves a "line-by-line editing" and demands an awareness of voice (122).

Of course, as Murray argues, all of these aspects must be kept in balance.

Unfortunately, many inexperienced writers, almost without exception, focus on the sentence-level, "line-by-line" editing process. To do otherwise feels overwhelming. One way of handling that feeling is to focus your revising process by writing at least three draft revisions of your essay: the first draft revision should focus on *content*, the second on *organization*, and the third on *grammar and style*. This process can be repeated as many times as necessary. It also helps to establish strategies that you use throughout the process:

- checking to make sure that your essay conforms to the requirements of the assignment,
- creating objective distance,
- asking questions,
- using a revision rubric, and
- using peer review.

Revision Strategies

This section first goes over some revision strategies and then provides guidelines for revising for content, organization, and grammar or style. Keep in mind that there are no hard and fast rules for the revising process, but you do need to revise your work thoroughly. This means that you need to find a process that works for you.

Conform to the Assignment Requirements

This is a common student error. You will lose valuable marks if you don't conform to the assignment requirements for focus, length, and form. Check the focus of the paper: Is it appropriate to the assignment? Does the topic relate directly to the questions asked by your instructor? Is the topic too big or too narrow? When you have written your paper, is it within the required essay length? Does it conform to the requirements of form: double spacing? Title page? Page numbers? Print size and font?

Create Objective Distance

To revise your paper, you need to be able to be critical of your own work. The best way of doing this is to print off a hard copy (problems that seem invisible on the screen will become apparent when you can see the entire paper in front of you) so that you can read your paper objectively. To do this, you need to imagine that you are not the writer of the essay but an ideal reader. An ideal reader for a first-year student would be a thoughtful, educated person, who is *not* familiar with the texts and the contexts you are analyzing. Part of your job is thus to provide summary, description, definition, and specific examples or quotations where appropriate to orient your reader. This will provide him or her with a framework for clearly understanding the text(s) you are analyzing and for understanding and being persuaded of the credibility of your argument.

Distance helps, so once you have written your first draft, put your paper aside for a day or for at least a few hours. That will help you to see it anew when you do return to it. Reading your paper out loud to an imaginary or real audience also helps. Your argument should be easy to understand and follow. If you are reading to an actual audience, ask for feedback. If you are told that your reader cannot understand or follow your argument, believe what they say and consider revising the relevant sections. When reading your paper out loud to yourself, read slowly sentence by sentence and try to listen to the argument as if you are hearing it for the first time. Trying to imagine questions your reader might ask about your argument will help you notice any lack of clarity, the need for more context, knowledge gaps, or inconsistencies.

As Peter Elbow advises, when reading out loud,

> [l]ook for places where you stumble or get lost in the middle of a sentence. These are obvious awkwardnesses that need fixing. Look for places where you get distracted or even bored—where you cannot concentrate. These are places where you probably lost focus or concentration in your writing. Cut through the extra words or vagueness or digression; get back to the energy. Listen even for the tiniest jerk or stumble in your reading, the tiniest lessening of your energy or focus or concentration as you say the words . . . A sentence should be alive and interesting, and if it is not, you will need to rework it. (*Writing with Power* 135)

Ask Questions

Asking questions that your reader might ask and then attempting to answer them will help you revise your essay more accurately. Once again, having a method for asking these questions will help you focus your revising process. Questions that address content, organization, and grammatical or stylistic errors are listed later in this chapter, but you could also come up with some questions of your own, particularly those that reflect your own weaknesses. For example, you could post the following questions above your computer:

- Have I checked my essay for comma splices?
- Have I gone off topic?
- Can I add more detail or evidence to support my argument?
- Remember, you need to make the revision process work for you. Only you know what really works best for you as a writer.

Work from a Hard Copy

Working from a hard copy and, if necessary, using scissors to cut up your paragraphs and reorder them are good strategies for organizing your work. Working on a computer does not allow you to see the larger picture of how your essay develops from beginning to end. Seeing it in hard copy, laid out on a table, will help you notice the gaps and inconsistencies in your logical development. Do not be afraid to rework your material, taking out words, sentences, and even paragraphs to make your main argument more focused and developed. If you are attached to some aspect of your paper that you discover does not relate appropriately to your main argument, do not throw it away by deleting it, but save it in a separate file to use later in another paper. This strategy helps you to release your attachment to that particular piece of writing. In my experience it can come in handy: it saves you significant time in future essays if you file it clearly and carefully on your computer.

Make an Outline

Another very important organizational strategy is outlining, which helps you because it allows you to see the kernel of your argument in a vertical presentation of the main points. Chapter 8 familiarized you with a variety of essay outlines so that you could organize your essay persuasively. Outlining your essay *after* you have written it can help you to see how you conformed to or diverged from your original or preliminary outline while also helping you to see the logic of your argument now that the essay has been written. By outlining the main points and sub-points of your essay, you should be able to see how your essay works logically to prove and support your argument. See chapter 8 for more information on outlining.

Watch for Logical Fallacies

Pay attention to logical fallacies at sentence level (see chapter 7). Pay particular attention to the most common student errors: begging the question (circular argument), non sequitur logic (recognizing any gaps in your argument that need filling in), generalizations, and cause and effect logic, where your argument does not follow logically from one point to the next.

STUDENT CONCERNS ABOUT THE REVISION PROCESS: SOME TYPICAL QUESTIONS

I don't know where or when to begin revising.
Use one or all of the revision strategies listed here and begin revising early, as soon as you have a complete draft. Your thesis statement should guide the argument you are making throughout your entire paper. Sometimes you will need to reorganize your points to help the reader follow your argument and sometimes you will need to add or delete material. This takes time, so do not leave your revising until the night before the essay is due.

I'm so busy with all of my other classes, I just don't have time to revise.
Make time. If you don't, you will not be able to write a paper that will conform to the standards expected of university students. Remember Donald Murray's statement: "Good writing is essentially rewriting" (121).

I revise as I write, so isn't that enough?
Although it can't hurt to revise as you go, this type of revision tends to be superficial, at the level of the individual word or phrase. You need to revise for content and organization as well and you need distance to perform this type of in-depth revision. You will not get the objective distance you need if you revise as you are writing your first draft. Moreover, performing focused revisions helps you see the big picture. Knowing how your argument develops is far better than focusing on commas and spelling mistakes at an early stage when the material may end up being cut as you continue revising.

When I revise, my paper just gets worse instead of better, then I get a bit depressed because I realize I don't know what a good paper is and I feel like an awful writer.
Worrying about perfection will not help you to become a better reviser; you will only become increasingly anxious. Your paper will improve if you follow a clear process, figure out what your particular problem areas are, and focus on your argument as you revise. Getting help from your instructor or participating in peer revision groups will also help you understand what you need to do, and this alone will build your confidence.

I put a lot of effort into my writing and I don't like deleting whole sections of it.
If you want to write well, you will eventually discover that sometimes you have to delete whole sections of what you write. When you first write a sentence or paragraph it can sometimes feel brilliant; however, in the revising process, you will, more often than not, realize that your writing is not as good as you first thought. It is important to realize that getting rid of some of these pieces of writing might well help the overall argument or structure of your essay. However, one strategy to avoid feeling as though you are trashing your own work is to put it in a separate file for future use. This way, you can acknowledge that your work is good while also acknowledging that it is not suitable for this particular argument. It can come in handy later if you file it clearly and carefully on your computer.

Use a Revision Rubric

Using a revision rubric means asking specific questions about your work. Here is a sample rubric:

1. Is it specific enough? Have I avoided generalizations and inaccurate or inappropriate words? Have I provided enough detail and specific context? Is my thesis specific and focused enough?
2. Is my essay clear? Is the meaning clear and focused? Is it logical, developing one point and then another so that the meaning flows? Could the meaning be expressed more clearly? Where is clarification needed?
3. Does my essay advance the meaning embedded in the thesis? Every sentence and paragraph should relate to and develop the meaning embedded in the main argument. Does this development flow? Is the reader ultimately concerned with *what* is said rather than *how* it is said?
4. Is the voice consistent? Does it focus on the knowledge rather than on what I think or believe? Is the diction formal? Is the tone objective and neutral? Do I use first or third person and avoid second person?

Use Peer Review

Oftentimes, your instructor will encourage you to work in small groups to read and revise your papers. If not, you can form your own revision groups outside of the classroom. This valuable strategy will allow you to get insight into the effectiveness of your paper from a "real" audience. If more than one person in the group has a problem with the same point, that is a good indication that more work needs to be done in this area. Sometimes, you will be asked to defend or explain your choices. This can be instructive, promoting thoughtful reflection. A by-product of peer review, of course, is that everyone benefits from it: the writer under review learns how to better revise his or her essay and the reviewers learn how to become better readers.

Problems that arise from peer review are usually the result of students not having a clear idea of how to engage in one-to-one critiques and/or their tendency to believe that they are not qualified to offer critiques. Regarding the latter point, having a clear idea of what is expected in terms of writing an academic essay will help the reviewers feel more confident, as will a feedback sheet (see Appendix B) that they can fill out and talk about. Following some general guidelines will help you engage in peer review successfully:

- Focus on what the writer does well, as well as what needs to be improved.
- Listen respectfully and constructively to everyone's comments and try to build on them: remember that no comment is a bad comment.
- Offer observations and suggestions, but don't try to rewrite the writer's essay.
- Be kind—you are here to help each other—but make sure that you do offer some points for improvement.
- Remember that the writer has the ultimate control over his or her essay: he or she can choose to incorporate your comments or ignore them.

More information regarding peer review can be found in Appendix B where you can find a sample peer-review evaluation questionnaire.

The above strategies can be applied at any part of the revising process. However, they are more effective if they are used with an ordered process, such as the following three-stage revision process. As you read the following suggestions for revising at the levels of content, organization, and grammar or style, experiment with some of the strategies outlined above as well. Quite simply, the more you revise, the better your work will be. However, you need to find what strategies work for you, so take the time to experiment with them all.

Holistic Revision Strategies

Revising holistically means revising for content, context, structure, and grammar. You might have noticed that this strategy was covered extensively in chapter 5 as a process for active reading. However, using this threefold process works at both the reading level, to help you with comprehension, and at the revising level, to help you to systematically and analytically revise your work.

Content

As you read through your draft, imagine that you are a member of your intended academic audience, who will be critically judging your essay with a view to improving it.

As you probably realized when you were first outlining and drafting your essay, the greatest challenge of writing an essay is finding a thesis or a central argument that will motivate your analysis and persuade your reader of your argument's validity. Your essay must develop an insight into its topic, a discovery that sheds *new* light on the text and content itself (Is there a knowledge gap?) and/or on the use of rhetoric: language, organization, bias, the use of emotion, logic, etc., offering your readers an awareness of something challenging or subtle that they would not have known themselves. If you realize, when carefully examining your essay, that you are simply repeating the argument made by the author of the text you are examining (the number one most common student mistake) or that your argument is insubstantial (ask yourself, why should I care about reading this essay?), then you need to rework your thesis statement and, of course, the corresponding argument in your body paragraphs and conclusion.

Context

The next area you need to focus on is *context*, which is necessarily part of your content. If you do not provide sufficient context for your readers, they will not understand the significance or the logic of your argument. It is thus important to ask yourself if there is any information that the reader needs and doesn't have, but you also need to avoid adding context if it is not directly related to your argument. Any information that takes your reader "outside" of the scope of your essay and argument will be considered "off topic."

Strategies for context rely mostly on summary. These summaries might be longer paragraph-length context about the larger situation or short summary sentences or quotes that provide evidence and context for your larger points. Your introduction will need to include some context to introduce your topic, text, and argument, and you will have to provide context as you develop your argument.

Exercise 9.5

REVISING FOR CONTENT AND CONTEXT

What follows are two examples of student writing that highlight content and context: the first example contextualizes Walter Ong's concept of orality to support an argument about communication between indigenous and non-indigenous peoples; the second paragraph is an example of student writing that goes "off-topic," using contextual information that is not relevant to the argument.

- Identify where the contextual information is.
- Make an argument (one paragraph) about how it supports the content or main argument.
- Discuss with your classmates.

Example 1:

In order to more clearly present the complexities hindering meaningful dialogue between Indigenous Canadians and non-Indigenous Canadians, some background in the history of language is warranted. Walter Ong, a language expert, notes that of the thousands of languages spoken in the course of human history, only 106 of these have been committed to writing, and producing, literature. Most languages have remained oral (Ong 7). In fact, even now, hundreds of languages are in active use that have never been committed to written language because linguists have failed to discover an effective way to interpret satisfactorily oral language. According to Ong, the rules governing oral language may be extracted and stated explicitly in written words only with great difficulty and never completely. Thus, Ong asserts, "Writing can never dispense with orality" (8).

Example 2:

There is a tendency in our society to place a mantle of superiority and distinction on popular media icons. Advertisers see the relationship between society and media icons as a powerful marketing tool. An example of advertisers capitalizing on this relationship is the Nation Milk Processor Board's Superman "Got milk?" advertisement. In this advertisement, Superman is featured flying above the clouds in full Superman apparel. He has an unyielding expression on his face and in contrast to his firm gaze is the recognizable milk moustache on his upper lip, the trademark feature that has made this series of advertisements so distinctive. Next to the image of the superhero is the familiar query, "Got milk?" The text in the advertisement explains the nutritional value of the calcium that milk contains

See the Exercise Answer Key in Appendix A for a sample analysis of these paragraphs.

and how it can help people develop "bones of steel." This advertisement is successful because Brandon Routh, who plays Superman, endorses the idea that we all need to drink milk. This paper will examine why milk is good for children and adults alike.

Above all, remember, you *must* focus on the knowledge and meaning you are attempting to communicate. At this stage, however, do *not* focus on grammar errors, typos, or spelling mistakes. If a sentence is constructed so poorly that its meaning is unclear, you might want to quickly reword it for clarity, but the majority of your editing and proofreading work should be done after you have first addressed revision at the content and organizational levels. Also, do not focus on voice (how authoritative you sound) at this stage: when you focus on the knowledge and your argument about the knowledge, your voice will emerge and develop as you become immersed in your argument. Once again, you can correct any errors in diction, tone, etc., at the later editing or proofreading stages. Here are some questions you might ask about content and context.

QUESTIONS TO ASK ABOUT CONTENT AND CONTEXT

- Do I have a clear, well-developed argument that my reader would want to read?
- Does my thesis make a thoughtful and provocative point?
- Does my thesis generalize instead of taking a specific position?
- Is my thesis clear? Should it be modified now that the paper is written and, possibly, go off in a different direction or include additional material?
- Why should I care about writing this argument? Why should my reader read it?
- Is there anything missing from the argument?
- Do I "buy" the argument the essay is making?
- Would my reader trust that I know what I am talking about?
- Is there sufficient background context?
- Is there sufficient and appropriate evidence? Are all my claims supported?
- Is the evidence developed in respect to the thesis or are the points left hanging, as if the argument should be self-evident?
- Does my conclusion summarize my main argument, completing the paper by ending on a reflective thoughtful note, or is it repetitive and unfocused?

Organization

The next area to focus your revision is your essay's organization. There is a very well-known saying in academic circles that form = content. This means that the form or organization of the essay must, as Murray argues, be "the hidden spine" that supports and holds the essay's argument together (122). One way to think about the relationship between content and form (structure/organization) is to think of the analogy of a commercial train that carries goods to a certain predefined destination. The goods on the train are the content that must be loaded and organized on the train so that the train is balanced and stabilized. This will maximize its pulling power so it can arrive at its destination.

Figure 9.2 shows another related analogy that might help you think about essay structure: would you want to buy this house after you have viewed it?

I cannot stress enough that you must not attempt to organize your essay using the five-paragraph structure. You can only create an in-depth, fully analyzed argument if you focus instead on meaning or the knowledge you are concerned with and ask questions about content: "What else needs to be said here? What have I left out?" Make sure that the content is closely related to your main point in that section. That will help your exploration of your argument to be logical and organized. Trust your ability to recognize the logical relationship between the ideas/points as they are presented. Ask yourself if the points in the body of your essay develop the main ideas expressed in the introductory paragraph and thesis of your essay. Do these points reflect why it is important for your reader to read this argument about your primary text? Or do your points simply summarize the primary text? Or work as a loosely connected list that makes no significant point?

Make sure that you outline your introduction, your thesis statement, and your entire essay at the paragraph level, but also make sure that you check the logic of your argument at the sentence level. Ask if the sentences in each paragraph flow from one point

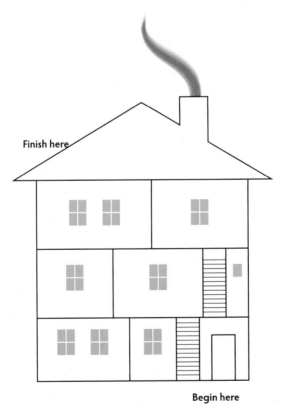

Finish here

You are now finished your tour of the house: What are your ultimate impressions? Like the smoke in the chimney, does the house leave you with something to think about?

The house has 3 floors: Each floor should make a statement that builds on the original impression when you first walked in the door.

Doorway into the house: Make a statement.

You are now entering the house: first impressions are important.

Begin here

Figure 9.2 ◆ Essay Structure: House Analogy
The bricks in the house are like the sentences in your essay. If they are not firmly interconnected, the house will not be strong and it will fall down.

to the next, logically developing the argument without making any leaps in another direction and without leaving gaps in your argument that cannot be accounted for. Return to this process as you revise your second and your third draft (and more if need be). You should return many times to specific sentences and paragraphs as you outline your argument and refine its logic.

As mentioned above, the writing process is recursive: the writer constantly moves back and forth between steps. While you're writing, you may come up with new ideas and directions, even some that require new research. You may also go back over a sentence and revise the wording choice and/or your meaning or syntax (the way the words create meaning); however, you should not get too caught up in grammar and mechanics during this stage. Working from a hard copy, outlining, and revising to correct any logical fallacies you have are all good strategies here.

QUESTIONS TO ASK ABOUT ORGANIZATION

- Does the introductory paragraph logically outline the argument made in the essay, either deductively, using a specific thesis, or inductively, using a hypothesis?
- Do the paragraphs logically develop the argument presented in the thesis, one point at a time (as a general rule, one point = one paragraph)?
- Are there any logical fallacies, such as begging the question or circular argument, non sequitur, cause-effect, hasty generalization, scare tactics, red herring, false authority, dogmatism, etc. (see chapter 7)?
- Sentence by sentence, does each paragraph logically develop the argument contained within each paragraph?
- Is my argument balanced? Do I spend too much time on one point and neglect to develop another point?
- Do the paragraph transitions move the argument smoothly and logically from one point to the next?
- Does the conclusion build from the preceding argument, summarizing the argument while pointing us forward to a larger consideration of the issues at hand?
- When I outline the written draft of the essay, does it accurately reflect the main points in my thesis? Would it work better if I moved some paragraphs or sentences around?

Revising for Grammar and Style

Revising for grammar errors and revising for style involve two completely different processes. The process you will probably be most familiar with is editing or revising for grammar errors, typos, and spelling mistakes. Given that computers have spellcheck, which makes correcting spelling mistakes easy, there is no reason for you to hand in a paper with spelling errors. Students who do hand in papers with a number of spelling mistakes or basic typos reveal not only their lack of professionalism but also the fact that they don't really care about the assignment or what they are writing.

Grammar mistakes, however, are a little more difficult for students to identify and assess. The grammar check is not always accurate, so you can't rely on that to fix your errors. Many students find the issue of grammar—errors of usage, punctuation, diction, etc.—immensely stressful. As one student stated, "How can I possibly remember all these rules and check my essay for everything? I'm overwhelmed."

You will need to identify the errors you make repeatedly and edit specifically for them. You will then begin to develop your critical eye for these mistakes. You might, for example, note that you consistently make comma splice and subject–verb agreement errors. When you know what these errors are and how to fix them, you can go through your paper with these errors in mind, look for instances where they appear, and correct them.

It is important, however, to perform this revision *after* you have taken care of your content and organization. Otherwise, you will become overwhelmed by the need to fix the small details and lose focus on the bigger overall meaning and structure of your argument. Also, correcting these editing mistakes at an early stage of the process is not time-effective: if you decide to throw out a complete paragraph or two, you will have wasted time editing a product you are not going to use in the final copy of your paper.

A consideration of style is important here. Style refers to *how* you write rather than *what* you write. Ideally, just as organization should support content, your writing style should support your content. Style has everything to do with careful word choice, sentence structure, and tone: the attitude of the writer toward his or her subject and audience. Academic writing demands a formal, objective, and logical tone. Although sentence variety is important in academic writing, there will be a tendency, depending on your discipline, to write sentences that are longer, with multiple modifying clauses, or to write sentences that are short and simple in construction. The sciences tend to use shorter, more factual, simple sentences, whereas the humanities tend to use longer, more complex sentences that reflect the complexity of the ideas presented.

Related to tone is voice, which is more closely related to what attitude the reader or listener perceives in the writer. Voice, or feeling compelled to develop a strong, confident voice, often worries students who feel they have to sound authoritative, intelligent, and confident. The key here is not to try to sound impressive; try, rather, to be clear and honest. You want your reader to trust you and you can only do this if you take the time and care enough about your subject to make sure your information is accurate, thoroughly researched (if necessary), contextualized, and detailed. You will need to be clear, concise, and specific, using accurate verbs and nouns, while avoiding contentious language or slang, clichés, and stereotypical phrases. You will also need to develop a consistent point of view (first or third person, but never second person) and use active voice (unless instructed otherwise).

What follows are guidelines for developing a strong sense of style. Please note that this guideline addresses issues at both the level of tone and voice. If you follow these guidelines, and focus on the knowledge, refraining from trying to sound important or authoritative, you should not have an issue with adopting an academic style.

BE CLEAR

Keep your focus on your need to communicate your knowledge and your argument to your reader. That will prevent you from losing focus and direction and confusing your reader (and possibly yourself). Don't try to sound impressive or authoritative, inflating your ideas in an attempt to sound important, but do make every sentence and every word as direct and simple as possible. Remember that academic writing is not conflated, convoluted, or creative writing, as many students believe. It is clear, simple writing that accurately and concisely expresses your point in as few words as possible.

BE CONCISE

One way of keeping your ideas clear and simple is, as William Zinsser argues in his essay "Simplicity," to cut out the clutter. In other words, cut out all repetition, "unnecessary words, circular constructions, pompous frills and meaningless jargon" (45). Play around with individual sentences and rephrase them to state your point more directly in fewer words.

BE DETAILED BUT SPECIFIC

Clear, detailed writing that does not leave any gaps for the reader to fill in and does not cloud the meaning with vague unclear words is good writing. Imagine a reader who does not know the situation or context surrounding your argument. Then edit your work to make sure that your meaning is specific and clear and that there is nothing you have left out. This doesn't mean that you have to add "filler," only that none of your points are obscure and that you use the best, most accurate words, including nouns and verbs, to convey your meaning.

AVOID GENERALIZING EXPRESSIONS

Writing is not easy; making your meaning clear and accurate demands vigilance. As Zinsser argues, you need to "clear [your] heads of clutter," and part of this clutter involves reworking or rethinking all the easy readily accessible stereotypes, generalizations, and clichéd expressions that come easily to us when we write (47). You will lose your reader's interest if your writing is full of sloppy, and, dare I say, lazy, well-used platitudes. When you find yourself using these types of sentences or phrases, ask yourself, "What am I trying to say here?" and rewrite them by rephrasing, using your own words (49). Let me assure you that it is well worth the effort.

TRUST

Trust that when you focus on developing a shared sense of knowledge in your writing, attempting to communicate and relate to your reader in a clear, knowledgeable, honest, and trustworthy way, you will also automatically communicate a voice and a sense of who you are related to your topic.

Last, in the editing and proofreading stage, you will need to fix all your formatting and documentation errors. Make sure that you have cited your sources accurately and that your font type and size, your page margins, title page, etc., conform to the assignment guidelines and documentation style manual you have been asked to use (MLA, APA, CSE, or CMS).

QUESTIONS TO ASK ABOUT REVISING FOR GRAMMAR AND STYLE

• Have I checked my paper for the grammar errors I repeatedly make?

- Have I checked my paper for spelling, typo, and diction (vocabulary) errors?
- Have I revised my paper for citation and formatting errors?
- Have I incorporated my quotes effectively?
- Does my writing make sense, establishing and developing a clear logical argument, sentence by sentence?
- Is my writing concise and yet detailed enough to include all necessary information?
- Have I eliminated all wordy, unclear, or repetitive constructions?
- Have I eliminated all generalizations, stereotypical representations, or clichés?
- Are the tone and formality of the language appropriate for my audience?
- Have I used active voice and a consistent academic point of view?

Exercise 9.6

REVISION

- Read the following student paragraph and see if you can notice where the student's writing style becomes inconsistent and unclear.
- See if you can rewrite the excerpt clearly and concisely, maybe cutting or combining sentences, words, vague references, or clichéd expressions.
- Compare the length of your revision with the original (it should be considerably shorter) and the voice in the original excerpt with your own emerging voice. Can you see that your voice comes through even though you have been focusing on the knowledge and clear communication rather than trying to affect a voice?

The way King structures his speech makes his speech more effective. The content of the speech is in a chronological order. King starts with the historic aspects, such as the Emancipation Proclamation. The Emancipation Proclamation was supposed to have taken them out of their captivity; however it did little to change anything. In the middle of the speech, King focuses on what needs to be done now in the present. Towards the end of the speech, there is a focus on what the future could hold for Americans. You can see that the chronological sequence is effective because at the end of the speech is where he will have the most impact on his audience.

Exercise 9.7

EDITING

- Read William Zinsser's "Simplicity" (see page 347 in the Reader) and compare a piece of your own editing with the editing Zinsser advocates. Do you think you need to do more editing?
- Using an example of your own writing, write a paragraph explaining how, in your work, "Clear thinking becomes clear writing; one can't exist without the other" (Zinsser 46) or, alternatively, write a paragraph relating Zinsser's statement that

"If the reader is lost, it's usually because the writer hasn't been careful enough" to your own work (46). Make sure that you follow the rules for clear, concise writing and paragraph structure and that your argument is not based on generalizations but on clear concise evidence taken either from Zinsser's essay or from your own writing.

- When you have written your paragraph, share it with your classmates and then trade your paragraphs and edit one paragraph for someone else. Hand it back and discuss the changes you have made, as well as the different sense of your emerging individual voices.

REVISING AN INTRODUCTORY PARAGRAPH

Exercise 9.8

1. Read the following student introduction, which is based on George Orwell's "Politics and the English Language." Are there ways that this introductory paragraph, focused on a critique of Orwell's essay, might be made clearer, more concise, and focused? Is the argument manageable? Why or why not?
2. Rewrite the paragraph so that it is clear and concise and has a manageable thesis statement or main argument.

In his article "Politics and the English Language." Orwell says the cause of the poor English state is due to politicians' use of tools, such as dying metaphors or pretentious dictions, that change the tone of his or her sentences (359). English writers' minds are corrupted by the political and economic styles of using the English language and so he or she cannot write effectively. Orwell makes the point that "language can also corrupt thought," (Orwell 361). Orwell's argument that politicians and the economy were the cause of the deterioration of the English language is not strong throughout his essay as he has not considered the impact that society has on politicians. This essay will discuss Orwell's lack of consideration to the people and their role in deteriorating and repairing English.

See my comments in the Exercise Answer Key in Appendix A.

ANALYZING AN INTRODUCTORY PARAGRAPH REVISION

Exercise 9.9

1. Now consider the student's revised introductory paragraph (revisions are italicized). Is it better? How and why? How does this revision compare with the revision you wrote? Did you have the confidence to make such extensive changes? Is your thesis, although most likely not the same, clear and manageable?
2. Write a short paragraph explaining how the revisions were made and why. Make sure you have an argument. Compare your paragraphs with your classmates' and discuss the choices for revision with them as well.

Continued

In his article "Politics and The English Language" George Orwell *argues that politicians are* the cause of the poor state *of the English Language* (359). *Because people from the general public imitate political and economic language, using* dying metaphors or pretentious diction, *their ability to write effectively and clearly is compromised, as is their ability to think clearly.* As Orwell states, "language can also corrupt thought" (361). This essay will discuss *how the structure of Orwell's essay forces the reader to think carefully and clearly. In this way,* Orwell *participates in the project, as he saw it in 1937 British culture, to repair a deteriorating English language.*

Exercise 9.10

REVISING

- Below are two before and after revisions of a student's introductory paragraph. They are taken from an argument about Sheridan's paper "The Silence before Drowning in Alphabet Soup" (see page 432 in the Reader). The revisions here are more subtle: can you spot some of the original problems in the "before" draft? How could you revise them? Is the thesis focused and manageable?
- Now read the revised draft and see if you could revise it yet again to make it clearer and more focused. Is there more detail now? Is the thesis statement or argument focused, clear, and manageable? Does the introductory paragraph lay out the organization of the entire essay?

BEFORE/EARLY DRAFT:

In "The Silence before Drowning In Alphabet Soup" Sheridan (1991) reviews the differences between orality and literacy, focusing on each culture's knowledge about and representation of silence, the self, the infinite, and subjective reality. In doing so, Sheridan condemns literacy for overshadowing orality, not only in our universal culture, but also in our education system. Although Sheridan makes a valid point, there are a few unintentional functions that ultimately weaken his argument. A particular damaging function is Sheridan's lack of evidence through primary research to support his claims; this leaves readers questionable of the author's credibility. Sheridan's failure to take into consideration the irony of his upbringing in a literate culture (with minimal direct experience of the oral culture) is another function that diminishes his ethos. Furthermore, in light of the reader's knowledge of Sheridan's questionable trustworthiness, one cannot help but question how such doubtful credibility could translate to Sheridan's over-generalizations of each culture.

Revised draft:

In "The Silence before Drowning in Alphabet Soup" Sheridan (1991) reviews the differences between oral and literate cultures, focusing on each culture's knowledge about and representation of silence. In making this comparison, Sheridan critiques literacy and the literate culture for its tendency to privilege mediated experience while negating orality, oral culture and its privileging of silence as a dominant way of knowing and understanding an individual's relationship to the earth and the divine. Although Sheridan makes a valid point when he argues that a literate culture should find balance by incorporating into its education system some oral techniques, such as silence, his lack of appropriate evidence, his failure to take into consideration his upbringing in a literate culture (with minimal direct experience of the oral culture), and his tendency to over-generalize ultimately weaken his argument and compromise his ethos.

You should be able to see that the revised paragraph in Exercise 9.10 is much stronger. The thesis is better organized, clearly outlining the step-by-step process by which the writer will make his or her argument. Do not be afraid, as in the first paragraph exercise, to radically revise your work, cutting out complete chunks of your writing if need be. It is only when you are prepared to cut and rework your essay repeatedly that you will be able to find what you want to say, and as Donald Murray notes, there is a certain satisfaction to be gained in being able to say what you want to say and saying it clearly and succinctly.

The following table shows a chart of common editing symbols that might be used by your instructor to comment on your work. There is also an assignment submission checklist, which will help you quickly review the steps for revising your essay before you hand it in to your instructor.

Table 9.3 ◆ Common Editing Symbols

Awk.	Awkward expression or construction	//	Parallel structure
W/C	Word choice	~	Transpose elements
D	Diction	/	Delete
Sp	Spelling error	⌣	Close up this space
Wordy	Wordy construction	Prep.	Preposition error
CS	Comma splice	Org.	Organization problems
Frag.	Sentence fragment	?	Clarify meaning
MC	Mixed construction	← → s.trans.	Sentence transition unclear
DM	Dangling modifier	p.trans. |	Paragraph transition unclear
MM	Misplaced modifier	G	Generalization
R-on	Run-on sentence	L	Logic unclear
TS	Tense shift	Rep.	Repetitive—revise
S-V	Subject–verb agreement	Cit.	Citation problem
P-A	Pronoun–antecedent agreement	Syntax	Word choice/meaning unclear
∧	Insert something	POV	Point of view unclear
₱	New paragraph		

ASSIGNMENT SUBMISSION CHECKLIST

Before submitting any assignment, make sure that you check the following checklist:

Structure and content:
- Make sure you have a strong *developed* thesis statement.
- Outline your argument to check for logical development.
- Check paragraph transitions.
- Check introductory and concluding paragraphs.

Editing:
- Check for grammar errors.
- Use spellcheck and then check for typos.
- Eliminate all contractions, abbreviations, and wordy constructions.

- Eliminate all vague unclear words or phrases and slang and eliminate or define jargon.
- Check for repetition of words and ideas.

Citation and formatting:
- Check formatting: double space, 1" margins, page #s, title page, etc., according to either MLA or APA formatting guidelines.
- Check that books, articles, films, etc., are cited correctly.
- Check that quotations are correctly cited, using quotation marks and parenthetical citations and correct punctuation.
- Reference sources in reference list (APA) or works cited (MLA) and make sure that each work is cited correctly.
- Staple or use a paper clip to secure pages.

Exercise 9.11

REVISION PROCESS

The following exercise asks you to write a paragraph or two outlining how your revision skills have progressed and what you still need to work on. This kind of self-evaluation is all part of the revising process. It will help you to develop a self-reflective critical and objective eye. Without that your writing is doomed to not improve. As Donald Murray stresses, "A piece of writing is never finished. It is delivered to a deadline, torn out of the typewriter on demand, sent off with a sense of accomplishment and shame and pride and frustration" (124). That is the nature of writing and to do well in academia, you must get used to the idea that rewriting is part of the process.

- Write two clear and concise double-spaced and typed pages in essay form, reviewing your revision methods and outlining a plan of action for future essays. Look at your previous essays and short assignments to see areas of growth, as well as areas that presented difficulties for you as a critical reader, thinker, writer, and reviser. Assess and state succinctly what was most difficult for you in the revising process, and show how you overcame or, conversely, failed to overcome, this problem.

- What has been most useful to you in this chapter and how you will revise your future essays? How will it help you in your future professional and academic work life? How will it help you in your personal life? Make sure you include evidence from this chapter and/or from your own essay revisions to support your statements.

- Outline what you still need to work on in your revising process and how you will go about doing this work. You might want to first focus on what you are doing well and then outline three areas where your revision practice still needs work. Compare notes with your classmates and then take turns using one of the strategies listed in this chapter to revise and edit each other's paragraphs.

CHAPTER SUMMARY

This chapter has focused on teaching you how to draft an essay and then revise it and stressed that all writing is recursive (as opposed to linear). You will need to draft, revise, and redraft your paper, and sections of your paper, multiple times until you are satisfied that it says what you want to say and successfully explores an argument about a topic. The features of successful versus unsuccessful essays have been outlined as well as a process for revising and useful strategies, such as asking questions, creating objective distance, identifying logical fallacies and errors that you make repeatedly, and using peer review. The chapter has stressed that it is important that you find your own process, as not all strategies and processes work for everyone. It is essential, though, that whatever process or strategies you follow, you do multiple revisions at the levels of content, organization, and grammar/style.

I cannot deny that revision is hard work. However, I must concur with Donald Murray when he points out that this process of revision, "of understanding, of making meaning clear" is ultimately where the real "fun" in writing is (123). There is a satisfying recognition and knowledge to be had when you know, without a doubt, that you have articulated what you have to say and that you have said or written it well to a community that will, no doubt, appreciate your work.

QUESTIONS FOR CONSIDERATION

1. What do I still need to know about drafting my essay? Is the process clear?
2. What do I still need to know about the process of revision? What is still unclear?
3. What process or strategies am I already using and are they as effective as they might be?
4. Are there any new strategies that I think will work for me? If so, which ones?
5. Did I have any difficulties with the exercises on paragraph revision? What were they? For example, am I comfortable cutting large sections of material from my paper? What strategies can I use to overcome my reluctance to do this?
6. How can I identify problems in my own writing and then outline some preliminary strategies that work for me?

10

Research Writing

LEARNING OBJECTIVES

In this chapter, you will learn:

◆ What research writing is and why it is essential to academia.

◆ The difference between informative (expository) research essays and argumentative research papers.

◆ Steps for writing a research essay, including how to find a topic, a research question, and a working thesis statement.

◆ Strategies for conducting and evaluating library research.

◆ Strategies for managing research writing: writing a research proposal, a critical response, and an annotated bibliography.

◆ The difference between primary and secondary sources.

◆ The importance of documentation and correctly citing your work.

◆ What plagiarism is and how to avoid it.

First-year students often fear that the research essay is beyond their abilities, believing it to be a genre that only experienced scholars can use properly. Students are concerned that they do not have the skills or the knowledge to engage competently in a critique of the existing knowledge on a topic, especially when they are reading essays written by professors who are experts in their field. They also fear that their writing skills are far below the level of the papers they are reading. What is important to remember here though is that experienced scholars did not begin their careers as accomplished academic writers. They began by learning how to write a critical paper and then an argumentative research

ACADEMIC FOCUS

ACADEMIC RESEARCH: SECONDARY BENEFITS

Besides learning how to write effectively for academia, there are secondary benefits to learning research writing skills. You will also learn how to

- become more aware and more critical of events, speeches, television shows, and such like in your everyday life;
- locate and evaluate information in the library and on the Internet;

- participate objectively, as opposed to personally, in a conversation about a topic;
- synthesize and organize a plethora of ideas and perspectives;
- document your sources accurately;
- plan and manage your time so that you are able to meet deadlines.

paper. It took them, as it will take you, many years to become accomplished writers who are comfortable engaging with the knowledge specific to their fields.

Rest assured, then, that your professors will not expect you to write as they do; they will, however, expect you to try on "a variety of voices and interpretive schemes" (Bartholomae 273), a variety of ways of speaking, writing, and reasoning that are consistent with a particular academic discipline. You will be expected to learn how to use language, analytical reasoning, and research to construct effective arguments that persuade academic audiences that your claims are valid.

What Is a Research Essay?

Most first-year students confuse the expository research essay with the argumentative research essay. The expository research essay is the research genre you are probably most familiar with as most of your high school research essays will have been expository essays. The **expository research essay** asks you to find, summarize, and make a statement about the existing research on a topic. Your claims will mostly be statements of fact, which you will organize in an attempt to provide a reliable and focused overview of the subject. For example, in high school you might be asked to write a short essay about the benefits of eating well. All of the research will be easily obtainable and probably point to the same conclusions. You might even be asked to write an expository research essay in a first-year university course if, for example, your history professor wants you to summarize several debates related to the American Civil War, and take a position on them (see chapter 2 for more on expository writing).

However, the majority of your essay writing at the university level will be of the argumentative kind, as in an **argumentative research essay**, which requires that you not

ARGUMENTATIVE RESEARCH ESSAYS

Report findings: What has already been said about the topic?

and

Add to the existing knowledge on a topic: What needs to be said?

and/or

Call the existing knowledge into question: How and why do
I disagree with what has been said?

only report your findings but analyze them, adding to the existing state of knowledge, providing original insight into a topic or an issue by calling into question that knowledge, and exposing "what hasn't been said, what needs to be said, or even what has been mistakenly said" (Giltrow 197).

Once you realize that you can comment on the existing knowledge by finding a small debatable point or gap in the writer's argument or by adding a related consideration to the existing argument that will strengthen or call the argument into question, you will begin to feel as though you are part of the academic community, sharing ideas and enjoying your newfound ability to participate in academic debate.

While it is true that research writing does involve a more intense engagement with your topic, it really is just an extension of other forms of writing we have already considered: summary and critical persuasive writing. As we have seen, the skills specific to summary writing help you to understand the topic or text clearly whereas the skills specific to persuasive critical writing involve learning how to read and respond analytically and persuasively to a text. The research essay simply takes this process one step further.

Your argument, then, is prefaced not only on your ability to make an argument *about* a text but also on your ability to contextualize your argument in relation to other relevant reliable information from experts in the field. You are thus demonstrating your ability to make a credible argument, locating, selecting, organizing, and synthesizing your sources to this end. In turn, this process, and the resulting end product, will demonstrate your ability to contribute to a body of established research and, ultimately, your own emerging academic expertise.

Figure 10.1 illustrates how scholarly knowledge is always building on what has come before it. This process "invents the university," as David Bartholomae argues, and the larger community, by producing new knowledge that other scholars/economists/scientists/activists, etc., can relate to and build on. Although these stages are not as static as this diagram illustrates, because the process is recursive, it provides a good approximation

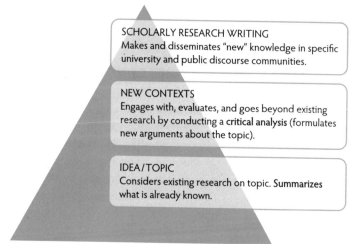

SCHOLARLY RESEARCH WRITING
Makes and disseminates "new" knowledge in specific university and public discourse communities.

NEW CONTEXTS
Engages with, evaluates, and goes beyond existing research by conducting a **critical analysis** (formulates new arguments about the topic).

IDEA/TOPIC
Considers existing research on topic. Summarizes what is already known.

Figure 10.1 ◆ Research Writing: Contexts and Process

of how academic research requires that we position ourselves in relation to other schol-ars and the knowledge itself.

Correcting Some Common Misperceptions

One common misconception about research writing, which has been covered already, is the tendency to confuse expository and argumentative research essays. You should not confuse them, though, if you remember that when writing an expository essay, you are merely summarizing the existing arguments (and maybe deciding which one is bet-ter), but when writing an argumentative essay, you are making a new point or argument about the existing research. If you are unclear about what type of research essay you have been asked to write, the best thing to do is to ask your instructor.

A research essay that is related to the expository essay is the **research report**. This type of research is usually conducted in courses related to the sciences, social sciences, engineering, and business and is an expository-style examination of or a report on a primary source. The audience for your essay might be your professor or your peers, but you might also direct it to a specific audience, such as a group of engineers or the board members of a specific company. In that case, the tone and language of the report would be geared to the specific audience that the report is aimed at.

For example, a report aimed at engineers might contain a considerable amount of jargon, but a report aimed at the board members of a local business might be far more accessible and easy to understand. The analysis might involve direct observation or field experimentation or constitute a close examination of secondary sources. Your research might be quantitative or qualitative (see chapter 3).

The report essay will most likely follow the quantitative inductive structure, but, like all research essays, it must clearly identify the secondary sources and contextualize them

ACADEMIC FOCUS

QUALITATIVE VERSUS QUANTITATIVE RESEARCH

Qualitative research aims to understand prevalent trends of thought, reasoning processes, and motivations; provide insight into the issue; and generate ideas and reflective consideration.

Quantitative research quantifies or measures data from a relatively large sample population, then generalizes the results and recommends a final course of action. It uses standardized techniques, such as questionnaires or interviews, and follows the rules and regulations for measuring statistical data.

in an organized and effective manner. Below is an example of an inductive research report outline. Your secondary research will likely appear in your introduction, methodology, discussion, and conclusion.

Research report outline:

1. **Title page:** first page of report; it contains the title, the name of writer, company (if applicable), name of who the report is intended for or the name of the course you are writing the report for.
2. **Abstract (summary) of paper:** an abridged version of the report, written, as clearly as possible, for a general audience; sometimes called an **executive summary**.
3. **Table of contents:** outline of report; shows how you are organizing the report according to title headings and subheadings and presents the related page numbers, and also includes a list of appendices.
4. **Introduction:** purpose and scope of paper, including hypothesis; any necessary background information or context and an overview of the existing research on the topic. Your hypothesis might appear here, but, if it does, it is usually reiterated or expanded on at the end of the methodology section that follows. Research might be introduced here, as in Catherine Schryer's paper, to show how your paper will build on existing research in your area.
5. **Methodology:** methods used to conduct research: comparison, questionnaires, etc., and purpose or scope of research. Engagement with other scholars will usually appear here as you establish your focus. Take a look at Schryer's paper: in her methodology section, she uses the theories of scholars who have engaged in genre theory and applies it to her own analysis. Your hypothesis, or a version of it, might appear here.
6. **Discussion:** main body of report: findings, data, and evidence are outlined,

categorized, and analyzed. Patterns are revealed and described in relation to your hypothesis. Research material is provided here to support your points.

7. **Conclusion:** summary of findings and conclusion arrived at from the discussion. Once again, research is provided as needed; you might find, however, that your work resonates with and builds on the work of one particular scholar. You might reiterate research mentioned earlier in the methodology section.

8. **Recommendations:** suggest a certain course of action.

9. **Appendices:** contain supporting data that are peripheral to the main argument. Including this material in the main body of the report would distract from the main data or argument. These data might include tables, charts, photographs, specifications, etc.

ACADEMIC FOCUS

RESEARCH ESSAY GENRES

EXPOSITORY ESSAY:

- Process: research information related to the topic; find a position or emphasis that effectively and accurately summarizes this information for you, and organize the information to reflect that position.

- Audience: scholarly, but geared to learning the forms of knowledge and the writing requirements of a specific academic discipline. Usually involves an assignment that requires you to demonstrate your thorough understanding of a particular event in history, process, theory, etc. Verbs used to describe this type of research include *describe, summarize, explain, compare, contrast, illustrate.*

REPORT ESSAY:

- Process: research information related to the topic. Find a position or emphasis that effectively and accurately summarizes this information for you and organize the information to reflect that position.

- Audience: this form of essay writing is often

designed to give you practice in writing to a specific professional audience, such as engineers, teachers, business executives, who have specific writing and stylistic requirements outside of academia. Usually involves an assignment that requires you to demonstrate your thorough understanding of a situation, process, theoretical problem, or issue. Verbs used to describe this type of research include *describe, summarize, explain, compare, contrast, illustrate.*

ARGUMENTATIVE ESSAY:

- Process: research information related to the topic, and analyze the information according to your stand on the topic. Explore the multiple complexities of the topic to convince your audience that your position is valid and reliable. Organize your information to effectively reflect your position.

- Audience: scholarly and discipline-specific. Verbs used to describe this type of research include *examine, evaluate, analyze, argue, persuade.*

For examples of the research report style, please see Research Proposal 3 later in this chapter (see page 257). This chapter, however, is more concerned with outlining the deductive, qualitative argumentative research essay because

(a) it is the format that you will use most often in your undergraduate studies; and

(b) it is a format that will provide you with a level of expertise that will allow you to transfer your essay writing skills to other formats, such as the expository essay or the research report.

This analysis of research genres leads to another common misconception, the belief that research is simply about providing sources to support your argument. This interpretation is too simplistic. If you follow this model, your argument will become one-sided, if not biased and ineffective. As in an essay using persuasive analysis, it is not enough to take a stand on an issue, identifying an issue or a situation, finding a knowledge gap, and then finding support for this stand

Your argument needs to be more nuanced than this. It needs to account as much as possible for the full spectrum of opinions and beliefs related to the topic. You must extend and refine your analysis to show the constraints, limits, and possibilities of a specific situation or analysis by adding layers of depth in the form of evidence, debate (counter-arguments, which might involve acknowledging that a different viewpoint might have some validity), and a reflective, considered tone.

When writing a research essay, you begin with a contextualized and thoughtful observation, asking questions and examining alternatives and possibilities. You then consider your argument and how it relates to the arguments other scholars are making on the same or a similarly related topic. This is how you will demonstrate your knowledge and your position as it relates to, challenges, and expands on the opinions and values of other scholars. Understand that your perceptions might be flawed and limited, and that you will be willing to revise them, while still taking and maintaining a strong scholarly position, when new perspectives are brought to your attention. Tyrell DaSilva does an excellent job of this in his essay at the end of this chapter.

As in the persuasive essay, you will have made an argument about some point in your primary text; in the research essay, though, to support your argument you will provide evidence not only from your primary text but also from your secondary sources or research material.

Primary versus Secondary Sources

One of the biggest problems students have is in identifying and using primary and secondary sources.

- **Primary sources** include literary texts, diaries, journals, historical documents, surveys, experiments, questionnaires, and interviews. They are the original sources for the issue at hand and constitute the text that you will analyze in your paper.

- **Secondary sources** include books, journal articles, and conference papers. They, directly or indirectly, comment on or critically examine the original primary sources.

A journal article, such as "Escaping the Silence: Diagnosis and Discourse in 'The Yellow Wallpaper'" by Paula A. Treichler, is a secondary source that examines how diagnosis and discourse is used in the primary text "The Yellow Wallpaper," a short story by Charlotte Perkins Gilman.

ACADEMIC FOCUS

A NOTE ON PRIMARY AND SECONDARY SOURCES

What is confusing about primary and secondary research is that what sometimes appears to be a primary source is actually a secondary source and vice versa. For example, sometimes a primary source is obvious, as in the book *Oryx and Crake* or *Generation X*, above, but sometimes a primary source might be used as a secondary source if, for example, a journal entry or a letter is used to support an argument. You might use the letters of a prominent author or philosopher as a primary source, using the letters as your "primary" object of analysis, but you might also use them as a secondary source to provide an example of the way a novel or theoretical concept developed.

The important point here is that you need to make sure that you are clear about what your primary source is—a text (or several texts) that you are using for your primary analysis—and what your secondary texts that you will use to help support (or refute) your analysis are. Your instructor will usually tell you the minimum number of secondary texts required.

PRIMARY AND SECONDARY SOURCES

Exercise 10.1

1. Identify the primary and secondary sources in the following academic journal articles.
2. See if you can identify the academic discipline.
3. Provide a brief description of what you think might be the article's argument:

   - "Gilman's Gothic Allegory: Rage and Redemption in 'The Yellow Wallpaper'" by G. Johnson.
   - "Model estimates of CO_2 Emissions from Soil in Response to Global Warming" by D.S. Jenkinson et al.

Continued

- "Margaret Atwood's *Oryx and Crake*: The Terror of the Therapeutic" by S. Dunning.
- "Community Study of Role of Viral Infections in Exacerbations of Asthma in 9–11-Year-Old Children" by S.L. Johnston et al.
- "The Politics of Marginalization at the Centre: Canadian Masculinities and Global Capitalism in Douglas Coupland's *Generation X*" by Kit Dobson.

Primary Research in the Sciences and Social Sciences

In the social sciences and sciences, primary research most often involves direct observation, questionnaires, surveys, interviews, experiments, or data gleaned from first-hand field experience; however, it might also involve indirect observation, in the form of literary resources. As an undergraduate student, you will, for the most part, use first-hand studies that have already been conducted by qualified professors working at a university, rather than conducting your own field experiments.

This is because valid questionnaires, interviews, and experiments have to be conducted under strict conditions with respect to sample size, impartiality, protection, and justice, etc. These conditions apply to all quantitative experiments involving human or animal participants and are designed to meet the core ethical principles that all ethics review boards are guided by. Because these review boards are so thorough in their requirements for quantitative participant studies, they require a considerable amount of time and expertise to establish.

However, as an exercise in traditional scientific methodologies, a professor might ask you to develop a research paper based on traditional quantitative scientific research. If this is the case, you will be immersed in observational research. This involves carefully observing an event, an activity, an interaction, a person, or a phenomenon and carefully documenting data. Observation might involve using your five senses, a questionnaire, a survey, and/or some form of technology, such as a video recorder, camera, or recording device.

Most important, you will need to make sure that you maintain strict and reliable standards so that the quantifiable findings related to your chosen site of study will be considered valid. This means that the situations or specimens you are observing would need to be a fair sample size and relate directly to the information you are testing or processing. You might, for example, be asked to document how many cars in a busy intersection at different times of the day obey the stop sign. Alternatively, if you are an education student, you might be asked to write a research paper documenting and describing the behaviour of several learning-disabled students in your student-teaching class, following some closely defined criteria.

As soon as you have these outlined criteria, as defined by the purpose of your experiment and your predictive hypothesis, you will need to decide how best to test your research subjects. Besides direct observation, questionnaires, surveys, and interviews can assist you in obtaining the knowledge you require. It is important to make sure that you document everything carefully. Keeping a detailed log of research data is essential, as is documenting and assessing your results. This detailed documentation needs to be completed as close to the research time as possible to ensure accuracy, even if your analysis is calculated at a later date.

Organizing and interpreting or evaluating your findings requires that you examine your main categories of data carefully, relating them to the context of your original research question and possibly describing the situation or specimen. For example, if you are analyzing the behaviour of several caged elephants and their young in a small zoo, you might want to outline the context—the particulars of the zoo and the cage in which they live—and describe the elephants themselves. Then you might analyze your categories of information according to your predictions and some specific contexts, such as the time of day and the elephants' sleeping, eating, and nurturing habits.

However, this information will not serve a purpose unless it is related to a clear hypothesis or argument. When analyzing your data, you must classify your examples into several categories that exemplify certain aspects of your hypothesis, but do not forget to account for those examples that challenge or even discount your hypothesis. Calculating and measuring this knowledge will help you see patterns and eventually arrive at some conclusions that might confirm or challenge your hypothesis, or suggest possibilities for future research.

Interviews, Questionnaires, and Surveys

Interviews, questionnaires, and surveys are used extensively in the "real" world and in academia: by companies for hiring purposes and advertising research, by police officers to interview suspects, by lawyers in courtroom defences, and by politicians canvassing their constituents. In academia, interviews and questionnaires are used by anthropologists, sociologists, psychologists, and scientists in an attempt to establish in detail the parameters of their primary research. An opportunity to practise these research genres will introduce you to this type of primary research and also help you to build organizational, analytical, and socializing skills.

Interviews, questionnaires, and surveys might be conducted via telephone, in a one-on-one conversation, over email, or in hard-copy formats. Whereas a journalist might spontaneously interview someone at the scene of a crime or an accident, an academic will be more likely to use a more formal, structured, and prepared format. If you are using a questionnaire or survey, you must provide directions for completing the questions as well as a reason for asking the respondent to fill out the form. Moreover, your respondent should always be made aware of the parameters of the study and that he or she can choose how to respond.

If you are conducting an interview, a questionnaire, or a survey as a primary source of your research, you will need to carefully prepare a list of questions that reflect your purpose or working hypothesis and provide the information you seek. These questions might be in a multiple-choice format, a simple yes/no/maybe format, or in a format that requires short written responses. More important, you will need to consider using open-ended questions so you can provide the opportunity for a carefully considered answer, as opposed to closed questions, which force your respondent to answer with a narrow, focused response (often a simple yes or no).

EXAMPLES OF OPEN-ENDED, CLOSED-ENDED, AND LEADING QUESTIONS

Open-ended question: What does happiness mean to you?

Closed-ended question: Are you happy?

Leading question: Many people think happiness is hard to achieve: do you agree?

Open-ended question: Do you believe that street drugs create societal problems?

Closed-ended question: Are street drugs bad?

Leading question: The severe social problems caused by the trade in street drugs have been thoroughly documented: do you think the use of street drugs should be more strictly policed?

The questions need to reflect your particular purpose: the biggest problem with many questionnaires is that the questions are too loosely related to the central purpose or are too narrow to be of any use. Leading questions that expect a certain answer should be avoided, as should questions that are not appropriate for your audience or situation because they are not as rigorous or valid as questions that reflect your purpose. See chapter 3 for more on questionnaires.

Please read chapter 3 on the social sciences for more information on this type of quantitative research.

As a short review, though, remember that

- quantitative research involves accurately recording and quantifying (counting and sorting the information into categories) your collected data; and
- qualitative research aims to understand the how and the why of human experience.

Primary Research in the Arts and Humanities

Examples of primary qualitative research include narration, storytelling, ethnography (social sciences), literature, diaries, legal documents, advertisements, political debates, critical theory, and philosophical treatises (in other words, any text you can read and analyze). Primary texts such as these are the texts that you will use to focus your analysis of the topic and provide you with the evidence you need to make your argument.

As previously stated, most of your essays as an undergraduate student will be qualitative, involving a close examination of, for example, a novel or an event, because of the constraints on conducting valid quantifiable research.

Research Writing: Plans, Processes, and Strategies

When your instructor assigns a research essay, he or she will most likely provide you with a broad choice of topics from which to choose. You will, however, need to come up with a plan for conducting your research, focusing and narrowing your topic to arrive at a workable argument, and possibly writing a research proposal. What follows is a step-by-step plan that will lead you through the process of writing a qualitative research essay.

Steps for Writing the Research Essay

Research writing can feel overwhelming at the beginning of the project. This is true for experienced and inexperienced writers alike. The difference is that experienced writers are aware that the research takes time and will need focusing and organizing whereas inexperienced writers often leave their research until the last minute and then immediately get lost in the huge amounts of information they find and have to organize and focus. Breaking down the process into steps that take you logically through the entire process, from finding a topic and working thesis statement right through to the research, writing, and documentation stages, can significantly help you to focus and complete your research essay assignment on time. Bear in mind that you will need at least a couple of weeks to write a research paper.

1. Decide on a Topic and a Primary Text

Ask yourself

- Is this topic viable?
- What specifically interests me in this topic?
- Will I be able to make a valid argument *about* it rather than simply repeating the current research?
- Do I have a primary text: a text I can use to focus and direct my analysis?

2. Establish a Working Thesis Statement

You can establish a working thesis statement by asking and answering a research question.

- Once you have a primary text, go through it, reading carefully and critically, looking for a knowledge gap: somewhere you can ask a question about what is missing in the text and needs to be addressed.
- Develop your thesis by answering your research question (for more on research questions see "Finding and Answering a Research Question" later in this chapter).
- Make sure your argument synthesizes your research with the information in your primary text.
- Even though your argument might change as you write and research, make sure you have a strong argument

- that other people can disagree with;
- that is manageable; and yet
- that is deep enough to reflect a thorough sustained engagement with an issue.

3. Go Online

- As soon as you have a primary text and a working thesis statement, search the library catalogue, using Boolean search terms (*and, or, not*) and subject headings, title information, and keywords to access material relevant to your analysis. For example, you might conduct direct searches related to your primary text or you might use keywords or subject headings taken from your working thesis statement (see "Library Catalogue" under "Finding Research" later in this chapter).
- You will be looking for articles related to your topic and/or your primary text that are written by scholars working at a credible university (see "Evaluating Sources" later in this chapter). Ask yourself: will I be able to find an appropriate number of background sources that pertain either directly or indirectly to my topic and primary text?

4. Expand Your Search

- Access specialized electronic databases, such as ERIC (Educational Resources Information Center) for education-related topics, MLA (Modern Language Association) for literature, and MEDLINE for medicine and bioscience information (See "Library Databases" under "Finding Research" later in this chapter).
- As you conduct your research, make sure you keep notes, either on the printed article or in a notebook. Keep your topic and primary text in mind as you read the article to help you refine and refocus your argument. At this point, be prepared for your argument to change somewhat, but keep in mind that you are trying to focus and make your larger topic manageable, according to what interests you about it and what patterns and connections you see with your primary text and working thesis statement.
- Thoroughly document all quotations and page numbers so that you do not have trouble finding the information when you cite your sources in your paper. These quotations might provide significant dates or offer a view that supports or refutes your position.

5. Develop a Working Outline of Your Essay

- Use either point or detailed form, so that you begin to see how your argument is developing logically.
- Make sure you can insert appropriate support and evidence. Keep checking to see that your outline is explicating some aspect directly connected to your thesis statement. See chapter 8 for more information on outlines.

6. Write Several Drafts of Your Essay

- When writing the first draft, you might choose to simply write the entire paper in one sitting and then refine it in the revisions. You might closely examine your outline or spend more time on the introductory paragraph, which outlines your argument and provides your thesis, to carefully establish your argument. No *one* way is right; you need to find out how you work best and go with that. Remember that you will need to make as many drafts and revisions as it takes to achieve an in-depth, persuasive research essay (see chapter 9 for revision strategies).
- Ask yourself if the interpretation takes into account the complexity of the work. If it is an argumentative paper, ask if your argument is insightful. Does the paper reflect a thorough and comprehensive engagement with other research?

7. Use a Revision Rubric

- A revision rubric will help you analyze the effectiveness of your paper. Revise either on your own or in a small-group workshop, where you will read and comment on each other's papers. Here is a sample revision rubric:

Revision Rubric

Revise by answering the following questions. Make sure you provide evidence for the points.

Clarity and organization

- Does the opening sentence grab my attention? Do I want to read on, or does it need work?
- Does the introduction accurately reflect the content of the essay? Does it outline the main points it will be developing in the essay in relation to a clearly defined topic or issue?
- Is the thesis clear? Is it interesting? Does it show innovative, original thinking?
- Do the *sentences* and the *paragraphs* in this piece of writing flow logically, picking up and developing the sentence/paragraph that came before? Do the sentences and paragraphs advance the argument, not repeat it?
- Does the conclusion summarize the essay without repeating the points exactly as they are written in the essay? Does the conclusion encourage a larger reflection on the topic?

Analysis and evidence

- Does the argument constitute a full and complete analysis of the topic?
- Are there any gaps in or illogical development of the analysis? Is the argument well supported with an appropriate amount of textual evidence?
- Does the paper engage with other researchers who have written on the same text and/or topic? Does it add to or refute their analysis?

- Does the interpretation take into account the context and period in which the work was written or the event happened?

Voice
- Is there a strong sense of voice in this writing?
- Is the language clear, focused, and confident or is it too forceful, bureaucratic, or timid?
- Do I trust this voice?
- Does the voice presuppose an academic audience?

Editing
- Check for grammar errors, typos, and spelling mistakes.
- Check that your format, documentation style, and quotations are accurate.
- Does your essay meet all the requirements of the assignment?

Now that you are aware of the process involved in writing a research essay, you need to focus more intently on each of the steps. Here is some information to help you focus and narrow your topic and find and answer research questions.

Focusing and Narrowing Your Topic

You have either been given or have found a broad essay topic that you want to explore. You will now need to focus your topic and continue to narrow, define, and redefine your position so that it is manageable. For example, if one of the choices presented to you is quite broad, as in the essay topic "Cultural differences and health care," you will need to narrow your focus to prevent your analysis from being too general and too broad. You might begin by asking such questions as, What cultural differences am I going to focus on? Which health care system? How do cultural differences and health care relate to each other? What primary text will I use to focus this analysis? What secondary research material might I use? What argument am I going to make?

Finding and Answering a Research Question

Coming up with a research question and attempting to answer it will help you arrive at an argument. For example, in relation to the above topic, you might ask something such as, "How is cultural difference addressed in the Canada Health Act, and how is this mandate implemented or managed in practice?" Answering this question will form the basis of your argument, providing you with a focus and a primary text. Using the above example, you can see that you now have a focus and a primary text: cultural difference as it appears in the Canada Health Act and its implementation in Canadian hospitals (this argument would probably use media or specific hospital report as primary texts).

However, you might also note that you don't have a specific argument yet. Asking what interests you about cultural difference can help, but you might also look for a knowledge gap. In the above example, for example, you might note that that a gap exists between what is intended in the Canada Health Act and what is implemented in practice.

Attempting to answer your research question and make it more specific will give you the material to write a tentative or working thesis statement. Using the above topic, your thesis might initially go something like this:

> Although the Canada Health Act accounts for cultural difference in its "universality" clause—a clause that guarantees accessibility—it does not in practice account for new immigrants, who do not receive equal health care delivery.

Now you have a specific topic (cultural difference, as it relates to new immigrants and health care delivery), a specific primary text (the "universality clause" in the Canada Health Act and health care delivery), and a specific argument: contrary to popular belief, the "universality clause" does not guarantee accessibility. This thesis will probably change considerably as you research and write your paper and find that you need to be more specific again.

Continually asking questions can help you, once again, to narrow your focus. For example, in relation to the above thesis, you might ask, what immigrants? Which city or cities? What does cultural difference have to do with accessibility? How is accessibility framed in the Canada Health Act? As you can see, these questions narrow your focus rather than broaden it; however, you also have to be careful that your thesis is not too narrow. If a topic is too current or too obscure it might not be covered in academic journals.

Remember, when choosing a topic or an issue, that it takes time for it to be researched and published. It will usually take at least a year for an event or an issue to manifest in academic publications, so keep this in mind if you are thinking of writing about a very recent event. Also, if the topic is concerned with a community, an issue, or a place that is too local and has no larger implications, it might not be considered relevant for academic coverage.

A good workable thesis is one that will provide the depth of analysis and specific focus that your instructor is looking for. Ultimately, it is only by asking and re-asking and attempting to answer your research question that you will arrive at an argument that is manageable and focused.

Now that you have considered how you might make your thesis focused and manageable, you might also want to think about how you might make it interesting. Because research is a lot of work, selecting a topic and a focus that interests you will not only make the amount of work more bearable but also spur you on to do a more thorough analysis.

If your instructor chooses your topic for you, find a way (an angle or an approach to the material) to make it interesting. Ask yourself, what could interest me about this topic? Sometimes your instructor will ask you questions when he or she assigns a topic. These questions are designed to help you ask the necessary questions that will help you

FOCUSING YOUR THESIS STATEMENT

To write effective thesis statements, you need to ask the following questions:

- Do I have an argument?
- Is my thesis too broad?
- Is my thesis too narrow?
- Is my thesis based on personal opinion?
- Can my thesis be supported by research and an in-depth analysis?

EXAMPLES:

Thesis too broad and no argument: Scientists agree that global warming is creating a huge problem in the world.

This thesis, as is, is expository because it suggests that you will simply be summarizing what scientists already know. Ask, which scientists? Where do you stand in relation to the arguments of these scientists? Is there a gap, an inconsistency, or a contradiction in their arguments that you can expose? Can you add to their arguments? The thesis is also too broad. You can't cover all aspects of global warming in a short essay, so clarify which aspect of global warming you are concerned with. What do you mean by "huge problem"? What is the problem, specifically? Is it the same problem for all parts of the world? Consider focusing your thesis on a particular problem in a particular part of the world.

Thesis too narrow: The proposed plan to start a fracking project in the Lethbridge area over the next two years is going to create environmental problems for local residents.

This thesis is too narrow. There won't be research on the actual project yet and what there is will be limited and speculative. You will need to be flexible in revising this thesis so it is workable. If you limit yourself to researching the environmental problems created by fracking, you will be writing an expository essay, but if you use the proposed Lethbridge plan as a primary text, you might not be able to find enough information. The danger is that you would generalize research that has already been done on the danger the Lethbridge fracking project poses to the environment without having a clear understanding of what this project entails.

Opinion-based thesis: There is no truth to global warming research that states global warming is harmful to the environment.

If you can answer your research question—is there any truth to the global warming issue?—with a simple yes or no, you are in the realm of unsupported and/or biased opinion. You must be able to account for the multiple complexities of an issue rather than simply taking a personal one-sided stand on the issue. Your thesis must be able to be supported by current research and an in-depth analysis.

narrow your topic and come up with a working thesis statement. Consider the following research essay topic, provided for the students of an English class:

> For Ludwig Wittgenstein, language is an activity that is tied to a culture's particular ways of seeing and relating to the world: "to imagine a language is to imagine a form of life." Analyze a text of your choice—a novel, a short story, a film, a legal case, a news article, an event, etc.—in terms of how the author is able to use language to imagine a certain "form" of life. Does this imagining challenge our perceptions about what is "normal" and/or "abnormal," "acceptable" and "unacceptable"? Does language, and maybe the genre and/or context, have the ability to change the way we see and relate to those considered Other? If you pick this option, you might want to consider some of the following topics: the family's website or media interpretations of the Ashley X case; film representations of "monsters" or "freaks" (*Frankenstein, Resident Evil, Godsend, The Mist, The Island, Pan's Labyrinth, Spider-Man*, or television shows, such as *Dexter, Carnivale*, or *Heroes*); representations of mental illness in the media; or robotics or genetic engineering. Make sure you consider the larger cultural context and how the text under consideration imagines not only a cultural Other but also a cultural norm against which the Other is imagined.

The instructor here has provided a focus for the essay, but within that focus there is a lot of choice. He or she has suggested several primary texts as available options and has asked many questions that will help students to narrow down an approach to the topic. In answering these questions, you should be able to significantly focus your argument, choosing a primary text to frame your argument. Here is one student's working thesis statement, written in response to the above essay assignment:

> In 1932, the film *Freaks* served as an educating medium, enforcing societal norms through the use of visual and verbal rhetoric.

This student has focused and made her argument manageable by naming a primary text—*Freaks*—and by outlining an approach she will be using in her analysis: an examination of visual and verbal rhetoric. The instructor has also provided the student who picked this topic with some potential research material by naming Ludwig Wittgenstein and by naming some key terms: *Other* and *norm*. Defining these terms will help the student find a way in to analyzing the film and, in the process, further establish her argument.

Here is another thesis statement, which includes Wittgenstein's theory:

> Ludwig Wittgenstein's theory that language is capable of creating a "form of life" can be applied to an analysis of the Ashley X case, where normal able-bodied experience is privileged over Ashley's dis-abled experience.

Exercise 10.2

FROM RESEARCH QUESTION TO THESIS STATEMENT

Below are some broad topics for a research essay.

- Read them through, pick one that interests you, and see if you can come up with a research question.
- Answer the research question to the best of your ability and use your answer to write a short working thesis statement.

1. Write a research essay exploring the media's role in influencing "ideal" body images, sizes, and lifestyles.
2. Walter Benjamin once wrote that "mankind's self-alienation has reached such a degree that it can experience its own destruction as an aesthetic pleasure of the first order." Keeping this quote in mind, analyze the media representation of the conflict in the Middle East. Here you will need to focus on a specific place (Iraq, Afghanistan), a specific event (9/11), and a specific representation (a specific newspaper's, journalist's, or photographer's representation). How does the representation distance us from the actual event? If Benjamin is right, and we are persuaded to see the horror and violence of war in aesthetic terms, is he also right in stating that the representation of war alienates us from war and, ultimately, from ourselves? You might make some larger conclusions here about the potential for art to incite social or political change.
3. Find two or three texts that deal with a specific animal rights issue (whaling, the containment of animals in zoos, animal agriculture, animal experimentation, etc.) and make an argument for the rhetorical effectiveness of the arguments made about the case. The texts that you address in this case will need to be closely connected either in theme (animal experimentation in the media, for example) and/or perspective (Greenpeace's take on whaling, for example).
4. The NHL and violence.

Once you have a topic, a research question, and a working thesis statement that answers your question, ask yourself the following questions:

- Do I have a primary text? Will the text enable me to perform a close analysis of the topic in question?
- Is my argument manageable? Will I be able to find enough existing research on some aspect of the topic? Is my topic narrow enough to explore in a short research paper?

Writing a Research Proposal

To help you keep your argument manageable and focused, your instructors will often assign a research proposal. Regardless of whether it is assigned or not, the research proposal is an excellent strategy and should be used. The research proposal, then, has the dual purpose of forcing you to think about your research essay far ahead of the due date, helping you manage your time, and enabling the instructor to assist you in focusing your topic.

The research proposal you will write for a research essay in class is similar to writing a research proposal for a scholarship or grant application in that your purpose is to show the reader your thorough background knowledge in the subject and your intention of doing something original and substantial with the material.

Although an undergraduate research essay does not have as much breadth as a scholarship or grant application, the underlying principle applies. If asked to write a research proposal for your essay, you must still make sure that you are following the guidelines your instructor has set out for you in your assignment. Your proposal will need to take into account the type of research essay you are writing. For example, if it is an expository essay or a report, your main focus will be to present and organize existing information on a focused topic, but if it is an argumentative essay, your proposal will need to show your willingness to explore the complexities of the topic and take a stand on a related issue.

Regardless of the form, though, you will be expected to thoroughly and concisely review the topic you intend to explore, and also to think seriously about the background issues. Remember that thinking critically involves being aware of the assumptions you are making about authors and their works and being aware that there may be more than one answer to the question. Keep in mind that your argument will become part of the dialogue on the subject in question.

The formal research proposal should always be typed and double-spaced using the standard academic Times New Roman 12-point font. It is usually short, approximately 350–450 words long (one to two pages). Your instructor will probably provide you with the format he or she requires, but, in general, a proposal should

- present your topic and primary text;
- identify the purpose of your paper;
- set out the research question and other central questions you want to address;
- propose a working thesis statement that attempts to answer your research question (be aware that this might change as you refine your responses);
- suggest the types of research you expect to do; and
- propose the dates by which you intend to have the various phases of your paper completed.

Here are three sample research proposals, written by first-year students.

Research Proposal 1

This proposal is written for an English class; it is well thought out and focused.

Topic and Primary Text: I am interested in writing on women's issues in Nancy Mairs's autobiographical book, *Remembering the Bone House*.

Research Question: How does Mairs establish a sense of community with other women? How does she use language to do this?

Detail and Context: Using *Remembering the Bone House* as my central text, I hope to bring to light the way language can establish female community and maybe incite social change (in the 1980s). Autobiography is a powerful medium for doing this. Specifically, I want to look at how Mairs uses pathos or emotion to challenge the male-centred world view, while at the same time empowering women to speak and act.

Central Questions: Is autobiography an effective medium for establishing community? Is pathos, as a tool for challenging the norm and establishing community, effective? If so, is it effective only on an individual level? Or is it also effective socially/culturally? Does Mairs present a model by which other women might live?

Working Thesis Statement: In *Remembering the Bone House*, Nancy Mairs uses pathos, in particular women's emotional experience and knowledge, to challenge a foundational male-centred world view and to promote female community.

Projected Research: I hope to supplement my current research with more journal articles. I have already looked at Plato's *Republic* and an essay by Mary Hawkesworth, titled "Feminist Rhetoric: Discourses on the Male Monopoly of Thought," which should be very useful. My research should be completed by November 18th, and the first draft should be completed by November 26th.

Research Proposal 2

This proposal could work for either a Native Studies or an English class; the writer here struggles to find a primary text that will help focus an analysis:

Topic: In this essay, I want to explore the notion that storytelling is healing.

Purpose: To address the way in which storytelling has been or might be used in First Nations' communities to heal troubled teenagers. I want to look at traditional methods for telling stories and compare them with psychological research on this same issue.

Central Questions: Has storytelling been used in First Nations' communities in Canada as a form of healing? If so, for what section of the Native population? How successful has it been? How might it help troubled teenagers? Would it provide them with a sense of community and a sense of self?

Primary Text: There is a problem here; I don't simply want to repeat existing research and the scope of this paper and my own experience won't allow me to do my own study of a Native community. I think I need to either find an existing model in a community and relate that model to its potential for other communities (even the dominant community) or look at how a novel—Eden Robinson's *Monkey Beach*—or poet might offer potential insights for how storytelling is healing.

Projected Research: There is information in the library on the psychological and medical benefits of storytelling. I will check these out and also look to see if there is any research that pertains specifically to a First Nations' perspective. I will also use Jerome Bruner's and Paula Gunn Allen's essays. Both of these essays will help me to think about healing and storytelling, as it might apply to First Nations' beliefs, values, and practices.

Schedule of Work to Be Completed:
- Complete Library Research: Nov. 16th
- Complete first draft: Nov. 18th
- Revise essay (#1): Nov. 30th
- Revise essay (#2): Dec. 3rd
- Submit completed essay: Dec. 10th

Research Proposal 3

This proposal could be written for an engineering or science class. While the first two proposals are argumentative, this proposal is an inductive expository, or report-style, essay.

Summary or Introduction: I want to argue that geothermal energy is key to our future.

Background and Context: I will provide a context for how geothermal energy has been used and how it might be used in the future.

Details: parameters and approach: I will look at how it is used in the western world with a focus on home and business use.

Details: evaluation and suggestions: I will argue that it is good for the environment and good for the economy.

Recommendations: action that needs to be taken. We need to use geothermal energy.

Attachments: supporting data, including cost analyses, spreadsheets, etc.

Exercise 10.3

PROPOSAL WRITING

- Write a one-page proposal that documents your understanding of research writing up to this point.
- Use your own writing experience and what you have learned so far from this text as your primary material. You will be expected to
  - know what a research paper is and to understand the different types of research papers that you could use;
  - demonstrate a familiarity with the process of research writing; and
  - be able to show that you are willing to refine the skills you do have by continuing to develop your understanding of research writing.

As a result, you will need to review your strengths and areas for improvement as well as noting how you might use your expertise and new knowledge in future assignments.

Finding Research

Now that you have found and narrowed your topic into a workable thesis statement, you will need to access your college or university library to begin gathering your research. Although much of your research will initially be online, you will need to go beyond a simple Google search, or even a Google Scholar search, to explore your library's web interface portal. This will include the library catalogue, databases, and non-library websites.

Library Catalogue

The more precise your search terms or keywords are, the more you will be able to narrow and focus your search. You can search by

- author;
- title;
- content;
- keyword; or
- subject.

A subject search is more precise than a keyword search, which will require you to focus and refocus your search according to keywords, phrases, or concepts.

You might also need to take your search further, finding alternative keywords or **synonyms** for your topic. For example, a keyword search based on the student thesis statement "Violence in hockey has become a national problem" might include the keywords *violence*, *hockey*, and *national*. These words, however, will probably provide you with too much information; the program will pull up all the sources related to *violence*, *hockey*, and *national*, but the topics might not be related. You might, for example, find that you have located texts highlighting *violence* in Afghanistan or *hockey* in the Olympics.

Neither of these texts will be useful for your particular analysis. To make things worse, your results will probably be in the thousands.

A Boolean search, common to all library interfaces, will help you narrow your search even further. Boolean searches allow you to relate your search terms using *and, or,* and *not*. Briefly, when searching using *and*, as in violence *and* hockey, you will be accessing all the articles or books that have both terms in the title, but when using *or* you will be accessing titles that include only one term or the other. If you want to exclude a term, use *not*, as in hockey *not* lacrosse. You might have to experiment with these terms, narrowing your key or subject terms until you find the focus you need.

Of course, if you know the title or the author of the text you are looking for, your search should be considerably easier, but this is not always the case.

Once you have found an article or a book that you think you might be able to use, you will be able to access either a full-text electronic copy or find the hard copy by locating the call number and going to the library shelves to retrieve it. Because library books are organized according to subject material, searching the shelves for similar books in the area where you find one source is a useful strategy. If the library does not carry the source you are looking for, you will be able to find it by using the interlibrary loan service.

Library Databases

Most of the information you will find will come from journal articles. These can be found on one of the specialized **library databases**. Some databases are general and cover different disciplines, but some are organized according to subject, that is, the material related to a specific academic discipline (anthropology, chemistry, art, education, etc.). Academic Search Premier is an example of a general database. It contains articles on history, math, education, psychology, English, etc. The MLA International Bibliography is a specialized database for English language and literature.

On the library interface, the databases should be listed alphabetically, as well as according to subject areas and academic disciplines. If in doubt, you can ask the librarian for help in navigating and searching material on appropriate databases.

FINDING RESEARCH

Exercise 10.4

1. Identify some keywords or concepts in the following student working thesis statements and then key them into your library catalogue.
2. Using subject terms and/or keywords, ask how you can refine your search to yield not more, but more specific results.
3. Find some synonyms for your keywords. For example, for the word *violence* you might also search for the synonyms, *abuse, brutality, force, onslaught, rampage, fight*. Did your search reveal some useful texts, appropriate to the argument embedded in the thesis statements?

Continued

THESIS STATEMENTS

Teenage body image has been affected by the modelling industry.

The oil industry must become aware of and act on ecologically meaningful principles.

Rosemarie Garland-Thomson's point that memorials tell "inherently controversial" stories is evident in the FDR Memorial and how it represents people with disabilities.

This essay will examine the role of silence in Joy Kogawa's *Obasan*.

It is important to remember that language really does matter when planning your search strategy. You need to be flexible and open to narrowing your search, looking for a specific aspect, time period, or perspective, or broadening it, looking for synonyms or broader terminology to help you relate your material to a larger argument.

Evaluating Sources

Because the sheer volume of research can be somewhat overwhelming, you will have to not only find but also evaluate the existing body of knowledge on your topic. Not all the information you find will be useful or even acceptable, so part of your job is to figure out not only how to use a library catalogue but also how to weed out the unreliable from the reliable or valid information. One of the first skills you will be required to learn is to be able to distinguish between academic and non-academic sources.

Distinguishing between Academic and Non-Academic Sources

Most sources are accessible either directly or indirectly through your university or college library, including books, academic and journalistic articles, newspapers, maps, music, and current or historical information in a variety of formats: hard or electronic copy, video, CD, etc.; however, while many of these sources will be academic, such as journal peer-reviewed articles or books, many of them will be non-academic, such as newspapers, web articles, etc. Being able to distinguish between academic and non-academic texts is crucial.

Your instructor will probably require that your essay cite a certain number of *academic* sources, but you might also use non-academic material for background or current information, statistics, and some quick facts. Remember, though, that it is the academic sources that will provide you with a considered and contextualized analysis of the material you are working with. Below is an overview of academic and non-academic research, along with an introduction to the type of information they will provide for your research:

Table 10.1 ◆ Academic versus Non-Academic Research: An Overview

Academic Research	*Non-Academic Research*
• Used to support an in-depth analysis of your topic. • If your instructor requires academic sources, you will be searching for material in this category.	• Used for context, statistics, and quick current information and facts. • Material in this category might also provide the material for a primary text (newspaper articles, magazines, etc.).
Academic journal articles: These will be your number one academic source. They offer original research related to a specific discipline and written by an academic scholar working in a recognized university. The best articles are peer-reviewed (critically evaluated by experts in the field) and range from about 24 to 35 pp. long.	**Newspapers and magazines:** These sources are reader-friendly and useful as primary texts or for providing information on current events, trends, etc., but they are not academic research. • See larger comparison on the difference between scholarly and popular journals in Table 10.2.
Books: Books are useful because they cover the issue or topic in more detail. Pay attention to the date of publication though: a book on web technologies written in 1975 will be out of date in 2015. However, some books are still valid for use in academic research. For example, Freud's *Interpretation of Dreams* is still considered valid research because the research is seminal, or key, to thinking about the psychology of dreams.	**Books:** Fiction, poetry collections, anthologies of short stories, and autobiographies might serve as primary texts (i.e., a text you can analyze to make an argument about it), but they would not fall into the category of academic research.
Web: Academic sources can be found on the web, but it is sometimes difficult to distinguish between academic and non-academic sources. Google Scholar has academic articles, but you can't always access the full text and not all the articles listed on the web are academic. Moreover, library information is selected, organized, and filtered for quality; web resources are unfiltered, unorganized, and unedited. Academic library databases are libraries of specialized information that you do not have access to on the web.	**Web:** There are thousands of sites to wade through when you use the web, academic and non-academic sources, but sometimes it is hard to distinguish between them. Full-text articles are hard to find, and, if you do find them, you are often expected to purchase them. The web is useful, however, for book and film reviews, statistics, current information, legal and government information, images, and non-profit websites.
Encyclopedias, dictionaries, almanacs, handbooks: Although these sources would *not* be considered an academic reference, they are a useful starting point. However, it is important, especially in the case of definitions, to go beyond what you might find in these sources. The *Oxford English Dictionary* is generally considered the best dictionary and can usually be accessed on the university or college library database.	**Encyclopedias, dictionaries, almanacs, handbooks:** Useful as a starting point for your research because they provide a short summary or overview and provide some quick facts. However, they do not provide enough information to allow an in-depth analysis, so never stop here. Wikipedia is not academic and because it is often inaccurate, you should check with your instructors about their policies on using Wikipedia.

Most commonly confused are scholarly journals and popular magazines. Below is a comparison of scholarly journals and popular magazines. Understanding the differences between these sources should help you to understand not only how the two exist separately as distinctive genres in their own right but also how and when to incorporate these sources into your paper.

Table 10.2 ◆ Scholarly Journals versus Popular Magazines

Scholarly Journals	Popular Magazines
Contain original research related to specific disciplines. Research is not current because of the time it takes to do in-depth research and publish.	**Contain** articles about current events, popular culture and topics, opinion, fiction, how-to, self-help, etc.
Written by a professor or researcher working at an established university.	**Written by** staff writers, freelance journalists, etc.
Read by academic scholars, researchers, students, etc. Technical information and jargon can make the material difficult to read.	**Read by** the general public according to individual interests.
Peer-reviewed: Articles critically evaluated by experts in field before publication.	**Reviewed by** non-specialists. Articles are selected by general editors.
Appearance: Plain cover, informative, black-and-white pictures, graphs, tables, charts. Very few, if any, advertisements. Non-profit, knowledge-driven. Use footnotes, bibliographies, methodologies, and data that point to further research. Use logic and correct grammar. Accessible in libraries.	**Appearance:** Glossy cover, colour photographs, easy to read layout, large print/fonts, lots of advertisements indicating profit-driven purposes. Informing and selling are often blurred. Use sensational and emotional language. Accessible in many different stores.

Exercise 10.5

EVALUATING SOURCES

1. Go to the library and find a journal that focuses on feminist or women's concerns. Evaluate it to make sure it is an academic journal. Check out the titles of the articles in the journal. Are these titles knowledge-driven?
2. Now find a magazine—it might be in the library, but if not you will find it in a local store—that also deals with feminism or women's issues. Check out the titles of the articles in the magazine. How would you characterize these titles?
3. Compare the two sources, according to the table above. List at least eight indicators of the different genres: academic and commercial.

Another problem is finding and using sources that are relevant not only to your topic but, most important, to the argument you are trying to make about your topic. Keeping your argument in mind, first ask these preliminary questions:

- Is the article academic or non-academic?
- Does the article or book chapter relate directly to my texts and my argument?

- Do I have the required number of academic sources?
- Is the article or book up to date?
- Is it objective, offering an in-depth coverage of the material?

Here are some steps for finding and evaluating your academic sources:

1. Before beginning your research, make sure you have a working thesis statement (a context for doing your research).
2. Brainstorm some search terms that might apply to your topic or main idea.
3. Use the appropriate databases to find an article that will address some of your identified search terms.
4. Evaluate the reliability of your sources. Check the publication date. How up to date is it? Is the author an expert in his or her field (check bibliography)? Is he or she affiliated with a university? Does he or she have a PhD? Has he or she written other publications in the same area? Is the article peer-reviewed, demonstrating that other scholars working in the same field have evaluated and approved the article's content?
5. Read the introduction or the abstract, if there is one. Get an overview of the researcher's argument. Ask what the writer's purpose/argument is. Is she or he working to correct a misconception, to fill or expose a gap, or to build on or extend the work of others? Is the author biased? Is the reasoning sound?
6. Examine the table of contents and the index, if it is a book. Consider the most relevant chapters to your topic or argument. Is the emphasis the same?
7. Check the notes and bibliographic references. Identify the authors referred to by a researcher and the titles of both books and articles. List the sources you might want to use in your own research. Do certain sources seem more important than others?
8. Skim deeper. Read chapter titles, headings, and topic sentences to determine the relevance of what you are reading. Ask if the focus is relevant to your topic, issue, question, or working thesis.
9. Take notes on what you are reading: document the key and possibly relevant points as you read; put them either in the margins of your book or in a notebook. A useful notebook strategy is to either split the page into two sections—content/my connections—or to use different-coloured pens: one for writing down the important key points, and one for your response. Also implement critical reading and writing techniques: freewriting, clustering, close reading guidelines, summary writing, and critical response writing.

You might also use the acronym CRAAP, which asks you to consider if the book or article is

- Current (When was it published? Is the information up to date?);
- Relevant (Does the information answer your research question? Does it meet the requirements for the assignment?);

- <u>A</u>uthoritative (Is the author an authority on the subject? Is he or she affiliated with a university? Is the article peer-reviewed?);
- <u>A</u>ccurate (Are there any false statements or inaccuracies?);
- <u>P</u>urposeful (Does the author have a clear purpose? Is he or she biased or use strong emotional language that detracts from an objective stance?).

Do not forget to take notes, keeping in mind your subject and thesis as you do so, making sure you document all your secondary sources, noting the author, the work, and the page number.

When reading, pay attention to the following points and ask the following questions:

- Read the introductory section and ask how this work relates to your primary text and the argument you are making about it.
- Find the thesis statement: how does it speak to your argument? Does it either challenge or confirm your argument?
- Are there any useful theories or theorists you can use in your own work? Check out the reference page at the end of the essay: are there any articles, books, or authors there that might help you with your argument?
- Read the conclusion or discussion at the end of the work: does it provide you with more insight into your own topic and argument?
- Pay attention to how the article is structured: how is the essay broken up into sections? Could you emulate this structure in your own work?

Critical Reading Strategies

These strategies will help you understand not only the secondary research source you are reading but also how the text relates to your argument. Other note-taking strategies include paraphrasing and summarizing, writing a critical response, and writing an annotated bibliography. All of these strategies will help you integrate the research into your own thinking about the topic and, more specifically, about your particular thesis statement or argument.

Paraphrasing and Summarizing

As stated in chapter 6, these two terms are often confused; they both involve putting someone else's ideas into your own words. A paraphrase is usually shorter than the original passage, but longer and more detailed than a summary. A summary is significantly shorter than the original because it focuses only on the main or key ideas in the passage. Use paraphrases when you want to convey a difficult concept or idea and need more detail to do this; use summaries to provide a quick and accurate overview of an author's main ideas, when they are simple and straightforward. Using paraphrasing and summarizing can help you to understand the main points or ideas of a passage. Just as important, they can be used when you are writing your essay to convey someone else's ideas in your own words.

When using summary or paraphrase, you must document your sources: both MLA and APA require you to document direct quotes and all summaries, paraphrases, and ideas that belong to someone else. Documenting all ideas that are not your own is a sign of your professionalism; if you do not document your sources, you will be considered unprofessional and, at the same time, risk a charge of plagiarism (see chapter 11: "Documentation Style"). Here is an example of an original quotation, followed by a sample paraphrase and summary of the quotation. Please note how and where citation is used in these examples.

Direct Quotation:

"The power of the audio visual revolution was enormously increased when television became widely available after the Second World War. Within an amazingly few years, television could be received in more than 90 percent of the homes in America, and the average American was spending several hours a day before the screen." —Dan Lacy, "Reading in an Audiovisual and Electronic Era" (457).

Paraphrase:

After the Second World War, television played an important part in creating and furthering the widespread popularity of audio visual technology (Lacy 457). This revolution allowed television to be accessed by more than 90 percent of Americans, most of whom were watching it for a few hours each day (457).

Summary:

In America, the "audio visual revolution" was furthered by the immense popularity of television after the Second World War (Lacy 457).

Critical Response

Critical response is a useful strategy for understanding and working with a secondary source. It incorporates both summary and analysis of a work to help you understand and critique it as you relate it to your own argument.

Critical response allows you to understand and articulate the difference between summary and critical persuasive analysis. It also asks you to think carefully about how you can expand your critical thinking on a specific text. Even if your assignments have varied formats, you will need to write both a summary and a critique of one article, and develop the critique by asking further questions about the topic. These questions might not automatically provide you with a thesis statement or an argument, but they will help you focus your thinking so that you can find an argument that appeals to you.

What follows is a sample student critical response based on the film *I Am Sam*. As you read the summary, critique, and the questions below, you might see an argument you could make about the film. You should also be able to see how you could directly or indirectly transfer this summary and critique to different parts of your essay. For example, you might use the summary of the film in the introduction to your essay or you might use some of your critique, as it relates to your main argument, in the body of your essay. However, please remember that when you transfer this information, you still need to cite all words, phrases, and ideas that are not your own.

Sample Critical Response: *I am Sam*. Dir. Jessie Nelson, 2001.

Summary:

In *I am Sam* Sean Penn portrays a man with autism and a low IQ. Penn is faced with the responsibility of raising his child, Lucy, on his own when the mother of the child disappears shortly after Lucy's birth. The necessary supports and resources are met for Lucy until her first year of school. At this point, Family and Social Services get involved, questioning Sam's ability to be a good father because of his cognitive problems. After an upset at Lucy's seventh birthday party, witnessed by a Social Services caseworker, Lucy is taken out of Sam's custody and a legal battle ensues. The legal battle reveals the strength of Sam's relationship with and love of his daughter.

Critique:

This film provides an interesting perspective on the role of disabled individuals in society, especially society's conception of their ability to fulfil responsible roles. In the film, Sam is seen by many people as completely incapable of fulfilling the role and responsibilities of a parent. However, by the end of the film most viewers have both empathized with Sam and found that their perception of "good" parenthood has been challenged. This film falls into the Hollywood cliché of the happy ending but the relationships in the film speak volumes about the acceptance of different kinds of disabilities in society.

Questions:

- Is there a difference in society's reaction between a mental and a physical disability?
- What does this movie tell us about responsible parenting stereotypes?
- This movie is based on a real-life experience and legal case. As a result, it forces us to ask if established support systems should be in place to allow for disabled individuals to experience roles and identities that might at first appear to be beyond their mental or physical capabilities. Should I bring this into my essay or will that make it unfocused?

Annotated Bibliography

Another excellent strategy for reading and relating to your academic research sources (your secondary material) is the annotated bibliography. It also helps you to keep track of your research material.

An annotated bibliography is useful because it requires that you read and consider the issues raised by a research article, book, or book chapter ahead of time. It helps you to figure out if the research will be useful, and, more important, which parts of the article, book, or book chapter directly relate to your argument. Once again, the process and form will vary, depending on your instructor's preferences, but you will need to list the articles and/or books as you would in your works cited or reference page, using either correct MLA or APA citation (see chapter 11: "Documentation Style"), then briefly annotate or summarize the major points of the essay *as they apply to your thesis.*

This means that you will directly relate the relevance of the article or book chapter to your essay topic and argument by writing a short paragraph for each citation. Remember that to avoid a charge of plagiarism, you are required to cite all your sources, including summaries, by referencing the source in parentheses and by enclosing all significant words and phrases that are not your own in quotation marks.

Complete an annotated bibliography by following these steps:

1. Find your research, keeping your working thesis statement in mind;
2. Evaluate your research according to the aforementioned steps for evaluating library sources; and
3. Write an annotated bibliography, as in the example below (taken from the sample research proposal), summarizing and explaining the usefulness of the academic source to your topic and argument.

The example below uses MLA citation to document the source.

Working Thesis Statement:

In *Remembering the Bone House,* Nancy Mairs uses pathos, in particular women's emotional experience and knowledge, to challenge a foundational male-centred world view and to promote female community.

Annotated Bibliography:

Hawkesworth, Mary E. "Feminist Rhetoric: Discourses on the Male Monopoly of Thought." *Political Theory.* 16.3. (Aug. 1988): 444–67.

This paper argues that because a patriarchal male-centred worldview tends to focus on "conquest, domination, [and] hierarchy," it is oppressive for women (445). Women and women's minds are constrained and limited within the traditional discourses, "voices, perspectives, interests, ideas and modes of dominant thinking" that are male centred (446). This paper will provide me with a foundation for

understanding exactly *what* particular male-centred worldview Mairs is attempting to challenge, while also enabling me to understand *how* she is challenging it.
Because this article focuses on the "rhetoric of oppression," it provides me with a
basis for understanding how Mairs uses emotion, as a form of rhetoric, to liberate
herself and all women from that oppression.

Once you have your secondary research sources and are clearly able to understand
how they relate to your primary text and argument, you can, as shown above in the
steps for writing a research paper, go on and outline your essay. The biggest challenge
at this stage is to synthesize your research with your primary text and argument so
that your argument logically and persuasively convinces your reader that your position is valid. Remember that your secondary sources will be used to support your
argument, add credibility to a point, expose a knowledge gap, or refute someone else's
argument. Therefore, your secondary research material must be incorporated carefully
into your argument.

Incorporating Your Research into Your Argument

As mentioned, it is essential that you learn how to accurately document your sources
by citing them both in the body of your paper and at the end in a works cited or reference page. However, this requirement is often ignored by many first-year students, who
have the mistaken idea that using someone else's ideas or words shows that they are
not thinking for themselves. The opposite is true, unless you use someone else's words
to the exclusion of your own argument. Interacting with others on the subject means
that you are engaging in a scholarly debate on a particular subject and, it is hoped, taking a position in relation to someone else who is concerned with the same knowledge.
Moreover, besides demonstrating that you are part of the scholarly community, you are
also supporting and adding authority to your argument.

As Giltrow argues, selective direct quotations—where you copy directly from the
text word for word—are important because they function as mini summaries of a larger idea. This lends authoritative support or evidence for your argument (27). However,
don't overuse direct quotations because eventually, if you do, you will feel as if you are
simply repeating the arguments other scholars have made about the topic. Whether you
are using direct quotes, paraphrasing, or summarizing, you need to make sure that the
focus is on *your* argument about the topic or issue. Where you use them depends on
the emphasis you want to make. Direct quotes carry more authority. Use direct quotes
when you feel you can't say it any better yourself. Paraphrase if you need to describe
something in detail, and summarize when you need a useful and concise way to add
support and credibility to your point.

I repeat, though: do *not* overuse quotations. A string of quotations in a paper indicate that the student is not taking responsibility for his or her own argument. Balance
is key to using quotations: use them, not to make your argument, but to support and

emphasize the importance of your argument. You might use summary or direct quotes to refute or disagree with someone else's ideas but that, too, will ultimately add credence to your own argument.

Equally important is how you integrate these quotations into your work. Reporting expressions are used to introduce or signal an upcoming quotation, which will integrate the words of someone else into your work (see chapter 2). Consider the following example: *Martha Kolin argues* that writing well involves learning how to use "the tools that our writing system has available" (3). *Martha Kolin* is the noun, although it could equally be a pronoun, and *argues* is the verb that objectively introduces her main point: that writing well is dependent on the ability of the writer to use grammatical "tools."

What follows are some general directions for integrating and citing the words of others.

Integrating Quotations, Paraphrase, and Summary

MLA and APA citation methods require that all words or phrases that are not your own be put in quotation marks and cited. There are three different ways to cite a source in the body of your paper.

APA citation methods prefer, and MLA citation methods require, that you cite not only direct quotations but also another person's ideas if they are not your own.

1. Include the quoted material as part of your sentence so that the quote is embedded in your words and ideas.
2. Make a general statement and then use a colon to introduce the quote as a specific example or evidence to support your statement.
3. Longer quotes—more than five lines for MLA and more than 40 words for APA citation (see chapter 11 for more specific directions)—must be separated from the main paragraph and indented from the left margin. The right-hand side of the text is never justified. Quotation marks are omitted, and the punctuation, which comes after the parenthesis in the body of the text, is reversed.

Here are some templates for using these citation methods:

1. QUOTATIONS INCORPORATED INTO YOUR SENTENCE

MLA: Smith argues that "all words that are not your own must be cited" (24).
APA: Smith (1999) argues that "all words that are not your own must be cited" (p. 24).

2. USING A GENERAL STATEMENT, A COLON, AND A SPECIFIC EXAMPLE

MLA: Smith makes an important point: "all words that are not your own must be cited" (24).
APA: Smith (1999) makes an important point: "all words that are not your own must be cited" (p. 24).

3. LONGER, INDENTED QUOTATION

Please note that after the indented quotation, also included is an example of a short significant phrase that is used to support the writer's point and an example of summary citation, where the ideas of the author, rather than the actual words, are cited. What follows are two identical examples using MLA and APA citation methods.

MLA: Writing about the importance of citation, Giltrow emphasizes:

> Citation—the attributing of a statement to another speaker—produces one of the distinctive sounds (and looks) of scholarly writing. The distinctiveness of this way of writing could lead to . . . [the view] that scholarly citations are a shortcut to 'authority', simply a way to support an argument. (14)

However, as Giltrow points out, although citation "is a salient feature" of scholarly writing, it is not unique to academia (21). We use citation continuously in everyday conversation (14).

APA: Writing about the importance of citation, Giltrow (2005) emphasizes:

> Citation—the attributing of a statement to another speaker—produces one of the distinctive sounds (and looks) of scholarly writing. The distinctiveness of this way of writing could lead to . . . [the view] that scholarly citations are a shortcut to 'authority', simply a way to support an argument. (p. 14)

However, as Giltrow points out, although citation "is a salient feature" of scholarly writing, it is not unique to academia (p. 21). We use citation in everyday conversation continuously (p. 14).

Chapter 11 on documentation style will provide you with more detailed information about using different citation systems, but for now you need to be aware that you must cite all words, phrases, or sentences that are not your own. To do otherwise is to risk a charge of plagiarism. Depending on the severity of the charge, this could result in receiving a zero on a paper, a fail on a course, or expulsion from the university.

Exercise 10.6

CHANGING QUOTES INTO SUMMARY STATEMENTS

1. Change the following passages, which are written as direct quotes, into summary statements. Make sure you alter the passages accurately and put any words that are not your own in quotation marks, followed by a page citation in parenthesis.
2. Cite the author and the page number where the quote or idea can be found according to MLA citation methods (as above).
3. Discuss the accuracy of your summaries and citation use with your classmates.

As Michael Stone stated, "New York State ordered about 250 STD, family-planning, and prenatal care clinics to provide free, voluntary testing for the AIDS virus. Five of these clinics are in New York City. In addition, the City Health Department operates two anonymous testing clinics and encourages people who fear they are at risk to get tested" (40).

In "Keeping Close to Home: Class and Education," bell hooks argues that "open, honest communication is the most important way we maintain relationships with kin and community as our class experience and backgrounds change. It is as vital as the sharing of resources. . . . Communication between black folks from various experiences of material privilege was much easier when we were all in segregated communities sharing common experiences in relation to social institutions. Without this grounding, we must work to maintain ties, connection" (24).

Writing about the nature of scientific reasoning, Bronowski argues that "[n]o scientific theory is a collection of facts. It will not even do to call a theory true or false in the simple sense in which every fact is either so or not so. The Epicureans held that matter is made of atoms two thousand years ago and we are now tempted to say that their theory was true. But if we do so we confuse their notion of matter with our own. John Dalton in 1808 first saw the structure of matter as we do today, and what he took from the ancients was not their theory but something richer, their image; the atom. Much of what was in Dalton's mind was as vague as the Greek notion, and quite as mistaken. But he suddenly gave life to the new facts of chemistry and the ancient theory together, by fusing them to give what neither had: a coherent picture of how matter is linked and built up from different kinds of atoms" (n. pag).

ACADEMIC FOCUS

A NOTE ABOUT FOOTNOTES AND ENDNOTES

Note that the student essay at the end of this chapter uses the MLA citation method and footnotes. These are consecutively numbered superscript Arabic numerals within the body of the text (1, 2, 3, etc.). These numbers refer to footnotes at the bottom of the relevant page or, alternatively, to endnotes, which are listed in a separate page at the end of the paper. Footnotes (and endnotes) are used to include comments about content that either amplifies or defines a point within the text. They differ from parenthetical documentation, which is used in the body of the text to explain a short contextual comment, definition, or aside for longer commentaries that are considered peripheral to the main logical developmental context and argument.

Your decision to use footnotes or endnotes depends on the method of citation you choose or are required to use. For example MLA and APA use footnotes while Chicago uses footnotes and endnotes.

Plagiarism

Plagiarism is the presentation of someone else's words, ideas, images, or data as your own. Whether deliberate or accidental, it is a serious academic offence; A charge of plagiarism can result in a fail on a particular assignment or on the entire course and can even lead to suspension or expulsion from the university or college that charges you.

Plagiarism means that you have deliberately

- copied a phrase, a sentence, or a passage from another source (print or electronic) and handed it in as if it is your own;
- summarized or paraphrased someone else's work without acknowledging the original source;
- handed in a paper you have bought, had someone else write, or copied from someone else.

Accidental plagiarism implies the following:

- carelessness in copying down your sources;
- omitting a source citation because you are either unaware of the need to document your sources or, when taking notes, forgot to mark that it was a citation;
- forgetting to place quotation marks around another writer's words;
- not realizing that you must cite summary and paraphrases as well as direct quotes;
- mistakenly thinking that if you rework the material into your own words, you will receive more credit from your instructor. This problem comes from not being aware of academic conventions that require you to engage with the work of other scholars in your discipline, thereby in privileging a "community" of scholars.

These accidental problems are easy to fix: vigilance is the key for most of them. For the last point, honesty and a sincere desire to engage with the knowledge and ideas of other scholars need to be developed in equal measure.

While cheating and outright copying someone else's work as your own are obvious plagiarism offences, students are often not aware that plagiarism also includes the following:

- Misrepresenting facts, which means that you take a small part of what someone else argues and twist it to meet your requirements. An easy way to fix this problem is to make sure that your reading and interpretation of another scholar or source are accurate. If in doubt, ask your professor for insight into your interpretation and how it might apply to your essay.
- Substantial editorial assistance: if you employ a tutor or an editor or even get a friend to look over your work, the work must remain in your control and

CITING CORRECTLY

To avoid plagiarism, quotation marks must be placed around the exact words of the source, as in the following MLA example:

> As Jean-Paul Sartre wrote, "[m]an is nothing else but what he makes of himself" (1193).

In the above example, the quotation is introduced by a reporting expression—"As Jean-Paul Sartre wrote"—and the exact words are enclosed within quotation marks. The first letter of the word man is enclosed in square brackets to indicate that a capital "M" has been changed to a lower-case "m," which is in keeping with the punctuation of the sentence. A page number is given at the end of the sentence (punctuation is placed after the page number parenthesis). There will be a corresponding bibliographic entry, which will include the author's name, the title of the work, the publisher, and the date of publication, on a separate page at the end of the paper.

If you were to summarize the previous sentence you might write something like the following:

> Jean-Paul Sartre points out that every man is responsible for his own existence (1193).

or

> He points out that every man is responsible for his own existence (Sartre 1193).

Please note that the first time you use a source, you need to include the full name, as in Jean-Paul Sartre, but in subsequent citings, you only include the last name (Sartre).

the argument yours and yours alone. Editors or tutors should not mark up or provide feedback for more than 10 per cent of your essay. There is an easy solution to this problem: do the work yourself. Get help if you need it, but maintain control of your ideas and your arguments. The final decision must be yours.

IDENTIFYING ACCIDENTAL PLAGIARISM

Exercise 10.7

Read the following examples of accidental plagiarism. Can you identify the problem in each of the passages and, more important, can you see how it might be fixed?

> M. Barker argues that we can understand comic books in terms of a contract between the reader and the text. The meaning of the text arises out of a social relationship the reader has with popular culture, and it is through this relationship that ideology is established.

Continued

See Exercise Answer Key in Appendix A for an analysis of this passage.

This conventional conception of "costs" is a result of our capitalist and materialist mentality, which Noam Chomsky (1999) describes as letting markets set [the] price and encouraging the government [to] get out of the way (p. 20). It is through these capitalist interpretations that we understand the implied meaning of the documented expenditures, such as "$18.1 billion [or] $1,500 for every household."

Paraphrasing presents a particular problem for plagiarism, mainly because it demands carefully translating the material into your own words. Only paraphrase if

- you need to translate technical material into simple language for lay people; or
- you need to translate a poem or a difficult concept into simple language so that your reader can understand any ambiguity that might arise in the text.

When paraphrasing, you thus need to be vigilant about accurately documenting small phrases or larger passages of the original source. Keep in mind, too, that when paraphrasing you *must* acknowledge the original source.

ACADEMIC FOCUS

CHECKLIST FOR AVOIDING PLAGIARISM

- Have you noted which words are yours, which words are common knowledge, and which words belong to someone else? The words that belong to someone else must be acknowledged in a citation both in the body of your paper and at the end in a works cited or references page.
- Have you carefully documented all of your quotations?
- Have you connected the right page numbers and sources to your quotations?
- Have you accurately cited all the *ideas* of someone else, whether they are summarized or paraphrased?
- Have you cited information you obtained from the Internet?
- Does your works cited or reference list include all the sources you used in your paper?

N.B. Keep your drafts: if there is evidence of plagiarism, you will be required to submit drafts/working copies that clearly indicate the stages of the work in question.

Sample Research Paper

What follows is a student research paper, the finished product of the research process. The essay is written in response to Joe Sheridan's "The Silence before Drowning in Alphabet Soup," (see page 432 in the Reader).

Read Sheridan's paper, then read the student paper below. Pay attention to how it engages with Sheridan's paper, presenting an original argument and successfully using secondary sources.

(Mis)Understanding Literate Culture: An Analysis of Joe Sheridan's "The Silence before Drowning in Alphabet Soup"

BY TYRELL DASILVA

1   In Joe Sheridan's work "The Silence before Drowning in Alphabet Soup," a metaphor of silence is used to describe the way in which oral and literate cultures understand nature, and thus reality (Sheridan 24). For Sheridan, both literate and oral culture understands nature and reality through a default to their respective literate or oral definition and interpretation of silence or sound. Sheridan believes that alphabetization (literate definition) cannot truly interpret nature because it is unable to represent silence or the unsayable (24). In stating this, Sheridan negates the literate definition of reality and describes the affects of literacy on orality as negative (31) without fully considering the role that orality and silence play in today's culture. It is not the case that silence is the key to understanding nature or saving oral tradition, but that sound-based literate invention (secondary orality) is an innovation with the same final cause, a cause aimed at developing characteristic understandings of nature and sensual experience, which is esteemed within oral culture (25).

2   The concepts of oral practice (speech), and oral values (sensation), are still regarded highly in contemporary literate culture[1] and are practiced in a number of mediums. Within these mediums, all of which have roots in radio broadcasting, silence/sound can be reconciled with contemporary literate values, and still impose the contemplative, qualitative moods that Sheridan believes literate culture is lacking (30).

3   Walter J. Ong recognized that oral practice and values have not been abandoned by literal culture but have been incorporated into it and still exist today. Sound, or an absence of it for that matter, is still representable through electronic media and has given way to a new form of orality, "which Ong has styled the world of 'Secondary Orality'" (Ong qtd in: Weeks and Hoogestratt 14). Secondary orality is the development and incorporation of oral values like sound sensation within literate culture. This incorporation was arguably made most easily with the invention of the broadcast radio and advanced later with personal music players and other devices. These devices allowed oral

---

1   Contemporary literate culture refers to technology based, or electronic media culture (i.e. television, radio, internet.)

Good title: goes from general to specific.

Good opening sentence: focused summary of Sheridan's essay.

Concise summary of the essay.

Tyrell takes issue with Sheridan's argument and presents his own thesis.

Tyrell's thesis: radio broadcasting can create silence and contemplation.

Good evidence and support for his argument (Walter Ong).

Definition of Ong's concept of secondary orality: a key term for Tyrell's paper.

expression and practice to develop within literate culture. Much like primary orality was an antecedent to writing, secondary orality and its consequences[2] are antecedent to an entirely new form of communication and oral practice within literate communities (Weeks 14–15).

4   With the invention of the radio, and development of a mediated oral experience, the incorporation of "oral tradition" within literate culture had been discovered, creating the potential for new paths of communication. As John Foley asserts in his work, "The bards audience is always more than fiction.... The reality of the situation, as derived from evidence submitted from societies worldwide, is that oral traditions are often practised by functionally literate people who somehow can manage a variety of verbal actions" (96). This discovery shows two things: The first being that literate individuals practice oral traditions, and the second being that literate individuals are diverse in their practices of these traditions and thus develop new forms of communication. Marshall McLuhan echoes this sentiment when stating his belief that radio, "could not possibly have failed to provide some new shapes for human experience" (257).

5   By utilizing diverse forms of communication, and specifically the radio, literate culture reconciled the connectivity of sensual experience, that for Sheridan is lacking within literate tradition. The role of silence/sound,[3] and the seemingly tribal-like sensual experiences it brings about are brought to light in Marshal McLuhan's work "Understanding Radio." McLuhan recognizes that radio strikes home to many of the same forgotten, and often sensual and thus personal, experiences (258), which Sheridan posits only orality provides (28). For McLuhan, radio "comes to us ostensibly with person-to-person directness that is private and intimate, while in more urgent fact, it is really a subliminal echo-chamber of the magical power to touch remote and forgotten chords" (258).

6   It is not surprising that McLuhan uses a sound-based metaphor to discuss direct personal experience. Much like for Sheridan, the importance placed on sound, and therefore its converse silence, is extremely evident. Similar to Sheridan, McLuhan understands that personally felt characteristic feelings of experience are based in the sensual realm of sound, as opposed to sight: "The ear is intolerant, closed, and exclusive, whereas the eye is open, neutral, and associative" (257). McLuhan shows that this auditory experience can invoke either tribal feelings, and/or lead us to seclude ourselves (31).[4]

---

2 The consequences of secondary orality refer to contemporary uses of radio or radio derivatives. These include iPods, podcasts, broadcast radio (CBC), and any other form of mass media accessible because of the popularity of radio.

3 Because silence and sound are conversely related, each is considered equally causal within oral tradition. Silence or sounds can both produce resonant or quale-like feelings.

4 Tribal feelings include the inspiration that human voice can bestow in a group of people. And seclusion in this regard refers to experiencing a specific personal auditory experience (radio), in the absence of all other sounds.

Margin annotations:

Good use of evidence here. Please note that Tyrell uses a good combination of direct quotes and summary.

Very good paragraph transition. Tyrell picks up on his previous point about communication and then develops his ideas by introducing sensual experience. He brings us back to Sheridan, diverging from his ideas. His argument here, which uses McLuhan's theories about radio communication, successfully challenges Sheridan's point about sensual experience and the negation of literate culture.

Good use of evidence (McLuhan) not only to confirm Sheridan's argument, but also to diverge from it in terms of radio communication.

Consider Tyrell's use of footnotes to expand on points that do not fit logically into the main argument.

7   This concept of a secluded individual ties into the metaphor of sound. An individual listening to the radio in isolation "shhim listening to the radio" is exposed to the dramatic pauses and changes in tone that a speaker uses. The absence of words or emphasis of words at key moments can develop a richer sense of experience. As William Stott states in his piece "Documenting Media," "All that the speaker left unspoken—found unspeakable—testified to the reality of his experience" (249). With an enriched experience, talented orators can affect large numbers of people by making each person feel individuated from the rest, as though it were face to face. When the listeners pictures themselves within the speaker's situation, while feeling as though the situation is unique to them, the listener is left with a characteristic feeling and understanding of what the speaker is saying (248).

> Tyrell further develops his argument using evidence from William Stott's work.

8   For McLuhan these characteristic feelings of silence, or resonance,[5] are tied closely to oral traditions and their value of sensual experience. In McLuhan's view, the ability to influence many people through the use of speech may be positive or negative. Sheridan believes that the affects of literacy are always negative and would agree with the position that McLuhan takes regarding evil. However, McLuhan shows that radio can be used for evil,[6] or it can be used for good. In the latter sense, McLuhan believes that radio is a way of maintaining oral traditions within literate culture: "the Israeli present an even more extreme stance of linguistic revival. They now speak a language that has been dead in books for centuries" (31). McLuhan's view of the radio as a tool is one literate culture should support, but only if this tool can yield characteristic understandings of experience and a true interpretation of reality.

> Good development here: Tyrell engages with Sheridan's argument while reinforcing his own argument about radio.

> The concept of "evil" is unclear; additionally, the reader is not clear about why the "Israeli" experience is introduced. This is a good example of a non sequitur.

9   Although it seems apparent at this point that Sheridan did not consider radio's ability and therefore literate culture's ability,[7] to develop new and exciting ways of incorporating oral values and traditions in contemporary culture. The issue still lies as to whether or not radio has the ability to truly embody the characteristic feelings actual face-to-face orality inspire. It would seem from Stott's view that the unspeakable is easily conveyed through radio, For McLuhan, however, it is the imagination of the listener that breeds this feeling: "all those gestural qualities that the printed page strips from language come back in the dark, and on the radio. Given only the 'sound' of a play, we have to fill in all the senses" (259). This point demonstrates a fact that Sheridan leaves out of his work: The fact that within an oral experience, primary or not, the

> This section functions as a summary of the argument thus far.

---

5 Resonance is used as a synonym for the affect silence or sound can have on an individual, a sort of "silent resonance": I sat there silently considering the gravity of the situation.

6 McLuhan uses Hitler and his successful radio propaganda methods on a German audience that was oral based to show evil. Using Plato's political dream (best leader is one everyone can hear), Nazi politics are used as an example of the negative consequences of radio.

7 Radio was developed through contextualized knowledge and without literate knowledge would not have been possible (Weeks & Hoogestratt).

onus is placed on the listener to develop their own picture of the scenario. The speaker may use silence or sound to help facilitate this feeling of experience; however, without a rich imagination words can fall on deaf ears.

10   If individuals within literate culture can use their silent and personal imagination, in combination with tools that yield a felt sensual experience, the reconciliation of oral tradition and values will not be hard. Nor will the revival of traditions that have been lost or the development of new oral traditions.[8] In terms of silence and the unsayable, Sheridan was wrong to assume literate culture will forget or abandon its oral heritage. In fact, with the invention of podcasts and other high streaming instant audio, the individuated experience of oral tradition is becoming even more "felt."

11   Literate individual's now have the ability to access specific broadcasts on any subject that appeals to their values and beliefs or to pick and choose orators who truly inspire them, or inspire a qualitative feeling. Internet radio and audio books are becoming increasingly more popular, and they are an excellent example of literate culture attempting to stay grounded in its oral history. It may be shown that literate culture has developed the ability to incorporate oral values, but those supporting an oral tradition, such as Sheridan, will argue that orality is based off a face-to-face contact and the experience of hearing the tale from the person who was in the situation.

12   However, if oral tradition or primary orality is based primarily in the realm of hearing the story first hand and visual knowledge is not a necessary condition to gain a characteristic understanding, then radio can achieve the same ends storytelling can. By using sound/silence, the speaker can help the literate listener connect with the material. By invoking the human imagination, self-perception and self-awareness, a talented radio broadcaster can insight deeply felt sensations and a true characteristic understanding of silence/sound, and its place in the world.

13   With new developments in "Secondary orality" and the way in which it is practiced, the question will not be whether or not literate culture can simulate or incorporate oral tradition and value, but if their simulation of orality is superior. It has been shown that the aesthetic or sensual experience of sound can be induced within literate practice; however, this often originates from written words.

14   Radio broadcasters as speakers within secondary orality are different from those speakers within primary orality. Radio people are often reading the ideas they have written, or ideas that have been written for them, and therefore any radio of this form comes from a silent source. Primary oralists differ in their expression from secondary oralists because they are reciting actual experience or knowledge gained directly through orality. This is not to say a radio broadcaster cannot reach his or her literate audience unless he or she was

---

8 An example of a new oral tradition would be cell or telephone etiquette and practice.

Tyrell exposes the gap in Sheridan's argument: the work that the imagination does.

Good analysis and objective tone.

Tyrell moves from abstractions to concrete evidence.

Good consideration of Sheridan's position here, which provides a counter-argument that Tyrell will now have to refute.

Tyrell's refutation that radio broadcasting can achieve the same ends by stimulating the listener's imagination.

Good reflective argument.

truly there in the midst of the situation, but shows that the experience is richer when he or she is.

15   It seems than that silence and sound are essential in order to gain a true characteristic understanding or felt sensation of reality. Sheridan assumed incorrectly that literate culture would desert its oral influenced values of sensation, and it is apparent at this point that these values (silence and sound) are still extremely influential on how we think and what we think about. Radio opened the door to entirely new forms of orality, and it achieved this by appealing directly to literate culture's ancestral, tribal, and oral history.

> Good conclusion: Tyrell reinforces his argument.

WORKS CITED

Weeks and Hoogestratt. "Introduction." *Time, Memory, and the Verbal Arts.* Editor: Dennis Weeks, Jane Hoogestraat London: Associated University Presses, 1998. 14–16. Print.

Foley, John. "The Bard's Audience is always More than Fiction." *Time, Memory, and the Verbal Arts.* Editor: Dennis Weeks, Jane Hoogestraat London: Associated University Presses, 1998. 94–7. Print.

McLuhan, Marshall. "Understanding Radio." *Communication in History.* Editor: David Crowley, Paul Heyer. New York: Longman, 1996. 256–9. Print.

Stott, William. "Documenting Media." *Communication in history.* Editor: David Crowley, Paul Heyer, New York: Longman, 1996. 247–50. Print.

Sheridan, Joe. "Silence before drowning in Alphabet Soup." *Canadian Journal of Native Education, 18 (1),* 1991. 23–31. Print.

> Tyrell correctly uses MLA citation.

General comment: DaSilva's essay is an excellent example of student writing. DaSilva effectively engages with and critiques Sheridan's argument while keeping an objective and measured tone. His argument effectively exposes a knowledge gap, which he effectively develops through analysis and relevant, contextualized research into an original and substantial argument. DaSilva's essay was awarded best student essay in the University of Lethbridge's academic writing competition in 2009.

CHAPTER SUMMARY

This chapter has introduced you to research reading and writing. The difference between expository or report writing and research writing has been explained and a process has been provided to help you find a topic, a research question, and a working thesis statement. The chapter also explained the difference between primary and secondary texts in the humanities, the social sciences, and sciences, and the difference between academic and non-academic research. You should now have a good understanding of how to locate and evaluate research sources in the library and how you might use some of the strategies outlined in this chapter for evaluating and using these sources. You should also have a clear idea of what constitutes plagiarism and how to avoid it in your writing assignments. The annotated student research essay should help you to recognize what constitutes a good student research paper and assess and understand what you need to do in your own research writing assignments.

As a final note, when writing a research essay, you will need to make sure you have a plan and a realistic schedule that will allow you time to find and incorporate your research material into a well-written and revised paper. Allow yourself time to

- find your topic and thesis;
- gather and evaluate your research;
- take notes;
- outline and draft your paper, using some of the strategies listed in this chapter;
- synthesize your secondary sources; and
- revise your essay at the level of content, organization, and style, including proofreading for grammar and citation errors.

QUESTIONS FOR CONSIDERATION

1. If I could reduce this chapter to three significant points that I need to remember about research writing, what would they be?
2. Is the research essay process outlined in this chapter clear to me? Can I use it to write a research essay?
3. What is the difference between academic and non-academic research? When and how would I use each?
4. Which evaluation strategy do I think would be most useful?
5. Do I understand the difference between primary and secondary texts and how to use them in different disciplines and in different essays?
6. Do I understand why citation is important and why plagiarism must be avoided at all costs?
7. What do I still need to know about research writing?

Documentation Style

LEARNING OBJECTIVES

In this chapter, you will learn:

◆ Why citation is crucial to academic writing.

◆ How to avoid plagiarism.

◆ How to cite using MLA citation methods.

◆ How to cite using APA citation methods.

Citation, documenting your sources, is a crucial component of academic writing. When you acknowledge someone else's ideas or words, you are demonstrating honesty, giving credit where it is due. You are allowing others to be responsible for their own knowledge-making activities and you are taking responsibility for your own engagement with the knowledge base related to your research area. In this way, you are participating in the conversations of a community of scholars. You acknowledge the work of others, engage critically with their work, and either add to or take issue with their ideas. While first-year students often express frustration with the numerous citation rules, their vigilance will not only help them become better, more professional, writers and scholars, it will also help them to be better able to engage critically with the ideas of others. Understanding citation will also help students avoid a charge of plagiarism.

Plagiarism

As stated in chapter 10, plagiarism is the unacknowledged use of someone else's intellectual work. This might involve intentionally or accidentally representing the words, ideas, phrases, sentences, arguments, summaries, paraphrases, or direct quotes of another as if they are your own. Plagiarism is a serious academic offence and might result in a failure on the assignment or the course, or expulsion from the college or university.

To avoid a charge of either intentional or accidental plagiarism you need to be diligent: you must clearly and accurately state and mark all sources that are distinct from your own work in every assignment you submit. Accidental plagiarism usually occurs when students do not understand the cultural conventions and citation methods of academic writing. The first convention is based on the idea that intellectual ideas and expressions can be owned. To copy these ideas or words without acknowledging them is tantamount to stealing. The second convention is an acknowledgement that writing is a concrete representation of a writer's intellectual skill. To misrepresent your knowledge and accomplishments in this respect is tantamount to fraud or cheating. Knowing the steps that can be taken to avoid plagiarizing other people's texts or words is important, so take some time to read the more complete explication of plagiarism in chapter 10. Also keep the following rules in mind:

1. When quoting a source, copy the words exactly as they appear in the original. If a change has to be made, it must be contained in square brackets (e.g., "she [went] to the store").
2. When dealing with difficult concepts or ideas be vigilant about quoting even short phrases that are not your own.
3. If an idea is not common knowledge, cite it.
4. When in doubt, cite your source. That will show your credibility and skill as an academic.
5. Document your sources as you take notes, but leave yourself enough time before your paper has to be handed in to document your sources accurately. Citing your sources, particularly when learning the conventions of a citation method, takes a considerable amount of time. Plan for it!

Citation Methods

Because academic writing requires that you document all secondary sources, there are several different citation systems in place to help you cite other people's ideas and quotations effectively and accurately. In this chapter, I present both the Modern Language Association (MLA) and the American Psychological Association's (APA) documentation style format in detail, explaining which disciplines use a particular citation method and illustrating the reasoning behind the particular form of citation. You will need to refer to the particular citation method required by your academic discipline or course requirement as you write and edit your essays. Use the templates of specific citations and the sample annotated essays in this chapter as models to help you with this requirement.

MLA Citation Style

Modern Language Association (MLA) style is typically reserved for writers and students preparing manuscripts in various humanities disciplines such as:

- English studies—language and literature
- foreign language and literature
- literary criticism
- comparative literature
- cultural studies
- philosophy
- religion
- business

The style guidelines set out by MLA provide students and professional scholars with a method of citing their sources so that they can

- provide evidence of their accountability;
- engage with other scholars who are conversant in the same areas of research;
- avoid any possible charges of plagiarism, which is the intended or accidental undocumented use of someone else's research.

These guidelines will cover MLA citation style as laid out in the seventh edition of the *MLA Handbook for Writers of Research Papers* and the third edition of the *MLA Style Manual and Guide to Scholarly Publishing*. First, I will provide an overview of the general formatting expectations for papers and then provide you with in-text and bibliographical citations, which in MLA format appears in the form of a Works Cited page that is included as a separate page at the end of your essay. I will then provide you with a student essay written in MLA format style.

MLA Formatting Guidelines

Students should observe the following criteria of format and usage in formal writing assignments. Remember that citation is required in colleges and universities. Disregarding these standards will result in a lowered or a failing grade; attention to them will count toward the grade awarded.

Manuscript

1. Type and double-spaced on standard-size white paper (8 1/2 × 11 inches). Type on one side of the page only.
2. Use black ink, Times New Roman (preferable) 12-point font, double space.
3. Set page margins at 1 inch on all sides.

4. Leave one space after periods and other punctuation marks.

5. Indent the first line of paragraphs 1/2 inch from the left margin (use the TAB key).

6. Do not leave extra spaces between paragraphs.

7. Use italics when citing the titles of books or plays (e.g., *Bleak House*) and quotation marks for smaller works, such as short stories, poems, and articles (e.g., "Jabberwocky").

8. Fasten the pages together with either a paper clip or a staple (ask your instructor).

9. Do not number the title page (if asked to submit one) or the first page of your essay. Number the pages consecutively beginning with page 2 of your essay. The number should go in the top right-hand corner along with your last name. For example: Smith-2.

10. On the first page of your essay, put your name, your instructor's name, the course, and the date (double spaced). Under this, centred in the middle of the page, put the title of your essay. Do not underline it or place it in quotation marks. Use standard capitalization (capitalizing the first letter of the word) and if mentioning the work of someone else, italicize the titles of books and put short stories or articles in quotation marks. Here is a sample MLA format of a first page:

Jane Smith
Professor Sally Hayward
English 101

12 August 2015

Hockey, Violence, and Canada's National Identity

Although other nations view Canada as a
peace-keeping nation in international affairs
and conflicts, the game that represents Canada
is accepted as being "notoriously violent"
(Robidoux 220). Fist-fights, which are
considered criminal acts outside of the sport, are
a norm in the game of hockey, which is violent
by nature. These fist-fights hold a place within
hockey and have since its early development
(Robidoux 219), but recently an on-ice
altercation has led to the first recorded death of a
hockey player directly resulting from a fist-fight

Figure 11.1 ◆ The First Page of an MLA Paper

Some instructors might require a more formal title page. If this is the case, include a separate title page for your essay and centre the title on the page using Times New Roman 14-point (maximum) font and standard capitalization. Once again, do not underline, but you can bold the title if you wish. Put your name, your professor's name, the name of the course and the date you submit the paper in the bottom right-hand corner. Do not number this page. The following page has no title or page number. This is where you begin your essay. Begin paginating on the page after this (the second page of your essay). Put your last name and the page number in the top right-hand corner. From this point on the pages are numbered consecutively.

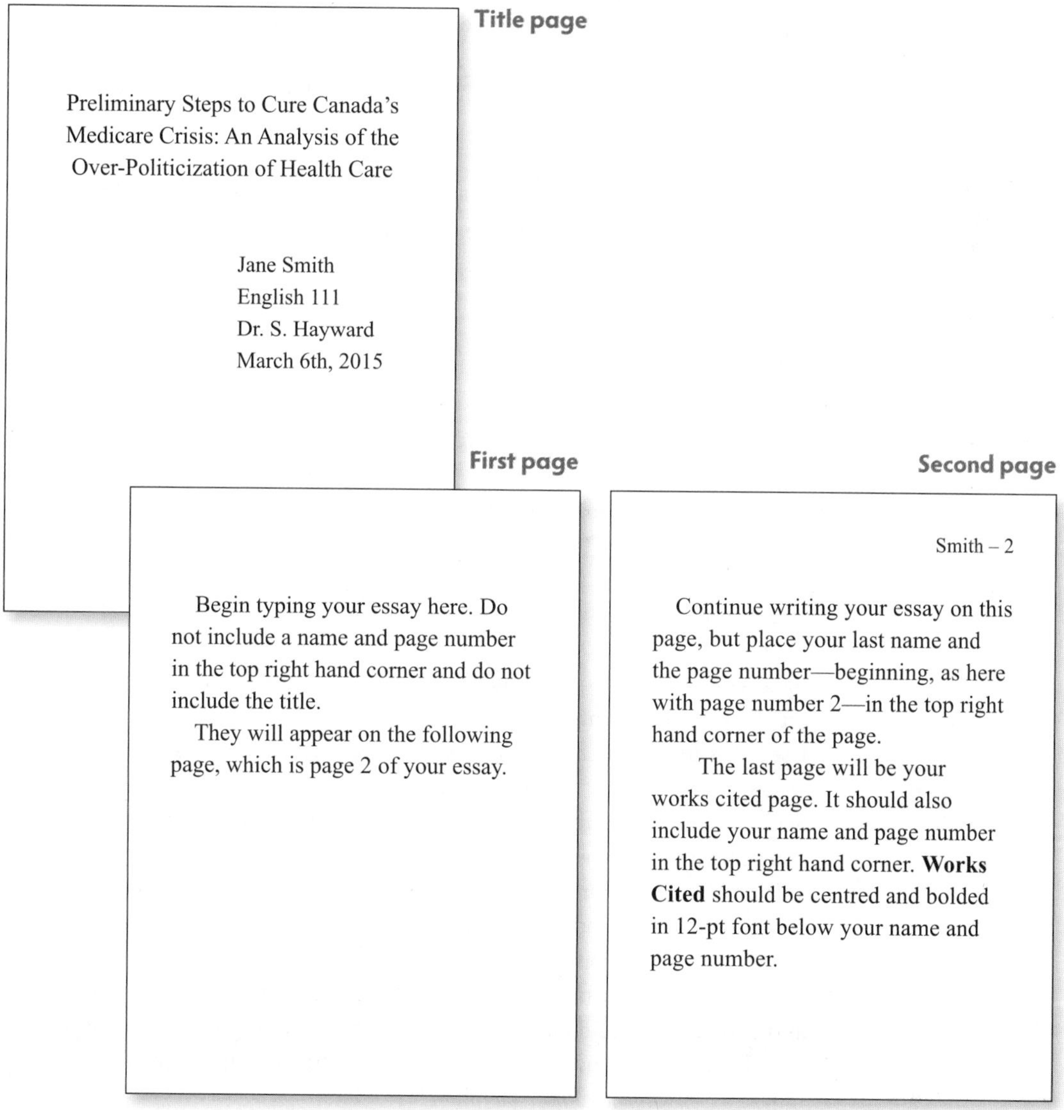

Title page

Preliminary Steps to Cure Canada's
Medicare Crisis: An Analysis of the
Over-Politicization of Health Care

Jane Smith
English 111
Dr. S. Hayward
March 6th, 2015

First page

Begin typing your essay here. Do not include a name and page number in the top right hand corner and do not include the title.

They will appear on the following page, which is page 2 of your essay.

Second page

Smith – 2

Continue writing your essay on this page, but place your last name and the page number—beginning, as here with page number 2—in the top right hand corner of the page.

The last page will be your works cited page. It should also include your name and page number in the top right hand corner. **Works Cited** should be centred and bolded in 12-pt font below your name and page number.

Figure 11.2 ◆ MLA Formatting with Title Page

Section Headings

MLA allows you to use section headings. These sections are used to improve the readability of your paper because they function as a logical outline of your paper. MLA recommends, but does not require, numbering your section headings. The introduction may or may not be included in these section headings. Make sure, however, that the section headings maintain an academic tone, are logical, and approximately of the same length and grammatical structure. Here is an example of section headings related to the title "Hockey, Violence, and Canada's National Identity":

1. The debate about hockey and violence
2. The Don Sanderson case: The place of fighting in hockey
3. Hockey and violence: A masculine stereotype?
4. Canada's national identity: Hyper-masculine and violent?

Conventions and Usage

When using MLA citation, you must cite or document any sources you have consulted, even if you presented the ideas from these sources in your own words. You need to cite to

- identify other people's ideas and information used in your essay;
- inform the reader of your paper where to look if they want to find the same sources.

A citation must appear in two places in your essay:

- in the body of your text (parenthetical or "in-text citations");
- in the works cited list (at the end of your paper).

Here are some additional conventions:

1. Italicize titles of books and plays and put titles of short stories, poems, and articles in quotation marks.
2. Use italics to emphasize a certain word. However, do *not* overuse italics in this way.
3. Spell out numbers consisting of one or two words, such as "four hundred." If you begin a sentence with a number, spell it out, even if it is a long number or a date. When using large numbers in the middle of a sentence, you can use a combination of numerals and words, such as "5.2 million." Spell out spans of time, such as "twentieth century."
4. Use hyphens (-) to form compound words when these words function together as an adjective to a noun. For example, the phrase *well known* does not need a hyphen, but when used together as one idea that modifies a noun, as in the phrase a *well-known author*, a hyphen is needed.

5. Use footnotes for explanatory or digressive information that does not belong in the main body of the paper. Footnotes are indicated by superscript Arabic numbers in the text itself, along with a corresponding reference at the foot of the page.

6. Do *not* use contractions, such as "don't" for "do not," and do not use abbreviations, such as "i.e.," "etc.," and "e.g."

7. Students are expected to be able to spell correctly. No student, for example, should have to be reminded of the difference between the possessive pronoun "its" and the contraction "it's" (for it is). Use the spell check on your computer, but note that the spell check will not pick up everything.

8. Be careful about punctuation, grammar, and structure. The quality of your essay depends not only upon the content but also on the form that you use to convey the content. Use the grammar check; it is particularly useful for highlighting the use of passive voice.

9. Be specific; avoid wordy constructions, and remember that clarity is the key.

To introduce other people's ideas in the text, use reporting expressions (sometimes called *signal phrases* because they signal the upcoming citation (see chapter 2)). Reporting expressions generally include the author's name (or pronoun) and an academic verb. Consider the following examples:

Richardson argues, refers to, explains, hypothesizes, compares, concludes, . . . etc.

As Littlewood and Sherwin demonstrated, proved, . . . etc.

Punctuation

Brackets: Use brackets to enclose words you insert into quotations. When you use quotations, you may have to change the form of a word or two to make the quotations fit the structure and grammar of your sentence.

Shuter reported "this trend [is] almost reversed in Italy" (305).

Ellipsis: Used to indicate a gap or an omission from a quotation. It consists of three spaced periods with a space on either end. Normal punctuation is used before an ellipsis. If you need to change a capital letter, put it in square brackets, as indicated below.

Although Paul Hewson argues that "Big Rock [beer] tastes fresh and crisp, . . . [s]atisfying Canadian beer-drinkers is always a challenge" (30).

Single quotation marks: When quoting someone else inside a quotation, put the quoted material in single quotation marks. In the example below the quote is taken from Robson, who quotes a line from Roch Carrier's story "The Hockey Sweater."

"The Hockey Sweater" tells the story of a boy who grows up idolizing professional hockey players, with dreams of playing in the National Hockey League himself one day. As Robson points out, "[m]uch of the story emphasizes the fascination and obsession that Canadians have with the game of hockey as the fictional protagonist narrates that '[t]he winters of my childhood were long, long seasons'" (64).

Parenthetical (in-text) Citations

You must include a citation in the body of your essay, when you cite or refer to a concept from a work. A citation looks like this: (author's last name or short title plus page #). Do not put a comma between the author's last name or your shortened version of the title and the page number: (Jones 8). Punctuation marks—commas, semicolons, colons, and periods—go after the parenthesis, but punctuation marks in a direct quote remain in the quotation. For example, a typical citation might look like this:

> In his ground-breaking book *Imagined Communities*, Benedict Anderson argues that the nation is "an imagined political community" (6).

Note that the book title is italicized and the page number follows at the end of the sentence after the direct quote to which the reference (6) refers.

Here are some more specific citation examples, beginning, like the example above, with a template for the citation format when the author is included in the body of the sentence. In-text citations look like this (citation underlined):

Author in Body of Sentence

> In *The History of Sexuality*, Michel Foucault argues that we have become a confessing society, compelled to confess our crimes sins, desires, illnesses, and sex lives (97).

The title of the book is italicized and the name of the author is named in full in the sentence the first time he or she is mentioned. The second time the author is mentioned, only use the last name (Foucault, in this case). The page number is included in parenthesis, with the period after the parenthesis.

Author Not in the Body of the Sentence

> He argues that we have become a confessing society (Foucault 97).

Try to include the citation in a way that will interfere the least with the flow of your sentence, such as immediately after the quotation, at the end of the sentence, or at the end of a clause (i.e., before a colon, semicolon, or possibly a comma).

After this scene, "Walsh felt angry and hurt" (Jones 319), but he refused to let anyone know.

After this scene, "Walsh felt angry and hurt," but he refused to let anyone know (Jones 319).

Page Numbers Are Cited for All MLA Citations

These include direct quotes, summaries, and paraphrases.

To scrutinize the safety of aspartame even further, it is important to look at the chemicals that together constitute aspartame (Naudé 454). Phenylalanine, which makes up "fifty percent of aspartame, [is] a known amino acid isolate" (455).

Consecutive Quotations by the Same Author

These require only page numbers (follows from Naudé example above).

Occurring naturally in the body, aspartame also plays an important role in amino acid metabolism, protein structuring and neurotransmitter regulation (455).

However, if the citation of another author interrupts the flow, you must clearly cite the author to whom the quote or summary belongs:

This limits "the amount of important amino acids entering the brain" (Naudé 455) and compromises dopamine production, . . . resulting in a lower concentration of dopamine. This lowering of dopamine concentration affects normal motor behaviour and may lead to "dyskinesia, dystonia, tics, obsessive–compulsive disorders and abnormal eye movements" (Herlenius and Langercrantz 64) and may be related to Parkinson's disease (Naudé 458). Consequently, excessive consumption of phenylalanine inhibits other important amino acids from reaching the brain, causing permanent damage to the body (458).

Citing Multiple Works by the Same Author

The following example shows a book reference followed by an essay:

Michel Foucault argues that confession was used in the eighteenth century to persuade individuals to "confess their sins" (History of Sexuality 97) so that the church could direct and control an individual's and, hence, a community's conscience ("Confession of the Flesh" 216).

Anonymous Author

If "Anonymous" is specified by the author, treat it as if it were a real name.

(Anonymous 67)

Direct Quotations of More Than Five Lines

Block indent the left-hand margin, omit the quotation marks, and reverse the punctuation at the end of the quotation (instead of putting the period on the right-hand side of the parenthesis, put it on the left-hand side):

> At this point, the themes under analysis become rich and complex. While the motivation for a reader to insert his or her own life material into the text is strong, the closeness of the critical reader is, I suggest, ideally a position where the context of the work itself and the social/material conditions is comes from, is of the primary focus. (Jones 219)

Citing Indirect Sources

When citing someone who is citing someone else, you must acknowledge the original citation. In the first example below, Samuel Johnson is the author who cited Boswell. MLA uses *qtd in* and the page number to acknowledge the secondary source. If there is no person named in the sentence, you must include the author in the parenthetical citation, in this case, Johnson.

> Samuel Johnson admitted that Burke was an "extraordinary man" (qtd in Boswell 45).

> He admitted that Burke was an "extraordinary man" (Johnson qtd in Boswell 45).

Citing Multiple Sources in the Same Parenthetical Reference

Use this format to identify multiple reference sources. Separate the citations by a semicolon, as in the example below:

> . . . as has been discussed elsewhere (Burke 3; Dewey 21).

Citing a Work by Multiple Authors: Three or Fewer Authors

Use this format to identify a work that is written by more than one person. In the body of the text, you must type out "and" rather than using an ampersand. Note the use of commas in the example below.

> They argue that advertising is a form of social control, designed to deflect attention (Johannason, Smith, and Jones 345).

Citing a Source with Three or More Authors

Et al. means "and others." Note that there is no punctuation after "et."

> Brayford, Latimer's lawyer deliberately courted the press (Janz et al. 5).

Use Line Numbers for Poems

In Cherry's poem, "Alzheimer's," the "crazy old man" has lucid moments (1), when he remembers "himself" as he was, "a younger man, . . . who loved music" (18–20).

Citing the Bible

Include the version of Bible, book (can be abbreviated, as in Ezek. for Ezekiel), chapter, and verse.

After sinning, "the eyes of them both were opened, and they knew that they *were* naked" (*King James Bible Online*, Genesis 3:7).

Works Cited

At the end of your paper, you must include an attached sheet with the words *Works Cited* centred at the top of the page. Each work that you cite in the paper should directly correspond to the citation in the works cited page. The list should be in alphabetical order by the primary author's last name, or the title if an author is not listed. Double space and indent each line by one inch after the first line of the citation. Use the following citations as templates. Observe how punctuation is used in your citations and follow this use strictly.

Basic Book Citation

Author's last name, First name. *Book Title*. City where published: Publishing company, year of publication. Publishing format (print, in this case).

Jones, Bridgett. *Mis-spent Ink; or, Writing Without Using Real Words*. Toronto: Penguin Canada, 2001. Print.

Book chapter: Author's last name, First name. "Article Title." *Book Title*. Editors' names, first then last names. Publication city: Publishing company, year of publication. Page range. Format.

Fish, Stanley. "Is There a Text in This Class?" *Critical Theory Since 1965*. Eds. Hazard Adams and Leroy Searle. Tallahassee: Florida State University Press, 1986. 524–33. Print.

Work in an Anthology

Author's last name, First name. "Title of Article or Poem." *Title of Anthology*. Edition. Editors' first, then last names. Publishing city or cities: Publishing company, year of publication. Page range. Format.

Poe, Edgar Allen. "The Raven." *Norton Anthology of Literature*. 9th ed. Ed. Alison Booth, J. Paul Hunter, and Kelly J. Mays. New York and London: W.W. Norton, 2005. 982–84. Print.

Article in a Journal

Author's last name, first name. "Essay Title." *Journal Title*. Volume.Issue number. (year of publication): page range. Format.

> Sheridan, Joe. "The Silence before Drowning in Alphabet Soup." *Canadian Journal of Native Education*. 18.1. (1991): 23–31. Print.

> Whitford, Andrew B, and Yates, Jeff. "Policy Signals and Executive Governance: Presidential Rhetoric in the 'War on Drugs.'" *The Journal of Politics*. 65.4. (Nov. 2003): 995–1012. Print.

Government Publication

Author or commissioning agency. *Title*. Publishing city: Agency, year. page range. Format.

> United Nations, Centre on Transnational Corporations. *Foreign Direct Investment, the Service Sector, and International Banking*. New York: United Nations, 1987. 4–6. Print.

Magazine

Author's last name, first name. "Title of Article." *Title of Magazine* Month and year of publication: page range. Format.

> Harrison, T. "Domestic Violence." *Psychology Today* Dec. 1993: 48–9. Print.

The Bible

Provide the name of the edition you are using, along with any editors, and publication information. Format (e.g., Print).

> *The Holy Bible: King James Version*. London and New York: Collins Press, 1923. Print.

A Lecture, a Speech, or an Address

Speaker's last name, first name. "Title of the presentation." The meeting. The sponsoring organization (if known). The location. The date. Format.

> Atwood, Margaret. "Silencing the Scream." Boundaries of the Imagination Forum. MLA Convention. Royal York Hotel, Toronto. 29 Dec. 1993. Presentation.

> Hyman, Earle. Reading of Shakespeare's *Othello*. Symphony Space, New York. 28 Mar. 1994. Presentation.

Online Sources

MLA lists electronic sources as Web Publications. Thus, when including the medium of publication for electronic sources, list the format as Web.

Abbreviations Commonly Used with Electronic Sources

Use *n.p.* (no publisher) to indicate that neither a publisher nor a sponsor name has been provided. Use *n.d.* (no date) when the Web page does not provide a publication date.

When an entry requires that you provide a page but no pages are provided in the source (as in the case of an online-only scholarly journal or a work that appears in an online-only anthology), use the abbreviation *n. pag.*

Basic Style for Citations of Electronic Sources (Including Online Databases)

Here are some common features you should try to find before citing electronic sources in MLA style. Not every Web page will provide all of the following information. However, collect as much of the following information as possible both for your citations and for your research notes:

- Author and/or editor names (if available)
- Article name in quotation marks (if applicable)
- Title of the website, project, or book in italics. (Remember that some print publications have Web publications with slightly different names. For example, they may include the additional information or otherwise modified information, such as domain names [e.g., .com or .net].)
- Any version numbers available, including revisions, posting dates, volumes, or issue numbers
- Publisher information, including the publisher name and publishing date
- Page numbers (if available)
- Medium of publication
- Date you accessed the material
- URL (if required, or for your own reference)

ACADEMIC FOCUS

IMPORTANT NOTE ON THE USE OF URLS IN MLA

MLA no longer requires the use of URLs in MLA citations. Because Web addresses change often and because documents sometimes appear in multiple places on the Web (e.g., on multiple databases), MLA explains that most readers can find electronic sources via title or author searches in Internet search engines. *For instructors or editors who still wish to require the use of* URLs, MLA suggests that the URL appear in angle brackets (< >) after the date of access.

Aristotle. *Poetics.* Trans. S.H. Butcher. *The Internet Classics Archive.* Web Atomic and Massachusetts Institute of Technology, 13 Sept. 2007. Web. 4 Nov. 2008. <http://classics.mit.edu/>.

Article in an Online Scholarly Journal

MLA requires a page range for articles that appear in scholarly journals. If the journal you are citing appears exclusively in an online format (i.e., there is no corresponding print publication) that does not make use of page numbers, use the abbreviation *n. pag* to denote that there is no pagination for the publication.

> Dolby, Nadine. "Research in Youth Culture and Policy: Current Conditions and Future Directions." *Social Work and Society: The International Online-Only Journal* 6.2 (2008): n. pag. Web. 20 May 2009.

Article in an Online Scholarly Journal That Also Appears in Print

Cite articles in online scholarly journals that also appear in print as you would a scholarly journal in print, including the page range of the article. Provide the medium of publication that you used (in this case, *Web*) and the date of access.

> Wheelis, Mark. "Investigating Disease Outbreaks Under a Protocol to the Biological and Toxin Weapons Convention." *Emerging Infectious Diseases* 6.6 (2000): 595–600. Web. 8 Feb. 2010.

An Article from an Online Database (or Other Electronic Subscription Service)

Cite articles from online databases (e.g., LexisNexis, ProQuest, JSTOR, Science Direct) and other subscription services just as you would print sources. Since these articles usually come from periodicals, be sure to consult the appropriate Works Cited references. Also provide the title of the database (italicized), the medium of publication, and the date of access.

> Junge, Wolfgang, and Nathan Nelson. "Nature's Rotary Electromotors." *Science* 29 Apr. 2005: 642–4. *Science Online*. Web. 5 Mar. 2012.

> Langhamer, Claire. "Love and Courtship in Mid-Twentieth-Century England." *Historical Journal* 50.1 (2007): 173–96. *ProQuest*. Web. 27 May 2011.

An Article in a Web Magazine

Author last name, first name. "Article Name." *Title of Web Magazine*. Publisher name, publication date. Medium of publication. Access date.

Remember to use *n.p.* if no publisher name is available and *n.d.* if not publishing date is given.

> Bernstein, Mark. "10 Tips on Writing the Living Web." *A List Apart: For People Who Make Websites*. A List Apart Mag., 16 Aug. 2002. Web. 4 May 2009.

Email (Including Email Interviews)

Provide the author of the message, followed by the subject line in quotation marks. State to whom the message was sent, the date the message was sent, and the medium of publication.

Kunka, Andrew. "Re: Modernist Literature." Message to the author. 15 Nov. 2000.
Email.

Neyhart, David. "Re: Online Tutoring." Message to Joe Barbato. 1 Dec. 2000. Email.

Citing an Entire Website

Editor. Author or compiler name (if available). *Name of Site*. Version number. Name of
institution/organization affiliated with the site (sponsor or publisher), date of resource
creation (if available). Medium of publication. Date of access.

Felluga, Dino. *Guide to Literary and Critical Theory*. Purdue University, 28 Nov. 2003.
Web. 10 May 2006.

A Page on a Website

For an individual page on a website, list the author or alias, if known, followed by the
information covered above for entire websites.

"How to Make Vegetarian Chili." *eHow.com*. eHow, n.d. Web. 24 Feb. 2009.

A Listserv, Discussion Group, or Blog Posting

Cite Web postings as you would a standard Web entry:
Editor, screen name, author, or compiler name (if available). "Posting Title." *Name of Site*.
Version number (if available). Name of institution/organization affiliated with the site
(sponsor or publisher), date of resource creation. Medium of publication. Date of access.

Include screen names as author names when author name is not known. If both
names are known, place the author's name in brackets.

Salmar1515 [Sal Hernandez]. "Re: Best Strategy: Fenced Pastures vs. Max Number of
Rooms?" *BoardGameGeek*. BoardGameGeek, 29 Sept. 2008. Web. 5 Apr. 2009.

An Image (Including a Painting, Sculpture, or Photograph)

Artist's last name, First name. *Name of Work of Art*. date of creation. Institution, city
where the work is housed. *Name of the Website*. Medium of publication. Access date.

Goya, Francisco. *The Family of Charles IV*. 1800. Museo Nacional del Prado, Madrid.
Museo Nacional del Prado. Web. 22 May 2006.

Film

List films (in theatres or not yet on DVD or video) by their title. Include the name of the
director, the film studio or distributor, and the release year. If relevant, list performer
names after the director's name. Use the abbreviation *perf.* to head the list of performer
names. List film as the medium of publication.

The Usual Suspects. Dir. Bryan Singer. Perf. Kevin Spacey, Gabriel Byrne, Chazz
Palminteri, Stephen Baldwin, and Benicio del Toro. Polygram, 1995. Film.

To Emphasize Specific Performers (Perf.) or Directors (Dir.)

Begin the citation with the name of the desired performer or director, followed by the appropriate abbreviation.

> Lucas, George, dir. *Star Wars Episode IV: A New Hope*. Twentieth Century Fox, 1977. Film.

Broadcast Television or Radio Program

"Title of Episode (if any)." *Title of Program* or series. Name of network, Call numbers (if any), city of local station (if any), Broadcast date. Medium (e.g., *Television, Radio*). For television episodes on videocassette or DVD, refer to the "Recorded films or movies" section below.

> "The Blessing Way." *The X-Files*. Fox. WXIA, Atlanta, 19 Jul. 1998. Television.

> "The One about the Monkey." *Friends*. National Broadcasting Company. WOAI, San Antonio. 6 Feb. 2005. Television.

Recorded Films or Movies

List films by their title. Include the name of the director, the distributor, and the release year. If relevant, list performer names after the director's name. Use the abbreviation *perf.* to head the list. End the entry with the appropriate medium of publication (e.g., DVD, VHS, Laser disc).

> *Ed Wood*. Dir. Tim Burton. Perf. Johnny Depp, Martin Landau, Sarah Jessica Parker, Patricia Arquette. Touchstone, 1994. DVD.

Sound Recordings

List sound recordings so they can easily be found by readers. Generally, citations begin with the artist name. They might also be listed by composers (comp.) or performers (perf.). Otherwise, list composer and performer information after the album title.

Use the appropriate abbreviation after the person's name and a comma, when needed. Put individual song titles in quotation marks. Italicize album names. Provide the name of the recording manufacturer followed by the publication date (or *n.d.*, if date is unknown). List the appropriate medium at the end of the entry (e.g., CD, LP, audiocassette). For MP3 recordings, see the "Digital Files" section below.

Note: If you know the recording date and want to list it, include this information before the manufacturer name. Use the abbreviation for "recorded" (*Rec.*) and list the recording date (dd mm year format) before the manufacturer name.

> Foo Fighters. *In Your Honor*. RCA, 2005. CD.

> Nirvana. "Smells Like Teen Spirit." *Nevermind*. Geffen, 1991. Audiocassette.

An Advertisement in a Magazine

Name of product, company, or institution. Descriptive label. *Magazine.* Publication date: Page numbers. Medium.

Miller Genuine Draft. Advertisement. *GQ.* 4 May 2003: 112. Print.

An Advertisement on Television

Name of product, company, or institution. Descriptive label. Channel. Date. Medium.

Pringles Potato Chips. Advertisement. MTV. 19 Jan. 2005. Television.

A Map, Chart, or Place

Name of Map or Chart. Form of document. Location of publisher: Publisher, year. Medium.

Michigan. Map. Chicago: Rand, 2000. Print.

Edmonton River Valley Trail. Graffiti Railing. Edmonton: 2005. Print.

A Performance (Play, Opera, Ballet, Concert)

Title. By name of author/composer. Dir. Name of director. Perf. Names of performers. Name of theatre, City. Date. Medium.

Hamlet. By William Shakespeare. Dir. John Gielgud. Perf. Richard Burton. Schubert Theatre, Boston. 4 Mar. 1964. Performance.

Sample Essay Using MLA Style

What follows is an annotated sample student essay using MLA citation format. This essay is an example of a reading of a video commercial. The student writer, Jenny Byford, examines the Conservative party video commercial *Our Country* in an effort to consider how the video either ignores or misrepresents health-related issues pertinent to all Canadians.

When reading this essay, ask

- How does this writer introduce her primary text?
- How does she engage consistently with the primary text throughout her entire essay?
- How does she use reporting expressions to introduce both her direct quotes and summaries?
- How does she use MLA citation: parenthetical and bibliographical?

Harper's Canada: Misleading the Canadian Public in the Conservative Campaign Video *Our Country*

BY JENNY BYFORD

The title page of this student essay is not included for space reasons. See Figure 11.2 for a sample MLA title page.

Jenny Byford
Professor Sally Hayward
English 101
14 February 2014

Good title: general statement and then uses a colon to introduce a more specific summary of the argument. Videos and films are italicized.

Harper's Canada: Misleading the Canadian Public in the
Conservative Campaign Video *Our Country*

Good opening sentence and effective summary of the overall context. Primary text: *Our Country*.

1   April 2011 marked the release of the Conservative campaign video *Our Country* in promotion of Prime Minister Stephen Harper's hopeful re-election into political office. Airing on television and spreading viral across the internet, *Our Country* was a key piece of Harper's *Here for Canada* campaign leading up to the May election. In aims of appealing to the masses, the one-minute video effectively combines imagery and music to create a strong sense of national pride. However, there is a discrepancy between the message portrayed in the video and actual political practices of the Conservative government. Evidence suggests that the video's techniques of emotional language and visual imagery create a misleading and even/perhaps dishonest message about Canadian health-related policies.

Description of the video.

Thesis statement.

2   *Our Country* was the final visual promotional piece released by the Conservative Party of Canada before the May 2011 federal election. Unlike other campaign components, this video was neither a smear advertisement towards competing political parties, nor a response to allegations by other parties. The video cast the Conservatives as a mature party with a high moral standing. After the election, *Our Country* was the only pre-election video not removed from the Conservative website. The message of the video was that an elected Conservative government would work towards protecting the character of Canada and its citizens. The Conservative party would make Canada an "example to the world" (*Our Country*). In the month leading up to the election, the intention of the video was to promote Stephen Harper as the political candidate of choice, gain voter support, and reinforce the idea that Canada is a country its citizens can be proud of.

Good background context. The film is cited in italics and parentheses.

3   Aesthetically appealing, *Our Country's* visual design exemplifies Canada and its people in an idyllic, positive manner. As an attempt to evoke emotions of pride, national identification and unity, very general images are chosen to forge a connection between the Conservatives and the viewers. A standard of identification is set with images of picturesque Canadian landscapes.

Byford – 2

Canadians recognize Alberta and Saskatchewan prairies, British Columbia mountain ranges, East and West coasts, and northern tundra. Integrated in this sequence of Canadian landmarks are motion clips of Canadian people participating in traditional cultural activities such as ice hockey, hiking, and family outings. Historical clips of the Canadian military as well as an Olympic torch runner are specific images associated with pride. Throughout these various scenes, images of Stephen Harper are included: he is shown standing in front of the Canadian flag, walking in Parliament, walking with his wife, visiting with supporters, speaking at political rallies, and presenting a speech at an international conference. This combination of visual images suggests that Stephen Harper is responsible for the pride with which Canadians value their country and lifestyle. By identifying with the images, viewers identify with Harper and the Conservative party.

> Very good description of the video here.

4   Accompanying the visual aesthetics, Stephen Harper and the Conservative party's positive image are reinforced with the use of pathos (emotion). Throughout the video, the audience emotionally identifies with the Conservative party's national pride. Dramatic orchestral music plays in the background, climaxing at the video's conclusion and ending on a triumphant note that bears the Conservative logo. Capturing audience attention, Harper's pronunciation is clear and his tone is passionate as he announces Canada is the greatest nation and should strive to be an international leader: "it must be great for all Canadians . . . a country of hope and an example to the world" (*Our Country*). He also flatters the audience, stressing that Canada must, like the Canadian people, demonstrate an honourable, faithful, and loyal character. With such proclamations, audience emotion is deliberately targeted as Canadians resonate with a desire to be "honourable," "faithful," and "loyal" to Canada, to each other, and the Conservative party (*Our Country*).

> Shift to analysis here: the video's use of emotion.

> Good use of in-text citation format

> Good focused description, evidence, and analysis of how the video specifically targets the viewer's emotions.

5   Similarly, the video plays on the viewers' emotions when it uses Stephen Harper's reputation as a political leader and previous prime minister of Canada to encourage them to place their trust in Harper's voice, believing his words are truthful and not the creation of the Conservative marketing team. Harper's repeated declaration that Canada and Canadian's are "great," along with his image as a central, unifying, and rallying leader effectively makes him seem more relatable and honest in the eyes of the Canadian public.

> Second point regarding the use of emotion.

6   However, this portrayal of Canada is misleading. Much information about the country and political party is left out or ignored. Firstly, the video's very vague statements are left to the interpretation of the individual viewer. When he argues that Canada must in all circumstances be a considered a "strong" and "free" country, a "true north" and "best" example for all other countries, he generalizes a concept of Canada as a "true north" (*Our Country*). Moreover, it is unknown what Stephen Harper intended by "strong," and "free" (*Our Country*). Such statements could mean different things to different

> Shift here to the crux of the analysis: the use of emotion is misleading in that it focuses on an ideal image of Canada and omits issues that would compromise this ideal vision.

> First point: vague statements.

> Good example of vague use of language here, and a good analysis of audience relevance.

> Second part of this analysis: vague statements are not grounded in Conservative policies.

> Second point: statements do not speak to all Canadians and all issues, specifically, Canadians who are ill or have disabilities, health care reform, and the export of asbestos. These specific points are only implied in the thesis. When using this method, the reader must not feel as though you are going off topic, so make sure the points are implicitly contained in your thesis.

> Context and suggested reasons for the omission of health care reform. Even though it would be easy to say too much and go off topic here, this analysis successfully stays on topic because it brings us back to a consideration of the video.

> Canada in parenthesis defines what is meant by "It."

people; one person may view the "best" country in the world as one advanced in economics, while another may view the best country as one focused on health promotion and treatment.

7   More importantly, each opinion or perspective would require a different form of governance and the actual Conservative policies are not directly addressed in the video. The ethos and general credibility of the video would have been enhanced by specific evidence of how, in their individual policies, the Conservative party interpreted "strong" and "free," along with how it intended to make Canada the "best" country in the world (*Our Country*). Instead, the video uses vague claims and statements to persuade the audience to believe Harper and the Conservative party want the same goals as each individual viewer, which generalize what the entire country desires.

8   Secondly, and maybe more importantly, the images selected for the video are not representative of the needs and desires of the entire population and the related issues. Of the thirty-two different images displayed, not one reflected the Canadian health care system, troubling health-related issues such as the exportation of asbestos, or any Canadian suffering from a disability or illness. The absence of health-related issues and ill or disabled people demonstrates the Conservative party's attempt to show only an ideal, rather than a fully accurate image of Canada. Lastly, this absence of health care coupled with evidence of false claims proves the campaign video *Our Country* is by omission dishonest.

9   Throughout the election campaign, Harper was heavily criticized by Liberal and NDP political opponents for the health care budget, as well as for his proposed plans for the future of the Canadian medical system. With rising negative attention from campaign attack advertisements, the Conservative choice to ignore the issue of health care in their last campaign video, *Our Country*, might well have been a political tactic to save voter support. Even so, the absence of health care disguises future Conservative plans.

10   Speculation of Harper's 2011 policy platform infers the Conservative government will not renew the Canada Health Accord in 2014. Provincial, territorial, and federal governments will not be bound by funding and health care service agreements if the act is not renewed. This could potentially spark competition within provinces and territories if private avenues are chosen to fund certain services to compensate for a decreasing in federal funding. More so, the portability of Canada's health care system would be lost in fragmented coverage systems that differed between provinces and territories.

11   By not renewing Canada's Health Accord, Canada's current medicare system that serves all Canadians will be altered. Such an action is not reflective of Harper's campaign, which states that "It (Canada) must be great for all Canadians; it must be a country of hope" (*Our Country*). A shift away from medicare will not be "great" for all Canadians; individuals with illnesses or disabilities and individuals without private insurance will suffer. Although the

Byford – 4

video's statements appear positive, unaddressed health concerns point to a less than ideal Canada: a reality that is deliberately omitted from the campaign video *Our Country*.

12   Similarly, the video fails to address where the Conservative party stands on the contentious issue of asbestos exports. Following the election in the fall of 2011, Canada's exportation of carcinogenic asbestos caught major media attention. Press coverage speculates Canada generates a profit of one-hundred million dollars annually on asbestos exports (Visser n. pag). While strict Canadian guidelines surround the handling and use of asbestos to protect Canadians, Canada still exports to countries like India, Algeria, and Indonesia, with less protective regulations. The World Health Organization (WHO) warns asbestos is known to cause lung cancer, cancer of the larynx, mesothelioma, and fibrosis of the lungs (n. pag). The WHO reports from 2004 cite that asbestos-related diseases are responsible for one hundred and seven thousand deaths, and over one million, five hundred thousand Disability Adjusted Life Years from occupational exposures worldwide (WHO n. pag). Such negative health consequences associated with asbestos exposure have been internationally known since 1977 much before the Conservative campaign video *Our Country* was created, let alone released (Office of the Auditor General of Canada n. pag).

13   In making the video, the Conservative party was well versed in Canada's asbestos trade practices and knew the associated health consequences the trade caused for others. Though Canada's trade in asbestos has lasted over a period of various leaders and federal governments, the 2011 Conservative video outwardly disregarded this issue in aims of creating voter appeal. Statements depicting Canada as "honourable in our dealings," "loyal to our friends," "a compassionate neighbour," and "a country of hope and an example to the world" are obvious contradictions to the Conservative government's position on asbestos regulations (*Our Country*). If Canada were, or intended to be, a global leader or a compassionate neighbour, its government would protect the health of citizens across the globe by ending asbestos exports.

14   Similarly, the failure to address this issue makes the portrayal of Stephen Harper as a global leader, speaking at an international conference; however, the type of leader is open for interpretation. Problematically, Canada was the first country to oppose adding Chrysotile Asbestos to the list of hazardous substances under the United Nations' Rotterdam Convention (Office of the Auditor General of Canada n. pag). Against evidence to the contrary, Canada and Conservative party leadership are not ethical global leaders of high moral standing. Asbestos exportation is a deliberate choice to privilege economic gain over global human welfare. Despite the noble claims of the video, the Conservative government does not address this very important issue. Canada's asbestos exports endanger millions of lives and threaten the health of the global community.

Second part of this analysis: asbestos exports

Last name of author plus *n. pag* (no page numbers).

No need to document Visser again as no other author is cited after the first mention.

WHO is cited because the individual author is unknown.

No author, no page citation.

Effective contextual background.

Good conclusion: summary of main points and a reiteration of her argument. Good objective tone of voice: it would be easy to make the ad hominem fallacy and slide into attack mode.

Good concluding sentence that encourages us to reflect on the argument.

15   A symbol of national pride, the Conservative campaign video *Our Country* manipulates audience emotion to gain voter support. In doing so, a misinterpretation and dishonest picture is created of Conservative practices towards Canadian and global health. Abstaining from typical political campaign attack antics, the Conservative party depicts itself as holding a high moral standing, yet evidence of past actions and potential future health policies suggest otherwise. At the local level, the Conservative party's potential plan to alter Canada's current universal health care system will create a division between Canadians and negatively affect population health. At the global scale, the Conservative's continuance of asbestos exports and resistance to international regulations harm the global community. Although it is possible Stephen Harper and the Conservative party support their claims in other ways, in health-related instances, Canada is not "great for all Canadians" and Canada is not "an example to the world" (*Our Country*). From an analytical health perspective, it would be appropriate to rename Harper's "Here for Canada" campaign to "Harper, here for just parts of Canada."

Byford – 6

Works Cited

Canada Conservative Party of Canada. *Our Country*. Online Video Clip. *YouTube*. 6 April 2011. Web. 10 February 2012.

Office of the Auditor General of Canada. "Canada's Policies on Chrysotile Asbestos Exports." *Government of Canada*. Web. 13 February 2012.

Visser, Josh. "Canada Mocked in U.S. for Asbestos 'Hypocrisy'." *CTV NEWS*. 2 July 2011. Web. 12 February 2012.

World Health Organization. "Asbestos." Web. 13 February 2012.

> Please note the citation of a video and government document citation in the Works Cited list.

General comments: Overall, this is a very good essay. Jenny provides a good description of the video and effectively addresses a knowledge gap, which involves an objective analysis of what the video omits to mention: the local and global Conservative policy on health care. Jenny uses evidence from the video, such as quotes from Harper himself, while also outlining the importance of the issues that have been omitted from the Conservative video Our Country. *In outlining these issues, she maintains the relevance of the topic to the video and the Conservative campaign without giving the impression that she is taking us in a different direction or off topic. Her use of* MLA *citation conforms to video citation expectations. Please note, however, that most of the citations are web-based and the analysis would have been strengthened by including some academic scholarship.*

Exercise 11.1

ANALYZING QUOTATION USE AND ARGUMENT

Consider how Jenny Byford uses MLA documentation style in this essay and answer the following questions:

1. Where does she use direct quotations and /or summary and how does she use them?
2. How do they support her analysis?
3. Do they accurately encapsulate the point she is trying to make?
4. How does she vary "tiny citations" with summary and/or paraphrase?
5. What is Byford's argument?
6. Is it fully supported with evidence from the primary text?
7. Is the argument, in your opinion, valid?
8. Can you outline a central syllogism for this essay?

American Psychological Association (APA) Citation Format

APA style describes rules for the preparation of manuscripts for writers and students in:

- social sciences, such as psychology, linguistics, sociology, economics, education, and criminology;
- business;
- nursing.

These guidelines will cover APA citation style as laid out in the sixth edition of the *Publication Manual of the American Psychological Association.* First, I will provide an overview of the general formatting expectations for papers and then provide in-text and bibliographical citations. In APA format, these appear in the form of a reference list that is included as a separate page at the end of your essay. I will then provide you with a student essay written in APA format style.

When you use APA format style, cite and document any sources that you have consulted, even if you presented the ideas from these sources in your own words.

You need to cite:

- to identify other people's ideas and information used within your essay;
- to inform the reader of your paper where they should look if they want to find the same sources.

A citation must appear in two places in your essay:

- in the body of your text ("in-text citations");
- in the reference list (at the end of your paper).

APA Guidelines

Essay Form

Students should observe the following criteria of format and usage in formal writing assignments. Consistent disregard of these standards could result in a charge of plagiarism or a lowered or failing grade. Attention to the standards will count toward the grade awarded.

Manuscript

1. Use white standard-size paper (8 1/2 × 11 inches).
2. Use black ink, Times New Roman 12-point font, double space, and type on one side of the page only.
3. Set page margins at 1 inch on all sides.
4. Indent the first line of paragraphs 1/2 inch from the left margin (use the TAB key).
5. Do not leave extra spaces between paragraphs.
6. Fasten the pages together with paper clips or staples.
7. There are four major sections you will need to complete: title page, abstract, main body, and references.
8. Page 1: Include a title page.
   a. Centre your title (in upper and lowercase letters), name, institutional affiliation, header (in left-hand margin), and date in the middle of the page.
   b. Add the words "running head," then a colon and the shorter title of your essay, capitalized, at the top of the page.
   c. Next to it, flush with the right-hand margin, add the short-form title and the page number. This running head must be put in the header so that it appears on every page of your paper. Do not underline or include any additional information, pictures, etc. on your title page.
9. Page 2: Include an abstract:
   a. Underneath the running head and page number, centre the title "Abstract."
   b. Below the title, provide the reader with a concise summary of your paper of approximately 150 to 250 words. It should contain your research questions, participants (if relevant), methods, results, and conclusion. You should also include any implications of your research for future work.
   c. Below the abstract, you might want or be required to list keywords, which will list the keywords in your essay. If you do this, you will need to indent as usual and then type *Keywords*, followed by a colon in the left-hand margin, then type your keywords.

10. Page 3: Underneath the running head and page number, centre the title at the top of the page. The running head, but not the title, appears on each consecutive page. Below is an example of the first two pages (the title page and the abstract):

Title page/First page

NATIONAL IDENTITY   1

Hockey, Violence, and
Canada's National Identity

Bruce Dennet

University of Lethbridge

May 2, 2012

Second page

NATIONAL IDENTITY   2

Abstract

Write a concise summary of your paper here. Include your research question, participant (if appropriate), methods, results, and conclusion. Your abstract should be between 150 and 250 words.

Keywords: Keywords from your paper are often listed below your abstract.

Figure 11.3 ◆ APA Formatting with Title Page and Abstract

Third page

NATIONAL IDENTITY   3

Hockey, Violence, and
Canada's National Identity

Begin writing the essay here. Make sure that you indent each paragraph five spaces. Do not right justify your margins, but do make sure that you double space your lines and use Times New Roman, 12-pt font. Your page should have one-inch margins.

Remember that for each new topic, you will need a new paragraph. The paragraphs should connect and develop some aspect of your main point or thesis statement. Do not put extra spaces between paragraphs.

Fourth page

NATIONAL IDENTITY   4

Continue writing here. The final page of your essay will have the same header, but will also include a title—References—centred in the middle of your page.

Figure 11.4 ◆ APA First and Consecutive Pages

Section Headings

APA allows you to use section headings. These sections are used to improve the readability of your paper because they function as a logical outline of your paper. The introduction may or may not be included in these section headings. However, make sure that the section headings maintain an academic tone, are logical, and are about the same length, with the same grammatical structure. Here is an example of section headings related to the title "Hockey, Violence, and Canada's National Identity":

1. The debate about hockey and violence
2. The Don Sanderson case: The place of fighting in hockey
3. Hockey and violence: a masculine stereotype?
4. Canada's national identity: hyper-masculine and violent?

Conventions and Usage

1. Italicize the titles of books and plays. Put the titles of short stories, poems, and articles in quotation marks.
2. You can also use italics to emphasize a certain word. However, do *not* overuse italics in this way.
3. Capitalize all words in a heading that are more than four letters long. Do not capitalize prepositions regardless of their length unless they are the first or last word of the title.
4. Capitalize the first word after a dash or colon: Hockey and Violence: An Examination of Canadian Identity.
5. Use hyphens (-) to form compound words when these words function together as an adjective to a noun. For example, the phrase *well known* does not need a hyphen, but when taken together as one idea that modifies a noun, a *well-known actor*, a hyphen is needed. In a title, capitalize both words in a hyphenated compound word.
6. APA does not recommend footnotes; they should be used sparingly only if absolutely necessary, for explanatory or digressive information that does not belong in the main body of the paper. Footnotes are indicated by superscript Arabic numbers in the text along with a corresponding reference at the foot of the page.
7. Do *not* use contractions, such as "don't" for "do not," and do not use abbreviations, such as "i.e.," "etc.," and "e.g."
8. Students are expected to be able to spell correctly. No student, for example, should have to be reminded of the difference between the possessive pronoun "its" and the contraction "it's" (for it is). Use the spell check on your computer, but note that it will not pick up everything. Look up the word in a dictionary if you are unsure of the spelling.
9. Be careful about punctuation, grammar, and structure. The quality of your essay depends not only upon the content but also on the form that you use to convey the content. Use the grammar check; it is particularly useful for highlighting the use of passive voice.

10. Be specific; avoid wordy constructions, and remember that clarity is the key.
11. To introduce other people's ideas in text, use reporting expressions:

Richardson argues, refers to, explains, hypothesizes, compares, concludes;

As Littlewood and Sherwin demonstrated, proved, . . . etc.

Punctuation

Brackets

Use brackets to enclose words that you insert into quotations. When you use quotations, you may have to change the form of a word or two to make the quotations fit the structure and grammar of your sentence.

Shuter (1997) reported "this trend [is] almost reversed in Italy" (p. 305).

Ellipsis

Use to indicate a gap or an omission from a quotation. An ellipsis consists of three spaced periods with a space on either end. Use normal punctuation before an ellipsis. If you need to change or add a letter, it should go in square brackets, as indicated below.

Although Paul Hewson (2004) argues that "Big Rock [beer] tastes fresh and crisp . . . , [s]atisfying Canadian beer-drinkers is always a challenge" (p. 30).

Single Quotation Marks

When quoting someone else inside a quotation, put the quoted material in single quotation marks. In the example below, the quote is taken from Robson, who quotes a line from Carrier's story "The Hockey Sweater."

"The Hockey Sweater" tells the story of a boy who grows up idolizing professional hockey players, with dreams of playing in the National Hockey League himself one day. As Robson (1999) points out, "[m]uch of the story emphasizes the fascination and obsession that Canadians have with the game of hockey as the fictional protagonist narrates that '[t]he winters of my childhood were long, long seasons'" (p. 64).

Parenthetical (in-text) Citations

In-text parenthetical citations identify the source of your material and enable readers to locate the source in a list of references at the end of the essay. A typical parenthetical citation includes the *author's name and the year of the publication*. Always provide *page numbers* for direct quotations; page numbers for a summary or paraphrase of an author's ideas are *preferred* but not essential. Titles of articles appear in quotation marks; titles of books are italicized.

For example, a typical citation might look like this:

> In his ground-breaking book *Imagined Communities,* Benedict Anderson (1991) argues that the nation is "an imagined political community" (p. 6).

Note that the book title is italicized, the publication year follows the author's name, and the page number follows at the end of the sentence after the direct quote to which the reference (p. 6) refers.

Here are some more specific examples, beginning, similar to the example above, with a template for the citation format when the author is included in the body of the sentence.

Author in Body of Sentence

If you are quoting from a work and the name of the person you are quoting is in the body of the sentence, you will need to introduce the quotation with a reporting expression, the author's last name, and the date of publication in parenthesis. There is no page number in this example because it is a summary and not a direct quotation.

> <u>Vernon (1978) found</u> that people with Type O blood are more likely to develop duodenal ulcers than people with Type A, B, or AB blood.

Author Not in Body of Sentence

If the author is not mentioned in the body of the sentence, you will need to put his or her last name, followed by a comma and the date, in parenthesis at the end of the sentence before the period. As in MLA style, the punctuation mark is placed after the parenthesis.

> People with Type O blood are more likely to develop duodenal ulcers than people with Type A, B, or AB blood <u>(Vernon, 1978).</u>

Page Numbers

APA uses page numbers to cite direct quotes (quotes taken directly from the original source and directly referenced in quotation marks).

> As Fukuyama (1995) points out, "[i]n Japan, no stigma attaches to adoption outside the kinship group" (p. 173).

Paragraph Numbers

When there are no page numbers, as in an electronic text, use paragraph numbers (para. 6) to help the reader find the cited text (Wallace, 2001, para. 5).

> Mazzolini (2003), borrowing Slaughter and Leslie's description, defines academic capitalism as "the phenomenon of universities' and faculty's increasing attention to market potential as research impetus" (para. 2).

When quoting an article in the text without page or paragraph numbers, you can use a section heading and specify the paragraph number as it appears under that heading:

In "Socialism" (1995), socialism and capitalism are compared: "Philosophers usually frame the argument between Capitalism and Socialism as a conflict between the needs of the individual vs. the needs of society" ("Which Is Right: Capitalism or Socialism?" para. 2).

Essays Without an Identified Author

If the author's name is not given, either use the first two or three words of the title in the parenthetical citation ("Strange Encounter," 1987) or use the complete title in a signal phrase.

In "Strange Encounter," the issue is raised as . . .

Anonymous Author

If "Anonymous" is specified by the author, treat it as if it were a real name.

(Anonymous, 1991)

Direct Quotes: Fewer Than 40 Words

Always place direct quotes within quotation marks. For quotations of fewer than 40 words, you must cite the author, date, and page number.

As Summers (1992) reported, "workplace stress occurs when jobs are high in stressors and low in controllability" (p. 56).

Long Quotations: More Than 40 Words

Quotations of more than 40 words are set off from the text by indenting five spaces from the left margin. Quotation marks are omitted. The parenthetical citation follows the period at the end of the quotation.

In "Body/Power," Foucault (1980) writes that he has attempted to analyse how, at the initial stages of industrial societies, a particular punitive apparatus was set up together with a system for separating the normal from the abnormal. To follow this up, it will be necessary to construct a history of what happens in the nineteenth century. (p. 61)

Citing Indirect Sources

When citing an author who is citing someone else, you must acknowledge it in your parenthetical citation by using "as cited in" to identify the original source.

Samuel Johnson (1986) admitted that Burke was an "extraordinary man" (as cited in Boswell, 1999, p. 45).

He admitted that Burke was an "extraordinary man" (Johnson et al., cited in Boswell, 1999, p. 45).

Multiple Sources

When citing two or more works by different authors, list the authors alphabetically, add the year, and separate the citations with semicolons.

(Bachnik, 1983; Fukuyama, 1995).

(Anderson, 1980; Fowers & Powell, 1993; Simonetti, 1998).

Multiple Authors: Two Authors

Use both names in all citations. Use the ampersand (&) in the citation, and spell out "and" in the text.

The outcome measures used in the study have been criticized (Campbell & Tsuang, 2001).

Campbell and Tsuang (2001) have criticized the outcome measures used in the study.

Three to Five Authors

Identify all authors in the signal phrase or in parenthesis the first time you cite the source.

(Caplow, Bahr, Chadwick, Hill, and Williamson, 1982).

In subsequent citations, use the first author's name followed by "et al." in either the signal phrase or parenthesis: (Caplow et al., 1982).

Six or More Authors

Use only the first author's name followed by "et al." in all citations.

(Berger et al., 1971).

Personal Communication

Cite conversations, memos, letters, and similar unpublished person-to-person communications by initials, last name, and precise date.

(L. Smith, personal communication, October 12, 1994).

Do not include personal communications in the list of references.

APA References

The reference list, titled *References,* starts on a separate page at the end of the essay. Entries in a reference list are arranged alphabetically by the surnames of the authors or editors. Reference entries that lack authors or editors are alphabetized by the first word of the title, excluding *a, an,* or *the.* Double spacing is used between and within entries throughout the list. APA uses the hanging-indent style.

Basic Book Citation

Last name, Initial of first name. (Year of publication). *Title with first letter only capitalized.* Place of publication: Publisher.

> McLeish, J. (1981). *The development of modern behavioural psychology.* Calgary: Detselig.

Article or Chapter in an Edited Book, Two Editors

Last name, First name initial. (year of publication). Article title with only first letter capitalized. In + editors, using first then last names (Eds.), *Book title with only first letter capitalized* (pp. + page range). Place of publication: Publisher.

> Fish, S. (1986). Is there a text in this class? In Hazard Adams and Leroy Searl (Eds.), *Critical theory since 1965* (pp. 524–533). Tallahassee: Florida State University Press.

Editors Who Author a Work

Last name(s), first initial(s). (Eds.). (year of publication.) *Title.* Place of publication: publisher.

> Sebeck, T. A., & Umiker-Sebeck, D. J. (Eds.). (1980). *Speaking of apes: A critical anthology of two-way communication with man.* New York: Plenum Press.

Two or More Authors and Edition

Last name(s), first initial(s) ampersand + second author. (Publication date). *Title.* (edition, as formatted below). Place of publication: publisher.

> Wiley, J., & Harzem, P. (1981). *Predictability, correlation, and continguity.* (2nd Canadian ed.). Toronto: J. Wiley.

Translation

Last name, first initial. (year of publication). *Title* (First initial, Last name, Trans.). Place of publication: publisher. (original work published + date)

> Miller, A. (1980). *The untouched key: Tracing childhood trauma in creativity and destructiveness* (H. and H. Hannum, Trans.). New York: Doubleday. (original work published 1988)

Work in an Anthology

Last name, first initials. (year of publication). Article title. In + editor's first initial and last name (Ed.). *Book title* (pp. = page range). Place of publication: Publisher.

> Basso, K. H. (1970). Silence in western Apache culture. In P. Giglioli (Ed.). *Language and social context* (pp. 67–86). Harmondsworth, England: Penguin.

Article in a Journal

Last name(s), first name initials. (publication date). Article title: Capitalize first letter and word that follows a colon. *Journal Title, Volume,* Page range.

> Buss, M. D., & Schmitt, D. P. (1993). Sexual strategies theory: An evolutionary perspective on human mating. *Psychological Review, 100,* 204–232.

Government Publication

Publishing body. Date. *Title of report* (catalogue or publishing no.). Place of publication: publishing details.

> Health Canada. (2002). *A report on mental illnesses in Canada* (Cat. No. 0-662-32817-5). Ottawa, Canada: Canada Cataloguing in Publication.

Magazine

Last name, first name initials. (year, month and day of publication). Article title with first word only capitalized. *Magazine italicized, Volume,* page range.

> Henry, W. A. (1990, April 9). Beyond the melting pot. *Time, 135,* 28–31.

Online Sources

As a way of providing stable online links to articles, APA recommends using a Digital Object Identifier (DOI), when available. This long alphanumeric code is used like a URL active link and can usually be found on the first page of the document. Use the title of the article if there is no author listed and use the abbreviation (n.d.) if there is no date listed.

Article in an Online Scholarly Journal with No DOI

Author's last name(s), initials. (Date of publication). Title of article. *Title of Journal, volume*(issue number), page range. Retrieved from http://www.journalhomepage.com/full/url/

> Strinati, D. (1992). Postmodernism and popular culture. *Sociology Review, 1*(4), 2–7. Retrieved from http://www.sociologyreview.com

Article in a Scholarly Journal Online with DOI Present

Author's last name(s) First name, initials only. (Date of publication). Title of article. *Title of Journal, volume*(issue number), page range. doi:0000000/000000000000 or http://dx.doi.org/10.0000/0000

Dussault, M., & Barnett, B. G. (2004). Peer-assisted leadership: Reducing educational managers' professional isolation. *Journal of Educational Administration, 34*(3), 5–14. doi:1132/76002889076009

Article from a Database

Provide the same information you would for a printed journal article and add a retrieval statement that gives the proper name of the database or its URL.

Eid, M., & Langeheine, R. (1999). The measurement of consistency and occasion specificity with latent class models. *Psychological Methods, 4,* 100–16. Retrieved from http://www.apa.org/journals/webref.html

Schredl, M., Brenner, C., & Faul, C. (2002). Positive attitude toward dreams: Reliability and stability often-item scale. *North American Journal of Psychology, 4,* 343–6. Retrieved from Academic Search Premier database.

Web Magazine or Newspaper with Author and Unknown Author

Author's last name and initials. (Publication year, month day). Article title. *Name of magazine or newspaper*. Retrieved from URL address.

Hutton, W. (2014, April 12). Capitalism simply isn't working and here are the reasons why. *The Guardian*. Retrieved from http://www.theguardian.com

Capitalism simply isn't working and here are the reasons why. (2014, April 12). *The Guardian*. Retrieved from http://www.theguardian.com

Emails, Letters, Etc.

Emails and similar personal communications are cited in the body of your text, but because they do not provide recoverable data, they are not included in the reference list. In the body of your text, cite emails as personal communications and provide the date of your communication.

(J. B. Barnes, personal communication, April 1, 2010)

Website

Author's last name(s), initials. (Publication date). Article title. Retrieved from publisher if known: URL. Retrieval dates are not included unless the source material may change over time (e.g., nonarchived social media pages).

If there is no author, begin with the title. If there is no date, use the abbreviation (n.d.).

Weldon, F. (n.d). Writing tips. Retrieved from http://www.fayweldon.co.uk

Capitalism. (n.d). Retrieved from http://www.capitalism.org

Painting, Photograph, or Image

There are no clear guidelines listed by APA regarding paintings or images. However, the following format is generally accepted: Painter's last name, first initials. (date produced). *Title* [Painting]. Retrieved from location if available and URL.

> Constable, J. (1829). *Hadleigh Castle* [Painting]. Retrieved from The Yale Centre for British Art, http://www.britishart.yale/edu/

Film, Video Recording, or DVD

Last name, first initial. (Director). (year of production). *Title of production* [Motion picture]. Place produced: Production company.

> Kubrick, S. (Director). (1980). *The shining* [Motion picture]. United States: Warner Brothers.

> Clement, M. (Producer). (1984). *A fighting chance* [DVD]. Toronto: Addiction Research Foundation.

Television or Radio Program

Last name, first initial (Job identification). (year, month, day of production). Title of episode [identification of type of program. In + first name initial, + last name (Producer), *Title of program*. Place of publication: Publisher.

> MacIntyre, L. (Reporter). (2002, January 23). Scandal of the century [Television series episode]. In H. Cashore (Producer), *The fifth estate*. Toronto: Canadian Broadcasting Corporation.

Sound Recordings

Songwriter's last name and initials. (Copyright date). Title [Recorded by artist if different from song writer]. On *Title of album* [Medium of recording]. Location: Label. (Recording date if different from copyright date).

> Stewart, R. (1988). Forever young. On *Out of order* [CD]. Burbank, CA. USA: Warner Bros.

Podcasts

Presenter. Publication date. Title [Form]. Producer. Program Title. URL.

> Sherman, N. (Presenter). (2009, October 20). The devil lives in Houston [Audio podcast]. In N. Sherman (Producer), *The drabblecast audio-fiction podcast*. Retrieved from https://itunes.apple.com/podcast/drabblecast

Advertisement

Place where published. Title of advertisement. (year, month, day of publication). Retrieved + date from URL.

Adbusters. Joe Chemo spoof advertisement. (2007, February 18). Retrieved February 1, 2008, from http://blog.americanfeast.com/images/chemo.jpg

Sample Essay Using APA Style

What follows is an annotated student essay, using APA format and citation style. It is not only a good example of APA format, it is also a good example of a student who uses research to support her argument about three primary texts.

Animal Rights: An Examination of Veterinary Educational Institutions

BY AILA CROWTHER-HAYWARD

Animal Rights: An Examination of Veterinary Educational Institutions

The title page is not included for space reasons. See Figure 11.3 for a sample APA title page.

Opening sentence: quite general, but the second sentence gets to the point.

Concise summary of her research and the abuse of animals.

Author in body of sentence.

Citation: Direct quote format with page number.

Summary of Carl Cohen's argument. Cohen's name is cited in full the first time and after that, only the last name is used.

Implicit thesis statement, using first person.

1   People who own and love their pets trust that they will be taken care of by people who have been taught to advocate for the rights of animals. However, many veterinarian schools, such as the University of Georgia, Brookhaven Technical School, and Ross Veterinarian school, are abusing the rights of animals. The abuse that is inflicted upon these animals can range anywhere from starvation and beating to inappropriate living conditions. The people who inflict this abuse and violation of animal rights can be the teachers, students or workers, and, sometimes, indirectly, through policies, rules, and regulations, the educational institutions who consider animals as property. Rights, as defined by Carl Cohen (1986), one of the most well-known and well published critics of the animal rights movement, "is a claim, or potential claim, that one party may exercise against another" (p. 633). As Cohen (1986) argues, animals do not have the mental reasoning to exercise a claim against another, and, therefore, they have no rights (p. 633). In this way, animals become objects and property, and humans, who do have reason, can do with them as they will. In this essay, I will first look at the opposing animal rights theories of Carl Cohen and Tom Regan, and then apply that to three examples of experimentation on and treatment of animals in veterinarian institutions.

2   In Cohen's (1986) "The Case for the Use of Animals in Biomedical Research," speciesism, the belief that humans are superior to animals because they are capable of engaging in "moral reflection" and "recognizing just claims against their own interest" (p. 637), means that there is a rational argument to

ANIMAL RIGHTS   2

be made for refusing animal rights and, thus, for allowing animals to experimented on by humans (p. 638). As Cohen (1986) argues, "rights arise, and can be intelligibly defended, only among beings who actually do, or can, make moral claims against one another. whatever else rights may be, therefore, they are necessarily human; their possessors are persons, human beings" (p. 633). Consequently, animals, who have a lack of capacity for free moral judgment and are incapable of exercising or responding to moral claims, have no rights (p. 634).

3   Contradicting Cohen's opinions, Tom Regan (1985) argues in "The Case for Animal Rights" that an animal is a "subject of a life" and, as such, does have moral rights (p. 623). He also points out that, as humans, we have an indirect duty regarding animals because we can do wrong acts that involve animals: "by way of illustration: suppose your neighbour kicks your dog. Then your neighbour had done something wrong. But not to your dog. the wrong that has been done is a wrong to you. After all, it is wrong to upset people" (p. 623). In this sense, he argues that animals' pain and suffering are consequences of a bigger problem: the idea that animals are our property and we may do what we want to them:

> What is wrong isn't the pain, isn't the suffering, isn't the deprivation. These compound what's wrong. Sometimes—often—they make it much, much worse. But they are not fundamentally wrong. The fundamentally wrong is the system that allows us to view animals as our resources, here for us—to be eaten, or surgically manipulated, or exploited for sport. (p. 622)

4   Regan (1985) stresses that if we accept animals as a resource, we lose all appreciation for them and start thinking of them as objects and not living, feeling subjects (p. 622). According to Regan (1985), we have a moral duty to acknowledge the rights of animals, which requires humans to cease using animals for any purpose, not just those associated with pain and suffering (p. 626).

5   The views expressed by Cohen and Regan can be seen in several examples of animal abuse in veterinarian educational institutions. My first example is an incident that happened at the University of Georgia, where Ashley Council, a student and lab technician at the veterinary hospital, was charged with seven counts of cruelty for beating a litter of puppies, aged between seven to eight weeks old, to death ("UGA Student Charged," 2009, para. 1). The puppies, who were found behind a convenience store in a box, had multiple bruising and open wounds, suggesting the puppies suffered. A University of Georgia's spokesman, Tracy Giese, said that Council is still employed at the university, but no longer has contact with animals (para. 7).

Summary of Cohen's argument. Note that the sentence beginning "Consequently, animals . . ." is a summary and is also cited (p. 634).

Summary of Regan's position. Aila uses several quotes from Regan's essay here: one is a hypothetical example, common to philosophy essays, and the other is a longer indented quote.

Format for summarizing a quote.

Aila has a good, clear structure: she has compared and contrasted Cohen's and Regan's views and she is now going to use them to analyze her three examples.

Aila's first example summarized. Media citation cites paragraph number because there are no page numbers (para.7).

6   The "fundamental wrong" in this example is that the university is still allowing Council to work at the animal hospital, caring for the animals. These two actions—Council killing the animals and the University allowing her to keep her job—ultimately negates the animals' value of life. The university is sending a clear message to Council and to others that this behaviour is acceptable. In this scenario, the animals become no more than objects, undeserving of the care we, as moral agents, are obligated to provide for those who cannot advocate for themselves (Regan, 1985, p. 623).

7   Cohen would echo this belief, arguing that we do have a sense of moral obligation to care for these animals, whether or not they have rights:

> Obligations may arise from differences of status: adults owe special care when playing with young children, and children owe special care when playing with young pets. Obligations may arise from special relationships: the payment of my son's college tuition is something to which he may have no right, although it may be my obligation to bear the burden if I reasonably can. (Cohen, 1986, p. 635)

8   Both Regan and Cohen might agree, then, that educational institutions should take more care to screen and manage their employees. It is their duty and obligation to care for these animals. Respecting the rights of these animals means implementing and following certain regulations that might compromise that duty. Screening employees for a history of animal abuse and having a policy in place that would allow the university to fire someone charged with animal abuse would help prevent further abuse.

9   My second example happened at Brookhaven Technical School where four students, enrolled in the pre-veterinarian course, were charged with torturing and killing several animals in their animal care class ("Four Teens Accused of Cruelty," 2009, para. 1). A few of the crimes included starving a caged dog to death over a period of three weeks, using mice as baseballs by hitting them with metal pipes, killing a pregnant guinea pig by throwing it against a wall, slashing hamsters with razor blades and using them as hackey sacks, juggling kittens causing one to break its leg, and repeatedly smashing ferrets' heads together (para. 2). Alan Goodman, the teacher of the class, took no action to stop the abuse. He was suspended with pay and was charged with animal cruelty. The students were permanently removed from the animal care class, but not the program (para. 4).

10   The four students and the teacher make the animals in the animal care class into lower "subjects of life" with a lower moral status (Regan, 1985, p. 629). Cohen (1986) would argue that the animals have no rights because they are morally inferior to humans, but he would also argue that those who do have

---

Annotations (margin notes):

- Here Aila presents Regan's view and uses it to support her argument. Good transition to the following paragraph, which picks up on this obligation from Cohen's perspective.

- Author not in body of sentence.

- Cohen's perspective.

- Summary of case using both Regan and Cohen. Aila presents a solution.

- Aila's second example, clearly and objectively summarized. Good examples/evidence.

- Citation: unidentified author and no page numbers.

ANIMAL RIGHTS   4

rights, the students and the teacher, must give reasons for their actions, especially when it comes to violating the animals: "[h]olders of rights must recognize possible conflicts between what is in their own interest and what is right" (Cohen, p. 634). The four students might have done these vicious acts because they believed in a self-interested way, that they were entertaining themselves, but that does not justify the acts that they did or make them morally right. This also goes for the teacher, who might have had his own interests in mind when he avoided a conflict between the school and the students by not reporting or stopping the abuse in his class. Once again, this self-interested behaviour does not mean that what the teacher was doing by allowing this abuse was just or morally right.

11   What is disturbing about this example is the extent and nature of the abuse. These animals were tortured extensively for the students' entertainment and the teacher, whose responsibility was not only to the students but also to the animals in his care, clearly believed the students' entertainment was more important than the animals' rights. Regan (1985) would argue that this particular example would be a perfect case of how humans constantly abuse animals and get away with it. In Regan's words, "What's wrong—fundamentally wrong—with the way animals are treated isn't the details that vary from case to case. It's the whole system" (p. 622). The governing institutions and laws and policies within the system, supporting the speciesist belief in human superiority, do not support or defend the abuse of animals because they are not holders of rights.

12   My last example happened at Ross University School of Veterinary Medicine, where People for the Ethical Treatment of Animals (PETA) accused Ross of invasive and deadly teaching procedures on dogs, donkeys, and sheep ("Ross Vet School," 2009, para. 1). The complaints and undercover photographs came from the students attending the veterinary school. They showed healthy dogs having their stomachs, intestines and urinary bladders needlessly cut open, sheep having tissue removed and suffering from infected wounds, donkeys having the nerves and ligaments in their feet and legs severed and fluid removed from their joints (para. 2). After these procedures, the animals were killed so the students could practice amputating the animals bones and drilling into their skulls. Ross ignored PETA's previous appeals to cease the alleged practices and also the suggestions for more humane procedures.

13   The animals at Ross University are subjected to being property of the university and therefore have no rights regardless of PETA's involvement and regardless of the pain that these animals experienced. The experiments that Ross perform are used to help teach students how to be veterinarians, but this does not mean that some of these experiments are necessary or right: "a good end does not justify and evil means" (Regan, 1985, p. 628). Generally speaking,

---

Aila uses Cohen here and his concept of self-interest to argue that these actions are wrong.

Second paragraph on the second example. Regan is used to support her analysis. Good paragraph transition.

Description of the last case using concrete evidence from primary text.

ANIMAL RIGHTS   5

Aila's critique, using Regan.

Ross University uses animals as a resources in order to teach their students how to become veterinarians, but they did not in any measure show any obligation, as an indirect duty demanded of human beings, to care for the animals, helping to avoid the pain and suffering of animals in their care.

14   In the three examples above, there is a violation of the animals' right to be cared for. In all three examples, the animals are considered objects of property and are consequently refused any rights—direct or indirect—and any acknowledgement that their lives have any value. Regan (1985) would argue that we must not just make things more "humane," we must abolish all use of "animals in science" (p. 621). Whether or not these animals are morally different to human beings, we must acknowledge animal rights because to treat them as anything other than "subjects of life" is to open them to abuse (p. 622). If, indeed, it is, as Cohen argues, necessary to use animals in veterinarian educational institutions for the benefit of veterinarian students and science, there must be certain rules and regulations that must be strictly enforced if we are to live up to the expectation and obligation of being human.

Aila's conclusion successfully uses Regan and Cohen to support her argument, opening up the conversation to larger questions about our responsibility as humans to care for animals.

ANIMAL RIGHTS 6

References

Cohen, C. (1986). The case for the use of animals in biomedical research. In *The Norton Reader* (pp. 633–643). New York: W. W. Norton.

Four teens accused of cruelty to animals in pre-vet class. (2009, April 3). *New York Daily News*. Retrieved from http://www.nydailynews.com

Regan, T. (1985). The case for animal rights. In *The Norton Reader* (pp. 621–633). New York: W. W. Norton.

Ross vet school accused of cruelty to animals. (2009). *SKN*. Retrieved from http://www.sknvibes.com

UGA student charged with killing puppies denies accusations. (2009). *Petfinder*. 2009. Retrieved April 5, 2009 from http://forums.petfinder.com

General comment: *This is a very good essay. Aila successfully uses three primary texts, two main research sources, APA citation, direct quotes, summary, analysis, and a logical compare–contrast structure to make a valid and original argument about our obligations to animals.*

> References include an article in an edited collection and a newspaper article.

Exercise 11.2

COMPARING COMPARE–CONTRAST TECHNIQUES

- Compare Aila's essay to Garth Forsyth's essay in chapter 8. Both essays are compare–contrast essays. However, whereas Garth presents a very good critique of Regan and Cohen, Aila uses Regan and Cohen as secondary support for her critique. Take note on how they engage differently with Regan and Cohen. What points or content does each writer focus on to make an argument? Outline both papers so you can see how they work logically to compare and contrast their material. Could you use these essays as model structures for your own analysis of two or more texts?
- Now compare Jenny Byford's essay with Diana Lim's essay in chapter 2. Both of these essays critique a visual text. Consider where and how they use summary and analysis. Outline both papers so you can see how they work logically to summarize and critique their primary texts. Could you use a similar structure when critiquing a visual text yourself?

Other Styles of Documentation

While MLA and APA styles of documentation are the two citation methods most consistently used in an academic context, some academic disciplines use other documentation styles. If required by your discipline and by the instructors in your specific courses, you will need to familiarize yourself with these other citation and documentation methods. Your library will have hard copy and online information for these citation methods, but you might also want to check out the following sources:

The Chicago Manual of Style. 16th ed. Chicago and London. University of Chicago Press, 2010. The Chicago Manual of Style online: www.chicagomanualofstyle.org/.

Scientific Style and Format: The CSE Manual for Authors, Editors, and Publishers. 7th ed. Cambridge: Cambridge University Press, 2006.

Council of Science Editors Online: www.councilscienceeditors.org/.

When using these sources, simply follow the directions for citing and documenting your research both in the body of the text and in a reference page at the end of the paper, as you have learned to do with MLA and APA citation.

CHAPTER SUMMARY

This chapter has provided an introduction to the importance of academic citation and stressed the need to avoid either intentionally or accidentally plagiarizing your sources. For that reason, a detailed overview of both MLA and APA citation style has been provided, including two sample student essays as models of each citation format. These critical essays—the first an example of a compare–contrast essay using MLA format, the second a compare–contrast research essay using APA format—are exemplary under-graduate essays that can be studied as models of effective writing. While there hasn't been room in this chapter to cover Chicago and the Council of Science Editors citation style formats, they can both be found in the online accompaniment to this book.

QUESTIONS FOR CONSIDERATION

1. Why, in your words, is citation important?
2. What do I still need to know about citation?
3. What method would I use, given my chosen discipline?
4. How might the two student essays presented in this chapter serve as models both of effective citation and effective argumentation?

PART III

THE READER

Introduction

Reading as a Call for Critical Response

The nineteen readings in The Reader have been carefully chosen to reflect the needs and concerns of students working across the different university disciplines. Not all disciplines are included in this collection, but there is a broad enough sampling for you to understand the similarities and differences in form and content that the individual disciplines demand. There are representative essays in the fields of science, philosophy, education, sociology, history, Native studies, disability studies, gender studies, cultural studies, English literature, and rhetoric and composition studies.

A large percentage of the essays are academic, with the exception of Donald M. Murray's and William Zinsser's essays, which are directed at a popular audience and are more journalistic in tone, and the essays by Richard Wagamese and Drew Hayden Taylor, who wrote short autographical commentaries about the 2008 Truth and Reconciliation Commission. Wayne C. Booth's essay, although published widely in academic texts, was written as a conference paper, so assumes a different audience. In addition, there are a number of primary texts, such as short stories and poems, that serve as a critical focus for analysis.

These works serve to emphasize the issue of genre, which is also a central concern of this book, the basic tenet being that when you are able to identify and understand how a text reflects a specific genre, with its own set of conventions and expectations, the more effectively you will be able to participate in the writing that the genre requires. Of course, the genre and focus that we are most concerned with is the writing that is produced in academia in general, and in the individual disciplines (the sub-genres) in particular. However, the focus on genre should also allow you to analyze other writing genres, such as the poem, the short story, the autobiography, or journalism, if that is where your interest lies.

The assumption throughout the collection is twofold:

1. Even though many of these primary readings are non-academic, our focus for reading them is strictly academic.
2. Because our intent is to critique these readings from an academic standpoint, considering their effectiveness and relatedness as disciplinary examples, a focus on language and rhetoric (persuasion) is central to our analysis.

These readings thus serve as models of effective writing, demonstrating for students the disciplinary requirements and conventions, as well as presenting some effective techniques students can incorporate into their own writing. It is hoped that the readings will also provide a varied and interesting critical focus for analysis.

In these readings, I have included a representative sampling of writing by male and female, American, British, and German authors, but, most important, I have focused on a significant number of Canadian writers who are either representative of Canada's literary heritage or who engage critically in topics of interest to Canadians. These topics include indigenous, educational, institutional, national, and identity-related issues (how we see ourselves as Canadians). The essays also focus on science, animal rights, politics, disability, and, most important for this collection, the practice and art of writing in the academic disciplines.

A major focus of this book is the incorporation of student academic writing examples. These vary from small excerpts to entire essays and are at the end of many of the chapters. While some of the essays are exceptional—for example, the innovative, award-winning essay on Sheridan and radio technology in chapter 10—they all demonstrate important features of good student writing: an effective thesis, language use, organization, and research. The following table lists the annotated student essays and shows which ones correspond to selections within The Reader.

The Annotated Student Essays

Location	Annotated Student Essay	Corresponding Selections in the Reader
Chapter 2	Delaney Blewett/The Unethical Use and Legalization of Aspartame: Poisoning the People, page 36	
	Diana Lim/The Role of the Media in Defining Beauty: An Analysis of the Dove Film *Evolution*, page 42	
Chapter 6	Savannah Simpson/Wayne Booth's "The Rhetorical Stance": A Summary, page 129	Wayne C. Booth/The Rhetorical Stance, page 335
Chapter 7	Brook Biesenthal/Catherine Schryer's "The Lab vs. the Clinic: Sites of Competing Genres": An Example of Bias?, page 162	Catherine F. Schyer/The Lab vs. the Clinic: Sites of Competing Genres, page 350
Chapter 8	Garth Forsyth/An Examination of Tom Regan's "The Case for Animal Rights" and Carl Cohen's "The Case for the Use of Animals in Biomedical Research": Fallacious Arguments?, page 202	Tom Regan/The Case for Animal Rights, page 378 Carl Cohen/The Case for the Use of Animals in Biomedical Research, page 369
Chapter 10	Tyrell DaSilva/(Mis)Understanding Literate Culture: An Analysis of Joe Sheridan's "The Silence before Drowning in Alphabet Soup," page 275	Joe Sheridan/The Silence before Drowning in Alphabet Soup, page 432
Chapter 11	Jenny Byford/Harper's Canada: Misleading the Canadian Public in the Conservative Campaign Video *Our Country*, page 298	
	Aila Crowther-Hayward/Animal Rights: An Examination of Veterinary Educational Institutions, page 316	Tom Regan/The Case for Animal Rights, page 378 Carl Cohen/The Case for the Use of Animals in Biomedical Research, page 369

To help you select which readings will be beneficial to you, the readings have been organized by theme, but you can also refer to the classifications according to genre, discipline, and analytical patterns that are listed on the inside covers of this book.

Each reading is prefaced by a short introductory and biographical note and followed by Questions for Discussion, and From Reading to Writing questions, where you will find suggestions for responding to each piece in written form.

To assist your response to these readings, I have included a review of critical reading and writing, which is outlined below.

Review of Critical Reading

As you are now aware, critical reading involves not simply summarizing the given text, but also responding to it in a thoughtful, reflective manner, making connections to other texts you have read and other contexts you are aware of or have researched. When formulating your critique, you need to focus on the following strategies:

- Remember that your focus as an academic should be on the knowledge: what and how the information is presented.
- Read the work at least twice, and take notes as you read by either annotating your text in the margins or by using a notebook and dividing the page in half with a summary of the work on one side and your response to the work on the other side. This response might involve asking questions, synthesizing the information with other works and contexts, or developing ideas for an argument of your own.
- Frame your reading with a research question that you want answered because it will give you a purpose for reading and help to focus your attention.
- Ask if there is a knowledge gap or deficit in the material you are reading: a place where something is presented inaccurately or where there is something that is not said that needs to be said. This deficit will provide you with a place to insert your argument in the text you are reading.
- Ask the following questions: What this work and the essay's development and organization, does well, in relation to the argument? What needs improvement? What is not accounted for?
- Relate your reading to other similar texts, situations, or contexts: what are the similarities and/or differences? What do these contexts reveal about the larger research questions you might ask?

Following these steps will help you to establish a strategy for reading critically that suits your study habits. Once again, it is important to find a method that works for you. In developing your critical thinking and reading skills, you will also be developing a more aware and open perspective about the world in which we live. In doing this, I want you not to simply passively consume the things you hear, see, know, and experience, but to actively and critically engage with them. You will thus not only become informed critical thinkers but successful and aware communicators in both spoken and written mediums.

From Reading to Writing

Note-taking is the first step in developing this communication. This begins with you and the author and text you are reading and extends to other readers of your primary text and the readers of your work. Remember that academic writing is about exchanging ideas between interested and knowledgeable experts. You might be concerned about challenging, revising, testing, or expanding on someone else's ideas, or you might be confident enough to apply what someone else has written and argued to a completely new but relevant context. In this way, you will be reviewing and analyzing the current state of knowledge on a specific topic and, at the same time, building on the existing research that is already out there.

You will do this, first, by analyzing your primary text, which could be any text in this reader, and the existing or original research that your primary text is discussing, paying careful attention to the detail for knowledge gaps and by comparing and contrasting the particular text you are analyzing to other related studies, concepts, or ideas. Second, you will formulate your argument, find evidence that supports (or refutes) your argument, and then structure it in a logical, persuasive way that your reader will find intellectually engaging and convincing.

As you refine your skills in academic reading and writing you will learn that you are then better equipped to read and analyze problems both in your own life and in the world in general. For example, you could take these skills and use them to become a more critical consumer of products and information or, alternatively, you could use them in your careers outside the university, particularly if you develop an interest in government, the law, public interest, or rights groups, or if you become involved in a media-related occupation. At the very least, you will become a better, more responsible, and more skilled reader and writer, which will help you immeasurably in every area of your life.

◆ ◆ ◆ ◆ ◆ Language and Communication ◆ ◆ ◆ ◆ ◆

Writing with Teachers: A Conversation with Peter Elbow
BY DAVID BARTHOLOMAE

INTRODUCTION

David Bartholomae is a professor of English at the University of Pittsburgh specializing in composition studies. "Writing with Teachers" was written in response to the conversation David Bartholomae and Peter Elbow (University of Massachusetts) had at the 1991 Conference on College Composition and Communication (CCCC) meeting in Boston. In the essay, Bartholomae argues in a traditional sense, that teachers must teach academic writing to first-year university students who learn to participate in the academic discourse community by learning and applying, through the process of imitation, the discipline-specific use of language and academic conventions. In making this argument, he takes issue with Peter Elbow's "expressivist" approach, which claims that writers learn to write for academia by writing, whether that writing is academic or personal (diaries, letters, poems, etc.). I have included it in the list of readings to help you to contextualize the arguments I have made about academic writing as a genre, as outlined in chapters 1 and 2.

1   Most discussions like the one we are about to have begin or end by fretting over the central term, academic writing. It is clear that this is not just a contested term, but a difficult one to use with any precision. If, for example, it means the writing that is done by academics, or the writing that passes as currency in the academy, then it is a precise term only when it is loaded: academic writing—the unreadable created by the unspeakable; academic writing—stuffy, pedantic, the price of a career; academic writing—pure, muscular, lean, taut, the language of truth and reason; academic writing—language stripped of the false dressings of style and fashion, a tool for inquiry and critique.

2   And so on. I don't need to belabor this point. Academic writing is a single thing only in convenient arguments. If you collect samples of academic writing, within or across the disciplines, it has as many types and categories, peaks and valleys, as writing grouped under any other general category: magazine writing, business writing, political writing, sports writing. Or, I could put it this way: Within the writing performed in 1990 under the rubric of English studies, writing by English professors, you can find writing that is elegant, experimental, sentimental, autobiographical, spare, dull, pretentious, abstract, boring, dull, whatever.

3 If I am here to argue for academic writing as part of an undergraduate's training, or as a form or motive to be taught/examined in the curriculum, I need to begin by saying that I am not here to argue for stuffy, lifeless prose or for mechanical (or dutiful) imitations of standard thoughts and forms. We need a different set of terms to frame the discussion. It is interesting, in fact, to consider how difficult it is to find positive terms for academic writing when talking to a group of academics, including those who could be said to do it for a living. It is much easier to find examples or phrases to indicate our sense of corporate shame or discomfort.

4 I don't have time to pursue this line of argument here, but I think it is part and parcel of the anti-professionalism Fish argues is a pose of both the academic right (for whom the prose in our journals is evidence of bad faith, of the pursuit of trends, an abandonment of the proper pursuit of humane values, great books), but also for the academic left (for whom professional practice is the busy work we do because we are co-opted). For both, academic writing is what you do when you are not doing your "real" work.

My Position, I Think

5 I want to argue that academic writing is the real work of the academy. I also want to argue for academic writing as a key term in the study of writing and the practice of instruction. In fact, I want to argue that if you are teaching courses in the university, courses where students write under your supervision, they can't not do it and you can't not stand for it (academic writing, that is) and, therefore, it is better that it be done out in the open, where questions can be asked and responsibilities assumed, than to be done in hiding or under another name.

6 To say this another way, there is no writing that is writing without teachers. I think I would state this as a general truth, but for today let me say that there is no writing done in the academy that is not academic writing. To hide the teacher is to hide the traces of power, tradition and authority present at the scene of writing (present in allusions to previous work, in necessary work with sources, in collaboration with powerful theories and figures, in footnotes and quotations and the messy business of doing your work in the shadow of others). Thinking of writing as academic writing makes us think of the page as crowded with others—or it says that this is what we learn in school, that our writing is not our own, nor are the stories we tell when we tell the stories of our lives—they belong to TV, to Books, to Culture and History.

7 To offer academic writing as something else is to keep this knowledge from our students, to keep them from confronting the power politics of discursive practice, or to keep them from confronting the particular representations of power, tradition and authority reproduced whenever one writes.

8 Now—I say this as though it were obvious. Students write in a space defined by all the writing that has preceded them, writing the academy insistently draws together: in the library, in the reading list, in the curriculum. This is the busy, noisy, intertextual space—one usually hidden in our representations of the classroom; one that becomes a subject in the classroom when we ask young writers to think about, or better yet, confront, their situatedness.

9   And yet, it is also obvious that there are many classrooms where students are asked to imagine that they can clear out a space to write on their own, to express their own thoughts and ideas, not to reproduce those of others. As I think this argument through, I think of the pure and open space, the frontier classroom, as a figure central to composition as it is currently constructed. The open classroom; a free writing. This is the master trope. And, I would say, it is an expression of a desire for an institutional space free from institutional pressures, a cultural process free from the influence of culture, an historical moment outside of history, an academic setting free from academic writing.

10   *Whose* desire? That is a hard question to answer, and I will finesse it for the moment. I don't want to say that it is Peter's; I think it is expressed in Peter's work.

11   I can, however, phrase this question: "Whose desire is this, this desire for freedom, empowerment, an open field?"—I think I can phrase the question in terms of the larger debate in the academy about the nature of discourse and the humanities. The desire for a classroom free from the past is an expression of the desire for presence or transcendence, for a common language, free from jargon and bias, free from evasion and fear; for a language rooted in common sense rather than special sense, a language that renders (makes present) rather than explains (makes distant). It is a desire with a particularly American inflection and a particular resonance at a moment in the academy when it has become harder and harder to cast any story, let alone the story of education, in a setting that is free, Edenic or Utopian.

12   "I have learned to relinquish authority in my classroom." How many times do we hear this now as the necessary conclusion in an argument about the goals of composition? "I want to empower my students." "I want to give my students ownership of their work." What could it mean—to have this power over language, history and culture? to own it?

13   Unless it means stepping outside of the real time and place of our writing—heading down the river, heading out to the frontier, going nowhere. Unless it means stepping out of language and out of time. I am arguing for a class *in* time, one that historicizes the present, including the present evoked in students' writing. Inside this linguistic present, students (with instruction—more precisely, with lessons in critical reading) can learn to feel and see their position inside a text they did not invent and can never, at least completely, control. Inside a practice: linguistic, rhetorical, cultural, historical.

14   As I am thinking through this argument, I read Peter's work as part of a much larger project to preserve and reproduce the figure of the author, an independent, self-creative, self-expressive subjectivity. I see the argument against academic writing, and for another writing, sometimes called personal or expressive writing, as part of a general argument in favor of the author, a much beleaguered figure in modern American English departments. This is one way that the profession, English, has of arguing out the nature and role of writing as a subject of instruction—Personal writing/academic writing—this opposition is the structural equivalent to other arguments, arguments about authorship and ownership, about culture and the individual, about single author courses, about the canon.

15   And these arguments are part of still other arguments, with different inflections, about production and consumption, about reading and writing, about presence and

transcendence, culture and individualism—arguments working themselves out in particular ways at conferences and in papers in many settings connected to the modern academy. The desire for an open space, free from the past, is a powerful desire, deployed throughout the discourses of modern life, including the discourses of education.

The Contact Zone

16   When we talk about academic writing at CCCC, I don't think we are talking about discourse—at least, after Foucault, as discourse is a technical term. We are not, in other words, talking about particular discursive practices and how they are reproduced or policed within the academic disciplines.

17   I would say that we are talking about sites, possible scenes of writing, places, real and figurative, where writing is produced. This is why so much time is spent talking about the classroom and its literal or metaphorical arrangement of power and authority—where do we sit, who talks first, who reads the papers. Whether we rearrange the furniture in the classroom or rearrange the turns taken by speakers in a discussion, these actions have no immediate bearing on the affiliations of power brought into play in writing. At worst, the "democratic" classroom becomes the sleight of hand we perfect in order to divert attention for the unequal distribution of power that is inherent in our positions as teachers, as figures of institutional/disciplinary authority, and inherent in the practice of writing, where one is always second, derivative, positioned, etc.

18   I am trying to think about the scene of writing as a discursive space. So let me say that we shouldn't think of ourselves as frontier guides but as managers, people who manage substations in the cultural network, small shops in the general production of readers and writers. We don't choose this; it is the position we assume as teachers. If, from this position, we are going to do anything but preside over the reproduction of forms and idioms, we have to make the classroom available for critical inquiry, for a critique that is part of the lesson of practice. We have to do more, that is, than manage.

19   If our goal is to make a writer aware of the forces at play in the production of knowledge, we need to highlight the classroom as a substation—as a real space, not as an idealized utopian space. There is no better way to investigate the transmission of power, tradition and authority than by asking students to do what academics do: work with the past, with key texts (we have been teaching Emerson, Rich, Simon Frith on rock and roll); working with other's terms (key terms from Rich, like "patriarchy," for example); struggling with the problems of quotation, citation and paraphrase, where one version of a student's relationship to the past is represented by how and where he quotes Rich (does he follow the block quotation with commentary of his own? can Rich do more than "support" an argument, can a student argue with Rich's words, use them as a point to push off from?).

20   I want this issue to be precise as well as abstract. You can teach a lot about a writer's possible relations with the past by looking at how and why she uses a passage from an assigned text. This is not, in other words, simply a matter of reproducing standard texts, but as using them as points of deflection, appropriation, improvisation, or penetration (those are Mary Louise Pratt's terms). But you can't do this without making foremost the situatedness of writing, without outlining in red the network of affiliations that constitute writing in the academy.

21   Let me do this another way. There is a student in my class writing an essay on her family, on her parents' divorce. We've all read this essay. We've read it because the student cannot invent a way of talking about family, sex roles, separation. Her essay is determined by a variety of forces: the genre of the personal essay as it has shaped this student and this moment; attitudes about the family and divorce; the figures of "Father" and "Mother" and "Child" and so on. The moment of this essay is a moment of the general problematics of writing—who does what to whom; who does the writing, what can an individual do with the cultural field? Of course we can help the student to work on this essay by letting her believe it is hers—to think that the key problem is voice, not citation; to ask for realistic detail rather than to call attention to figuration. Almost two hundred years of sentimental realism prepares all of us for these lessons. We can teach students to be more effective producers of this product. We can also teach them its critique. Perhaps here is a way of talking about the real issues in the debate over academic writing? How can you not reproduce the master narrative of family life? How might a student writer negotiate with the professional literature? How and what might it mean to talk back to (or to talk with) Adrienne Rich about family life? What does it mean for a student to claim that her own experience holds equivalent status with Rich's memories as material to work on?

Source: Excerpted from Bartholomae, David. "Writing with Teachers: A Conversation with Peter Elbow." *College Composition and Communication* 46.1 (Feb. 1995): 62–71. Print. Published by: National Council of Teachers of English. Copyright 2014 by the National Council of Teachers of English. Reprinted with permission.

QUESTIONS FOR DISCUSSION

1. In this essay, Bartholomae distinguishes between his and Peter Elbow's ideas about how writing should be taught in academia. How do the ideas of these two scholars differ?
2. Whose methodology do you primarily agree with and why? Would it be possible to use both methodologies?
3. What does teaching have to do with writing, according to Bartholomae? What role do tradition, power, and authority play in academic writing? What role does freedom play?
4. Chapter 2 of this book presents a genre-specific analysis of academic writing. How does the analysis in chapter 2 conform to or diverge from Bartholomae's analysis?

FROM READING TO WRITING

What is academic writing, according to David Bartholomae? Write a short paragraph defining academic writing. Make sure you include key terms, processes, and definitions. Discuss with your classmates. Do you agree with this definition? How might you revise it to conform to your understanding of what academic writing is?

The Rhetorical Stance

BY WAYNE C. BOOTH

INTRODUCTION

Wayne C. Booth was a distinguished professor of English at the University of Chicago. His major works include *The Rhetoric of Fiction* and *The Company We Keep: An Ethics of Fiction,* which reflected his long-standing interest in the ethical relationship between the writer and reader.

"The Rhetorical Stance," originally written in 1963 as a conference paper, expresses a similar concern with the writer and reader. It argues that to establish a clear communication with your audience, you must present a clear argument in an appropriate voice. This essay is a useful study for undergraduate students in that it stresses what academic writers should and should *not* do: write in a pedantic style, advertise, or attempt to entertain their readers.

See chapter 6 for directions on how to read Booth's essay, followed by a sample student summary.

1   Last fall I had an advanced graduate student, bright, energetic, well-informed, whose papers were almost unreadable. He managed to be pretentious, dull, and disorganized in his paper on *Emma,* and pretentious, dull, and disorganized on *Madame Bovary.* On *The Golden Bowl* he was all these and obscure as well. Then one day, toward the end of term, he cornered me after class and said, "You know, I think you were all wrong about Robbe-Grillet's *Jealousy* today." We didn't have time to discuss it, so I suggested that he write me a note about it. Five hours later I found in my faculty box a four-page polemic, unpretentious, stimulating, organized, convincing. Here was a man who had taught freshman composition for several years and who was incapable of committing any of the more obvious errors that we think of as characteristic of bad writing. Yet he could not write a decent sentence, paragraph, or paper until his rhetorical problem was solved—until, that is, he had found a definition of his audience, his argument, and his own proper tone of voice.

2   The word "rhetoric" is one of those catch-all terms that can easily raise trouble when our backs are turned. As it regains a popularity that it once seemed permanently to have lost, its meanings seem to range all the way from something like "the whole art of writing on any subject," as in Kenneth Burke's *The Rhetoric of Religion,* through "the special arts of persuasion," on down to fairly narrow notions about rhetorical figures and devices. And of course we still have with us the meaning of "empty bombast," as in the phrase "merely rhetorical."

3　I suppose that the question of the role of rhetoric in the English course is meaningless if we think of rhetoric in either its broadest or its narrowest meanings. No English course could avoid dealing with rhetoric in Burke's sense, under whatever name, and on the other hand nobody would ever advocate anything so questionable as teaching "mere rhetoric." But if we settle on the following, traditional, definition, some real questions are raised: "Rhetoric is the art of finding and employing the most effective means of persuasion on any subject, considered independently of intellectual mastery of that subject." As the students say, "Prof. X knows his stuff but he doesn't know how to put it across." If rhetoric is thought of as the art of "putting it across," considered as quite distinct from mastering an "it" in the first place, we are immediately landed in a bramble bush of controversy. Is there such an art? If so, what does it consist of? Does it have a content of its own? Can it be taught? Should it be taught? If it should, how do we go about it, head on or obliquely?

4　Obviously it would be foolish to try to deal with many of these issues in twenty minutes. But I wish that there were more signs of our taking all of them seriously. I wish that along with our new passion for structural linguistics, for example, we could point to the development of a rhetorical theory that would show just how knowledge of structural linguistics can be useful to anyone interested in the art of persuasion. I wish there were more freshman texts that related every principle and every rule to functional principles of rhetoric, or, where this proves impossible, I wish one found more systematic discussion of why it is impossible. But for today, I must content myself with a brief look at the charge that there is nothing distinctive and teachable about the art of rhetoric.

5　The case against the isolability and teachability of rhetoric may look at first like a good one. Nobody writes rhetoric, just as nobody ever writes writing. What we write and speak is always *this* discussion of the decline of railroading and *that* discussion of Pope's couplets and the other argument for abolishing the poll-tax or for getting rhetoric back into English studies.

6　We can also admit that like all the arts, the art of rhetoric is at best very chancy, only partly amenable to systematic teaching; as we are all painfully aware when our 1:00 section goes miserably and our 2:00 section of the same course is a delight, our own rhetoric is not entirely under control. Successful rhetoricians are to some extent like poets, born, not made. They are also dependent on years of practice and experience. And we can finally admit that even the firmest of principles about writing cannot be taught in the same sense that elementary logic or arithmetic or French can be taught. In my first year of teaching, I had a student who started his first two essays with a swear word. When I suggested that perhaps the third paper ought to start with something else, he protested that his high school teacher had taught him always to catch the reader's attention. Now the teacher was right, but the application of even such a firm principle requires reserves of tact that were somewhat beyond my freshman.

7　But with all of the reservations made, surely the charge that the art of persuasion cannot in any sense be taught is baseless. I cannot think that anyone who has ever read Aristotle's *Rhetoric* or, say, Whateley's *Elements of Rhetoric* could seriously make the charge. There is more than enough in these and the other traditional rhetorics to provide structure and content for a year-long course. I believe that such a course, when planned and carried through with intelligence and flexibility, can be one of the most important of all educational experiences. But it seems obvious that the arts of persuasion cannot be learned in one year, that a good teacher will continue to teach them regardless of his subject matter, and that we as English teachers have a special responsibility at all levels to get certain basic rhetorical principles into all of our writing assignments. When I think back over the experiences which have had any actual effect on my writing, I find the great good fortune of a splendid freshman course, taught by a man who believed in what he was doing, but I also find a collection of other experiences quite unconnected with a specific writing course. I remember the instructor in psychology who penciled one word after a peculiarly pretentious paper of mine: *bull*. I remember the day when P. A. Christensen talked with me about my Chaucer paper, and made me understand that my failure to use effective transitions was not simply a technical fault but a fundamental block in my effort to get him to see my meaning. His off-the-cuff pronouncement that I should never let myself write a sentence that was not in some way explicitly attached to preceding and following sentences meant far more to me at that moment, when I had something I wanted to say, than it could have meant as part of a pattern of such rules offered in a writing course. Similarly, I can remember the devastating lessons about my bad writing that Ronald Crane could teach with a simple question mark on a graduate seminar paper, or a penciled "Evidence for this?" or "Why this section here?" or "Everybody says so. Is it true?"

8   Such experiences are not, I like to think, simply the result of my being a late bloomer. At least I find my colleagues saying such things as "I didn't learn to write until I became a newspaper reporter," or "The most important training in writing I had was doing a dissertation under old *Blank*." Sometimes they go on to say that the freshman course was useless; sometimes they say that it was an indispensable preparation for the later experience. The diversity of such replies is so great as to suggest that before we try to reorganize the freshman course, with or without explicit confrontations with rhetorical categories, we ought to look for whatever there is in common among our experiences, both of good writing and of good writing instruction. Whatever we discover in such an enterprise ought to be useful to us at any level of our teaching. It will not, presumably, decide once and for all what should be the content of the freshman course, if there should be such a course. But it might serve as a guideline for the development of widely different programs in the widely differing institutional circumstances in which we must work.

9   The common ingredient that I find in all of the writing I admire—excluding for now novels, plays and poems—is something that I shall reluctantly call the rhetorical stance, a stance which depends on discovering and maintaining in any writing situation a proper balance among the three elements that are at work in any communicative effort: the available arguments about the subject itself, the interests and peculiarities of the audience, and the voice, the implied character, of the speaker. I should like to suggest that it is this balance, this rhetorical stance, difficult as it is to describe, that is our main goal as teachers of rhetoric. Our ideal graduate will strike this balance automatically in

any writing that he considers finished. Though he may never come to the point of finding the balance easily, he will know that it is what makes the difference between effective communication and mere wasted effort.

10   What I mean by the true rhetorician's stance can perhaps best be seen by contrasting it with two or three corruptions, unbalanced stances often assumed by people who think they are practicing the arts of persuasion.

11   The first I'll call the pedant's stance; it consists of ignoring or underplaying the personal relationship of speaker and audience and depending entirely on statements about a subject-that is, the notion of a job to be done for a particular audience is left out. It is a virtue, of course, to respect the bare truth of one's subject, and there may even be some subjects which in their very nature define an audience and a rhetorical purpose so that adequacy to the subject can be the whole art of presentation. For example, an article on "The relation of the ontological and teleological proofs," in a recent *Journal of Religion*, requires a minimum of adaptation of argument to audience. But most subjects do not in themselves imply in any necessary way a purpose and an audience and hence a speaker's tone. The writer who assumes that it is enough merely to write an exposition of what he happens to know on the subject will produce the kind of essay that soils our scholarly journals, written not for readers but for bibliographies.

12   In my first year of teaching I taught a whole unit on "exposition" without ever suggesting, so far as I can remember, that the students ask themselves what their expositions were for. So they wrote expositions like this one—I've saved it, to teach me toleration of my colleagues: the title is "Family relations in More's *Utopia*." "In this theme I would like to discuss some of the relationships with the family which Thomas More elaborates and sets forth in his book, *Utopia*. The first thing that I would like to discuss about family relations is that overpopulation, according to More, is a just cause of war." And so on. Can you hear that student sneering at me, in this opening? What he is saying is something like "you ask for a meaningless paper, I give you a meaningless paper." He knows that he has no audience except me. He knows that I don't want to read his summary of family relations in *Utopia*, and he knows that I know that he therefore has no rhetorical purpose. Because he has not been led to see a question which he considers worth answering, or an audience that could possibly care one way or the other, the paper is worse than no paper at all, even though it has no grammatical or spelling errors and is organized right down the line, one, two, three.

13   An extreme case, you may say. Most of us would never allow ourselves that kind of empty fencing? Perhaps. But if some carefree foundation is willing to finance a statistical study, I'm willing to wager a month's salary that we'd find at least half of the suggested topics in our freshman texts as pointless as mine was. And we'd find a good deal more than half of the discussions of grammar, punctuation, spelling, and style totally divorced from any notion that rhetorical purpose to some degree controls all such matters. We can offer objective descriptions of levels of usage from now until graduation, but unless the student discovers a desire to say something to somebody and learns to control his diction for a purpose, we've gained very little. I once gave an assignment asking students to describe the same classroom in three different statements, one for

each level of usage. They were obedient, but the only ones who got anything from the assignment were those who intuitively imported the rhetorical instructions I had overlooked—such purposes as "Make fun of your scholarly surroundings by describing this classroom in extremely elevated style," or "Imagine a kid from the slums accidentally trapped in these surroundings and forced to write a description of this room." A little thought might have shown me how to give the whole assignment some human point, and therefore some educative value.

14   Just how confused we can allow ourselves to be about such matters is shown in a recent publication of the Educational Testing Service, called "Factors in Judgments of Writing Ability." In order to isolate those factors which affect differences in grading standards, ETS set six groups of readers—business men, writers and editors, lawyers, and teachers of English, social science and natural science—to reading the same batch of papers. Then ETS did a hundred-page "factor analysis" of the amount of agreement and disagreement, and of the elements which different kinds of graders emphasized. The authors of the report express a certain amount of shock at the discovery that the median correlation was only .31 and that 94% of the papers received either 7, 8, or 9 of the 9 possible grades.

15   But what *could* they have expected? In the first place, the students were given no purpose and no audience when the essays were assigned. And then all these editors and business men and academics were asked to judge the papers in a complete vacuum, using only whatever intuitive standards they cared to use. I'm surprised that there was any correlation at all. Lacking instructions, some of the students undoubtedly wrote polemical essays, suitable for the popular press; others no doubt imagined an audience, say, of *Reader's Digest* readers, and others wrote with the English teachers as implied audience; an occasional student with real philosophical bent would no doubt do a careful analysis of the pros and cons of the case. This would be graded low, of course, by the magazine editors, even though they would have graded it high if asked to judge it as a speculative contribution to the analysis of the problem. Similarly, a creative student who has been getting A's for his personal essays will write an amusing colorful piece, failed by all the social scientists present, though they would have graded it high if asked to judge it for what it was. I find it shocking that tens of thousands of dollars and endless hours should have been spent by students, graders, and professional testers analyzing essays and grading results totally abstracted from any notion of purposeful human communication. Did nobody protest? One might as well assemble a group of citizens to judge students' capacity to throw balls, say, without telling the students or the graders whether altitude, speed, accuracy or form was to be judged. The judges would be drawn from football coaches, hai-lai experts, lawyers, and English teachers, and asked to apply whatever standards they intuitively apply to ball throwing. Then we could express astonishment that the judgments did not correlate very well, and we could do a factor analysis to discover, lo and behold, that some readers concentrated on altitude, some on speed, some on accuracy, some on form—and the English teachers were simply confused.

16   One effective way to combat the pedantic stance is to arrange for weekly confrontations of groups of students over their own papers. We have done far too little

experimenting with arrangements for providing a genuine audience in this way. Short of such developments, it remains true that a good teacher can convince his students that he is a true audience, if his comments on the papers show that some sort of dialogue is taking place. As Jacques Barzun says in *Teacher in America*, students should be made to feel that unless they have said something to someone, they have failed; to bore the teacher is a worse form of failure than to anger him. From this point of view we can see that the charts of grading symbols that mar even the best freshman texts are not the innocent time savers that we pretend. Plausible as it may seem to arrange for more corrections with less time, they inevitably reduce the student's sense of purpose in writing. When he sees innumerable W13's and P19's in the margin, he cannot possibly feel that the art of persuasion is as important to his instructor as when he reads personal comments, however few.

17   This first perversion, then, springs from ignoring the audience or overreliance on the pure subject. The second, which might be called the advertiser's stance, comes from *under*valuing the subject and overvaluing pure effect: how to win friends and influence people.

18   Some of our best freshman texts—Sheridan Baker's *The Practical Stylist*, for example—allow themselves on occasion to suggest that to be controversial or argumentative, to stir up an audience is an end in itself. Sharpen the controversial edge, one of them says, and the clear implication is that one should do so even if the truth of the subject is honed off in the process. This perversion is probably in the long run a more serious threat in our society than the danger of ignoring the audience. In the time of audience-reaction meters and pre-tested plays and novels, it is not easy to convince students of the old Platonic truth that good persuasion is honest persuasion, or even of the old Aristotelian truth that the good rhetorician must be master of his subject, no matter how dishonest he may decide ultimately to be. Having told them that good writers always to some degree accommodate their arguments to the audience, it is hard to explain the difference between justified accommodation—say changing *point one* to the final position—and the kind of accommodation that fills our popular magazines, in which the very substance of what is said is accommodated to some preconception of what will sell. "The publication of *Eros* [magazine] represents a major breakthrough in the battle for the liberation of the human spirit."

19   At a dinner about a month ago I sat between the wife of a famous civil rights lawyer and an advertising consultant. "I saw the article on your book yesterday in the Daily News," she said, "but I didn't even finish it. The title of your book scared me off. Why did you ever choose such a terrible title? Nobody would buy a book with a title like that." The man on my right, whom I'll call Mr Kinches, overhearing my feeble reply, plunged into a conversation with her, over my torn and bleeding corpse. "Now with my *last* book," he said, "I listed 20 possible titles and then tested them out on 400 business men. The one I chose was voted for by 90 percent of the businessmen." "That's what I was just saying to Mr Booth," she said. "A book title ought to grab you, and *rhetoric* is not going to grab anybody." "Right," he said. "My *last* book sold 50,000 copies already; I don't know how this one will do, but I polled 200 businessmen on the table of contents, and . . ."

20   At one point I did manage to ask him whether the title he chose really fit the book. "Not quite as well as one or two of the others," he admitted, "but that doesn't matter, you know. If the book is designed right, so that the first chapter pulls them in, and you *keep* 'em in, who's going to gripe about a little inaccuracy in the title?"

21   Well, rhetoric is the art of persuading, not the art seeming to persuade by giving everything away at the start. It presupposes that one has a purpose concerning a subject which itself cannot be fundamentally modified by the desire to persuade. If Edmund Burke had decided that he could win more votes in Parliament by choosing the other side—as he most certainly could have done—we would hardly hail this party-switch as a master stroke of rhetoric. If Churchill had offered the British "peace in our time," with some laughs thrown in, because opinion polls had shown that more Britishers were "grabbed" by these than by blood, sweat, and tears, we could hardly call his decision a sign of rhetorical skill.

22   One could easily discover other perversions of the rhetorician's balance—most obviously what might be called the entertainer's stance—the willingness to sacrifice substance to personality and charm. I admire Walker Gibson's efforts to startle us out of dry pedantry, but I know from experience that his exhortations to find and develop the speaker's voice can lead to empty colorfulness. A student once said to me, complaining about a colleague, "I soon learned that all I had to do to get an A was imitate Thurber."

23   But perhaps this is more than enough about the perversions of the rhetorical stance. Balance itself is always harder to describe than the clumsy poses that result when it is destroyed. But we all experience the balance whenever we find an author who succeeds in changing our minds. He can do so only if he knows more about the subject than we do, and if he then engages us in the process of thinking—and feeling—it through. What makes the rhetoric of Milton and Burke and Churchill great is that each presents us with the spectacle of a man passionately involved in thinking an important question through, in the company of an audience. Though each of them did everything in his power to make his point persuasive, including a pervasive use of the many emotional appeals that have been falsely scorned by many a freshman composition text, none would have allowed himself the advertiser's stance; none would have polled the audience in advance to discover which position would get the votes. Nor is the highly individual personality that springs out at us from their speeches and essays present for the sake of selling itself. The rhetorical balance among speakers, audience, and argument is with all three men habitual, as we see if we look at their non-political writings. Burke's work on the Sublime and Beautiful is a relatively unimpassioned philosophical treatise, but one finds there again a delicate balance: though the implied author of this work is a far different person, far less obtrusive, far more objective, than the man who later cried *sursum corda* to the British Parliament, he permeates with his philosophical personality his philosophical work. And though the signs of his awareness of his audience are far more subdued, they are still here: every effort is made to involve the *proper* audience, the audience of philosophical minds, in a fundamentally interesting inquiry, and to lead them through to the end. In short, because he was a man engaged with men in the effort to solve a human problem, one could never call what he wrote dull, however difficult or abstruse.

24 Now obviously the habit of seeking this balance is not the only thing we have to teach under the heading of rhetoric. But I think that everything worth teaching under that heading finds its justification finally in that balance. Much of what is now considered irrelevant or dull can, in fact, be brought to life when teachers and students know what they are seeking. Churchill reports that the most valuable training he ever received in rhetoric was in the diagramming of sentences. Think of it! Yet the diagramming of a sentence, regardless of the grammatical system, can be a live subject as soon as one asks not simply "How is this sentence put together," but rather "Why is it put together in this way?" or "Could the rhetorical balance and hence the desired persuasion be better achieved by writing it differently?"

25 As a nation we are reputed to write very badly. As a nation, I would say, we are more inclined to the perversions of rhetoric than to the rhetorical balance. Regardless of what we do about this or that course in the curriculum, our mandate would seem to be, then, to lead more of our students than we now do to care about and practice the true arts of persuasion.

Source: Booth, Wayne C. *College Composition and Communication* 14.3, Annual Meeting, Los Angeles, 1963: Toward a New Rhetoric. Oct. 1963, 139–45. Published by: National Council of Teachers of English. Copyright 2014 by the National Council of Teachers of English. Reprinted with permission.

QUESTIONS FOR DISCUSSION

1. Was this essay easy to read: if not, why not? Consider the audience, organization, and voice when answering this question.
2. Who, in your opinion, is Booth's main audience here?
3. How well does the anecdote work in Booth's opening paragraph?
4. Booth's thesis statement appears in two places in the essay. The first time it appears it is not as well defined. Can you find both instances?
5. Did you find Booth's points about how not to write—the pedant's, advertiser's, and entertainer's stances—useful? Do you recognize any of these stances in your own writing? How might you avoid using these stances in your future writing assignments?

FROM READING TO WRITING

Can you find one or two selections in The Reader that would exemplify Booth's definition of good writing? Write a short paragraph-length summary defending your choices and share it with your classmates.

The Maker's Eye: Revising Your Own Manuscripts

BY DONALD M. MURRAY

INTRODUCTION

Donald M. Murray was a professor emeritus of English at the University of New Hampshire and a journalist. In 1954, he won the Pulitzer Prize for editorials he had written for the *Boston Globe*. He has published novels, poetry, and many books on the art of writing and teaching writing. For Murray, writing, which includes pre-writing, writing, and rewriting, is about discovering and clarifying meaning: saying exactly what you want to say.

In the following essay, first published in *The Writer* in 1973, Murray emphasizes the importance of revision. Comparing the revision methods and attitudes of student writers with those of professional writers, he emphasizes his point that "good writing is essentially rewriting." This essay is particularly useful because it identifies some common student misconceptions about revision, while also providing a number of useful strategies for completing the revision process.

1   When students complete a first draft, they consider the job of writing done—and their teachers too often agree. When professional writers complete a first draft, they usually feel that they are at the start of the writing process. When a draft is completed, the job of writing can begin.

2   That difference in attitude is the difference between amateur and professional, inexperience and experience, journeyman and craftsman. Peter F. Drucker, the prolific business writer, calls his first draft "the zero draft"—after that he can start counting. Most writers share the feeling that the first draft, and all of those which follow, are opportunities to discover what they have to say and how best they can say it.

3   To produce a progression of drafts, each of which says more and says it more clearly, the writer has to develop a special kind of reading skill. In school we are taught to decode what appears on the page as finished writing. Writers, however, face a different category of possibility and responsibility when they read their own drafts. To them the words on the page are never finished. Each can be changed and rearranged, can set off a chain reaction of confusion or clarified meaning. This is a different kind of reading which is possibly more difficult and certainly more exciting.

4   Writers must learn to be their own best enemy. They must accept the criticism of others and be suspicious of it; they must accept the praise of others and be even more suspicious of it. Writers cannot depend on others. They must detach themselves from their own pages so that they can apply both their caring and their craft to their own work.

5   Such detachment is not easy. Science-fiction writer Ray Bradbury supposedly puts each manuscript away for a year to the day and then rereads it as a stranger. Not many writers have the discipline or the time to do this. We must read when our judgment may be at its worst, when we are close to the euphoric moment of creation.

6   Then the writer, counsels novelist Nancy Hale, "should be critical of everything that seems to him most delightful in his style. He should excise what he most admires, because he wouldn't thus admire it if he weren't . . . in a sense protecting it from criticism." John Ciardi, the poet, adds, "The last act of the writing must be to become one's own reader. It is, I suppose, a schizophrenic process, to begin passionately and to end critically, to begin hot and to end cold; and, more important, to be passion-hot and critic-cold at the same time."

7   Most people think that the principal problem is that writers are too proud of what they have written. Actually, a greater problem for most professional writers is one shared by the majority of students. They are overly critical, think everything is dreadful, tear up page after page, never complete a draft, see the task as hopeless. The writer must learn to read critically but constructively, to cut what is bad, to reveal what is good. Eleanor Estes, the children's book author, explains: "The writer must survey his work critically, coolly, as though he were a stranger to it. He must be willing to prune, expertly and hard-heartedly. At the end of each revision, a manuscript may look....worked over, torn apart, pinned together, added to, deleted from, words changed and words changed back. Yet the book must maintain its original freshness and spontaneity."

8   Most readers underestimate the amount of rewriting it usually takes to produce spontaneous reading. This is a great disadvantage to the student writer, who sees only a finished product and never watches the craftsman who takes the necessary step back, studies the work carefully, returns to the task, steps back, returns, steps back, again and again. Anthony Burgess, one of the most prolific writers in the English-speaking world, admits, "I might revise a page twenty times." Roald Dahl, the popular children's writer, states, "By the time I'm nearing the end of a story, the first part will have been reread and altered and corrected at least 150 times . . . Good writing is essentially rewriting. I am positive of this."

9   Rewriting isn't virtuous. It isn't something that ought to be done. It is simply something that most writers find they have to do to discover what they have to say and how to say it. It is a condition of the writer's life.

10   There are, however, a few writers who do little formal rewriting, primarily because they have the capacity and experience to create and review a large number of invisible drafts in their minds before they approach the page. And some writers slowly produce finished pages, performing all the tasks of revision simultaneously, page by page, rather than draft by draft. But it is still possible to see the sequence followed by most writers most of the time in rereading their own work.

11   Most writers scan their drafts first, reading as quickly as possible to catch the larger problems of subject and form, and then move in closer and closer as they read and write, reread and rewrite.

12   The first thing writers look for in their drafts is *information*. They know that a good piece of writing is built from specific, accurate, and interesting information. The writer must have an abundance of information from which to construct a readable piece of writing.

13   Next writers look for *meaning* in the information. The specifics must build to a pattern of significance. Each piece of specific information must carry the reader toward meaning. Writers reading their own drafts are aware of *audience*. They put themselves in the reader's situation and make sure that they deliver information which a reader wants to know or needs to know in a manner which is easily digested. Writers try to be sure that they anticipate and answer the questions a critical reader will ask when reading the piece of writing.

14   Writers make sure that the *form* is appropriate to the subject and the audience. Form, or genre, is the vehicle which carries meaning to the reader, but form cannot be selected until the writer has adequate information to discover its significance and an audience which needs or wants that meaning.

15   Once writers are sure the form is appropriate, they must then look at the *structure*, the order of what they have written. Good writing is built on a solid framework of logic, argument, narrative, or motivation which runs through the entire piece of writing and holds it together. This is the time when many writers find it most effective to outline as a way of visualizing the hidden spine by which the piece of writing is supported.

16   The element on which writers spend a majority of their time is *development*. Each section of a piece of writing must be adequately developed. It must give readers enough information so that they are satisfied. How much information is enough? That's as difficult as asking how much garlic belongs in a salad. It must be done to taste, but most beginning writers underdevelop, underestimating the reader's hunger for more information.

17   As writers solve development problems, they often have to consider questions of *dimension*. There must be a pleasing and effective proportion among all the parts of the piece of writing. There is a continual process of subtracting and adding to keep the piece of writing in balance.

18   Finally, writers have to listen to their own voices. *Voice* is the force which drives a piece of writing forward. It is an expression of the writer's authority and concern. It is what is between the words on the page, what glues the piece of writing together. A good piece of writing is always marked by a consistent, individual voice.

19   As writers read and reread, write and rewrite, they move closer and closer to the page until they are doing line-by-line editing. Writers read their own pages with infinite care. Each sentence, each line, each clause, each phrase, each word, each mark of punctuation, each section of white space between the type has to contribute to the clarification of meaning.

20   Slowly the writer moves from word to word, looking through language to see the subject. As a word is changed, cut or added, as a construction is rearranged, all the words used before that moment and all those that follow that moment must be considered and reconsidered.

21   Writers often read aloud at this stage of the editing process, muttering or whispering to themselves, calling on the ear's experience with language. Does this sound right—or that? Writers edit, shifting back and forth from eye to page to ear to page. I find I must do this careful editing in short runs, no more than fifteen or twenty minutes at a stretch, or I become too kind with myself. I begin to see what I hope is on the page, not what actually is on the page.

22   This sounds tedious if you haven't done it, but actually it is fun. Making something right is immensely satisfying, for writers begin to learn what they are writing about by writing. Language leads them to meaning, and there is the joy of discovery, of understanding, of making meaning clear as the writer employs the technical skills of language.

23   Words have double meanings, even triple and quadruple meanings. Each word has its own potential of connotation and denotation. And when writers rub one word against the other, they are often rewarded with a sudden insight, an unexpected clarification.

24   The maker's eye moves back and forth from word to phrase to sentence to paragraph to sentence to phrase to word. The maker's eye sees the need for variety and balance, for a firmer structure, for a more appropriate form. It peers into the interior of the paragraph, looking for coherence, unity, and emphasis, which make meaning clear.

25   I learned something about this process when my first bifocals were prescribed. I had ordered a larger section of the reading portion of the glass because of my work, but even so, I could not contain my eyes within this new limit of vision. And I still find myself taking off my glasses and bending my nose toward the page, for my eyes unconsciously flick back and forth across the page, back to another page, forward to still another, as I try to see each evolving line in relation to every other line.

26   When does this process end? Most writers agree with the great Russian writer Tolstoy, who said, "I scarcely ever reread my published writings, if by chance I come across a page, it always strikes me: all this must be rewritten; this is how I should have written it."

27   The maker's eye is never satisfied, for each word has the potential to ignite new meaning. This article has been twice written all the way through the writing process [...]. Now it is to be republished in a book. The editors made a few small suggestions, and then I read it with my maker's eye. Now it has been re-edited, re-revised, re-read, and re-re-edited, for each piece of writing to the writer is full of potential and alternatives.

28   A piece of writing is never finished. It is delivered to a deadline, torn out of the typewriter on demand, sent off with a sense of accomplishment and shame and pride and frustration. If only there were a couple more days, time for just another run at it, perhaps then...

Source: Murray, Donald M. "The Maker's Eye: Revising Your Own Manuscripts." *Language Awareness: Readings for College Writers*. Ed. Paul Eschholz, Alfred Rosa, and Virginia Clark. 8th ed. Boston: Bedford/ St. Martin's, 2000. 161–5. Print.

QUESTIONS FOR DISCUSSION

1. Do you agree with Murray when he states, "Good writing is essentially rewriting"? What does rewriting mean to you?

2. Which of Murray's strategies did you find most useful? Can you use Murray's strategies to come up with a plan for revising your work?

3. Murray suggests that there are often practical constraints that prevent the practice of revision. Do you agree? If so, how might you overcome those constraints so that you are able to fully revise your work?

FROM READING TO WRITING

Go through Murray's essay and, using two columns, list the common practices of student and professional writers. Which category do you fall into? If you identify more with the practices of student writers, how might you change your thinking and your practices to emulate the practices of professional writers? Come up with a strategic revision plan and a method of ensuring that you use it.

Simplicity

BY WILLIAM ZINSSER

INTRODUCTION

William Zinsser is an American essayist, journalist, and writing instructor. He has worked as a journalist for the *New York Herald Tribune* and taught writing at both Yale and Columbia university. Reflecting his focus on a variety of different writing genres (non-fiction, memoir, and journalism), Zinsser has written books on writing, including *On Writing Well, Write to Learn,* and *Write About Your Life.*

"Simplicity," a chapter in *On Writing Well,* foregrounds Zinsser's economical approach to revision: the elimination of "clutter," which includes "unnecessary words, circular constructions, pompous frills and meaningless jargon." I have included it in The Reader because it complements Murray's revision process by providing a focus on editing or proofreading at the level of the individual clause, phrase, and word.

1   Clutter is the disease of American writing. We are a society strangling in unnecessary words, circular constructions, pompous frills, and meaningless jargon.

2   Who can understand the viscous language of everyday American commerce: the memo, the corporation report, the business letter, the notice from the bank explaining its latest "simplified" statement? What member of an insurance or medical plan can decipher the brochure explaining his costs and benefits? What father or mother can put together a child's toy from the instructions on the box? Our national tendency is to inflate and thereby sound important. The airline pilot who announces that he is

presently anticipating experiencing considerable precipitation wouldn't think of saying it may rain. The sentence is too simple—there must be something wrong with it.

3   But the secret of good writing is to strip every sentence to its cleanest components Every word that serves no function, every long word that could be a short word, every adverb that carries the same meaning that's already in the verb, every passive construction that leaves the reader unsure of who is doing what—these are the thousand and one adulterants[1] that weaken the strength of a sentence. And they usually occur in proportion to education and rank.

4   During the late 1960s the president of my university wrote a letter to mollify[2] the alumni after a spell of campus unrest. "You are probably aware," he began, "that we have been experiencing considerable potentially explosive expressions of dissatisfaction on issues only partially related." He meant that the students had been hassling them about different things. I was far more upset by the president's English than by the students' potentially explosive expressions of dissatisfaction. I would have preferred the presidential approach taken by Franklin D. Roosevelt when he tried to convert into English his own government' memos, such as this blackout order of 1942:

> Such preparations shall be made as will completely obscure all Federal buildings and non-Federal buildings occupied by the Federal government during an air raid for any period of time from visibility by reason of internal or external illumination.

5   "Tell them," Roosevelt said, "that in buildings where they have to keep the work going to put something across the windows."

6   Simplify, simplify. Thoreau[3] said it, as we are so often reminded, and no American writer more consistently practiced what he preached. Open *Walden* to any page and you will find a man saying in a plain and orderly way what is on his mind:

> I went to the woods because I wished to live deliberately, to front only the essential facts of life, and see if I could not learn what it had to teach, and not, when I came to die, discover that I had not lived.

7   How can the rest of us achieve such enviable freedom from clutter? The answer is to clear our heads of clutter. Clear thinking becomes clear writing: one can't exist without the other. It is impossible for a muddy thinker to write good English. He may get away with it for a paragraph or two, but soon the reader will be lost, and there is no sin so grave, for he will not easily be lured back.

8   Who is this elusive creature the reader? The reader is someone with an attention span of about 30 seconds—a person assailed by many forces competing for attention.

---

1   *adulterants*: unnecessary ingredients that taint the purity of something.

2   *mollify*: to soothe in temper; appease.

3   *Henry David Thoreau* (1817–1862): American essayist, poet, and philosopher activist. *Walden*, his masterwork, was published in 1854.

At one time those forces were relatively few: newspapers, magazines, radio, spouse, children, pets. Today they also include a galaxy of electronic devices for receiving entertainment and information—television, VCRs, DVDs, CDs, video games, the Internet, e-mail, cell phones, BlackBerries, iPods—as well as a fitness program, a pool, a lawn, and that most potent of competitors, sleep. The man or woman snoozing in a chair with a magazine or book is a person who was being given too much unnecessary trouble by the writer.

9   It won't do to say that the reader is too dumb or too lazy to keep pace with the train of thought. If the reader is lost, it is usually because the writer has not been careful enough. The carelessness can take any number of forms. Perhaps a sentence is so excessively cluttered that the reader, hacking through the verbiage, simply doesn't know what it means. Perhaps a sentence has been so shoddily constructed that the reader could read it in several ways. Perhaps the writer has switched pronouns in midsentence, or has switched tenses, so the reader loses track of who is talking or when the action took place. Perhaps Sentence B is not a logical sequel to Sentence A; the writer, in whose head the connection is clear, hasn't bothered to provide the missing link. Perhaps the writer has used a word incorrectly by not taking the trouble to look it up.

10   Faced with such obstacles, readers are at first tenacious. They blame themselves—they obviously missed something, and they go back over the mystifying sentence, or over the whole paragraph, piecing it out like an ancient rune, making guesses and moving on. But they won't do that for long. The writer is making them work too hard, and they will look for one who is better at the craft.

11   Writers must therefore constantly ask: what am I trying to say? Surprisingly often they don't know. Then they must look at what he has written and ask: have I said it? Is it clear to someone encountering the subject for the first time? If it's not, some fuzz has worked its way into the machinery. The clear writer is someone clear-headed enough to see this stuff for what it is: fuzz.

12   I don't mean that some people are born clearheaded and are therefore natural writers, whereas others are naturally fuzzy and will never write well. Thinking clearly is a conscious act that writers must force upon themselves, as if they were working on any other project that requires logic: making a shopping list or doing an algebra problem. Good writing doesn't come naturally, though most people seem to think it does. Professional writer are constantly bearded[4] by strangers who say they'd like to "try a little writing sometime"—meaning when they retire from their real profession, like insurance or real estate, which is hard. Or they say, "I could write a book about that." I doubt it.

13   Writing is hard work. A clear sentence is no accident. Very few sentences come out right the first time, or even the third time. Remember this in moments of despair. If you find that writing is hard, it's because it *is* hard.

Source: Excerpted from pp. 6-11 of *On Writing Well: An Informal Guide to Writing Non-Fiction* by William Zinsser. Copyright © 1976, 1980, 1985 by William Zinsser. Reprinted by permission of HarperCollins Publishers.

4   *bearded*: confronted boldly.

The Lab vs. the Clinic: Sites of Competing Genres

BY CATHERINE F. SCHRYER

INTRODUCTION

Catherine Schryer is a professor at the University of Waterloo, in Waterloo, Ontario, Canada specializing in composition, rhetoric, and genre theory, has published in journals, and has co-written, with Laurence Steven, *Contextual Literacy: Writing Across the Curriculum* and *Towards Writing Across the Curriculum.*

In "The Lab vs. the Clinic," Schryer considers how and why the reporting methods of veterinary clinicians and researchers differ. Schryer examines how the hierarchical privileging of research over clinical practice is embedded in clinicians' respective reporting methods. Indirectly, she points to the power of language to dictate how we view the world.

This excerpt is an exemplary model of inductive research writing. As you read, pay attention to the title (which outlines the basic argument), the abstract ("Voices"), which provides a summary of the essay, and the headings, which outline the logical structure of the argument.

In chapter 7, there is an excellent student essay on this reading by Schryer.

Voices

Dr W (pathologist): Personally I dread it when a clinician dumps a manuscript on my desk for my comments. I know it's going to be badly written.

Dr B (biomedical science): The clinicians are not scientists. They are practitioners. They feel threatened by a mindset that is geared towards research. There are virtually no people in the clinics with advanced degrees. Such purely applied people can only write reviews. They lack the sort of curiosity needed for research.

Dr K (clinician): The traditional way, IMRDS [Introduction, Methods, Results, Discussion, and Summary], can lead to boredom, and it suggests that there is a finite amount of information which can be memorized by role memory. But we're trying to emphasize problem solving—the ability to dig out data and then transfer towards plans.

G (first year student): On the one side is the faculty and on the other side are the clinicians. The faculty deal with basic science and clinicians with practical information. Both views are important, but the practical is more important. When we graduate we are going to have to trade and barter with information, and we will benefit from the practical experience they provide.

Dr F (biomedical science): The writing in the clinic is different. In the basic sciences we have a different mandate. We're interested in long term proposals and ongoing research problems. It is exactly the opposite in the clinics. They have to solve problems instantly.

1   The above voices, taken from a study of literacy[1] at a veterinary school (Schryer 1989) were not located in the same time and space. Yet these different voices articulate a conversation that haunts professions such as medicine and engineering that attempt to unite research and practice. As this constructed conversation reveals, researchers and practitioners often have deeply shared prejudices about each other's activities. Schön (1983), a thoughtful observer of professional education, identified a dominant epistemology of practice that he called "technical rationality" (p. 21) as the source of this division. Technical rationality is the belief that "professional activity consists in instrumental problem solving made rigorous by the application of scientific theory and technique" (p. 21). In Schön's view, the hierarchy involved in this model, the fact that scientific theory and technique are perceived as more "rigorous" than "instrumental problem solving," has led to a serious devaluation of practitioners' skills and abilities. Practitioners' artistry, the ability of some expert practitioners to address complex, "messy" (p. 42) problems, is being ignored, Schön suggests. Yet an understanding of this artistry is clearly needed to address the complicated problems that such professions as engineering, medicine, social work and teaching actually encounter. Schön calls for a practitioner-oriented model of education that would require practitioners to become

more reflective of their own activities. Practitioner artistry is often tacit, Schön (1987) argues. By becoming aware of the strategies and tactics that actually work, practitioners will improve their own performance, pass on their skills to neophyte practitioners, and include their clients or patients in the problem solving process.

2   Schön's project is humane and liberating, but this chapter contends that his enterprise is more difficult than he might imagine. The worlds of the lab and clinic (research and practice) have been in conflict for several hundred years. This tension is expressed in their genres, their recurrent ways of representing their problem solving and knowledge construction. This chapter will focus on two central genres characteristic of research and practice in a medical, specifically a veterinary medical, context: the experimental article, expressed as Introduction, Methods, Results, Discussion and Summary (IMRDS), and the medical record keeping system, the Problem Oriented Veterinary Medical Record (POVMR). These genres reflect and help to maintain a research-practice division characteristic of disciplines like medicine. Furthermore, these genres exist in a hierarchy in which one genre, IMRDS, is more highly valued than the other. Thus, one of the forces continuing to keep researchers and practitioners apart is their information producing and recording systems, their central genres. In my view, researchers in professional writing and writing instructors associated with professional programs such as applied health, engineering or computer science need to be aware of the complex, competing values associated with different writing practices—especially those related to competing genres.

Methods

[Editor's note: In this omitted section, Schryer outlines the methodology of a prior study that led to her present study. It constituted, in Schryer's words, "a study of literacy at a veterinary school."]

Theory

3   In an effort to explain this relationship between groups and their discursive practices I turned to genre theory and developed the following definition (Schryer 1993). The concept of genre can help researchers describe a "stabilized enough site of social and ideological action" (p. 200). This definition reflects my agreement with Miller (1984; revised version Chapter 2, this volume) who defines genre as "recurrent, significant action" (p. 165). Each of these three terms—recurrent, significant and action—reflect key insights. As a recurrent phenomenon, a genre represents a series of texts sharing features at the levels of content, form and style. These, discursive practices shape their users while at the same time users affect the genre. This notion of recurrence also involves the social actors who construct the genre. Only those involved can interpret a situation and any possible responses as recurrent and significant. Consequently, genre researchers must consult the users of discursive practices to see if these practices are

both recurrent and significant. Most importantly, Miller, and Bazerman (1988), observe that rhetorical genres are forms of social action. A genre coordinates work—from the simplest action of constructing a shopping list to the complex activity involved in conducting scientific research.

4   Bakhtin (1981) acknowledges that genres are not only sites of social action—they are also sites of ideological action. As Bakhtin makes clear these discourse structures are imbued with "concrete value judgments." He suggests, "They knit together with specific objects and with the belief systems of certain genres of expression and points of view peculiar to particular professions" (p. 289). Genres express deeply held values or, to echo Williams (1983), the tacit sets of shared values that constitute common sense for particular groups (p. 38).

5   Bakhtin's (1986) most important contribution, however, to this reconceptualization of genre is his paradoxical observation that genres are sites of both stability and instability. Speech genres are in Bakhtin's term of "utterances," and the boundaries of an utterance are determined by a *change of speaking subjects* (p. 71, original emphasis). Consequently, built into his notion of genre is a sense of "addressivity" or attitude to the audience. This audience has a rich repertoire of utterances at its disposal. These genres or utterances are in a dialectric with each other and thus constantly influencing and changing each other. Bakhtin pointed out, for example, that both secondary and primary speech genres exist (p. 62). Secondary genres, such as the novel or research paper, are in a constant process of subsuming more primary genres such as letters or lists. From Bakhtin's perspective even the most monologic and thus ideological genres such as scientific articles or medical records are sites of struggle between the centripetal and centrifugal forces within language.

6   In this chapter, then, genres are viewed as stabilized-for-now or stabilized-enough sites of social and ideological action. This definition builds in a sense of genres as simultaneously diachronic and synchronic. All genres have a complex set of relation with past texts and with other present texts: genres come from somewhere and are transforming into something else. Because they exist before their users, genres shape their users, yet users and their discourse communities constantly remake and reshape them. Most importantly, genres are inherently ideological; they embody the unexamined or tacit way of performing some social action. Hence they can represent the ways that a dominant élite does things. This theoretical perspective allows researchers to ask the following kinds of questions: Where does this genre come from? What are the stabilizing (recurrent conventions and structures) features that characterize these texts? What are the destabilizing features? What are the values and beliefs instantiated within a set of practices? Who can or cannot use this genre? How does this genre affect its users?

History: The Larger Context

7   There is no doubt that divisions between research and practice extend well beyond the bounds of the college I studied. In *Educating the Reflective Practitioner*, Schön

(1987) explores the normative curriculum that governs professions such as medicine which insist that "instrumental problem solving is grounded in systematic, preferably scientific knowledge" (p. 8). Such a curriculum implies the following hierarchy of knowledge:

- basic science,
- applied science,
- technical skills of day-to-day practice (p. 9).

8   Within even such minor (according to Schön) professions as social work and education, proximity to research, basic science or the making of theoretical, prepositional knowledge brings both prestige and power. Between professions, those disciplines which present themselves as "rigorous practitioners of a science-based knowledge" (p. 9) generally have a higher status. Schön and others interested in professional education are radically questioning this model of education. They ask whether "the prevailing concepts of professional education ever yield a curriculum adequate to the complex, unstable, uncertain and conflictual worlds of practice" (p. 12). They point to the gaps existing between the professional schools and the workplace, between research and practice. Schön advocates the development of a "reflective practicum" (p. 18), a practicum aimed at helping students "acquire the kinds of artistry essential to competence in the indeterminate zones of practice" (p. 18).

[Editor's note: In this omitted section, Schryer outlines the historical context of the researcher-practioner divide, citing Latour's analysis of the "struggle between research and practice" over the past hundred years in the discipline of medicine.]

History: The Local Context

9   The diverse belief structure that both Schön and Latour identify was at work in the college that I studied. It was clearly evident that researchers and clinicians (the group most closely associated with practitioners) viewed themselves as distinct groups. Researchers in the biomedical sciences, pathology or immunology had doctorates. To achieve their degrees they worked closely with a senior researcher who supervised both their research and their writing. One researcher who supervised graduate students spoke in detail about her students' papers and the suggestions she provided to make them publishable. As a group, researchers valued doctorates since this research represented their initial contribution to the knowledge or theory development of their disciplines.

10   This value placed on contributing knowledge to the discipline was echoed in a curious way in an undergraduate ethics course. A panel of speakers representing both researchers and clinicians was addressing the issue of using live animals in experimentation. The one hundred or so undergraduate students in the course were deeply concerned about this issue. In several of their other courses they were learning surgical techniques using live animals, and many found themselves in an ethical dilemma, especially since the previous semester the anaesthetic they had been using in the "bunny labs" had not worked effectively. The clinicians on the panel understood the concern for a better anaesthetic but not the revulsion at using live animals. Knowing how live animals responded to surgery would prevent future errors in the students' own surgeries, the clinicians argued. The researchers, however, did sympathize. A prominent biomedical researcher told the students, "I am very uneasy about the ethical implications of using animals to add to your own data banks. In research, it is more defensible since you are adding to information banks, not just improving your own expertise." In other words, it was ethical to "sacrifice" animals if their deaths led to new knowledge, but not appropriate if their deaths only served to enhance the students' surgical skills.

11   This belief in the greater value of collective knowledge was also reflected in the teaching strategies of these researchers. They believed strongly that they provided the "basics," the fundamental knowledge that students needed in order to solve individual clinical problems. These "basics" included all the fundamental systems of anatomy, biochemistry, physiology, etc. "Basic" information, of course, was valid, collective knowledge that originally derived from empirical research. Students were expected to memorize these fundamentals. The material itself was often presented through lectures characterized by massive amounts of handouts, overheads and slides. In veterinary medicine in particular this emphasis on the "basics" is becoming problematic. Veterinary students have traditionally studied every biological entity except humankind. From the students' perspective the effect of this massive inundation of information was "overwhelmosis."

12   The value placed on developing new information was matched by the value placed on the ability to write up and publish such information. It was on this level that many researchers critiqued clinicians and practitioners. One pathologist observed that he would like to see the students more involved in writing, but lamented that students were too influenced by the clinicians, and that clinicians did not research or publish. Another pointed to a clinician-oriented journal and complained that the worst writing appeared in such journals—not only was the writing sloppy, but even worse, the research was derivative. Other commentators were fairer in their assessment. They pointed out that clinicians lacked training in research and writing and more importantly perhaps the time required for such activities.

13   Of course, the clinicians had a different perspective. Students can memorize "like stink" the clinician told me, but they are lost in their books, and they cannot solve clinical problems. This individual described herself as a clinician first, then a teacher, then an administrator and finally as a researcher. Her training did not include a dissertation and a doctorate. Rather she had passed a series of board exams for which she had read five years of recent journal articles. She had completed an intense multiple choice exam (five to six hours) and written a series of short reports explaining solutions to medical problems. Her work day was also very different from a researcher's. When she was not teaching, she was in the clinic on call for at least eight to 10 hours and always supervising the actions of a group of four to six students.

14   Like most clinicians, she lacked the freedom to control her own time. Like other clinicians, she also seemed to prefer ambiguity to certainty. In medical and surgical rounds, students were constantly warned that nothing was black and white and that most rules were only rules of thumb to be adjusted to a specific case. Her teaching techniques were distinct as well. As a third year student described,

> I like her clinical approach. She presents us with cases and says here's a picture of this case. And then she asks us questions. I'm tired of a pure science approach, frustrated with copious scientific material which we have to memorize immediately.

15   Like many clinicians, however, she may not get her tenure, since she may not publish enough to remain at the college.

16   This perceived difference between research and practice and the hierarchy at work is nowhere more evident than in a set of definitions found in documents of particular interest to the college. Veterinary colleges across the North American continent are restructuring their programmes in response to recent social and economic changes. While I was at the college, a report on the Purdue plans for reformulating their program was circulated among faculty. Essentially the report advocating educating rather than training new veterinarians. According to the report, "*Education* is the instruction in and cultivation of an understanding of the system of ideas and conviction which are valued by society, including the philosophy and method of science. Education is generalizing, expanding." On the other hand, "*Training* is the mastery of knowledge and skills by practice and apprenticeship and is aimed at the identification and solution of problems. Training is focused." The value system at work in these definitions is self-evident. Education means medical research; training means medical practice.

17   Latour (1987) and Schön's insights as well as events and documents at the college suggest that a set of binary opposition traverses professional contexts that attempt to unite research and practice. The list below attempts to summarize these competing interests and values:

Research	**Practice**
Science	Medicine
Information development	Case problem solving
Memorization of facts	Problem or case-oriented teaching
Communalistic	Individualistic
Long-term	Short-term, immediate
Validity	Ambiguity and complexity
Methods	Skills
Education	Training

18   It would be simplistic to suggest that all health professions divide simply and easily along these lines. Several faculty members worked in both research and clinical areas. Both researchers and practitioners would also contend that they engage in problem solving, but each group defines problems quite differently. In her study of biomedical researchers, Adams-Smith (1984) quotes her researcher informants as acknowledging that problems are the life-blood of research projects. One of her informants then explained:

Biomedical research . . . is not a matter of problem-solving. Rather it is the observation of something interesting that does not seem to fit the pattern, followed by the observation of this phenomenon over a period of time, and the recording and explanation of the findings. (pp. 19–20)

19   In fact, researchers identify and choose to work on particular problems, and they can work towards simplifying and controlling the variables with their problem. Practitioners, especially clinicians, must work with the complex, often interrelated problems that a particular case presents. Neither clinicians nor practitioners can choose their problems, and, in fact, the art of practice might exist in actuality recognizing problems that characterize a case. This essential difference in task and the socialization process used to prepare students for their careers is deeply embedded within the profession's basic genres.

Competing Genres

20   The above insights gathered during an ethnographic study of a veterinary college reflect a research-practice division characteristic of many disciplines such as medicine. Commentators such as Donald Schön suggest that some rapprochement is possible to span the growing fault lines between researchers and practitioners. Research gathered during this study, however, indicates that power relations in fields such as veterinary medicine are often expressed through genres related to research or practice. These genres are distinctly polarized in their epistemology, their values, their organizational structure, their purpose and their perceived validity. Depending on key career decisions, students will be deeply socialized into either of these competing traditions located in the lab or the clinic.

21   A genre choice indicates the nature of the writer's own socialization. In the veterinary college that forms the basis of this study, students training to be practitioners were rarely taught to be producers of research. They were, however, always taught to be consumers of research. On several occasions student-practitioners were referred to as "databanks" or were directed to file information in their data banks. The only students specifically taught research skills and supervised as to the writing up of their results were graduate students in either the basic sciences or in the clinical areas of the college. However, different research traditions existed for each of these groups—one based on the experimental article (Introduction, Methods, Results, Discussion, Summary or IMRDS) and the other on medical problem solving systems, specifically the Problem Oriented Medical Record (POMR) system. These two systems capture the paradigmatic difference in world view between two traditions, that of the lab and that of the clinic.

Experimental Genre

22   The IMRDS approach to presenting information is so ubiquitous and pervasive that it is difficult to isolate it and see its history, the social action that it enacts, its inherent values, and epistemology. On the surface IMRDS appears a simple heuristic. The introduction defines the problem (why?); the methods section explains how the problem will be

analysed (how?); the results relate what was discovered (what?); the discussion reveals the significance of the results (so what?); and the summary reduces the content found in the above structure into a microcosm again answering why, how, what and so what.

23 As Bazerman (1988) reminds us, the experimental article has a complex history. From its beginning as narrative accounts of experiments embedded within letters exchanged between the experimenters, the research article has evolved into a "logical and empirical juggernaut, with every step in the reasoning backed up with carefully described experimental experiences precisely related to the formal proposition" (p. 121). In his seminal account of the experimental article Bazerman points out the constructed nature of the rhetorical strategies that provide this sense of inevitable logic and order. For example, he points to Isaac Newton's brilliant invention of the second person imperative in the method section (pp. 115–6). As Swales (1990) observes, this tactic turns readers into virtual witnesses (p. 111) compelled to cooperate with the writer in reconstructing the experiment.

24 Accounts of the purpose of social action that IMRDS enacts exist at various levels. At the college, graduate students in the biomedical sciences were sometimes directed to handbooks such as *A Guide to Scientific Writing* by Lindsay (1984), an animal scientist at the University of Western Australia. From Lindsay's perspective, the article is "no more and no less than an objective and accurate account of a piece of research" (p. 3). Several research studies (Latour and Woolgar 1979, 1988; Knorr-Cetina 1981; Gilbert and Mulkay 1984) challenge this perspective by documenting the relationship between an article and the research on which it was based. In her study of a large research centre, for example, Knorr-Cetina (1981) observes that published account was a reversed version of the actual research process. Prelli (1989) agrees that research reports routinely suppress false leads or unsuccessful procedures. He suggests, in fact, that:

> Research articles are thus more persuasive because the articles present an image of determinacy in science and obscure the influences of historical and situational circumstances and possibilities of alternate approaches and judgments. (p. 103)

25 As Swales recognizes, the research article is in fact a very different genre than the laboratory report (1990:118). The real task of IMRDS, Swales argues, is to provide "complexly distanced reconstructions of research activities" (p. 175). Because they are so driven by the need to anticipate audience reactions, these reconstructions are filled with rhetorical strategies at all levels. Bazerman would add that the real task of IMRDS is to provide symbolic representations of the phenomenal world (1988:187). These representations are expressions of the need for order and control of the natural world.

26 This need for order and control is central to the common-sense belief structures or ideologies that pervade much of the empirical research tradition and its genres. In his generative work on scientific ethos, Merton identifies the institutional norms of universalism, communality, disinterestedness, organized scepticism, originality and humility that govern science and facilitate "the establishment and extension of certified objective knowledge of the physical world" (Prelli 1989:105). The scientific article with its emphasis on inductive style, a style that Prelli suggests "implies that claims were

found through impartial investigation of phenomena that have independent, objective, and undeniable existence" (p. 103) is the ideological vehicle for such values.

27 The ideological or common-sense system of beliefs embedded with IMRDS is nowhere more apparent than in its organizational structure, an arrangement which Gross (1990) identifies as epistemological (p. 85). The sequence of introduction, methods, results, and discussion Gross insists is essential to mirror the transition of contingent laboratory events to the necessity of natural processes (p. 89). Introductions work to "recreate a theoretical world in which the otherwise contingent events of the laboratory will attain their significance as scientific experiments, instantiations of particular natural laws" (p. 90). However, introductions, as Swales observes, must create this theoretical world in relation to other current work and researchers. Introductions, in fact, have to create a research space which accomplishes three tasks or moves:

1. establish the relevance of the research field itself;
2. locate the specific research project in relation to the field; and
3. occupy and defend a particular niche in the field by means of the research project (Swales 1990:142).

28 Lindsay also advises neophyte article writers to create space for their research in their introductions. He advices his readers to construct carefully their hypotheses or focal points. Lindsay is clear in his definition of the hypothesis. "It is not a statement of fact," he announces, "but a statement which takes us just beyond known facts and anticipates the next logical step in a sequence of facts" (1984:7). A good hypothesis exists on the cutting edge between the old and the new, past and future fact. It creates new space.

29 Method sections, because they embody the deeply shared value placed on replication, continue to be obligatory in most scientific disciplines. Yet much research (Knorr-Cetina 1981) suggests that such replication is not really possible. Laboratory skills have become so complex and background knowledge so specialized that methods have become in Swales's terms "highly abstracted reformulations of final outcomes in which an enormous amount is taken for granted" (1990:121). In explaining the methods section, Lindsay suggests, the only criterion is that a knowledgeable colleague should be able to repeat procedures. In fact, the art of writing methods sections exists in knowing what one can safely omit. Methods are inherently rhetorical enthymeme structures built on current knowledge and beliefs about procedures. For example, the following methods section taken from a research article in a veterinary journal presumes extensive knowledge of accepted procedures:

> For the clitoral fossa, Culturette swabs (Canlab, Toronto, Ontario) were used; a disposable sterile "guarded culture instrument" (Kalayjin Industries Inc., Long Beach California) with a protective sheath capped at the tip was used to collect vaginal, cervical, and uterine samples. Swabs were taken by the technique Higgins *et al.* (p. 11). Bermundez *et al.* 1987:520)

30   Only the initiated would recognize a "guarded culture instrument" or the Higgins technique.

31   Deeply enacted in the results section is the attempt to create a "reader-environment in which the tentative facts can be allowed to 'speak for themselves'" (Swales 1990:121). Lindsay supports this normative position when he advises his reader that only results should appear in the results section. Results must preserve their "objectivity" and remain aloof from the interpretation found in the discussion section. Of course, as Lindsay admits, "Most data requires some treatment" (1984:15), and the data of most relevance to the hypothesis and consequently the discussion must be highlighted.

32   The task of the discussion sections is to align the results with the theoretical frame of the introduction and thus create and defend the new research niche. Or as Gross, reflecting Bazerman, notes, "in the Discussion the data from Results will be transformed into candidate knowledge by adducing in their favor their close correspondence to the report's claim" (1990:90). Gross comments, too, that the data of results and the claims of discussions derive from two different worlds: the world of the lab and the world of nature. The essential task of the discussion is to convince readers that the data are consistent with the already known, constraining "facts" about nature and that the article is making a valid claim to knowledge production. Appropriately then in his advice regarding discussions, Lindsay is at his most overtly rhetorical. If the writer has planned his or her introduction and results carefully, he suggests, the reader need only be guided gently "by logical steps to see things from your point of view" (p. 18) and with careful positioning of arguments and evidence and precise management of style "you can manipulate the reader into ranking the priorities of your arguments in the same way as you have" (p. 22).

Recording Genre

33   When genres are perceived as stabilized sites of social action, then professional record keeping, the formalized accounts of doctors, social workers, police, etc., also assume a special importance. The sociologist Dorothy E. Smith (1984) explored the impact of such practices both on the organizations that construct and use them and on larger social interests. Our lives, she said are "infused with a process of inscription" (p. 59) or the rendering of an event or object in documentary form (p. 65). Documents such as records are the very fabric of organizations, their fact-making mechanisms. From both the perspective of genre conceived as social action and from Smith's critical account of the function of professional records, it is clear that the social processes which produce records need to be examined as well as their impact on both their producers and the larger community.

34   The Problem Oriented Veterinary Medical Record (POVMR) is a variant of the Problem Oriented Medical Record system developed in the 1960s for human medicine by Dr Lawrence Wed (1969) in an effort to make medical records more readable, more open to monitoring, evaluation and standardization.[2] Prior to Weed, record keeping had been generally haphazard but basically dominated by the Source-Oriented Record (SOR) system. In the SOR system the practitioner records the presenting complaint, a review of symptoms, and physical exam results. This is followed by "a statement of the most likely provisional diagnosis, often accompanied by one or more differential diagnoses" (Tugwell and Dok 1985:148). The investigation and management of the case are then listed together below the diagnosis. Progress notes follow the same format with no standardized approach for recording.

35   Weed was intensely critical of the SOR system. He believed that the system encouraged physicians to jump to diagnostic conclusions and to ignore the complex problems that could afflict a patient. He saw that medical records, because of their failure to break problems down into manageable units, and their failure to connect those problems to subsequent investigation and treatment, were often comprehensible only to their initial writers. This meant that medical records could not be used for either evaluation or research purposes, and were sources of mismanagement when more than one health care provider was involved in a case. Finally, he wanted to redesign records to mirror the medical problem solving process itself. They could become "audits of action" (introduction). From a rhetorical perspective, we might add that his system offers new physicians a heuristic that reflects the actual problem solving structures that Weed believed many experienced physicians employed.

36   [Figure 1] illuminates Weed's project. It is a visual depiction of his system as it is presented to veterinary students at the college I studied. During the early 1980s, younger clinicians converted the animal hospital's record system from the SOR to a

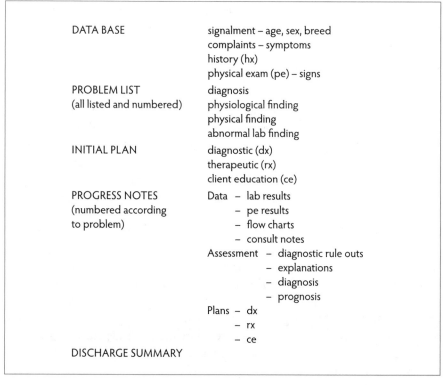

DATA BASE	signalment – age, sex, breed
	complaints – symptoms
	history (hx)
	physical exam (pe) – signs
PROBLEM LIST	diagnosis
(all listed and numbered)	physiological finding
	physical finding
	abnormal lab finding
INITIAL PLAN	diagnostic (dx)
	therapeutic (rx)
	client education (ce)
PROGRESS NOTES	Data – lab results
(numbered according	– pe results
to problem)	– flow charts
	– consult notes
	Assessment – diagnostic rule outs
	– explanations
	– diagnosis
	– prognosis
	Plans – dx
	– rx
	– ce
DISCHARGE SUMMARY	

Figure 1 ◆ **Problem Oriented Veterinary Medical Record System (POVMR)**

variant of Weed's POMR, a variant they call the Problem Oriented Veterinary Medical Record system (POVMR).[3]

37 For rhetoricians, the recursive nature of the system is particularly interesting. The data is analysed and used to create a hierarchical set of "problems." These problems are a clustered set of symptoms, observations or laboratory results. During their training, students are taught to recognize and name provisionally these configurations. At this stage in the process, the experienced practitioner might hazard a diagnosis, but veterinary students are urged to keep their options open and thus prevent premature and often incorrect diagnoses. Instead these related configurations are named as "problems."

38 After an initial plan for the management of the case is drawn up, practitioners put their plans into action and then observe the results of their intervention through progress notes. These notes are central to Weed's contention that records could be audits of thought and action. Instead of a haphazard collection of action, observations and data, the POVMR notes are organized according to the problems identified in the initial assessment of the case. Under each problem, the practitioner lists data, assessment and plans. As the initial intervention is put into action, symptoms should change and laboratory results will arrive. These results become data. As the data changes, the practitioner's assessment or explanation of the disease or metabolic processes at work will also change. The practitioner might even reach a diagnosis. All this interrelation of data and the practitioner's knowledge of physiology and medicine is recorded in the assessment section. Finally, as the practitioner's understanding of a case increases, so will the plans change. These changes in plans, of course, produce more data. Progress notes record this recursive interaction of data, assessment and plans until the problem is resolved.

IMRDS vs. POVMR

39 A comparison between IMRDS and POVMR as genres reveals some areas of similarity but also some startling differences. Both genres as found in medicine use similar technical language. In fact, one of the main aims of medical education is to teach both researchers and practitioners the precise meanings of technical terms. Both genres are also problem solving heuristics. IMRDS is meant to be a linguistic reconstruction of the research process. POVMR is meant to be an audit of action, a representation of the problem-solving techniques used by experienced physicians.

40 However, their differences outweigh their similarities in terms of purpose, audience and epistemology. IMRDS is essentially a reporting rather than a recording genre. In composing a report, the writer looks back in time towards a set of events. The writer has the opportunity to select and control the kinds of material that go into the report. IMRDS does not reflect the possibly messy, recursive nature of scientific research. Research is essentially an effort of "bricolage"; yet IMRDS turns it into a work of "engineering." In the report, a problem is identified, variables are controlled, and a hypothesis is tested. In fact, the purpose of the experimental article is, as Law notes (1986b), to act as a funnel of interests. Experimental articles begin with as broad a focus as possible and then through a series of interconnecting arguments ("interessements") draw or channel readers into accepting a specific finding. Law explains:

> The mouth of such a funnel is broad in order to suck in as wide an audience as possible, focused on a particular series of points. Interests are thus channelled and flow along a course that is determined by the linked series of interessements. These are deployed by the authors in order to prevent escapes—to ensure that the reader reaches the approved conclusion and then moves with this back to the general once more. (Law 1986b: 77)

41   The article wants to compel acceptance of its findings and thus is inherently argumentative in its purpose.

42   POVMR, in contract, is essentially a recording genre, even though it sometimes appears in article format. Practitioners cannot afford the luxury of looking back on events. As little time as possible must elapse between events and their recording, their translation into identifiable problems. Practitioners have little choice as to the complexity of problems they deal with. They often deal with "zebra" cases, cases with multiple and rare interacting problems. The work of "bricolage," the recursive often messy nature of problem solving, is entirely evident. Variables cannot be eliminated; they can only be discovered, identified and managed. In fact, the purpose of records is quite distinct. Records not only document events and cases (animals or people), they are records of intervention. Records order treatments—diagnostic, pharmaceutical or surgical. Records act immediately to change phenomenological events. Finally in today's litigious world, records are acts of justification. Practitioners need to be able to reconstruct their actions in order to defend their interventions.

43   The two genres differ in their addressivity as well. IMRDS writers are hyper-aware of a critical audience both during the research and writing process. Law suggests (1986a), in fact, that particular problems are selected and refined as they are of interest to particular audiences. During the research process, researchers are on the lookout for publishable results—results that will interest their projected audience. Much current research suggests that the experimental article, despite its claims to objectivity, is, as noted earlier, an inherently rhetorical act. Even methods sections, according to Latour and Bastide (1986) are polemical. Methods are filled with passwords (one word descriptions of techniques which those in the know realize must be done if a procedure is to work) and secret recipes (certain procedures are omitted since those in-the-know know that such procedures are always performed). Methods sections are carefully written to prevent objections from critical readers.

44   Records, on the other hand, have a different sense of audience and audience awareness. Records are written for a narrower audience of those involved in a case and those socialized into reading records. Records themselves are extraordinarily elliptical in their sentence structure and style. In my earlier research (1993), I noted the effect of this elliptical quality on the students and faculty—the deeply shared conventions that make communications rapid but exclusive—only for those in the know (p. 224).

These shared conventions also extend to organizational patterns even when records lie behind published articles. The following paragraph, written by two clinicians, appeared in the clinician/practitioner oriented journal produced by the college. This paragraph follows the signalment (information regarding the animal's age, sex and breed), initial data regarding the history and physical exam results, and identification of the main presenting problem, "a grade III lameness, with a short anterior phase of the stride in the affected left forelimb." The paragraph reads:

> Radiographs of the left shoulder demonstrated a focal osteolysis restricted to the proximal physis and greater tubercle of the humerus. The cartilaginous space of the scapulohumeral joint was widened and indistinct, a finding that was consistent with a diagnosis of septic arthritis accompanying physeal osteomyelitis.

45　　Those who read records would recognize not only the sections devoted to history and physical exam results and the focus on the presenting problem or problems but would also recognize the interaction between data, assessment and plans echoed above. In the first sentence a plan, a radiographic test, produces data, evidence regarding "osteolysis." An assessment emerges from the data—a possible diagnosis of "septic arthritis accompanying physeal osteomyelitis." The action of DAPing a case or the interaction of data, assessment and plans is the central problem solving and reading strategy of users of the POVMR. Yet the main moves of this organizational structure are never signalled in these kinds of texts with heading or with any other typographical feature.

46　　In the rest of this journal, basically devoted to research articles, the structure of IMRDS was always visually identified by means of headings. The main moves, the problem identification structures, were always identified, but more importantly perhaps is the narrow range of interests or "interessements" covered by POVMR articles. This is evident both in their introductions and references. IMRDS articles begin with a large funnel of interests so as to attract as many interested researchers as possible. POVMR articles often begin with a narrowly defined case. This narrowness is nowhere more evident than in the reference section. IMRDS articles normally have extensive bibliographies in order to align the interests of the lab with other researchers and labs. POVMR articles rarely have extensive reference sections.

47　　This pattern of restricting the POVMR to narrow interests and thus limited audience extends to oral presentation as well. During my research at the college I observed graduate students from both the biomedical and clinical areas presenting their research in progress at grand rounds. Those trained in IMRDS's tradition not only used the IMRDS's structure but always connected their research to wider interests in their disciplines. Graduate students in the clinical areas had a harder time. They usually presented in the POVMR format, and rarely connected their cases either to other cases or to wider research interests. As a result they were often critiqued, even by clinicians. Their research was seen as unsubstantial and invalid.

48　　Finally the epistemological assumptions and status assigned to the production of knowledge in each genre differ. At the college, knowledge produced by IMRDS was simply deemed more valid, more "real" (i.e. scientific), than information produced by POVMR. As a genre, IMRDS allows its users to select and narrow problems, to control variables, to present results as the work of "engineering" rather than "bricolage," and to align the interests of a specific lab to the wider research community. These strategies are inherently more persuasive than the strategies available in the POVMR. The strategies embedded within IMRDS allow researchers to instantiate the central ideology of science—the need to order and control the natural world. The strategies involved in the POVMR reflect practitioners' inability to select and simplify problems and their consequent need to respond to problems as they emerge and develop.

49 In my view, the consequences of this division between research and practice, a division partially held in place by competing genres, are serious for professions like veterinary medicine. Before I left the college, I wrote a report for the Curriculum Committee. The report echoed many of the divisive comments also found in this chapter and explored with college members the possibility that the research-practice split had important implications for the college. In particular, I noted that the students disliked intensely the lecture-driven "basic" pedagogy characteristic of the first two years and that this pedagogy stood in sharp contrast to the problem-oriented, case-driven pedagogy of later years. The labelling of students as "data banks" into which information would be poured was also problematic. The metaphor assumed that students were passive and that as practitioners they would never produce valid "data" themselves or, in other words, contribute to the knowledge basis of the profession. In fact, one of the problems this college faces is that after graduation most of its students, do not contribute to the college's development. In my view, the very socializing genres at the college were working to maintain this division. I recommended to the college that they consider two actions. Entry level instructors, mostly researchers in the basic sciences, needed to be aware of the case method as expressed in the POVMR and could develop simple cases to illustrate their points. The assessment section in the POVMR was also a part of the record keeping system that research-oriented faculty could use in their pedagogy because during assessment practitioners test their judgments against known medical knowledge. At the same time, I advised the college that all students should be exposed to both kinds of genres and traditions. A new option is opening up in veterinary medicine—consultancy work in which veterinarians will need both sets of skills. Consultants will not be working on individual cases, but will be hired to identify and prevent problems occurring in large groups of animals. Thus they will need to be able to diagnose from a complex set of problems (the practitioner's skill), gather and test data (the researcher's ability) and develop a plan to prevent future problems. The information consultants produce will be valuable both to researchers and practitioners.

50 The college is slowly moving to implement these suggestions, although not perhaps because I identified this set of problems. Rather the tensions in disciplines that attempt to link research and practice are so high that solutions, even temporary ones must be found to alleviate the pressure. However, change, in my view, will come very slowly indeed to professions like medicine and engineering. In these professions, their genres, their ways of speaking, writing, reading and listening, deeply enact their ideology. And in professions with research and practice traditions, the genres of research instantiate far more closely the central ideology of science—the belief in order and controlling the natural world.

51 In conclusion, recent research on genre has suggested that genres conceived as stabilized sites of social action coordinate the work of groups and organizations. The research gathered in this study contributes to this notion by illustrating some of the work that certain genres can and cannot do. IMRDS and POVMR perform different tasks. This study adds to the growing work on genre by illuminating some of the inherent ideological and socializing forces at work within genres. These forces can define groups and the work they can do; they can even keep members of apparently the same discourse, community separate and apart. Clinicians and practitioners who speak and write only the POVMR will not be able to complete as effectively as those socialized into IMRDS. Research will continue to dictate to practice in disciplines such as medicine and engineering, despite the efforts of reformers such as Donald Schön, as long as groups are socialized into different genres, especially when one genre is more highly valued.

ACKNOWLEDGEMENT

52 I am grateful to the organizers of the Rethinking Genre Conference for comments and suggestions on the original draft of this paper. I extend particular thanks to Carolyn Miller who provided useful comments on the final version.

NOTES

1 The college and all participants in this study remain anonymous.
2 An extended version of this account of medical record keeping appears in Schryer (1993).
3 The main difference between the POMR and POVMR lies in the structure of the progress notes. Medical doctors "SOAP" a case. They collect Subjective and Objective data, Assess the data, and arrive at a Plan. Subjective data is what the patient tells the doctor. Objective data is what the physician actually sees. Veterinarians, on the other hand, "DAP" a case. They cannot collect subjective data because animals cannot talk. So they only collect data. The actions of assessment and planning remain the same in both systems.

REFERENCES

Adams-Smith, D.E. (1984) "Medical Discourse: Aspects of Author's Comment." *The ESP Journal*, **3**, pp. 25–36.

Bakhtin, M.M. (1981) "Discourse in the Novel," *The Dialogic Imagination: Four Essays*, (trans. C. Emerson and M. Holquist, ed. M. Holquist) Austin, TX: University of Texas Press, pp. 259–422.

Bakhtin, M.M. (1986) "The Problem of Speech Genres," *Speech Genres and Other Late Essays*, (trans. V.W. McGee, ed. C. Emerson and M. Holquist) Austin, TX: University of Texas Press, pp. 60–102.

Bazerman, C. (1988) *Shaping Written Knowledge: The Genre and Activity of the Experimental Article in Science*, Madison, WI: University of Wisconsin Press.

Bermudez, V., Miller, R., Johnson, W., Rosendal, S. and Ruhnke, L. (1987) "Recovery of Mycoplasma ssp. from the Reproductive Track of the Mare During the Estrous Cycle," *Canadian Veterinary Journal*, **28**, pp. 519–22.

Fetterman, D. (1984) *Ethnography in Educational Evolution*, Beverly Hills, CA: Sage.

Gilbert, G.N. and Mulkay, M. (1984) *Opening Pandora's Box: A Sociological Analysis of Scientists' Discourse,* Cambridge: Cambridge University Press.

Glaser, B. and Strauss, A.L. (1967) *The Discovery of Grounded Theory: Strategies for Qualitative Research,* Chicago, IL: Aldine.

Gross, A. (1990) *The Rhetoric of Science,* Cambridge, MA: Harvard University Press.

Heath, S. (1983) *Ways With Words: Language, Life and Work in Communities and Classrooms,* Cambridge University Press.

Knorr-Cetina, K.D. (1981) *The Manufacture of Knowledge.* Oxford: Pergamon.

Latour, B. (1987) *Science in Action: How to Follow Scientists and Engineers Through Society,* Milton Keynes, Bucks: Open University Press.

Latour, B. (1988) *The Pasteurization of France,* (trans. A. Sheridan and J. Law) Cambridge, MA: Harvard University Press.

Latour, B. and Bastide, F. (1986) "Writing Science—Fact and Fiction: The Analysis of the Process of Reality Construction Through the Application of Socio-Semiotic Methods to Scientific Texts" in Callon, M., Law, J. and Rip, A. (eds) *Mapping the Dynamics of Science and Technology,* London: Macmllian, pp. 51–66.

Latour, B. and Woolgard, S. (1979) *Laboratory Life: The Social Construction of Scientific Facts,* Beverly Hills, CA: Sage.

Law, J. (1986a) "Laboratories and Texts," in Callon, M., Law, J. and Rip, A. (eds) *Science and Technology,* London: Macmillan, pp. 35–55.

Law, J. (1986b) "The Heterogeneity of Texts," in Callon, M., Law, J. and Rip, A. (eds) *Mapping the Dynamics of Science and Technology,* London: Macmillan, pp. 67–83.

Levine, K. (1986) *The Social Context of Literacy,* London: Routledge and Kegan Paul.

Lindsay, D. (1984) *A Guide to Scientific Writing: Manual for Students and Research Workers,* Melbourne: Longman Cheshire.

Lynch, M. and Woolgar, S. (1988) "Introduction: Sociological Orientation to Representational Practice in Science," *Human Studies,* **11,** pp. 99–116.

Miller, C.R. (1984) "Genres as Social Action," *Quarterly Journal of Speech,* **70,** pp. 151–57.

Prelli, L.J. (1989) *A Rhetoric of Science: Inventing Scientific Discourse,* Columbia, SC: University of South Carolina Press.

Schön, D.A. (1983) *The Reflective Practitioner: How Professional Think in Action,* New York: Basic Books.

Schön, D.A. (1987) *Educating the Reflective Practitioner,* San Francisco, CA: Jossey-Bass.

Schryer, C.F. (1989) "An Ethnographic Study of Literacy at a Veterinary College: A Consultancy Model of Research," doctoral dissertation, University of Louisville, KY (Dissertation Abstracts International, 51, 9026449).

Schryer, C.F. (1993) "Records as Genre," *Written Communication,* **10,** pp. 200–34.

Smith, D.E. (1984) "Textually Mediated Social Organization," *International Social Science Journal,* **36,** pp. 59–75.

Street, B. (1984) *Literacy in Theory and Practice,* Cambridge: Cambridge University Press.

Swales, J.M. (1990) *Genre Analysis: English in Academic and Research Settings,* Cambridge: Cambridge University Press.

Tugwell, P. and Dok, C. (1985) in Neufeld, V.R. and Norman, G.A. (eds) *Assessing Clinical Competence,* New York: Springer, pp. 142–82.

Weed, L.L. (1969) *Medical Records, Medical Education and Patient Care: The Problem-Oriented Record as a Basic Tool,* Chicago, IL: Year Book Medical Publisher.

Williams, R. (1983) *Keywords: A Vocabulary of Culture and Society,* New York: Oxford University Press.

Source: Excerpted from Schryer, Catherine. "The Lab vs. the Clinic: Sites of Competing Genes" in *Genre and the New Rhetoric,* eds., Aviva Freedman and Peter Medway (London: Taylor & Francis, 1994), 105–124. Print. Reproduced by permission of Taylor & Francis Books UK.

QUESTIONS FOR DISCUSSION

1. What is the significance of the "Voices" section?
2. What are Schryer's primary texts? How does she use them?
3. What is Schryer's hypothesis?
4. What research is Schryer primarily engaging with to frame her argument?
5. How do the two veterinary reporting models become focus points in a battle of values and relationships of power?
6. What conclusion does Schryer come to?
7. Review Schryer's references at the end of the essay. Can you identify how she uses these references to support her theory or her analysis of history, for example?

FROM READING TO WRITING

1. Outline Schryer's inductive argument by paying attention to her headings, and in a few words summarize what each section contains. Can you see the logic of her argument?
2. Identify how Schryer uses background context, description, and argument. How does she balance this information?
3. Write a short paragraph summarizing Schryer's concluding comments.

◆ ◆ Animal Rights ◆ ◆ ◆ ◆ ◆ ◆ ◆ ◆ ◆ ◆ ◆ ◆ ◆ ◆ ◆ ◆ ◆ ◆ ◆

The Case for the Use of Animals in Biomedical Research

BY CARL COHEN

INTRODUCTION

Carl Cohen, a philosophy professor at the University of Michigan, co-authored the *Animal Rights Debate* with Tom Regan. In this particular essay, Cohen argues that animals do not have rights because rights are necessarily confined to human beings, who are capable of making moral claims. Human beings do have obligations toward animals, but this does not imply that animals have rights.

This essay is an excellent example of philosophical writing. Cohen presents a logical, reasoned defence of his claim, a refutation of an opposing claim, and appropriate evidence, reasons, examples, and a contextualized examination of other theoretical claims.

Cohen's and Regan's essays can be compared and contrasted for their conflicting views on animal rights. See also Garth Forsyth's student essay, which critiques the logic of Cohen's and Regan's essays (chapter 8), and Aila Crowther-Hayward's student essay, which uses Cohen's and Regan's essays to support her argument about the treatment of animals in veterinary institutions (chapter 11).

1   Using animals as research subjects in medical investigations is widely condemned on two grounds: first, because it wrongly violates the rights of animals,[1] and second, because it wrongly imposes on sentient creatures much avoidable *suffering*.[2] Neither of these arguments is sound. The first relies on a mistaken understanding of rights; the second relies on a mistaken calculation of consequences. Both deserve definitive dismissal.

Why Animals Have No Rights

2   A right, properly understood, is a claim, or potential claim, that one party may exercise against another. The target against whom such a claim may be registered can be a single person, a group, a community, or (perhaps) all humankind. The content of rights claims also varies greatly: repayment of loans, nondiscrimination by employers, noninterference by the state, and so on. To comprehend any genuine right fully, therefore, we must know *who* holds the right, *against whom* it is held, and *to what* it is a right.

3   Alternative sources of rights add complexity. Some rights are grounded in constitution and law (e.g., the right of an accused to trial by jury); some rights are moral but give no legal claims (e.g., my right to your keeping the promise you gave me); and some rights (e.g., against theft or assault) are rooted both in morals and in law.

4   The differing targets, contents, and sources of rights, and their inevitable conflict, together weave a tangled web. Notwithstanding all such complications, this much is clear about rights in general: they are in every case claims, or potential claims, within a community of moral agents. Rights arise, and can be intelligibly defended, only among beings who actually do, or can, make moral claims against one another. Whatever else rights may be, therefore, they are necessarily human; their possessors are persons, human beings.

5   The attributes of human beings from which this moral capability arises have been described variously by philosophers, both ancient and modern: the inner consciousness of a free will (Saint Augustine[3]); the grasp, by human reason, of the binding character of moral law (Saint Thomas[4]); the self-conscious participation of human beings in an objective ethical order (Hegel[5]); human membership in an organic moral community (Bradley[6]); the development of the human self through the consciousness of other moral selves (Mead[7]); and the underivative, intuitive cognition of the rightness of an action (Prichard[8]). Most influential has been Immanuel Kant's emphasis on the universal human possession of a uniquely moral will and the autonomy its use entails.[9] Humans confront choices that are purely moral; humans—but certainly not dogs or mice—lay down moral laws, for others and for themselves. Human beings are self-legislative, morally *auto-nomous*.

6   Animals (that is, nonhuman animals, the ordinary sense of that word) lack this capacity for free moral judgment. They are not beings of a kind capable of exercising or responding to moral claims. Animals therefore have no rights, and they can have none. This is the core of the argument about the alleged rights of animals. The holders of rights must have the capacity to comprehend rules of duty, governing all including themselves. In applying such rules, the holders of rights must recognize possible conflicts between what is in their own interest and what is just. Only in a community of beings capable of self-restricting moral judgments can the concept of a right be correctly invoked.

7   Humans have such moral capacities. They are in this sense self-legislative, are members of communities governed by moral rules, and do possess rights. Animals do not have such moral capacities. They are not morally self-legislative, cannot possibly be members of a truly moral community, and therefore cannot possess rights. In conducting research on animal subjects, therefore, we do not violate their rights, because they have none to violate.

8   To animate life, even in its simplest forms, we give a certain natural reverence. But the possession of rights presupposes a moral status not attained by the vast majority of living things. We must not infer, therefore, that a live being has, simply in being alive, a "right" to its life. The assertion that all animals, only because they are alive and have interests, also possess the "right to life"[10] is an abuse of that phrase, and wholly without warrant.

9   It does not follow from this, however, that we are morally free to do anything we please to animals. Certainly not. In our dealings with animals, as in our dealings with other human beings, we have obligations that do not arise from claims against us based on rights. Rights entail obligations, but many of the things one ought to do are in no way tied to another's entitlement. Rights and obligations are not reciprocals of one another, and it is a serious mistake to suppose that they are.

10   Illustrations are helpful. Obligations may arise from internal commitments made: physicians have obligations to their patients not grounded merely in their patients' rights. Teachers have such obligations to their students, shepherds to their dogs, and cowboys to their horses. Obligations may arise from differences of status: adults owe special care when playing with young children, and children owe special care when playing with young pets. Obligations may arise from special relationships: the payment of my son's college tuition is something to which he may have no right, although it may be my obligation to bear the burden if I reasonably can; my dog has no right to daily exercise and veterinary care, but I do have the obligation to provide these things for her. Obligations may arise from particular acts or circumstances: one may be obliged to another for a special kindness done, or obliged to put an animal out of its misery in view of its condition—although neither the human benefactor nor the dying animal may have had a claim of right.

11   Plainly, the grounds of our obligations to humans and to animals are manifold and cannot be formulated simply. Some hold that there is a general obligation to do no gratuitous harm to sentient creatures (the principle of nonmaleficence); some hold that there is a general obligation to do good to sentient creatures when that is reasonably within one's power (the principle of beneficence). In our dealings with animals, few will deny that we are at least obliged to act humanely—that is, to treat them with the decency and concern that we owe, as sensitive human beings, to other sentient creatures. To treat animals humanely, however, is not to treat them as humans or as the holders of rights.

12   A common objection, which deserves a response, may be paraphrased as follows:

> If having rights requires being able to make moral claims, to grasp and apply moral laws, then many humans—the brain-damaged, the comatose, the senile— who plainly lack those capacities must be without rights. But that is absurd. This proves [the critic concludes] that rights do not depend on the presence of moral capacities.[11]

13   This objection fails; it mistakenly treats an essential feature of humanity as though it were a screen for sorting humans. The capacity for moral judgment that distinguishes humans from animals is not a test to be administered to human beings one by one. Persons who are unable, because of some disability, to perform the full moral functions natural to human beings are certainly not for that reason ejected from the moral community. The issue is one of kind. Humans are of such a kind that they may be the subject of experiments only with their voluntary consent. The choices they make freely must be respected. Animals are of such a kind that it is impossible for them, in principle, to give or withhold voluntary consent or to make a moral choice. What humans retain when disabled, animals have never had.

14 A second objection, also often made, may be paraphrased as follows:

> Capacities will not succeed in distinguishing humans from the other animals. Animals also reason; animals also communicate with one another; animals also care passionately for their young; animals also exhibit desires and preferences. Features of moral relevance—rationality, interdependence, and love—are not exhibited uniquely by human beings. Therefore [this critic concludes], there can be no solid moral distinction between humans and other animals.

15 This criticism misses the central point. It is not the ability to communicate or to reason, or dependence on one another, or care for the young, or the exhibition of preference, or any such behavior that marks the critical divide. Analogies between human families and those of monkeys, or between human communities and those of wolves, and the like, are entirely beside the point. Patterns of conduct are not at issue. Animals do indeed exhibit remarkable behavior at times. Conditioning, fear, instinct, and intelligence all contribute to species survival. Membership in a community of moral agents nevertheless remains impossible for them. Actors subject to moral judgment must be capable of grasping the generality of an ethical premise in a practical syllogism. Humans act immorally often enough, but only they—never wolves or monkeys—can discern, by applying some moral rule to the facts of a case, that a given act ought or ought not to he performed. The moral restraints imposed by humans on themselves are thus highly abstract and are often in conflict with the self-interest of the agent. Communal behavior among animals, even when most intelligent and most endearing, does not approach autonomous morality in this fundamental sense.

16 Genuinely moral acts have an internal as well as an external dimension. Thus, in law, an act can be criminal only when the guilty deed, the *actus reus,* is done with a guilty mind, *mens rea.* No animal can ever commit a crime; bringing animals to criminal trial is the mark of primitive ignorance. The claims of moral right are similarly inapplicable to them. Does a lion have a right to eat a baby zebra? Does a baby zebra have a right not to be eaten? Such questions, mistakenly invoking the concept of right where it does not belong, do not make good sense. Those who condemn biomedical research because it violates "animal rights" commit the same blunder.

In Defense of "Speciesism"

17 Abandoning reliance on animal rights, some critics resort instead to animal sentience—their feelings of pain and distress. We ought to desist from the imposition of pain insofar as we can. Since all or nearly all experimentation on animals does impose pain and could be readily forgone, say these critics, it should be stopped. The ends sought may be worthy, but those ends do not justify imposing agonies on humans, and by animals the agonies are felt no less. The laboratory use of animals (these critics conclude) must therefore be ended or at least very sharply curtailed.

18 Argument of this variety is essentially utilitarian, often expressly so[12]; it is based on the calculation of the net product, in pains and pleasures, resulting from experiments on animals. Jeremy Bentham, comparing horses and dogs with other sentient creatures, is thus commonly quoted: "The question is not, Can they reason? nor Can they talk? but, Can they suffer?"[13]

19 Animals certainly can suffer and surely ought not to be made to suffer needlessly. But in inferring, from these uncontroversial premises, that biomedical research causing animal distress is largely (or wholly) wrong, the critic commits two serious errors.

20 The first error is the assumption, often explicitly defended, that all sentient animals have equal moral standing. Between a dog and a human being, according to this view, there is no moral difference; hence the pains suffered by dogs must be weighed no differently from the pains suffered by humans. To deny such equality, according to this critic, is to give unjust preference to one species over another; it is "speciesism." The most influential statement of this moral equality of species was made by Peter Singer:

> The racist violates the principle of equality by giving greater weight to the interests of members of his own race when there is a clash between their interests and the interests of those of another race. The sexist violates the principle of equality by favoring the interests of his own sex. Similarly the speciesist allows the interests of his own species to override the greater interests of members of other species. The pattern is identical in each case.[14]

21 This argument is worse than unsound; it is atrocious. It draws an offensive moral conclusion from a deliberately devised verbal parallelism that is utterly specious. Racism has no rational ground whatever. Differing degrees of respect or concern for humans for no other reason than that they are members of different races is an injustice totally without foundation in the nature of the races themselves. Racists, even if acting on the basis of mistaken factual beliefs, do grave moral wrong precisely because there is no morally relevant distinction among the races. The supposition of such differences has led to outright horror. The same is true of the sexes, neither sex being entitled by right to greater respect or concern than the other. No dispute here.

22 Between species of animate life, however between (for example) humans on the one hand and cats or rats on the other—the morally relevant differences are enormous, and almost universally appreciated. Humans engage in moral reflection; humans are morally autonomous; humans are members of moral communities, recognizing just claims against their own interest. Human beings do have rights; theirs is a moral status very different from that of cats or rats.

23 I am a speciesist. Speciesism is not merely plausible; it is essential for right conduct, because those who will not make the morally relevant distinctions among species are almost certain, in consequence, to misapprehend their true obligations. The analogy between speciesism and racism is insidious. Every sensitive moral judgment requires that the differing natures of the beings to whom obligations are owed be considered. If all forms of animate life—or vertebrate animal life?—must be treated equally, and if therefore in evaluating a research program the pains of a rodent count equally with the pains of a human, we are forced to conclude (1) that neither humans nor rodents possess rights, or (2) that rodents possess all the rights that humans possess. Both alternatives are absurd. Yet one or the other must be swallowed if the moral equality of all species is to be defended.

24   Humans owe to other humans a degree of moral regard that cannot be owed to animals. Some humans take on the obligation to support and heal others, both humans and animals, as a principal duty in their lives; the fulfillment of that duty may require the sacrifice of many animals. If biomedical investigators abandon the effective pursuit of their professional objectives because they are convinced that they may not do to animals what the service of humans requires, they will fail, objectively, to do their duty. Refusing to recognize the moral differences among species is a sure path to calamity. (The largest animal rights group in the country is People for the Ethical Treatment of Animals; its codirector, Ingrid Newkirk, calls research using animal subjects "fascism" and "supremacism." "Animal liberationists do not separate out the human animal," she says, "so there is no rational basis for saying that a human being has special rights. A rat is a pig is a dog is a boy. They're all mammals."[15])

25   Those who claim to base their objection to the use of animals in biomedical research on their reckoning of the net pleasures and pains produced make a second error, equally grave. Even if it were true—as it is surely not—that the pains of all animate beings must be counted equally, a cogent utilitarian calculation requires that we weigh all the consequences of the use, and of the nonuse, of animals in laboratory research. Critics relying (however mistakenly) on animal rights may claim to ignore the beneficial results of such research, rights being trump cards to which interest and advantage must give way. But an argument that is explicitly framed in terms of interest and benefit for all over the long run must attend also to the disadvantageous consequences of not using animals in research, and to all the achievements attained and attainable only through their use. The sum of the benefits of their use is utterly beyond quantification. The elimination of horrible disease, the increase of longevity, the avoidance of great pain, the saving of lives, and the improvement of the quality of lives (for humans and for animals) achieved through research using animals is so incalculably great that the argument of these critics, systematically pursued, establishes not their conclusion but its reverse: to refrain from using animals in biomedical research is, on utilitarian grounds, morally wrong.

26   When balancing the pleasures and pains resulting from the use of animals in research, we must not fail to place on the scales the terrible pains that would have resulted, would be suffered now, and would long continue had animals not been used. Every disease eliminated, every vaccine developed, every method of pain relief devised, every surgical procedure invented, every prosthetic device implanted—indeed, virtually every modern medical therapy—is due, in part or in whole, to experimentation using animals. Nor may we ignore, in the balancing *process*, the predictable gains in human (and animal) well-being that are probably achievable in the future but that will not be achieved if the decision is made now to desist from such research or to curtail it.

27   Medical investigators are seldom insensitive to the distress their work may cause animal subjects. Opponents of research using animals are frequently insensitive to the cruelty of the results of the restrictions they would impose. Untold numbers of human beings—real persons, although not now identifiable—would suffer grievously as the consequence of this well-meaning but short-sighted tenderness. If the morally relevant differences between humans and animals are borne in mind, and if all relevant considerations are weighed, the calculation of long-term consequences must give overwhelming support for biomedical research using animals.

Concluding Remarks

Substitution

28   The humane treatment of animals requires that we desist from experimenting on them if we can accomplish the same result using alternative methods—*in vitro* experimentation, computer simulation, or others. Critics of some experiments using animals rightly make this point.

29   It would be a serious error to suppose, however, that alternative techniques could soon be used in most research now using live animal subjects. No other methods now on the horizon or perhaps ever to be available—can fully replace the testing of a drug, a procedure, or a vaccine, in live organisms. The flood of new medical possibilities being opened by the successes of recombinant DNA technology will turn to a trickle if testing on live animals is forbidden. When initial trials entail great risks, there may be no forward movement whatever without the use of live animal subjects. In seeking knowledge that may prove critical in later clinical applications, the unavailability of animals for inquiry may spell complete stymie. In the United States, federal regulations require the testing of new drugs and other products on animals, for efficacy and safety, before human beings are exposed to them.[16,17] We would not want it otherwise.

30   Every advance in medicine—every new drug, new operation, new therapy of any kind must sooner or later be tried on a living being for the first time. That trial, controlled or uncontrolled, will be an experiment. The subject of that experiment, if it is not an animal, will be a human being. Prohibiting the use of live animals in biomedical research, therefore, or sharply restricting it, must result either in the blockage of much valuable research or in the replacement of animal subjects with human subjects. These are the consequences—unacceptable to most reasonable persons—of not using animals in research.

Reduction

31   Should we not at least reduce the use of animals in biomedical research? No, we should increase it to avoid when feasible the use of humans as experimental subjects.

Medical investigations putting human subjects at some risk are numerous and greatly varied. The risks run in such experiments are usually unavoidable, and (thanks to earlier experiments on animals) most such risks are minimal or moderate. But some experimental risks are substantial.

32 When an experimental protocol that entails substantial risk to humans comes before an institutional review board, what response is appropriate? The investigation, we may suppose, is promising and deserves support, so long as its human subjects are protected against unnecessary dangers. May not the investigators be fairly asked, *Have you done all that you can to eliminate risk to humans by the extensive testing of that drug, that procedure, or that device on animals?* To achieve maximal safety for humans we are right to require thorough experimentation on animal subjects before humans are involved.

33 Opportunities to increase human safety in this way are commonly missed, trials in which risks may be shifted from humans to animals are often not devised, sometimes not even considered. Why? For the investigator, the use of animals as subjects is often more expensive, in money and time, than the use of human subjects. Access to suitable human subjects is often quick and convenient, whereas access to appropriate animal subjects may be awkward, costly, and burdened with red tape. Physician-investigators have often had more experience working with human beings and know precisely where the needed pool of subjects is to be found and how they may be enlisted. Animals, and the procedures for their use, are often less familiar to these investigators. Moreover, the use of animals in place of humans is now more likely to be the target of zealous protests from without. The upshot is that humans are sometimes subjected to risks that animals could have borne, and should have borne, in their place. To maximize the protection of human subjects, I conclude, the wide and imaginative use of live animal subjects should be encouraged rather than discouraged. This enlargement in the use of animals is our obligation.

Consistency

34 Finally, inconsistency between the profession and the practice of many who oppose research using animals deserves comment. This frankly *ad hominem* observation aims chiefly to show that a coherent position rejecting the use of animals in medical research imposes costs so high as to be intolerable even to the critics themselves.

35 One cannot coherently object to the killing of animals in biomedical investigations while continuing to eat them. Anesthetics and thoughtful animal husbandry render the level of actual animal distress in the laboratory generally lower than that in the abattoir. So long as death and discomfort do not substantially differ in the two contexts, the consistent objector must not only refrain from all eating of animals but also protest as vehemently against others eating them as against others experimenting on them. No less vigorously must the critic object to the wearing of animal hides in coats and shoes, to employment in any industrial enterprise that uses animal parts, and to any commercial development that will cause death or distress to animals.

36   Killing animals to meet human needs for food, clothing, and shelter is judged entirely reasonable by most persons. The ubiquity of these uses and the virtual universality of moral support for them confront the opponent of research using animals with an inescapable difficulty. How can the many common uses of animals be judged morally worthy, while their use in scientific investigation is judged unworthy?

37   The number of animals used in research is but the tiniest fraction of the total used to satisfy assorted human appetites. That these appetites, often base and satisfiable in other ways, morally justify the far larger consumption of animals, whereas the quest for improved human health and understanding cannot justify the far smaller, is wholly implausible. Aside from the numbers of animals involved, the distinction in terms of worthiness of use, drawn with regard to any single animal, is not defensible. A given sheep is surely not more justifiably used to put lamb chops on the supermarket counter than to serve in testing a new contraceptive or a new prosthetic device. The needless killing of animals is wrong; if the common killing of them for our food or convenience is right, the less common but more humane uses of animals in the service of medical science are certainly not less right.

38   Scrupulous vegetarianism, in matters of food, clothing, shelter, commerce, and recreation, and in all other spheres, is the only fully coherent position the critic may adopt. At great human cost, the lives of fish and crustaceans must also be protected, with equal vigor, if speciesism has been forsworn. A very few consistent critics adopt this position. It is the *reductio ad absurdum* of the rejection of moral distinctions between animals and human beings.

39   Opposition to the use of animals in research is based on arguments of two different kinds—those relying on the alleged rights of animals and those relying on the consequences for animals. I have argued that arguments of both kinds must fail. We surely do have obligations to animals, but they have, and can have, no rights against us on which research can infringe. In calculating the consequences of animal research, we must weigh all the long-term benefits of the results achieved—to animals and to humans—and in that calculation we must not assume the moral equality of all animate species.

REFERENCES

1   Regan T. *The case for animal rights*. Berkeley, Calif.: University of California Press, 1983.
2   Singer P. *Animal liberation*. New York: Avon Books, 1977.
3   St. Augustine. *Confessions*. Book Seven. 397 A.D. New York: Pocketbooks. 1957: 104–26.
4   St. Thomas Aquinas. *Summa theological*. 1273 A.D. Philosophic texts. New York: Oxford University Press. 1960: 353–66.
5   Hegel GWF. *Philosophy of right*. 1821. London: Oxford University Press, 1952: 105–10.
6   Bradley FH. Why should I be moral? 1876. In: Meldon AI, ed. *Ethical theories*. New York: Prentice-Hall, 1950: 345–59.
7   Mead GH. The genesis of the self and social control. 1925. In: Reck AJ, ed. *Selected writings*. Indianapolis: Bobbs-Merrill. 1964:264–93.
8   Prichard HA. Does moral philosophy rest on a mistake? 1912. In: Cellars W, Hospers J, eds. *Readings in ethical theory*. New York: Appleton-Century-Crofts, 1952: 149–63.
9   Kant I. *Fundamental principles of the metaphysic of morals*. 1785. New York: Liberal Arts Press, 1949.

10 Rollin BE. *Animal rights and human morality*. New York: Prometheus Books, 1981.

11 Hoff C. Immoral and moral uses of animals. *N Engl J Med* 1980: 302: 115–18.

12 Jamieson D. Killing persons and other beings. In: Miller HB. Williams WH, eds. *Ethics and Animals*. Clifton, N.J.: Humana Press, 1983: 135–46.

13 Singer P. *Ten years of animal liberation*. New York Review of Books. 1985: 31:46–52.

14 Bentham J. *Introduction to the principles of moral and legislation*. London: Athlone Press. 1970.

15 McCabe K. Who will live, who will die? *Washington Magazine*. August 1986: 115.

16 U.S. Code of Federal Regulations. Title 21. Sect. 505(i). Food, drug, and cosmetic, regulations.

17 U.S. Code of Federal Regulations, Title 16, Sect. 1500. 40–2. Consumer product regulations.

Source: Cohen, Carl. "The Case for the Use of Animals in Biomedical Research." Reprinted from the *New England Journal of Medicine*. Vol. 315, 2 Oct 1986: 865–70.

QUESTIONS FOR DISCUSSION

1. Do you agree with Cohen's argument that animals do not have rights? Why or why not?
2. What hypothetical evidence does Cohen provide to support his argument?
3. Cohen refutes other arguments. Provide some examples. Are these refutations convincing in your opinion? Why or why not?
4. How does Cohen use logic and emotion to make his argument? Is it effective?
5. In attacking his opponents as being hypocritical, Cohen makes a logical fallacy. Can you name it (see chapter 7)?

FROM READING TO WRITING

1. Are there any terms or concepts you do not understand? If so, look up their definitions and then think about how an understanding of these terms increases your understanding of the text.
2. Using the technique of freewriting, write a response to Cohen's argument. Spend five minutes writing without stopping. Share your responses with your classmates. Do these responses help you to understand and form a position in relation to the essay?

The Case for Animal Rights

BY TOM REGAN

INTRODUCTION

Tom Regan, a professor emeritus at North Carolina State University, is a philosopher who specializes in the theory of animal rights. His argument, articulated here and in his seminal book of the same name, states that non-human animals are, like humans, "subjects of a life." If we ascribe value to *all* human beings regardless of their rational capacity, then we must ascribe it to *all* non-human animals.

This essay is an example of philosophical writing. As such, it uses logic, pathos, hypothetical syllogisms, and a sustained engagement with other theories and theorists.

See Garth Forsyth's student essay in chapter 8 for a comparison of Cohen's and Regan's rhetorical strategies. Also see chapter 11 where Aila Crowther-Hayward uses Regan and Cohen to support her analysis of the treatment of animals in veterinary institutions.

1   I regard myself as an advocate of animal rights—as a part of the animal rights movement. That movement, as I conceive it, is committed to a number of goals, including:

- the total abolition of the use of animals in science;
- the total dissolution of commercial animal agriculture;
- the total elimination of commercial and sport hunting and trapping.

2   There are, I know, people who profess to believe in animal rights but do not avow these goals. Factory farming, they say, is wrong—it violates animals' rights—but traditional animal agriculture is all right. Toxicity tests of cosmetics on animals violates their rights, but important medical research—cancer research, for example—does not. The clubbing of baby seals is abhorrent, but not the harvesting of adult seals. I used to think I understood this reasoning. Not anymore. You don't change unjust institutions by tidying them up.

3   What's wrong—fundamentally wrong—with the way animals are treated isn't the details that vary from case to case. It's the whole system. The forlornness of the veal calf is pathetic, heart wrenching; the pulsing pain of the chimp with electrodes planted deep in her brain is repulsive; the slow, tortuous death of the raccoon caught in the leg-hold trap is agonizing. But what is wrong isn't the pain, isn't the suffering, isn't the deprivation. These compound what's wrong. Sometimes—often—they make it much, much worse. But they are not the fundamental wrong.

4   The fundamental wrong is the system that allows us to view animals as *our resources*, here for us—to be eaten, or surgically manipulated, or exploited for sport or money. Once we accept this view of animals—as our resources—the rest is as predictable as it is regrettable. Why worry about their loneliness, their pain, their death? Since animals exist for us, to benefit us in one way or another, what harms them really doesn't matter—or matters only if it starts to bother us, makes us feel a trifle uneasy when we eat our veal escalope, for example. So, yes, let us get veal calves out of solitary confinement, give them more space, a little straw, a few companions. But let us keep our veal escalope.

5   But a little straw, more space and a few companions won't eliminate—won't even touch—the basic wrong that attaches to our viewing and treating these animals as our resources. A veal calf killed to be eaten after living in close confinement is viewed and

treated in this way: but so, too, is another who is raised (as they say) "more humanely." To right the wrong of our treatment of farm animals requires more than making rearing methods "more humane"; it requires the total dissolution of commercial animal agriculture.

6   How we do this, whether we do it or, as in the case of animals in science, whether and how we abolish their use—these are to a large extent political questions. People must change their beliefs before they change their habits. Enough people, especially those elected to public office, must believe in change—must want it—before we will have laws that protect the rights of animals. This process of change is very complicated, very demanding, very exhausting, calling for the efforts of many hands in education, publicity, political organization and activity, down to the licking of envelopes and stamps. As a trained and practising philosopher, the sort of contribution I can make is limited but, I like to think, important. The currency of philosophy is ideas—their meaning and rational foundation—not the nuts and bolts of the legislative process, say, or the mechanics of community organization. That's what I have been exploring over the past ten years or so in my essays and talks and, most recently, in my book, *The Case for Animal Rights*. I believe the major conclusions I reach in the book are true because they are supported by the weight of the best arguments. I believe the idea of animal rights has reason, not just emotion, on its side.

7   In the space I have at my disposal here I can only sketch, in the barest outline, some of the main features of the book. It's main themes—and we should not be surprised by this—involve asking and answering deep, foundational moral questions about what morality is, how it should be understood and what is the best moral theory, all considered. I hope I can convey something of the shape I think this theory takes. The attempt to do this will be (to use a word a friendly critic once used to describe my work) cerebral, perhaps too cerebral. But this is misleading. My feelings about how animals are sometimes treated run just as deep and just as strong as those of my more volatile compatriots. Philosophers do—to use the jargon of the day—have a right side to their brains. If it's the left side we contribute (or mainly should), that's because what talents we have reside there.

8   How to proceed? We begin by asking how the moral status of animals has been understood by thinkers who deny that animals have rights. Then we test the mettle of their ideas by seeing how well they stand up under the heat of fair criticism. If we start our thinking in this way, we soon find that some people believe that we have no duties directly to animals, that we owe nothing to them, that we can do nothing that wrongs them. Rather, we can do wrong acts that involve animals, and so we have duties regarding them, though none to them. Such views may be called indirect duty views. By way of illustration: suppose your neighbour kicks your dog. Then your neighbour has done something wrong. But not to your dog. The wrong that has been done is a wrong to you. After all, it is wrong to upset people, and your neighbour's kicking your dog upsets you. So you are the one who is wronged, not your dog. Or again: by kicking your dog your neighbour damages your property. And since it is wrong to damage another person's property, your neighbour has done something wrong—to you, of course, not to your dog. Your neighbour no more wrongs your dog than your car would be wronged if the windshield were smashed. Your neighbour's duties involving your dog are indirect duties

to you. More generally, all of our duties regarding animals are indirect duties to one another—to humanity.

9   How could someone try to justify such a view? Someone might say that your dog doesn't feel anything and so isn't hurt by your neighbour's kick, doesn't care about the pain since none is felt, is as unaware of anything as is your windshield. Someone might say this, but no rational person will, since, among other considerations, such a view will commit anyone who holds it to the position that no human being feels pain either—that human beings also don't care about what happens to them. A second possibility is that though both humans and your dog are hurt when kicked, it is only human pain that matters. But, again, no rational person can believe this. Pain is pain wherever it occurs. If your neighbour's causing you pain is wrong because of the pain that is caused, we cannot rationally ignore or dismiss the moral relevance of the pain that your dog feels.

10   Philosophers who hold indirect duty views—and many still do—have come to understand that they must avoid the two defects just noted: that is, both the view that animals don't feel anything as well as the idea that only human pain can be morally relevant. Among such thinkers the sort of view now favoured is one or other form of what is called *contractarianism*.

11   Here, very crudely, is the root idea: morality consists of a set of rules that individuals voluntarily agree to abide by, as we do when we sign a contract (hence the name contractarianism). Those who understand and accept the terms of the contract are covered directly; they have rights created and recognized by, and protected in, the contract. And these contractors can also have protection spelled out for others who, though they lack the ability to understand morality and so cannot sign the contract themselves, are loved or cherished by those who can. Thus young children, for example, are unable to sign contracts and lack rights. But they are protected by the contract none the less because of the sentimental interests of others, most notably their parents. So we have, then, duties involving these children, duties regarding them, but no duties to them. Our duties in their case are indirect duties to other human beings, usually their parents.

12   As for animals, since they cannot understand contracts, they obviously cannot sign; and since they cannot sign, they have no rights. Like children, however, some animals are the objects of the sentimental interest of others. You, for example, love your dog or cat. So those animals that enough people care about (companion animals, whales, baby seals, the American bald eagle), though they lack rights themselves, will be protected because of the sentimental interests of people. I have, then, according to contractarianism, no duty directly to your dog or any other animal, not even the duty not to cause them pain or suffering; my duty not to hurt them is a duty I have to those people who care about what happens to them. As for other animals, where no or little sentimental interest is present—in the case of farm animals, for example, or laboratory rats—what duties we have grow weaker and weaker, perhaps to vanishing point. The pain and death they endure, though real, are not wrong if no one cares about them.

13   When it comes to the moral status of animals' contractarianism could be a hard view to refute if it were an adequate theoretical approach to the moral status of human beings. It is not adequate in this latter respect, however, which makes the question of

its adequacy in the former case, regarding animals, utterly moot. For consider: morality, according to the (crude) contractarian position before us, consists of rules that people agree to abide by. What people? Well, enough to make a difference—enough, that is, *collectively* to have the power to enforce the rules that are drawn up in the contract. That is very well and good for the signatories but not so good for anyone who is not asked to sign. And there is nothing in contractarianism of the sort we are discussing that guarantees or requires that everyone will have a chance to participate equally in framing the rules of morality. The result is that this approach to ethics could sanction the most blatant forms of social, economic, moral and political injustice, ranging from a repressive caste system to systematic racial or sexual discrimination. Might, according to this theory, does make right. Let those who are the victims of injustice suffer as they will. It matters not so long as no one else—no contractor, or too few of them—cares about it. Such a theory takes one's moral breath away ... as if, for example, there would be nothing wrong with apartheid in South Africa if few white South Africans were upset by it. A theory with so little to recommend it at the level of the ethics of our treatment of our fellow humans cannot have anything more to recommend it when it comes to the ethics of how we treat our fellow animals.

14   The version of contractarianism just examined is, as I have noted, a crude variety, and in fairness to those of a contractarian persuasion it must be noted that much more refined, subtle and ingenious varieties are possible. For example, John Rawls, in his *A Theory of Justice*, sets forth a version of contractarianism that forces contractors to ignore the accidental features of being a human being—for example, whether one is white or black, male or female, a genius or of modest intellect. Only by ignoring such features, Rawls believes, can we ensure that the principles of justice that contractors would agree upon are not based on bias or prejudice. Despite the improvement a view such as Rawls's represents over the cruder forms of contractarianism, it remains deficient: it systematically denies that we have direct duties to those human beings who do not have a sense of justice—young children, for instance, and many mentally retarded humans. And yet it seems reasonably certain that, were we to torture a young child or a retarded elder, we would be doing something that wronged him or her, not something that would be wrong if (and only if) other humans with a sense of justice were upset. And since this is true in the case of these humans, we cannot rationally deny the same in the case of animals.

15   Indirect duty views, then, including the best among them, fail to command our rational assent. Whatever ethical theory we should accept rationally, therefore, it must at least recognize that we have some duties directly to animals, just as we have some duties directly to each other. The next two theories I'll sketch attempt to meet this requirement.

16   The first I call the cruelty-kindness view. Simply stated, this says that we have a direct duty to be kind to animals and a direct duty not to be cruel to them. Despite the familiar, reassuring ring of these ideas, I do not believe that this view offers an adequate theory. To make this clearer, consider kindness. A kind person acts from a certain kind of motive—compassion or concern, for example. And that is a virtue. But there is no guarantee that a kind act is a right act. If I am a generous racist, for example, I will be inclined to act kindly towards members of my own race, favouring their interests above those of others. My kindness would be real and, so far as it goes, good. But I trust it is too obvious to require argument that my kind acts may not be above moral reproach—may, in fact, be positively wrong because rooted in injustice. So kindness, notwithstanding its status as a virtue to be encouraged, simply will not carry the weight of a theory of right action.

17 Cruelty fares no better. People or their acts are cruel if they display either a lack of sympathy for or, worse, the presence of enjoyment in another's suffering. Cruelty in all its guises is a bad thing, a tragic human failing. But just as a person's being motivated by kindness does not guarantee that he or she does what is right, so the absence of cruelty does not ensure that he or she avoids doing what is wrong. Many people who perform abortions, for example, are not cruel, sadistic people. But that fact alone does not settle the terribly difficult question of the morality of abortion. The case is no different when we examine the ethics of our treatment of animals. So, yes, let us be for kindness and against cruelty. But let us not suppose that being for the one and against the other answers questions about moral right and wrong.

18 Some people think that the theory we are looking for is utilitarianism. A utilitarian accepts two moral principles. The first is that of equality: everyone's interests count, and similar interests must be counted as having similar weight or importance. White or black, American or Iranian, human or animal—everyone's pain or frustration matter, and matter just as much as the equivalent pain or frustration of anyone else. The second principle a utilitarian accepts is that of utility: do the act that will bring about the best balance between satisfaction and frustration for everyone affected by the outcome.

19 As a utilitarian, then, here is how I am to approach the task of deciding what I morally ought to do: I must ask who will be affected if I choose to do one thing rather than another, how much each individual will be affected, and where the best results are most likely to lie—which option, in other words, is most likely to bring about the best results, the best balance between satisfaction and frustration. That option, whatever it may be, is the one I ought to choose. That is where my moral duty lies.

20 The great appeal of utilitarianism rests with its uncompromising *egalitarianism*: everyone's interests count and count as much as the like interests of everyone else. The kind of odious discrimination that some forms of contractarianism can justify—discrimination based on race or sex, for example—seems disallowed in principle by utilitarianism, as is speciesism, systematic discrimination based on species membership.

21 The equality we find in utilitarianism, however, is not the sort an advocate of animal or human rights should have in mind. Utilitarianism has no room for the equal moral rights of different individuals because it has no room for their equal inherent value or worth. What has value for the utilitarian is the satisfaction of an individual's interests, not the individual whose interests they are. A universe in which you satisfy your desire for water, food and warmth is, other things being equal, better than a universe in which these desires are frustrated. And the same is true in the case of an animal with similar desires. But neither you nor the animal have any value in your own right. Only your feelings do.

22 Here is an analogy to help make the philosophical point clearer: a cup contains different liquids, sometimes sweet, sometimes bitter, sometimes a mix of the two. What has value are the liquids: the sweeter the better, the bitterer the worse. The cup, the container, has no value. It is what goes into it, not what they go into, that has value. For the utilitarian you and I are like the cup; we have no value as individuals and thus no equal value. What has value is what goes into us, what we serve as receptacles for; our feelings of satisfaction have positive value, our feelings of frustration negative value.

23   Serious problems arise for utilitarianism when we remind ourselves that it enjoins us to bring about the best consequences. What does this mean? It doesn't mean the best consequences for me alone, or for my family or friends, or any other person taken individually. No, what we must do is, roughly, as follows: we must add up (somehow!) the separate satisfactions and frustrations of everyone likely to be affected by our choice, the satisfactions in one column, the frustrations in the other. We must total each column for each of the options before us. That is what it means to say the theory is aggregative. And then we must choose that option which is most likely to bring about the best balance of totalled satisfactions over totalled frustrations. Whatever act would lead to this outcome is the one we ought morally to perform—it is where our moral duty lies. And that act quite clearly might not be the same one that would bring about the best results for me personally, or my family or friends, or for a lab animal. The best aggregated consequences for everyone concerned are not necessarily the best for each individual.

24   That utilitarianism is an aggregative theory—different individuals' satisfactions or frustrations are added, or summed, or totalled—is the key objection to this theory. My Aunt Bea is old, inactive, a cranky, sour person, though not physically ill. She prefers to go on living. She is also rather rich. I could make a fortune if I could get my hands on her money, money she intends to give me in any event, after she dies, but which she refuses to give me now. In order to avoid a huge tax bite, I plan to donate a handsome sum of my profits to a local children's hospital. Many, many children will benefit from my generosity, and much joy will be brought to their parents, relatives and friends. If I don't get the money rather soon, all these ambitions will come to naught. The once-in-a-lifetime opportunity to make a real killing will be gone. Why, then, not kill my Aunt Bea? Oh, of course I *might* get caught. But I'm no fool and, besides, her doctor can be counted on to co-operate (he has an eye for the same investment and I happen to know a good deal about his shady past). The deed can be done . . . professionally, shall we say. There is *very* little chance of getting caught. And as for my conscience being guilt-ridden, I am a resourceful sort of fellow and will take more than sufficient comfort—as I lie on the beach at Acapulco—in contemplating the joy and health I have brought to so many others. Suppose Aunt Bea is killed and the rest of the story comes out as told. Would I have done anything wrong? Anything immoral? One would have thought that I had. Not according to utilitarianism. Since what I have done has brought about the best balance between totalled satisfaction and frustration for all those affected by the outcome, my action is not wrong. Indeed, in killing Aunt Bea the physician and I did what duty required.

25   This same kind of argument can be repeated in all sorts of cases, illustrating, time after time, how the utilitarian's position leads to results that impartial people find morally callous. It is wrong to kill my Aunt Bea in the name of bringing about the best results for others. A good end does not justify an evil means. Any adequate moral theory will have to explain why this is so. Utilitarianism fails in this respect and so cannot be the theory we seek.

26   What to do? Where to begin anew? The place to begin, I think, is with the utilitarian's view of the value of the individual—or, rather, lack of value. In its place, suppose we consider that you and I, for example, do have value as individuals—what we'll call *inherent value.* To say we have such value is to say that we are something more than, something different from, mere receptacles. Moreover, to ensure that we do not pave the way for such injustices as slavery or sexual discrimination, we must believe that all who have inherent value have it equally, regardless of their sex, race, religion, birthplace and so on. Similarly to be discarded as irrelevant are one's talents or skills, intelligence and wealth, personality or pathology, whether one is loved and admired or despised and loathed. The genius and the retarded child, the prince and the pauper, the brain surgeon and the fruit vendor, Mother Teresa and the most unscrupulous used-car salesman—all have inherent value, all possess it equally, and all have an equal right to be treated with respect, to be treated in ways that do not reduce them to the status of things, as if they existed as resources for others. My value as an individual is independent of my usefulness to you. Yours is not dependent on your usefulness to me. For either of us to treat the other in ways that fail to show respect for the other's independent value is to act immorally, to violate the individual's rights.

27 · Some of the rational virtues of this view—what I call the rights view—should be evident. Unlike (crude) contractarianism, for example, the rights view *in principle* denies the moral tolerability of any and all forms of racial, sexual or social discrimination; and unlike utilitarianism, this view *in principle* denies that we can justify good results by using evil means that violate an individual's rights—denies, for example, that it could be moral to kill my Aunt Bea to harvest beneficial consequences for others. That would be to sanction the disrespectful treatment of the individual in the name of the social good, something the rights view will not—categorically will not—ever allow.

28 The rights view, I believe, is rationally the most satisfactory moral theory. It surpasses all other theories in the degree to which it illuminates and explains the foundation of our duties to one another—the domain of human morality. On this score it has the best reasons, the best arguments, on its side. Of course, if it were possible to show that only human beings are included within its scope, then a person like myself, who believes in animal rights, would be obliged to look elsewhere.

29 But attempts to limit its scope to humans only can be shown to be rationally defective. Animals, it is true, lack many of the abilities humans possess. They can't read, do higher mathematics, build a bookcase or make *baba ghanoush*. Neither can many human beings, however, and yet we don't (and shouldn't) say that they (these humans) therefore have less inherent value, less of a right to be treated with respect, than do others. It is the *similarities* between those human beings who most clearly, most non-controversially have such value (the people reading this, for example), not our differences, that matter most. And the really crucial, the basic similarity is simply this: we are each of us the experiencing subject of a life, a conscious creature having an individual welfare that has importance to us whatever our usefulness to others. We want and prefer things, believe and feel things, recall and expect things. And all these dimensions of our life, including our pleasure and pain, our enjoyment and suffering, our satisfaction and frustration, our continued existence or our untimely death—all make a difference to the quality of our life as lived, as experienced, by us as individuals. As the same is true of those animals that concern us (the ones that are eaten and

trapped, for example), they too must be viewed as the experiencing subjects of a life, with inherent value of their own.

30   Some there are who resist the idea that animals have inherent value. "Only humans have such value," they profess. How might this narrow view be defended? Shall we say that only humans have the requisite intelligence, or autonomy, or reason? But there are many, many humans who fail to meet these standards and yet are reasonably viewed as having value above and beyond their usefulness to others. Shall we claim that only humans belong to the right species, the species *Homo sapiens*? But this is blatant speciesism. Will it be said, then, that all—and only—humans have immortal souls? Then our opponents have their work cut out for them. I am myself not ill-disposed to the proposition that there are immortal souls. Personally, I profoundly hope I have one. But I would not want to rest my position on a controversial ethical issue on the even more controversial question about who or what has an immortal soul. That is to dig one's hole deeper, not to climb out. Rationally, it is better to resolve moral issues without making more controversial assumptions than are needed. The question of who has inherent value is such a question, one that is resolved more rationally without the introduction of the idea of immortal souls than by its use.

31   Well, perhaps some will say that animals have some inherent value, only less than we have. Once again, however, attempts to defend this view can be shown to lack rational justification. What could be the basis of our having more inherent value than animals? Their lack of reason, or autonomy, or intellect? Only if we are willing to make the same judgment in the case of humans who are similarly deficient. But it is not true that such humans—the retarded child, for example, or the mentally deranged—have less inherent value than you or I. Neither, then, can we rationally sustain the view that animals like them in being the experiencing subjects of a life have less inherent value. *All* who have inherent value have it *equally*, whether they be human animals or not.

32   Inherent value, then, belongs equally to those who are the experiencing subjects of a life. Whether it belongs to others—to rocks and rivers, trees and glaciers, for example—we do not know and may never know. But neither do we need to know, if we are to make the case for animal rights. We do not need to know, for example, how many people are eligible to vote in the next presidential election before we can know whether I am. Similarly, we do not need to know how many individuals have inherent value before we can know that some do. When it comes to the case for animal rights, then, what we need to know is whether the animals that, in our culture, are routinely eaten, hunted and used in our laboratories, for example, are like us in being subjects of a life. And we do know this. We do know that many—literally, billions and billions—of these animals are the subjects of a life in the sense explained and so have inherent value if we do. And since, in order to arrive at the best theory of our duties to one another, we must recognize our equal inherent value as individuals, reason—not sentiment, not emotion—reason compels us to recognize the equal inherent value of these animals and, with this, their equal right to be treated with respect.

33   That, very roughly, is the shape and feel of the case for animal rights. Most of the details of the supporting argument are missing. They are to be found in the book to which I alluded earlier. Here, the details go begging, and I must, in closing, limit myself to four final points.

34   The first is how the theory that underlies the case for animal rights shows that the animal rights movement is a part of, not antagonistic to, the human rights movement. The theory that rationally grounds the rights of animals also grounds the rights of humans. Thus those involved in the animal rights movement are partners in the struggle to secure respect for human rights—the rights of women, for example, or minorities, or workers. The animal rights movement is cut from the same moral cloth as these.

35   Second, having set out the broad outlines of the rights view, I can now say why its implications for farming and science, among other fields, are both clear and uncompromising. In the case of the use of animals in science, the rights view is categorically abolitionist. Lab animals are not our tasters; we are not their kings. Because these animals are treated routinely, systematically as if their value were reducible to their usefulness to others, they are routinely, systematically treated with a lack of respect, and thus are their rights routinely, systematically violated. This is just as true when they are used in trivial, duplicative, unnecessary or unwise research as it is when they are used in studies that hold out real promise of human benefits. We can't justify harming or killing a human being (my Aunt Bea, for example) just for these sorts of reason. Neither can we do so even in the case of so lowly a creature as a laboratory rat. It is not just refinement or reduction that is called for, not just larger, cleaner cages, not just more generous use of anaesthetic or the elimination of multiple surgery, not just tidying up the system.

36   It is complete replacement. The best we can do when it comes to using animals in science is—not to use them. That is where our duty lies, according to the rights view.

37   As for commercial animal agriculture, the rights view takes a similar abolitionist position. The fundamental moral wrong here is not that animals are kept in stressful close confinement or in isolation, or that their pain and suffering, their needs and preferences are ignored or discounted. All these *are* wrong, of course, but they are not the fundamental wrong. They are symptoms and effects of the deeper, systematic wrong that allows these animals to be viewed and treated as lacking independent value, as resources for us—as, indeed, a renewable resource. Giving farm animals more space, more natural environments, more companions does not right the fundamental wrong, any more than giving lab animals more anaesthesia or bigger, cleaner cages would right the fundamental wrong in their case. Nothing less than the total dissolution of commercial animal agriculture will do this, just as, for similar reasons I won't develop at length here, morality requires nothing less than the total elimination of hunting and trapping for commercial and sporting ends. The rights view's implications, then, as I have said, are clear and uncompromising.

38   My last two points are about philosophy, my profession. It is, most obviously, no substitute for political action. The words I have written here and in other places by themselves don't change a thing. It is what we do with the thoughts that the words express—our acts, our deeds—that changes things. All that philosophy can do, and all I have attempted, is to offer a vision of what our deeds should aim at. And the why. But not the how.

39   Finally, I am reminded of my thoughtful critic, the one I mentioned earlier, who chastised me for being too cerebral. Well, cerebral I have been: indirect duty views, utilitarianism, contractarianism—hardly the stuff deep passions are made of. I am also reminded, however, of the image another friend once set before me—the image of the ballerina as expressive of disciplined passion. Long hours of sweat and toil, of loneliness and practice, of doubt and fatigue: those are the discipline of her craft. But the passion is there too, the fierce drive to excel, to speak through her body, to do it right, to pierce our minds. That is the image of philosophy I would leave with you, not "too cerebral" but *disciplined passion*. Of the discipline enough has been seen. As for the passion: there are times, and these not infrequent, when tears come to my eyes when I see, or read, or hear of the wretched plight of animals in the hands of humans. Their pain, their suffering, their loneliness, their innocence, their death. Anger. Rage. Pity. Sorrow. Disgust. The whole creation groans under the weight of the evil we humans visit upon these mute, powerless creatures. It is our hearts, not just our heads, that call for an end to it all, that demand of us that we overcome, for them, the habits and forces behind their systematic oppression. All great movements, it is written, go through three stages: ridicule, discussion, adoption. It is the realization of this third stage, adoption, that requires both our passion and our discipline, our hearts and our heads. The fate of animals is in our hands. God grant we are equal to the task.

Source: Regan, Tom. "The Case for Animal Rights" from *In Defense of Animals* by Singer, Peter Albert David. Reproduced with permission of HarperTrade in the format Republish in a book via Copyright Clearance Centre.

QUESTIONS FOR DISCUSSION

1. The argument in this essay can be compared and contrasted with the argument in Carl Cohen's essay. In your opinion, which essay presents the most reasonable, logical argument? Provide reasons for your answer.
2. How does Regan use pathos or emotion? Is it effective, in your opinion?
3. Can you outline a valid syllogism used by Regan in this essay (see chapter 7)?
4. Can you identify any logical fallacies in Regan's argument (see chapter 7)?

FROM READING TO WRITING

1. Write a short paragraph summarizing either utilitarianism or contractarianism, as Regan presents these theories. Discuss with your classmates to clearly define the terms and theories and to understand how Regan is using them.
2. Regan argues that the "rights view" is the most satisfactory moral theory. Write a paragraph summarizing this view and then state whether or not you agree with it. Use Cohen's argument to provide reasons and evidence for your argument.

Identity and Difference

Shape Structures Story: Fresh and Feisty Stories about Disability [1]

BY ROSEMARIE GARLAND-THOMSON

INTRODUCTION

Rosemarie Garland-Thomson is a professor of women's studies at Emory University in Atlanta, Georgia. She specializes in feminist theory, American literature, and disability studies. In "Shape Structures Story," Garland-Thomson engages with and departs from the work of Caroline Walker Bynum to argue that stories about people with disabilities revise and challenge normative stories or narratives. She goes on to provide and analyze four diverse examples of how this revision happens.

The theory in this essay can be used, similar to the way Garland-Thomson uses it herself, to frame an argument about other stories or situations. For example, you might use it to make an argument about Raymond Carver's "Cathedral" or Susan Musgrave's "Arctic Poppies," pointing out that the blind man or the hunchback revise how we see and think about "normal" people and situations.

1   In her deeply wise meditation on the question of continuity in human identity, the medieval historian Caroline Walker Bynum offers us the elegant concept that "shape carries story."[2] Her inquiry arose from her own personal experience of observing her father's shift in identity over 10 years of living with progressive dementia. Bynum acknowledges three aspects of identity: individual personality, ascribed or achieved group affiliation, and spatio-temporal integrity, which is the sense of identity upon which she focuses. Her fundamental question is, "How can I be the same person I was a moment ago?" In other words, she asks how we can maintain a continuous sense of self as our bodies change over time. Being an historian, Bynum frames this issue as a historical one; being a literary critic, I am going to frame this question as a narrative one. That different framing leads me to adapt Bynum's phrase and refer to shape "structuring" rather than "carrying" story. Narrative is a way of constructing continuity over time; it is a coherent knitting of one moment to the next. Bynum's wisdom is to understand the narrative link between time and space, more precisely perhaps, between time and human materiality. A clunkier explication of this formulation is that the configuration and function of our human body determines our narrative identity, the sense of who we are to ourselves and others. In Bynum's words, "Story spreads out through time the behaviors or bodies—the

shapes—a self has been or will be, each replacing the one before. Hence story has before and after, gain and loss. It goes somewhere.... Moreover, shape or body is crucial, not incidental, to story. It carries story; it makes story visible; in a sense it is story. Shape (or visible body) is in space what story is in time.... Identity is finally shape carrying story." In a sense, I want to extend Bynum's claim by suggesting that shape not only carries story but also leads to certain structures for stories about the connection between disability and identity. Indeed, I would like to suggest that shape structures story is the informing principle of disability identity.

2　　One of our most tenacious cultural fantasies is a belief in bodily stability, more precisely the belief that bodily transformation is predictable and tractable. Our cultural story of proper human development dares not admit to the vagaries, variations, and vulnerabilities that we think of as disability. This refusal to recognize the contingency of human bodies has its benefits and its liabilities, a point I have discussed at length elsewhere. One of its disadvantages is the social bias it creates toward people whose way of being and appearing in the world offer evidence against the myth of certainty and compliancy in regard to human bodies. Another way of talking about this larger cultural imagining is to say that we would prefer to believe that story is independent from shape, perhaps we would even prefer to go so far as to claim that story structures shape. Indeed, one of the fundamental propositions of what I call Cultural Disability Studies is that the modern impulse to standardize the body through medical technology enacts our conviction that story structures shape. Another way of saying this is that both our bodies and the stories we tell about them are shaped to conform to a standard model of human form and function that is called normal in medical-scientific discourses, average in consumer capitalism, and ordinary in colloquial parlance. The measure of all things human, normal is the central concept governing the status and value of people in late modernity. It is the abstract principle toward which we are all herded by a myriad of institutional and ideological forces. According to Ian Hacking, it is "the centre from which deviation departs"(164).[3] Normalcy, as Lennard Davis tells us, is "enforced." It is the destination to which we all hasten and the stick used to drive us there. We are obliged to act, feel, look and be normal—at any cost. And normal does cost. The anxious demand to achieve the right clothes, cars, toys, faces, bodies creates enormous commercial markets that fuel consumer capitalism. Thus, we use the cultural story that we call normalcy to structure our shapes.[4]

3　　In contrast to this, disability insists that shape structures story. The story structured by the shape we think of as disability is not imagined as a pretty one. This story of despair, catastrophe, loss, excess, suffering, and relentless cure-seeking that we tell about disability is being retold, however. Fresh, feisty stories about disabled shapes and acts abound these days. In what follows, I will offer four examples that recast traditional disability plots. In other words, these are narratives where the shape we think of as disability structures positive instead of negative stories. The examples come from conventional narrative genres—film, poetry, memoir, exposition. Each of these stories is about disability as an occasion for exuberant flourishing. Such a rendering of disability sharply contradicts the usual stories of misery, diminishment, and calamity to which we are accustomed. My brief analysis of these four exemplary stories exposes two narrative currents which are seldom included in the usual stories we tell about disability: sexuality and community. Plots involving suffering, catastrophe, isolation, overcoming, or pity abound in our stereotypical disability narratives. Think, for example, about telethons or charity campaigns. Stories about disabled sex or communal affiliation are scarce.

4   One of the principal fonts of exuberant human flourishing is the erotic, which often is not part of the disability narrative. Indeed, one aspect of disability discrimination in our culture is what Harlan Hahn calls the "asexual objectification" of people with disabilities. A second primary site of exuberant flourishing are the human communities that form through deliberate or situational association in which shared experience bonds people together in mutually sustaining groups. Disability is seldom understood in our culture as the kind of experience that would lead to circles of supportive association based on commonality. Because we think of disability as at once individualized and isolating rather than communal and shared, the concept of a disability community in which one might thrive seems counterintuitive. To introduce sexuality and community into a disability narrative, then, is to make a new story.

5   In the 2005 documentary film *Murderball*, the shapes that we think of as disability structure a revisionist narrative of sexuality and community. The presenting plot concerns the outcome of a sport competition among quadriplegic rugby teams. *Murderball* is the hyped-up, suggestively ironic, name for this extreme sport. The film's conventional suspense-driven emplotment presents the competition between the American and Canadian rival national quad rugby teams and who will win the 2002 World Championship in Sweden and the 2004 Paralympics in Athens. But knitted into this raucous and predictable surge of incidents is the unusual story of how the players on "our" American team became disabled and how their bodies now operate. Because bodies shaped by sport are usually the most regularized we encounter, the particular inflections of these rugby players' impairments add unexpected variegation to both their appearance and functioning. The film is admirably restrained in its answering of the conventional "what-happened-to-you?" narrative mandate of disability stories. More important, the film refuses the expected narrative of overcoming that infuses almost every positive story about disability. We learn that young men are a reckless lot, and with measured drama, their impairment stories unfurl. The impairments that their testosterone-driven antics produce seem catastrophic at the onset but transform through the logic of competitive sport into compelling mechanical challenges that heighten the pleasure of the game for both players and spectators.

6   *Murderball* invites us to relish along with the players how adaptability and innovation produces a new sport—quad rugby—to which their new bodies are perfectly suited. Cyborgs composed of steel fused with flesh—like pumped-up golfers—these men perform ultra-masculinity with disabled bodies, working against the stereotype of sidelined and dejected injured athletes. Thus, the film is a guy story about exuberant flourishing made possible because of rather than in spite of disability. What *Murderball* captures is the counterintuitive idea that disability can provide a meaningful life in which one thrives rather than languishes. Disability provides an unanticipated opportunity for boys to come into themselves as athletes and men.

7　　Sport culture typically provides men with a masculine heterosexual identity and homosocial community, which is precisely what quad rugby players get. For the Murderballers, disability intensifies rather than attenuates these anchors of masculinity, but it also equips them with new bodies. The shapes that impairment endows the quad rugby players' bodies with produce what Judith Halberstam calls an alternative masculinity. The shared experience which underpins the masculine community partakes of the dominant sport model of cooperation among peers in coalition against a common competitor. At the same time, the alternative experience of medicalized impairment and disability struggle bonds the team members. The sport brings together what would be isolated, individualized cases of impairment as disqualification and forges them together into a communal and mutually supportive cohort of friends and colleagues who flourish through their positive masculinized identities as quad rugby players. As a testament to the cultural work of quad rugby, the film's main character, Mark Zupan, said in a *Washington Post* interview that before becoming disabled he was a lost and confused college dropout and now he's a respected athlete, a famous movie star, and an advocate for his community.

8　　Virile and vibrant heterosexuality also defines the masculine athlete. As with sport community, the quad rugby players perform an alternative masculine heterosexuality in the film. A major suspense-provoking narrative subtext in the film turns on the question that everybody has about paralyzed guys: Can they *do it*? And if they do, *how* do they *do it*? Much typical testosterone banter drives this subplot, which climaxes—so to speak—in an interview with an appealing blond kid on the team who is finally required through the conventions of the documentary to reveal the mechanics of the sexuality that haunts all of the hypermasculine repartee. In my view, it is the film's most successful moment, played with precisely the right degree of economy and irony. Seated in his wheelchair, this charming young rugby player smiles sweetly and slyly and says, "I like to eat pussy." The film manages to distance itself from the vulgar and raw aspect of this typical big boy boast by intimating that he has adapted by developing an innovative, non-phallic, alternative sexuality that is a source of pride rather than shame. This irreverent and endearing moment breaks the tension of the implicit question about the sexual story a quadriplegic male body structures. Rather than being obscene, it comes off as life-affirming.[5] As such, the film becomes a counter argument to the stereotypical idea that disability ruins a life, obliterates sexual activity and appeal, prevents meaningful work, and isolates one from others. While all of these benefits are imagined as accruing to a successful athlete, seldom are they taken as central to the life of disabled people. Becoming a hot jock is not what something we imagine life with a disability can get you. This is the cultural work of *Murderball*.[6]

9　　If *Murderball* is a guy story, the poem called "I Am Not One of The . . ." by Cheryl Marie Wade is a parallel girl story from a different genre that narrates exuberant flourishing made possible because of rather than in spite of disability. Announcing herself as a fully erotic "woman with juice," Wade eschews the euphemisms for people with disabilities, insisting instead on a list of alternative feminine descriptors which structure a disabled female subjectivity that decidedly departs from convention. Here is the entire poem:

I Am Not One of the

I am not one of the physically challenged—

I'm a sock in the eye with gnarled fist
I'm a French kiss with cleft tongue
I'm orthopedic shoes sewn on the last of your fear

I am not one of the differently abled—

I'm an epitaph for million imperfect babies left untreated
I'm an ikon carved from ones in a mass grave at Tiergarten, Germany
I'm withered legs hidden with a blanket

I am not one of the able disabled—

I'm a black panther with green eyes and scars like a picket fence
I'm pink lace panties teasing a stub of milk white thigh
I'm the Evil Eye

I'm the first cell divided
I'm mud that talks
I'm Eve I'm Kali
I'm The Mountain That Never Moves
I've been forever I'll be here forever
I'm the Gimp
I'm the Cripple
I'm the Crazy Lady

I'm The Woman With Juice

10   Although the poem contains no narrative in the strict sense of emplotment through causally linked events, the rapid fire of descriptive images creates a vital character study. Instead, the poem achieves generic hybridity by making a series of identity claims that allude to broader narratives. Wade's self-assertion here draws on archetypes of transgressive, powerful, and threatening quasi-female figures such as "Eve," "Kali," "The Evil Eye," "mountains," "panthers," "primordial mud," and "serpents." Interlaced are stereotypical disability images such as "gnarled fist," "orthopedic shoes," "withered legs," "stub," "Gimp," "Cripple," and "Crazy Lady." The poem is thus a character study and a strong assertion of lyric emotion, both of which depend upon the speaker and audience sharing some understanding of the large narratives alluded to by "a sock in the eye with gnarled fist" and the other "I am" statements.

11   Sexuality and community interweave in this sketch to flesh out, so to speak, the emergent figure of "The Woman with Juice." Wade's French kisses, "pink lace panties," and the "milk white thigh" directly but delicately eroticize this self-portrait and conventionally feminize it. Yet the predictable feminine images of French kisses and white thighs are crossed with inflections such as a cleft tongue and a stub that might be said

to "cripple" them, to disable these archetypal female allusions. Although the "I am" statements seem at first individualized, the speaker opens out to a communal identity which contains multitudes of "withered legs," "imperfect babies," "cripple[s]," "gimp[s]," and crazies, all of which she claims affiliation with under a single "I."[7] The broadest allusion to communal identity that anchors the poetic subject forged here is the "mass grave at Tiergarten, Germany," that refers to the eugenic euthanasia of people with disabilities under the Nazis.[8] The physical traits which define disability, from "crazy" to "cripple," became the markers of a social group destined for incarceration and elimination under the eugenic ideology and regime of Nazi Germany. As with many segregated and subordinated groups, a sense of communal identity arises from the material consequences of persecution. If any disabled people were eugenic targets in Nazi Germany, the poem insists on connecting this woman with juice to the long dead victims whose shapes and functions destined them for the gas chambers, mass graves, and crematoria. The poem's assertion, then, of Wade's fleshly being as a disabled woman is key to the poem's identity politics. Similar to *Murderball*, this "Woman with Juice" tells a new story, a new disability narrative, in which shape structures story.

12   The memoir *My Body Politic*, written by arts consultant and activist Simi Linton, offers a fresh narrative of life lived by a disabled body. Nowhere in Linton's narrative is the usual disability story of suffering and overcoming we have come to expect. Her book emanates from a disability community narratively constructed through the strategic reference to disabled people as "we" rather than "they." Like *Murderball* and Wade's poem, Linton's is a story not about tragedy, pity, and suffering but about a "robust and excitable" young woman's transition from "the walking world" into the unfamiliar world of disability. Linton emerges from a traumatic accident with a new body, re-entering the world via her wheelchair and her peers from the disability community. Linton details with wit and passion how a new shape gave her a new story, how she transformed into the "substantial person" that disability makes her. She learns, in this story, to "absorb disability," to pilot a new and interesting body and uncover a fresh perspective on her life. This perspective is not one of loss but of wonder, a discovery of her body's pleasures, hungers, surprises, hurts, strengths, limits, and uses, a new discovery of a body we characteristically think of as disabled.

13   Like *Murderball* and Wade's poem, Linton's memoir is about redemption, but not through cure. Rather it is about redemption through community. Both Linton and the men in *Murderball* on the quad rugby team develop a new sense of themselves as they experience the world through their new bodies. Yet their identities as disabled people do not emerge as the heroic individual struggle against adversarial forces. Rather, the men forge disability identity in conjunction with their team members, just as Linton develops her sense of self as a disabled woman through and with other members of her new community. Theirs is a process that involves replacing stereotypical and oppressive conceptions of disability with different understandings rooted in the experience of a new embodiment. Linton writes eloquently of the process of identification through experience:

I have become a disabled woman over time. I certainly would have rejected such a title in the beginning.... It took many people to bring me into the fold. To help me move toward disability.... My advancement was due to other disabled people.... This new cadre of disabled people has come out of those special rooms set aside just for us. Casting off our drab institutional garb, we now don garments tailored for work and play, love and sport. Indeed, as an indicator of our new social standing, the high-toned among us even appear in television commercials wearing such finery. While many of us have obvious disabilities—we wield that white cane or ride that wheelchair or limp that limp—we don't all necessarily, as I didn't in my early years, ally with the group. And all the others, those whose characteristics are more easily masked, come to the surface even more gradually, determining how, when, and to whom to declare their membership.

14   Linton's explication here of what she calls "claiming disability" occurs through a willed entrance into a positive-identity communal experience. This experience begins for her, however, with the acquisition of a new shape. Although her new shape is instantaneous, the new sense of self develops as a process of simultaneous growth and healing. The recently impaired body pulls along the new sense of self, which resists and struggles as it reforms itself within a new community based on a shared sense of being in and relating to the world. This process of identification is an arduous birthing, attended by a circle of collaborators who ease the way. The identity she ultimately claims is a new story which gives narrative coherence to her new shape.

15   My final example of fresh and feisty disability narratives is one I offer from my own communal experience of how shared shape structures shared story. My story of collective disability identity is structured by the received conventions we think of as "ethnicity." Thus, I have put together a hybrid narrative which draws from the familiar story of ethnicity in order to create a fresh story about disability which I want to offer as a replacement to the familiar story of disability as tragedy.

16   I've always been vaguely envious of "ethnicity" as it is romanticized in movies and novels. You know the scenes I mean: celebrations—mostly weddings, sometimes funerals—where gaggles of communally bonded, funkily chic folks get down to extravagant feasting, dancing, and conversing in charming and exotic ways that express their collective quirkiness. The scenes evoke a sense of belonging based on distinctness: you know, everyone talking together with their hands and sharing bottles of Chianti on Italian holidays; fiddling and dancing jigs at the Irish wedding, the down home flavor of the African American family picnic; whole villages in Provence eating chocolates together. Such narratives of communal identity are intended to fuel a nostalgic desire for a sustaining group membership that offers unequivocal belonging and positive identity to those who qualify as the elect.

17   For ethnicity to emerge as colorful and sharp, of course, it must somehow be distinguished from the ordinary, safe, and dull way of being that we academics call "the dominant order." As a white, Anglo girl growing up, I felt bereft of what I imagined as a distinctive ethnic community that would provide the sense of belonging and validation that the compelling stereotypes created for me. I also grew up as a disabled girl. Even though I had lots of friends and identified strongly with women's culture, I still longed to be enfolded in a community that affirmed something more particular to me:

my disability. It took me years to find the distinct culture of the disabled community: to find my part of the one that Linton writes about and that *Murderball* presents.

18   As is often the case with identity communities, I both found and created a cadre of supportive peers who have much in common with me. They are other disabled academics and activists who work together toward the goal of making the world a more receptive and equitable place for people with disabilities. This work is at once gratifying and isolating because there are so few other academics who are willing to identify as disabled. Often, I feel the burden of being the only one, the one who always has to explain, the one who is different.

19   My community gathers every June at the Society for Disability Studies (SDS) Annual Convention. We get much good academic work done there, coming together in innovative ways that accommodate our various impairments. Conference rooms abound with a motley assortment of aids that keep us connected to one another and facilitate our scholarly tasks: wheelchairs, sign language interpreters, personal assistants, closed captioning screens, white canes, speech synthesizers, crutches, service dogs. There's a sense that much more is going on here than at more ordinary conferences where everybody just sits quietly and unobtrusively in rows of chairs, staring intently at a placid speaker behind the podium.

20   But the communal gathering that most fully fulfills my fantasy for a fierce sense of ethnic belonging is the annual SDS dance. Now, academics, for the most part, aren't much for dancing. We are a head-centered lot; flamboyance is an anomaly among professors. Not at the SDS dance, however. Here in the shelter of our mutual acceptance, we extravagantly flaunt the bodies that most of us would never expose at the chic discos where what we call the "norms" (those who think of themselves as nondisabled) hang out.

21   Like the conference rooms, the dance floor is a tangle of equipment and human variation—only here it's all roused to the beat of the music. Some of us lunge around; others glide smoothly on wheels; crutches prop some of us and stomp to the rhythm; still others fan white canes around them as if marking turf; the dogs rest quietly under the tables; people sip alternately on cocktails and wheelchair puff sticks to move around the room. Sign language criss-crosses the room, reaching through the loud music. Those of us with plenty of involuntary movement, the kind they struggled to keep under wraps in the workaday world, let it go where it may at the dance, twitching, bobbing, and jerking in distinctive patterns that anywhere else would make them targets of derision. One very chic young woman who looks like a model has unstrapped both of her prosthetic legs and cast them in a pile under table so she can more freely and expressively use her body out on the dance floor. The legs lay unremarked in a heap under the chairs, looking like cast off storeroom mannequin parts designed to display the high fashion stilettos that grace their ends. Someone has covered the dance floor with bubble wrap that pops insistently as the wheels move over it. There's plenty of eros. One woman spins her chair around topless because it's so hot. A few guy chair-users are benefiting from authentic "lap dancing," as they put the moves on the girls snuggled erotically in along with them in their wheelchairs. Everybody dances with everybody else—all partners in this lively violation of ordinary dance decorum. We proudly parade our differences with abandon.

No self-consciousness here. Bring on the anthropologists—this is disability culture.

22   At the SDS (a gesture to the 60's radical Students for a Democratic Society) dance, we've developed our very own ethnic folk dance. It's "tongue dancing," a form of expression that arises out of our collective identity, history, and experience. Tongue dancing got started by one of our forty-something colleagues, John Kelly, a quadriplegic sociologist who's a theory genius. John uses the SUV equivalent of a wheelchair—a big, bright red, motorized one, complete with hand tray in front, puff stick, high back, and straps across his limbs and chest for support. It looks a lot like a high tech throne. John dances with his tongue because that's the part of his body that he can move. His face is incredibly animated as he goofily and seductively bobs his tongue from side to side to the beat of the music. He's got as many moves as Fred Astaire—some graceful, others playful, most erotic. His tongue curls, extends, sways, touches his nose, undulates, thickens, and wiggles. It stirs with a variety and grace unimagined by those of us who move more parts of our bodies than John does. Our tongues are underutilized, almost vestigial compared to John's expressive organ. Of course, the eroticism of tongue dancing is lost on none of us. On the dance floor, John leads and the rest of us follow, discovering the exquisite oral pleasure of watching his alternately phallic and labial movements and simultaneously feeling our own awkward tongues explore new shapes and spaces. Our tongues wear out, but like the old time marathon dancers, John keeps up the stunts.

23   So we all dance the night away in our peculiar ways. It's our culture, our ethnic distinctiveness. Tongue dancing is our jig, our tango, our hora, our Virginia reel. And like the macherena, it's our contribution to mainstream culture. With its erotic quirkiness, tongue dancing may just catch on faster than the twist or the limbo ever did, once it gets out. One of the "norms" at the conference, a cute, very hip, young guy who has just finished a theater studies project on freak performance, can't wait to introduce tongue dancing to the discos in Seattle. I figure that very soon somebody will do a sequel to the 1987 movie *Dirty Dancing*, set at the Society for Disability Studies Conference. It might have starred Christopher Reeve as our imperturbable leader, John Kelly; but now we have Mark Zupan to do Patrick Swayze on wheels. They'll have to get us as extras because no norm actors could match us for cultural authenticity. The Academy Award nominations then will go to the genuine ethnics. No Jon Voight from *Coming Home*, Tom Cruise from *Born on the Fourth Of July*, Daniel Day Lewis from *My Left Foot*, Dustin Hoffman from *Rain Man*, Tom Hanks from *Forrest Gump* or *Philadelphia*, Geoffrey Rush from *Shine*, Russell Crowe from *A Beautiful Mind*, Sean Penn from *I Am Sam*, Hilary Swank from *Million Dollar Baby*, or Javier Bardem from *The Sea Inside* will walk away with Oscars for this film. Tongue dancing can overturn all that Telethon sentimentality and make disability as cool as all those other trendy ethnicities. Our unorthodox dancing is a response to the demands of our bodies. Our shapes, in all their uncontained variation, structure our stories.

24   Narratives do cultural work. They frame our understandings of raw, unorganized experience, giving it coherent meaning and making it accessible to us through story. By turning the experience of the dance into a narrative, I can extend the celebration of the community enacted by the dance. This story is a way then to provide access to some elements of my community to both disabled and nondisabled audiences alike.

ENDNOTES

1 I gratefully acknowledge the support of a senior fellowship at The Emory University Center for Humanistic Inquiry that enabled me to write this essay. It is expanded from the Disability, Narrative, and the Law Conference at OSU, May 2006.

2 See Bynum's National Endowment for the Humanities Jefferson Lecture in the Humanities.

3 For discussions of normalcy, also see Georges Canguilhem's *The Normal and the Pathological*.

4 Queer theory has similarly challenged the primacy of normal. Both disability and homosexuality are embodiments that have been pathologized by modern medicine. Robert McRuer has theorized this affinity most thoroughly in *Crip Theory* in his useful neologism "Compulsory Ablebodiedness," which alludes to Adrienne Rich's germinal concept of Compulsory Heterosexuality." Also see Michael Warner's *The Trouble with Normal*.

5 This scene of alternative phallic heterosexual narrative follows the disability tradition first initiated in Hal Ashby's 1978 film *Coming Home,* in which Jon Voight, who plays a quadriplegic Vietnam War veteran, provides Jane Fonda, who plays a disenchanted war wife, with her first orgasm. The sexual narratives in *Coming Home* and *Murderball* are in contradistinction to the erotic narrative told by Alejandro Amenabar's 2004 feature film *The Sea Inside,* whose quadriplegic hero intransigently insists that he can have no post-impairment sexual life, even though several fabulous women offer themselves up to him as lovers in the film. The film actually suggests that his dogmatic asexuality is one of the chief motivations of his decision to commit suicide.

6 I argue that the film moderates the rugby players' raucous adolescent sexuality by achieving a critical distance inherent in the documentary form. The audience understands the film is not endorsing the masculinist perspective here, but rather it is revealing the undiminished life force behind it. The film allows the players to expose their own liabilities; for example, one young player expresses disability prejudice, even while he claims disability pride, when he says that the Paralympics is superior to the Special Olympics, which is for people that he calls "retarded."

7 This poetic convention of using an expansive communal "I" to etch group identity from multitudinous particular individuals comes from Walt Whitman's "Song of Myself," the paradigmatic poem of American identity formation.

8 Wade exercises literary license here in the interest of poetic economy. In fact, Tiergarten is not the location of a mass grave, but is instead the street name in Berlin of the place where the planning and directives for the plan to eliminate Germany's disabled population originated. The building's address, Tiergartenstrasse 4, provided the name for the euthanasia program, T-4. Beginning in September 1939, T-4 was carried out in a network of hospitals throughout Germany which were turned into killing centers for the disabled. At these hospitals, the Nazis developed the bureaucratized methods of mass murder. They eliminated thousands of people by using gas chambers disguised as showers, cremation of bodies, mass graves, and an entire sham medical apparatus, including doctors who directed murders. These procedures, including personnel and equipment, which was developed at the hospital killing centers early in the war was later transferred to the Eastern concentration camps where it was used to kill the Jewish population and other targeted groups. For historical accounts of Nazi eugenic euthanasia, see Aly, Friedlander, and Kuhl, among many others.

WORKS CITED

Bynum, Caroline Walker. "National Endowment for the Humanities Jefferson Lecture in the Humanities." Concert Hall of the Kennedy Center for the Performing Arts, Washington, D.C. March 22, 1999.

Canguilhem, Georges. *The Normal and the Pathological.* Translated by Carolyn R. Fawcett and Robert S. Cohen. New York: Zone Books, 1989.

Coming Home. DVD. Directed by Hal Ashby. Hollywood: MGM/UA, 1978.

Davis, Lennard J. *Enforcing Normalcy: Disability, Deafness, and the Body.* New York: Verso, 1995.

Garland-Thomson, Rosemarie. *Extraordinary Bodies: Figuring Physical Disability in American Culture and Literature.* New York: Columbia Univ. Press, 1997.

Gerhart, Ann. "Paralyzed Into Action: The Men Of 'Murderball.'" *Washington Post.* July 24, 2005.

Hacking, Ian. *The Taming of Chance.* Cambridge: Cambridge Univ. Press, 1990.

Halberstam, Judith. *Female Masculinity.* Durham: Duke Univ. Press, 1998.

Linton, Simi. *My Body Politic: A Memoir.* Ann Arbor, MI: Univ. of Michigan Press, 2005.

McRuer, Robert. *Crip Theory: Cultural Signs of Queerness and Disability.* New York: New York Univ. Press, 2006.

Murderball. DVD. Directed by Dana Adam Shapiro and Henry-Alex Rubin. New York: Think Film Co.,2005.

The Sea Inside. DVD. Directed by Alejandro Amenábar. Hollywood: Fine Line Features, 2004.

Wade, Cheryl Marie. "A Woman with Juice." http://www.brava.org/Pages/Archives/Juice.html. Accessed 27 July 2006.

Warner, Michael. *The Trouble with Normal: Sex, Politics, and the Ethics of Queer Life.* Cambridge: Harvard Univ. Press, 2000.

Source: Garland-Thomson, Rosemarie. "Shape Structures Story: Fresh and Feisty Stories about Disability." *Narrative* 15.1 (Jan 2007) pp. 113–23. Print. Published by Ohio State University Press. Reprinted with permission.

QUESTIONS FOR DISCUSSION

1. Use a dictionary to look up any terms from the reading that you don't understand or use the surrounding context to understand them. Is the meaning clearer now?

2. Does Garland-Thomson's argument work toward "making the world a more receptive and equitable place for people with disabilities?" Provide reasons for your opinion.

3. Does storytelling challenge and possibly revise how we see those who are different? Provide evidence.

4. What function does the detailed description of the SDS dance play in this paper? How is this primary text different from the other primary texts Garland-Thomson analyzes?

FROM READING TO WRITING

1. Outline the way Garland-Thomson has logically organized the main points and evidence in her essay. Does this outline help you to better understand the essay?

2. How does Garland-Thomson use endnotes? What information does she convey and how do these endnotes inform her argument? Write a paragraph outlining her use of endnotes; discuss with your classmates.

Cathedral

BY RAYMOND CARVER

INTRODUCTION

Raymond Carver was an American short-story writer. "Cathedral," published in the collection of the same name in 1983, is often considered his best short story. In the story, Carver's minimalist focus on ordinary people and mundane everyday situations serves as a backdrop for an exploration of difference. In this story, the unnamed narrator and his wife's normative reality is disturbed by the arrival of the blind man, Robert. Both the narrator and his wife stereotype Robert, each of them making negative assumptions about his non-normal life as a blind man. The wife pities and tries to take care of him while the narrator finds his presence threatening and disturbing.

When reading this story, think about how Carver subverts normal perceptions to challenge stereotypical notions about normality and what it means to live with a disability.

1   This blind man, an old friend of my wife's, he was on his way to spend the night. His wife had died. So he was visiting the dead wife's relatives in Connecticut. He called my wife from his in-laws'. Arrangements were made. He would come by train, a five-hour trip, and my wife would meet him at the station. She hadn't seen him since she worked for him one summer in Seattle ten years ago. But she and the blind man had kept in touch. They made tapes and mailed them back and forth. I wasn't enthusiastic about his visit. He was no one I knew. And his being blind bothered me. My idea of blindness came from the movies. In the movies, the blind moved slowly and never laughed. Sometimes they were led by seeing-eye dogs. A blind man in my house was not something I looked forward to.

2   That summer in Seattle she had needed a job. She didn't have any money. The man she was going to marry at the end of the summer was in officers' training school. He didn't have any money, either. But she was in love with the guy, and he was in love with her, etc. She'd seen something in the paper: HELP WANTED—*Reading to Blind Man*, and a telephone number. She phoned and went over, was hired on the spot. She'd worked with this blind man all summer. She read stuff to him, case studies, reports, that sort of thing. She helped him organize his little office in the county social-service department. They'd become good friends, my wife and the blind man. How do I know these things? She told me. And she told me something else. On her last day in the office, the blind man asked if he could touch her face. She agreed to this. She told me he touched his fingers to every part of her face, her nose—even her neck! She never forgot it. She even tried to write a poem about it. She was always trying to write a poem. She wrote a poem or two every year, usually after something really important had happened to her.

3   When we first started going out together, she showed me the poem. In the poem, she recalled his fingers and the way they had moved around over her face. In the poem,

she talked about what she had felt at the time, about what went through her mind when the blind man touched her nose and lips. I can remember I didn't think much of the poem. Of course, I didn't tell her that. Maybe I just don't understand poetry. I admit it's not the first thing I reach for when I pick up something to read.

4   Anyway, this man who'd first enjoyed her favors, the officer-to-be, he'd been her childhood sweetheart. So okay. I'm saying that at the end of the summer she let the blind man run his hands over her face, said goodbye to him, married her childhood etc., who was now a commissioned officer, and she moved away from Seattle. But they'd kept in touch, she and the blind man. She made the first contact after a year or so. She called him up one night from an Air Force base in Alabama. She wanted to talk. They talked. He asked her to send him a tape and tell him about her life. She did this. She sent the tape. On the tape, she told the blind man about her husband and about their life together in the military. She told the blind man she loved her husband but she didn't like it where they lived and she didn't like it that he was a part of the military-industrial thing. She told the blind man she'd written a poem and he was in it. She told him that she was writing a poem about what it was like to be an Air Force officer's wife. The poem wasn't finished yet. She was still writing it. The blind man made a tape. He sent her the tape. She made a tape. This went on for years. My wife's officer was posted to one base and then another. She sent tapes from Moody AFB, McGuire, McConnell, and finally Travis, near Sacramento, where one night she got to feeling lonely and cut off from people she kept losing in that moving-around life. She got to feeling she couldn't go it another step. She went in and swallowed all the pills and capsules in the medicine chest and washed them down with a bottle of gin. Then she got into a hot bath and passed out.

5   But instead of dying, she got sick. She threw up. Her officer—why should he have a name? he was the childhood sweetheart, and what more does he want?—came home from somewhere, found her, and called the ambulance. In time, she put it all on a tape and sent the tape to the blind man. Over the years, she put all kinds of stuff on tapes and sent the tapes off lickety-split. Next to writing a poem every year, I think it was her chief means of recreation. On one tape, she told the blind man she'd decided to live away from her officer for a time. On another tape, she told him about her divorce. She and I began going out, and of course she told her blind man about it. She told him everything, or so it seemed to me. Once she asked me if I'd like to hear the latest tape from the blind man. This was a year ago. I was on the tape, she said. So I said okay, I'd listen to it. I got us drinks and we settled down in the living room. We made ready to listen. First she inserted the tape into the player and adjusted a couple of dials. Then she pushed a lever. The tape squeaked and someone began to talk in this loud voice. She lowered the volume. After a few minutes of harmless chitchat, I heard my own name in the mouth of this stranger, this blind man I didn't even know! And then this: "From all you've said about him, I can only conclude—" But we were interrupted, a knock at the door, something, and we didn't ever get back to the tape. Maybe it was just as well. I'd heard all I wanted to.

6   Now this same blind man was coming to sleep in my house.

7   "Maybe I could take him bowling," I said to my wife. She was at the draining board doing scalloped potatoes. She put down the knife she was using and turned around.

8   "If you love me," she said, "you can do this for me. If you don't love me, okay. But if you had a friend, any friend, and the friend came to visit, I'd make him feel comfortable." She wiped her hands with the dish towel.

9   "I don't have any blind friends," I said.

10   "You don't have *any* friends," she said. "Period. Besides," she said, "goddamn it, his wife's just died! Don't you understand that? The man's lost his wife!"

11   I didn't answer. She'd told me a little about the blind man's wife. Her name was Beulah. Beulah! That's a name for a colored woman.

12   "Was his wife a Negro?" I asked.

13   "Are you crazy?" my wife said. "Have you just flipped or something?" She picked up a potato. I saw it hit the floor, then roll under the stove. "What's wrong with you?" she said. "Are you drunk?"

14   "I'm just asking," I said.

15   Right then my wife filled me in with more detail than I cared to know. I made a drink and sat at the kitchen table to listen. Pieces of the story began to fall into place.

16   Beulah had gone to work for the blind man the summer after my wife had stopped working for him. Pretty soon Beulah and the blind man had themselves a church wedding. It was a little wedding—who'd want to go to such a wedding in the first place?—just the two of them, plus the minister and the minister's wife. But it was a church wedding just the same. It was what Beulah had wanted, he'd said. But even then Beulah must have been carrying the cancer in her glands. After they had been inseparable for eight years—my wife's word, *inseparable*—Beulah's health went into a rapid decline. She died in a Seattle hospital room, the blind man sitting beside the bed and holding on to her hand. They'd married, lived and worked together, slept together—had sex, sure—and then the blind man had to bury her. All this without his having ever seen what the goddamned woman looked like. It was beyond my understanding. Hearing this, I felt sorry for the blind man for a little bit. And then I found myself thinking what a pitiful life this woman must have led. Imagine a woman who could never see herself as she was seen in the eyes of her loved one. A woman who could go on day after day and never receive the smallest compliment from her beloved. A woman whose husband could never read the expression on her face, be it misery or something better. Someone who could wear makeup or not—what difference to him? She could, if she wanted, wear green eye-shadow around one eye, a straight pin in her nostril, yellow slacks, and purple shoes, no matter. And then to slip off into death, the blind man's hand on her hand, his blind eyes streaming tears—I'm imagining now—her last thought maybe this: that he never even knew what she looked like, and she on an express to the grave. Robert was left with a small insurance policy and a half of a twenty-peso Mexican coin. The other half of the coin went into the box with her. Pathetic.

17   So when the time rolled around, my wife went to the depot to pick him up. With nothing to do but wait—sure, I blamed him for that—I was having a drink and watching the TV when I heard the car pull into the drive. I got up from the sofa with my drink and went to the window to have a look.

18   I saw my wife laughing as she parked the car. I saw her get out of the car and shut the door. She was still wearing a smile. Just amazing. She went around to the other side

of the car to where the blind man was already starting to get out. This blind man, feature this, he was wearing a full beard! A beard on a blind man! Too much, I say. The blind man reached into the back seat and dragged out a suitcase. My wife took his arm, shut the car door, and, talking all the way, moved him down the drive and then up the steps to the front porch. I turned off the TV. I finished my drink, rinsed the glass, dried my hands. Then I went to the door.

19 My wife said, "I want you to meet Robert. Robert, this is my husband. I've told you all about him." She was beaming. She had this blind man by his coat sleeve.

20 The blind man let go of his suitcase and up came his hand. I took it. He squeezed hard, held my hand, and then he let it go.

21 "I feel like we've already met," he boomed.

22 "Likewise," I said. I didn't know what else to say. Then I said, "Welcome. I've heard a lot about you." We began to move then, a little group, from the porch into the living room, my wife guiding him by the arm. The blind man was carrying his suitcase in his other hand. My wife said things like, "To your left here, Robert. That's right. Now watch it, there's a chair. That's it. Sit down right here. This is the sofa. We just bought this sofa two weeks ago."

23 I started to say something about the old sofa. I'd liked that old sofa. But I didn't say anything. Then I wanted to say something else, small-talk, about the scenic ride along the Hudson. How going *to* New York, you should sit on the right-hand side of the train, and coming *from* New York, the left-hand side.

24 "Did you have a good train ride?" I said. "Which side of the train did you sit on, by the way?"

25 "What a question, which side!" my wife said. "What's it matter which side?" she said.

26 "I just asked," I said.

27 "Right side," the blind man said. "I hadn't been on a train in nearly forty years. Not since I was a kid. With my folks. That's been a long time. I'd nearly forgotten the sensation. I have winter in my beard now," he said. "So I've been told, anyway. Do I look distinguished, my dear?" the blind man said to my wife.

28 "You look distinguished, Robert," she said. "Robert," she said. "Robert, it's just so good to see you."

29 My wife finally took her eyes off the blind man and looked at me. I had the feeling she didn't like what she saw. I shrugged.

30 I've never met, or personally known, anyone who was blind. This blind man was late forties, a heavy-set, balding man with stooped shoulders, as if he carried a great weight there. He wore brown slacks, brown shoes, a light-brown shirt, a tie, a sports coat. Spiffy. He also had this full beard. But he didn't use a cane and he didn't wear dark glasses. I'd always thought dark glasses were a must for the blind. Fact was, I wished he had a pair. At first glance, his eyes looked like anyone else's eyes. But if you looked close, there was something different about them. Too much white in the iris, for one thing, and the pupils seemed to move around in the sockets without his knowing it or being able to stop it. Creepy. As I stared at his face, I saw the left pupil turn in toward his nose while the other made an effort to keep in one place. But it was only an effort, for that eye was on the roam without his knowing it or wanting it to be.

31 I said, "Let me get you a drink. What's your pleasure? We have a little of everything. It's one of our pastimes."

32 "Bub, I'm a Scotch man myself," he said fast enough in this big voice.

33 "Right," I said. Bub! "Sure you are. I knew it."

34 He let his fingers touch his suitcase, which was sitting alongside the sofa. He was taking his bearings. I didn't blame him for that.

35 "I'll move that up to your room," my wife said.

36 "No, that's fine," the blind man said loudly. "It can go up when I go up."

37 "A little water with the Scotch?" I said.

38 "Very little," he said.

39 "I knew it," I said.

40 He said, "Just a tad. The Irish actor, Barry Fitzgerald? I'm like that fellow. When I drink water, Fitzgerald said, I drink water. When I drink whiskey, I drink whiskey." My wife laughed. The blind man brought his hand up under his beard. He lifted his beard slowly and let it drop.

41 I did the drinks, three big glasses of Scotch with a splash of water in each. Then we made ourselves comfortable and talked about Robert's travels. First the long flight from the West Coast to Connecticut, we covered that. Then from Connecticut up here by train. We had another drink concerning that leg of the trip.

42 I remembered having read somewhere that the blind didn't smoke because, as speculation had it, they couldn't see the smoke they exhaled. I thought I knew that much and that much only about blind people. But this blind man smoked his cigarette down to the nubbin and then lit another one. This blind man filled his ashtray and my wife emptied it.

43 When we sat down at the table for dinner, we had another drink. My wife heaped Robert's plate with cube steak, scalloped potatoes, green beans. I buttered him up two slices of bread. I said, "Here's bread and butter for you." I swallowed some of my drink. "Now let us pray," I said, and the blind man lowered his head. My wife looked at me, her mouth agape. "Pray the phone won't ring and the food doesn't get cold," I said.

44 We dug in. We ate everything there was to eat on the table. We ate like there was no tomorrow. We didn't talk. We ate. We scarfed. We grazed that table. We were into serious eating. The blind man had right away located his foods, he knew just where everything was on his plate. I watched with admiration as he used his knife and fork on the meat. He'd cut two pieces of meat, fork the meat into his mouth, and then go all out for the scalloped potatoes, the beans next, and then he'd tear off a hunk of buttered bread and eat that. He'd follow this up with a big drink of milk. It didn't seem to bother him to use his fingers once in a while, either.

45 We finished everything, including half a strawberry pie. For a few moments, we sat as if stunned. Sweat beaded on our faces. Finally, we got up from the table and left the dirty places. We didn't look back. We took ourselves into the living room and sank into our places again. Robert and my wife sat on the sofa. I took the big chair. We had us two or three more drinks while they talked about the major things that had come to pass for them in the past ten years. For the most part, I just listened. Now and then I joined in. I didn't want him to think I'd left the room, and I didn't want her to think I was feeling left out. They talked of things that had happened to them—to them!—these past ten years. I waited in vain to hear my name on my wife's sweet lips: "And then my dear husband came into my life"—something like that. But I heard nothing of the sort. More talk of Robert. Robert had done a little of everything, it seemed, a regular blind jack-of-all-trades. But most recently he and his wife had had an Amway distributorship, from which, I gathered, they'd earned their living, such as it was. The blind man was also a ham radio operator. He talked in his loud voice about conversations he'd had with fellow operators in Guam, in the Philippines, in Alaska, and even in Tahiti. He said he'd have a lot of friends there if he ever wanted to go visit those places. From time to time, he'd turn his blind face toward me, put his hand under his beard, ask me something. How long had I been in my present position? (Three years.) Did I like my work? (I didn't.) Was I going to stay with it? (What were the options?) Finally, when I thought he was beginning to run down, I got up and turned on the TV.

46   My wife looked at me with irritation. She was heading toward a boil. Then she looked at the blind man and said, "Robert, do you have a TV?"

47   The blind man said, "My dear, I have two TVs. I have a color set and a black-and-white thing, an old relic. It's funny, but if I turn the TV on, and I'm always turning it on, I turn on the color set. It's funny, don't you think?"

48   I didn't know what to say to that. I had absolutely nothing to say to that. No opinion. So I watched the news program and tried to listen to what the announcer was saying.

49   "This is a color TV," the blind man said. "Don't ask me how, but I can tell."

50   "We traded up a while ago," I said.

51   The blind man had another taste of his drink. He lifted his beard, sniffed it, and let it fall. He leaned forward on the sofa. He positioned his ashtray on the coffee table, then put the lighter to his cigarette. He leaned back on the sofa and crossed his legs at the ankles.

52   My wife covered her mouth, and then she yawned. She stretched. She said, "I think I'll go upstairs and put on my robe. I think I'll change into something else. Robert, you make yourself comfortable," she said.

53   "I'm comfortable," the blind man said.

54   "I want you to feel comfortable in this house," she said.

55   "I am comfortable," the blind man said.

56   After she'd left the room, he and I listened to the weather report and then to the sports roundup. By that time, she'd been gone so long I didn't know if she was going to come back. I thought she might have gone to bed. I wished she'd come back downstairs. I didn't want to be left alone with a blind man. I asked him if he wanted another drink, and he said sure. Then I asked if he wanted to smoke some dope with me. I said I'd just rolled a number. I hadn't, but I planned to do so in about two shakes.

57   "I'll try some with you," he said.

58   "Damn right," I said. "That's the stuff."

59   I got our drinks and sat down on the sofa with him. Then I rolled us two fat numbers. I lit one and passed it. I brought it to his fingers. He took it and inhaled.

60   "Hold it as long as you can," I said. I could tell he didn't know the first thing.

61   My wife came back downstairs wearing her pink robe and her pink slippers.

62   "What do I smell?" she said.

63   "We thought we'd have us some cannabis," I said.

64   My wife gave me a savage look. Then she looked at the blind man and said, "Robert, I didn't know you smoked."

65   He said, "I do now, my dear. There's a first time for everything. But I don't feel anything yet."

66   "This stuff is pretty mellow," I said. "This stuff is mild. It's dope you can reason with," I said. "It doesn't mess you up."

67   "Not much it doesn't, bub," he said, and laughed.

68   My wife sat on the sofa between the blind man and me. I passed her the number. She took it and toked and then passed it back to me. "Which way is this going?" she said. Then she said, "I shouldn't be smoking this. I can hardly keep my eyes open as it is. That dinner did me in. I shouldn't have eaten so much."

69   "It was the strawberry pie," the blind man said. "That's what did it," he said, and he laughed his big laugh. Then he shook his head.

70   "There's more strawberry pie," I said.

71   "Do you want some more, Robert?" my wife said.

72   "Maybe in a little while," he said.

73   We gave our attention to the TV. My wife yawned again. She said, "Your bed is made up when you feel like going to bed, Robert. I know you must have had a long day. When you're ready to go to bed, say so." She pulled his arm. "Robert?"

74   He came to and said, "I've had a real nice time. This beats tapes doesn't it?"

75   I said, "Coming at you," and I put the number between his fingers. He inhaled, held the smoke, and then let it go. It was like he'd been doing it since he was nine years old.

76   "Thanks, bub," he said. "But I think this is all for me. I think I'm beginning to feel it," he said. He held the burning roach out for my wife.

77   "Same here," she said. "Ditto. Me, too." She took the roach and passed it to me. "I may just sit here for a while between you two guys with my eyes closed. But don't let me bother you, okay? Either one of you. If it bothers you, say so. Otherwise, I may just sit here with my eyes closed until you're ready to go to bed," she said. "Your bed's made up, Robert, when you're ready. It's right next to our room at the top of the stairs. We'll show you up when you're ready. You wake me up now, you guys, if I fall asleep." She said that and then she closed her eyes and went to sleep.

78   The news program ended. I got up and changed the channel. I sat back down on the sofa. I wished my wife hadn't pooped out. Her head lay across the back of the sofa, her mouth open. She'd turned so that her robe slipped away from her legs, exposing a juicy thigh. I reached to draw her robe back over her, and it was then that I glanced at the blind man. What the hell! I flipped the robe open again.

79   "You say when you want some strawberry pie," I said.

80   "I will," he said.

81   I said, "Are you tired? Do you want me to take you up to your bed? Are you ready to hit the hay?"

82   "Not yet," he said. "No, I'll stay up with you, bub. If that's all right. I'll stay up until you're ready to turn in. We haven't had a chance to talk. Know what I mean? I feel like me and her monopolized the evening." He lifted his beard and he let it fall. He picked up his cigarettes and his lighter.

83   "That's all right," I said. Then I said, "I'm glad for the company."

84   And I guess I was. Every night I smoked dope and stayed up as long as I could before I fell asleep. My wife and I hardly ever went to bed at the same time. When I did go to sleep, I had these dreams. Sometimes I'd wake up from one of them, my heart going crazy.

85   Something about the church and the Middle Ages was on the TV. Not your run-of-the-mill TV fare. I wanted to watch something else. I turned to the other channels. But there was nothing on them, either. So I turned back to the first channel and apologized.

86   "Bub, it's all right," the blind man said. "It's fine with me. Whatever you want to watch is okay. I'm always learning something. Learning never ends. It won't hurt me to learn something tonight, I got ears," he said.

87   We didn't say anything for a time. He was leaning forward with his head turned at me, his right ear aimed in the direction of the set. Very disconcerting. Now and then his eyelids drooped and then they snapped open again. Now and then he put his fingers into his beard and tugged, like he was thinking about something he was hearing on the television.

88   On the screen, a group of men wearing cowls was being set upon and tormented by men dressed in skeleton costumes and men dressed as devils. The men dressed as devils wore devil masks, horns, and long tails. This pageant was part of a procession. The Englishman who was narrating the thing said it took place in Spain once a year. I tried to explain to the blind man what was happening.

89   "Skeletons," he said. "I know about skeletons," he said, and he nodded.

90   The TV showed this one cathedral. Then there was a long, slow look at another one. Finally, the picture switched to the famous one in Paris, with its flying buttresses and its spires reaching up to the clouds. The camera pulled away to show the whole of the cathedral rising above the skyline.

91   There were times when the Englishman who was telling the thing would shut up, would simply let the camera move around the cathedrals. Or else the camera would tour the countryside, men in fields walking behind oxen. I waited as long as I could. Then I felt I had to say something. I said, "They're showing the outside of this cathedral now. Gargoyles. Little statues carved to look like monsters. Now I guess they're in Italy. Yeah, they're in Italy. There's paintings on the walls of this one church."

92   "Are those fresco paintings, bub?" he asked, and he sipped from his drink.

93   I reached for my glass. But it was empty. I tried to remember what I could remember. "You're asking me are those frescoes?" I said. "That's a good question. I don't know."

94   The camera moved to a cathedral outside Lisbon. The differences in the Portuguese cathedral compared with the French and Italian were not that great. But they were there. Mostly the interior stuff. Then something occurred to me, and I said, "Something has occurred to me. Do you have any idea what a cathedral is? What they look like, that is? Do you follow me? If somebody says cathedral to you, do you have any notion what they're talking about? Do you know the difference between that and a Baptist church, say?"

95 He let the smoke dribble from his mouth. "I know they took hundreds of workers fifty or a hundred years to build," he said. "I just heard the man say that, of course. I know generations of the same families worked on a cathedral. I heard him say that, too. The men who began their life's work on them, they never lived to see the completion of their work. In that wise, bub, they're no different from the rest of us, right?" He laughed. Then his eyelids drooped again. His head nodded. He seemed to be snoozing. Maybe he was imagining himself in Portugal. The TV was showing another cathedral now. This one was in Germany. The Englishman's voice droned on. "Cathedrals," the blind man said. He sat up and rolled his head back and forth. "If you want the truth, bub, that's about all I know. What I just said. What I heard him say. But maybe you could describe one to me? I wish you'd do it. I'd like that. If you want to know, I really don't have a good idea."

96 I stared hard at the shot of the cathedral on the TV. How could I even begin to describe it? But say my life depended on it. Say my life was being threatened by an insane guy who said I had to do it or else.

97 I stared some more at the cathedral before the picture flipped off into the countryside. There was no use. I turned to the blind man and said, "To begin with, they're very tall." I was looking around the room for clues. "They reach way up. Up and up. Toward the sky. They're so big, some of them, they have to have these supports. To help hold them up, so to speak. These supports are called buttresses. They remind me of viaducts, for some reason. But maybe you don't know viaducts, either? Sometimes the cathedrals have devils and such carved into the front. Sometimes lords and ladies. Don't ask me why this is," I said.

98 He was nodding. The whole upper part of his body seemed to be moving back and forth.

99 "I'm not doing so good, am I?" I said.

100 He stopped nodding and leaned forward on the edge of the sofa. As he listened to me, he was running his fingers through his beard. I wasn't getting through to him, I could see that. But he waited for me to go on just the same. He nodded, like he was trying to encourage me. I tried to think what else to say. "They're really big," I said. "They're massive. They're built of stone. Marble, too, sometimes. In those olden days, when they built cathedrals, men wanted to be close to God. In those olden days, God was an important part of everyone's life. You could tell this from their cathedral-building. I'm sorry," I said, "but it looks like that's the best I can do for you. I'm just no good at it."

101 "That's all right, bub," the blind man said. "Hey, listen. I hope you don't mind my asking you. Can I ask you something? Let me ask you a simple question, yes or no. I'm just curious and there's no offense. You're my host. But let me ask if you are in any way religious? You don't mind my asking?"

102 I shook my head. He couldn't see that, though. A wink is the same as a nod to a blind man. "I guess I don't believe in it. In anything. Sometimes It's hard. You know what I'm saying?"

103 "Sure, I do," he said.

104 "Right," I said.

105   The Englishman was still holding forth. My wife sighed in her sleep. She drew a long breath and went on with her sleeping.

106   "You'll have to forgive me," I said. "But I can't tell you what a cathedral looks like. It just isn't in me to do it. I can't do any more than I've done."

107   The blind man sat very still, his head down, as he listened to me.

108   I said, "The truth is, cathedrals don't mean anything special to me. Nothing. Cathedrals. They're something to look at on late-night TV. That's all they are."

109   It was then that the blind man cleared his throat. He brought something up. He took a handkerchief from his back pocket. Then he said, "I get it, bub. It's okay. It happens. Don't worry about it," he said. "Hey, listen to me. Will you do me a favor? I got an idea. Why don't you find us some heavy paper? and a pen. We'll do something. We'll draw one together. Get us a pen and some heavy paper. Go on, bub, get the stuff," he said.

110   So I went upstairs. My legs felt like they didn't have any strength in them. They felt like they did after I'd done some running. In my wife's room, I looked around. I found some ballpoints in a little basket on her table. And then I tried to think where to look for the kind of paper he was talking about.

111   Downstairs, in the kitchen, I found a shopping bag with onion skins in the bottom of the bag. I emptied the bag and shook it. I brought it into the living room and sat down with it near his legs. I moved some things, smoothed the wrinkles from the bag, spread it out on the coffee table.

112   The blind man got down from the sofa and sat next to me on the carpet.

113   He ran his fingers over the paper. He went up and down the sides of the paper. The edges, even the edges. He fingered the corners.

114   "All right," he said. "All right, let's do her."

115   He found my hand, the hand with the pen. He closed his hand over my hand. "Go ahead, bub, draw," he said. "Draw. You'll see. I'll follow along with you. It'll be okay. Just begin now like I'm telling you. You'll see. Draw," the blind man said.

116   So I began. First I drew a box that looked like a house. It could have been the house I lived in. Then I put a roof on it. At either end of the roof, I drew spires. Crazy.

117   "Swell," he said. "Terrific. You're doing fine," he said. "Never thought anything like this could happen in your lifetime, did you, bub? Well, it's a strange life, we all know that. Go on now. Keep it up."

118   I put in windows with arches. I drew flying buttresses. I hung great doors. I couldn't stop. The TV station went off the air. I put down the pen and closed and opened my fingers. The blind man felt around over the paper. He moved the tips of his fingers over the paper, all over what I had drawn, and he nodded.

119   "Doing fine," the blind man said.

120   I took up the pen again, and he found my hand. I kept at it. I'm no artist. But I kept drawing just the same.

121   My wife opened up her eyes and gazed at us. She sat up on the sofa, her robe hanging open. She said, "What are you doing? Tell me, I want to know."

122   I didn't answer her.

123   The blind man said, "We're drawing a cathedral. Me and him are working on it. Press hard," he said to me. "That's right. That's good," he said. "Sure. You got it, bub, I can tell. You didn't think you could. But you can, can't you? You're cooking with gas now. You know what I'm saying? We're going to really have us something here in a minute. How's the old arm?" he said. "Put some people in there now. What's a cathedral without people?"

124   My wife said, "What's going on? Robert, what are you doing? What's going on?"

125   "It's all right," he said to her. "Close your eyes now," the blind man said to me.

126   I did it. I closed them just like he said.

127   "Are they closed?" he said. "Don't fudge."

128   "They're closed," I said.

129   "Keep them that way," he said. He said, "Don't stop now. Draw."

130   So we kept on with it. His fingers rode my fingers as my hand went over the paper. It was like nothing else in my life up to now.

131   Then he said, "I think that's it. I think you got it," he said. "Take a look. What do you think?"

132   But I had my eyes closed. I thought I'd keep them that way for a little longer. I thought it was something I ought to do.

133   "Well?" he said. "Are you looking?"

134   My eyes were still closed. I was in my house. I knew that. But I didn't feel like I was inside anything.

135   "It's really something," I said.

Source: Carver, Raymond. "Cathedral." 1981. Web. Copyright © 1981, 1982, 1983 by Raymond Carver. Used by permission of Alfred A. Knopf, an imprint of the Knofp Doubleday Publishing Group, a division of Random House LLC. All rights reserved.

QUESTIONS FOR DISCUSSION

1. Applying Rosemarie Garland-Thomson's understanding of how stories about disability challenge the norm, might we argue that "Cathedral" is "a fresh story about disability" that replaces "the familiar story of disability as tragedy?" How does Carver use the story to do this?

2. What is the significance of the cathedral in this story?

3. Why do you think the narrator and his wife remain nameless?

FROM READING TO WRITING

Draw a line down the centre of your notebook. On one side, write "normal" and on the other side write "abnormal." Let "normal" stand for the narrator and his wife and let "abnormal" represent the blind man, Robert. Then write down all the adjectives, nouns, verbs, phrases, or sentences associated with the normal/abnormal juxtaposition. Is there a clear-cut division here? Does Carver subvert the juxtaposition of normal/abnormal in this story?

Voices

BY ALICE MUNRO

INTRODUCTION

Alice Munro is an acclaimed Canadian short-story writer. She received the 2009 Man Booker International Prize for her lifetime body of work, and in 2013 she was awarded the Nobel Prize in literature for her work as "master of the contemporary short story."

Her semi-autobiographical story "Voices," printed in her latest anthology, *Dear Life,* is a coming-of-age story that documents the young Alice's emergence from childhood innocence to adult experience and sexuality. This work, similar to Munro's other stories, poses questions about what it is to be human. What does it mean to grow up in small town Ontario? What does it mean to be a woman—a daughter, a mother, a prostitute—in all its various guises? This story considers the girl's emerging identity in relation to the formative class and gender distinctions about which the story revolves.

1   When my mother was growing up, she and her whole family would go to dances. These would be held in the schoolhouse, or sometimes in a farmhouse with a big enough front room. Young and old would be in attendance. Someone would play the piano—the household piano or the one in the school—and someone would have brought a violin. The square dancing had complicated patterns or steps, which a person known for a special facility would call out at the top of his voice (it was always a man) and in a strange desperate sort of haste which was of no use at all unless you knew the dance already. As everybody did, having learned them all by the time they were ten or twelve years old.

2   Married now, with three of us children, my mother was still of an age and temperament to enjoy such dances if she had lived in the true countryside where they were still going on. She would have enjoyed too the round dancing performed by couples, which was supplanting the old style to a certain extent. But she was in an odd situation. We were. Our family was out of town but not really in the country.

3   My father, who was much better liked than my mother, was a man who believed in taking whatever you were dealt. Not so my mother. She had risen from her farm girl's life to become a schoolteacher, but this was not enough, it had not given her the position she would have liked, or the friends she would have liked to have in town. She was living in the wrong place and had not enough money, but she was not equipped anyway. She could play euchre but not bridge. She was affronted by the sight of a woman smoking. I think people found her pushy and overly grammatical. She said things like "readily" and "indeed so." She sounded as if she had grown up in some strange family who always talked that way. And she hadn't. They didn't. Out on their farms, my aunts and uncles talked the way everybody else did. And they didn't like my mother very much, either.

4   I don't mean that she spent all her time wishing that things weren't as they were. Like any other woman with washtubs to haul into the kitchen and no running water and a need to spend most of the summer preparing food to be eaten in the winter, she was kept busy. She couldn't even devote as much time as she otherwise would have done in being disappointed with me, wondering why I was not bringing the right kind of friends, or any friends at all, home from the town school. Or why I was shying away from Sunday School recitations, something I used to make a grab at. And why I came home with the ringlets torn out of my hair—a desecration I had managed even before I got to school, because nobody else wore their hair the way she fixed mine. Or indeed why I had learned to blank out even the prodigious memory I once had for reciting poetry, refusing to use it ever again for showing off.

5   But I am not always full of sulks and disputes. Not yet. Here I am when about ten years old, all eager to dress up and accompany my mother to a dance.

6   The dance was being held in one of the altogether decent but not prosperous-looking houses on our road. A large wooden house inhabited by people I knew nothing about, except that the husband worked in the foundry, even though he was old enough to be my grandfather. You didn't quit the foundry then, you worked as long as you could and tried to save up money for when you couldn't. It was a disgrace, even in the middle of what I later learned to call the Great Depression, to find yourself having to go on the Old Age Pension. It was a disgrace for your grown children to allow it, no matter what straits they were in themselves.

7   Some questions come to mind now that didn't then.

8   Were the people who lived in the house giving this dance simply in order to create some festivity? Or were they charging money? They might have found themselves in difficulties, even if the man had a job. Doctor's bills. I knew how dreadfully that could fall upon a family. My little sister was delicate, as people said, and her tonsils had already been removed. My brother and I suffered spectacular bronchitis every winter, resulting in doctor's visits. Doctors cost money.

9   The other thing I might have wondered about was why I should have been chosen to accompany my mother, instead of my father doing that. But it really isn't such a puzzle. My father maybe didn't like to dance, and my mother did. Also, there were two small children to be looked after at home, and I wasn't old enough yet to do that. I can't remember my parents ever hiring a babysitter. I'm not sure the term was even familiar in those days. When I was in my teens I found employment that way, but times had changed by then.

10   We were dressed up. At the country dances my mother remembered, there was never any appearance in those sassy square dance outfits you would see later on television. Everybody wore their best, and not to do so—to appear in anything like those frills and neckerchieves that were the supposed attire of country folk—would have been an insult to the hosts and everybody else. I wore a dress my mother had made for me, of soft winter wool. The skirt was pink and the top yellow, with a heart of the pink wool sewn where my left breast would be one day. My hair was combed and moistened and shaped into those long fat sausage-like ringlets that I got rid of every day on the way to school. I had complained about wearing them to the dance on the grounds that nobody else wore them. My mother's retort was that nobody else was so lucky. I dropped the complaint because I wanted to go so much, or perhaps because I thought that nobody from school would be at the dance so it didn't matter. It was the ridicule of my school fellows that I feared always.

11 My mother's dress was not homemade. It was her best, too elegant for church and too festive for a funeral, and so hardly ever worn. It was made of black velvet, with sleeves to the elbows, and a high neckline. The wonderful thing about it was a proliferation of tiny beads, gold and silver and various colors, sewn all over the bodice and catching the light, changing whenever she moved or only breathed. She had braided her hair, which was still mostly black, then pinned it in a tight coronet on top of her head. If she had been anybody else but my mother I would have thought her thrillingly handsome. I think I did find her so, but as soon as we got into the strange house I had to notice that her best dress was nothing like any other woman's dress, though they must have put on their best too.

12 The other women I'm speaking of were in the kitchen. That was where we stopped and looked at things set out on a big table. All sorts of tarts and cookies and pies and cakes. And my mother too set down some fancy thing she had made and started to fuss around to make it look better. She commented on how mouthwatering everything looked.

13 Am I sure she said that—mouthwatering? Whatever she said, it did not sound quite right. I wished then for my father to be there, always sounding perfectly right for the occasion, even when he spoke grammatically. He would do that in our house but not so readily outside of it. He slipped into whatever exchange was going on—he understood that the thing to do was never to say anything special. My mother was just the opposite. With her everything was clear and ringing and served to call attention.

14 Now that was happening and I heard her laugh, delightedly, as if to make up for nobody's talking to her. She was inquiring where we might put our coats.

15 It turned out that we could put them anywhere, but if we wanted, somebody said, we could lay them down on the bed upstairs. You got upstairs by a staircase shut in by walls, and there was no light, except at the top. My mother told me to go ahead, she would be up in a minute, and so I did.

16 A question here might be whether there could really have been a payment for attending that dance. My mother could have stayed behind to arrange it. On the other hand, would people have been asked to pay and still have brought all those refreshments? And were the refreshments really as lavish as I remember? With everybody so poor? But maybe they were already feeling not so poor, with the war jobs and money that soldiers sent home. If I was really ten, and I think I was, then those changes would have been going on for two years.

17 The staircase came up from the kitchen and also from the front room, joining together into one set of steps that led up to the bedrooms. After I had got rid of my coat and boots in the tidied-up front bedroom, I could still hear my mother's voice ringing out in the kitchen. But I could also hear music coming from the front room, so I went down that way.

18   The room had been cleared of all furniture except the piano. Dark green cloth blinds, of the kind I thought particularly dreary, were pulled down over the windows. But there was no dreary sort of atmosphere in the room. Many people were dancing, decorously holding on to each other, shuffling or swaying in tight circles. A couple of girls still in school were dancing in a way that was just becoming popular, moving opposite each other and sometimes holding hands, sometimes not. They actually smiled a greeting when they saw me, and I melted with pleasure, as I was apt to do when any confident older girl paid any attention to me.

19   There was a woman in that room you couldn't help noticing, one whose dress would certainly put my mother's in the shade. She must have been quite a bit older than my mother—her hair was white, and worn in a smooth sophisticated arrangement of what were called marcelled waves, close to her scalp. She was a large person with noble shoulders and broad hips, and she was wearing a dress of golden-orange taffeta, cut with a rather low square neck and a skirt that just covered her knees. Her short sleeves held her arms tightly and the flesh on them was heavy and smooth and white, like lard.

20   This was a startling sight. I would not have thought it possible that somebody could look both old and polished, both heavy and graceful, bold as brass and yet mightily dignified. You could have called her brazen, and perhaps my mother later did—that was her sort of word. Someone better disposed might have said, stately. She didn't really show off, except in the whole style and color of the dress. She and the man with her danced together in a respectful, rather absent-minded style, like spouses.

21   I didn't know her name. I had never seen her before. I didn't know that she was notorious in our town, and maybe farther afield, for all I knew.

22   I think that if I was writing fiction instead of remembering something that happened, I would never have given her that dress. A kind of advertisement she didn't need.

23   Of course, if I had lived in the town, instead of just going in and out every day for school, I might have known that she was a notable prostitute. I would surely have seen her sometime, though not in that orange dress. And I would not have used the word prostitute. Bad woman, more likely. I would have known that there was something disgusting and dangerous and exciting and bold about her, without knowing exactly what it was. If somebody had tried to tell me, I don't think I would have believed them.

24   There were several people in town who looked unusual and maybe she would have seemed to me just another. There was the hunchbacked man who polished the doors of the town hall every day and as far as I know did nothing else. And the quite proper looking woman who never stopped talking in a loud voice to herself, scolding people who were nowhere in sight.

25   I would have learned in time what her name was and eventually found out that she really did the things I could not believe she did. And that the man I saw dancing with her and whose name perhaps I never knew was the owner of the pool room. One day when I was in high school a couple of girls dared me to go into the poolroom when we were walking past, and I did, and there he was, the same man. Though he was balder and heavier now, and wearing shabbier clothes. I don't recall that he said anything to me, but

he did not have to. I bolted back to my friends, who were not quite friends after all, and told them nothing.

26   When I saw the owner of the pool room, the whole scene of the dance came back to me, the thumping piano and the fiddle music and the orange dress, which I would by then have called ridiculous, and my mother's sudden appearance with her coat on that she had probably never taken off.

27   There she was, calling my name through the music in the tone I particularly disliked, the tone that seemed to specially remind me that it was thanks to her I was on this earth at all.

28   She said, "Where is your coat?" As if I had mislaid it somewhere.

29   "Upstairs."

30   "Well go and get it."

31   She would have seen it there if she herself had been upstairs at all. She must never have got past the kitchen, she must have been fussing around the food with her own coat unbuttoned but not removed, until she looked into the room where the dancing was taking place and knew who that orange dancer was.

32   "Don't delay," she said.

33   I didn't intend to. I opened the door to the stairway and ran up the first steps and found that where the stairs took their turn some people were sitting, blocking my way. They didn't see me coming—they were taken up, it seemed, with something serious. Not an argument, exactly, but an urgent sort of communication.

34   Two of these people were men. Young men in Air Force uniforms. One sitting on a step, one leaning forward on a lower step with a hand on his knee. There was a girl sitting on the step above them, and the man nearest to her was patting her leg in a comforting way. I thought she must have fallen on these narrow stairs and hurt herself, for she was crying.

35   Peggy. Her name was Peggy. "Peggy, Peggy," the young men were saying, in their urgent and even tender voices.

36   She said something I couldn't make out. She spoke in a childish voice. She was complaining, the way you complain about something that isn't fair. You say over and over that something isn't fair, but in a hopeless voice, as if you don't expect the thing that isn't fair to be righted. Mean is another word to be made use of in these circumstances. It's so mean. Somebody has been so mean.

37   By listening to my mother's talk to my father when we got home I found out something of what had happened, but I was not able to get it straight. Mrs Hutchison had shown up at the dance, driven by the pool room man, who was not known to me then as the pool room man. I don't know what name my mother called him by, but she was sadly dismayed by his behavior. News had got out about the dance and some boys from Port Albert—that is, from the Air Force base—had decided to put in an appearance as well. Of course that would have been all right. The Air Force boys were all right. It was Mrs Hutchison who was the disgrace. And the girl.

38   She had brought one of her girls with her.

39   "Maybe just felt like an outing," my father said. "Maybe just likes to dance."

40 My mother seemed not even to have heard this. She said that it was a shame. You expected to have a nice time, a nice decent dance within a neighborhood, and then it was all ruined.

41 I was in the habit of assessing the looks of older girls. I had not thought Peggy was particularly pretty. Maybe her make-up had rubbed off with her crying. Her rolled up mousey-colored hair had got loose from some of its bobby pins. Her fingernails were polished but they still looked as if she chewed them. She didn't seem much more grown up than one of those whiny, sneaky, perpetually complaining older girls I knew. Nevertheless the young men treated her as if she was someone who deserved never to have encountered one rough moment, someone who rightfully should be petted and pleasured and have heads bowed before her.

42 One of them offered her a ready-made cigarette. This in itself I saw as a treat, since my father rolled his own and so did every other man I knew. But Peggy shook her head and complained in that hurt voice that she did not smoke. Then the other man offered a stick of gum, and she accepted it.

43 What was going on? I had no way of knowing. The boy who had offered the gum noticed me, while rummaging in his pocket, and he said, "Peggy? Peggy, here's a little girl I think wants to go upstairs."

44 She dropped her head so I couldn't look into her face. I smelled perfume as I went by. I smelled their cigarettes too and their manly woollen uniforms, their polished boots.

45 When I came downstairs with my coat on they were still there, but this time they had been expecting me, so they all kept quiet while I passed. Except that Peggy gave one loud sniffle, and the young man nearest to her kept stroking her upper leg. Her skirt was pulled up and I saw the fastener holding her stocking.

46 For a long time I remembered the voices. I pondered over the voices. Not Peggy's. The men's. I know now that some of the Air Force men stationed at Port Albert early in the war had come out from England, and were training there to fight the Germans. So I wonder if it was the accent of some part of Britain that I was finding so mild and entrancing. It was certainly true that I had never in my life heard a man speak in that way, treating a woman as if she was so fine and valued a creature that whatever it was, whatever unkindness had come near her, was somehow a breach of a law, a sin.

47 What did I think had happened to make Peggy cry? The question did not much interest me at the time. I was not a brave person myself. I cried when chased and beaten with shingles on the way home from my first school. I cried when the teacher in the town school singled me out, in front of the class, to expose the shocking untidiness of my desk. And when she phoned my mother about the same problem and my mother hanging up the phone herself wept, enduring misery because I was not a credit to her. It seemed as though some people were naturally brave and others weren't. Somebody must have said something to Peggy, and there she was snuffling, because like me she was not thick-skinned.

48 It must have been that orange-dressed woman who had been mean, I thought, for no particular reason. It had to have been a woman. Because if it had been a man, one of her Air Force comforters would have punished him. Told him to watch his mouth, maybe dragged him outside and beaten him up.

49   So it wasn't Peggy I was interested in, not her tears, her crumpled looks. She reminded me too much of myself. It was her comforters I marvelled at. How they seemed to bow down and declare themselves in front of her.

50   What had they been saying? Nothing in particular. All right, they said. It's all right, Peggy, they said. Now, Peggy. All right. All right.

51   Such kindness. That anybody could be so kind.

52   It is true that these young men, brought to our country to train for bombing missions on which so many of them would be killed, might have been speaking in the normal accents of Cornwall or Kent or Hull or Scotland. But to me they seemed to be unable to open their mouths without uttering some kind of blessing, a blessing on the moment. It didn't occur to me that their futures were all bound up with disaster, or that their ordinary lives had flown out the window and been smashed on the ground. I just thought of the blessing, how wonderful to get on the receiving end of it, how strangely lucky and undeserving was that Peggy.

53   And, for I don't know how long, I thought of them. In the cold dark of my bedroom they rocked me to sleep. I could turn them on, summon up their faces and their voices— but oh, far more, their voices were now directed to myself and not to any unnecessary third party. Their hands blessed my own skinny thighs and their voices assured me that I, too, was worthy of love.

54   And while they still inhabited my not yet quite erotic fantasies they were gone. Some, many, gone for good.

QUESTIONS FOR DISCUSSION

1. Garland-Thomson argues that "normal is the central concept governing the status and value of people." How does this concept of normal inform this story? How is normal "enforced" and at what cost?

2. How does the story raise questions about the difference between men, women, and different types of women? How does the girl, caught between an identification with the mother and the prostitute, resolve this difference?

3. How does the erotic work in this story? Consider the conclusion when the young girl imagines the young men "[blessing her] own skinny thighs." How do questions of agency, power, and powerlessness inform this analysis?

FROM READING TO WRITING

Pick one of the questions above and try to answer it in a short essay.

- Find places in the short story that speak to the question.
- Find patterns in the examples that will help you form an argument.
- Find evidence to support your argument.

Arctic Poppies

BY SUSAN MUSGRAVE

INTRODUCTION

Susan Musgrave is a Canadian poet, fiction, non-fiction, and children's writer. She published her first collection of poems, *Songs of the Sea Witch,* in 1970 when she was eighteen. In 1996, Musgrave received the Tilden Canadian Literary Award for poetry. She now teaches at the University of British Columbia in the MFA creative writing program. "Artic Poppies" was published in the 1996 anthology *Things that Keep and Do Not Change.*

This poem reflects common themes that we have seen already about what we consider normal and abnormal. Musgrave's strong imagery and contemplative language puts into perspective the profoundly fragile and sacred relationship between nature and human existence.

> After a week of rough seas the ship docked
> at Hopedale. The weather was no good but still
> I struggled ashore and climbed to the desecrated
> churchyard, determined to take away something
> 5   of a memory, to photograph the white Arctic
> poppies. Each time I framed a shot, my hands
> steady at last, a hunchback on crutches teetered
> into sight, as if innocently waiting for the fog
> to lift, the rain to let up, the light
> 10   to throw open its dingy overcoat and expose
> itself to my nakedness. My eye, my whole body
> had been saving itself for this, but every time
> he humped into view, I thought of you, the best
> man I'd ever left, lips tasting of whatever you'd had
> 15   to eat: spicy eggplant baba ghanouj, jumbo
> shrimp in garlic and Chablis, your mother's
> meat pie with a dash of cinnamon
> and cloves. When the sun broke
> through I'd have those wild flowers posed,
> 20   I'd be poised to shoot and then the stooped
> shadow would fall as if to say beauty
> without imperfection was something to be
> ashamed of, as if he could be my flaw.
> Crouched beside an abandoned grave

25   I tried to focus on those white
poppies in light that went on failing,
seeing your perfect body in his
crippled gaze. I could have taken him
back to my cabin aboard the ship, laid

30   his crutches down, bathed him, bent over
his grateful body and licked the smell
of smoked trout and caribou hide from his
thighs. Perhaps this is what he hoped for,
and then to be called beautiful afterwards.

35   I took his photograph. He'd wanted that, too
and suddenly I felt blessed, I felt
I'd been taken the way I liked it best: sex
in the head on sacred ground that has been
roughed up a little, a graveyard full

40   of ghostly poppies choking out the dead.

Source: Musgrave, Susan. "Arctic Poppies." Copyright © 1999 by Susan Musgrave. Published in Canada by McClelland and Stewart. Reprinted by permission of the author.

QUESTIONS FOR DISCUSSION

1. Does Musgrave's poem qualify, in Rosemarie Garland-Thomson's terms, as a "fresh, feisty story about disabled shapes and acts?" If so, how?

2. What role does the "hunchback on crutches" play in this poem? How does he disturb the narrator's view and attempt to make permanent the scene through the camera's lens?

3. How is the narrator's erotic engagement with the imaginary and real scene before her speak to the line, "beauty/without imperfection [is] something to be/ashamed of?" Can you summarize the narrator's ethical standpoint here?

4. What is the significance of the narrator's attempt to capture a picture of the Arctic poppies?

FROM READING TO WRITING

1. Define the word *beautiful*. Keeping in mind Musgrave's notion that when writers write and readers read poetry they find out about themselves, use the words and images from your definition to write a poem that expresses what the word *beautiful* means to you.

How to Write the Great American Indian Novel

BY SHERMAN ALEXIE

INTRODUCTION

Sherman Alexie is an acclaimed Native American poet, novelist, performer, and filmmaker. He grew up on the Spokane Indian Reservation, and his poetry, novels, short stories, and films, including the well-known film *Smoke Signals,* produced in 1998, tend to focus on the plight, powerlessness, and despair of Native Americans living on reservations. To this end, Alexie typically employs irony, humour, satire, and hyperbole.

"How to Write the Great American Indian Novel" employs all of these strategies as it exposes, from an outsider's predominantly white perspective, how Indians appear to the dominant culture. When reading this poem think about what Sherman Alexie is saying about the role story plays in creating potentially harmful stereotypes. Compare this poem with Richard Wagamese's and Drew Hayden Taylor's autobiographical responses to the Truth and Reconciliation Commission's response to residential schools (see pages 427 and 422). Are there commonalities in how First Nations' peoples are represented?

All of the Indians must have tragic features: tragic noses, eyes, and arms.
Their hands and fingers must be tragic when they reach for tragic food.
The hero must be a half-breed, half white and half Indian, preferably
from a horse culture. He should often weep alone. That is mandatory.

5   If the hero is an Indian woman, she is beautiful. She must be slender
and in love with a white man. But if she loves an Indian man
then he must be a half-breed, preferably from a horse culture.
If the Indian woman loves a white man, then he has to be so white
that we can see the blue veins running through his skin like rivers.

10   When the Indian woman steps out of her dress, the white man gasps
at the endless beauty of her brown skin. She should be compared to nature:
brown hills, mountains, fertile valleys, dewy grass, wind, and clear water.
If she is compared to murky water, however, then she must have a secret.
Indians always have secrets, which are carefully and slowly revealed.

15   Yet Indian secrets can be disclosed suddenly, like a storm.
Indian men, of course, are storms. They should destroy the lives
of any white women who choose to love them. All white women love

Indian men. That is always the case. White women feign disgust
at the savage in blue jeans and T-shirt, but secretly lust after him.

20   White women dream about half-breed Indian men from horse cultures.
Indian men are horses, smelling wild and gamey. When the Indian man
unbuttons his pants, the white woman should think of topsoil.
There must be one murder, one suicide, one attempted rape.
Alcohol should be consumed. Cars must be driven at high speeds.

25   Indians must see visions. White people can have the same visions
if they are in love with Indians. If a white person loves an Indian
then the white person is Indian by proximity. White people must carry
an Indian deep inside themselves. Those interior Indians are half-breed
and obviously from horse cultures. If the interior Indian is male

30   then he must be a warrior, especially if he is inside a white man.
If the interior Indian is female, then she must be a healer, especially if she is inside
a white woman. Sometimes there are complications.
An Indian man can be hidden inside a white woman. An Indian woman
can be hidden inside a white man. In these rare instances,

35   everybody is a half-breed struggling to learn more about his or her horse culture.
There must be redemption, of course, and sins must be forgiven.
For this, we need children. A white child and an Indian child, gender
not important, should express deep affection in a childlike way.
In the Great American Indian novel, when it is finally written,

40   all of the white people will be Indians and all of the Indians will be ghosts.

Source: "How to Write the Great American Indian Novel." Reprinted from *The Summer of Black Widows* © 1996 by Sherman Alexie, by permission of Hanging Loose Press.

QUESTIONS FOR DISCUSSION

1. Although Sherman Alexie is Native American himself, he employs an outsider's perspective in this poem in an attempt to objectify Native Americans. Why do you think he does this? How does this objectification reflect the way Native Indians have been objectified and treated by the dominant culture? Is this strategy effective?

2. How does Alexie both employ and subvert conventional stereotypes of Native Indians?

3. In representing his own people, rather than being represented, Alexie raises questions as to whether representation can be accurate. Does it matter, then, who is doing the representing?

FROM READING TO WRITING

1. In this poem, Alexie uses a combination of repetition, irony, hyperbole, and/or humour. Write a paragraph explaining how these techniques work in the poem. Are these techniques effective? Why?

continued

2. Are there commonalities between Alexie's poem and the concerns raised by Richard Wagamese and Drew Hayden Taylor? Write a paragraph highlighting these common concerns. Do stories offer any possible solutions?

Cry Me a River, White Boy

BY DREW HAYDEN TAYLOR

INTRODUCTION

Drew Hayden Taylor is an Ojibway First Nations award-winning essayist, play-wright, newspaper columnist, and short-story writer. He uses humour to write about the Aboriginal world-view and First Nations' identity. The autobiographical essay or commentary "Cry Me a River, White Boy" is written in response to Canada's Truth and Reconciliation Commission (TRC), established in 2008 to expose the "truth" of the Indian residential school system and help heal First Nations peoples. On 11 June 2008, Stephen Harper, Canada's prime minister, delivered a formal apology to First Nations people.

However, many First Nations people, including Drew Hayden Taylor, have been critical of the TRC. In 2009, the Aboriginal Healing Foundation published *Response, Responsibility, and Renewal: Canada's Truth and Reconciliation Journey* to explore issues related to the TRC.

Drew Hayden Taylor's response in this collection focuses on the historical relevance of Harper's apology.

1   *Aabwehyehnmigziwin* is the Anishnawbe word for apology. That is what Prime Minister Stephen Harper delivered in the House of Commons on the eleventh of June 2008 to the Survivors of Canada's residential school system.[1] Quoting the immortal words of singer Brenda Lee, who put it so eloquently,

> I'm sorry, so sorry...
> Please accept my apology...
> You tell me mistakes
> Are part of being young
> But that don't right
> The wrong that's been done

2   Harper said, "We are Sorry." Sorry. Surprising words from a surprising source. Brenda had put it much more eloquently. But the First Nations people of Canada listened. There were thousands of Aboriginal people on the front lawn of the Parliament buildings, eager to hear this historic admission of responsibility. Televisions were set

up in community centres, band offices, halls, and schools in Aboriginal communities all across the country. And then the people cried. They cried at the memory of what had been done, and what was being said. This event made a lot of people cry, and for many, it was a good cry—a cathartic one. Psychiatrists and Elders will tell you that.

3   Since the late 1800s, over 150,000 Aboriginal children were forcibly taken away from their families and shipped off to one of 130-plus schools scattered across seven provinces and two territories. There, they were robbed of their language, their beliefs, their self-respect, their culture, and, in some cases, their very existence in a vain attempt to make them more Canadian. The key phrase I kept hearing during the apology and in the opposition responses was the misguided belief that *in order to save the child, you must destroy the Indian.* How on earth did those two thoughts become entwined? Another fine example of an un-researched and unintelligent government policy like the Chinese head tax[2] or sending a small Inuit community five hundred kilometres further north in an attempt to establish Arctic sovereignty. The thought processes of many a politician can truly be baffling when it comes to people of another race.

4   The official *Aabwebyebnmigziwin* was a long time in coming, and hopefully it will close the chapter on this unfortunate part of First Nations history so that an entirely new book can begin, hopefully, this time with Aboriginal people as co-authors. All of the churches who ran residential schools—Roman Catholic, United, Anglican, and Presbyterian—have issued their own version of *aabwebyebnmigziwin* over the years. In 1998, the Liberals offered a kind of watered down, wimpy, anemic version. Essentially, it was something about having "profound regrets."[3] I have a lot of regrets too. Most people do. For instance, I have had sincere regrets about some of my past relationships, but that does not mean I apologize for them. Big difference.

5   Perhaps it is my working-class origins and artsy nature, but I do find it odd that it was the Conservative government who found the balls to issue the *aabwebyebnmigziwin.* It makes one wonder why the Conservative lawyers saw this as possible when ten years earlier, an army of government lawyers under the Liberals likely advised against it. You would think the residential school system would be something the Conservatives would admire. On the surface, it fits into their political and economic agenda. The government promised, in a number of treaties, to educate the youth from over 600 reserves across the world's second biggest country. They managed to download the cost of educating these youth by transferring it to the four main religious groups and their churches. Sounds like a sound economic decision, does it not?

6   In 2005, the Liberal government was all set to adopt the Kelowna Accord and address many of the serious issues plaguing First Nations communities. Then prime minister Paul Martin had long been concerned with Aboriginal issues. Yet no apology. Fast forward to 2006 when the Conservatives took power and offered Canada a new way of doing business, which basically involved shelving the Kelowna Accord and hiring Tom Flanagan, author of the controversial book *First Nations? Second Thoughts,* as a top Conservative advisor. Things did not look good for First Nations communities in this new century. Then came Harper's 180-degree turn. One could almost hear the snow falling in hell. Perhaps the official bean counters had taken into account the fact that

an official apology would be in their best interest, as it would shift responsibility to the Aboriginal communities. The government could then wash a lot of it off their hands.

7 How could the federal government know the whole issue of accountability for residential schools would later be classified as—and I love this term frequently used to describe screwed up governmental policies—a boondoggle? It has literally come back to bite them in their fish-belly white asses. On average, over 1.9 billion dollars[4] has already been paid out to many of the approximately 80,000 Survivors of Manifest Destiny High. That is a hell of an expensive education. And the price tag is still rising. Canadian tax-payers will be buying bandages for the physical and psychological wounds their ancestors inflicted for generations.[5]

8 It had been obvious for a long time that apologizing was not high on the Liberals to-do list. Pierre Trudeau did not want to bother with an *aabwehyehnmigziwin*. I think he felt it would just open the floodgates to more apologies that would quickly become unfortunate road bumps on the highway of proud Canadian history. I think he would have been right. Jean Chretien did not believe current social beliefs should be applied to past issues, yet it was Brian Mulroney's Conservatives who issued an apology to Japanese Canadians for the country's misdoings during World War II.[6] And now, Harper is regretting the Aboriginal people's historical treatment. Who would have thunk it? In all fairness, it should be mentioned that it was the Conservatives that gave Aboriginal people the right to vote in 1960. Way to go Progressive Conservatives! . . . a phrase I thought I would never say. Though many would argue old-school Conservatives are substantially different from the New World Conservatives. Personally, I think Diefenbaker could whip Harper's ass. Still, Harper is the current boss and I guess that is why the jibways call him the *Kichi Toodooshaabowimiijim*, which translates to "the Big Cheese" or, perhaps even more literally, to "Much Sour Milk."

9 Of course, there is always one spoilsport at every party, a pisser in the pool, known as the Conservative *brain trust* a.k.a. Pierre Poilievre and his amazingly insensitive comments about Survivors just needing a stronger work ethic and his opinion that giving these people reparation money was a waste of time. Otherwise, things might have been just fine and dandy. Evidently, Harper took the boy out to the proverbial woodshed, and a new and different apology by a contrite Poilievre soon followed. It should have been expected, just like there is one drunk at every party, one ex-girlfriend at every powwow, and one veggie burger at every barbecue. It was bound to happen in the volatile world of Canadian politics, somebody was going to pee in the pool. Conservative politicians are seldom known for their subtlety.

10 Was the *aabwehyehnmigziwin* sincere and do I buy it? Yes, I suppose it was sincere enough for me to buy it, however naïve that may sound. I suppose something is better then nothing. I also know that, by very definition, politicians should not be trusted nor believed any more than a Jerry Springer guest, especially when it comes to commitments to Aboriginal people. But Harper looked sincere, as did Dion, Duceppe, and Layton—all privileged white men apologizing for the actions of other privileged white men and also eager to curry First Nation favour. It is amazing how good education can make you the empathetic leader of a federal party and a bad education can get you an *aabwehyehnmigziwin.* They probably listened to Brenda Lee and her apologetic song. They are of that generation. Brenda probably knew little or nothing about Canadian politics or Aboriginal issues, though nobody could apologize like her.

11 I know a lot of people who were a little cynical about the sincerity of the apology. That is their right. If an abusive husband apologizes to his abused wife and kids, however sincere it might sound, some may doubt the authenticity of that apology. Same as in this situation, an admission of responsibility is as good a place as any to start. Ask any lawyer. But the healing must start somewhere.

12 I am very fortunate. Neither I nor any of my immediate relatives attended a residential school. Instead, we were schooled at the Mud Lake Indian Day School located directly on the Curve Lake Reserve in eastern Ontario. Still, many of the residential school policies extended to the communities. My mother tells of not being allowed to speak Anishnawbe on school grounds, which were located just a few hundred metres from where she lived. Just the other night, I heard her reminiscing with one of her sisters about how they made sure they never played under the windows of the school so the teacher would not hear them speaking in Anishnawbe. One usually does not think of one's seventy-seven-year old shy mother as a rebel. Maybe that is why Anishnawbe is still her first language and English a distant second.

13 There is a lot of collateral damage from that era as well. Hot on the heels of residential school Survivors are those who went through the Sixties Scoop, where Aboriginal kids were taken away by various social services and farmed out for adoption, usually to white families, sometimes to Europe and to the United States. They were part of the same larger, overall policy of eliminating Aboriginal culture by wiping away the memories and heritage of Aboriginal children and Canadianizing them. If you cannot get them through the front door, try the back, or even the window.

14 Interestingly, many Aboriginal people watching the historic *aabwehyehnmigziwin* were not actual students of residential schools. But I think it is safe to say that they were all affected by the practice in some way. Most Aboriginal people who watched knew somebody or several somebodies who attended residential school or were descended from, or a relative of, a Survivor. As a result, they were forced to deal with the repercussions of that experience. It now permeates our culture. Harper and Canada's apology was for all of us—those who attended the schools and those who are living with the fallout. Just as all Jewish people were affected by the Holocaust in some way (if I may be allowed to say this), all Aboriginal people were victims of what happened in those institutions. It is collateral damage in sort of an intergenerational way.

15 What happens now? I do not know. Maybe Phil Fontaine and the gang should contact Maher Arar. He might have some suggestions. If memory serves me correctly, Mr Arar was kidnapped suddenly for no logical reason, taken far away from his family for a long period of time, beaten, starved, and terrified for the greater good. He finally returned to his family a changed man and is now seeking justice. Geez, you would think he was an Aboriginal kid or something.

16 As the similarly sympathetic Connie Francis who, like Brenda Lee, was neither Aboriginal nor a residential school Survivor, also sang many years ago, "I'm sorry I made you cry." Did Harper get his words right (that were chosen for him by lawyers)? Harper had said, "We are sorry . . . We apologize for having done this." He must not forget that there is still a Canadian issue here that all Canadians need to address as part of an ongoing relationship. Closing the book on residential schools does not mean that the "Aboriginal problem" has been solved—at least not in the eyes of the government. Thus, I will let Connie Francis finish with her poignant lyrics:

> I'm sorry I made you cry
> Won't you forget, won't you forgive
> Don't let us say goodbye

17   I'm just glad Harper did not try to sing the *aabwehyehnmigziwin*.

NOTES

1   *See* Appendix 2.
2   For a brief review of the history of the Chinese head tax, please see pages 238–9 of Bradford W. Morse's article "Reconciliation Possible? Reparations Essential" in Castellano, Marlene Brant, Linda Archibald, and Mike DeGagné (2008). *From Truth to Reconciliation: Transforming the Legacy of Residential Schools*. Ottawa, ON: Aboriginal Healing Foundation: 233–56.
3   Government of Canada (1998). *Statement of Reconciliation*. Ottawa, ON: Indian and Northern Affairs Canada. Presented on 7 January 1998 by The Honourable Jane Stewart, Minister of Indian and Northern Affairs Canada. Retrieved 8 May 2014 from https://www.aadnc-aandc.gc.ca/eng/1100100015725/1100100015726.
4   Indian and Northern Affairs Canada (no date). Indian Residential Schools Resolution Canada 2007–2008 Departmental Performance Report. Retrieved 31 March 2009 from http://www.tbs-sct.gc.ca/dpr-rmr/2007-2008/inst/ira/ira-eng.pdf.
5   *See*: Bowlus, Audra, Katherine McKenna, Tanis Day and David Wright (2003). *The Economic Costs and Consequences of Child Abuse in Canada*. Ottawa, ON: The Law Commission of Canada; *and* Native Counselling Services of Alberta (2001). *A Cost-Benefit Analysis of Hollow Water's Community Holistic Circle Healing Process*. Ottawa, ON: Solicitor General Canada and Aboriginal Healing Foundation.
6   For a brief review of the apology and redress to Japanese Canadians, please see pages 237–8 of Bradford W. Morse's article "Reconciliation Possible? Reparations Essential" in Castellano, Marlene Brant, Linda Archibald, and Mike DeGagné (2008). *From Truth to Reconciliation: Transforming the Legacy of Residential Schools*. Ottawa, ON: Aboriginal Healing Foundation: 233–56.

Source: From *Response, Responsibility and Renewal: Canada's Truth and Reconciliation Journey*. Eds. Younging et al. Ottawa: Aboriginal Healing Foundation Research Series, 2009. 99–109.

QUESTIONS FOR CONSIDERATION

1.   Why does Drew Hayden Taylor frame this essay with song lyrics? What point is he trying to make?
2.   Hayden Taylor is "cynical about the sincerity of the apology." Identify the passages, sentences, or particular words where this becomes evident?

3. According to Hayden Taylor, what is the "fallout" of the residential school system? Has justice been done? Does he propose any solutions?

4. The "apology" is a genre that typically involves a defence or self-justification. Find Harper's apology and see if it meets these basic requirements. Is Hayden Taylor's critique, in your opinion, justified?

FROM READING TO WRITING

1. Omitting his use of humour, write a paragraph summarizing Hayden Taylor's response to Harper's apology. Now write a short critical response to Hayden Taylor.

2. Write a paragraph describing Hayden Taylor's tone. How does he use language and rhetoric to persuade the reader that Harper's apology is insufficient to the task?

Returning to Harmony

BY RICHARD WAGAMESE

INTRODUCTION

Richard Wagamese is one of Canada's foremost Ojibway First Nations poets, novelists, and journalists. He was born in 1955 in Northwestern Ontario and was raised in foster homes until he was adopted. Some of his books include *Indian House, Ragged Company, Keeper'n Me,* and *One Native Life.*

This essay, "Returning to Harmony," was also included in the Aboriginal Healing Foundation's *Response, Responsibility, and Renewal: Canada's Truth and Reconciliation Journey.* It appears in a section titled "Reconciliation, Restitution, and Rhetoric," and it documents the long-term effects of residential schools and his own experience with the child welfare system. Wagamese stresses the importance of "personal reconciliation" (8).

1   I am a victim of Canada's residential school system. When I say victim, I mean something substantially different than "survivor." I never attended a residential school, so I cannot say that I survived one. However, my parents and my extended family members did. The pain they endured became my pain, and I became a victim.

2   When I was born, my family still lived the seasonal nomadic life of traditional Ojibwa people. In the great rolling territories surrounding the Winnipeg River in Northwestern Ontario, they fished, hunted, and trapped. Their years were marked by the peregrinations of a people guided by the motions and turns of the land. I came into

the world and lived in a canvas army tent hung from a spruce bough frame as my first home. The first sounds I heard were the calls of loon, the snap and crackle of a fire, and the low, rolling undulation of Ojibwa talk.

3   We lived communally. Along with my mother and siblings, there were my matriarchal grandparents, aunts, uncles, and cousins. Surrounded by the rough and tangle of the Canadian Shield, we, moved through the seasons. Time was irrelevant in the face of ancient cultural ways that we followed.

4   But there was a spectre in our midst.

5   All the members of my family attended residential school. They returned to the land bearing psychological, emotional, spiritual, and physical burdens that haunted them. Even my mother, despite staunch declarations that she had learned good things there (finding Jesus, learning to keep a house, the gospel), carried wounds she could not voice. Each of them had experienced an institution that tried to scrape the Indian off of their insides, and they came back to the bush and river raw, sore, and aching. The pain they bore was invisible and unspoken. It seeped into their spirit, oozing its poison and blinding them from the incredible healing properties within their Indian ways.

6   For a time, the proximity to family and the land acted as a balm. Then, slowly and irrevocably, the spectre that followed them back from the schools began to assert its presence and shunt for space around our communal fire. When the vitriolic stew of unspoken words, feelings, and memories of their great dislocation, hurt, and isolation began to bubble and churn within them, they discovered that alcohol could numb them from it. And we ceased to be a family.

7   Instead, the adults of my Ojibwa family became frightened children. The trauma that had been visited upon them reduced them to that. They huddled against a darkness from where vague shapes whispered threats and from where invasions of their minds, spirits, and bodies roared through the blackness to envelope and smother them again. They forgot who they were. They struck back vengefully, bitterly, and blindly as only hurt and frightened children could do.

8   When I was a toddler, my left arm and shoulder were smashed. Left untreated, my arm hung backwards in its joint and, over time, it atrophied and withered. My siblings and I endured great tides of violence and abuse from the drunken adults. We were beaten, nearly drowned, and terrorized. We took to hiding in the bush and waited until the shouting, cursing, and drinking died away. Those nights were cold and terrifying. In the dim light of dawn, the eldest of us would sneak back into camp to get food and blankets.

9   In the mid-winter of 1958 when I was almost three, the adults left my two brothers, sister, and me alone in the bush camp across the bay from the tiny railroad town of Minaki. It was February. The wind was blowing bitterly and the firewood ran out at the same time as the food. They were gone for days, drinking in Kenora sixty miles away. When it became apparent that we would freeze to death without wood, my eldest sister and brother hauled my brother, Charles, and me across the bay on a sled piled with furs.

10   They pulled us across that ice in a raging snowstorm. We huddled in the furs on the leeward side of the railroad depot cold, hungry, and crying. A passing Ontario provincial policeman found us and took us to the Children's Aid Society. I would not see my mother or my extended family again for twenty-one years.

11   I lived in two foster homes until I was adopted at age nine. I left that home at age sixteen; I ran for my safety, my security, and my sanity. The seven years I spent in that adopted home were filled with beatings, mental and emotional abuse, and a complete dislocation and disassociation from anything Indian or Ojibwa. I was permitted only the strict Presbyterian ethic of that household. It was as much an institutional kidnapping as a residential school.

12   For years after, I lived on the street or in prison. I became a drug user and an alcoholic. I drifted through unfulfilled relationships. I was haunted by fears and memories. I carried the residual trauma of my toddler years and the seven years in my adopted home. This caused me to experience post-traumatic stress disorder, which severely affected the way I lived my life and the choices I would make.

13   The truth of my life is that I am an intergenerational victim of residential schools. Everything I endured until I found healing was a result of the effects of those schools. I did not hug my mother until I was twenty-five. I did not speak my first Ojibwa word or set foot on my traditional territory until I was twenty-six. I did not know that I had a family, a history, a culture, a source for spirituality, a cosmology, or a traditional way of living. I had no awareness that I belonged somewhere. I grew up ashamed of my Native identity and the fact that I knew nothing about it. I was angry that there was no one to tell me who I was or where I had come from.

14   My brother Charles tracked me down with the help of a social worker friend when I was twenty-five. From there, I returned to the land of my people as a stranger knowing nothing of their experience or their pain. When I rejoined my people and learned about Canada's residential school policy, I was enraged. Their political and social history impelled me to find work as a reporter with a Native newspaper. As a writer and a journalist, I spoke to hundreds of residential school Survivors. The stories they told, coupled with my family's complete and utter reticence, told me a great deal about how my family had suffered. I knew that those schools were responsible for my displacement, my angst, and my cultural *lostness*.

15   For years I carried simmering anger and resentment. The more I learned about the implementation of that policy and how it affected Aboriginal people across the country, the more anger I felt. I ascribed all my pain to residential schools and to those responsible. I blamed churches for my alcoholism, loneliness, shame, fear, inadequacy, and failures. In my mind I envisaged a world where I had grown up as a fully functioning Ojibwa, and it glittered in comparison to the pain-wracked life I had lived.

16   But when I was in my late forties, I had enough of the anger. I was tired of being drunk and blaming the residential schools and those responsible. I was tired of fighting against something that could not be touched, addressed, or confronted. My life was slipping away on me and I did not want to become an older person still clinging to a disempowering emotion like the anger I carried.

17   So one day I decided that I would visit a church. Churches had been the seed of my anger. I had religion forced on me in my adopted home and it was the churches that had run the residential schools that shredded the spirit of my family. If I were to lose my anger, I needed to face the root of it squarely. I was determined that I would take myself there and sit and listen to the service. As much as I knew that I would want to

walk out and as much as my anger would direct me to reject it all, I would force myself to sit and listen and try to find something that I could relate to. I chose a United Church because they had been the first to issue an apology for their role in the residential school debacle. They had been the first to publicly state their responsibility for the hurt that crippled generations. They were the first to show the courage to address wrongdoing, abuse, forced removal, and shaming. They had been the first to make tangible motions toward reconciliation. It put them in a more favourable light with me.

18   I was uncomfortable at first. No one spoke to me as I took my seat in a pew near the back. There were no other Native people there and I used that fact as a denunciation. When the service began, I heard everything through the tough screen of my rage. Then I noticed the old woman beside me sitting with her eyes closed as the minister spoke. She looked calm and peaceful, and there was a glow on her features that I coveted. So I closed my eyes too and tilted my head back and listened.

19   I ceased to hear the liturgy that day. I could not hear doctrine, semantics, proselytizations, or judgment. Instead, with my eyes closed, all I could hear was the small voice of the minister telling a story about helping a poor, drug-addicted woman on the street despite his fear and doubt. All I heard was the voice of compassion. All I heard was a spiritual, very human person talking about life and confronting its mysteries.

20   So I went back the next week. I went back and took my seat, and I listened with my eyes closed. After the scriptural text was read, the minister analyzed it by placing it in the context of his impatience and the lessons he had learned in the grocery line and in the freeway traffic. Here was a man responsible for directing the lives of a congregation talking about facing his own spiritual shortcomings. There was no self-aggrandization, no inferred superiority. There was only a man telling us how hard it was to behave like a spiritual being.

21   I went back to that church for many weeks. The messages I heard were all about humanity and about the search for innocence, comfort, and belonging. I do not know just exactly when my anger and resentment disappeared. I only know that there came a time when I could see that there was nothing in the message that was not about healing. I heard about compassion, love, kindness, trust, courage, truth, and loyalty and an abiding faith that there is a God, a Creator. There was nothing to be angry about in any of that; in fact, there was nothing different from what Native spirituality talks about. After I came home to my people I sought out teachers and healers and ceremonies. I had committed myself to learning the spiritual principles that allowed our peoples to sustain, define, and perpetuate themselves through incredible changes. I had adopted many of those teachings into my daily life, and every ceremony I attended taught me more and more about the essence of our spiritual lives. What I heard from that minister those Sunday mornings was not any different from the root message of humanity in our teachings. With my eyes closed there was no white, no Indian, no difference at all; the absence of anger happened quietly without fanfare.

22   It has been a few years now since I sat in that church. I have not receded back into the dark seas of resentment, rage, or old hurt. Instead, I have found a peace with churches and, in turn, with residential schools, with Canada. See, that church changed my personal politics. Sure, there are genuine reasons to be angry. The hurt caused by

the residential school experience, both of the Survivors and of those like me who were victimized a generation or more later, are huge, real, and overwhelming. But healing happens if you want it bad enough, and that is the trick of it, really. Every spiritually enhancing experience asks a sacrifice of us and, in this, the price of admission is a keen desire to be rid of the block of anger.

23   When the Truth and Reconciliation Commission makes its tour of the country and hears the stories of people who endured the pain of residential schools, I hope it hears more stories like mine—of people who fought against the resentment, hatred, and anger and found a sense of peace. Both the Commission and Canada need to hear stories of healing instead of a relentless retelling and re-experiencing of pain. They need to hear that, despite everything, every horror, it is possible to move forward and to learn how to leave hurt behind. Our neighbours in this country need to hear stories about our capacity for forgiveness, for self-examination, for compassion, and for our yearning for peace because they speak to our resiliency as a people. That is how reconciliation happens.

24   It is a big word, *reconciliation*. Quite simply, it means to create harmony. You create harmony with truth and you build truth out of humility. That is spiritual. That is truth. That is Indian. Within us, as nations of Aboriginal people and as individual members of those nations, we have an incredible capacity for survival, endurance, and forgiveness. In the reconciliation with ourselves first, we find the ability to create harmony with others, and that is where it has to start—in the fertile soil of our own hearts, minds, and spirits.

25   That, too, is Indian.

Source: Wagamese, Richard. "Returning to Harmony." *Response, Responsibility and Renewal: Canada's Truth and Reconciliation Journey.* Eds. Younging et al. Ottawa: Aboriginal Healing Foundation Research Series, 2009. 139–48. Web.

QUESTIONS FOR DISCUSSION

1. What is Richard Wagamese's argument?
2. How does the presentation of the ideal Ojibwa lifestyle create a background context for Wagamese's argument? How does this contextualization change how we perceive Wagamese's abuse?
3. Wagamese proposes several solutions for healing. What are they?
4. How does Wagamese's use of language, the flow of sentences and his word choices, support the emotion that Wagamese is trying to express?

FROM READING TO WRITING

1. Define community, as Wagamese sees it. Now compare it with Rosemarie Garland-Thomson's definition. How are they the same and/or different? What would your definition be?
2. Stories helped Wagamese begin his healing process. How does this attest to the value of storytelling? What stories do your family tell? Think of two or three and write one of them down, and reflect on the way your family also survives, endures, loves, and finds harmony in difficult situations?

The Silence before Drowning in Alphabet Soup

BY JOE SHERIDAN

INTRODUCTION

Joe Sheridan is a professor in the Faculties of Environmental Studies and Education at York University. His current research focuses on indigenous knowledge and its relevance to environmental thought and education.

"The Silence before Drowning in Alphabet Soup" examines differences in cosmologies between literate and oral cultures. Sheridan argues that education prioritizes literacy and refuses orality's focus on the self, silence, and direct unmediated experience. These latter experiences are necessary for learning.

Although this essay includes personal experience, as told by Drew Hayden Taylor and Richard Wagamese, its main thrust is academic, theorizing personal experience and making an argument about the cultural and educational ramifications of these diverse and polarized experiences. See also the related award-winning student essay written by Tyrell DaSilva in chapter 10. This essay is an excellent example of critical thinking: Tyrell has found and developed a knowledge gap that challenges Sheridan's privileging of orality.

1   The comparison in this discussion is between cosmologies and contexts, not between groups of people. The argument is not about abstracted cosmologies and idealized cultural contexts, though, because the cosmologies affect real people, and that is really what this article is about. It is not an absolutely cultural-determinist argument. To speak or write of a culture based on orality and another based on literacy does not define indigenous cultures as simply "oral" and settler culture as uniformly "literate," with consequent attribution of cognitive properties or patterns to members of either culture.

2   The attachment of "oral" and "literate" to a distinction between cultures is a shorthand reference to two related things, history and legitimacy. For hundreds of years, knowledge and ways of knowing in most of settler culture (and longer, for some sectors of it) have included alphabetized, literate media. For thousands of years there has been an oral tradition in indigenous cultures. That is history. There is also a history of attitude here. Literacy and orality are valued and legitimized differently, and the difference in how we have valued those is part of our joint history. Schools teach literacy. There is no question that literacy is a good thing. The issue is the consequence of assuming that literate definition has priority.

3   This article is written from the perspective of a fourth-generation Irish-Canadian, deeply influenced by Judaism. I grew up next to the Ojibway reserve of Parry Island, Ontario. Into my teens I was guided in knowing the bush by an elder Ojibway woman and a grandfather who was a trapper. My father ran the supply store servicing the area's hunters and fishermen, and my mother taught me to read and told the Irish stories that had survived our immigration. This article is written from that perspective and from the

perspectives provided by postgraduate training in the academic traditions of folklore and mythology, education (reading and language), and communication (media studies).

4   Writing about oral cultures first requires accepting the irony of substituting the map for the territory. Employing the alphabet to describe cultures that do not use the alphabet is the requirement of this article. Writing about the cognitive complexities of oral cultures glosses over and ignores what the alphabet on the page cannot communicate. Writing is about seeing and believing in symbols that are substitutes for sensual reality. The page, decorated with permutations of the alphabet, cannot represent smell, taste, touch, space, the teachings of the six directions, and earth. Most importantly, the alphabet is incapable of representing silence.

5   A book, in other words, always has something to communicate. Even blank books beg for the inscription of words or pictorial representations. To read is in essence the entry point into an exclusively symbolic reality at the cost of the reality it represents. To get a divinity degree, a person reads theology. Having a divinity degree is more about mastering the language that describes divinity and less about knowing the divine. One of the names for God in the Judeo-Christian tradition is The Word. That Word was spoken for a long time before it was written down. In the history of that tradition, God speaks and can be heard, but is invisible except as symbolized in text. In somewhat the same way, orality is not easily given to literate description. Orality is made physically visible only through literate description and in so doing, removing "the ear from the page" (to borrow a phrase from Illich & Saunders, 1988).

6   Fundamental to literacy is the alphabet. Deciding to subject reality to representation in 26 letters reflects a decision that reality can be represented in 26 letters. Schooling, in the context of that decision, cultivates the ability to think in sentences, and to represent sentences structurally as grammar, the formal expression of which reflects this alphabetization of thought.

7   Orality, in its purest sense, is not about thinking as sentences and alphabets dictate. Schools ask for thought to resemble sentences rather than for sentences to resemble thought. In education, sentences, and therefore literacy, are techniques from which thought is assumed to derive and subscribe. In a literate culture, cognition and literacy are conceived of as functions of each other.

8   There is an historical and ontological primacy to orality as a concomitant of cognition. If orality reflects how a mind in fact behaves, it is vital to recognize the veneration in which silence is esteemed in oral cultures. Keeping in mind that the alphabet records only sounds, literate people regard silence as time unrepresentable in print or writing, and as an absence of meaningful sound. Writers, unlike storytellers, do not use silence because the structure of print will not allow silence. Nor can time be alphabetically represented without description of its actualization. However, not making sounds does not imply absence of thought. Silently thinking like a moose, or with a moose, means having an identity with the moose—it is a nonsemantic reference—and the spell of being in mooseness is broken upon thinking in alphabetic language. Unfortunately, silence in education is conceived of primarily as the absence of words, rather than as a belonging to realms of stillness and the unsayable. In the realm of the unsayable and in the silence of the human voice, oral culture still hears, smells, touches, and tastes the wind, waves,

and rain. Thought is not constrained to lexically referential. Self-reflective conceptual thought, in silence and unmediated by symbolic representation, is constrained to refer to the physical self in physical context, the context of the Earth; the constraint is that no matter how abstract the flight, or how many levels of metaphor or abstraction, the physical self in physical context is the point of return.

9   Self-reflective conceptual thought that is mediated by alphabetized thought can displace the physical self, and the reflexivity can remove focus from the physical self to a conceptualized, symbolized self. With the physical self objectified and removed from this discourse of one, "self"-reflection can lead to a kind of conceptual looping, with no anchor to the world. One thought inevitably leads to another as surely as one literate sentence compulsively leads to another. This need not be considered bad but is surely a psychic attribute of symbolic environments.

10   Take, for example, contemporary people arising from sleep and turning on the television, so flickers of technicoloured light fill the room while accompanying background noise creates an ambient and habitual atmosphere of chronic hyperstimulation in the home. This hyperstimulation becomes subsequently manifested in things like Walkmans, vision processed through psychedelic tinted sunglasses, and neon clothing. Together they create a portable and prophylactic aural and visual hyperstimulation that cancels unmediated reality by emulating the electronic environment. This preference for replicating hyperreality is, in part, coming to terms with urban reality itself as a hyperreality. Which is to say, that the experience of reality as a mediated experience is preferential to accepting the sensual experience of *experience* on its own terms. This is a roundabout way of saying that reality as a perceptual, sensual experience is preferred when it is boosted into a mediated and therefore conceptual experience. Why else would joggers listen to a Phil Collins tape, dress in neon yellow, and wear purple sunglasses, unless the experience of running was somehow enhanced by these accoutrements? Marshall McLuhan (1964) was right when he said that media creates consciousness in its own image.

11   Like literacy, there are aural and visual hyperrealized stimulations that are homogeneous and universal signals. Michael Jackson tapes are essentially the same no matter where in the world they are played. Similarly, the essence of Karl Marx's thought is understood by adherents in Cuba as thoroughly as in Albania. Point being, when thoughts derived from literature race through the mind, or when our ears are busied by musical distractions, and when this becomes the predominant experience, the immediate physical environment becomes displaced as primary. Earth no longer serves to centre us and to nurture our place within nature. Earth becomes taken for granted as the point of departure from which we blast off into orbits of distractions from the guiding forces of the Earth. We launch imbalanced and complex expeditions that prevent us from knowing the Earth and ourselves, because we would otherwise be compelled to listen to the Earth and know ourselves. Distraction breeds distraction.

12   If oral cultures are conceived to be composed of people who are primarily aware of their immediate physical environment, it is because their sensual acuity is highly developed, because of this requirement of oral culture: however many levels of symbolized representation we employ, unmediated physical experience of the environment is the point of return. Oral cultures recognize abstraction for what it is: abstraction. Oral

people must be good listeners, seers, smellers, feelers, and tasters. Their experience of reality is acute because their senses work together harmoniously and equitably. They are not lost in mediation.

13   Aboriginal, and therefore primarily oral, attention to nature or sensual reality, has created complex and elaborate understandings of the elements of earth, sky, water, and living things. By putting nature in mind and mind in nature, aboriginal culture conceived of silence and the unsayable. It did what alphabetic culture could not. Through alphabetization, the experience of silence has meant silent reading and therefore looking at words rather than the experiencing of the things words describe with the five senses. Oral culture can be conceived of as the resistance against seeing the written representation of things as complete and genuinely conceived without using all the senses. Alphabetization is the acculturation and preference of conception over perception. So alphabetization is also the displacement of local knowledge through the force of universal curricula.

14   There is a difference between oral cultures and literate cultures in the way that the Infinite is conceived of. That difference is related to the way that microcosms are systematically contextualized within infinitely larger systems. Literate cultures standardized the idea of God (representable by the printed word; metaphorically, "The Word") and with this concept celebrated their monotheism. Literate cultures could not accept the idea that the Sacred was allied with and manifested in the natural environment, for that deconceptualized God for literate cultures, and alienated the infinite from the word. Movable type even removed the concept of God as picture, and standardized Him as printed word. The biblical God is a concept that can have currency worldwide because, like the alphabet, it is portable. However, many biblical proselytizers seem to insist that knowing religion is primarily knowing religious semantics. It would be inconceivable to them that a person can be taught about the Infinite and sacredness by the bush. Oral cultures, on the other hand, can recognize the way that the biblical God deals with creation, because of their knowledge of their ecosystem. They know—from sensed experience of the environment in microcosm—many properties of infinitely greater systems and domains.

15   From the specific meanings gained through understanding the bush, the oral mind created principles for recognizing infinity, the totality of all things in totality. This is immensely distinct, as Ivan Illich and Barry Saunders (1988) note, from literate knowing deriving "Infinite meanings without specific meanings" (p. 122). The understanding of microcosm as preliminary to understanding macrocosm is a common sense transition and, while centring the knower, reminds him and her of the great wisdom of being centred. As Jo-ann Archibald (1990) notes in a recent article quoting Chief Luther Standing Bear of the Lakota Nation,

> The Lakota was a true naturalist—a lover of nature. He loved the earth and all things of the earth, the attachment growing with age. The old people came literally to love the soil and they sat or reclined on the ground with a feeling of being close to a mothering power. . . . For him, to sit or lie upon the ground is to be able to think more deeply and to feel more keenly; he can see more clearly into the mysteries of life and come closer in kinship to other lives about him. (p. 74)

16   To fathom the transition from one microcosm to macrocosm is to ponder awe and wonder; it is to be silent, tranquil, and reverential in knowing the sacred. The enormous centredness learned by the elder from lessons of the earth allows the elder to know when to talk, and further to know when to listen and when another person is ready for these lessons. Perhaps this is the reason oral cultures recognized the auspiciousness of silence, for silence was the space between stages of development that kept the stages from blurring together. Books and electronic media place all information within the scope of the reader, and require no elder to judge preparedness for the next step in spiritual development. Thinking about written religious education is all the more curious when one considers that the oldest writings of the Middle East are accountancy records (Gelb, 1952). It is no wonder God first entrusted his words to a worthy listener and wrote his own tablets.

17   When sacredness and the infinite were first graphically represented, they apparently were not initially conceived of digitally—in letters or numbers—but ideographically in pictographs. With the evolution of the alphabet, the sacred became digitally represented and was eventually formalized as text. For the Egyptian, whose hieroglyphic or ideographic concept of divinity was not digital but analogical, the holy of holies was the chamber in the depths of the Great Pyramid where complete silence prevailed. This room was the architectural equal of Zen no-mind, a place where the coursing of the blood could be heard and perhaps the coursing of the universe.

18   Silence may describe a kind of nonconceptual cognition. Many thinkers have tried to express that observation in words and it is a precept of several traditions. Allan Watts warned, "To hear anything other than itself the mind must learn to be quiet," (1958, p. 5). Perception may be similarly argued to be nonconceptual. Jamake Highwater (1981), in his influential *The Primal Mind: Vision and Reality in Indian America*, argues that perception is not limited by the senses, but rather that the entire body is an organ of perception independent of the literary domain. Similarly, bodily knowledge in Western culture is historically addressed in Morris Berman's (1989) *Coming To Our Senses: Body and Spirit in the Hidden History of the West*. The no-mind of Zen is the dismissal of alphabetic consciousness. Oral minds are not bridled by conceptual thought as thoroughly as minds that are exclusively dominated by books and the built environment because they admit to the legitimacy, both of the concept—the abstraction—and to the return to the sensual, physical experience. The conceptualized experience is not the "real" one. In other words, this is not to say that oral minds are not conceptual thinking minds, but rather that in learning the lessons of thinking as the forest thinks, the oral mind is not divisive nor abstractly self-reflexive like literate minds, which seem ever attempting to heap more commentary upon smaller aspects of symbolic reality.

19   For example, books are written on books written about books and in our own lifetimes we can witness the information explosion caused by the computer which has doubled the amount of recorded knowledge every ten years. The forest, and the oral mind which lives within it, pay attention to where and what it is now—orality is sensual life and its recognition. Oral cultures are more likely to have reflection implosion rather than information explosion.

20   Literacy, on the other hand, is ideational and is always at least once removed from the experience of reality. Illich and Saunders (1988) seem to have described the tension

between the "we" which describes the oral reflection implosion and the "I" of literate information explosion when they say

> The alphabetization of silence has brought about the new loneliness of the "I," and an analytic "we." *We* is now one line in a text brought into being by communication. Not the silence before words but the absence of messages in a chaos of noises. (p. 123)

21   I do not claim that the grandfathers who knew the land did not resort to abstract words or representations, but Edmund Carpenter (1972) described the osmosis between world and word knowledge thus, "Once they venture to tell of the outer world, geography gives way to cosmography" (p. 13). The abstractions of oral cultures are derived from knowing reality; there is not a chaos of noises in the bush, for each sound is a lesson of the earth. Literate abstractions are derived from knowing symbols about reality. The chaos of noises is the inability to find meaning in the cacophony of the technological roar in the built environment. Answering the eternal questions of who are we, where did we come from, and where are we going, is difficult in both oral and alphabetic cultures. However, finding the answers in libraries or cities can lead to mechanistic explanations. Science tells us that we are here because of a cosmic explosion and live on a rock that will be destroyed before long when the sun explodes. Capitalism and materialism advise us that in the meanwhile we should be comforted through producing and consuming goods. This explanation of our beginnings sustains hopeless and desperate behaviour because it is a poor metaphor, unable to communicate the wisdom of earth. Jo-ann Archibald (1990) offers a sustaining story drawn from Crowfoot's knowing the earth; he says, "From nowhere we came: into nowhere we go. What is life? It is the flash of the firefly in the night. It is the breath of the buffalo in the winter time. It is the little shadow that runs across he grass and loses itself in the sunset" (p. 74). Culture out of contact with the earth becomes a stranger to the comforting lessons of wisdom and mystery that inform everyone living in sensitive relationship to the earth.

22   Orality brings you face to face with your traditions while literacy encourages privatization of conception and substitutes verisimilitude of description in language as appropriate substitution for reality. Literacy implies not only that symbols can represent knowledge but that symbols *are knowledge*. This puts the onus on people to always make sounds in order to be considered wise; silence is unworthy. Yet in silence we ultimately hear the earth and ourselves, and confront the immensity of what cannot be said, what cannot be translated into sound. Sounds and words ask us to explore what we already know and rarely ask us to explore what we cannot and do not know except in terms of what can be said.

23   Alphabetized minds insist on speaking themselves. They work on the idea that human sounds are better and wiser than either the language of the spirit or silence. Alphabetized minds are not inclined to hold their tongues and pens and keyboards, and to say nothing. On the page, saying nothing means having nothing to say. Since alphabetic thought enshrines only the sounds we can make, alphabetized minds compulsively make these sounds. Alphabetized culture has virtually ceased, except in jest, in

the story, and in the poem, to venerate the sounds of rolling thunder or the west winds of autumn; and when we do we rarely accord them a presence of wisdom in our writing and talk, for they are not human sounds. What if the world, as it well could, ceased to have anything but the sounds of alphabetized minds and machines communicating as books or tapes or televisions or computers?

24   It is alphabetized minds that do not see that every thing on the land is connected to every other thing, because sentences and books and even sight itself select and present things in isolation for examination. In oral cultures, hearing and smell, senses that are inclusive rather than selective, incorporate everything in their presence. Living in sensitive relationship with the land means oral cultures knew the land through all of their senses. Furthermore, there is little opportunity to mistake the map for the territory because oral cultures are surrounded by the things their words can and cannot symbolize. Overdependence on conceptually segmented sight as the sense most worthy for understanding the world isolates things and processes and becomes habitual in its repetitive and reinforced knowing of the world as a purely visual phenomenon. Alphabetized minds are mediated minds and prefer to write about the sunset, or photograph it, or interpret it in guitar riffs. These are preferred to experiencing the sunset on its own terms.

25   Alphabetized and mediated minds want to wring images and words from a sunset that is grandly illiterate. Ultimately these symbols come to assume greater importance than the sunset itself. One need only watch people in cars going to view sunsets to see how the image of the sunset occupies them more than the experience of the sunset. Once the sunset is on film it is transported into living rooms to be replayed as evidence that people were there. Mediated minds attempt to become closer to nature by spending more time in front of televisions witnessing on the screen what they originally experienced through the lens they used to experience the sunset in the first place.

26   Education conceived in terms of the words and images we can wring from these experiences asks us to busy ourselves always, and to displace silent and still experiencing of the earth. Alphabetized culture sees and hears itself experiencing the images and language about nature rather than experiencing nature itself; a sort of "this is me doing this" attitude is encouraged. Our meditations become the creation of images and records testifying that we were there and that we saw something. It is memory externalized. The great difficulty, of course, is that there is no elder teaching the story of the sunset. Videotapes are memory without mind and are at least for literate minds far sexier presentations than storytelling. Recording these experiences on film removes us from nature by making our presence there only a reference to the recorded event.

27   It is not going too far to say that mediated minds conceive of their behaviour as images in reference not to the place where they are, but in reference to how they will be recorded. One need only watch the behaviour of tourists playing to the camera or rock climbers in neon Spandex conceiving of themselves as images, behaving as though they were movies or photographs of themselves doing something so spectacular that they deserve to be filmed. Photographic culture conceives of itself as a narcissistic spectacle, one step beyond the writer as conceptual observer and two steps beyond the oral mind, that does not remark upon itself to itself, and lose itself in the remark.

28   The representation of reality has been a crucial issue in Western education since Socrates decried to Plato the effects of the technology of literacy on true learning and memory, "Your instruction will give them only a semblance of truth, not truth itself. You will train ignorant know-it-alls, nosey nothings, boring wiseacres" (Illich & Saunders, 1988, p. 26). Illich and Saunders add to this debate the origin of the idea of representing reality through the technology of writing, "Appropriate description of reality began as a jurisprudential method before it became the foundation of the natural sciences" (p. 36). The alphabetization of thought became the institution of education, yet the effects of the alphabet on nonalphabetic oral cultures have until recently, been rarely discussed. Literacy has been made visible because the age of electronic imagery brought it to light. Traditional orality and its connection to the earth are the best defence against the effects of both the alphabet and electronic imagery, and may arise as a respected art form. Literacy, like orality subscribes to the proverbial wisdom of Marshall McLuhan (1964) who said that he didn't know who discovered water, but that we could be sure that it wasn't a fish. We discovered what literacy was only when it arrived and when it is on its way out. If nothing else, literacy has warped the oral conception that truth resides within, as interior, by favouring truth and belief on the page as outside, or exterior to the spirit and mind. This reconceives the wisdom of silence as the quality of the know-nothing and the ignoramus. Illich and Saunders (1988) point out the effect of the transition to literacy.

> My *oath is my truth* into the twelfth century.... Only in the thirteenth century does Continental canon law *make the judge into a reader of the accused man's conscience*, an inquisitor into truth ... Truth ceases to be displayed in surface action and is now perceived as the *outward expression of inner meaning accessible only to the self.* (italics added, p. 85)

29   Literacy is biased toward absolutism. Under its influence reality is conceived as singular, because it is represented as singular. In oral cultures reality is composed of many realities in balance and unison, and is known by one's ability to become these realities. Oral reality does not favour print because its economy of expression appears to circumvent lengthy analysis and logical argument. The tremendous economy of expression of oral stories encourages silent reflection on its truth and therefore blesses the listener with a resonant silence as familiar and thankful as the quiet of the earth. The map is incidental to an unalphabetized culture able to silence the mind to hear the territory. As Neihardt (1979) quotes Black Elk, remembering a childhood experience of healing, Black Elk reflects on the vision which at nine years of age established the ontology that would transcend the realm of written symbols:

> Also, as I lay there thinking of my vision, I could see it all again and feel the meaning with a part of me like a strange power glowing in my body; but when the part of me that talks would try to make words for the meaning, it would be like fog and get away from me.

I am sure now that I was then too young to understand it all, and that I only felt it. It was the pictures I remembered and the words that went with them; for nothing I have ever seen with my eyes was so clear and bright as what my vision showed me; and no words that I have ever heard with my ears were like the words I heard. I did not have to remember these things; they have remembered themselves all these years. It was as I grew older that the meanings came clearer and clearer out of the pictures and the words; and even now I know that more was shown to me than I can tell. (p. 49)

30   Alphabetization has threatened the silence required to know the world on its own terms and so to explore its delicate balance. The technology of the alphabet does for the mind of the observer what a swarm of bees does for a picnic, the letters will not leave the mind alone. Tremendous authors have written powerful words, yet for all of their power these words can and often do lead away from the centring influence of the earth.

31   As teachers I believe we must be aware of the effects of both alphabet and media, and we must encourage reflection, stillness, quiet, and sensory awareness to compensate for the compulsive mind created by the map. In Eastern culture, Zen Bhuddism and Yoga are potent techniques for quieting the mind and spirit in highly populated lands no longer easily able to experience nature. Native oral culture on the land was a balance of words and the things they represent—aware that balanced senses were necessary for the representation and, more importantly, the experiencing of reality. Native oral culture prevented the cultural mistake that happens when learning occurs under the domination of the eye's appreciation of the visual symbol alone—believing the symbol and the thing it symbolizes are one. It is imperative to again know the territory as did our grandfathers, before the traditional balance and power in perception was subjected to the solipsism of conception. Before drowning in alphabet soup.

REFERENCES

Archibald, Jo-ann. (1990). Coyote's Story About Orality and Literacy. *Canadian Journal of Native Education*, 17(2), 66–81.

Berman, Morris. (1989). *Coming to our senses: Body and spirit in the hidden history of the West*. New York: Simon and Schuster.

Carpenter, Edmund. (1972). *Oh what a blow that phantom gave me*. New York: Holt, Rinehart and Winston.

Gelb, I. (1952). *The study of writing*. Chicago: University of Chicago Press.

Highwater, Jamake. (1981) *The primal mind: Vision and reality in Indian America*. New York: Harper & Row.

Illich, Ivan, & Saunders, Barry. (1988). *A, B, C: The alphabetization of the popular mind*. San Francisco, CA: North Point Press.

McLuhan, Marshall. (1964). *Understanding media*. New York: McGraw-Hill.

Neihardt, John G. (1979). *Black Elk speaks: Being the life story of a holy man of the Oglala Sioux*. Lincoln: University of Nebraska Press.

Watts, Alan. (1958). *Nature, man, and woman*. New York: Vintage Books.

Source: Sheridan, Joe. "The Silence before Drowning in Alphabet Soup." *Canadian Journal of Native Education* 18.1, (1991): 23–31. Print.

QUESTIONS FOR DISCUSSION

1. While Alexie, Hayden Taylor, and Wagamese use story to convey the problems related to First Nations culture, Sheridan's essay uses an academic critique. Are both perspectives necessary? How and why?

2. How does the first paragraph create an ethos of credibility for Sheridan?

3. Reread the places in the text where Sheridan inserts his personal experience, and make an argument for how it makes his thesis more or less effective.

4. Is the dichotomy of oral and literate cultures as fixed as Sheridan implies? Is he guilty of stereotyping and bias?

FROM READING TO WRITING

Sheridan writes that "The page, decorated with permutations of the alphabet, cannot represent . . . silence." Find three examples of writing that convey a sense of silence, then write three sentences of your own, using language and punctuation to create silence. Read them out loud and silently. How are these readings different?

What Is an Elementary Particle?

BY WERNER HEISENBERG

INTRODUCTION

Werner Heisenberg was awarded the Nobel Prize for Physics in 1932 for his work on quantum mechanics, but he is also well known for his theories on quantum uncertainty and the "uncertainty principle." This states that when an observer observes something, the more precise the measurement of one particle, the less precise the measurement of another associated particle. This principle revolutionized the way we think about nature and our limited ability to understand it.

Similarly, when attempting to define and understand the physics of elementary particles, Heisenberg asserts that our understanding is uncertain. In Heisenberg's words, "the atoms or elementary particles . . . form a world of potentialities or possibilities rather than one of things or facts." This fundamental uncertainty exposes how our language and thinking, which stem from traditional philosophy, are inadequate to the task of quantum physics. Consequently, Heisenberg insists that only the scientific "dynamics of matter" count.

1   The question "What is an elementary particle?" must naturally be answered above all by experiment. So I shall first summarize briefly the most important experimental findings of elementary particle physics during the last fifty years, and will try to show that, if the experiments are viewed without prejudice, the question alluded to has already been largely answered by these findings, and that there is no longer much for the theoretician to add. In the second part I will then go on to enlarge upon the philosophical problems connected with the concept of an elementary particle. For I believe that certain mistaken developments in the theory of elementary particles—and I fear that there are such—are due to the fact that their authors would claim that they do not wish to trouble about philosophy, but that in reality they unconsciously start out from a bad philosophy, and have therefore fallen through prejudice into unreasonable statements of the problem. One may say, with some exaggeration, perhaps, that good physics has been inadvertently spoiled by bad philosophy. Finally I shall say something of these problematic developments themselves, compare them with erroneous developments in the history of quantum mechanics in which I was myself involved, and consider how such wrong turnings can be avoided. The close of the lecture should therefore be more optimistic again.

2   First, then, to the experimental facts. Not quite fifty years ago, Dirac, in his theory of electrons, predicted that in addition to electrons there would also have to exist the appropriate anti-particles, the positrons; and a few years later the existence of positrons, their origin in pair-creation, and hence the existence of so-called anti-matter, was experimentally demonstrated by Anderson and Blackett. It was a discovery of the first order. For till then it had mostly been supposed that there are two kinds of fundamental particle, electrons and protons, which are distinguished above all others by the fact that they can never be changed, so that their number is always constant as well, and which for that very reason had been called elementary particles. All matter was supposed in the end to be made up of electrons and protons. The experimental proof of pair-creation and positrons showed that this idea was false. Electrons can be created and again disappear; so their number is by no means constant; they are not elementary in the sense previously assumed.

3   The next important step was Fermi's discovery of artificial radioactivity. It was learnt from many experiments that one atomic nucleus can turn into another by emission of particles, if the conservation laws for energy, angular momentum, electric charge, etc., allow this. The transformation of energy into matter, which had already been recognized as possible in Einstein's relativity theory, is thus a very commonly observable phenomenon. There is no talk here of any conservation of the number of particles. But there are indeed physical properties, characterizable by quantum numbers—I am thinking, say, of angular momentum or electric charge—in which the quantum numbers can then take on positive and negative values, and for these a conservation law holds.

4   In the thirties there was yet another important experimental discovery. It was found that in cosmic radiation there are very energetic particles, which, on collision with other particles, say a proton, in the emulsion of a photographic plate, can let loose a shower of many secondary particles. Many physicists believed for a time that such showers can originate only through a sort of cascade formation in atomic nuclei; but it later turned out that, even in a collision between a single pair of energetic particles, the theoretically conjectured multiple production of secondary particles does in fact occur. At the end of the forties, Powell discovered the pions, which play the major part in these showers. This showed that in collisions of high-energy particles, the transformation of energy into matter is quite generally the decisive process, so that it obviously no longer makes sense to speak of a splitting of the original particle. The concept of "division" had come, by experiment, to lose its meaning.

5   In the experiments of the fifties and sixties, this new situation was repeatedly confirmed: many new particles were discovered, with long and short lives, and no unambiguous answer could be given any longer to the question about what these particles consisted of, since this question no longer has a rational meaning. A proton, for example, could be made up of neutron and pion, or λ-hyperon and kaon, or out of two nucleons and an anti-nucleon; it would be simplest of all to say that a proton just consists of continuous matter, and all these statements are equally correct or equally false. The difference between elementary and composite particles has thus basically disappeared. And that is no doubt the most important experimental finding of the last fifty years.

6   As a consequence of this development, the experiments have strongly suggested an analogy: the elementary particles are something like the stationary states of an atom or a molecule. There is a whole spectrum of particles, just as there is a spectrum, say, of the iron atom or a molecule, where we may think, in the latter case, of the various stationary states of a molecule, or even of the many different possible molecules of chemistry. Among particles, we shall speak of a spectrum of "matter." In fact, during the sixties and seventies, the experiments with the big accelerators have shown that this analogy fits all the findings so far. Like the stationary states of the atom, the particles, too, can be characterized by quantum numbers, that is, by symmetry- or transformation-properties, and the exact or approximately valid conservation principles associated with them decide as to the possibility of the transformations. Just as the transformation properties of an excited hydrogen atom under spatial rotation decide whether it can fall to a lower state by emission of a photon, so too, the question whether a ϕ-boson, say, can degenerate into a ρ-boson by emission of a pion, is decided by such symmetry properties. Just as the various stationary states of an atom have very different lifetimes, so too with particles. The ground state of an atom is stable, and has an infinitely long lifetime, and the same is true of such particles as the electron, proton, deuteron, etc. But these stable particles are in no way more elementary than the unstable ones. The ground state of the hydrogen atom follows from the same Schrödinger equation as the excited states do. Nor are the electron and photon in any way more elementary than, say, a λ-hyperon.

7   The experimental particle-physics of recent years has thus fulfilled much the same tasks, in the course of its development, as the spectroscopy of the early twenties. Just as, at that time, a large compilation was brought out, the so-called Paschen-Götze tables, in which the stationary states of all atom shells were collected, so now we have the annually supplemented *Reviews of Particle Properties,* in which the stationary states of matter and its transformation-properties are recorded. The work of compiling such a comprehensive tabulation therefore corresponds, say, to the star-cataloging of the astronomers, and every observer hopes, of course, that he will one day find a particularly interesting object in his chosen area.

8   Yet there are also characteristic differences between particle physics and the physics of atomic shells. In the latter we are dealing with such low energies, that the characteristic features of relativity theory can be neglected, and nonrelativistic quantum mechanics used, therefore, for description. This means that the governing symmetry-groups may differ in atomic-shell physics on the one hand, and in particles on the other. The Galileo group of shell physics is replaced, at the particle level, by the Lorentz-group; and in particle physics we also have new groups, such as the isospin group, which is isomorphic to the SU_2 group, and then the SU_3 group, the group of scaling transformations and still others. It is an important experimental task to define the governing groups of particle physics, and in the past twenty years it has already been largely accomplished.

9   Here we can learn from shell physics, that in those very groups which manifestly designate only approximately valid symmetrics, two basically different types may be distinguished. Consider, say, among optical spectra, the O_3 group of spatial rotations, and the $O_3 \times O_3$ group, which governs the multiplet-structure in spectra. The basic equations of quantum mechanics are strictly invariant with respect to the group of spatial rotations. The states of atoms having greater angular momenta are therefore severely degenerate, that is, there are numerous states of exactly equal energy. Only if the atom is placed in an external electromagnetic field do the states split up, and the familiar fine structure emerge, as in the Zeeman or Stark effect. This degeneracy can also be abolished if the ground state of the system is not rotation-invariant, as in the ground states of a crystal or ferro-magnet. In this case there is also a splitting of levels; the two spin-directions of an electron in a ferro-magnet are no longer associated with exactly the same energy. Furthermore, by a well-known theorem of Goldstone, there are bosons whose energy tends to zero with increasing wavelength, and, in the case of the ferro-magnet, Bloch's spin-waves or magnons.

10   It is different with the group $O_3 \times O_3$, from which result the familiar multiplets of optical spectra. Here we are dealing with an approximate symmetry, which comes about in that the spin-path interactions in a specific region are small, so that the spins and paths of electrons can be skewed counter to each other, without producing much change in the interaction. The $O_3 \times O_3$ symmetry is therefore also a useful approximation only in particular parts of the spectrum. Empirically, the two kinds of broken symmetry are most clearly distinguishable in that, for the fundamental symmetry broken by the ground state, there must, by the Goldstone theorem, be associated bosons of zero rest mass, or long-range forces. If we find them, there is reason to believe that the degeneracy of the ground state plays an important role here.

11   Now if these findings are transferred from atomic-shell physics to particle physics, it is very natural, on the basis of the experiments, to interpret the Lorentz group and the SU_2 group, the isospin group, that is, fundamental symmetries of the underlying law of nature. Electromagnetism and gravitation then appear as the long-range forces associated with symmetry broken by the ground state. The higher groups, SU_3, SU_4, SU_6, or $SU_2 \times SU_2$, $SU_3 \times SU_3$ and so on, would then have to rank as dynamic symmetries, just like $O_3 \times O_3$ in atomic-shell physics. Of the dilatation or scaling group, it may be doubted whether it should be counted among the fundamental symmetries; it is perturbed by the existence of particles with finite mass, and by the gravitation due to masses in the universe. Owing to its close relation to the Lorentz group, it certainly ought to be numbered among the fundamental symmetries. The foregoing assignment of perturbed symmetries to the two basic types is made plausible, as I was already saying, by the experimental findings, but it is not yet possible, perhaps, to speak of a final settlement. The most important thing is that, with regard to the symmetry groups that present themselves in the phenomenology of spectra, the question must be asked, and if possible answered, as to which of the two basic types they belong to.

12   Let me point to yet another feature of shell-physics: among optical spectra there are non-combining, or more accurately, weakly combining term-systems, such as the spectra of para- and ortho-helium. In particle physics we can perhaps compare the division of the fermion spectrum into baryons and leptons with features of this type.

13   The analogy between the stationary states of an atom or molecule, and the particles of elementary particle physics, is therefore almost complete, and with this, so

it seems to me, I have also given a complete qualitative answer to the initial question "What is an elementary particle?" But only a qualitative answer! The theorist is now confronted with the further question, whether he can also underpin this qualitative understanding by means of quantitative calculations. For this it is first necessary to answer a prior question: What is it, anyway, to understand a spectrum in quantitative terms?

14 For this we have a string of examples, from both classical physics and quantum mechanics alike. Let us consider, say, the spectrum of the elastic vibrations of a steel plate. If we are not to be content with a qualitative understanding, we shall start from the fact that the plate can be characterized by specific elastic properties, which can be mathematically represented. Having achieved this, we still have to append the boundary conditions, adding, for example, that the plate is circular or rectangular, that it is, or is not, under tension, and from this, at least in principle, the spectrum of elastic or acoustic vibrations can be calculated. Owing to the level of complexity, we shall certainly not, indeed, be able to work out all the vibrations exactly, but may yet, perhaps, calculate the lowest, with the smallest number of nodal lines.

15 Thus two elements are necessary for quantitative understanding: the exactly formulated knowledge, in mathematical terms, of the dynamic behavior of the plate, and the boundary conditions, which can be regarded as "contingent," as determined, that is, by local circumstances; the plate, of course, could also be dissected in other ways. It is like this, too, with the electrodynamic oscillations of a cavity resonator. The Maxwellian equations determine the dynamic behavior, and the shape of the cavity defines the boundary conditions. And so it is, also, with the optical spectrum of the iron atom. The Schrödinger equation for a system with a nucleus and 26 electrons determines the dynamic behavior, and to this we add the boundary conditions, which state in this instance that the wave-function shall vanish at infinity. If the atom were to be enclosed in a small box, a somewhat altered spectrum would result.

16 If we transfer these ideas to particle physics, it becomes a question, therefore, of first ascertaining by experiment the dynamical properties of the matter system, and formulating this in mathematical terms. As the contingent element, we now add the boundary conditions, which here will consist essentially of statements about so-called empty space, i.e., about the cosmos and its symmetry properties. The first step must in any case be the attempt to formulate mathematically a law of nature that lays down the dynamics of matter. For the second step, we have to make statements about the boundary conditions. For without these, the spectrum just cannot be defined. I would guess, for example, that in one of the "black holes" of contemporary astrophysics, the spectrum of elementary particles would look totally different from our own. Unfortunately, we cannot experiment on the point.

17 But now a word more about the decisive first step, namely the formulation of the dynamical law. There are pessimists among particle physicists, who believe that there simply is no such law of nature, defining the dynamic properties of matter. With such a view I confess that I can make no headway at all. For somehow the dynamics of matter has to exist, or else there would be no spectrum; and in that case we should also be able to describe it mathematically. The pessimistic view would mean that the whole of particle physics is directed, eventually, at producing a gigantic tabulation containing the maximum number of stationary states of matter, transition-probabilities and the like, a "Super-Review of Particle Properties," and thus a compilation in which there is nothing more to understand, and which therefore, no doubt, would no longer be read by anyone. But there is also not the least occasion for such pessimism, and I set particular store by this assertion. For we actually observe a particle spectrum with sharp lines, and so, indirectly, a sharply defined dynamics of matter as well. The experimental findings, briefly sketched above, also contain already very definite indications as to the fundamental invariance properties of this fundamental law of nature, and we know from the dispersion relations a great deal about the level of causality that is formulated in this law. We thus have the essential determinants of the law already to hand, and after so many other spectra in physics have finally been understood to some extent in quantitative terms, it will also be possible here, despite the high degree of complexity involved. At this point—and just because of its complexity—I would sooner not discuss the special proposal that was long ago made by myself, together with Pauli, for a mathematical formulation of the underlying law, and which, even now, I still believe to have the best chances of being the right one. But I would like to point out with all emphasis, that the formulation of such a law is the indispensable precondition for understanding the spectrum of elementary particles. All else is not understanding; it is hardly more than a start to the tabulation project, and as theorists, at least, we should not be content with that.

18   I now come to the philosophy by which the physics of elementary particles is consciously or unconsciously guided. For two and a half millennia, the question has been debated by philosophers and scientists, as to what happens when we try to keep on dividing up matter. What are the smallest constituent parts of matter? Different philosophers have given very different answers to this question, which have all exerted their influence on the history of natural science. The best known is that of the philosopher Democritus. In attempting to go on dividing, we finally light upon indivisible, immutable objects, the atoms, and all materials are composed of atoms. The position and motions of the atoms determine the quality of the materials. In Aristotle and his medieval successors, the concept of minimal particles is not so sharply defined. There are, indeed, minimal particles here for every kind of material—on further division the parts would no longer display the characteristic properties of the material—but these minimal parts are continuously changeable, like the materials themselves. Mathematically speaking, therefore, materials are infinitely divisible; matter is pictured as continuous.

19   The clearest opposing position to that of Democritus was adopted by Plato. In attempting continual division we ultimately arrive, in Plato's opinion, at mathematical forms: the regular solids of stereometry, which are definable by their symmetry properties, and the triangles from which they can be constructed. These forms are not themselves matter, but they shape it. The element earth, for example, is based on the shape of the cube, the element fire on the shape of the tetrahedron. It is common to all these philosophers, that they wish in some way to dispose of the antinomy of the infinitely small, which, as everyone knows, was discussed in detail by Kant.

20   Of course, there are and have been more naive attempts at rationalizing this anti-nomy. Biologists, for example, have developed the notion that the seed of an apple contains an invisibly small apple tree, which in turn bears blossom and fruit; that again in the fruit there are seeds, in which once more a still tinier apple tree is hidden, and so *ad infinitum*. In the same way, in the early days of the Bohr-Rutherford theory of the atom as a miniature planetary system, we developed with some glee the thesis that upon the planets of this system, the electrons, there are again very tiny creatures living, who build houses, cultivate fields and do atomic physics, arriving once more at the thesis of their atoms as miniature planetary systems, and so *ad infinitum*. In the background here, as I said already, there is always lurking the Kantian antinomy, that it is very hard, on the one hand, to think of matter as infinitely divisible, but also difficult, on the other, to imagine this division one day coming to an enforced stop. The antinomy, as we know, is ultimately brought about by our erroneous belief that we can also apply our intuition to situations on the very small scale. The strongest influence on the physics and chemistry of recent centuries has undoubtedly been exerted by the atomism of Democritus. It permits an intuitive description of small-scale chemical processes. The atoms can be compared to the mass-points of Newtonian mechanics, and such a comparison leads to a satisfying statistical theory of heat. The chemist's atoms were not, indeed, mass-points at all, but miniature planetary systems, and the atomic nucleus was composed of protons and neutrons, but electrons, protons, and eventually even neutrons could, it was thought, quite well be regarded as the true atoms, that is, as the ultimate indivisible building-blocks of matter. During the last hundred years, the Democritean idea of the atom had thus become an integrating component of the physicist's view of the material world; it was readily intelligible and to some extent intuitive, and determined physical thinking even among physicists who wanted to have nothing to do with philosophy. At this point I should now like to justify my suggestion, that today in the physics of elementary particles, good physics is unconsciously being spoiled by bad philosophy.

21   We cannot, of course, avoid employing a language that stems from this traditional philosophy. We ask, "What does the proton consist of? Can one divide the electron, or is it indivisible?" "Is the light-quantum simple, or is it composite?" But these questions are wrongly put, since the words *divide* or *consist of* have largely lost their meaning. It would thus be our task to adapt our language and thought, and hence also our scientific philosophy, to this new situation engendered by the experiments. But that, unfortunately, is very difficult. The result is that false questions and false ideas repeatedly creep into particle physics, and lead to the erroneous developments of which I am about to speak. But first a further remark about the demand for intuitability.

22   There have been philosophers who have held intuit ability to be the precondition for all true understanding. Thus here in Munich, for example, the philosopher Hugo Dingler has championed the view that intuitive Euclidean geometry is the only true geometry, since it is presupposed in the construction of our measuring instruments; and on the latter point, Dingler is quite correct. Hence, he says, the experimental findings which underlie the general theory of relativity should be described in other terms than

those of a more general Riemannian geometry, which deviates from the Euclidean; for otherwise we become involved in contradictions. But this demand is obviously extreme. To justify what we do by way of experiment, it is enough that, in the dimensions of our apparatus, the geometry of Euclid holds to a sufficiently good approximation. We must therefore come to agree that the experimental findings on the very small and very large scale no longer provide us with an intuitive picture, and must learn to manage there without intuitions. We then recognize, for example, that the aforementioned antinomy of the infinitely small is resolved, among elementary particles, in a very subtle fashion, in a way that neither Kant nor the ancient philosophers could have thought of, namely inasmuch as the term *divide* loses its meaning.

23   If we wish to compare the findings of contemporary particle physics with any earlier philosophy, it can only be with the philosophy of Plato; for the particles of present-day physics are representations of symmetry groups, so the quantum theory tells us, and to that extent they resemble the symmetrical bodies of the Platonic view.

24   But our purpose here was to occupy ourselves not with philosophy, but with physics, and so I will now go on to discuss that development in theoretical particle physics, which in my view sets out from a false statement of the problem. There is first of all the thesis, that the observed particles, such as protons, pions, hyperons and many others, are made up of smaller unobserved particles, the quarks, or else from partons, gluons, charmed particles, or whatever these imagined particles may all be called. Here the question has obviously been asked, "What do protons consist of?" But it has been forgotten in the process, that the term *consist of* only has a halfway clear meaning if we are able to dissect the particle in question, with a small expenditure of energy, into constituents whose rest mass is very much greater than this energy-cost; otherwise, the term *consist of* has lost its meaning. And that is the situation with protons. In order to demonstrate this loss of meaning in a seemingly well-defined term, I cannot forebear from telling a story that Niels Bohr was wont to retell on such occasions. A small boy comes into a shop with twopence in his hand, and tells the shopkeeper that he would like two-pence-worth of mixed sweets. The shopkeeper hands him two sweets, and says: "You can mix them for yourself." In the case of the proton, the concept "consist of" has just as much meaning as the concept of "mixing" in the tale of the small boy.

25   Now many will object to this, that the quark hypothesis has been drawn from empirical findings, namely the establishing of the empirical relevance of the SU_3 group; and furthermore, it holds up in the interpretation of many experiments on the application of the SU_3 group as well. This is not to be contested. But I should like to put forward a counter-example from the history of quantum mechanics, in which I myself was involved; a counter-example which clearly displays the weakness of arguments of this type. Prior to the appearance of Bohr's theory, many physicists maintained that an atom must be made up of harmonic oscillators. For the optical spectrum certainly contains sharp lines, and they can only be emitted by harmonic oscillators. The charges on these oscillators would have to correspond to other electromagnetic values than those on the electron, and there would also have to be very many oscillators, since there are very many lines in the spectrum.

26   Regardless of these difficulties, Woldemar Voigt constructed at Gottingen in 1912 a theory of the anomalous Zeeman effect of the D-lines in the optical spectrum of sodium, and did so in the following way: he assumed a pair of coupled oscillators which, in the absence of an external magnetic field, yielded the frequencies of the two D-lines. He was able to arrange the coupling of the oscillators with one another, and with the external field, in such a way that, in weak magnetic fields, the anomalous Zeeman effect came out correct, and that in very strong magnetic fields the Paschen-Back effect was also correctly represented. For the intermediate region of moderate fields, he obtained, for the frequencies and intensities, long and complex quadratic roots; formulae, that is, which were largely incomprehensible, but which obviously reproduced the experiments with great exactness. Fifteen years later, Jordan and I took the trouble to work out the same problem by the methods of the quantum-mechanical theory of perturbation. To our great astonishment, we came out with exactly the old Voigtian formulae, so far as both frequencies and intensities were concerned and this, too, in the complex area of the moderate fields. The reason for this we were later well able to perceive; it was a purely formal and mathematical one. The quantum-mechanical theory of perturbation leads to a system of coupled linear equations, and the frequencies are determined by the eigen values of the equation-system. A system of coupled harmonic oscillators leads equally, in the classical theory, to such a coupled linear equation-system. Since, in Voigt's theory, the most important parameter had been cancelled out, it was therefore no wonder that the right answer emerged. But the Voigtian theory contributed nothing to the understanding of atomic structure.

27   Why was this attempt of Voigt's so successful on the one hand, and so futile on the other? Because he was only concerned to examine the D-lines, without taking the whole line-spectrum into account. Voigt had made phenomenological use of a certain aspect of the oscillator hypothesis, and had either ignored all the other discrepancies of this model, or deliberately left them in obscurity. Thus he had simply not taken his hypothesis in real earnest. In the same way, I fear that the quark hypothesis is just not taken seriously by its exponents. The questions about the statistics of quarks, about the forces that hold them together, about the particles corresponding to these forces, about the reasons why quarks never appear as free particles, about the pair-creation of quarks in the interior of the elementary particle—all these questions are more or less left in obscurity. If there was a desire to take the quark hypothesis in real earnest, it would be necessary to make a precise mathematical approach to the dynamics of quarks, and the forces that hold them together, and to show that, qualitatively at least, this approach can reproduce correctly the many different features of particle physics that are known today. There should be no question in particle physics to which this approach could not be applied. Such attempts are not known to me, and I am afraid, also, that every such attempt which is presented in precise mathematical language would be very quickly refutable. I shall therefore formulate my objections in the shape of questions: "Does the quark hypothesis really contribute more to understanding of the particle spectrum, than the Voigtian hypothesis of oscillators contributed, in its day, to understanding of the structure of atomic shells?" "Does there not still lurk behind the quark hypothesis the notion, long ago refuted by experiment, that we are able to distinguish simple and composite particles?"

28   I would now like to take up briefly a few questions of detail. If the SU_3 group plays an important part in the structure of the particle spectrum, and this we must assume on the basis of the experiments, then it is important to decide whether we are dealing with a fundamental symmetry of the underlying natural law, or with a dynamic symmetry, which from the outset can only have approximate validity. If this decision is left unclear, then all further assumptions about the dynamics underlying the spectrum also remain unclear, and then we can no longer understand anything. In the higher symmetries, such as SU_4, SU_6, SU_{12}, $SU_2 \times SU_2$ and so on, we are very probably dealing with dynamic symmetries, which can be of use in the phenomenology; but their heuristic value could be compared, in my view, with that of the cycles and epicycles in Ptolemaic astronomy. They permit only very indirect back-inferences to the structure of the underlying natural law.

29   Finally, a word more about the most important experimental findings of recent years. Bosons of relatively high mass, in the region of 3–4 GeV, and of long lifetime, have lately been discovered. Such states are basically quite to be expected, as Dürr in particular has emphasized. Whether, owing to the peculiarity of their long lifetime, they can be regarded to some degree as composed of other already known long-lived particles, is, of course, a difficult dynamical question, in which the whole complexity of many-particle physics becomes operative. To me, however, it would appear a quite needless speculation, to attempt the introduction of further new particles *ad hoc,* of which the objects in question are to consist. For this would again be that misstatement of the question, which makes no contribution to understanding of the spectrum.

30   Again, in the storage-rings at Geneva, and in the Batavia machine, the total action cross-sections for proton-proton collisions at very high energies have been measured. It has turned out that the cross-sections increase as the square of the logarithm of the energy, an effect already long ago surmised, in theory, for the asymptotic region. These results, which have also been found, meanwhile, in the collision of other particles, make it probable, therefore, that in the big accelerators the asymptotic region has already been reached, and hence that there, too, we no longer have any surprises to expect.

31   Quite generally, in new experiments, we should not hope for a *deus ex machina* that will suddenly make the spectrum of particles intelligible. For the experiments of the last fifty years already give a qualitatively quite satisfying, noncontradictory and closed answer to the question "What is an elementary particle?" Much as in quantum chemistry, the quantitative details can be clarified, not suddenly, but only by much physical and mathematical precision-work over the years.

32   Hence I can conclude with an optimistic look ahead to developments in particle physics which seem to me to give promise of success. New experimental findings are always valuable, of course, even when at first they merely enlarge the tabulated record; but they are especially interesting when they answer critical questions of theory. In theory, we shall have to endeavor, without any semi-philosophical preconceptions, to make precise assumptions concerning the underlying dynamics of matter. This must be taken with complete seriousness, and we should not, therefore, be content with vague hypotheses, in which most things are left obscure. For the particle spectrum can be understood only if we know the underlying dynamics of matter; it is the dynamics that count. All else would be merely a sort of word-painting based on the tabulated record, and in that case the record itself would doubtless be more informative than the word-painting.

Source: "What Is an Elementary Particle" from *Tradition in Science* by Werner Heisenberg. Copyright © 1983 by Werner Heisenberg. Reprinted by permission of HarperCollins Publishers.

QUESTIONS FOR DISCUSSION

1. In this essay, Heisenberg considers the role language plays in science. Is Heisenberg arguing, like Sheridan, that mediation of any form is inadequate to an immediate perception of scientific fact? Discuss.

2. Heisenberg points out that the central question of science is whether or not the theorist can "underpin [a] qualitative understanding by means of quantitative calculations." How and why does a qualitative understanding pose a problem for quantum physics?

FROM READING TO WRITING

1. There is a lot of scientific language, or jargon, in this essay. Do you have to understand the scientific theories to be able to understand the central message? Freewrite for three minutes in response to the following sentence starter: "Heisenberg's essay argues…." Discuss.

2. Following the inductive form, this essay is broken up into three main parts: a hypothesis, context, and a discussion. Can you identify them?

Molecular Structure of Nucleic Acids: A Structure for Deoxyribose Nucleic Acid

BY J.D. WATSON AND F.H.C. CRICK

INTRODUCTION

Francis Harry Compton Crick studied physics at University College, London and later worked at the Medical Research Council Unit at Cambridge University. James Dewey Watson studied at the University of Chicago and took a position at Cambridge University in 1951, where he met Francis Crick and began working with him on the structure of DNA. Watson and Crick, along with Maurice Wilkins, shared the 1962 Nobel Prize in Medicine for their discovery of DNA.

This paper articulates and contextualizes this discovery in the research of others. Arguing why their model of the structure of DNA should be accepted as the correct and primary model, the authors refute the claims made by earlier researchers in clear and accessible language.

See chapter 4 for an analysis of how language and metaphor are used strategically in this essay.

1   We wish to suggest a structure for the salt of deoxyribose nucleic acid (D.N.A.). This structure has novel features that are of considerable biological interest.

2   A structure for nucleic acid has already been proposed by Pauling and Corey.[1] They kindly made their manuscript available to us in advance of publication. Their model consists of three intertwined chains, with the phosphates near the fibre axis, and the bases on the outside. In our opinion, this structure is unsatisfactory for two reasons: (1) We believe that the material which gives the X-ray diagrams is the salt, not the free acid. Without the acidic hydrogen atoms it is not clear what forces would hold the structure together, especially as the negatively charged phosphates near the axis will repel each other. (2) Some of the van der Waals distances appear to be too small.

3   Another three-chain structure has also been suggested by Fraser (in the press). In his model the phosphates are on the outside and the bases on the inside, linked together by hydrogen bonds. This structure as described is rather ill-defined, and for this reason we shall not comment on it.

4   We wish to put forward a radically different structure for the salt of deoxyribose nucleic acid. This structure has two helical chains each coiled round the same axis (see diagram). We have made the usual chemical assumptions, namely, that each chain consists of phosphate diester groups joining β-D-deoxyribofuranose residues with 3',5' linkages. The two chains (but not their bases) are related by a dyad perpendicular to the

This figure is purely diagrammatic. The two ribbons symbolize the two phosphate sugar chains, and the horizontal rods the pairs of bases holding the chains together. The vertical line marks the fibre axis.

fibre axis. Both chains follow right-handed helices, but owing to the dyad the sequences of the atoms in the two chains run in opposite directions. Each chain loosely resembles Furberg's[2] model No. 1; that is, the bases are on the inside of the helix and the phosphates on the outside. The configuration of the sugar and the atoms near it is close to Furberg's "standard configuration," the sugar being roughly perpendicular to the attached base. There is a residue on each chain every 3·4 A. in the z-direction. We have assumed an angle of 36° between adjacent residues in the same chain, so that the structure repeats after 10 residues on each chain, that is, after 34 A. The distance of a phosphorus atom from the fibre axis is 10 A. As the phosphates are on the outside, cations have easy access to them.

5   The structure is an open one, and its water content is rather high. At lower water contents we would expect the bases to tilt so that the structure could become more compact.

6   The novel feature of the structure is the manner in which the two chains are held together by the purine and pyrimidine bases. The planes of the bases are perpendicular to the fibre axis. They are joined together in pairs, a single base from one chain being hydrogen-bonded to a single base from the other chain, so that the two lie side by side with identical z-co-ordinates. One of the pair must be a purine and the other a pyrimidine for bonding to occur. The hydrogen bonds are made as follows: purine position 1 to pyrimidine position 1; purine position 6 to pyrimidine position 6.

7   If it is assumed that the bases only occur in the structure in the most plausible tautomeric forms (that is, with the keto rather than the enol configurations) it is found that only specific pairs of bases can bond together. These pairs are: adenine (purine) with thymine (pyrimidine), and guanine (purine) with cytosine (pyrimidine).

8   In other words, if an adenine forms one member of a pair, on either chain, then on these assumptions the other member must be thymine; similarly for guanine and cytosine. The sequence of bases on a single chain does not appear to be restricted in any way. However, if only specific pairs of bases can be formed, it follows that if the sequence of bases on one chain is given, then the sequence on the other chain is automatically determined.

9   It has been found experimentally[3,4] that the ratio of the amounts of adenine to thymine, and the ratio of guanine to cytosine, are always very close to unity for deoxyribose nucleic acid.

10   It is probably impossible to build this structure with a ribose sugar in place of the deoxyribose, as the extra oxygen atom would make too close a van der Waals contact.

11   The previously published X-ray data[5,6] on deoxyribose nucleic acid are insufficient for a rigorous test of our structure. So far as we can tell, it is roughly compatible with the experimental data, but it must be regarded as unproved until it has been checked against more exact results. Some of these are given in the following communications. We were not aware of the details of the results presented there when we devised our structure, which rests mainly though not entirely on published experimental data and stereochemical arguments.

12   It has not escaped our notice that the specific pairing we have postulated immediately suggests a possible copying mechanism for the genetic material.

13   Full details of the structure, including the conditions assumed in building it, together with a set of co-ordinates for the atoms, will be published elsewhere.

14   We are much indebted to Dr Jerry Donohue for constant advice and criticism, especially on interatomic distances. We have also been stimulated by a knowledge of the general nature of the unpublished experimental results and ideas of Dr M.H.F. Wilkins, Dr R.E. Franklin and their co-workers at King's College, London. One of us (J.D.W.) has been aided by a fellowship from the National Foundation for Infantile Paralysis.

> J.D. Watson
> F.H.C. Crick
> Medical Research Council Unit for the Study of the
> Molecular Structure of
> Biological Systems,
> Cavendish Laboratory, Cambridge,
> April 2.

NOTES

1   Pauling, L., and Corey, R. B., *Nature*, 171, 346 (1953); *Proc. U.S. Nat. Acad. Sci.*, 39, 84 (1953).
2   Furberg, S., *Acta Chem. Scand.*, 6, 634 (1952).
3   Chargaff, E., for references see Zamenhof, S., Brawerman, G., and Chargaff, E., *Biochim. et Biophys. Acta*, 9, 402 (1952).
4   Wyatt. G. R., J. *Gen. Physiol.*, 36, 201 (1952).
5   Astbury, W. T., Symp. Soc. Exp. Biol. 1, Nucleic Acid, 66 (Camb. Univ. Press, 1947).
6   Wilkins, M. H. F., and Randall, J. T., *Biochim. et Biophys. Acta*, 10, 192 (1953).

Source: Reprinted by permission from Macmillan Publishers Ltd: *Nature*, Francis Crick and James D. Watson, "Molecular Structure of Nucleic Acids", vol. 171, pp. 737-738 (April 25, 1953).

QUESTIONS FOR DISCUSSION

1. Is the self-effacing tone in the first sentence—"we wish to suggest"—consistent with the magnitude of the claim? Is the tone in the twelfth paragraph consistent with the tone in the rest of the essay? Does the clarity of the language make the discovery accessible to a larger audience?

2. Analyze how Watson and Crick present and refute the research of other researchers. How do they use research to support their own hypothesis?

3. How does the diagram work to affirm and make accessible their discovery? What do they mean when they point out that "this figure is purely diagrammatic"?

4. How do the acknowledgments work at the end of the essay?

FROM READING AND WRITING

This essay is a model of inductive writing. Outline the essay and its logical development. Do the number of short paragraphs blur the boundaries between academic and non-academic essays?

Democratic Rule

Modern Democracy

BY CARL L. BECKER

INTRODUCTION

Carl Becker was an American historian and philosopher who taught and researched at the University of Kansas and at Cornell University from 1902 to 1941. Differing from many historians of his time, he didn't believe that there was one unchanging view of history. He believed instead in a relativistic view, which changed in response to new knowledge. "The past," Becker wrote, "is a kind of screen upon which each generation projects his vision of the future." However, the Second World War and the rise of Hitler caused him to revise his belief in progress and human perfectibility. As a result, he called for a reassertion of morality in historical writing.

He wrote *Modern Democracy* in 1941. In this excerpt, Becker discusses the conditions necessary for a democracy to survive and flourish, while also pointing to the problems and prospects for democratic rule in a troubled time.

1   Democracy, like liberty or science or progress, is a word with which we are all so familiar that we rarely take the trouble to ask what we mean by it. It is a term, as the devotees of semantics say, which has no "referent"—there is no precise or palpable thing or object which we all think of when the word is pronounced. On the contrary, it is a word which connotes different things to different people, a kind of conceptual Gladstone bag which, with a little manipulation, can be made to accommodate almost any collection of social facts we may wish to carry about in it. In it we can as easily pack a dictatorship as any other form of government. We have only to stretch the concept to include any form of government supported by a majority of the people, for whatever reasons and by whatever means of expressing assent, and before we know it the empire of Napoleon, the Soviet regime of Stalin, and the Fascist systems of Mussolini and Hitler are all safely in the bag. But if this is what we mean by democracy, then virtually all forms of government are democratic, since virtually all governments, except in times of revolution, rest upon the explicit or implicit consent of the people. In order to discuss democracy intelligently it will be necessary, therefore, to define it, to attach to the word a sufficiently precise meaning to avoid the confusion which is not infrequently the chief result of such discussions.

2   All human institutions, we are told, have their ideal forms laid away in heaven, and we do not need to be told that the actual institutions conform but indifferently

to these ideal counterparts. It would be possible then to define democracy either in terms of the ideal or in terms of the real form—to define it as government of the people, by the people, for the people; or to define it as government of the people, by the politicians, for whatever pressure groups can get their interests taken care of. But as a historian I am naturally disposed to be satisfied with the meaning which, in the history of politics, men have commonly attributed to the word—a meaning, needless to say, which derives partly from the experience and partly from the aspirations of mankind. So regarded, the term democracy refers primarily to a form of government, and it has always meant government by the many as opposed to government by the one—government by the people as opposed to government by a tyrant, a dictator, or an absolute monarch. This is the most general meaning of the word as men have commonly understood it.

3   In this antithesis there are, however, certain implications, always tacitly understood, which give a more precise meaning to the term. Peisistratus, for example, was supported by a majority of the people, but his government was never regarded as a democracy for all that. Caesar's power derived from a popular mandate, conveyed through established republican forms, but that did not make his government any the less a dictatorship. Napoleon called his government a democratic empire, but no one, least of all Napoleon himself, doubted that he had destroyed the last vestiges of the democratic republic. Since the Greeks first used the term, the essential test of democratic government has always been this: the source of political authority must be and remain in the people and not in the ruler. A democratic government has always meant one in which the citizens, or a sufficient number of them to represent more or less effectively the common will, freely act from time to time, and according to established forms, to appoint or recall the magistrates and to enact or revoke the laws by which the community is governed. This I take to be the meaning which history has impressed upon the term democracy as a form of government.

Source: Excerpted from Becker, Carl. *Modern Democracy*. Yale University Press: New Haven, 1941. Web.

QUESTIONS FOR DISCUSSION

1. As stated in chapter 2, definition provides a baseline for discussion and suggests the parameters of your argument. Outline Becker's logical reasoning process as he arrives at his definition of democracy. What is this definition? Summarize it in your own words.
2. How does Becker's theory of historical relativism appear in this short definition? Provide evidence.
3. Becker has been praised for his keen sense of style. Do you agree? Think about how he uses language and find three points that illustrate his technique and way with words. This might involve his use of analytical patterns, parallelism, diction, etc.

continued

FROM READING TO WRITING

Review the information on definition in chapter 2, then write an extended definition of not more than a page of an abstract political term. Using the technique of imitation, emulate some of Becker's paragraph and/or sentence structure, and word choice.

Democracy

BY E.B. WHITE

INTRODUCTION

E.B. White was an American novelist (*Charlotte's Web*, *Stuart Little*, *Here is New York*), poet, essayist, and journalist. Besides writing prolifically and winning many awards, he worked for United Press International and the American Legion News Service in 1921 and 1922 and as a reporter for the *Seattle Times* and contributing editor for *The New Yorker* magazine.

Franklin D. Roosevelt had established the Writer's War Board during the Second World War to persuade the public to support the war effort. In 1943, the Board sent E.B. White a letter, requesting a statement on the meaning of democracy. Instead of giving a dictionary definition or an extended analytical definition, as Carl Becker did, White creatively used metaphor to elicit readers' emotions.

1   We received a letter from the Writers' War Board the other day asking for a statement on "The Meaning of Democracy." It presumably is our duty to comply with such a request, and it is certainly our pleasure.

2   Surely the Board knows what democracy is. It is the line that forms on the right. It is the don't in don't shove. It is the hole in the stuffed shirt through which the sawdust slowly trickles; it is the dent in the high hat. Democracy is the recurrent suspicion that more than half of the people are right more than half of the time. It is the feeling of privacy in the voting booths, the feeling of communion in the libraries, the feeling of vitality everywhere. Democracy is a letter to the editor. Democracy is the score at the beginning of the ninth. It is an idea which hasn't been disproved yet, a song the words of which have not gone bad. It's the mustard on the hot dog and the cream in the rationed coffee. Democracy is a request from a War Board, in the middle of a morning in the middle of a war, wanting to know what democracy is.

Source: White, E. B. "Democracy." *New Yorker* (July 3, 1943). Print. © Conde Nast.

QUESTIONS FOR DISCUSSION

1. This definition was written in the middle of the Second World War on 3 July 1943. How does this occasion influence White's opinions about democracy?

2. How does White expand on the dictionary definition of democracy?

3. White uses a string of creative metaphors to describe democracy. How effective is this use of metaphorical language? Translate the metaphors into plain English. Is there something lost in this translation?

FROM READING TO WRITING

1. Emulate White's metaphorical technique for writing definitions and write a definition of an abstract term, such as justice, liberty, insanity, maturity, or joy.

2. Write a short essay comparing White's definition of democracy with Becker's. Make sure you take into account that although they were written at a similar time in response, at least in part, to the Second World War, they also represent two different genres: academic in the case of Becker and more journalistic and popular in the case of White.

PART IV

THE HANDBOOK

This handbook begins with the premise that students do not need to know all the rules and conventions of English grammar to be able to write well. Being able to name and recognize a variety of grammatical terms and concepts is useful only to the extent that you can apply this knowledge to your writing assignments and to the writing that you do in your lives outside of academia.

My aim in chapter 12 is to teach you how to *use* grammar. There is a grammar pretest, exercises to help you identify and correct your grammatical errors, and a post-test to help you assess your awareness of your errors and your ability to fix them. To familiarize you with the conventions of formal academic English, most of the examples (and the required responses) are academic. Many of the exercises in this chapter have answers in the Exercise Answer Key in Appendix A. It is important to realize, however, that the answers represent only one suggestion among many.

Chapter 13 asks you to think about how you might use your grammatical choices to enhance your meaning, to think about writing style and your commitment to clear communication. If you think about *what* you write, as well as *how* you write it, you will find a sense of your own voice emerging. And, hopefully, when you begin to get a sense of your own voice, you will agree that good, clear writing is a skill well worth having and developing.

Improving both your basic grammatical skills and your awareness of style will help you become more effective academic writers and more effective communicators in all areas of your life. If you apply what you learn in these chapters, everything you write will be more effective: academic essays, reports, resumes, cover letters, personal letters, emails, memos, company notices, and reports.

12

Grammar

LEARNING OBJECTIVES

In this chapter, you will learn:

- How to identify a sentence.
- The difference between everyday writing and academic writing at the level of language and grammar.
- Some basic academic conventions and how they appear at the basic sentence/language level.
- Ten of the most common student errors and how to correct them in your own writing.
- How to edit your paper for errors.

This chapter provides you with a useful guide to some of the most common grammar principles and the ten most common errors. It begins by outlining the parts of speech in detail, explaining how they function both in sentences and in relation to academic conventions. It then shows you how to identify a sentence, outlines the different types of sentences, and explains how these sentences are punctuated. If you understand how sentences are formed and punctuated, you should be able to avoid most grammatical errors.

However, an outline of the ten most common student errors with instructions for how to fix them has also been included. There is a pretest and a post-test to help you analyze how your skills have improved and exercises and quizzes, with a corresponding answer key in Appendix A, to assist you in improving your grammar skills. There is also instruction in how to detect these errors in your own writing. Most of the examples are academic ones to help you become familiar with the use of grammar in academic sentence constructions and conventions. This practical, inductive bottom-up approach to grammar instruction is based on the belief that the best way to understand grammar is to use it.

GRAMMAR PRETEST

This pretest is designed to provide you with an indication of your present ability to use grammar correctly. If you understand the terms outlined in the directions, it is all well and good, but it is more important for you to be able to use grammar and punctuation accurately and effectively. Questions 1 to 5 focus on sentence construction, while question 6 asks you to apply your understanding of sentences and common grammatical errors to a revision of a paragraph-length passage.

When you have finished the pretest, check your answers in the Exercise Key in Appendix A. Keep in mind that the questions or grammatical errors you have problems with indicate a problem with a particular grammatical concept that you will need to address in your writing assignments. Note these problem errors down in a journal and pay attention to them when reading and completing the exercises in this chapter.

1. **Finding subjects and verbs:** Underline the subjects and circle the verbs:

   Example: Heisenberg (wrote) about the uncertainty principle in 1921.

   a. Democracy protects the rights of all citizens.
   b. According to Schryer, researchers are privileged.
   c. Animal rights advocates propose that animals should be treated as persons, not property.
   d. Leonard Cohen is a poet and a musician.

2. **Recognizing independent (main) and dependent (subordinate) clauses:** Underline the independent clauses and circle the dependent clauses in the following sentences:

   Example: (Although revision is a time-consuming practice), it is essential to good writing.

   a. Many Americans objected when Bill Clinton signed the Kyoto Accord.
   b. Because there was strong opposition from Albertans, Canada was also reluctant to ratify the Accord.
   c. While outdated research denies human responsibility for global warming, current research reinforces that human pollution is its ultimate cause.

3. **Recognizing coordination and subordination:** Below are four different pairs of sentences. Use either coordinating conjunctions—*for, and, nor, but, or, yet, so*— or subordinating conjunctions—*after, although, because, before, as, so, when,* or *while*—to combine the sentences to make *one* sentence. Please note that there are a variety of options that will make sense; these options include changing the structure of the sentence, as in the example below.

Continued

Example: Genetic engineering threatens our ecosystems. Genetically engineered foods should be banned.

Genetically engineered foods should be banned *because* genetic engineering threatens our ecosystems.

a. Poetry is important. It is not particularly popular.
b. Quantitative research conforms to a set of measurable guidelines. Qualitative research attempts to uncover underlying theoretical assumptions and opinions.
c. A literature review assesses the published information on a particular subject area. Sometimes, this assessment is related to a specific time period.
d. Literature comments on human life. It enables readers to empathize with other people's life situations.

4. Use an appropriate adverbial conjunction and semicolon to connect the following pairs of sentences. Some frequently used adverbial conjunctions include the following words: *furthermore, however, moreover, nevertheless, consequently, therefore,* and *likewise.* Make sure that the word you use makes a logical connection between the sentences and ideas.

Example: The US economy is suffering a serious downturn. Many people are losing their jobs.

The US economy is suffering a serious downturn; consequently, many people are losing their jobs.

a. The songs of Leonard Cohen reflect his skill as a poet. His skill as a poet does not negate his skill as a songwriter.
b. Plagiarism is a serious academic offence. It is considered to be a form of stealing and may result in expulsion.
c. Language is important to culture. One culture's communication does not necessarily translate to another's.

5. **Finding restrictive (essential) and non-restrictive (non-essential) modifiers:** Underline the restrictive modifiers and circle the non-restrictive modifiers in the following sentences:

Examples:
Genetic engineering, which has been used to genetically modify foods threatens our ecosystem.

Anyone who has been to Greece knows that Greece is the best holiday location.

a. Randy Bachman, a Canadian singer-songwriter, is legendary in the rock-and-roll industry.

b. Diana Krall is a Canadian who sings and performs jazz music.

6. Fix the common errors in the following paragraph, rewriting the paragraph so that it makes sense. Pay attention to the following errors: comma splice, dangling modifier, run-on or fused sentence, apostrophe, mixed construction, and a fragment.

The Adbusters advertisement spoof "Beauty Is Averageness" critiques the beauty industry, it argues that traditional ideas about beauty are unrealistic and impossible. The advertisement shows a girl who is "undoubtedly" beautiful, but the text printed all over her face tells us that she is non-existent: she is in fact a compilation of many different women's faces. The text tells us this by pointing out that this beautiful woman is a representation of many average women, who are the real victims of the beauty industry.

See the Exercise Answer Key in Appendix A to see how you did on the pretest.

Do not worry if you didn't understand these terms or found these questions difficult. The purpose of the pretest and post-test is to reveal your strengths, and ultimately, to help you to eliminate your weaknesses.

Pay attention to your areas of strength, acknowledging what you can do well, and pay particular attention to your areas of weakness. Note these areas as you read this chapter, making sure you complete all the exercises in these areas. When you have read the chapter, make sure you do the post-test to see how your understanding of a particular grammatical error has improved.

What Is Grammar?

If you are a native English speaker, you follow the rules of English grammar without having to think about them. For example, you automatically know the general meaning of the following sentence, taken from Lewis Carroll's "The Jabberwocky" because, without thinking, you apply these grammatical rules:

'Twas brillig, and the slithy toves / Did gyre and gimble in the wabe.

Although the poem uses nonsense words—*brillig, slithy toves, gyre, gimble, wabe*—we know that the slithy toves is a reference to some kind of animal that is "slithy" ("slithy" is the adjective or describing word, followed by the noun, "toves"). Likewise, we understand that the fact that they "did gyre and gimble" indicates some kind of action (verbs) and that the "wabe" is the place where they performed their action (noun). "'Twas brillig," is probably a reference to the time of day or a special day or time of the year that the "slithy toves" were gyreing and gimbling or, in my interpretation, dancing, in "the wabe." There might be several interpretations of these nonsense words, but we make sense of this passage, despite ourselves, because we instinctively understand grammar and how it works.

At a basic level, then, what constitutes grammar is a set of conventions that govern the words or linguistic units of a sentence in an attempt to communicate meaning to a listener or reader. Central to this communication is where these words are placed and the relationship between them. When the order of the words is mixed up, we become confused, but if the basic conventions remain, we can understand the sentence whether or not we understand the individual words.

It is important to realize, though, that the rules and conventions of grammar depend on who uses them, where they are used, and for what purpose. Language use evolves and changes over time and in relation to a specific situation, place, or context. For example, the nonsense writing above is suitable for Lewis Carroll's fantasy situation in *Alice in Wonderland,* but if you talked like that in everyday conversation, nobody would understand you. Similarly, the everyday language you use with your friends or with certain groups of friends (texting, or when listening to rap music, for example) would not be suitable for your academic writing assignments. The academic context demands an awareness of and, more importantly, an ability to use formal, edited English. When you understand how grammar is used in an academic sentence, you will be better able to understand it and use it.

Parts of Speech

To be able to write grammatically correct sentences, you will need to review the parts of speech. Here, then, are the nine parts of speech and their definitions and usage in an academic context.

Nouns	Verbs	Prepositions
Pronouns	Adverbs	Conjunctions
Adjectives	Articles	Interjections

Nouns

Commonly known as "naming" words, nouns name a person (*John, Susan, engineer, writer*), place (*Toronto, ocean, lake, city*), thing (*bookcase, chair, computer*), or abstract quality (*joy, pain, beauty, fear*). Nouns are further divided into common and proper nouns. Common nouns are nouns that refer to general persons or things, such as farmer, field, university, dog, cat, whereas proper nouns make specific reference to people's names or titles and, as such, begin with a capital letter: Michael Jackson; Carleton University; Reverend Thomas; Molly, the dog.

Nouns can function as the **subject** or **object** of a sentence. To be able to identify the subject in a sentence, ask who or what the sentence is about. For example, in the sentence "John writes," John is the subject because the sentence is about him.

To identify the object of the sentence, which is also a **noun**, consider what the subject is acting on. For example, "John writes a book" contains the noun object, "book," which John is writing. Consider the following sentence, "Charles Dickens wrote *Bleak House*." This sentence contains two nouns. Charles Dickens is the subject of the sentence—it is the proper noun that is performing the action of writing—and *Bleak House* is the object of the sentence because it names the object that Charles Dickens wrote. *Bleak House* is also a proper noun because it names a specific novel that Dickens wrote.

Academic Context

In academia, you are expected to capitalize nouns correctly.
Follow these rules:

- Capitalize the first word of every sentence, unless it follows a semicolon or a colon.
- Capitalize proper nouns, which name specific persons, places, or things: *Canada, Saskatchewan, World War II, Stephen Hawking, Christmas, Monday, Kyoto Accord.*
- Capitalize proper adjectives, which are formed from proper nouns: *Canadian, Shakespearean, Aboriginal, Christian.*
- Capitalize common nouns, which are used in conjunction with proper nouns: *Charlton Road, Saskatchewan River, Lake Huron, Professor Smith.*
- Don't capitalize common nouns—nouns that are preceded by *a, an,* or *the* and represent a group of similar things: *the dog* (one particular dog of many dogs), *a dog* (any representative dog), *mother, brother, spring, summer, rose, book,* etc.
- Capitalize most words, with the exception of *a, an, the, to,* and short connecting words, such as *and, but,* etc., in titles and subtitles of works: *Romeo and Juliet,* "Memories of Christmas," *Oryx and Crake,* "The Case for Animal Rights," "Once More to the Lake." Always capitalize the first word, even if it begins with the exempted words: *The Bone People,* "An Examination of Pharmaceutical Advertising."
- If you change the capitalization in someone else's quotation, you must indicate the change by enclosing the letter in square brackets, as in the following example.

> **Original quote:** "Serious problems arise for utilitarianism when we remind ourselves that it enjoins us to bring about the best consequences" (Regan 627).

> **Integrated quote:** As Regan argues, "[s]erious problems arise for utilitarianism when we remind ourselves that it enjoins us to bring about the best consequences" (627).

The current tendency is to use fewer capitals, so be careful not to overcapitalize. Following these basic rules in your papers should help. Be sure to use these rules in every form of communication you use. Although some people capitalize words in emails to make a point, it is considered rude. Keep your voice and tone professional at all times by following the standard rules for capitalization in all communication.

Pronouns

A **pronoun** is a word that stands in place of a noun. Like a noun, it is used as the subject or object of a sentence.

Pronouns can be *subjective* (I, you, he, she, it, we, they), *objective* (me, you, him, it, her, us, them), *possessive* (mine, yours, his, hers, its, ours, yours, theirs), *demonstrative* (that, this, these, those), *indefinite* (all, both, each, everyone, anyone, either, etc.), *interrogative* (who, which, what, etc.), *relative* (who, which, that, whom, etc.), *reflexive* (myself, yourself, themselves, etc.), or *intensive* (I myself, you yourself, etc.). What you need to remember here, though, are that these words take the place of the noun.

Exercise 12.2

See the Exercise Answer Key in Appendix A for possible answers to these questions.

FINDING NOUNS

Highlight the nouns (proper and common) and the pronouns that represent the nouns in the following sentences:

> Buzz Aldrin, who was the second man to walk on the moon, wrote an autobiography called *Reaching for the Moon* that documents his lifelong ambition to walk on the moon.

Pronouns also indicate point of view. Please note the following chart and the relationship between point of view and personal pronoun use:

Table 12.1 ◆ Point-of-View and Personal Pronoun Use

Personal Pronoun = Point of View	Subjective	Objective	Possessive	Possessive Adjectives: not pronouns because they *modify* nouns but do not *replace* them
Singular				
1st person	I	me	mine	my
2nd person	you	you	yours	your
3rd person	he, she, it	him, her, it	his, hers, its	his, her, its
Plural				
1st person	we	us	ours	our
2nd person	you	you	yours	your
3rd person	they	them	theirs	their

Relative pronouns: who, whom, whose, which, that, what, whoever, whichever

Demonstrative pronouns: this, that, these, those

Indefinite pronouns: all, both, each, one, nothing, no one, nobody, anything, anybody, anyone, something, somebody, someone, everything, everybody, everyone

Academic Context

As a general rule pronouns should directly follow the nouns that they represent. It is important to note that academic writing uses first- or third-person point of view; it never uses second person, which is considered too subjective, because it puts the emphasis on the reader rather than, objectively, on the knowledge. The second person is, however, common in journalism and fiction.

Adjectives

Adjectives are describing words. They modify, describe, or add additional information or detail to a noun or pronoun. They appear most often before a noun, but sometimes they can appear after the noun (predicate adjective), as in the film title *The Matrix Reloaded*.

In academic writing, you need to avoid clichéd or archaic expressions of these types of adjectives, for example proof positive, time immemorial, times past, treasure trove, etc.

Consider the following sentences:

The yellow bicycle was stolen from outside the grocery store.

In 1969, Margaret Atwood wrote a feminist novel called *The Edible Woman*.

In the first sentence, *yellow* and *grocery* are the adjectives that tell us something more about the nouns they modify: the bicycle and the store. In the second sentence, *feminist* is the adjective that tells us what type of novel Atwood wrote. The book, *The Edible Woman*, is the noun, which is capitalized according to the conventional rules of capitalization. As an aside, *In 1969* is called a prepositional phrase.

Please note that *this, that, these, each, either, some, all, both, which, what,* and *whose* can be adjectives when placed before a noun.

Academic Context

In academic writing, adjectives are used only if they embody essential information that we need to know to understand the meaning of the text. For example, we might not need to know that the bicycle was yellow (so we can eliminate this adjective), but we might need to know that *The Edible Woman* was both a novel and a feminist one.

Articles

Articles are particular kinds of adjectives. The articles *the, a,* and *an* are adjectives because they modify a noun. They tell us which one, what quality, or how many.

Consider the following sentences:

He wrote ***the*** letter.

He wrote ***a*** letter.

It took him ***an*** hour to write it.

In the first sentence, the article *the* modifies the noun *letter* and indicates a specific letter. In the second sentence, the article *a* modifies the noun *letter*, but here it indicates any letter: a letter that is not specified. In the third sentence, *an* is used to modify the noun *hour*. The article *an* is used before words beginning with a silent *h* or a vowel (*an elephant* or *an octopus*, for example).

Academic Context

In academic writing, second-language users often have problems when they use *a* or *an* to describe non-countable nouns (nouns that cannot be broken up into separate elements), such as *water, love, happiness, or music*. For example, we can't write, "a music was interesting," but we can write "*a* piece of music was interesting" or, alternatively, "we went to *a* music festival."

Verbs

Verbs are action words. They express an action (*runs, studied, flew*) or a state of being (*seemed, existed, appears*). Verbs can be infinitive, transitive, intransitive, linking, helping, or participles.

Infinitive

The infinitive form of the verb is its pure form and can function as a noun, an adjective, or an adverb. The infinitive consists of the word *to* and the unchanged verb, e.g., *to run, to be, to teach*, etc. However, when an infinitive follows *can, could, may, might, must, should, shall, would,* or *will,* it can function without being preceded by the word *to*, e.g., she must *go* home; he should *take* a class.

Please note that when a word is placed between the two words in the infinitive form, it is called a split infinitive, which, in academic writing, is a stylistic error. An example would be *to freely run*, which should be rephrased as *to run freely*. Because we don't talk or write like this when conforming to other genres and styles of writing, this construction can feel awkward. If you consider that it is simply one of the conventions that academic writing demands, it is easier to get used to.

Transitive

Transitive verbs are action verbs with a direct object that receives the action of the verb: Smith *wrote* an article; she *enjoys* her English class.

Intransitive

Intransitive verbs do not require objects and are used when the action is not directed toward some receiver: lightning *strikes*; mother *drives*. While this construction might feel awkward, it is important to know that it constitutes a grammatically correct independent sentence (see sentence structure later in this chapter).

Linking Verbs

These verbs link the subject of a sentence with a word or words that describe or define the subject: Dorothy *is* my sister; she *became* ill. Linking verbs often use forms of the verb *to be*: *is, are, was were, be, have been*. Other linking verbs include *appear, grow, seem, taste, become, look, smell, feel, remain, sound*.

Auxiliary Verbs (Helping Verbs)

These verbs help create verb phrases that help other verbs. For example, in the following sentences, the verbs *will* and *be* help make the verbs *finished* and *go* make sense: the assignment *will be finished* today; she *will go* to school. Auxiliary or helping verbs often use the following words, which, once again, include forms of the verb *to be*: *am, is, were, have, had, are, was, will, has, been, am, must*.

Participle Verb

A participle is a word formed from a verb that can be used as an adjective. Participle verbs indicate tense: the time the action takes place (past, present, etc.). The present participle ends in *–ing* while the past participle ends in *–ed, –d, –t, –en,* or *–n*. For example, Susan *is studying* for her exam or Susan *studied* for her exam.

Verb Tense

Verbs indicate the tense or the time the action takes place: present, past, future, and subcategories of this main timeline. Here are some sample present, past, and future tenses:

PAST TENSE

He **wrote** his paper. (simple past: the action happened in the past)

He **had written** his paper but he realized he **had forgotten** to hand it in. (past perfect: two actions or conditions that occurred in the past, one before the other)

The autobiography **was released** in January 2012. (past progressive: ongoing action that began in the past)

PRESENT TENSE

She writes. (simple present: the action is happening now)

The instructor **decided to give** her students grammar tests. (present perfect: an action that began in the past and continues into the present)

The instructor **will be teaching** the class for the next two terms. (future progressive: a helping verb and a participle relating ongoing actions)

FUTURE TENSE

The students **will study** two hours a day for their exam. (simple future: actions that will only occur in the future)

The students **will have written** many exams by the time they leave university. (future perfect: current actions that will be completed at a specific time in the future)

The students **will graduate** next month. (future progressive: actions that will occur in the future)

Past	Present	Future
Past Perfect Describes a completed action that occurred before another point also in the past		
Example: Helen *had worked* at the hospital for ten years before she moved away.		
Helen worked at the hospital for ten years. Then she moved away.		
	Present Perfect Starts in the past and contiues to the present time.	
Example: Helen *has worked* at the hospital for ten years.		
Helen began working at the hospital ten years ago.	Helen still works at the hospital.	
		Future Perfect Describes an action that will be completed in the future at the time of another action or event.
Example: By the time she turns thirty, Helen *will have worked* at the hospital for ten years.		
Helen has been working at the hospital.	Helen currently works at the hospital.	Helen will continue to work at the hospital when she turns thirty.

Figure 12.1 ◆ Diagram of Tenses

Table 12.2 ◆ **Verb Tenses (active voice)**

	Past	Present	Future
	An action that occurred before the present time.	An action that occurs now, occurs repeatedly, or is generally true.	An action that will occur in the future.
Simple	Form: past tense form (–e or –ed).	Form: regular word or –s form.	Form: regular word, plus *will*.
	I/she/it *danced.* You/we/they *danced.*	I *dance.* You/we/they *dance.* He/she/it *dances.*	I/you/he/she/it/we/they *will dance.*
Progressive	Form: *was* or *were*, plus –*ing* form.	Form: *am*, *is*, or *are*, plus –*ing* form.	Form: *will be* plus –*ing* form.
	I/she/he/it *was dancing.* You/we/they *were dancing.*	I *am dancing.* You/we/they *are dancing.* He/she /it *is dancing.*	I/you/she/he/it/we/they *will be dancing.*

	Past Perfect Progressive	Present Perfect Progressive	Future Perfect Progressive
	An action in the past that was completed before another action in the past.	An action that began in the past and is still happening in the present.	An action that will end before another future action begins.
Perfect	Form: *had* plus past participle (–*ed* or –*d*).	Form: *have* or *has* plus past participle (–*ed* or –*d*).	Form: *will have* plus past participle (–*ed* or –*d*).
	I/you/he/she/it/we/they *had danced.*	I/you/we/they *have danced.* He/she/it *has danced.*	I/you/she/he/it/we/they *will have danced* all night by the time Chris arrives.
Perfect Progressive	Form: *had been* plus –*ing* form.	Form: *have been* or *has been* plus –*ing* form.	Form: *will have been* plus –*ing* form.
	I/you/he/she/it/ we/they *had been dancing.*	I/you/we/they *have been dancing.* He/she/it *has been dancing.*	I/you/he/she/it/they/ we/they *will have been walking* all morning by the time they stop for lunch.

There are about two hundred verbs in the English language that take an irregular form when conjugated in the past tense. For example, the plain or present form of the verb *begin* becomes *began* in the past tense and *begun* in the past participle. If you are unsure about verb forms, you might want to check your dictionary because it will list the verb and its various forms: the plain, past, and past participle form. If there are only two forms of the verb, as in *lend, lent,* then the past and the past participle are the same.

Table 12.3 ◆ Common Irregular Verbs

Below is a list of some of the most common irregular verbs (some allow for two choices):

Plain Form	Past Tense	Past Participle
arise	arose	arisen
become	became	become
begin	began	begun
blow	blew	blown
burst	burst	burst
choose	chose	chosen
come	came	come
do	did	done
draw	drew	drawn
dream	dreamed/dreamt	dreamed/dreamt
drink	drank	drunk
drive	drove	driven
eat	ate	eaten
fall	fell	fallen
flee	fled	fled
fly	flew	flown
get	got	got/gotten
go	went	gone
grow	grew	grown
hide	hid	hidden
know	knew	known
lend	lent	lent
lie	lay	lain
ride	rode	ridden
ring	rang	rung
rise	rose	risen
run	ran	run
see	saw	seen
shake	shook	shaken
shrink	shrank/shrunk	shrunk
sing	sang/sung	sung
sink	sank/sunk	sunk
think	thought	thought
write	wrote	written

Verb use: Active and Passive Voice

Voice has everything to do with the verb of a sentence. If the subject of the sentence performs the action of the verb, it is the active voice; if the subject is acted on by the verb, it is the passive voice. Active voice uses the form *subject–verb–object,* as in

Stuart Hall pioneered the discipline of cultural studies in the 1970s.

Stuart Hall is the noun or subject and *pioneered* is the verb: the subject is performing the action of pioneering when he speaks. *Cultural studies* is the object of the sentence.

Passive voice reverses the subject and object of the sentence, so the form is *object–verb–subject.* It also uses forms of the verb *to be* and the preposition *by,* which is sometimes implied.

Changing the above example to passive voice, you would get something like the following:

Cultural studies was pioneered by Stuart Hall in the 1970s.

In the above sentence, *Stuart Hall,* who is the subject who acts (*pioneers*) in this sentence, is put in the position of the object and is being acted upon. The form of the verb *to be* is paired with the past participle of pioneer—*was pioneered*—and the preposition *by.*

Active voice is the dominant academic voice. However, occasionally passive voice is used to provide emphasis. For example, if you want to emphasize cultural studies, you might leave this sentence in the passive voice; however, you need to be aware that *Stuart Hall* gets hidden in the middle of this sentence, so if your focus is on him, then he needs to be moved to the front of the sentence in his rightful position as the subject of the sentence.

Changing passive voice to active voice is easy. You simply identify the verb, the subject, and the object and then reverse the subject and object. Take the following passive sentence:

The mysteries of the universe are explored by Stephen Hawking in *The Grand Design.*

Are explored is the past participle passive construction of the verb *explore. Stephen Hawking* is the subject of the sentence (it is Stephen Hawking who is doing the exploring or acting) and the *mysteries of the universe* is the object (what he is exploring). Reworking this in the active voice you get the following sentence:

In *The Grand Design,* Stephen Hawking explores the mysteries of the universe.

The main sentence here, written in the active voice, is *Stephen Hawking* (subject) *explores* (verb) *the mysteries of the universe* (object). "In *The Grand Design*" is a prepositional phrase telling us where Hawking explores these mysteries.

More information on passive and active voice can be found in chapter 2. Exercises on passive and active voice can be found in the common errors section of this chapter.

Verb Use: Mood

Mood is also indicated by the verb you use in your writing. There are three types of mood: the indicative, the imperative, and the subjunctive.

THE INDICATIVE MOOD

The indicative mood states an opinion or a fact or asks a question.

> This book is boring. (opinion)

> This book has sixteen chapters. (fact)

> Will you read this book? (question)

THE IMPERATIVE MOOD

The imperative mood commands or gives direction. It omits the implied second-person subject of the sentence, you.

> Go and fetch my coat. (command)

> Turn right at the next crossroads. (direction)

THE SUBJUNCTIVE MOOD

This mood makes a suggestion or states a requirement, a desire, or an imaginary or hypothetical condition.

> In *A History of Sexuality*, Michel Foucault suggests that sexuality has been managed so that people comply with the norm. (suggestion/statement)

> This compliance was enforced by the requirement to confess one's sins. (requirement)

> If religion had not been so powerful, individuals might not have felt such an obligation to conform to sexual mores and norms. (hypothetical condition)

Academic Context

Verbs are the most important part of the academic sentence; however, academic writing does not use the sensational, emotional, or vivid verbs that you might see in creative or journalistic writing (*cried, jumped, swinging, banging, etc.*). It uses objective, intellectual verbs, such as *analyze, examine, posit, predict, debate, discuss, summarize, concede, agree, clarify, emphasis, interpret, speculate,* etc. Please see chapter 2 for a chart of common academic verbs and their possible contexts in a sentence.

Besides articles and prepositions, verbs and the correct application of verb tenses present some difficulties for students, particularly students for whom English is a second language. If this is the case, an awareness of irregular verb tenses can help, as can using the dictionary. An explanation of tense errors and exercises on tense, including subject–verb agreement, can be found in the common errors section of this chapter. If you are a visual learner, it sometimes helps to draw a chart depicting the tenses you are using. If in doubt, ask your instructor, set up a study and writing group, and be sure to thoroughly edit your work.

Although academic writing might contain personal opinion, the *indicative mood* is always contextualized in an objective and factual analysis. Questions that are left hanging or ask the reader to answer are inappropriate for academic writing. Any questions you do ask should be used sparingly and always answered by you, the writer. Academic writing never uses the imperative mood but often uses the subjunctive mood.

Adverbs

Adverbs modify verbs, adjectives, other adverbs, and sometimes entire clauses to add meaning. They let the reader know *how* and in *what way* the action is being performed.

He ran **fast**. (*fast* modifies the verb *ran*)

She sang **very loudly**. (*loudly* modifies the verb *sang* and *very* modifies the adverb *loudly*)

Camus's study of the Sisyphus myth is a critique that has been applauded **widely**. (*widely* modifies the verb *applauded*)

Academic Context

Like adjectives, adverbs should be used sparingly in an academic context. For example, if we do not need to know that the man ran fast, the woman sang loudly, or that Camus's study was applauded widely, then we omit the adverb.

Please note that placing an adverb between the particle *to* and the *verb* (infinitive verb = to + verb, as in *to run, to think,* etc.), as in *to quickly run, to carefully think,* etc., is a stylistic error called the *split infinitive.* Avoid placing words between the two parts of an infinitive verb.

Prepositions

Prepositions are connecting words that show the relationships between nouns or pronouns and other words in a sentence. A preposition can signal space and time (*above, below, near, after, before, until*), as in "*in* April, *under* the orange umbrella," or exclusion (*except, but*), as in "everyone *except* John signed the petition." Below are a list of common prepositions:

about	before	considering	near	since
above	behind	down	of/off	through
across	below	excluding	on/onto	to
after	beneath	following	opposite	toward
against	beside	for	outside	under
among	between	from	over	underneath
around	beyond	in	past	up/upon
as	by	inside	regarding	with/within
at	concerning	into	round	without

Here are some typical examples of how prepositions work in a sentence:

The boy stood **under** the tree.

Jane stood **beside** her boyfriend.

The plane flew **over** the baseball game, tipping its wings to the people **below**.

Consider the following paragraph, as you are directed on a tour of a house, and all the associated prepositions (the prepositions are bolded and italicized):

Before you go **into** the house, you can stand **with** me and look **around** the garden, stand **beside** the fence and look **at** the walls and the roof. If you so desire, you can walk **across** the lawn, climb **up** the ladder and **onto** the roof **of** the house. **From** there you can look **across** the roof **to** your neighbour's roof. When you have done this, go **inside** the house and look **around**. Walk **through** the entrance way, **by** the big hallway mirror, and **into** the kitchen. Go **past** the table and walk **between** the two counters **to** the refrigerator. Take **out** a drink, sit **at** the table **on** a stool and relax. Then you go **out of** the house, walking **away from** the house, and go home.

Please note that some words that function as prepositions also function as other parts of speech. To check whether a word is a preposition, see how it functions in its sentence.

The mountain climbers have not radioed in **since** yesterday. (preposition)

Since they have left the base camp, the climbers can communicate with us only by radio. (subordinating conjunction)

At first I was not worried, but I have **since** changed my mind. (adverb)

It is also important to know that phrasal, or compound, verbs often combine with prepositions to deliver their meaning. Sometimes these compound verbs can be separated from the preposition without interfering with the meaning. For example, the compound verb *throw away* can be changed to *I threw it away*, introducing an object between *threw* and *away*. Other examples include *bring back* (bring *love* back), *leave out* (leave *her* out), *hand in* (hand *the assignment* in), *look over* (look *the essay* over), and *figure out* (figure *it* out). Acceptable academic phrasal verbs (compound verbs) include *believe in, benefit from, concentrate on, consist of, depend on, dream of, dream about, insist on, participate in, access to, opposed to,* and *prepare for.*

Academic Prepositions

While students generally understand how prepositions can position someone or something in space in relation to something else, it is not as easy to understand the function of prepositions when dealing with abstract ideas or knowledge. The Academic Focus box on page 481 lists the academic prepositions, including *of, from, about, for, to, of, with,* and *in,* and how they are typically used in academic sentences. A good point to remember is that regardless of the preposition used, the meaning must be clear.

ACADEMIC FOCUS

COMMON ACADEMIC PREPOSITIONS

About	comments about	research about	issues about	a theory about	an argument about
Between	a comparison between	a distinction between	a connection between	a partnership between	
By	preceded by	written by	received by	analyzed by	
For	difficult for	criteria for	problematic for	strategies for	
From	excluded from	derived from	removed from	a deviation from	
In	to engage in	to fill in	an error in	inherent in	participation in
Into	an investigation into	to look into			
Of	an awareness of	an analysis of	a summary of		
On	to do research on	to comment on	to focus on	imposed on	a perspective on
To	to object to	adjacent to	to apply to	a commitment to	with attention to due to
With	to agree with	to argue with	to coincide with	compared with	to be consistent with

Academic Context

Students whose first language is not English often have problems with prepositions, such as *in, at,* and *on.* For example, we lie *in* bed but we also lie *on* the couch.

When referencing *time,* use *in* when referring to a year or month (in 2001; in May); use *in* also when referring to a period of time (in a few months) or a period of the day (in the morning; in the evening), but use *at* when referring to the night (at night). Use *on* when referring to a specific day (on Friday; on my birthday) and *at* when referring to a specific time (at noon; at takeoff; at breakfast).

When referencing a *place,* use *in* when referring to a location surrounded by something else (in Alberta; in the kitchen; in the bathtub), *at* when referring to a specific location (at your house; at the bank), and *on* when referring to the top or the surface of something (on page 10; on the second floor (but in the attic or in the basement)).

Conjunctions

Conjunctions, commonly called "joining" words, are words that join words or groups of words, making the relationship between the words and clauses clear. There are three types of conjunctions: coordinating, correlative, and subordinating conjunctions.

Coordinating Conjunctions

Coordinating conjunctions join sentence elements of equal rank. They can be remembered by the acronym FANBOYS:

<u>F</u>or   <u>A</u>nd   <u>N</u>or   <u>B</u>ut   <u>O</u>r   <u>Y</u>et   <u>S</u>o

Correlative Conjunctions

Correlative conjunctions come in pairs: either . . . or; neither . . . nor; not . . . but; not only . . . but also; both . . . and. If you leave out one half of these correlative pairs, you will have a grammatical error.

It is important to use ***either*** a coordinating conjunction ***or*** a correlative conjunction.

Learning the basic rules of grammar is ***not only*** a requirement ***but also*** essential if you want to learn how to write well.

Conjunctive Adverbs

Conjunctive adverbs are used to indicate the relationship between two independent clauses. Some common conjunctive adverbs include *however, therefore, nevertheless, moreover, in fact, consequently, hence, accordingly.*

A period can be used to join two independent clauses and a conjunctive adverb; ***however,*** a semicolon is also a good choice.

Subordinating Conjunctions

Subordinating conjunctions introduce subordinate or dependent elements and join them to the main or independent part of the sentence. Some sample subordinating conjunctions include the words *because, if, whether, while, unless, although, as, before, after,* and *until.*

> **Although** he disliked grammar intensely, he realized he had to learn the rules *if* he wanted to learn how to write well.

> She completed all the grammar exercises **because** she wanted to become a better writer.

Interjections

Interjections are exclamatory words, such as *oh, ouch, please, why, hey,* and *wow.* They are used to express strong feelings or to command attention, and they typically use exclamation marks (!).

> As her son ran out in front of the oncoming bus, she screamed, "Stop! Stop!"

Academic Context

Academic writing *never* uses interjections. They work well in advertising and creative writing, but unless you are quoting someone who is using them, do not use them in your academic writing.

FREEWRITE

Exercise 12.3

Now that you have completed the pretest and have a basic idea of how academic writing uses the parts of speech, it will be useful before reading about sentence construction to think about what areas of grammar you might struggle with. Write non-stop for three or four minutes on the following sentence starter:

The part of grammar that I think I have most trouble with is . . .

When you have finished, review what you have written and highlight the points that you think might create problems for you in your academic writing assignments. As you go through this chapter and the exercises, refer back to this assessment from time to time. It will most likely accurately reveal the problems you have with grammar. These might be specific repeated grammar problems, which might have become a bad habit, or simply reflect a lack of confidence in your writing skills.

Understanding what a sentence is and knowing how it uses the parts of speech will not only help you correct any bad habits or misconceptions you have accumulated but also help you to feel more confident in your ability to to write correct and meaningful academic sentences.

What Is a Sentence?

When I ask students what a **sentence** is, they often answer that it is a complete thought. While this is true, that definition is a little unclear. If asked, you might think the every-day sentences you speak are complete thoughts, but if you were to write them out, you would most likely discover that many of them are not, even though you and your friends or family would implicitly understand what these sentences mean:

Consider the following examples: Would they qualify as complete thoughts and/or complete sentences?

Lunch?

Want to skip class?

Going to school now.

See you later.

The answer is no, they wouldn't, because technically the subject and/or the verb of each of these sentences is missing. We hear them, even though they are not there. Consider the following sentences:

"Want to watch a movie?"

"Do *you* want to watch a movie?"

Both examples above might be considered complete thoughts, but the second is the only one that is a complete, grammatically correct, sentence. The first sentence is not complete because the subject of the sentence (you) is missing. It is not clear, in other words, *who* might want to watch a movie. In this respect, it is a sentence fragment.

Academic writing *always* uses complete sentences. Being able to identify a sentence and being able to understand sentence patterns will enable you to write grammatically correct, clearly constructed, and meaningful sentences. Your writing, whether it is for English courses, engineering reports, or business proposals, will need to be varied, interesting, emphatic, and, above all, persuasive.

How is it possible, then, to make sure that you are using complete sentences in your academic writing assignments? Technically speaking, a sentence is an *independent clause*. It contains a subject and a verb or a **predicate**, which is the verb and all of its modifiers. In the example, *John runs to the store*, *John* is the subject and *runs* is the verb. *Runs to the store* is the predicate because it tells us where John is running. Students often have trouble identifying sentences because they are often not this simple. For example, there might be more than one subject—as in *John and Bill run to the store*—and more than one subject modifier, as in *Big John and Bill, who was getting old, run to the store*. Similarly, the predicate might only contain one verb, as in *John runs*, or more than two verbs, as in *John ran and skipped to the store*. The sentence might also contain more than one independent clause and several **dependent clauses**. However, when you can identify a sentence and its component parts, understanding how these parts work in relation to each other, you will also be able to understand how to use grammar and punctuation.

How to Identify a Sentence

A sentence is an independent clause and contains a subject and a predicate (a verb and its modifiers). It can stand alone as a sentence, or it can form part of a more complex sentence that contains both independent and dependent clauses. Being able to recognize grammatically correct, complete sentences in other people's writing will also help your own writing.

To be able to identify an independent clause or, in other words, a simple sentence—subject–verb–object—you need to be able to find the subject (the noun that is performing an action) and the verb in a sentence. Understanding how objects work can also help.

Finding the Subject

To find the subject of the sentence, ask *who* or *what* the sentence is about.

John runs to the store.

The sentence is about John, who runs to the store. John is the simple subject of the sentence because there is only one subject who acts here.

The store was closed.

The sentence is about the store. The store is the subject of the sentence.

John's parents told him to come home.

The sentence is about John's parents, who told John to come home.

They didn't need the groceries.

The sentence is about "they." The pronoun *they*, refers to the noun *parents*, already mentioned.

John and his friend went to the park.

The sentence is about John and his friend. It has what is called a compound subject because there is more than one subject in this sentence.

WHAT IS A SENTENCE?

Sentence = an independent clause
An independent clause = a subject + a predicate (a verb and its modifiers)
Simple sentence = subject + verb or subject + verb + object

Exercise 12.4

See the Exercise Answer Key in Appendix A for the answers to these questions.

FINDING SUBJECTS

Underline the subjects in the following sentences.

Simon and Peter were covered in snow.

They struggled to their feet.

A few people, who were skiing by, stopped to help them.

Someone on a snowmobile came and gave them a ride down the hill.

The above examples, however, are not academic. In academic writing, sentences are often denser and more abstract. Consider the following academic example:

Considerable debate concerning the ethics of the Food and Drug Administration seems to have centred around harmful additives.

The language here is more difficult, but the principle is the same. As you might have identified, *debate* is the subject here. It is modified, or made more specific, with additional information about the nature of the debate: the ethics of the FDA.

Finding the Verb

The verb is often considered the most important part of the sentence: it indicates the action that is being performed by the subject and the time (past, present, future, etc.) when the action is being performed (verb tense). To find the verb of a sentence, ask what the subject is doing. The verb tells us what action the subject is performing, and when it is being performed. Keep in mind that linking verbs, such as *is, was,* etc., are used to describe or define the subject.

Susan writes.

- *Writes* is the verb here that tells us what Susan is doing (this is a simple predicate because it contains the verb only).

She is a very good writer.

- The verb *is* defines (tells us more about) the subject, *she*. It is a linking verb.

She practises every day.

- The verb, *practises*, tells us what Susan does every day. It is in the present tense. *Every day* is the part of the predicate that modifies how often Susan practises (complete predicate).

FINDING VERBS

Underline the verbs in the following sentences.

His mother drives him to the interview.

David reads.

David responds skillfully to the interview questions.

The interviewers appreciate and acknowledge David's knowledge.

Exercise 12.5

See the Exercise Answer Key in Appendix A for the answers to these questions.

Here is an academic sentence with the verbs italicized: Griers *intended to use* the documentary form to *introduce* and *explain* international events to Canadians.

Your ability to identify direct and indirect objects is also essential to your ability to recognize and use grammatically correct sentences.

Identifying Direct Objects

A direct object is a noun or noun equivalent that completes and receives the action of the verb. Just as the subject answers the question who or what is performing the action, so the direct object answers the question of who or what is receiving the action expressed in the verb.

Consider the following sentence:

The girl rode the horse.

Girl is the subject here and *rode* is the verb that tells us what the girl was doing. *Horse* is the direct object of rode because it tells us what is being ridden.

Identifying Indirect Objects

An indirect object denotes the person or thing indirectly affected by the action of the verb. Consider the following sentence:

> We gave her the dog.

Her is the indirect object of the verb *gave*. The indirect object answers the question "to (for) whom or what." Another way of writing this is "We gave the dog to her."

ACADEMIC FOCUS

PATTERNS FOR DIRECT AND INDIRECT OBJECTS

Direct object = subject–verb–object (S–V–O).
Indirect objects = subject–verb–object–indirect object (S–V–O–IO)
Indirect objects = subject–verb–indirect object–object (S–V–IO–O)

Exercise 12.6

DIRECT AND INDIRECT OBJECTS

Underline the direct and indirect objects in the following sentences.

Everyone loves a circus.

Ruth ordered pancakes and sausages for breakfast.

Steve cooked us a quiche.

He painted his car yellow.

My little sister cannot drink milk.

See the Exercise Answer Key in Appendix A for the answers to these questions.

To review, **independent clauses** or simple sentences contain a subject and a verb (or subjects and verbs), but they also contain other information that modifies what we know about the subject and verb. The subject might be modified by additional information, as might the verb.

SUBJECTS, VERBS, AND OBJECTS

Exercise 12.7

See the Exercise Answer Key in Appendix A for the answers to these questions.

Now that you have a basic understanding of what constitutes a simple sentence (also called an independent clause), see if you can identify the subjects or compound subjects (more than one), the verbs, and the objects (direct and/or indirect) in the following academic sentences:

Canadians conceive of a just and equitable Canada.

The Charter of Rights and Freedoms acknowledges women's rights, children's rights, and the rights of individuals with disabilities.

Section 15 of the Charter outlines equality rights for people with disabilities.

Using Complex Sentences

As you are probably aware, these simple sentences are relatively easy to identify. However, if we only ever used simple sentences, as in the following example, our writing would not be very interesting and it would not enable us to logically follow the main point of the passage:

Sue Rodriguez was diagnosed with amyotrophic lateral sclerosis in 1991. She was diagnosed with it when she was forty-one years old. The disease causes progressive muscle atrophy, paralysis, and death. She decided to commit suicide. In 1992, she petitioned the courts for the right to die. She argued that she would need the help of a physician to commit suicide.

This short paragraph outlines Sue Rodriguez's story chronologically. However, it is difficult to read because the short simple sentences are repetitive because they are all very similar in length. It reads as a list of facts, but the point the writer is trying to make is not clear. Sentence variety is highly valued in all forms of writing but in academic writing in particular.

Combining some of these sentences and subordinating and/or emphasizing some of the information would not only eliminate the repetition but would also give the passage direction.

Consider this revision:

Sue Rodriguez was diagnosed with amyotrophic lateral sclerosis in 1991 **when** she was forty-one years old. **Because** the disease causes progressive muscle atrophy, paralysis, and death, she decided to commit suicide. **Realizing** that she would need the help of a physician to do this, she decided, in 1992, to petition the courts for the right to die.

By combining some of these sentences and moving the last two sentences around so that the passage ends with Rodriguez's petition for the right to die, we now have a logical progression, without, repetition that emphasizes her decision to petition the courts.

For your writing to be persuasive, then, you need to do more than use simple sentences. In each sentence in your writing, you may use more than one independent clause, more than one dependent or subordinate clause, and more than one phrase (a group of words that cannot stand alone because it does not include both a subject and a verb). You may also have additional information that serves to modify (define and/or describe) the subject, verb, or object. As a first step, learning how to distinguish between independent and dependent clauses will help you to learn how to use commas and organize your ideas into logically parallel or subordinate relationships.

Independent and Dependent Clauses

Similar to an **independent clause**, a **dependent clause** contains a subject and a verb, but it begins with a coordinating or subordinating conjunction—*and, but, for, when, who, although, because, until, after*, etc.—that explains either the equal/coordinate or subordinate relationship between the independent and dependent clause. Coordinating and subordinating these clauses allows you to create meaning and emphasis in your writing. What follows is an explanation of coordination and subordination, with examples, to help you understand how you can use these patterns to make meaning. It is important to know that you have choice: no *one* option is correct. You *must,* however, follow the grammatical patterns, using the correct punctuation, as highlighted in the following methods.

Combining Sentences Using Coordinate Clauses

Use coordinate clauses whenever you have two related independent clauses (containing a subject and a predicate) that are of equal importance. There are two main ways to combine independent clauses. The first way is by using a coordinating conjunction, such as *and, but, or,* etc.; the second way is to use a semicolon or a semicolon with a conjunctive adverb such as *therefore, however, nevertheless* etc.

The pattern, including punctuation requirements, is as follows:

independent clause + comma + coordinating conjunction + independent clause

He joined the independent clauses with conjunctions, **and** he placed a comma between them.

Here is an example of two independent clauses that are combined using a coordinating conjunction: *for, and, nor, but, or, yet, so* (remember FANBOYS).

Independent clause: Information on the benefits received from proper exercise and nutrition is widely available.

Independent clause: Youth are not educated properly in these areas.

Combined sentence: Information on the benefits received from proper exercise and nutrition is widely available, **but** youth are not educated properly in these areas.

The coordinating conjunction *but* expresses the relationship between the two sentences or independent clauses. It indicates contradiction in that the second part of the sentence contradicts the first part. The word *yet* also indicates contradiction.

It is important to remember that you need *two* independent clauses, containing a subject and a verb, on either side of the comma and coordinating conjunction. The clause that is connected to the coordinating conjunction is considered to be *dependent* upon the independent clause. Here is the above pattern revised to acknowledge the dependent clause:

independent clause + comma + [coordinating conjunction + independent clause]
= independent clause + dependent clause

Many illnesses are the result of poor nutrition, **so** it is important to eat good food.

As you can probably see from the examples, using the correct words to establish meaning is essential. In general, *but* and *yet* express contradiction, *and* expresses a relationship based on addition, and *for* and *so*, as in the above example, convey a relationship of cause and effect. In the example above, the independent clause: "many illnesses are the result of poor nutrition"—provides the causal basis for understanding the ideas expressed in the dependent clause: "so it is important to eat good food." The dependent clause cannot stand on its own as a complete sentence: it depends on the independent clause for its meaning and grammatical correctness. On its own, the dependent clause— "so it is important to eat good food"—is a sentence fragment.

The second way of combining clauses using coordination is by using a semicolon and a conjunctive adverb.

USING THE SEMICOLON AND A CONJUNCTIVE ADVERB TO COORDINATE SENTENCES

Use a semicolon, or a semicolon and a conjunctive adverb, such as *therefore, however, nevertheless*, etc., to coordinate sentences.

The following is a list of common conjunctive adverbs:

however	indeed	nevertheless
consequently	thus	therefore
moreover	furthermore	hence

The pattern, including punctuation requirements, is as follows:

independent clause + [semicolon + conjunctive adverb + comma + independent clause]
= independent clause + dependent clause

Independent clauses can stand alone; **however**, dependent clauses must be joined to an independent clause.

Here is an example of two independent clauses that are combined using a semicolon and a conjunctive adverb to form an academic sentence.

Independent clause: Obesity is a national problem.

Independent clause: Something needs to be done about it.

Combined sentence: Obesity is a national problem; **consequently,** something needs to be done about it.

The conjunctive adverb, *consequently,* expresses a relationship based on cause and effect: because obesity is a national problem, something needs to be done about it.

USING A SEMICOLON TO COMBINE SENTENCES

Semicolons are not periods. They should be used sparingly and carefully to coordinate two independent clauses that are closely related in meaning and grammatical structure. The pattern, including punctuation requirements, is as follows:

independent clause + semicolon + independent clause

Independent clauses can stand alone; dependent clauses must be joined to an independent clause.

Figure 12.2 shows how the two independent clauses must be closely balanced in length, form, and meaning either side of the semicolon.

Here is an example of two independent clauses that are combined using a semicolon.

Independent clause: At best this approach adds investment value.

Independent clause: At worst it appears to be performance neutral.

Combined sentence: At best this approach adds investment value; at worst it appears to be performance neutral.

| Independent clause | ; | Independent clause |

Figure 12.2 ◆ Semicolon Use: The Teeter-Totter Example

This sentence is balanced in length and in parallel grammatical structure (at best . . . at worst). As a word of warning, do not overuse these types of sentences. They should be used to emphasize a point or an idea. Note that there is no capital letter following the semicolon.

Combining Sentences Using Subordinate Clauses

Use subordinate clauses when you have two independent clauses but want to show that one idea or clause is more important. The most important idea will appear in the main clause, and the subordinate idea will appear in the dependent or subordinate clause. You can identify this clause because it will start with a subordinating conjunction. Another way of looking at this is to argue that if a clause contains a subject and a verb, *and also* begins with one of the subordinating conjunctions, it is dependent and cannot stand alone.

Following is a list of common subordinating conjunctions. These words indicate the beginning of a dependent clause. Memorizing these words and how they are used will not only help you to develop clearer, more logical ideas but will also help prevent grammatical errors (especially sentence fragments).

The subordinating pattern, including punctuation requirements, is as follows:

[subordinating conjunction + independent clause] + comma + independent clause
= dependent clause + independent clause

or

independent clause + [subordinating conjunction + independent clause]
= independent clause + dependent clause

ACADEMIC FOCUS

COMMON SUBORDINATING CONJUNCTIONS

after	although	as
as if	as long as	as though
because	before	even if
even though	if	in order that
once	provided that	rather than
since	so that	though
unless	until	when
whenever	where	whereas
wherever	whether	while

If you begin a sentence with a dependent clause using a subordinating conjunction, there is *always* a comma between the dependent and the main or independent clause.

A comma is not necessary **when** the main clause occurs first.

When the main clause occurs last, a comma is necessary.

Below is an example of two pairs of independent clauses that are combined using subordinating conjunctions.

Independent clause: First Nations and Inuit people have lived in Canada for thousands of years.

Independent clause: They did not make contact with European explorers until the late fifteenth century.

Combined sentence: **Although** First Nations and Inuit people have lived in Canada for thousands of years, they did not make contact with European explorers until the late fifteenth century.

Although is the subordinating conjunction that indicates that the first independent clause is the subordinate clause. The main clause here—*they did not make first contact with European explorers until the late fifteenth century*—appears at the end of the sentence.

Independent clause: European explorers, missionaries, and teachers enforced their beliefs and values.

Independent clause: They believed their worldview was superior.

Combined sentence: European explorers, missionaries, and teachers enforced their beliefs and values **because** they believed their worldview was superior.

Because is the subordinating conjunction. The comma is omitted because the dependent clause is essential to the main idea of the sentence.

Exercise 12.8

REVIEW OF COORDINATE AND SUBORDINATE CLAUSES

PART A

Below are two pairs of independent clauses. Combine them by using a comma and one of the following coordinating conjunctions: *and, but, for, yet, or, so*. Make sure that you put the sentences in an order that makes sense (you can switch them around, putting the second one first if it makes more sense to do this). It is important to remember that when using any of these methods of combine sentences, no ONE way is correct.

1. **Independent clause:** He joined the independent clauses with conjunctions.
   Independent clause: He placed a comma between them.
2. **Independent clause:** Lack of physical activity in adolescents can cause health issues.
   Independent clause: Physical activity and proper nutrition in adolescents is important.

PART B

Combine the following sentences using a semicolon and a conjunctive adverb: *however, furthermore, consequently, nevertheless, moreover, therefore, indeed, hence, thus*. Remember that meaning is central to the choices you make.

1. **Independent clause:** Shamanism is a spiritual healing art.
   Independent clause: Shamans heal through rituals that connect them to the spirit world.
2. **Independent clause:** Al Gore argues that global warming is specifically relevant to Americans.
   Independent clause: All countries and all people are responsible for fixing this problem.

PART C

Combine the pairs of sentences below by using a subordinating conjunction. Make sure that you arrange the order of the sentences so that they make sense.

1. **Independent clause:** Conceptions of motherhood are at the centre of public controversy today.
   Independent clause: Stereotypes about motherhood will never change.
2. **Independent clause:** A British government report asserted that the melting of the ice caps has far-reaching, undesirable consequences for our future.
   Independent clause: Some scientists argue that the magnitude of the problem has been exaggerated.

See Exercise Answer Key in Appendix A for the answers to these questions.

Combining Sentences Using Relative Pronouns

Relative pronouns modify a noun or a pronoun. Similar to a pronoun, a relative pronoun stands for or replaces a noun/subject. The dependent relative pronoun clause generally falls immediately after the word it modifies. Relative pronoun clauses are either restrictive (essential to the meaning of the sentence) or non-restrictive (not essential to the meaning of the sentence).

Here is a list of common relative pronouns: *who, whom, whose, which, that.*

Restrictive vs Non-Restrictive Relative Pronouns

If the clause beginning with one of the above words is essential to the meaning of the sentence, it is not enclosed in commas. If the clause is not essential to the sentence, adding additional meaning or expanding on the meaning or context that is not central to our understanding of the sentence, it is enclosed in commas (one on either side of the non-restrictive clause).

Pay attention to the following examples:

The researcher **who was studying diabetes** had a breakthrough. (restrictive or essential clause)

The researcher**, who was studying diabetes,** had a breakthrough. (non-restrictive or non-essential clause)

A non-restrictive modifier does not have to include a relative pronoun because the relative pronoun is implied. Commas are used to signal that the non-restrictive phrase is not essential to the meaning of the sentence.

Pay attention to the following examples:

Wayne Booth, **a professor of rhetoric,** wrote an essay called "The Rhetorical Stance."

"The Rhetorical Stance," **an essay I loved,** was written by Wayne Booth.

Below is an example of two pairs of independent clauses that are combined using relative pronouns. Please note that, as always, the meaning you want to create will determine your choices. Only one choice of many has been presented.

Independent clause: People often use food to help them cope.

Independent clause: People work long hours at demanding jobs.

Combined restrictive sentence: People **who often use food to help them cope** work long hours at demanding jobs.

Combined non-restrictive sentence: People**, who work long hours at demanding jobs,** often use food to help them cope.

Independent clause: Crystal Lee Clark is a Canadian Aboriginal artist.

Independent clause: She blurs the boundaries between tradition and technology.

Combined restrictive sentence: Crystal Lee Clark is a Canadian Aboriginal artist **who blurs the boundaries between tradition and technology.**

Who is the relative pronoun here that replaces *she* in the second independent clause. The *who* in this sentence stands for Crystal Lee Clark, the Aboriginal artist. There is no comma before the *who* because the information that follows is essential to the sentence.

You could just as easily make this combined sentence non-restrictive. In this way, the non-restrictive clause could be lifted out of the sentence without changing the meaning of the main clause.

> Combined non-restrictive sentence: Crystal Lee Clark, **who is a Canadian Aboriginal artist,** blurs the boundaries between tradition and technology.

REVIEW OF COORDINATE, SUBORDINATE, AND RELATIVE PRONOUN CLAUSES

Exercise 12.9

So far, you have learned how to identify and use a simple sentence and how to create variety in your sentences by combining them, using coordinate, subordinate, and relative pronoun clauses. What follows are a number of exercises that will help you practise these skills, using the relevant and correct punctuation for the particular sentence pattern.

COORDINATE CLAUSES

Coordinate the following pairs of sentences using a coordinating conjunction (*and, for, but, yet, so, as*), a correlative conjunction (*either . . . or; not only . . . but also*; etc.), or a semi-colon and a conjunctive adverb (*however, therefore, consequently*, etc.):

1. **Independent clause:** The findings indicate that we should not be occupied with social exclusion.
   Independent clause: We should be looking at how to enable inclusion.
2. **Independent clause:** Many people look back nostalgically at close-knit communities.
   Independent clause: Communal farms and urban settlements are becoming popular.

SUBORDINATE CLAUSES

Subordinate the following pairs of sentences using a subordinating conjunction. (See page 492 for a list of subordinating conjunctions.)

3. **Independent clause:** They have been confronted with an unequal labour market.
   Independent clause: They will adopt a default position that favours low-wage policies.
4. **Independent clause:** Inequalities could be minimized by the welfare state.
   Independent clause: They had to address areas of intense deprivation.

Continued

See the Exercise Answer Key in Appendix A for the answers to these questions.

RELATIVE PRONOUNS

Combine the following pair of sentences using a relative pronoun. Make sure that you use commas to identify a non-restrictive (non-essential) phrase or clause.

5. **Independent clause:** The worldwide exodus grew steadily.
   Independent clause: This exodus coincided with the rapid mechanization of agriculture.

Phrases

A phrase is a group of words that function as a noun, verb, or modifier. Phrases cannot stand alone because they do not include both a subject and a predicate (a verb and its modifiers).

Phrases include *noun, verb, adverb,* and *adjective* phrases, which refer to the dominant emphasis of the phrase (to define, describe, etc.). There are also **absolute phrases** (using a noun or pronoun and the *–ing* or *–ed* form of the verb), **prepositional** (indicating position or place), **appositive phrases** (renaming or identifying a noun), **participle phrases** (using a participle form of the verb), **verbal phrases** (using verb forms that function as adjectives, adverbs, or nouns), and **gerund phrases** (using the *–ing* form). Phrases are sometimes offset by commas when adding additional information to the sentence, but they can be essential to the sentence and appear without commas.

What is important to remember here, however, is how to use phrases correctly. This means that you have to know how to punctuate them. Once again, this comes down to being in control of your syntax or meaning. Ask yourself if the phrase is essential to the meaning of the sentence or if it could be taken out, as in a non-restrictive modifier. If it is essential to the meaning of the sentence—as in "The man turned *to see the woman*"—commas are not needed; if it is non-essential, commas are needed: *According to my professor,* I need a comma in this sentence.

Please note that phrases punctuated as if they are sentences—for example, *according to my professor*—create sentence fragments, which are serious grammatical errors.

From behind the window, a face appeared. (prepositional phrase—modifies where the face was seen. Non-restrictive phrase)

He laughed *at the clown*. (prepositional phrase—modifies what he was laughing at. Restrictive phrase)

Being somewhat surprised, I jumped backwards. (participle/noun phrase—modifies the subject, I. Non-restrictive phrase)

The woman, *a real lady*, greeted me at the door. (appositive phrase—modifies "the woman." This phrase is non-restrictive in that it can be taken out of the sentence without changing the sentence.)

The shaman **with long, dark hair** danced **around the room**. (adjectival phrase followed by a prepositional phrase. Restrictive or essential to the sentence)

High blood pressure can be avoided **with consistent daily exercise**. (prepositional phrase. Restrictive)

According to Cheryl Glenn, a feminist scholar and expert in the theory of rhetoric, these narratives have traditionally favoured men. (prepositional phrase followed by an appositive phrase that modifies Cheryl Glenn)

Building a Sentence

A good and enjoyable exercise that helps you learn how to use independent and dependent clauses, phrases, etc., is to look at sentence structure as a building project. Begin with a simple basic sentence. By the time you add a dependent clause, a phrase, restrictive, and non-restrictive modifiers, your sentence will be much more detailed and interesting. Pay attention to the following example. Additions to the combined following sentences are in bold italics.

Start with an independent clause/simple sentence: Susan wrote the test.

Add a phrase*: **Feeling terrified**, Susan wrote the test.

Add a restrictive modifier: Feeling terrified, Susan wrote the test **that she had not studied for**.

Add a non-restrictive modifier: Feeling terrified, Susan, **who had always been bad at English**, wrote the test that she had not studied for.

Add a dependent, coordinating conjunction clause: Feeling terrified, Susan, who had always been bad at English, wrote the test that she had not studied for, **and she passed it**.

Add a non-restrictive modifying phrase: Feeling terrified, Susan, who had always been bad at English, wrote the test that she had not studied for, and, **to her surprise**, she passed it.

SENTENCE BUILDING

Exercise 12.10

- Using the example above, pick a simple sentence at random, such as the one above (Susan wrote the test). Examples might include, She works as a model; he hit the ball; the dog howled, etc. When you have picked a sentence, build it in a way similar to the way I built the example above.

Continued

- Challenge yourself to make the sentence as long as you possibly can, using coordination, subordination, non-restrictive modifiers, phrases, etc. (using the appropriate punctuation of course). Keep in mind that the relationship between the components must be logical. In other words, it needs to make sense.
- Share your sentences with your classmates or friends. You might be surprised how much you enjoy this exercise. How useful do you think this exercise would be in helping you add sentence variety in your papers?

Exercise 12.11

REVIEW: IDENTIFYING SENTENCE STRUCTURES AND PUNCTUATING SENTENCES

1. Identify the phrases and the subordinate, coordinate, and non-restrictive modifier clauses in the following passage. Place commas where appropriate.

   When students complete a first draft, they consider the job of writing done. . . . When professional writers complete a first draft, they usually feel that they are at the start of the writing process. When a draft is completed, the job of writing can begin. . . . Most writers share the feeling that the first draft, and all of those which follow, [is an opportunity] to discover what they have to day and how best they can say it. (Murray 120).

2. Place commas where appropriate, so that the phrases, and the subordinate, coordinate, and relative pronoun clauses are clearly delineated.

   News is a high-status television genre. Its claimed objectivity and independence from political or government agencies is as many theorists would argue essential for the workings of democracy. Television companies who are in the process of applying for renewal of their licences use their news programs as evidence of their social responsibility. However news is also a commodity. It is expensive to gather and distribute and it must produce an audience of the right size. Although the national news is primarily masculine culture it often ends with a "softer" item that is intended for a female audience. The news more importantly is a discourse a set of conventions that strives to control and limit the meanings of events. Theories of news which foreground questions of accuracy bias and objectivity can provide insight into the ideology of the news makers. (Fiske, John. *Television Culture 87*)

See Exercise Answer Key in Appendix A for the answers to these questions.

Sentence Types

An awareness of the different types of sentences can function as another way of thinking about and practising how clauses, phrases, and their appropriate punctuation are used in a sentence. These types, illustrated by academic examples, are as follows:

The Simple Sentence

The simple sentence is a single independent clause. It has one subject and one verb or predicate; however, you need to remember that the sentence components might be compounded; that is, one simple sentence might have multiple or compound subjects, objects, and verbs.

Example: Robert and John washed and polished their new car.

Academic example: Rhetoric is the art of effective expression and communication

The Compound Sentence

The compound sentence contains at least two independent clauses (underlined).

Example: John, who was really frightened, ran to the house, but he was too late.

Academic example: Both women take issue with a hegemonic male-centred rhetoric, and they consider women's appropriate response to it.

The Complex Sentence

The compound sentence contains one independent clause and one or more dependent clauses (independent clauses are underlined; dependent clauses are bolded and italicized).

Example: The doll's house *that you gave Molly for her birthday* is broken.

Academic example: This model informs and supports a popular understanding of masculine power, *which attempts to make central rational, legal, and political language.*

The Compound-Complex Sentence

The compound-complex sentence has at least two independent clauses and one or more dependent clauses (independent clauses are underlined; dependent clauses are italicized).

Example: We spent the morning looking for the home of the woman *who paints landscapes*, but we were unable to find it.

Academic example: For Lorde, individual identities are formed through difference, and these differences are important *because they form an even more fundamental gender distinction* and *because they may allow us to bring about genuine change.*

Punctuation

As you have probably realized already, understanding how a sentence works will help you understand how to punctuate the sentence. Instead of seeing sentence structure and punctuation as two separate exercises, you will be able to understand punctuation through your ability to combine clauses and phrases in relation to the meaning you want to convey. Knowing how the rules of punctuation relate to and support your meaning is an essential first step. In other words, you can't break the rules—for example, mostly leaving punctuation out—before you thoroughly understand them.

Commas

Students seem to have the most problems with commas. Knowing how to punctuate clauses and phrases should fix any of your comma problems. As you should know now, commas are not used when you need "to take a breath," and they are not, like decorative flowers, sprinkled throughout your paragraphs as you feel necessary. Rather, their use conforms to strict rules of grammar. Once you know these rules, you can use commas more sparingly to help you create meaning.

Here, then, are the most important comma rules:

1. Use a comma after a short phrase or introductory word at the beginning of a longer sentence.

   > In a cosmopolitan culture, traditional attitudes and practices are interrogated.

   > Consequently, Fish argues that it is situation and the norms, the "purposes and goals" of institutions, that determine meaning.

2. Use a comma after a phrase or clause beginning with a subordinating conjunction IF the phrase or clause occurs at the beginning of the sentence (if the word occurs in the middle of the sentence, no comma is required). (For a list of subordinating conjunctions, see page 492.)

3. Don't join complete sentences with commas. This is called a comma splice.

   > ✗ She joined the sentences with commas, her instructor went crazy.

   > ✓ She joined the sentences with commas. Her instructor went crazy.

   > ✓ At first, she joined the sentences with commas; eventually, she learned to use a semicolon.

4. Place a comma <u>before</u> *and, but, nor, or, so,* and *yet* when they join two independent clauses.

> She joined the sentences with commas, and her instructor went crazy.

5. Use a comma in a list of items.

> He brought a toothbrush, a comb, and a razor.

6. Put commas around short modifying phrases in the middle of a sentence and before a short phrase before the end of a sentence.

> While Abrams stressed that there should be one meaning, Fish, in turn, argued for many meanings.

> She wanted a dog to protect her house, which was filled with expensive things.

7. Use commas with appositive constructions (<u>except</u> for reflexive pronouns):

> Mel Gibson himself autographed the book.

> Mel Gibson, an actor who has been in many films, autographed the book.

> The book, which was well written, documented Mel Gibson's life.

8. Do not add commas or other punctuation in the middle of a sentence's component parts. Never separate

   - the subject from the verb;
   - the direct object from the object complement (the object's modifying information);
   - the indirect object from the subject complement; or
   - the verb from the direct object.

Academic Context

I am often asked if it is correct to use the Oxford comma (also called the Harvard or serial comma), which is placed before *and* in a list of items. For example, *Regan argues for abolition of the use of animals in science, agriculture, and sport hunting.* I prefer to use the Oxford comma because it helps clarify meaning. For example, the sentence, "Thanks go to my parents, Sylvia and God" is ambiguous. It would seem that Sylvia and God are the person's parents. However, if the comma is placed after Sylvia, then we have a simple list. Neither way is completely wrong, but I suggest you ask your instructor, and make sure you are consistent with your usage of commas.

ACADEMIC FOCUS

THE TWO-MILLION-DOLLAR COMMA

For those of you who still doubt the importance of following comma rules, read this real-life example of a case where a missing comma resulted in enormous costs:

In August of 2006, Rogers Communications Inc. had to pay an extra $2.13 million to Aliant to use the utility poles in the Maritimes after the placement of a comma in a contract permitted the deal's cancellation.

Here is the disputed sentence:

"This agreement shall be effective from the date it is made and shall continue in force for a period of five years from the date it is made, and thereafter for successive five year terms, unless and until terminated by one year prior notice in writing by either party."

From Rogers's perspective, the contract is good for five years and is automatically renewed for successive five-year terms unless one-year notice is given. From the perspective of Aliant, the second comma in the non-restrictive clause (*and thereafter for successive five-year terms*) means that the clause is non-restrictive and, therefore, non-essential to the contract (it can be lifted out of the sentence without changing the meaning of the main contract). Aliant argued that conditions for cancelling the contract applied to the initial five-year term only. Despite the higher electricity rates, Rogers was locked in for another five years, which cost it two million dollars.

Exercise 12.12

The original passage is in the Exercise Answer Key in Appendix A, but please note that there is no one way to write this. You need to make sure that your meaning is clear and your comma use is grammatically correct.

COMBINING SIMPLE SENTENCES

Use coordinate and subordinate clauses to make this string of simple sentences more readable and understandable. In order to do this, you can

- Add or delete words (but do not change the meaning).
- Make lists.
- Use coordinating conjunctions, semicolons, and subjunctive adverbs or subordinating conjunctions.

Communication is essential to science. Undergraduate and graduate students are apprentices. They are apprentices to the discipline of science. Learning to communicate in writing is important. It is important for scholars to write about their research. The publication of scientific results is most important. They must submit them to public scrutiny. They must distribute them widely. They must strive for excellence at all stages of the research and writing process. Students need guidance to learn how to meet the standards of scholarly research and writing.

Colons

The colon is used to introduce a quote or point, defining or adding to what comes before, always moving from the general to the specific. The colon is always preceeded by an independent clause (subject and predicate); it can be followed by an independent or dependent clause, a phrase, a quote, or even a list.

Here is the pattern:

> independent clause/general statement + colon + specific example
> (independent clause: dependent clause with phrase, list, quote)

Pay attention to the following examples:

Many pets are quite small: cats, mice, and iguanas. (independent clause + colon + list with commas)

Shakespeare uses figurative language to develop his characters: "Love all, trust a few, do wrong to none." (to introduce a quote: independent clause + colon + quote in quotation marks)

Lorde's autobiographical writing suggests that we are all responsible for change: women must transform language into action, and men must listen more to women's needs. (independent clause + colon + independent clause + independent clause)

Semicolons

The semicolon separates elements of equal importance, joining independent clauses of the same length and grammatical structure. Semicolon use follows strict grammatical rules: do not use semicolons as if they are commas.

Here is the pattern (see coordinating conjunctions and diagram of semicolon use earlier in this chapter):

> independent clause + semicolon + independent clause
>
> or
>
> independent clause + semicolon + adverbial conjunction + comma + independent clause

Here are some examples:

"Ask not what your country can do for you; ask what you can do for your country" (Kennedy). (independent clause + semicolon + independent clause)

Booth's essay was interesting; however, it was hard to understand. (independent clause + semicolon + adverbial conjunction + comma + independent clause)

Colons, Commas, Semicolons, and Lists

Colons and commas or semicolons are often used together to give order to a list of items:

> This model is important for two reasons: (a) because it suggests another mode of communication, and (b) because this form of rhetoric privileges the reader.

Commas can be replaced with semicolons in a complex list when using commas would confuse the meaning.

> The high school reunion attracted a wide variety of people: Mai, who loves to party; Samantha, who loves to study; and Dave, who loves to sleep.

Dashes

Dashes indicate an interruption in a train of thought or an interruption in the structure of the sentence. In academic writing dashes come in pairs. They create an air of informality and so should be used sparingly in formal writing. Use the dash for the following purposes:

1. To set off abrupt shifts in thought and non-essential material.

> Michel Foucault's theory of biopolitics—the theory that suggests the manipulation of life and material practices are at the base of modern power politics—has transformed the way we think about hegemonic power relations.

2. To set off a list when it comes in the middle of a sentence.

> She established her goals in life—to become a vet, to go to graduate school at a university, and to travel the world—before she was sixteen.

N.B. When the list comes at the end of a sentence, use a colon.

> Before she was sixteen, she had established her goals in life: to become a vet, to go to graduate school at a university, and to travel the world.

Remember that your choice of sentence structure will depend upon what meaning you want to create and what words or ideas you want to emphasize. (In the above example, that would be the fact that she established her goals or the goals themselves.)

Parenthesis

Parenthesis allows writers to interrupt a sentence's structure to add additional information. Parentheses function like dashes; however, unlike dashes—which tend to make interruptions stand out—parentheses tend to de-emphasize what they enclose. Use parentheses sparingly because their overuse can be distracting.

Postmodernism (a twentieth-century movement) constitutes an attempt to understand a world threatened by nuclear war, the environmental destruction of the planet, and rampant capitalism.

Although other cities (Dresden, for instance) had been destroyed in World War II, never before had a single weapon been responsible for such destruction.

ACADEMIC FOCUS

A COMPARISON OF NON-RESTRICTIVE ELEMENTS: DASHES, COMMAS, AND PARENTHESES

Dashes: Many scientists—*especially those concerned about global warming*—will attend the Kyoto Conference. (most emphatic)

Commas: Many scientists, *including biologists and physicists,* are concerned about global warming. (less emphatic)

Parentheses: The Kyoto Accord *(signed in Japan in 1977)* is controversial.

Remember that a restrictive or essential phrase or clause (material that cannot be deleted without changing the meaning of the sentence) does not use the above punctuation.

Example: Scientists who are concerned about global warming recommend more research in this area.

Ten Common Errors

So far, this chapter has dealt with sentence structure, which includes basic sentence punctuation. If you learn how to write a grammatically correct sentence, most of your errors will disappear. However, if you have picked up some bad writing habits (and we all do), then you will need to identify your particular errors and fix them. What follows is a freewriting exercise that will help you identify your errors, and a list of ten common errors, an explanation of what they are, and suggestions for how to fix them. Here are the most common student errors:

1. sentence fragments
2. comma splices
3. run-on or fused sentences

4. mixed constructions
5. dangling, misplaced, and limiting modifiers
6. subject–verb agreement
7. pronoun–antecedent agreement
8. tense shifts
9. apostrophe errors
10. comma, semicolon, and colon use

Exercise 12.13

GRAMMAR ERROR FREEWRITE

Follow the sentence starter and write for five minutes non-stop without thinking too much, in a stream of consciousness style. Here is the sentence starter:

What worries me most about my own writing is . . .

- When you have written for five minutes, stop and read through what you have written, paying careful attention to your sentence structure. If you have read the sentence structure part of this chapter carefully, you should be able to identify where your sentence structure is not as it should be—even if it is not completely clear to you.
- Underline the areas that seem like particular problems for you, and refer back to them as you read about common errors.
- See if you can pick out the error(s) that you might have made in the freewriting exercise. If you can, you might want to try to fix it. Most people constantly misuse one particular error or another, so once you have identified an error you have made, you will need to watch for it in your other writing assignments, particularly in the editing stage.

Here are the ten most common errors.

1. SENTENCE FRAGMENTS

A sentence fragment occurs when a portion of a sentence is punctuated as if it is a complete sentence. There is either a missing subject or a missing verb; sometimes the writer mistakes a dependent clause for a complete sentence.

Fragment: John to the store. (missing verb)

Revised: John **walked** to the store.

Fragment: walked to the store. (missing subject)

Revised: **John** walked to the store.

Fragment: John walked to the store because. (dependent clause with subordinating conjunction)

Revised: John walked to the store because **he needed to buy groceries**.

2. COMMA SPLICES

A comma splice happens when the writer joins two independent clauses with a comma.

She loved to write, she took a writing course.

3. RUN-ON SENTENCES

Run-on sentences (also called *fused sentences*) occur when there is *no punctuation* between two independent clauses.

She loved to write she took a writing course.

There are three ways to fix a comma splice and/or a run-on sentence:

1. Use a period to separate the independent clauses:

   She loved to write. She took a writing course.

2. Use a semicolon:

   She loved to write; she took a writing course.

3. Use a comma, and a coordinating conjunction:

   She loved to write, **so** she took a writing course.

4. MIXED CONSTRUCTIONS

A mixed construction starts in one direction with a particular structure but, confusingly, goes off in a different direction, shifting to a different structure. These are probably the most difficult errors to fix because there is no specific rule to fix them. To revise these errors, be clear about what you want to say. Identifying your main idea in the sentence and then eliminating wordy constructions or any unnecessary or superfluous words or ideas will help you fix this problem.

Example: By learning how to fix my grammar errors, will give me better grades.

Revised: Learning how to fix my grammar errors will give me better grades. (This sentence begins with a prepositional phrase, but there is no subject or person doing the fixing here. Removing the preposition is an easy solution here.)

Example: Because the grammar errors that the instructor wants me to correct or sentence structure will make me a better writer. (The problem here occurs, in part, because the subordinate clause (beginning with "because") needs a subject to complete it; in part, the writer is simply not clear about what he or she is trying to say.)

Revised: The instructor pointed out that correcting my grammar or sentence structure errors will make me a better writer.

5. DANGLING MODIFIERS

A dangling modifier does not sensibly modify the subject or noun it is related to in the sentence. Fix this error by making sure that you follow the modifying phrase or clause directly by the subject that it is intended to modify.

Example: Walking down the street, the houses became visible.

The modifying phrase seems to describe houses, but houses do not walk down the street. We need to know who was walking down the street. Who saw the houses?

Revised: Walking down the street, she saw the houses.

Example: After spending hours writing my essay, the instructor gave me a failing mark. (The instructor didn't write the essay: who did?)

Revised: After spending hours writing my essay, *I* was disappointed when my instructor gave me a failing mark.

Revised: The instructor gave me a failing mark on my essay even though I had spent hours writing it. (revision using a subordinate clause)

Misplaced modifiers. A misplaced modifier falls in the wrong place in a sentence. Readers tend to link a modifier to the nearest word it could modify. If the modifier does not clearly refer to the correct antecedent, it is a misplaced modifier. Fix this error by moving the misplaced modifier closer to the word it is modifying.

Example: The actress was photographed with her boyfriend in a blue bikini.

Revised: The actress, who wore a blue bikini, was photographed with her boyfriend. (It is the actress who wore the blue bikini, not her boyfriend).

Example: He said it was going to snow on the news today.

Revised: The news reporter said it was going to snow today.

Limiting modifiers. A limiting modifier, such as *almost, even, always, exactly, hardly, just, merely, nearly, only,* and *simply,* must be placed immediately before the word or word group that it is intended to limit. Placing the modifier in the wrong place changes the meaning of the sentence. In the first example below, the writer wants to articulate that they had been married almost ten years. In the first example, the modifying word, *almost,* does not modify the years but states that they were *almost married.*

Example: They were **almost** married ten years.

Revised: They were married **almost** ten years.

Example: I am **only** buying organic meat from now on.

Revised: I am buying **only** organic meat from now on.

6. SUBJECT–VERB AGREEMENT

Subjects and their related verbs should agree in number. This means that singular subjects take singular verbs and plural subjects take plural verbs.

Consider the following sentences:

Students enjoy writing papers. (plural)

The teacher enjoys marking them. (singular)

Keep the following hints in mind when proofreading your papers:

- Do not be misled by words or phrases intervening between the *subject* and the *verb.*

     The **repetition** of the vowels *helps* to stir emotion. (Repetition is the subject here, not vowels, which simply tell us what kind of repetition this is.)

- As a rule, the subject (whether it is singular or plural) is not changed by the addition of expressions beginning with words or phrases, such as *accompanied by, along with, as well as, in addition to, including, no less than.*

     Individual counselling **as well as** group discussions helps the recovery process.

In the above example there is still only one subject—individual counselling—so the sentence would read as follows: individual counselling *helps* the recovery process. You might include the point about group discussions in a variety of ways. For example, you could use terms such as *along with* or *as well as,* as in the above example or you could add another sentence that makes a point about group discussions. If you wanted to make group discussions and individual counselling of equal importance, you could use *and*: individual counselling *and* group discussions *help* the recovery process. Please note that if you do this, you now have two subjects (individual counselling and group discussions) and the verb is now plural and becomes *help* instead of *helps*.

- Subjects joined by "and" are usually plural.

  My mother and father **do** not understand.

  Exception: Occasionally, a compound subject takes a singular verb because the subject denotes one person or a single unit.

- Indefinite pronouns, such as *everyone, everybody, all*, or *each*, call for a singular verb.

  Everyone **is** going to the game.

  All **was** lost.

7. PRONOUN AGREEMENT (ANTECEDENT OR REFERENT PROBLEMS)

Pronouns have to agree in number and gender with the nouns (sometimes called antecedents or referents) they represent or refer to. If there is a pronoun in a sentence, it must refer directly back to the noun it is modifying. This can result in a dangling modifier error.

Example: While **Susan**, like other anorexics, realizes that anorexia is dangerous, **they find** it hard to recover.

Revised: While **Susan**, like other anorexics, realizes that anorexia is dangerous, **she finds** it hard to recover.

N.B. Please note that when the pronoun changes (*they* and *she* in the above example), the corresponding verb will also change (*find* and *finds*).

Example: Every company has **their** own way of interviewing new applicants.

Revised: Every company has **its** own way of interviewing new applicants.

8. TENSE SHIFTS

Do not shift verb tenses (moving from past to present, for example) as you write unless you intend to change the time of the action.

Example: I **asked** (past tense) her to go to the party, and she **says** (present tense) yes.

Revised: I **asked** (past tense) her to go to the party, and she **said** (past tense) yes.

Change tenses only if you are changing the logical time of the verb's action:

> The students **had worked** (past-perfect tense) on their papers all night long because their assignments **were** (past tense) due the following morning. (The first action occurred before the second one.)

See the charts on tense earlier in the chapter.

9. APOSTROPHE MISUSE

Apostrophes appear to be an increasing problem with first-year university students. The rules for apostrophe use, however, are quite simple. The apostrophes that we are mostly concerned with in academic writing are those that are used to indicate possession.

Apostrophes in the possessive case signal that one noun possesses another.

> Susan's dog = the dog that belongs to Susan (singular possessive: apostrophe goes before the *s*)

> Students' concerns = the concerns that belong to the students (plural possessive: the apostrophe goes after the *s*)

Specific placements. The following specific variations often confuse students, but, once again, the rules are relatively simple. Consciously correct your apostrophe use in your final edit, especially if you have identified it as a problem.

- Add –'s to a singular nouns that end with *s*.

  > Oliver Sacks's book *The Awakenings* was made into a film.

- Some singular nouns ending in an an *s* or a sound are hard to pronounce with an additional *s* sound on the end. There is no firm usage rule in this case, but the additional possessive *s* is sometimes omitted.

  > **Moses's** commandments have become central to the religious life.

  > The **dress's** waistline was too low for her body type.

- Collective nouns usually operate as singular nouns.

  > The **Navy's** ships were docked in the bay.

- If two or more nouns possess something, only the last noun in the list gets the apostrophe.

  > The party was at **John and Ashley's house**. (John and Ashley shared the house.)

- If the two nouns possess separate things, however, they each take an apostrophe.

  We'll go to the party in ***David's and George's cars***. (They are taking two cars: one car belongs to David, and one car belongs to George.)

- In hyphenated words, only the last word takes an apostrophe.

  She wanted a ride in ***my brother-in-law's car***.

- The its/it's error is probably the most common apostrophe error. The word *its*, as opposed to the contraction *it's (it is)*, is a possessive adjective and does not need an apostrophe.

  The dog buried ***its*** bone. (If you use an apostrophe here, as in *it's*, the sentence would read "the dog buried it is bone," which obviously doesn't make sense.

N.B. An apostrophe is also used for contractions, which indicates the omission of a letter or letters in *wouldn't* for *would not*; *can't* for *cannot*; *we'd* for *we would*.

You do not have to worry about mixing these up with possessive apostrophe use because academic writing *does not* use contractions.

10. COMMA, SEMICOLON, AND COLON CONFUSION

These punctuation marks are not interchangeable. They each have a specific role or purpose to play in your writing. Explanations for the semicolon and colon were presented in the sentence structure part of this chapter. To reiterate:

- Use a semicolon to join main clauses when the ideas are closely related and there is no coordinating conjunction (*and, but, for, or, nor, so, yet*) to join the clauses.

  John was an idealist; Susan was a pragmatist.

- Use a semicolon to join two clauses when the second clause begins with a conjunctive adverb (*therefore, thus, hence, furthermore, moreover, however*, etc.)

  The semicolon is an important punctuation mark; however, it is often mistakenly used as a comma or a colon.

- Do *not* use a semicolon to join a main clause and a subordinate clause.

  ✗ The restaurant switched to Fair Trade coffee; because the manager knew that customers would buy it. (Check the rules for subordinating sentences: no punctuation, not even a comma, is needed here.)

- Do *not* use a semicolon as if it is a colon.

  ✕ She went to the store to buy groceries; eggs, milk, bacon, and hashbrowns. (Use a colon here instead.)

- Use a colon to indicate that what follows is a more specific example of what has already been generally stated. The items following the colon should be grammatically parallel.

  There are many different types of fruits: apples, oranges, and pears.

  Car manufacturers have introduced several improvements: better restraint systems, better pollution-controlling devices, and better rust-proofing.

- Use a colon to introduce a phrase or clause that explains the preceding statement.

  She wanted only one outcome in the course: to get an A.

- Use a colon to introduce a quotation. Both the quotation and the sentence that introduces it must be grammatically complete.

  In 1947, E.B. White wrote a letter to *The New York Herald Tribune* objecting to the US government's oppression of individual freedom of expression: "It is not a crime to believe anything at all in America" (835).

- Do not use a colon when the list begins with *such as* or *for example*.

  ✕ Car manufacturers have introduced several improvements: such as better restraint systems, better pollution controlling devices, and better rust-proofing. (Use a comma here instead.)

ASSESSING YOUR WRITING

Exercise 12.14

Now that you have considered the most common student errors, take another look at your freewrite. Can you identify your particular error now?

When you have done this, find some of your old marked writing assignments, and see what error or errors your instructor or high school teacher highlighted for your attention. Was it the same error that you noticed in your freewrite? If you had fewer errors in your freewrite, you might be second-guessing your choices when writing in a more formal situation, especially when marks are at stake.

Identifying the errors you make consistently and using the rules in this chapter to fix them is essential to your academic writing success.

Editing Strategies

You will correct your errors most effectively when you actively edit your work with these errors in mind. Here are some strategies for editing your work:

1. Put your particular error or errors and the rules associated with them on a sticky note beside your computer and refer to it regularly when you edit.
2. Go through your entire paper looking specifically for and editing your particular grammatical errors.
3. Create distance by using the following strategies:
   - Leave yourself enough time to be able to put your work aside for a day or so. When you come back to it, you will be able to see errors that were seemingly invisible before.
   - Read your work out loud, slowly, listening to what you are actually arguing (when you stumble, you have probably made a grammatical error).
   - Read your essay to a friend who will tell you truthfully when she doesn't follow your argument. This is particularly useful if your error is using mixed constructions.
   - Above all, remember that learning the rules and how they apply to your own writing will help you become a better, more accomplished, writer.

Exercise 12.15

GRAMMAR POST-TEST

Complete the following post-test. Remember or refer to the rules of basic grammar, and remember that there is no one acceptable solution (you always have the choice, for example, to use coordination or subordination, use a relative pronoun, etc.). When you have finished, compare your results with your understanding of grammar in the pretest. Do you have a better understanding of how you might use grammar now to improve your writing so that your meaning and emphasis are clearer? As you probably now realize, clarity of meaning is the ultimate purpose of grammar.

1. Combine the following sentences, using coordinate or subordinate clauses, to make one sentence:

   Language is both arbitrary and fixed. It resists at the same time as it conforms to the dominant societal conventions, rules, and traditions.

   Emily Brontë distances her readers from Lockwood. She emphasizes his superficial and hypocritical actions.

   Schryer is concerned with the competing genres in veterinary institutions. She is not concerned with animal rights.

2. Combine or rearrange the following sentences with the use of an appropriate relative pronoun:

Non-Native Canadians must assist in decolonization. Decolonization is good for all Canadians.

Tricia Rose is the author of *Black Noise*. This is perhaps the most important study of rap music.

Coyle works for a market research firm. She asks if direct-to-consumer advertising is ethical given how it broadens the domain of medicine.

3. Correct the following comma splice, run-on, or sentence fragment errors:

The word *accommodate* is often misspelled remember to use the two c's and the two m's.

When I sat down. She stood up.

Knowledge about disability is socially produced, this knowledge upholds existing practices.

The AIDS pandemic has been addressed; by gay organizations they attempt to address the extreme homophobia around the disease.

4. Fix the following subject–verb agreement errors by choosing one of the verbs in parenthesis.

Kinga and Auren (discuss / discusses) their favourite issues.

The teacher, along with her students, (hope / hopes) to make the trip.

The action of the supervisor (was / were) deemed inappropriate.

The reading club along with the writing club (is / are) growing by the hour.

5. Correct the following subject–verb agreement errors:

Woolf encourage her readers to identify with women's position in a male-dominated culture.

Smith along with Johnson and Coombes argue that the far north must be protected.

Continued

In "The Politics of the English Language," Orwell equate bad writing with poor thinking. He points out that everyone are responsible for correcting this problem.

Lee Maracle, writing on behalf of all native writers, object to the appropriation of native stories.

6. Correct the following pronoun/antecedent agreement errors by choosing one of the pronouns in parenthesis:

   In Israel, everyone must do (his or her / their) army duty.

   Joan was worried that someone had not received (his or her / their) invitation.

   Each one of us had to present (his or her / their) piece of ID at the door.

7. Correct the following pronoun/antecedent agreement errors by making the ambiguous reference clear:

   In "The Goods on the Tube," Mark Kingwell points out that TV fans feel embarrassed about his or her love of superficial shows.

   Today, primary oral cultures in a strict sense hardly exist since it is immersed in dominant literary cultures.

8. Rewrite the following sentences to eliminate the misplaced, limiting, and dangling modifiers:

   That summer, Roxanne almost went swimming every day.

   I jumped out of bed as the radio alarm went off in my bare feet.

   Last week, I found a box containing an old health care card, which was made of beautifully carved mahogany.

   Nostrils flaring, I watched the wild black stallion speed away.

   Knowing that it is important to respect the language of indigenous people, is not the same as actually practising it in everyday life, Johnston insists.

   Writing from Birmingham Jail, the impassioned use of rhetoric is used by King to invoke the moral conscience of the nation.

9. Correct the verb tense errors in the following passage:

Alice Walker was born in 1944. She was the eighth and youngest child of Willie Lee and Minnie Grant Walker who were sharecroppers in Eatonton, Georgia. Walker did well in school, encouraged by her teachers and her mother, who loves her stories. For two years, Walker attended Spelman College, then she studies at Sarah Lawrence College, where she began her writing career and becomes active in the civil rights movement. Today, she is one of the best-known fiction writers in the world.

10. Fix the following common grammar and punctuation errors. Please note that these errors might include agreement (subject–verb, pronoun-antecedent), comma splice, fragments, run-ons, dangling modifier errors, mixed constructions, colon and semicolon errors, or errors in verb tense:

Jogging down the street in a blue suit, the truck came out of nowhere and almost hit me.

Fukuyama, Kass, and their allies has the president's ear.

Each of the languages has idioms of their own.

The customer asked the pharmacist for the prescription, but the pharmacist tells the customer that the ingredients had been ordered.

In any non-violent campaign; there are three basic steps such as: negotiation, self-purification, and direct action.

The students bought books; papers; and printer cartridges.

The travel agent's advice proved correct, Amsterdam was an entertaining city.

11. Edit the following student paragraph, fixing the common errors and the punctuation errors so that the paragraph makes better sense.

The Camel Cigarette Company relies on marketing a "Western Lifestyle" to sell it's cigarettes. The "Western Lifestyle" that Camel portrays. That of "freedom, integrity and self-sufficiency" is at the centre of Camels marketing scheme. The "Camel Filter" advertisement depicts a rugged hard-working man, he is smoking a refreshing "Camel Filter" in the wilderness. It is a prime example of the marketing ploys that Camel effectively utilize to sell its cigarettes. Many people agrees that tobacco smoking is a deadly habit, and that tobacco companies, including Camel gain prosperity at the expense of its dying patrons. Acknowledging this, Camel is effective in selling the appearance of rugged individualism, healthy masculinity and upholding the "American Dream" of freedom integrity and self-sufficiency however it also sacrifices ethics for corporate gain.

See the Exercise Answer Key in Appendix A for possible answers to these questions. Can you see an improvement in your grammar skills? Have you been able to identify your particular grammar error(s)? Do you feel you now have the ability to fix your error(s)?

CHAPTER SUMMARY

This chapter has introduced you to the basic rules of grammar and punctuation. I have argued that, first, you need to be aware of the parts of speech and how they function grammatically in a sentence, specifically in an academic sentence. Second, I have presented you with ten of the most common student errors and encouraged you to figure out which errors you make in your own work. By identifying the errors that you make, you should be better able to correct them and work toward being a better, more accomplished academic writer.

QUESTIONS FOR CONSIDERATION

1. What are the parts of speech, and how do they function in a sentence?
2. What is a sentence? How is it constructed?
3. Do I know what my particular grammar error or errors are?
4. Do I feel comfortable and confident that I will be able to fix them?
5. What strategies do I intend to use to help me with this process of editing my grammar errors?
6. What do I still need to work on to refine my grammar skills?
7. What do I still not understand about these grammar basics?

Style

LEARNING OBJECTIVES

In this chapter, you will learn:

- The importance of the word and language in spoken or written communication.

- The difference between learning the rules of grammar and using language and sentence structure to support and emphasize meaning or your main argument.

- How to use grammar persuasively (rhetorically).

- Strategies for developing your own voice.

- How style supports and enhances content and structure.

- How style appears in qualitative and quantitative research.

Once you have learned the basic rules of grammar, you are ready to expand your skills and start using grammar and sentence structure to enhance your meaning. As previously stated, choice is essential to the construction of meaning. In making these choices, you will develop your own style of writing, your own particular way of using language to make sense and meaning of the world. To begin with, though, let's revisit what a sentence is, beginning with its most basic component: the word.

When we look at the world in which we live, we can see that the word is far from neutral. The word can make us buy hamburgers, cars, makeup, books, holidays, insurance policies, and televisions; it can also make us believe certain philosophies and political perspectives (communism, democracy, capitalism, etc.) or conform to or rebel against certain persuasive or didactic programs. Just as eighteenth-century romantic poets used the words in their poetry to help us believe in beauty and love, Hitler used words and propaganda to convince millions of people that "Aryans" were a superior master race that deemed Jewish people inferior.

Ideally, the academic word is the objective word; it, too, creates reality by transforming the way we think and act, but it also suggests that the speaker's or writer's argument is a fair and just one. It does not attempt to manipulate or move you emotionally but uses your rational faculty to consider the existing argument. Academic writing also assumes that the relationship with a reader or audience will be reflective and the arguments themselves consistently open to revision. These arguments, and the knowledge contained in them, are indeed constrained by the present context: how the relevant words, ideas, sentences, and arguments have been reconfigured through time, across geographical and psychological space, and in relation to other academic work.

What Is a Sentence: Revisited

As we have seen, a sentence is simply a group of words organized according to rules that help create meaning. These rules require that there be a subject and a predicate, and also perhaps a cluster of simple and compound-complex clauses and phrases, punctuated according to convention. If you understand how these components fit together, like a jigsaw, you should be able to avoid grammatical errors.

However, a sentence is far more than the words or the rules that dictate its use. It is also far more than a means to an end: more than a necessary rule-bound construction that helps you convey to your instructor, your business manager, or the general public what you want to say. The sentence is, as Stanley Fish argues, "nothing less than lessons and practice in the organization of the world." Sentences and the language they use cannot be divorced from real-world contexts: they are the central or primary matter in how we construct the world around us.

Sentences must be organized logically according to what you want to communicate. To do this well, you must get a feel for your sentences, for the words and the rhythm. And you must do this in a way that does not draw attention to you, but, rather, emphasizes your knowledge and what you have to say about it. We, your readers, must trust you to take us on this argumentative journey, sentence by sentence, to your logical conclusion, and we must say, at the end of it, that we believe what you have to say, that your argument is effective and persuasive.

Bearing Witness to Good Sentences

As Stanley Fish noted in *How to Write a Sentence*, the ability to appreciate and create a good sentence are acquired "in tandem" (8). In other words, reading and listening to good sentences somehow transforms you as a person into a writer of good sentences. The key word here, though, is "acquired." Learning how to write well does not automatically happen: you have to be prepared to read, listen, and pay attention to how language works in your own reading and writing practices.

To this end, I have titled this section "Bearing Witness to Good Sentences" because reading good sentences is a kind of bearing witness to the good writing that is in them. According to this conception then, witnessing is not simply seeing the sentence but listening to and experiencing the nuances and the silence (the silence a comma makes, for example) present in the language of the sentence. When you see a sentence in this way, you will *attest* to the true meaning, the essence of what the writer is trying to convey. In witnessing the sentence, the reader is transformed and begins to know, and to feel, his or her own relationship with language and thus his or her own voice.

FOUND SENTENCES

Exercise 13.1

- Keep a journal of sentences you find and enjoy. These *found* sentences will not only help you to be more aware of how language is used but also help you to use sentences, and language in general, more consciously and more effectively in your own writing.
- You might want to cover your journal and title it to make it personal. You might also want to organize your journal into sections that explore different genres of creative writing (short story, poetry, autobiography, etc.), journalistic writing, Shakespeare, humour, science, marketing, or academic writing, etc., unless, of course, you already know your preferred discipline and want to focus on that.
- Use these sentences as models for future use. At the very least, bear witness to these sentences: write briefly why you like them: how they relate to the content and how they create rhythm or emphasis. This can be particularly useful for academic sentences, which rely heavily on the logical relationship between clauses and sentences. Look back on these sentences intermittently to see how your own appreciation for and skill in reading—and writing—sentences is improving.
- Write a separate journal or include a section on *how not to write* sentences, keeping a record of some of the worst sentences you have ever read. These sentences could include pretentious, bureaucratic language, or overt marketing slogans, but many of your examples may simply be examples of bad grammar. Identifying grammar errors in this writing, such as sentence fragments or modifier errors, will strengthen your ability to recognize errors in your own writing.
- Refer back to your journal frequently. It will help immerse you in the sound and feel of good (and bad) language and help you to know the difference.

To give you a feel for some of the sentences you might include in your journal, as well as presenting you with a model for analyzing these sentences, some examples of creative, literary, and academic sentences you should *not* want to write, followed by examples of sentences you possibly *would* want to write are listed below. I have also analyzed briefly why these sentences can be considered good or bad.

Ouch, or the How Not to Write Examples

1. The first example was written for the 2012 Bulwer-Lytton Fiction Contest by Cathy Bryant. The challenge was to write "the worst opening of an imaginary novel."

> As he told her that he loved her she gazed into his eyes, wondering, as she noted the infestation of eyelash mites, the tiny deodicids burrowing into his follicles to eat the greasy sebum therein, each female laying up to 25 eggs in a single follicle, causing inflammation, whether the eyes are truly the windows of the soul; and, if so, his soul needed regrouting.

It is the juxtaposition of the language of science and the language of love (and building) that makes this long opening sentence funny. The lesson here is focus: there is a time and a place for outlining the social and medical facts pertaining to eyelash mites if, of course, you feel the need to highlight them at all. You don't have to provide all the facts: some information should not be communicated.

2. Rodney Reed, the 2011 runner-up in this competition, also provides humour in his anti-climactic finish to the following sentence:

> As I stood among the ransacked ruin that had been my home, surveying the aftermath of the senseless horrors and atrocities that had been perpetrated on my family and everything I hold dear, I swore to myself that no matter where I had to go, no matter what I had to do or endure, I would find the man who did this . . . and when I did, when I did, oh, there would be words.

Taken out of context, this sentence could be critiqued for its vague use of words—"senseless horrors and atrocities" that do not give a clear picture of what happened. It does, however, reveal the person's character in an amusing way by creating a sense of suspense and then undercutting it with a weak final response. The success of this piece would depend on whether you wanted your reader to laugh at this point or not.

3. This sentence, written by *New York Times* journalist Jackie Calmes, was highlighted by Megan McArdle in an article in *The Atlantic* (2009):

> And as his aspiration of putting aside petty politics has met the necessity of winning legislative votes—no more than two or three Senate Republicans are expected to support him, which is two or three more than did so in the House—he has gone through a public evolution that has left him showing sharper edges when it comes to the ways of Washington. (Calmes 2009)

Although if you break this sentence up, it is grammatically correct, the long non-restrictive dash clause in the middle of the sentence provides information that seems to take us in another direction. The meaning shifts from a focus on the development of the politician to a focus on who in the Senate is supporting him. There is no clear connection between these two different perspectives. Also, vague clichéd phrases, such as *petty politics, public evolution*, and *sharper edges*, do not help this sentence.

4. Here are several rather wordy, confusing, and, in Orwell's terms, pretentious academic sentences. They are both taken from Denis Dutton's *Philosophy and Literature* Bad Writing Contest:

> The move from a structuralist account in which capital is understood to structure social relations in relatively homologous ways to a view of hegemony in which power relations are subject to repetition, convergence, and rearticulation brought the question of temporality into the thinking of structure, and marked a shift from a form of Althusserian theory that takes structural totalities as theoretical objects to one in which the insights into the contingent possibility of structure inaugurate a renewed conception of hegemony as bound up with the contingent sites and strategies of the rearticulation of power. (Butler 13)

> If, for a while, the ruse of desire is calculable for the uses of discipline soon the repetition of guilt, justification, pseudo-scientific theories, superstition, spurious authorities, and classifications can be seen as the desperate effort to "normalize" *formally* the disturbance of a discourse of splitting that violates the rational, enlightened claims of its enunciatory modality. (Bhaba 130–1)

Although these sentences, written by leading academics, are taken out of context, they are undoubtedly difficult. We could say that the complexity of their writing reflects the complexity of their ideas and concepts; however, regardless of how famous you are in the academic world, good writing *is* clear writing. As a word of warning, do not try and write like some of the theorists you might read in your classes.

WOW, or the Want to Write Like That Examples

I have kept a journal for many years now, and I still refer back to it for inspiration. Here are examples of two of my favourite sentences, along with explanations as to why.

> (1) It was a queer, sultry summer, the summer they electrocuted the Rosenbergs, and I didn't know what I was doing in New York.

This sentence opens Sylvia Plath's *The Bell Jar*. Using a non-restrictive modifier about an electrocution at the centre of the sentence, halfway between a "queer" summer and the narrator's sense of feeling lost or discombobulated not only foreshadows her own breakdown and suicidal behaviour but also demonstrates how much work a single sentence can perform. I love, too, how the "sultry" rhythm of this sentence increasingly breaks down until we, as readers, are able to identify with the emotion Sylvia Plath is attempting to create.

> (2) Often Miss Stein would have no guests and she was always very friendly and for a long time she was affectionate.

This sentence was taken from Ernest Hemingway's *A Moveable Feast*. It consists of three independent clauses—Miss Stein would have no guests; she was always very friendly; she was affectionate—joined by the coordinating conjunction *and*. In this way, the sentence constitutes a simple list, telling us three things about Miss Stein.

However, notice that Hemingway has left out the prerequisite commas that would have separated and delineated Miss Stein's characteristics. He thus forces the reader to pay careful attention to each feature. In omitting the commas, Hemingway increases the speed of the action and makes us see Miss Stein more holistically: she is all of these things, all at once. However, the modifying word *often* at the beginning of the sentence and the prepositional phrase *for a long time* provide the reader with a sense of doubt, implying that Miss Stein did indeed change her attitude and behaviour. I love this sentence because it says so much in such a short space.

> (3) So we beat on, boats against the current, borne back ceaselessly into the past.

This sentence comes from F. Scott Fitzgerald's *The Great Gatsby*. It is the last sentence in the novel. I like it because the use of the coordinating conjunction *so* forces us to think about what came before (the novel up to this point). Paradoxically, there is no ending here because "we beat on, . . . ceaselessly"; however, the movement is deceptive: it is not forward, but backwards into the past. The use of the pronoun *we* also forces us to identify with the narrator while also reflecting on our own past and present lives.

In contrast to the convoluted academic writing seen in the "ouch" comparison of writing styles, consider the following academic sentence, written by Michel Foucault, another academic heavyweight:

> (4) I don't claim at all that the State apparatus is unimportant, but it seems to me that among all the conditions for avoiding a repetition of the Soviet experience and preventing the revolutionary process from running into the ground, one of the first things that has to be understood is that power isn't localized in the State apparatus and that nothing in society will be changed if the mechanisms of power that function outside below and alongside the State apparatuses, on a much more minute and everyday level, are not also changed. ("Body/Power" Foucault 60)

While this sentence is very long, and while the ideas are quite complex, it is relatively easy to follow if you break it down according to the information contained within the major comma breaks and the less important non-restrictive modifying clauses. Moreover, Foucault's voice is not lost in the abstractions but, rather, firmly rooted in his thinking process ("it seems"). Consequently, we trust this writer.

The following excerpt, containing two academic sentences, is also an example of good (i.e., clearly written) academic writing.

> (5) The history of industrialization has always been a continuing struggle (which today takes an even more marked and vigorous form) against the element of "animality" in man. It has been an uninterrupted, often painful and bloody process of subjugating natural (i.e. animal and primitive) instincts to new, more complex and rigid norms and habits of order, exactitude and precision which can make possible the increasingly complex forms of collective life which are the necessary consequence of industrial development. (Gramsci 286)

Even though this is a short excerpt, these sentences clearly articulate Antonio Gramsci's argument. The shorter first sentence states that industrialization has struggled against the animal-like aspects of man. The second sentence provides more specific detail concerning the way in which man's animal nature has been subjugated. It is also a good example of sentence variety.

IMITATION

Exercise 13.2

- Find a paragraph that appeals to you: it might appeal because of the topic, the language, or the concepts contained in it, or it might appeal because of the genre. For example, if you are interested in writing a novel, you might pick a paragraph that deals specifically with character development or setting. Alternatively, you might pick a particularly difficult academic paragraph—similar to the ones above written by Homi Bhaba and Judith Butler—and work to figure out the logical development of the concepts.
- Outline the sentence structure in the paragraph. Note how each sentence logically connects to the following sentence. Also consider the overall direction that the author is working toward. Notice how the use of phrases and dependent clauses, punctuation, and the actual words themselves are used, and ask what work they do in your particular paragraph.
- Pick a topic, and write a similar paragraph. Imitate as closely as possible the same sentence structure as your original. This exercise also works well for poetry, helping the imitator to learn the rhythms and subtle shifts in language and attention to image that are typical of poetry writing.
- Share your paragraph (or poem) with your classmates. Do you have a better feel now for how you might use language to persuade the reader?

Strategies for Crafting Good Sentences

Imitation, as in the above exercise, is one particularly effective way of learning how to write well, but it is only one way of teaching you how to use language to coordinate, subordinate, and combine your sentences to create the meaning you want to convey in the most effective way possible. Of course, as you did in the chapter on grammar, you must learn the rules, but once you have learned them, you need to find a way of using language and grammar that will enable you to communicate clearly and effectively and, in doing so, find your own **voice**. To be able to write well, you have to become an observant reader and a careful and aware writer.

In *How to Write a Sentence,* Stanley Fish argues that you need to become aware of the individual components that make up a sentence as well as their logical relationship to each other. In this respect, he suggests an exercise where you pick several verbs and modal auxiliaries (*would, could, might,* etc.) and put them together to make up a sentence.

What follows is a sample exercise, similar to the one suggested by Fish. I have chosen five nouns, two verbs, and one modal auxiliary. The first example is fashioned for a less formal audience and then expanded to use in an academic context. Think about how the two sentences differ. How are the extra words, phrases, and clauses (subordinate, coordinate) used?

Nouns: hockey, game, Canada, identity, man/men

Verbs: *fight/fighting, play/playing*

Modal auxiliary: *might*

General (personal opinion):
Because I live in Canada, I frequently see men and children *playing* hockey either in the streets or on television; however, it bothers me to think that the repetitive *fighting* in the game *might* negatively affect a young man's identity.

Academic (objective, larger concerns):
This recent incident concerning Don Sanderson's death reignites the age-old discussion, much debated by the men who *play* and watch hockey, about the place of *fighting* in professional hockey. More importantly, the privileging of this violent behaviour *might* speak to the Canadian national identity. While Canada purports to be a peaceful country, the game of hockey, which is central to the way Canadians see themselves, raises questions that need to be addressed.

As you can see in the two examples above, the sentence in the first more general and personal example is not as detailed and developed as the sentences and ideas in the second example. In the academic example, the meaning is expanded from the personal to take into consideration a specific event (Don Sanderson's death) and a more detailed questioning of how this violence in hockey reflects what it means to be Canadian.

BUILDING SENTENCES

This exercise, which is adapted from the one Stanley Fish recommends, will help you learn how to write effective sentences.

- Pick five related items (nouns), and then randomly pick two verbs and a modal auxiliary, such as *would, could, should, will, might*, etc.
- Use any other words you deem appropriate and put them together into one or two sentences.
- Ask yourself, what idea are these sentences anchored in? What is the nature of the relationship that I am creating with these words? What feeling does the rhythm of the sentences create?
- When you have completed these sentences and reflected on the logical relationship between the words, see if you can make the meaning more formal, as in the example above. Are you fascinated by the way meaning can be made out of such a small amount of primary material: mere words?

Can you see how you might take your personal writing and things you're interested in to a more developed academic concern, simply by focusing on developing your ideas within a logical sentence structure? Compare your writing with that of your classmates.

Becoming aware of the words you use and how you structure them in your sentences is, then, an important first step. Understanding how words work is important. A brief introduction to syntax, semantics, and diction can help you understand the importance of paying close attention to the words you use.

Syntax and Semantics

Syntax refers to the way in which words are put together to form the units of a sentence. **Semantics** refers to the way in which your words make meaning. As an academic writer, you will be concerned with both syntax and semantics. However, every sentence you write must logically develop the meaning you are trying to convey. Punctuation is important to finding a syntax that works rhythmically and effectively to enhance your meaning. Keeping your argument in mind as you craft your sentences to enhance your meaning is essential to your success. As an aside, never assume that your reader will be able to fill in the missing parts of your argument. You need to make sure that you concisely and clearly articulate your argument so that your reader is able to follow your thinking every step of the way.

Diction

Effective diction, or word choice, is crucial to creating an effective sentence and a coherent and intelligent meaning for a particular audience. If in doubt, don't guess at a word. Use a dictionary or thesaurus diligently to find the perfect word for what you are trying to say, but be careful to keep your words as clear, simple, and concise as possible.

George Orwell addresses this issue in "Politics and the English Language," when he warns against using "the *–ize* and *de-* formations," such as *defamiliarize, deregionalize,* or *rationalize.* recommending instead the use of concrete, direct verbs. He also cautions against complex or pretentious words that "dress up simple statements" or cloud clear thought or meaning (356), including words that appear impartial and scientific, such as *phenomenon, constitute, categorical, exhibit, veritable*; words that reflect their Greek or Latin roots (*expediate, ameliorate, extraneous, subaqueous*); foreign words, such as *ancient regime, status quo,* and *weltanschauuung,* that try too hard to provide an "air of culture and elegance;" and abstract words, such as *beautiful, sentimental, natural, romantic,* which are so general that they are essentially meaningless.

The tendency to use these pretentious or vague words reflects the belief, held by many first-year students, that writing at the academic level means that you have to use big words, large abstractions, and generalizations. This is not the case. In general, academic writing is clear, concise, and straightforward. Every word contributes to your meaning and argument. If you have a problem with diction, take Orwell's recommendations at the end of his essay, and put them on a piece of paper by your writing desk:

> Never use a metaphor, simile or other figure of speech which you are used to seeing in print.
> Never use a long word where a short one will do.
> If it is possible to cut a word out, always cut it out.
> Never use the passive where you can use the active.
> Never use a foreign phrase, a scientific word or a jargon word if you can think of an everyday English equivalent. (362–3)

The Importance of Verbs

In the example related to Stanley Fish's exercise above, verbs are important because they describe the action of the sentences: it is the playing and the fighting that create a context for thinking about the concrete nouns (men, game) and the more abstract nouns, such as identity. When using the active voice, the subjects and verbs are closely positioned, making the sentence not only clear but also emphatic. The subject and the verb are the most important parts of a sentence. When they are not clearly connected in the sentence, the sentence will be passive, wordy, and un-emphatic. Paying attention to how subjects or nouns and verbs work together will help your writing be more emphatic. Here are some basic recommendations:

Whenever Possible, Use the Active Voice

The use of the passive and active voice has been covered extensively in other areas of this book (see chapters 4 and 12). To review, though, *voice* refers to a verb's ability to show whether a subject acts or receives the action named by the verb. English has two voices: active and passive. Academic writing generally uses the *active* voice.

- Active voice: In the active voice, the subject performs the action.

  Most good writers believe it is important to read.

  In this sentence, the subject (*writers*) acts: writers *believe*.
- Passive voice: In the passive voice, the subject is acted upon, and the person or thing doing the acting often appears as the object of the preposition *by*.

  Reading is believed to be important by most good writers.

  In this sentence, the subject (*reading*) is acted upon by writers, the object of the preposition *by*.

In the above example, the emphasis is now on reading when it should be on writers or what writers believe about reading. While passive voice does have a role to play in academic writing (seen mostly in the sciences), it is generally avoided.

Avoid Nominalization

Nominalization is the use of adjectives and verbs as nouns. When nominalizations are used, the action either stops or is completely obscured. Nominalization is also, as Orwell points out, a feature of political or bureaucratic writing, its function to abstract and obfuscate the real meaning and subject of the sentence. These nouns include intention (from intend), proposal (from propose), decision (from decide), expectation (from expect), argument (from argue), and inclusion (from include). As you might have noted, these nominalizations take an adjective or verb (the verb *intend*, for example) and by adding a suffix, such as *ity, ion, tion, ize,* or *ism* (e.g., intention), create a noun. These nouns take concrete and active verbs or adjectives and make them abstract and passive, thereby impeding communication. Worse still, they often obliterate the acting subject in the sentence (the I that speaks). Consider the following examples:

Unemphatic nominal style: A **decision** to lay off workers was reached by the company managers, who **recognized** the need to effect an economic **stabilization** of company resources, thereby reducing the impact of the recent recession.

Emphatic active style: The company managers **decided** to lay off workers because of financial problems resulting from the recent recession.

As you can see from the above comparison, the emphatic active style is clearer, more direct, and much shorter. The following exercises should help you to develop the skills to recognize nominalization and eliminate it from your writing.

Exercise 13.4

AVOIDING NOMINALIZATION

The following passages are overloaded with nominalizations, creating an abstract convoluted style.

Rewrite the passages so that they are more active, emphatic, readable, and accessible. However, do not change the meaning of the sentence. Asking "who is performing the action here?" can help address passive abstractions. Make sure that you use the active voice so that the subject or agent performing the action is clear.

1. The first passage is taken from an article titled "Zombie Nouns," written by Helen Sword in *The New York Times* (23 July 2012).

   The proliferation of nominalizations may in a discursive formation be an indication of a tendency toward pomposity and abstraction.

2. The second passage is taken from the Husky Oil Company's website:

   Husky is committed to responsible corporate citizenship. This includes the integration of social, environmental and economic considerations into its core businesses while engaging key stakeholders and conducting business in a manner that maximizes positive impacts on current and future generations.

See the Exercise Answer Key in Appendix A for sample revised passages.

Exercise 13.5

FOUND NOMINALIZATIONS

Find a business or government letter or report, an article in a newspaper, a memo from an organization, or a speech that contains examples of nominalization and pretentious and inflated diction.

1. Identify the examples.
2. Rewrite the passage to make the writing clearer and more active.

Do you think the writer is intentionally keeping the language obscure? Discuss your examples and revisions with your classmates.

Use Subordination

The subordinate style of writing is probably the most effective and logical style for academic writing. Subordination means that some elements in a sentence are less important to your meaning than others. It tends to presuppose a cause–effect relationship between its component parts (oranges are better than tangerines because...) and distinguishes between the importance of different elements (events, time, situations, etc.).

If the meaning contained within the subordinate clause is essential to your sentence, rewrite it so that it is not subordinate. In other words, don't subordinate information that is essential to your meaning. In the following examples, the first example demonstrates a string of main clauses with no emphasis or subordination; the second example takes the first sentence and revises it for subordination and emphasis:

Original: Ernest Hemingway used clear, simple, direct prose, and he used short and long cumulative sentences, and these sentences quickened or slowed the pace of the action, and, in this way, he created dramatic effect.

Revised: In order to create dramatic effect, Ernest Hemingway used clear, simple, direct prose, consisting of short and long cumulative sentences to quicken or slow the pace of the action.

The first original example illustrates an additive style, typical of Ernest Hemingway, that allocates equal importance to all the points in the sentence. While this writing serves a purpose, it is hard to understand what the main points are. The second example uses the same information but focuses it on the main point: *Ernest Hemingway used clear, simple, direct prose... to quicken or slow the pace of the action.* As you can see, not only is this sentence shorter, it is also easier to understand. This is because some of the information has been subordinated, making it less important. The middle part of the sentence—consisting of short and long cumulative sentences—has been subordinated. It is now a non-restrictive modifier, which means that it could be omitted and the sentence would not change. The last clause—*he created dramatic effect*—has also been subordinated and is now a phrase that introduces rather than concludes the sentence, thus providing a framework for our overall understanding of the sentence.

Constructing a clear focus or meaning is essential when using non-restrictive modifying clauses: clauses that are contained within commas and contain non-essential information. In this case, emphasis comes from keeping the important information in the main clause (underlined), and subordinating the less important details. Please note that keeping your subjects and verbs close together helps to avoid confusion. Consider the following example:

A clock, <u>chiming in the middle of the night,</u> drives me to distraction.

This sentence uses a non-restrictive modifying clause—*chiming in the middle of the night*—to subordinate the more specific information about the clock. However, if we take out the non-restrictive modifying clause, the sentence no longer makes sense: A clock drives me to distraction (rarely would a clock on its own drive someone to distraction).

Revised: A clock chiming in the middle of the night drives me to distraction.

Focusing on what information is important and omitting and/or subordinating information that does not reflect your meaning can help you write effective, meaningful sentences.

Pay Attention to Rhythm

This section relates to the idea of bearing witness to good sentences. In hearing, reading, and learning how to write good sentences, we find a sense of our own internal rhythm. Another way of saying this is that our internal rhythm or personal style manifests itself in how our words appear on a page or are spoken. All language, not just poetry, has a rhythmic beat. This is also known as the intonation pattern of a sentence and refers to the degrees of stress that we place on different words, clauses, and phrases.

The main emphasis of a sentence is usually at the end, the predicate: it is what we are left with and it is what we remember. What we see first—the beginning of a sentence—is second in importance. And the middle of a sentence is, sadly, the more easily forgotten. Advertisers are experts at manipulating this language to emphasize their main messages. Take, for example, the following Heineken beer commercial slogan:

Heineken refreshes the parts other beers cannot reach.

The advertisement is effective because it articulates a slogan—"Heineken refreshes"—that we will remember and because it leaves us reaching back, figuratively, to the beginning of the sentence. In this way, the slogan comes full circle, leaving the "parts" in the middle to hang ambiguously and humorously in the air between the two.

Consequently, you need to be aware of what is most and least important in your sentences and structure them accordingly. Of course, no sentence stands on its own so this meaningful construction has to take the context into consideration and the relationship a sentence has with the sentence immediately preceding and following it, as well as the other sentences in the paragraph.

Exercise 13.6

RHYTHM AND STRESS

- Read the following passage.
- Listen carefully to the intonation of each sentence.
- Identify the words that get the most stress, and then consider how this stress is reflected and maybe emphasized in the passage as a whole.
- If the normal pattern of stress diverges, as in a word or an idea that stops or distracts you, why do you think this is the case?
- Discuss your reading with that of your classmates.

I tell the class. "I am legally blind." There is a pause, a collective intake of breath. I feel them look away uncertainly and then look back. After all, I just said I couldn't see. Or did I? I had managed to get there on my own—no cane, no dog, none of the usual trappings of blindness. Eyeing me askance now, they might detect that my gaze is not quite focused. My eyes are aimed in the right direction but the gaze seems to stop short of touching anything. But other people do this, sighted people, normal people, especially in an awkward situation like this one, the first day of class. (Kleege 390)

You might have noticed in the previous exercise that the emphasis doesn't always follow the normal pattern: not all sentences are alike and not all sentences put the emphasis in the predicate or end of the sentence. Sometimes, the emphasis is placed elsewhere. Where you place specific words can make a difference. Words, such as *now, did, specifically, there,* etc., can point to a word or clause we want to emphasize in a sentence. For example, the sentence "Hemingway did want to omit commas" puts the focus on *did* and makes us understand that, despite what others might think, his omission was intentional.

ANALYZE YOUR OWN WRITING

Exercise 13.7

- Find a paragraph or two of your own writing.
- Look for places where you have placed stress in your own sentences.
- Ask: Are my sentences as effective as they could be? Have I used interrupting words, phrases, and clauses effectively? Have I developed this stress, which emphasizes and affirms my meaning, across sentences and, possibly, paragraphs? How might I improve this writing to make it more effective?

Parallel Structure

Parallel structure is similar to the concept of parallel lines in geometry, and calls for the use of equivalent grammatical forms to express ideas of equal importance. When you are expressing ideas of equal weight in your writing, parallel sentence structures can echo that fact and offer you a writing style that uses balance and rhythm to help deliver your meaning. Parallel structures may be as simple as groups of single words (nouns, adjectives, verbs, etc.) or as complicated as groups of phrases or clauses within a sentence. Sometimes the parallel structures appear as pairs, sometimes as lists or series. They are often connected with correlative conjunctions, such as *both … and; not only … but also, either … or,* etc. Below are examples of effective parallel structure:

Recommended exercise includes running, swimming, and cycling. (the *–ing* words are parallel in structure and equal in importance)

Exercise helps people to maintain healthy bodies and to handle mental pressure. (the *to* phrases are parallel in structure and equal in importance)

People exercise because they want to look healthy, because they need to have stamina, or because they hope to live longer. (the *because* subordinate clauses are parallel in structure and equal in importance)

Consider the following examples, which compare the effective and ineffective use of parallel structure in different grammatical structures:

PARALLEL WORDS IN A LIST AND SENTENCE LENGTH

Ineffective: Her complaints were *boring, childish,* and *showed how ignorant she was.*

Effective: Her complaints were *boring, childish,* and *ignorant.*

CORRELATIVE CONJUNCTIONS

Ineffective: She said that there were two options: he could either come to the house or not.

Effective: She said that there were two options: either he could come to the house, or they could meet at the bank.

INFINITIVE PHRASES

Ineffective: She worked late in the evening not only *to catch up on her studies* but also *writing her paper.*

Effective: She worked hard late in the evening not only *to catch up on her studies* but also *to write her paper.*

DEPENDENT CLAUSES

Ineffective: Williams pointed out that the author correctly used logos but not pathos.

Effective: Williams pointed out that the author correctly used logos but that his use of pathos was incorrect.

INDEPENDENT CLAUSES

Ineffective: You can ask what your country can do for you or the other way around.

Effective: Ask not what your country can do for you; ask what you can do for your country.

This last sentence, a quote from John F. Kennedy, is effective because it uses parallel-structured sentences (independent clauses) separated by a semicolon. However, do not overuse this structure. Occasionally this strategy is very effective, but if used too much it will lose its effectiveness, and feel repetitive and a little didactic.

Nevertheless, parallel structure can greatly increase your emphasis and at the same time create an effective balance and sense of rhythm in your writing. Consider the following sentence:

> To assign unanswered letters their proper weight, to free us from the expectations of others, to give us back to ourselves—here lies the great, the singular power of self-respect. (Didion 218)

This parallel, balanced list of infinitive phrases—to assign, to free, to give—are presented as causes of the effect in the sentence conclusion: self-respect. The sentence is clear, concise, and rhythmical. Significantly, though, this is a sentence that Didion uses for special effect. She does not continually repeat this structure. One or two parallel sentences in your essay will make the ideas stand out, but if you overuse them, you will lose the effect.

Tone, Audience, Purpose

This point about balance—the need to carefully construct and use it for effect in both your words and your sentences—brings us to an analysis of tone.

Tone has everything to do with the way you use your words (diction) and sentences, but, more specifically, it provides a sense of who you are, the attitude you take in relation to yourself, your reader (audience), your topic, and your knowledge or purpose for writing. For example, if you were writing a letter to your best friend, the language would probably be informal, even playful, and use colloquial, slang words, sentence fragments, and short, loosely framed, paragraphs; however, if you were writing an essay for an academic science course, your language would be formal and use objective language, balanced and complete sentence structures, and longer fully developed and logical paragraphs. Obviously, here we are concerned with developing an objective academic tone, given that your readers will mostly be other academic peers and professors.

What follows are four versions of a single message: the first is a verse from the Old Testament book in the Bible of Ecclesiastes, the second (written by George Orwell) rephrases the verse in a parody of the style of official government documents, the third (written by Keith Waterhouse) translates the message into the style of the *Daily Mirror*. The fourth is an academic translation written by me. The first three appear in Waterhouse's book *Daily Mirror Style*.

> I returned, and saw under the sun, that the race is not to the swift, nor the battle to the strong, neither yet bread to the wise, nor yet riches to men of understanding, nor yet favour to men of skill; but time and chance happeneth to them all. (Ecclesiastes 9:11)

> Objective consideration of contemporary phenomena compels the conclusion that success or failure in competitive activities exhibits no tendency to be commensurate

with innate capacity, but that a considerable element of the unpredictable must invariably be taken into account. (Orwell 358)

Using your loaf won't fill your bread-bin, a mystery preacher warned in a pulpit blast yesterday.

And punters will be pipped to know that though the horse they backed is first past the post—they won't pick up their winnings. HE-men have had it, according to the no-holds-barred sermon. (Waterhouse)

The Old Testament book of Ecclesiastes uses a poetic style to emphasize that physical prowess, wisdom, skill, youth, and wealth are not, on their own, an indication of success. Rather, these skills, and the success that they might enable, are always subject to fate.

The tone in the above examples—poetic, bureaucratic, journalistic, and academic, respectively—directly reflect the attitudes held toward events, issues, characters, plot, context etc. However, in addition, tone, as the above examples show, is influenced by the discipline that you are in and the way you feel about the subject. Academic writing across the disciplines requires an objective, clear, and concise tone. The focus is on the information or knowledge and audience the writer is versed in and familiar with.

However, please note that if you are studying business or engineering, you might be expected to adapt your tone for a specialized audience outside of academia. The following examples, taken from Lisa Moretto's *Technically Write* (18), illustrate how tone might be adapted for a specific audience. For example, a report geared toward electronics engineers who specialize in radar-equipped airfields might have a certain amount of jargon attached to it:

We modified the MTI by installing a K-59 double-decade circuit. This brightened moving targets by 12% and reduced ground clutter by 23%.

The same report to the airport manager might read:

We modified the radar set's Moving Target Indicator by installing a special circuit known as the K-59. This increased the brightness of responses from aircraft and decreased returns from fixed objects on the ground.

The same report written to describe improvements in the airport's air traffic control system for the local Chamber of Commerce might read:

We have modified the airfield radar system to improve its performance, which has helped us to differentiate more clearly between low-flying aircraft and high objects on the ground.

Once again, an awareness of audience is key to writing in any discipline or in any context inside or outside of academia.

AUDIENCE

- Read the following passages and then rewrite *one* of them for at least one other intended audience.
- Define the audience and make sure that you highlight why it needs to know this information. The key here is to make the academic language accessible to another audience, but please note that the length of your revision might be considerably shorter (or longer) than the original.
- Compare your passages with those of your classmates.

EXCERPT 1

When are new firms innovative? Organizational researchers have long studied this question, but mixed findings have emerged from these studies. Some scholars have suggested that new firms, which cannot use existing firm knowledge (Cohen & Levinthal, 1990) and resources (Teece, 1996), have trouble innovating. However, other authors have argued exactly the opposite: New firms are highly innovative because their innovative efforts do not cannibalize their existing products (Arrow, 1982) or require them to filter new knowledge through organizational routines and structures that are ill-suited to that purpose (Henderson & Clark, 1990).

[…]

Our study seeks to examine the environmental characteristics that give rise to innovation in new firms, building on the recommendations of resource-based theorists to consider the relationship between resources and the environmental context in which they are used (Miller & Shamsie, 1996; Priem & Butler, 2001).

From Katila, R. & Shane, S. (2005). When Does Lack of Resources Make New Firms Innovative?

EXCERPT 2

The influence of culture on the development of eating disorders such as anorexia nervosa (AN) and bulimia nervosa (BN) has been long appreciated. These syndromes are more prevalent in industrialized and often Western cultures and are far more common among females than males, mirroring cross-cultural differences in the importance of thinness for women (Miller & Pumariega, 2001; Pate, Pumariega, Hester, & Garner, 1992). Furthermore, eating disorders seem to have become more common among younger females during the latter half of the twentieth century, during a period when icons of American beauty (Miss America contestants and *Playboy* centerfolds) have become thinner and women's magazines have published significantly more articles on methods for weight loss (Garner, Garfinkel, Schwartz, & Thompson, 1980; Owen & Laurel-Seller, 2000; Rubinstein & Caballero, 2000; Wiseman, Gray, Mosimann, & Ahrens, 1992).

Keel, P.K. & Klump, K.L. (2003). Are Eating Disorders Culture-Bound Syndromes? Implications for Conceptualizing Their Etiology.

Continued

- Which audiences did you choose to focus on?
- Was writing for an audience that was not academic easier than writing for an academic audience? If so, why do you think this might be?
- What was the process of revision like?
- Discuss the difficulties and particular problems you had with your classmates.

Revising for Style

As the chapter on revision emphasizes, to write well, you need to be able to organize your argument logically and use language in such a way that it supports your argument. If your sentences do not develop logically from idea to idea and your language isn't appropriate to the audience and occasion, then your argument will fall apart. This means that you must revise your work at two levels:

a.   at the level of the logical development of your argument; and
b.   at the level of your word use, sentence structure, and tone, always, of course, keeping your argument in mind as you revise.

Once again, using Orwell's questions to ask yourself about your work at this latter level can prove useful. I have adapted them for an academic writing focus, below (see square brackets):

1.   What am I trying to say?
2.   What words will express it?
3.   What [evidence,] image, or idiom will make it clearer?
4.   Is this [evidence or] image [valid, concrete, and] fresh enough to have an effect? [...]
5.   Could I put it more concisely?
6.   Have I said anything that is avoidably ugly [awkward, vague, or pretentious]? (359)

Editing

While revising deals with questions of content and structure, editing and proofreading deal with the more particular details of sentence structure, grammar, spelling, diction, and citation accuracy. The editing process usually comes after the revision stage, although you might revisit this entire process recursively many times. Editing your work means that you pay attention to detail, cutting, adding, and rearranging words to make better sense of your clauses and sentences as they exist in relationship to your main argument and the requirements of academic essay writing (manuscript length, page margins, citation, conventions, etc.). When editing for clarity of meaning, pay particular attention to generalizations, wordiness, and repetition, and, of course, any grammar errors you have made, such as errors in parallelism, voice, etc.

Generalizations

Although academics do make generalizations about certain forms of knowledge, they do this by focusing on the specifics of some aspect of the knowledge. When students misunderstand this focus on generalization, they tend to use large generalizations incorrectly. Some examples of this include since the beginning of time; women are made to be caregivers in the home; all people love and want to care for animals. While these generalizations point to a possible argument, they are far too large to produce any meaningful analysis. Narrowing down your focus can help you make your generalization more manageable. For example, instead of trying to analyze something from "the beginning of time," pick a specific century, decade, or, preferably, a year, that is representative of the knowledge you are considering.

Repetition

Repetition, if used well, can give emphasis to your ideas, words, or grammatical constructions. It can be used to stress or reinforce a certain point and create cohesion and order. Consider the following example in *Hamlet*, "To be or not to be, that is the question." The repetition of "to be" reinforces Hamlet's pending life and death decision. Everything hangs on the intervening words "or not" between them.

Here is an another example, by Plutarch: "They are wrong who think that politics is like an ocean voyage or a military campaign, something to be done with some end in view, something which levels off as soon as that end is reached. It is not a public chore, to be got over with; it is a way of life" (qtd in Schell 855). Here, the repetition of "something" adds to the intensity and condemnation of those who are "wrong" about politics. It intensifies the list of things that are wrong. The repetition of "it is" in "it is not ... it is" helps emphasize what politics *is* while also providing a parallel construction in the final sentence.

However, repetition without a clear purpose is simply redundant and should not be used. If your repetition is not adding emphasis or cohesion, then you need to find an alternative word to replace one of your repetitions. As an aside, do not overdo repetition, even if it is being used for emphasis.

Wordiness and Redundancy

Using too many words or words that are redundant can obscure your thinking and your argument. In academia, your writing needs to be precise and concise. If you can take a word out, then do so. If you can use a simple word instead of a long and convoluted word, then do it. Keep your focus on your argument and convey it as simply, concisely, and clearly as you possibly can. William Zinsser's essay in the Reader addresses this issue and provides you with excellent strategies for making your writing more concise.

ACADEMIC FOCUS

EDITING CHECKLIST FOR GRAMMAR, PUNCTUATION, AND STYLE

GRAMMAR ERRORS

- Have I checked my work for the following errors (focusing on the errors I commonly make)?
  - Tense shifts; agreement errors (pronoun/antecedent, subject/verb); modifier errors (misplaced/dangling); mixed constructions; parallel structure; sentence fragments, run-on sentences, comma splices.

PUNCTUATION

- Have I checked for apostrophe, colon, semicolon, and comma errors?
- If I have used dashes or parenthesis, have I used them correctly?

STYLE

- Does incorrect or awkward word usage (diction) interfere with the reader's comprehension?
- Is the writing direct, clear, and concise (not wordy, but detailed and full of explanation)?

- If I have used repetition, have I used it effectively?
- Is my tone objective and formal enough for an academic paper?
- Is there a confident, strong voice?
- Is the tone appropriate and consistent?
- Have I documented my sources and used quotations appropriately and accurately?

FORM AND CONTENT

- Does the essay have a clear thesis statement?
- Is the progression of the argument clearly outlined in the thesis, introduction, and the entire essay?
- Do the sentences logically develop my argument, or are the transitions between sentences awkward?
- Are the paragraphs unified in content, or do they skip from topic to topic without preparing the reader for what comes next?
- Are there transitions between paragraphs?
- Is there a progression or order in the paper's presentation of its main points?

Style Conventions: The Importance of Citation

Chapter 11 provided you with more specific information on citation and, in particular, the two major citation methods: APA (American Psychological Association) and MLA (Modern Languages Association).

Plagiarism is covered in more depth in chapter 10, research essay writing, but it is important to reiterate the importance of citing all sentences, words, concepts, and ideas that are not your own. A failure to cite ideas, words, or summaries has serious consequences in academia. Plagiarized work will usually result in a failing grade for the assignment and can result in failing the course, academic suspension, or expulsion.

Overview of Other Style Conventions

Citation is just one of many academic conventions. As outlined in chapter 2, other conventions include the use of

- an established research position;
- logic and objectivity;
- first or third person;
- active voice (unless requested otherwise);
- reporting expressions;
- quotations; and
- obvious and limiting expressions or statements.

You are also required to know and use the correct formats for university essay writing (what constitutes a report, an expository essay, etc.) and develop a sustained engagement with the data and/or knowledge. If you do not conform to these conventions as you familiarize yourself with academic writing as a specific genre, you will not do well on your writing assignments.

Apart from the academic conventions that pertain to the documentation and citation of sources—the correct incorporation of quotations and the use of reporting verbs and reporting expressions—keep in mind that academic writing requires a self-reflective tone and the use of conventions, such as limiting expressions and direct statements of fact (see chapter 2).

Quantitative versus Qualitative Research: A Question of Style

Additionally, the tone you use will depend on whether you are writing an essay for a course in the hard sciences, which value more **quantitative research**, or a humanities or arts course, which values more **qualitative research**.

Quantitative Research

Research performed in the hard sciences values a broad sampling of research and the corresponding data, statistics, facts, and numbers, which are assumed to carry more objective, rhetorical, or persuasive force. The focus is on objective hard facts and data. For writers working in the hard sciences or even the social sciences, it is this type of information that will persuade your readers of the validity of your argument.

Quantitative studies often use shorter sentences that get to the point, or the facts, of the matter. Sentences tend to be more direct and factual although sentence variety is still required. Traditionally, quantitative methods have used third person (*he, she, they*) passive-voice sentence constructions that omit the subject of the sentence who is performing the action. However, this use of the passive voice is now being challenged by recent calls for scientific responsibility and the active voice is now more common.

TYPICAL QUANTITATIVE RESEARCH SENTENCES

The experimental control proved statistically that all variables conformed to expectations.

Overall, the data shows that 40% of the participants were successful when they studied one hour per day over a period of four weeks.

Group X were given two Aspirin tablets a day and group Y were given two placebo tablets a day.

Table 2 combines the data for the 25 essays, indicating the distribution of topic sentences of each type (Braddock 177).

We gathered information from 156 studies concerning animal extinction and global warming for our meta-analysis.

The balance of evidence strongly suggests that global warming has been exaggerated.

Qualitative Research

In contrast, qualitative research, often labelled soft or self-reflexive research, differs from quantitative research in that it replaces the broad example (as many cases as possible, which are open to statistical interpretation) with one or several examples. These examples are analyzed in detail and researchers search for patterns, associations, and commonalities. In making an argument about their examples (primary texts), researchers need to be aware of their own position or perspective (where they stand; what biases they have, etc.) in relation to the research topic.

Qualitative studies often use longer and more compound-complex sentences that require multiple clauses. This is because the disciplines that use qualitative research are more concerned with the complexities pertaining to the knowledge than with results.

TYPICAL QUALITATIVE RESEARCH SENTENCES

Faced with evidence of the inaccuracy of this patriarchal doctrine, many boys and men are re-evaluating gender construction. I found repeated evidence of this shift in my curatorial research: I did not find any artists producing images of iconic or celebratory masculinity. (Garneau 56)

"As the media often 'detextualize' events by focusing on sensational aspects of a protest—indeed, are compelled to do so by the dynamics of news reportage—a situation may arise in which the actions of a small minority may come to represent in the eyes of the public, an entire movement" (Kruse qtd in Mika 921).

"In this chapter, I argue that though Mister Sandman conflates homosexuality and disability in potentially constructive ways, exposing the impossibility and incomprehensibility of a normative, heterosexual existence, this representation is compromised by Gowdy's tendency to metaphorically appropriate disability rather than explore it as a valid and equal subject position" (Hayward 216).

QUALITATIVE VS QUANTITATIVE STYLE

Exercise 13.9

Compare the following two excerpts and answer the following questions:

1. Which excerpt demonstrates primarily quantitative data? Which one demonstrates qualitative data?
2. Can you identify the discipline for each example?
3. Identify some of the stylistic requirements of writing in this discipline, as it appears in the examples.
4. Which writing sample appeals to you most? Which sample more consistently reflects your own writing style?

EXCERPT 1

The problem of deep oceanic convection induced by localized surface cooling has received considerable attention in the last years. Results from field observations (e.g. in the Greenland Sea or Gulf of Lions), laboratory experiments, and numerical simulations have led to some theoretical predictions concerning the structure of the convective region like plume scale, chimney scale, and rim current by, for example, Klinger and Marshall[1], Send and Marshall[2], and Viseck et al.[3]. The comparison of these scaling arguments with real ocean data on deep convection is somewhat restricted due to the lack of detailed measurements of convective plumes and chimneys, although field experiments have provided very impressive cases of deep ocean convection (eg. Morawitz et al.[4]).

(Raasch and Etling 1786)

EXCERPT 2

Literature in English is an increasingly international, even global phenomenon. Writers all over the world, from the Pacific, Asia, Africa, and the West Indies as well as from traditional centres in the British Isles and the United States, use English as a medium for fiction and poetry. One consequence has been that literature in English has become increasingly cross- or multi-cultural, as writing about a given culture is destined—because of its language, English, and its place of publication, usually London or New York—to have readers of many other cultures. . . . Over the last generation there has been such an explosion in writing from a global range of cultures that, arguably, multicultural literature dominates literature in English today.

(Dasenbrock 10)

Exercise 13.10

READING STYLE

- Choose two works from the Reader that are similar or comparable and discuss in a short two-page paper how they differ in style.
- Establish your criteria for comparing the essays' style and then take a position on these papers, arguing that one is more effective and persuasive than the other. You might address how the style of these works supports the content and argument that the author is trying to make.

CHAPTER SUMMARY

This chapter has looked at style as a way of refining meaning and making your writing more persuasive. In particular, the chapter has covered how to read and work with sentences to make them more interesting, effective, and reflective of the arguments and meaning you are trying to create. In this respect, parallel structure, subordination, tone, sentence rhythm, and active and passive voice have also been covered. There is a section on how to edit for style and a section on how style conventions appear in both quantitative and qualitative research. Numerous writing exercises should help you refine your own writing style in relation to the purpose for your writing and your audience, along with a checklist to help you with the editing process.

QUESTIONS FOR CONSIDERATION

1. How do I feel about the sentences I read and write?
2. Are there some specific examples of good sentences that I can use as models for my own writing?
3. Have I written some good sentences that I can say I am proud of? Can I identify them?
4. What do I still need to know about some of the strategies for crafting good sentences?
5. Which strategy appeals most to me? Which strategy do I think I have the most trouble with in my own writing?
6. Do I feel comfortable editing for style? Will I use the checklist to help me?
7. Can I use the section on quantitative and qualitative research to help me understand how the different disciplines use style to support their content?

Exercise Answer Key

Please note that for the most part the answers given here are suggestions and your responses may vary. There is no one "correct" answer.

CHAPTER 1

Exercise 1.1

Although each piece of writing deals with the same topic, animal experimentation, each piece points to a different situation, purpose, audience, and genre.

Example 1: The journalistic article

This article refers to a specific situation (the abusive treatment of animals in the entertainment industry and science) and a specific audience (the readers of a local city newspaper). Its aim or purpose is to persuade readers that animal abuse, particularly of chimpanzees, is wrong. Stylistically, the article uses journalistic writing conventions: it tells a story about the chimpanzee and equates the chimpanzee's experience with human experience by helping readers to relate emotionally to human needs (e.g., she is given a name, loves to carry a purse, and has a passion for necklaces). The story of Sue Ellen's treatment is presented with emotion-laden sentences and phrases, such as "she had her teeth knocked out with a crowbar" and "shot over and over again." These visual sentences draw a picture for readers, helping them to feel appropriate shock and disgust. Automatically, we know that this journalist has a purpose: to persuade the reader that animal abuse is unethical.

Example 2: The Twitter entry

Here we have a couple of undocumented facts tweeted by Animal Awareness, an online site for animal lovers. Because Twitter restricts the letter count to 140 words per entry, there is only room for essential information. Consequently, Animal Awareness communicates its purpose—the cost of animal experimentation—to an audience used to receiving information in small chunks, using short factual sentences, figures, and a direct address (yours), which helps the reader relate to the specific purpose or message (to not support animal testing). Twitter participants can get more information by exploring the Animal Awareness website.

Example 3: A PETA advertisement

PETA is an animal rights organization that has often been criticized for its controversial advertising campaigns. This advertisement plays on the viewer's emotions by putting a picture of a caged baboon in the centre. The baboon, which has fresh scars on its head, is staring at the viewer with lifeless eyes. The brutality of the treatment is highlighted with a description of the removal of the baboon's left eye and the clamping of an artery to induce a stroke. A quiz asks the viewer to participate and take a stand about who is responsible for the testing performed on these baboons. The purpose of this advertisement is to persuade a sympathetic audience to act on the belief that animal experimentation is ethically wrong. At the bottom of the advertisement there is a website address the viewer can go to for further information.

Exercise 1.3

Passage 1

Confusing academic writing with high school writing. In academic terms, the student understands that he or she has to engage with the primary text and Schaefer's concept of "soundscapes." The student also understands that he or she needs to quote Schaefer and engage analytically with her ideas. Unfortunately, however, the student begins to focus not on the knowledge presented in the text, but on his or her own personal experience. In particular, the student narrates an experience he or she had with the grandmother's dog. Formal academic conventions are replaced with informal colloquialisms ("Nanny's dog" instead of "grandmother's dog"), clichés ("[t]hen came the beginning of the end"), inappropriate, sensationalistic verbs ("tapping"), repetitive vague generalizations ("moments in their past that were happy, sad, exciting or boring"), and unprofessional errors, such as capitalization errors and spelling mistakes ("rufus/Rufus" and "pert store" for "pet store") that should have been addressed and fixed in a final edit.

Passage 2

Academic essay writing. The focus is on the knowledge that Milton engages with (divorce and love) and the tone is objective. The student writer smoothly transitions her reader from Milton's general "need to both live and write virtuously" to a more specific examination of *The Doctrine and Discipline of Divorce* and Milton's conception of conjugal love. The writer embeds relevant quotes and uses limiting expressions—seems—and academic verbs: insists, writes. The writer uses first person, has a clear thesis statement, and uses language that is clear, direct, and focused.

Passage 3

Confusing journalism and academic writing. While there is a clear introduction to and summary of the basic plot of the book, the student falls into the common error of trying to advertise or "sell" the book to the reader. This journalistic strategy is evident in the use of adjectives—"sensational book," "moving and disturbing story," "fantastic read"—and in the insistence that this book must "not be missed."

Passage 4

The belief that academic writing is convoluted, wordy, authoritative, and pretentious. Although this writer attempts to provide the reader with an argument—how Findley addresses women's equality—the use of "big words" ("deconstruction," "militarism," "authoritarianism") and concepts ("binary constructs," and "bureaucratic patriarchal power structure") is confusing. The focus is not on a clear argument about the knowledge, as it should be, but on the writer, who is clearly trying to impress the reader with a broad and pretentious engagement with ideas. Additionally, the writer uses second person—"you"—which contributes to the inappropriate, subjective, and, in Bartholomae's words, "teacherly" tone.

Passage 5

Academic writing as an extension of high school creative writing. While the writer provides the reader with an accurate plot summary of *The Adventures of Alice in Wonderland,* he or she embellishes this summary with adjectives—"pretty great girl," "lovely, beautiful gardens"—and adverbs—"incredibly tired"—that attempt to make the story more interesting for the reader. In academic terms, these words are not necessary to our understanding of the story and, therefore, should not be used. Moreover, these abstract adjectives, such as "lovely" and "beautiful," confuse the meaning with their vagueness. For example, *beautiful* means many different things to different people. Moreover, this writer's attempt to use repetition to embellish the story—the repetition of "down," for example—confuses creative writing with academic writing, which uses repetition sparingly and only in the context of improving the logic of an argument.

CHAPTER 2

Exercise 2.3

1. Medical research shows that vitamin B12 is essential to good health.

2. One global warming myth presupposes that all countries will experience warmer weather.

3. Legally, divorced or separated mothers have a right to apply for and receive child support from the fathers of their children.

Exercise 2.4

Please note that the academic version is shorter because in communicating only the essential information, all unnecessary words have been omitted.

> When entering the teaching profession, student teachers have to learn to be professional. Standards, such as classroom discipline and mutual respect, must be upheld. Additionally, children should be taught to maintain and take pride in achieving a high standard of work.

Exercise 2.5 Identifying Academic Conventions

Please note that the appropriate convention is placed in square brackets after the relevant information, which is underlined for your attention.

> Orientalism is never far from what Denys Hay has called [*reporting expression and verb*] the idea of Europe, a collective notion identifying "us" Europeans as against all "those" non-Europeans, [*definition and summary citation*] and indeed it can [*limiting expression*] be argued that the major component in European culture is precisely [*limiting expression*] what made that culture hegemonic both in and outside Europe: the idea of European identity as a superior one in comparison with all the non-European peoples and cultures. [*restatement of the "major component in European Culture"*] There is in addition the hegemony of European ideas about the Orient, themselves reiterating European superiority over Oriental backwardness, [*summary of dominant ideas about Orient*] usually overriding the possibility that a more independent, or more skeptical, thinker might have had different views on the matter. [*shift to the writer's subject position*]
> —Edward Said, *Orientalism* (7)

Audience: academic scholars, possibly from the disciplines of philosophy, history, or English.

Exercise 2.7

Introduction I

Topic: effective speech writing

Context: World War II and the context for and reception of Winston Churchill's (England) and Adolf Hitler's (Germany) speeches.

Argument: This paper will compare Adolf Hitler's speech given in Munich on 24 February 1941 and Winston Churchill's famous "House of Many Mansions" speech given from London on 20 January 1940. An analysis of the rhetorical devices used by both

Churchill and Hitler will reveal how the rhetorical tools used in politics transcend different cultural and political backgrounds.

Summary of existing knowledge: Churchill and Hitler's cultural and political backgrounds; political rhetoric.

New knowledge: How Churchill and Hitler use political rhetoric in their speeches (two specific speeches form the basis of this analysis.

Summary sentence: This essay examines two speeches, given by Churchill and Hitler in the Second World War, to examine how political rhetoric crosses cultural and political contexts [why it is important].

Research: Cultural and political background of both Churchill and Hitler; techniques of speech writing and political rhetoric; Second World War as a context; Wolfgang Mieder (academic) and Paul Scheffer (journalism).

Introduction II

Topic: Healing the problems created by the colonization of indigenous Canadians.

Context: Colonization of Native Peoples in Canada; Blackfoot culture; autobiography.

Argument: An examination of where and how Bastien uses Blackfoot language suggests that Bastien believes that Blackfoot knowledge may heal this rift in Canadian society.

Summary of existing knowledge: The colonization of indigenous peoples; autobiography.

New knowledge: How Betty Bastien's autobiography contributes to healing the rift created by colonization.

Summary sentence: In her autobiography, *Blackfoot Ways of Knowing,* Betty Bastien uses Blackfoot language and knowledge in an attempt to heal the rift between indigenous and non-idigenous peoples created by colonization.

Research: Colonization and its effects on indigenous peoples: poverty, genocide, and the extinction of their traditional way of life. Autobiography and the role it plays in truth-telling and healing.

Exercise 2.8

Introduction I

Introduction I, The youth Fit for Life Protocol, is an expository research essay. The Fit for Life Protocol is summarized in depth and well-researched, using APA documentation style and a number of credible sources, such as Annesi, Tennant, Westcott, Faigenbaum, and Smith. However, it is an expository essay because the argument simply repeats the aims of the The Fit for Life Protocol, which is designed to be "a solution to the rising health problems in youth."

Introduction II

Introduction II, the analysis of the movie *Spider-Man*, is a research essay. The writer summarizes the film and uses several research sources (Garland-Thompson, Raimi, and Wittgenstein) to make an argument about how language is used to assign the label "freak" to Peter Parker. The argument that Parker's difference is created by "socially constructed meanings and norms that... negatively label individuals as social Others" is original.

CHAPTER 3

Exercise 3.7

Please note that the appropriate convention is placed in square brackets after the relevant information, which is underlined.

> For <u>many</u> [*limiting expression*] African Americans, <u>including those who do not particularly</u> [*limiting expression*] <u>like [Michael] Jackson's music</u> [*further defining or specifying the broad generalization of "many African Americans"*], his achievement retains a special significance. While Jackson was preceded by <u>many</u> [*limiting expression*] <u>vastly</u> [*limiting expression / adverb*] talented African-American musicians and entertainers, his achievement in shattering the sales records for an album in any music category was a long-awaited moment for African Americans. Jackson was told that there was a ceiling for black stars in America—the biggest black star still could not surpass the biggest white star. When Jackson, irked by the fact that <u>"They call Elvis [Presley] the King,"</u> asked <u>"Why don't they call me that"</u> he was advised to curb his ambition because <u>"the white man will never let you be bigger than Elvis" (445)</u>. [*citation*] When Jackson <u>actually</u> [*limiting expression/adverb*] surpassed Presley in record sales, it was a signal event in American cultural history.
>
> —Yuan, David D. "The Celebrity Freak: Michael Jackson's 'Grotesque Glory'."

CHAPTER 4

Exercise 4.5

Change the following passive sentences into active sentences:

1. The researcher designed the experiment.

2. Scientists experienced difficulty when attempting to separate the fluids.

3. They agreed that the experiment should be supervised.

4. Researchers working in the North Pole examined evidence of global warming.

CHAPTER 5

Exercise 5.1

Passage 1

Passage one is journalistic; it is easier to read passively because the information is designed to give the reader a quick and easy overview of the subject. Labrecque is writing for an interested general public that does not have specialized knowledge of the area, so he makes the reading accessible, using everyday clichéd expressions, such as "thrown their hats into the ring." Although Labrecque does use some terms that are not easy to understand—anterior cingulate cortex and ventromedial prefrontal cortex—the reader can understand them in context. A careful reader might also note that while the relationship between the brain and "wisdom" is an interesting concept, it is not fully explicated in the article.

Passage 2

This passage is academic. It uses academic conventions, such as an objective engagement with knowledge and discipline-specific jargon. As this dense and unfamiliar language indicates, this excerpt is more difficult to read, requiring an active engagement with the material. This difficulty is a consequence of the intended academic audience, who are immersed in a discipline-specific language. The sheer number of inaccessible words and expressions make this reading inaccessible to the average reader without research and a good medical dictionary. It is possible, however, to understand the general context: the functional organization of the brain and the roles that the different parts of the brain play in "cognitive control."

Exercise 5.2

As you might have noted, this excerpt is taken from an academic essay and originates in the discipline of psychology. The study is interdisciplinary in that it considers how religious practice can inform a psychological study. The argument, which examines the practice of sukha to see how it can inform a psychological perspective, is organized around two research directions: an examination of the biological responses of Buddhist practitioners who achieve sukha and the "reliability of self-report." In terms of style conventions, the essay uses APA citation style, first-person plural pronoun, "we," and limiting expressions, such as *some, may, presumably, most,* etc. It also uses analytical patterns. The most obvious pattern here is definition: "*sukha* is an enduring trait that arises from a mind in a state of equilibrium and entails a conceptually unstructured and unfiltered awareness of the true nature of reality." Ekman also uses compare–contrast when comparing religious and psychological responses and cause-and-effect when considering the parameters and possible results of the study.

CHAPTER 6

Exercise 6.1

Passage 1

An everyday conversation with a friend. The speaker is attempting to repeat information he or she saw on a television program, but the summary is not accurate: the details are generalized and there is no attempt to cite the sources accurately or provide specific information (What was the program? Who made the claim?). Although this information is interesting, it has no authority and is not verifiable.

Passage 2

Journalism. The passage is taken from a review in *The Guitarist* magazine. The writer summarizes the preferences for guitarists in the '80s and provides enough information to convince us that he is a knowledgeable source. However, his use of colloquial language, such as "mind-boggling" and "halcyon pre-Nevermind days" sets a scene that is current and emotional. From an academic perspective, the appeal to emotion along with the convention of not citing sources makes the information less trustworthy.

Passage 3

Academic. The writer begins by summarizing "what scholars have suggested," providing specific points about the knowledge that is already in circulation, and, using APA citation style, cites the sources of this information (DiPrete & Bachman, 2006; Goldin et al., 2006). The writer then goes on to summarize why the position taken by these scholars might not accurately reflect the entire situation. In doing this, the writer exposes a knowledge gap—"these explanations do not fully account for why women surpassed men" (824)—that she then goes on to address by stating her own position ("this study examines..."), which functions as a summary of the argument.

Exercise 6.3

The appropriate strategy is placed in square brackets after the relevant information.

> In *Oedipus the King*, Oedipus possesses his mother and takes her to his bed as his wife, [*summary*] but the whole plot revolves around the fact that this is unconscious. He is characterized by non-knowing. [*interpretation*] He "knows nothing" about his origins, his parentage, or his present circumstances (474). As Teiresias informs him, "even [his] own words / miss the mark" (348–9). In not knowing who he is, Oedipus is a curse to both himself and his kin (460). He destroys his family and ends up as a blind outcast himself. [*summary*] This focus in the play is historically consistent with, as R.W. Connell states, the belief that men's knowledge hinges not on familial relations, but on an identification with a "fixed, true masculinity" that remains unquestioned (45). [*interpretation*]

CHAPTER 7

Exercise 7.4

Example 1

The International Tree Federation's website. This excerpt is a good example of how the media uses pathos to encourage readers that the topic is important. Readers are encouraged to think about trees as being "immeasurably precious." Moreover, readers are encouraged to read on, incited by the bolded words to see how trees actually "save lives." From an academic perspective, however, this excerpt is not effective because it relies on sensation and emotion to persuade the reader. It does not provide any actual evidence, preferring to rely on the use of adjectives ("healthy, abundant") and sensational verbs, such as "enhance [and] save."

Example 2

Charles Darwin's *The Origin of Species*. Although this excerpt uses a lot of descriptive adjectives, in this context they serve to provide the kind of detail that the reader needs, in the days before photography, to get a clear picture of the specimen under consideration. As an example of nineteenth-century scientific writing, this example captures the reader's interest by encouraging him or her to feel and envision the beauty of the growing tree. However, by today's academic standards, the use of words such as *beautiful* would not be acceptable and a reliance on description, while being useful for conveying context, would not substitute for analysis.

Example 3

"Effects of Urban Tree Management and Species Selection on Atmospheric Carbon Dioxide" by David J. Nowak et al. This excerpt is factual and objective. There is no emotional language. The authors have cited their sources (APA), and they have used clear, focused language. This example is typical of a science essay.

Exercise 7.5

Example 1

This example does not demonstrate that the writer has a thorough knowledge of his or her topic. He or she does not use any evidence, replacing specific, concrete evidence and examples with a string of generalizations about the topic. You will note that there is no clear argument here either, so the writer does not appear knowledgeable and we do not trust him or her. Additionally, the tone is informal. The writer generalizes—"all the time . . . constantly" and uses the subjective, direct address ("you"), rather than an objective, neutral tone.

Example 2

This example is stronger. The writer uses evidence (Susan Sontag and some specific examples), showing that he or she is aware of the larger context encompassing his or her argument. The tone is formal, which enables the reader to surmise that this writer is trustworthy and knowledgeable.

Exercise 7.6

Example 1

This example illustrates a student writer who has not learned to develop his or her points logically. The claims that he or she makes are too general (Which author? What is the good idea? Which problem? Which solution? What examples?), and there is no specific evidence. Additionally, the logic of the argument does not flow smoothly from one point to the next, but, rather, appears to jump from topic to topic. We don't trust this writer to present us with an argument that we can believe or trust.

Example 2

This writer logically develops, point by point, his or her initial statement that a self-reflective teaching practice is challenging. By elucidating *how* this practice is challenging, by providing specific detailed evidence (updating and adapting), by logically connecting his or her main points, and moving the argument forward by adding more depth (teachers—the importance of self-reflection—challenging—adapt methods to needs of students—especially children with learning disabilities), the author more successfully persuades the reader of the validity of the argument.

Exercise 7.8

Humans, as "experiencing subjects of life," have rights.
Animals are "experiencing subjects of life."
Therefore, animals have rights

Exercise 7.9

1. Hasty Generalization.

   Many people report that taking the time each day to meditate is beneficial for insomnia, improving study habits, or just overall relaxing.

2. Circular Argument.

   The connection oral speakers have with nature is often transferred to the larger cultural environment.

3. Non Sequitur.

   Sheridan states, "Literate cultures could not accept the idea that the sacred was allied with and manifested in the natural environment" (26). Refusing this direct connection between the sacred and nature, literate cultures interpreted the sacred indirectly through written language or, more specifically, the alphabet.

4. Ad Hominem.

   Adding the "United Colors of Benetton" logo at the bottom of the advertisement reinforces the importance of the charitable cause while also promoting Benetton products.

CHAPTER 8

Exercise 8.2

Text A

The Down syndrome advertisement taken from a blog written by Shannon Roberts and titled "An end to Down syndrome in New Zealand?" This advertisment advocates for the rights of Down syndrome children and their parents. The advertisement, which is geared to the general public, successfully uses a biased, personal testimony designed to change the viewer's perspective that living with a Down syndrome child is difficult. The repetition of "my life" and the use of words and expressions, such as "brighter," "wonderful," and "filled with love" juxtaposed against the expectant, happy face of a young Down syndrome child convinces the viewer of the value of these children. The advertisement's credibility rests upon the viewer's willingness to take *one* personal opinion to stand for many (*all* parents of Down syndrome children) and to be emotionally moved by the personal testimony that works in conjunction with the appealing, even "adorable" blond child. The web link on the side of the advertisement in the bottom-right corner (everydayfamily.com) lends authority to the advertisement. It lets us know that we can go to this site for more information while also adding to the emotional pull by telling us that the issue presented here has relevance to "everyday" families.

Text B

Written in 1994 by J. Jenish and T. Fennell in an article for *Maclean's* magazine, titled "What Would You Do: In Saskatchewan, a Wrenching Verdict of Murder Reignites a Long-Simmering Debate about Mercy Killing." The authors of this article are clearly biased, as they do not present a balanced argument, providing arguments for and against Robert Latimer's actions, but, rather, one that chooses to show Latimer, the man who killed his disabled daughter, Tracy, in a positive light. This bias is present in the title of the article, which presents the verdict as "wrenching" and the murder as a "mercy killing."

In the body of the article, Jenish and Fennell appear to present an objective account, but a careful examination reveals that these facts are designed to present Latimer as a conscientious farmer: someone the reader can identify with and respect. Moreover, by using descriptive adjectives, such as *typical, hard-working, clean-living,* and *self-reliant,* to create the image of an upstanding, responsible, law-abiding man, Jenish and Fennell carefully construct an argument that encourages the reader to identify with Latimer, "Laddie" to many, a "friend" to many in the community, and "an ordinary person faced with extraordinary hardship" (Janz). Although this excerpt does not directly support Latimer's decision to end his daughter's life, the way the article encourages the reader to identify and sympathize with Latimer does imply an albeit left-wing sympathy that may or may not be displaced.

Text C

Excerpted from Heidi Janz's academic article "Disabling Images and the Dangers of Public Perception." Janz uses the support of experts in their field, not personal opinion or story, as in the news article, to support her argument. There are direct quotes that reflect and support Janz's own argument that the public sympathy for Robert Latimer is misplaced. Janz raises two significant and related questions—Tracy's disability and pain—and calls into question the ethics of killing a handicapped child versus an able-bodied child. Note that while Janz clearly feels strongly about this issue, her argument remains objective and couched in important questions about the ethical treatment of disabled persons. *The Constitutional Forum* is a respected academic journal, which adds further credibility to her argument.

Exercise 8.3

1. This thesis is too general: What does the writer mean by "In recent years?" What specific period of time frames the writer's research? A specific example (or two) of Facebook bullying would provide evidence and support for this argument. Can the writer prove the vulnerability of certain students?

2. This thesis needs to be more specific: which Christian perspective? Which text is being used to support this argument? If it is the Bible, then which books? As is, this is an expository essay. This argument has already been made. The writer needs to find a way to insert his or her own argument. For example, an argument about "rights" might make this argument interesting or, alternatively, the argument might be further developed by considering how this "right" relates to animal experimentation.

3. Once again, this is an expository essay thesis statement. The writer is not telling us anything we don't already know. The writer might ask *why* this argument is

important to write about. *How* will this writer manage this very broad argument: which quantum physicists, which texts? This argument could be made original by applying a scientific reading of string theory and multi-dimensionality to a novel or a film.

4. This writer has two texts for a compare–contrast essay. However, he or she does not have an argument yet: ask *why The Hurt Locker* is a better Iraq war film than *Stop-Loss*.

5. This is an expository argument. The writer is telling us a well-known fact rather than making an argument about the case or the consequences of the ruling since 1973. To make this argument persuasive and original, the writer would need to apply the 1973 United States Roe vs Wade abortion case to an event or a situation either in the United States or in another country, such as Canada. The writer might also consider some pertinent cases to examine the negligable boundaries between legal and illegal abortion.

6. This thesis is quite good: the writer has two primary texts that he or she intends to compare and contrast and an argument (the privileging of able-bodied fetuses). The argument is not obvious on first examination, which is good.

Exercise 8.8

Excerpt 1

This paragraph provides a clear context and description of the advertisement. The tone is objective, and it has a clear thesis statement: the advertisement uses generalizations to manipulate viewers into believing that it is beneficial to drink milk. The focus is on the advertisement, not on drinking milk. Consequently, the evidence is directly related to and taken from an analysis of the advertisement.

Excerpt 2

This paragraph is not as clear. The writer assumes that the advertisement's claim is true—milk makes people feel "super" and "strong"—and slips into a teacherly tone when using second person (you) to address the viewer. The thesis goes beyond the primary text, effectively ignoring the advertisement, to focus on the benefits of drinking milk. In other words, the evidence in this paragraph takes us away from the actual advertisement to further develop the advertisement's claim that it is beneficial to drink milk. The writer of this paragraph will have to do research about the benefits of drinking milk to find evidence. This writer, then, would be considered "off topic" and would need to rethink his or her use of evidence with the advertisement in mind. This latter problem is one of the most common errors made by first-year students.

Exercise 8.10

Excerpt 1

This paragraph makes the most common first-year student mistake: it stays at the level of generality. This writer needs to incorporate concrete evidence to support the large, general statements. In other words, Regan's "various ways . . . his use of emotion . . . numerous verbs" and his "vision" all require concrete evidence to add depth to the larger generalizations. The illogical leap from emotion to verbs is confusing, so the writer needs to learn how to fully develop one point before making connections and moving on to the next point. This paragraph is not, at this time, engaging in a critical analysis that tells her readers something new about Regan's work.

Excerpt 2

This paragraph is a better attempt at a critical analysis, but the writer also fails to support the large generalizations with concrete evidence. Examples of where and how both writers use logic and "straightforward and strong evidence" would make this writing considerably stronger. Likewise, the reader needs to know how and why, with concrete examples, "their analyses are well thought out." At the end of the paragraph, the reader is not clear about what the mentioned "technique" is, so this illogical development needs to be clarified in the body of the paragraph.

Excerpt 3

The last paragraph is much stronger because it does achieve a balance between large abstractions and concrete evidence. It provides the example (the black-and-white thinking of some animal activists) and the logical fallacy that this thinking implies, defines the fallacy, and then uses hypothetical examples to call this type of thinking into question. It also tells us something "new" about the essays that we might not have noticed before (the fallacy of false dilemma).

CHAPTER 9

Exercise 9.5

Example 1

This paragraph is a good example of a writer who provides appropriate and focused context. In this case, the writer uses Walter Ong and his privileging of oral communication to provide a context for thinking about possible dialogues between indigenous (orality) and non-indigenous (literacy) peoples.

Example 2

This paragraph is an example of student work that appears, at the beginning of this paragraph, to be focused, providing the reader with a good summary of the advertisement and stating the writer's intention of examining how advertisers capitalize on media icons. However, the writer goes off-topic in the thesis when it appears that he or she intends instead to examine the benefits of drinking milk. Rather than being central to the analysis, the advertisement thus becomes a lead into a discussion about the benefits of drinking milk. The focus should stay on the primary text—the Superman advertisement—and develop an argument and a context that is clearly related to that.

Exercise 9.8

My comments:

This introduction needs focusing. It clearly lets the reader know what the primary text is— George Orwell's "Politics and the English Language"—but although the writer points to the role of politicians, the introduction does not seem to have a clear workable argument. Evidence for an argument *must* be found in the primary text and it is not clear how the writer intends to do this without generalizing about what politicians "do" or conflating time periods (when Orwell wrote this essay and now). To solve this problem, be specific: which society? Which politicians? Ask "How can I make generalizations more specific by adding concrete, supportive evidence?" Related to this point, the argument needs to be structured so that one point logically builds on the previous point and leads to a far more specific thesis than the one outlined here. Moreover, this over-generalized thesis takes the reader "outside" Orwell's argument and requires extensive research as to how and why he omits the role of society and its impact on the English language. Last, the essay needs to be checked for wordy constructions, repetition, tense, modifying errors ("cause of the poor English state"), and agreement errors (politicians/writers→ his/her, etc.).

My revision

> In his article "Politics and the English Language," Orwell writes that the poor state of the English language is due to politicians who misuse rhetorical tools, such as dying metaphors or pretentious diction, that change the tone of a sentence (359). According to Orwell, the mind of the English writer is corrupted by an unclear or pretentious political and economic writing style. In other words, "language can . . . corrupt thought," (Orwell 361). Orwell's argument that politicians and the language they use are the cause of the deterioration of the English language is, however, complicated by the impact that society has on politicians. This essay will examine Orwell's blind spot and consider how certain aspects of society can play a role in both deteriorating and repairing English.

Compare this revised paragraph with your own: how is it similar or different? What changes have I made and why have I made them? Please note that, as is, the thesis is implicit. Because "society" is a broad term, the writer will be expected to clearly define what these "certain aspects" are in the body of the paper.

CHAPTER 10

Exercise 10.7

1. Although this student cites his source, M. Barker, he or she does not use any other form of citation method to identify whether these ideas, clearly originating with Barker, are hisor her complete summarized ideas or if some of the material should be contained within quotation marks. For example, Barker is mentioned in relation to the idea that comic books constitute a contract between the text and the reader, but the writer of this passage forgets to document where he or she got this information. The second sentence here extends Barker's theory, but this sentence is not documented at all. Therefore, it is not clear if they are the writer's words and ideas or Barker's. One of citation's main roles is to ensure that you distinguish between your words and views and the words and views of others. All words and ideas that are not your own *must* be cited.

2. The second example illustrates another example of accidental plagiarism. The writer clearly intends to document his or her sources, using APA style to quote Chomsky's theory. However, this writer forgets to put quotation marks around the direct quote—"letting markets set [the] price and encouraging the government [to] get out of the way" (p. 20)—even though he or she does remember to document the page number and use square brackets to indicate changes to the quote. The second sentence includes a direct quote that has quotation marks around it, but the source is not mentioned. As is, the quote reads as if it is Chomsky's words, but this is not the case. Scholars who want to identify the sources of these quotes will quickly become confused. Paying attention to detail will help correct these errors.

CHAPTER 12

Exercise 12.1: Grammar Pretest

1. Find the subjects and verbs: underline the subjects and circle the verbs.
   A. Democracy protects the rights of all citizens.
   B. According to Schryer, researchers are privileged. [*linking verb*]
   C. Animal rights advocates propose that animals should be treated [*verb phrase = helping verb + be + main verb*] as persons, not property.
   D. Leonard Cohen is a poet and a musician.

2. Recognizing independent (main) and dependent (subordinate) clauses: underline the independent clauses and circle the dependent clauses in the following sentences.

    A. Many Americans objected when Bill Clinton signed the Kyoto Accord.

    B. Because there was strong opposition from Albertans, Canada was reluctant to ratify the Accord.

    C. While outdated research denies human responsibility for global warming, current research reinforces that human pollution is its ultimate cause.

3. Recognizing and using coordination and subordination.

    A. Poetry is important, ***but*** it is not particularly popular.

    B. Qualitative research attempts to uncover underlying theoretical assumptions and opinions ***while*** quantitative research conforms to a set of measurable guidelines.

    C. A literature review assesses the published information on a particular subject area, ***and***, sometimes, this assessment is related to a specific time period.

    D. ***Because*** literature comments on human life, it enables readers to empathize with other people's life situations.

4. Use an appropriate adverbial conjunction and semicolon to connect the following pairs of sentences.

    A. The songs of Leonard Cohen reflect his skill as a poet; ***however,*** his skill as a poet does not negate his skill as a songwriter.

    B. Plagiarism is a serious academic offence; ***in fact,*** it is considered a form of stealing and may result in expulsion.

    C. Language is important to culture; ***nevertheless,*** one culture's communication does not necessarily translate to another's.

5. Finding restrictive (essential) and non-restrictive (non-essential) modifiers: underline the restrictive and circle the non-restrictive modifiers in the following sentences.

    A. Randy Bachman, a Canadian singer-songwriter, is legendary in the rock-and-roll industry.

    B. Diana Krall is a Canadian who sings and performs jazz music.

6. Fix the common errors in the following student paragraph, rewriting the paragraph so that it makes sense.

The ***Adbuster's*** advertisement spoof "Beauty Is Averageness" critiques the beauty industry, ***arguing*** that traditional ideas about beauty are unrealistic and impossible. The advertisement shows a girl who is "undoubtedly" beautiful. The text, ***which*** is printed all over her face, tells us that she is non-existent ***because*** she is ***merely*** a compilation of many different women's faces. This beautiful woman is a representation of many average women who are the real victims of the beauty industry.

Exercise 12.2

Buzz Aldrin and the book's title, *Reaching for the Moon,* are proper nouns. They are capitalized because they represent a specific example of a larger category (people and books). Note, though, that *for* and *the* are not capitalized in the title, according to the rules for capitalizing titles. The common nouns are *man, moon, book*, and *ambition*. The pronouns are *who* (relative pronoun that stands for Buzz Aldrin) and *it* (stands for the book, *Reaching for the Moon).*

Exercise 12.4

Underline the subjects in the following sentences.

1. Simon and Peter were covered in snow.

2. They struggled to their feet.

3. A few people, who were skiing by, stopped to help them.

4. Someone on a snowmobile came and gave them a ride down the hill.

Exercise 12.5

Underline the verbs in the following sentences.

1. His mother drives him to the interview.

2. David reads.

3. David responds skilfully to the interview questions.

4. The interviewers appreciate and acknowledge David's knowledge.

Exercise 12.6

Underline the direct [D] and indirect objects [ID] in the following sentences.

1. Everyone loves a circus. [D]

2. Ruth ordered pancakes and sausages [D] for breakfast. [ID]

3. Steve cooked us [ID] a quiche. [D]

4. He painted his car yellow. [D]

5. My little sister cannot drink milk. [D]

Exercise 12.7

Identify the subjects or compound subjects (more than one), the verbs, and the objects (direct and/or indirect) in the following academic sentences:

1. Canadians [*noun/subject*] conceive [*verb*] of a just and equitable Canada [*object*].

2. The Charter of Rights and Freedoms [*noun/subject*] acknowledges [*verb*] women's rights, children's rights, the rights of individuals with disabilities [*object is compound here: 3 sets of rights*].

3. Section 15 of the Charter [*noun/subject*] outlines [*verb*] equality rights [*direct object*] for people with disabilities [*indirect object*].

Exercise 12.8

Part A

Combine the following two pairs of independent clauses.

1. He joined the independent clauses with conjunctions, ***and*** he placed a comma between them.

2. Lack of physical activity in adolescents can cause health issues, ***so*** physical activity and proper nutrition in adolescents is important.

Part B

Combine the following sentences using a semicolon and a conjunctive adverb:

1. Shamanism is a spiritual healing art; ***consequently,*** Shamans heal through rituals that connect them to the spirit world.

2. Al Gore argues that global warming is specifically relevant to Americans; ***however,*** all countries and all people are responsible for fixing this problem.

Part C

Combine the pairs of sentences below by using a subordinating conjunction.

1. Stereotypes about motherhood will never change ***even though*** conceptions of motherhood are at the centre of public controversy today.

2. ***Although*** a British government report asserted that the melting of the ice caps has far-reaching, undesirable consequences for our future, some scientists still argue that the magnitude of the problem has been exaggerated.

Exercise 12.9

Coordinate clauses

Coordinate the following pairs of sentences using a coordinating conjunction, a correlative conjunction, or a semicolon plus conjunctive adverb.

1. The findings indicate that we should not be occupied with social exclusion, *but* we should be looking at how to enable inclusion.

   Another way of writing this might be:

   The findings indicate that we should *not only* be occupied with social inclusion *but also* be looking at how to enable inclusion.

2. Many people look back nostalgically at close-knit communities, *so* communal farms and urban settlements are becoming popular.

Subordinate clauses

Subordinate the following pairs of sentences using a subordinating conjunction.

3. *Because* they have been confronted with an unequal labour market, they will adopt a default position that favours low-wage policies.

4. *Although* inequalities could be minimized by the welfare state, they had to address areas of intense deprivation.

Relative pronouns

Combine the following pair of sentences using a relative pronoun.

5. The worldwide exodus, *which grew steadily,* coincided with the rapid mechanization of agriculture.

Exercise 12.11

1. Most importantly, [*phrase*] when students complete a first draft, [*subordinate*] they consider the job of writing done. [*main clause*]…When professional writers complete a first draft, [*subordinate*] they usually feel that they are at the start of the writing process. [*main clause*] When a draft is completed, [*subordinate*] the job of writing can begin. [*main clause*]…Most writers share the feeling that the first draft, and all of those which follow, [*relative pronoun clause*] is an opportunity to discover what they have to say. [*main clause*] (Adapted from Donald Murray's "The Maker's Eye," 120.)

2. News is a high-status television genre. Its claimed objectivity and independence from political or government agencies is[,] as many theorists would argue[,] essential

for the workings of democracy. Television companies[,] who are in the process of applying for renewal of their licences[,] use their news programs as evidence of their social responsibility. However[,] news is also a commodity. It is expensive to gather and distribute[,] and it must produce an audience of the right size. Although the national news is primarily masculine culture[,] it often ends with a "softer" item that is intended for a female audience. The news[,] more importantly[,] is a discourse[,] a set of conventions that strives to control and limit the meanings of events. Theories of news[,] which foreground questions of accuracy bias and objectivity[,] can provide insight into the ideology of the news makers. (Taken from John Fiske's *Television Culture* (87).)

Exercise 12.12

Communication is essential to science. Undergraduate and graduate students are apprentices to the discipline of science*; **therefore,*** learning to communicate in writing is important. The publication of scientific results is most important, ***so*** it is important for scholars to write about their research. They must submit their research to public scrutiny, distribute it widely, ***and*** strive for excellence at all stages of the research and writing process. ***Consequently,*** students, ***who are not familiar with these expectations,*** need guidance to learn how to meet the standards of scholarly research and writing.

Exercise 12.15: Grammar Post-Test

Remember to compare your results with your understanding of grammar as evidenced in the pretest. Do you have a better understanding of how you might use grammar now to improve your writing so that your meaning and emphasis are clearer? As you should now realize, clarity of meaning is the ultimate purpose of grammar.

1. Combine the following sentences, using coordination *or* subordination, to make one sentence.
    a. ***Because*** language is both arbitrary and fixed, it resists at the same time as it conforms to the dominant societal conventions, rules, and traditions.
    b. Emily Brontë distances her readers from Lockwood ***when*** she emphasizes his superficial and hypocritical actions.
    c. Schryer is concerned with the competing genres in veterinary institutions, ***but*** she is not concerned with animal rights.

2. Combine or rearrange the following sentences with the use of an appropriate relative pronoun.
    a. Non-Native Canadians must assist in decolonization, ***which*** is good for all Canadians.

    b. Tricia Rose is the author of *Black Noise,* **which** is perhaps the most important study of rap music.

    c. Coyle, **who** works for a market research firm, asks if direct-to-consumer advertising is ethical given how it broadens the domain of medicine.

3. Correct the following comma splice, run-on, or sentence fragment errors.

    a. The word *accommodate* is often misspelled. Remember to use the two c's and the two m's.

    b. When I sat down, she stood up.

    c. Knowledge about disability is socially produced, and this knowledge upholds existing practices.

    d. The AIDS pandemic has been addressed by gay organizations who attempt to address the extreme homophobia around the disease.

4. Fix the following subject–verb agreement errors by choosing one of the verbs in parenthesis.

    a. Kinga and Auren *discuss* their favourite issues.

    b. The teacher, along with her students, *hopes* to make the trip.

    c. The action of the supervisor *was* deemed inappropriate.

    c. The reading club along with the writing club *is* growing by the hour.

5. Correct the following subject–verb agreement errors.

    a. Woolf encourage<u>s</u> her readers to identify with women's position in a male-dominated culture.

    b. Smith, along with Johnson and Coombes, argue<u>s</u> that the Far North must be protected.

    c. In "The Politics of the English Language," Orwell equate<u>s</u> bad writing with poor thinking. He points out that everyone <u>is</u> responsible for correcting this problem.

    d. Lee Maracle, writing on behalf of all Native writers, object<u>s</u> to the appropriation of Native stories.

6. Correct the following pronoun/antecedent agreement errors by choosing one of the pronouns in parenthesis.

    a. In Israel, everyone must do *his or her* army duty.

    b. Joan was worried that someone had not received *his or her* invitation.

    c. Each one of us had to present *his or her* piece of ID at the door.

7. Correct the following pronoun/antecedent agreement errors by making the ambiguous reference clear.

    a. In "The Goods on the Tube," Mark Kingwell points out that TV fans feel embarrassed about *their* love of superficial shows.

    b. Today, primary oral cultures in a strict sense hardly exist since *they are* immersed in dominant literary cultures.

8. Rewrite the following sentences to eliminate the *misplaced, limiting,* and *dangling* modifiers.
   a. That summer, Roxanne went swimming *almost* every day.
   b. I jumped out of bed *in my bare feet* as the radio alarm went off.
   c. Last week, I found a box, *which was made of beautifully carved mahogany*, containing an old health care card.
   d. I watched the wild black stallion, *who, with nostrils flaring,* sped away.
   e. Knowing that it is important to respect the language of indigenous people is not the same as actually practising *respect* in everyday life, Johnston insists.
   f. Writing from Birmingham Jail, *King uses* an impassioned rhetoric to invoke the moral conscience of the nation.

9. Correct the verb errors in the following passage.

   Alice Walker was born in 1944. She *was* the eighth and youngest child of Willie Lee and Minnie Grant Walker who were sharecroppers in Eatonton, Georgia. Walker did well in school, encouraged by her teachers and her mother, who *loved* her stories. For two years, Walker attended Spelman College, then she *studied* at Sarah Lawrence College, where she began her writing career and *became* active in the civil rights movement. Today, she *is* one of the best-known fiction writers in the world.

10. Fix the following common grammar and punctuation errors.
    a. *I was* jogging down the street in a blue suit when the truck came out of nowhere and—almost hit me.
    b. Fukuyama, Kass, and their allies *have* the president's ear.
    c. Each of the languages has idioms of *its* own.
    d. The customer asked the pharmacist for the prescription, but the pharmacist *told* the customer that the ingredients had been ordered.
    e. In any non-violent campaign, there are three basic steps, such as negotiation, self-purification, and direct action.
    f. The students bought books, papers, and printer cartridges.
    g. The travel agent's advice proved correct. Amsterdam was an entertaining city.

11. Edit the following student paragraph, fixing the common errors and the punctuation errors so that the paragraph makes better sense.

    The Camel Cigarette Company relies on marketing a "Western Lifestyle" to sell its cigarettes. The "Western Lifestyle," *one that portrays "freedom, integrity, and self-sufficiency,"* is at the centre of Camel's marketing scheme. The "Camel Filter" advertisement, *which* depicts a rugged hard-working man smoking a refreshing "Camel Filter" in the wilderness, is a prime example of the marketing ploys that

Camel effectively utilize*s* to sell its cigarettes. Many people *agree* that tobacco smoking is a deadly habit and that tobacco companies, including Camel, gain prosperity at the expense of *their* dying patrons. ***Although I acknowledge that this is an important consideration, it cannot be denied that*** Camel is effective in selling the appearance of rugged individualism, healthy masculinity and the "American Dream" of freedom, integrity, and self-sufficiency. ***Unfortunately, however,*** it also sacrifices ethics for corporate gain.

CHAPTER 13

Exercise 13.4

1. Writers who overload their sentences with nominalizations tend to sound pompous and abstract (Sword).

2. Husky as a corporation is committed to its concept of responsible citizenship. While considering how social, environmental, and economic concerns might impact its core businesses, of primary concern is maximizing the profits for its key stakeholders, both now and in the future.

Peer-Review Guidelines

As stated in chapter 9, working with your peers in and out of class works extremely well if you can establish genuine support and commitment from all group members. Peer-group work, whether it is in pairs or in larger groups, up to six members, can help you with any reading, writing, and speaking difficulties related to your work in any college or university course. Here are some of the benefits of this kind of peer-group work:

- You will all become better, more effective, readers and writers.
- You will have a "real" audience that can give you feedback on your interpretation of a specific reading and on the content, structure, and general effectiveness of your paper.
- Because the process encourages you to think about your choices, you will become a deeper, more thoughtful, critical thinker.
- The process can help build confidence by providing you with a safe place to share your ideas and your work, first with the group members and later, possibly, with the whole class.
- It can help establish community with other writers, as you identify with their difficulties and strengths while also coming up with solutions.

ESTABLISHING PEER-REVIEW GROUPS

Peer review can be used for reading or writing. It can work well to help you review and understand a difficult text. Usually, your instructor sets this up with some focused reading questions that can be discussed within the groups, and follows up with an exercise in or out of class to develop the discussion. My focus here though is to provide you with information for setting up and using an effective writing peer-review group. This information might help you understand the process when you see it in your writing class or it can be used to help you establish a peer-review group out of class.

Some General Rules and Expectations

Difficulties with the peer-review process are usually the result of students not having a clear idea of how to engage in one-to-one critiques and/or their tendency to believe they are not qualified to offer critiques. This latter point is not true: as readers, you can offer invaluable feedback to other students and, in turn, improve your own ability to critique your own work.

More problematic is understanding how to offer a productive critique of another student's work. This problem can be alleviated, first, by having a clear idea of what is expected in your writing assignment. This is easily resolved by reading the assignment sheet carefully and by understanding the conventions of the expected form (essay, literature review, etc.). Your instructor should provide you with this information, but if anything is not clear you *must* clarify the expectations with your instructor. Second, you will need to understand the process and set up some clear expectations and rules of exchange. Here are some guidelines:

- Focus on what the writer does well, as well as on what needs to be improved.
- Don't monopolize the discussion. Everyone's comments need to be heard.
- Listen respectfully and constructively to everyone's comments, and try to add to and build on them: remember that no comment is a bad comment.
- Offer observations and suggestions, but don't try to rewrite the writer's essay.
- Be kind—you are here to help each other—but make sure that you do offer some points for improvement.
- Focus on the writing, not the writer.
- Don't get off track and start talking about related content or issues.
- Remember that the writer has the ultimate control over his or her essay: he or she can choose to incorporate your comments or ignore them.

Establishing a Group: Group Size

Peer-review groups work best if they are limited to between three and six students. Working in pairs can work well for a detailed close reading of another student's work, but the advantage of larger groups is that there is more feedback. Any more than six to a group can diffuse the focus and allow shyer students to sit back and not participate. It is also easier for several students to start up a conversation and get off track.

You need as much feedback as you can get. When working in pairs, you get a response from one student, but when working in larger groups, you can get feedback from a number of students. While all responses to your work must be considered as potential problems, consistently similar responses from a number of students should let you know there is a clear area of difficulty that needs to be addressed. Similarly, a number of positive responses can affirm that you are, indeed, on the right track. Here are some suggested groupings for response:

Group of Three
Reviewer Student A
Reviewer Student B   →   Listening and responding to Writer Student C

Group of Four
Reviewer Student A
Reviewer Student B   →   Listening and responding to Writer Student D
Reviewer Student C

Keep in mind, though, that effective peer-reviewing takes time. Each student must receive an equal number of responses to their work, so set an allocated time for each reading and response. Ten to fifteen minutes is usually appropriate for each student.

The Peer-Review Process

The following process has worked best for me in class, but there are several variations that can be implemented. For example, you might choose to all read the work silently or simply listen and respond without taking notes. As I have stressed throughout this book, find out what works best for you and your group.

- Student A, who is having his or her work critiqued, establishes a focus for the reading. He or she might want the responders to pay attention to structure, content, evidence, etc.
- Student A then reads his or her writing (an essay or part of an essay that he or she needs feedback on: introduction, conclusion, etc.) out loud. Read slowly and clearly. Do not stop to make comments.
- As Student A reads, the responders (Students B and C, for example) follow along with either a copy of the work that is being read or a peer-review questionnaire. If they use the actual essay, they can make quick comments or underline important ideas or points, but if they use a peer-review form, they will have to write notes in the specific content areas. Most important, they must allow the writer/reader to continue without stopping him or her to ask questions.
- When the writer (Student A) has finished reading, each respondent takes a turn in providing their response to the work: they must say something they like about the work as well as indicating something that can be improved. At this point, the writer does not comment but simply takes note of the responses.
- When everyone has given their responses, the writer/reader can now respond to the comments of the respondents and a discussion of the work can begin. The writer/reader can ask questions and receive feedback at this point. It is important to stay open to suggestions and not get caught up in defending your work. All responses should be given to the writer at the end of each student's turn, so the writer can take the responses home and incorporate them appropriately into the writer's thinking about his or her work.
- Make sure you keep your eye on the time: appointing one member of the group to be a timekeeper can help. If you are in class, your instructor will manage this.

To work well, the group work must be focused and organized. What follows are some general rules to help you do this.

Rules for Writer and Respondents

Here are some specific rules for both the writer and the respondents.

For writers

- Direct the focus of your listeners/respondents to areas you believe might be problematic: some aspect of your work that needs attention (content, structure, grammar, the clarity of a particular concept, etc.).
- Read your work slowly and clearly; pause slightly where you have punctuated with commas; pause for a longer period of time where you have a semicolon or period.
- When it is your respondents' turn to comment, listen attentively and take notes of anything you consider important (look for patterns in these responses).
- Do not interrupt or disagree with the respondents when they are making their comments.
- Solicit more information after they have given their responses, asking questions or asking for help with a specific area of difficulty.
- Trust your readers and be open to changing your ideas, but, at the same time, keep control of your own work and ideas.

For respondents/listeners

- Listen carefully and attentively: be interested in the writing.
- Do not interrupt the writer's reading: instead, make brief notes for later clarification on a piece of paper or on the writer's work that you are following as he or she reads.
- After the work is read, respond first to the piece as a whole. Make sure you say something positive at this point, then respond to the area that you see needs improvement.
- Use "I" statements—"I think…"; "I believe…"; etc.—while keeping the focus on the writing not the writer: "I think this topic sentence could connect more logically with the concluding sentence of the previous paragraph," for example.
- Respond mostly to content and organization, but do highlight a grammar error that *consistently* appears in the writer's work.

PEER-EDITING WORKSHEETS AND PROCESSES

While having a copy of the writer's essay is a good strategy for effective response, you might also choose to use a peer-editing response questionnaire. These questionnaires or response forms, which can be used with or without the corresponding writer's essay, can help you focus your response in relation to specific areas of concern. Here are several sample peer-review sheets:

Peer-Review Worksheet

This worksheet works well with the outlined process above. It can be used in conjunction with the writer's essay or it can be used on its own. Simply listen attentively as the writer reads his or her paper out loud, filling in the appropriate sections of the review sheet as you listen. Once again, your responses would be brief so that you could continue to follow the writer's meaning. With this process, however, you would be advised to take a few minutes after the reading to fill out your form in more detail. The following form is designed to elicit a written and spoken response to an entire essay:

PEER-REVIEW FORM

Writer/Reader: _____   **Respondent:** _____

Introduction and Thesis

❑ Is the opening sentence effective? Is it too general or too unfocused?
❑ Is the introduction logical? Are there any points that shouldn't be there?
❑ Did I get lost at any point? Try and note the place where you couldn't follow the argument.
❑ Is the thesis clear? Do I understand what argument the writer is trying to make? What is it?

_____

_____

Content and Context

❑ Is the argument clear and focused? Is it clearly developed throughout the entire paper?
❑ Are there any points where the writer goes off-topic?
❑ Is there an effective context established for this analysis? What is it?

_____

_____

Organization

❑ Is the argument organized logically throughout the paper?
❑ Do the sentences and paragraphs flow logically from one point to another? Highlight points where you got lost or couldn't follow the argument.

_____

_____

Conclusion

❑ Does the conclusion round up the main argument, providing a review of the main points of the essay without repeating them?
❑ Does it make a larger point about the significance of the issues expressed in the essay?

_____

_____

Voice

❑ Is there a strong sense of voice here?
❑ Is the language appropriate to the audience?
❑ Is the language logical and self-assured without being "teacherly," forceful, or too timid?

_____

_____

Metaphor

If you were to come up with a metaphor for this entire paper, what would it be? Explain how your metaphor is relevant to the paper. Some examples include a "steam train," where the paragraphs all logically follow each other and move the argument forward, or a "wild flower garden," where the language is pretty but lacks order and substance.

_____

_____

PEER-REVIEW PROCESS I

This process is relatively simple. It demands that you ask questions of the essay you are peer-reviewing as you silently read it. Here are the questions:

1. First, read the essay quickly: underline points, ideas, sentences that strike you as being particularly good; put a squiggly line underneath points, ideas, or sentences that are unclear or illogical.

2. Go back to the beginning of the essay and read more carefully. Pay attention to the introduction and the thesis (or hypothesis). Summarize the essay in three to five sentences.

3. Outline the essay, keeping the thesis in mind. Focus on overall development (big picture). Does the argument go off track anywhere? Does the conclusion effectively round out the introduction and thesis?

4. Examine the writer's use of evidence and analysis, keeping the thesis in mind. (small picture: focus on paragraphs and sentences). Is there enough evidence? Is it appropriate and focused? Is there an appropriate amount of analysis to support the evidence?

5. Have you placed any squiggly lines under grammar errors? Does the writer consistently make the same errors? Can you identify them?

6. Write a short paragraph-length summary of your analysis: make sure you first focus on what is working well in the essay, as well as focusing on what needs work, in your opinion. Give the analysis to the writer and discuss your response with him or her.

Peer-Review Process II

This evaluation questionnaire works best for an in-depth paired reading of a student's work. The student respondent will need to keep this alongside the writer's actual paper when evaluating and commenting on the work. I would allow more time for this type of review (15–20 minutes), which could be followed by a short discussion of the paper.

PEER-REVIEW EVALUATION

Writer's name: _____

Peer editor's name: _____

Use the form below to guide you in your evaluation of a peer's work. Identify both strengths and weaknesses, and provide comments that might help the author to improve his or her work. Evaluate for structural problems (grammar, punctuation, sentence-level errors) as well as content and organization (idea development, persuasive appeals, cohesion, etc.). You need to respond meaningfully to the paper you are reviewing. DO NOT make any corrections to the work; your job is to point out strengths and weaknesses and make suggestions for improvements; it is the writer's job to implement the changes.

Introduction

- ❑ Does the introduction grab your interest? Why or why not?
- ❑ Does it announce the subject and provide sufficient background information before giving the thesis statement?
- ❑ Does the thesis statement contain the author's opinion and purpose (how the author will develop it)?
- ❑ Does the author establish his or her ethos? How?

_____

_____

_____

_____

Body Paragraphs

- ❑ Does the order of the paragraphs seem logical?
- ❑ Are any paragraphs too long or too short?
- ❑ Does each paragraph support the thesis statement?
- ❑ Does each paragraph have a topic sentence that is developed within the paragraph?
- ❑ Is each paragraph cohesive? Which ones are not? Why?
- ❑ Are there appropriate transitions between sentences linking them together?
- ❑ Is there evidence of the writer's opinion in every paragraph?
- ❑ Is the use of logos effective? Does the evidence support the central argument?
- ❑ Are the ideas focused?

_____

_____

_____

_____

Conclusion

- ❑ Does the conclusion synthesize and interpret the author's views rather than just reword the thesis?
- ❑ Does the author show how or why his/her argument and conclusions are valid and relevant?
- ❑ Has the essay left you with a lasting impression?

_____

_____

_____

_____

Continued

Mechanics

❏ Is the essay free of comma splices, run-on sentences, and sentence fragments?
❏ Is the essay in correct grammatical format?
❏ Are sentences parallel in structure?
❏ Is the essay written in first or third person?
❏ Is the wording concise, clear, and direct?
❏ Is the essay free of spelling errors?
❏ Is the language professional, avoiding slang, idioms, and casual jargon?

_____

_____

_____

_____

_____

Citation

❏ Does the essay contain both parenthetical citations AND reporting expressions?
❏ Do the citations follow a documentation style format (i.e., MLA/APA or CSE)?
❏ Do the source citations support the thesis?
❏ Are the sources relevant and credible?
❏ Has the author used the required number of academic sources?
❏ Is there an over-reliance on any source(s)?
❏ Does the author seem familiar with the sources?
❏ Is there too much reliance on the sources?

_____

_____

_____

_____

_____

Content

❏ Does the author seem credible? Trustworthy?
❏ Has the author conveyed knowledge and defended an assertion?
❏ Has the author used a variety of rhetorical tools to increase your understanding?
❏ Is the author impartial, objective, non-judgmental?

_____

_____

_____

_____

Provide written comments below and on as many attached pages as necessary. The more criticism you provide, the more helpful it will be to the writer.

_____

_____

_____

_____

_____

_____

_____

Detailed Peer-Review Process

This response sheet is a bit too detailed for a large group peer-review workshop in class, but it works well for a paired silent reading when students can take the time to respond either in class, at home, or online. If the response is online, the responses might be public, on a class site, or private. In any case, a strict adherence to appropriate, respectful responses is crucial to the success of the exercise. What follows is an effective process for engaging with a more focused and detailed peer-review questionnaire.

This peer-edit questionnaire is based on Nancy Sommers's "Revision Strategies of Student Writers and Experienced Adult Writers." It begins with a summary of her essay, and then uses Sommers's insights about inexperienced writers to formulate appropriate and, ideally, helpful questions.

PEER-REVIEW QUESTIONNAIRE

Writer's name: _____   **Peer-editor's name:** _____

Nancy Sommers's essay, "Revision Strategies of Student Writers and Experienced Adult Writers," compares "the revision strategies of student writers and experienced writers to see what role revision played in their writing processes" (344). Sommers found that students were rule-driven rather than content- or meaning-driven and tended to focus mainly on vocabulary or the revision process she calls a "rewording activity" (345) because they were most afraid of repeating words, rather than concepts. Structure or form, rather than being content- or meaning-driven, was reduced to the "rule" that an essay must have an "introduction, a body, and a conclusion" (348). The following workshop is adapted from and builds on Sommers's analysis of experienced writers and what they do when they revise their work.

Summary
— What is the "kernel" of the essay here? In other words, what is the argument about?
— Is there an *original* argument that engages with a primary text and the current knowledge on a specific topic, either adding to that knowledge or challenging it?
— Does the thesis disturb or create dissonance (352)?
— Can you change the language to make the argument (thesis) more effective?
— Provide specific feedback.

Context
— Is there a summary or description of the primary text?
— Does the writer provide the necessary context for understanding the argument?

Thesis/essay development
— Do the introduction and the thesis statement indicate the "form or the shape of [the] argument" as it is laid out in the essay? In other words, does the argument or larger "why" of the argument central to the entire paper appear and get developed in each of the paper's main points (remember, one point per paragraph) and are these paragraphs logically developed, moving the argument forward to the argument's conclusion?
— Keeping your partner's thesis in mind, outline your partner's argument. Does the thesis indicate a clear framework of analysis?

Evidence/analysis
— Are there any sentences, ideas, examples, evidence, topics here that do not fit? Can they be moved to a different section, put aside for another essay, or deleted?
— Are there any illogical gaps in the argument: places where more evidence, analysis, or detail is needed?

Continued

— Does the argument constitute a full and complete analysis of the topic?
— Does the analysis have depth, fully analyzing each point or quote that it uses, or does it merely skim the surface?
— Is the analysis developed logically from the evidence and from the larger "why" of the argument?
— Does the writer consider the larger "why" in the conclusion of the essay, showing the importance of this analysis, and possibly how this analysis might be extended, recontextualized, or used by other researchers? Show page numbers.

Writing

— Does the writer revise words, dropping, substituting, reordering them, and adding to them if need be?
— Does the writer cut enough unnecessary words? Are the sentences meaning-driven? In other words, is the writer asking whether the sentence says exactly what she or he wants it to say?

Voice

— Is there a sense of voice here: does the writer conform to academic conventions and maintain an objective tone?
— Ask, "does this sound academic," without being overbearing, pompous, teacherly, or timid? Reading the essay out loud can help here.

Audience

— Is there a clearly defined audience here?
— Does the writer keep in mind "the anticipation of a reader's judgment" and does that judgment prompt "a feeling of dissonance when the writer recognizes incongruities between" what they intend to write and what they actually do write?

Style

— Is there an emerging sense of style: a sense of "form, balance, rhythm, or communication"?
— Look at sentence and paragraph structure here: the use of balanced paragraph and sentence transitions, etc.

Exercise: Peer Review for Grammar/Editing Skills

This exercise asks you to take a close look at your grammar usage and style, to identify the problems you might have with grammatical structures or punctuation, audience, tone, or voice. It also asks you to formulate a plan for addressing these issues in your next essay.

Working in small groups, exchange your latest draft essays with other students in your group. Working silently:

1. Read the essay and identify something that is working in the writing: something that the writer is doing well.

2. Identify three specific writing problems the writer has in the areas of grammar (a common error, such as fragments, comma splice, etc.), punctuation, audience, tone, or voice. Highlight two or three examples of these errors.

3. See if you can find a solution to *three* of the problems identified, along with a process for handling them when revising the essay. For example, you might suggest editing the paper for comma-splice errors or editing the essay for inappropriate diction.

absolute phrases A noun and its modifiers that interrupt the main clause. For example, *The woman, a skilled orator, spoke confidently to her audience.*

abstract A summary of the contents of an essay or article. Often expected in inductive science or social science essays. Synonymous with synopsis, summary, and précis.

abstractions Language that refers to ideas, qualities, and attitudes. Scholars work with large intellectual ideas, but they always ground them in *concrete* information (objects, events, places, cases).

active/passive voice *See* **voice**.

active reading Critically engaging with the content to understand and evaluate it.

ad hominem A logical fallacy that involves an attack on the opponent's character rather than his or her argument.

adjective Commonly known as a "describing word," qualifies, or makes more specific, the noun it modifies. The adjective usually precedes the noun, as in *the old man*, but occasionally it follows the noun, as in *time immemorial* or in *this chocolate is scrumptious.*

adverb Words used to modify a verb (*to run quickly*), an adjective (*only two essays*), another adverb (*she read quite slowly*). Academic writing uses adverbs *only* if they are necessary to the meaning of the sentence.

analogy An analytical pattern that compares two objects or ideas that are not normally associated with one another. It is most effective when the unfamiliar terms are explained in terms of the familiar. For example, *rhetoric is war* is an analogy that might be developed to analyze a combative rhetorical style.

analysis The separation or division of a subject into its parts. Analysis is fundamental to critical thinking and academic work in general.

analytical patterns Patterns used to *analyze* and *organize* material to allow you to generate and deepen your insights, e.g., compare and contrast, classification and division, cause and effect, description, and definition.

appositive A noun or noun phrase that identifies or renames a noun or pronoun. The appositive is placed next to the noun or pronoun it modifies and can take the non-restrictive or restrictive form. If it takes the restrictive form, the appositive phrase is contained in commas: *Alice Munro, the author of* Runaway, *is a Canadian writer.*

argument A debatable and logical reason given to support a main idea, statement, or theory, e.g., *Academic argumentation is highly persuasive.*

argumentative research essay Uses secondary sources to support or refute a specific argument about a topic or issue, thereby adding to, challenging, or exposing a deficit in the existing information or perspectives on the topic that are already debated by scholars working in the same area or discipline. *See* **expository essay** *and* **research essay**.

articles The words *a, an,* and *the. A* signals a non-particular noun (*a dog,* i.e., any dog), *an* is used when the following noun begins with a vowel or vowel sound (*an object* or *an honour*), and *the* is used to indicate a particular noun (*the dog,* i.e., not just any dog). Second-language users often have problems with article use.

audience, purpose, and occasion All three terms compose the rhetorical context of a piece of writing. *Audience* refers to the writer's consideration of his or her readers, *purpose* to the writer's reason for writing, and *occasion* to the specific and larger context of the writing, as well as to the form or organizational structure of the writing. For a work to be persuasive, all three aspects should be duly weighed and considered.

author In one sense, this term simply refers to someone who writes books, essays, etc. Historically, however, the term has been a subject of debate. For example, the author's intention in writing the text has been considered the main or even fixed source of meaning when it comes to understanding a text. This perspective has been revised by Michel Foucault who argues that the author can tell us a lot about the text's historical and cultural reception, which includes the creation of a certain type of **reader**. Expanding on this notion of the reader, Roland Barthes, in his essay "The Death of the Author," argues that the creation of meaning, which is always in play and indeterminate, lies solely with the reader.

bias A perspective that demonstrates prejudice by refusing to acknowledge equally valid alternatives or perspectives. If a person is biased, he or she is considering only one aspect of a situation or person. For example, a journalist who presents a biased perspective of a government election will side with one political party at the expense of presenting a full and accurate account of the other party's politics.

brainstorming A technique for generating information about a topic that involves listing everything you know about a topic, using only a few words for each point.

case study An in-depth analysis of an individual or a group of individuals within a specific situation and/or location, using a variety of methods, including direct observation, interviews, documents (letters, records), description, etc., to develop and answer a specific hypothesis. Often used in the social sciences.

categorical syllogism A form of argument that consists of three categorical propositions: a major premise, a minor premise, and a conclusion.

cause and effect An analytical pattern that involves examining the logical outcomes and reasons for those outcomes (the causes).

citation Documenting the sources used to make an argument; essential to academic writing. Some common citation systems include the American Psychological Association (APA), the Modern Languages Association (MLA), the Chicago Manual of Style (CMS), and the Council of Science Editors (CSE).

classification and division An analytical pattern that organizes information into categories and then analyzes them by breaking the information into smaller units and parts.

clause A group of words that contain both a subject and a predicate (a verb and its modifiers). An **independent clause** can stand on its own as a sentence; a **dependent clause**, which modifies the independent clause, cannot.

clustering A technique for generating ideas about a topic. The main idea is placed in the centre of the page and circled; the other related ideas surround the central idea and are usually circled and pointed to with a line expanding out from the central idea.

codes A specific or broad set of shared rules or conventions that structure "normal" communication.

comma splice A grammatical error that occurs when two main or independent clauses are separated by a comma instead of a period.

commonplaces A rhetorical term that indicates a shared understanding of a statement or piece of knowledge.

comparison and contrast An analytical pattern that considers the similarities (compare) and differences (contrast) between two or more topics.

complex sentence *See* **sentence.**

compound sentence *See* **sentence.**

compound–complex sentence *See* **sentence.**

concrete reference points Balance and provide evidence for the abstract ideas used by academics.

conjunctions Words that link different parts of a sentence.

Coordinating conjunctions (*for, and, nor, but, or, yet, so*) connect clauses of equal grammatical weight: *An independent clause can stand on its own, <u>but</u> a dependent clause cannot.* **Correlative conjunctions** (*either . . . or; neither . . . nor; not only . . . but also*) work together to connect clauses: *A clause is <u>either</u> independent <u>or</u> it is dependent.* **Subordinating conjunctions** (*after, although, however, because, when, while,* etc.) join clauses of unequal weight. The subordinated clause is introduced by a subordinating conjunction: *<u>While</u> independent clauses can stand on their own, dependent clauses cannot.*

content *What* you are going to write about: the subject matter, information, experiences, and associated contexts used to analyze a topic and make an argument about it. Content might also include language and persuasive rhetorical strategies that are used to make the argument. In this way, content must consistently reflect the expectations of the genre.

context The situation that surrounds or relates to your topic and argument. An understanding of context is crucial to academic writing. *See* **rhetorical context.**

conventions A set of shared rules, standards, and norms shared by a particular community. Understanding and being able to reproduce these conventional rules or expectations is essential to successful interaction with academia.

critical analysis Crucial to academic reading, thinking, and writing; Effective critical analysis involves taking apart a concept, idea, or topic to discern meaning and/or relationships that exist below the surface. Critical analysis often has negative undertones, but equally it can involve a positive interpretation. A critical persuasive essay is an essay that uses critical analysis, judging and discerning what lies below the surface of a topic, a concept, or an idea, to persuade a clearly defined audience of the validity of your argument.

dangling modifier A grammatical error that occurs when a modifying phrase or clause does not modify what it is supposed to. Example: *Hoping to finish the operation on time, the patient was quickly sedated* (the patient is not the person who was operating, as this construction implies). Revised: *Hoping to finish the operation on time, the doctor quickly sedated the patient.*

deduction Arguing from the general to the specific. The form of argument most often used in the humanities and arts.

definition An analytical pattern used to outline the characteristics of something to define what it is and is not. Essential to academic writing.

dependent clause *See* **clause.**

description An analytical pattern that uses the reader's senses (sight, sound, smell, taste, and touch) to communicate the writer's perceptions of a person, a place, or an object.

direct object *See* **object.**

discourse A form of communication or debate, spoken or written. The linguistic definition refers to the way in which a connected form of utterances create a common ground for the speakers or writers. Michel Foucault extended this definition by considering how discourses generate knowledge and self-governing rules and ways of seeing and knowing the world that create reality. **Discourse analysis** studies the relations between these texts and related worldviews.

dogmatism A logical fallacy that claims the issue at hand is beyond argument and that the solution is self-evident.

drafting The initial stages in the writing process. Involves writing a complete or nearly complete essay that contains a thesis, developed ideas, and a logical paragraph structure.

editing Usually the last step, before proofreading, in revising a text for clarity, grammatical correctness, and tone.

ethos The rhetorical (persuasive) appeal to ethics or writer credibility or trustworthiness. To establish credibility with an academic audience, a writer must be reasoned and present a well-considered or reflective engagement with the knowledge.

evidence Information used to support assertions. Evidence might include facts, examples, expert opinions, and logical constructions.

example An analytical pattern that uses illustrations to support the main idea. Examples are highly effective; they provide a reader with concrete, specific information or evidence to support an analysis.

executive summary A summary of a business or management report or proposal. Like other summaries or abstracts, it is placed at the beginning of the document.

expository essay Offers a clear description and explanation of a topic or process, thus setting forth information to expose or display the topic for the reader's attention. An expository research essay uses research sources to support and add depth to the exposition.

expressivist writing Writing that is personal and subjective, rather than neutral and objective, that reflects the writer's experiences, opinions, thoughts, and feelings. This writing, where a sense of "self" is central to the process, might include journal writing, personal letter writing, and autobiographical narratives. Composition study theorists, such as Peter Elbow, argue that expressivist writing, as a process-based way of teaching writing, allows students to grow in confidence, developing skills and generating ideas that will allow them to discover meaning.

false authority A logical fallacy that attempts to persuade an audience by using the testimony of an unqualified "expert." Also called *Ipse Dixit* (Latin for "He himself said it.").

figures of speech words or phrases used in a different way to change the meaning and create a specific effect. Examples include personification (endowing a non-human object with human qualities: *the flowers danced in the meadow*) and hyperbole (exaggerated statement used for emphasis: *guilt is killing her*).

fragment An incomplete sentence (missing a subject or a verb/predicate) or a subordinate, dependent clause punctuated as if it is a complete sentence.

form The organizing structure of a piece of writing; works at both the sentence and paragraph level. The form of a piece of writing is driven by the meaning or the main message you want to convey. The form should reflect and even enhance the content or subject matter.

freewriting A technique for generating ideas and information involving writing non-stop for a fixed amount of time on a particular topic.

generalization *See* **hasty generalization.**

genre A term traditionally used to categorize different types of writing to organize course offerings in educational institutions.

genre theory The study of how form (the medium and language) dictates and is dictated to by genre-specific situational conventions and expectations. Examples of genre understood in this way include religious doctrine, advertising, and, of course, academic writing.

gerund verbal phrases A phrase consisting of a **gerund** (a verbal phrase that ends in –*ing* and functions as a noun) and its modifiers: e.g., *working late*.

gist Presents the main points or substance of a text or an action.

gist outline Presents the main points of a text to provide a general summary of the text's general message.

hasty generalization A logical fallacy that generalizes a conclusion from insufficient evidence. For example, it would be difficult to argue that *all women love children* because it would be impossible to prove.

hegemony The dominance of one group of people or one nation over another. In *Prison Notebooks*, Antonio Gramsci uses the term to refer to class relations and suggests that these relations are maintained not only by force but also by consent.

hyperbole Deliberate exaggeration that is used for effect.

hypothesis A proposed explanation or speculation that is tested and proved through further examination or experimentation.

ideal reader An imaginary reader who would, ideally, understand and respond appropriately to every word, phrase, allusion, etc.

imitation A rhetorical exercise that involves copying the form of an original work while supplying new content.

implied author and reader The *implied author* refers to the character a reader may give to an author, regardless of the author's real personality. The *implied reader* can be distinguished from a "real" reader: a reader who has specific needs and characteristics that the writer accounts for. Like the implied author, the implied reader is invented by the writer to suit his or her purposes in writing the text.

independent clause A clause that can stand alone as a sentence and contains both a subject and verb/predicate.

indirect object *See* **object**.

induction Arguing from a specific premise to a general conclusion.

jargon The specialized language of a group of people, e.g., the academic disciplines, who share specialized terms and expressions. Academic writing should, however, be as clear and concise as possible.

knowledge gap or deficit A deficit in the established knowledge. The writer engages with this gap in an attempt to find evidence that provides the basis for an argument.

lab report Most often used in the scientific disciplines to record the findings of a laboratory experiment. The common organizational structure of a lab report is known by the acronym IMRAD: Introduction, Methods/ Materials, Results, and Discussion.

library databases Your library catalogue has links to a variety of discipline-related electronic databases that will provide you with access to electronic and hard-copy journal articles, books, and other resources.

limiting expressions Expressions such as *usually, most, some, many, in part,* and *generally* added to statements to qualify or limit statements or generalizations. For example, arguing that *Generally, women are paid less than men in the job market* is arguing that while this is mostly true, it is not always the case.

literature review Documents, synthesizes, and summarizes the published information on a particular topic or in a particular subject area. In an academic research paper, a literature review can support an argument by tracing the progression of intellectual thought in the subject area, thereby providing a basis for research.

logical fallacies Errors in argument. While a writer or speaker might use an invalid line of argument simply out of ignorance and a lack of experience, it is important to recognize that, all too often, writers and speakers use fallacies of argument by design, from a conscious intent to deceive, distract, and manipulate their audience. This is particularly true in advertising and in politics. Learning to detect such fallacies can make us more aware consumers of products and ideas. This awareness can also make us more ethical communicators, by using sound reasoning while, at the same time, refusing to use these fallacies to manipulate our audience.

logos The rhetorical (persuasive) appeal to logic or reason. Academic writing is highly logical.

metacognitive A higher order reasoning skill that means knowing about knowing. It involves thinking about your thinking or reasoning processes, which will make you better able to analyze and learn.

misplaced modifier Sometimes called a squinting modifier, a misplaced modifier indicates that a word or phrase does not accurately modify the word it is supposed to. An example would be as follows: Last night my house was robbed in my sleep. Also see **squinting modifier**.

mixed construction A sentence that is not logically consistent, whose logical development or use of grammar appears confused.

Modernism An early-twentieth-century literary movement, Modernism broke with many of the Victorian traditions and conventions, including Realism. Although it was known for its creative and often revolutionary experimentation, it was ultimately criticized for its tendency to reinscribe traditional attitudes under the guise of experimental forms.

narration An analytical pattern that explains the narrative or story of what happened. Usually written in chronological sequence.

New Criticism This American literary movement, which was popular from the 1930s to the 1960s, argued for an objective, autonomous approach to reading literature. The **New Critical approach** emphasized that a work should speak intrinsically for itself without taking into account any biographical or historical contexts. This approach, which typically examines how the form and the content of a work are interrelated, constitutes the basis of the "close reading" that students are often asked to complete in college or undergraduate university courses.

nominalization The transformation of a verb or adjective into a noun. Often used in bureaucratic or political language to obfuscate an action. For example, *movement* from *move*, *failure* from *fail*, *investigation* from *investigate*.

non sequitur A logical fallacy in which one point does not follow logically from another.

noun Also called a naming word. A noun names a person, a place, a thing, a quality, or an idea.

null hypothesis Assumes that there is no relationship between two measurable phenomena. Disproving the null hypothesis and thereby arguing that there is a measurable relationship between two things is one of the central tasks of science.

object A noun, pronoun, or group of words that receives the action of a verb. A **direct object** directly receives the action of the verb and usually immediately follows it in a sentence (*We went to Toronto*); an **indirect object** indirectly shows for or to whom the action is aimed: *We went to Toronto to see the ball game*.

occasion *See* **audience, purpose, and occasion**.

paraphrase The restatement of original source material, putting all the main ideas in your own words; paraphrases must always be cited.

particle A preposition or an adverb in a double verb: *drive forth*; *look up*.

participle phrases *See* **phrase**.

passive reading A reading that passively absorbs the material, assuming a certain truth without participating in any analysis or critical thinking.

pathos The rhetorical (persuasive) appeal to emotion. Academic writing rarely uses pathos.

persuasion Involves synthesizing the insights gleaned from an analysis into a well-reasoned and valid argument.

phrase A group of words that cannot stand on their own as a sentence because they lack either a subject or a verb/predicate. Phrases can be **prepositional** (*under the book*; *over the top*); **participle or noun phrases**, which function as an adjective to modify the noun in the sentence (*Running to the store, John tripped*); and **verbal** (*Reading the book is important*).

point of view The vantage point or perspective from which the author presents the action of the story. Point of view includes first person (I, me, we), second person (you), third person (he, she, they), omniscient (all knowing), limited-omniscient (has access to some but not all of the character's thoughts, events, etc.), intrusive (comments on action, etc.), unintrusive, reliable, unreliable (causes us to doubt the reliability of the perspective), and self-reflective. Academic writing uses first and third person, never second person.

postmodernism Postmodernism, a literary movement that took issue with the central tenets of Modernism,

constitutes an attempt to understand the world in the latter half of the twentieth century. In a world threatened by nuclear war, the environmental destruction of the planet, rampant capitalism and individualism, and increased technology, postmodernism can be seen as an attempt to understand the meaning of community.

pragmatic Taking a realistic or practical approach to a topic or an issue: *Susan took a pragmatic approach to studying for her exams*.

précis A summary that reproduces the logic, organization, and emphasis of the original source in a much shorter form. Often used in technological or business reports.

predicate The part of the sentence that includes the verb and its modifiers.

premise A statement from which another statement is inferred or follows; more specifically, a logical step used in an argument to justify a conclusion. Two premises that lead to a logical conclusion form the basis of an argumentative structure called a syllogism.

prepositional phrases *See* **phrases**.

primary text The text used to analyze and make an argument about a larger related topic. It presents a specific instance (evidence) for analysis of this topic.

probability The measure of the likeliness that an event will occur.

process analysis An analytical pattern that shows how something happens or explains a process. It can take the form of instructions (as in a recipe or instructions on how to quit smoking) or it can involve more complex processes that address the depth of the subject being analyzed. Often seen in expository essays.

pronoun A word that stands in place of a noun. There are eight types of pronouns: **personal** (*he, she, it, we, they, you*), **indefinite** (*everybody, somebody, anybody, some*), **relative** (*who, whom, which, that*), **interrogative** (*who, which, what*), **intensive** (*himself, herself*), **reflexive** (*themselves*, as in *they hurt themselves*), **demonstrative** (*this, that, such*), or **reciprocal** (*each other, one another*).

proofreading Correcting a final draft for errors and omissions in text and visual layout.

purpose *See* **audience, purpose, and occasion**.

qualitative research Examines phenomena, issues, and relationships, replacing the large research examples found in quantitative research with a small number of examples. It is used mostly by the humanities, arts, and social science disciplines.

quantitative research Uses empirical (experiential) analysis to explain phenomena. It collects and analyzes large numbers of numerical data and statistics. Primarily used in the social sciences and sciences.

reader *See* **author.**

realism A literary movement and style of writing that offers a realistic or an accurate representation of reality. Although realism is still a popular form today, its high point was in the mid- to late-nineteenth century, when many writers saw themselves as confronting, describing, and documenting "new" truths about society. Scientific investigation, industrialization, and imperialism contributed to the belief that, through the representation of authentic "ordinary" experience in realistic narratives, the "truth" could be known.

reliable evidence Relevant, dependable, provable evidence. Findings are more reliable or valid if they can be accurately repeated.

reporting expressions Also called signal phrases. Used to introduce the words of someone else, either in a summary, paraphrase, or direct quotation.

representation Taking the place of something or someone else, e.g., in politics, a politician represents or stands for the people and their needs; in literature, the writing itself stands for the reality it seeks to represent.

research The systematic study of a topic or an idea using secondary sources to establish new conclusions and arguments.

research question A point of departure that allows the writer to define a focus and a methodology related to his or her topic of interest. By answering a specific research question, the writer can arrive at a working thesis statement that will further narrow and focus the writer's exploration of a topic.

research essay A thorough exploration of a topic that requires an original engagement with the issues, material, and external sources (work written by other scholars who are interested in the same topic).

research report Comprises an in-depth coverage of the material and provides an account of the information gained from the research and presented to interested readers. It is most often used in the social sciences, the sciences, and business.

rhetor A person who produces rhetoric to communicate and persuade. A rhetor might be a speaker, a writer, a cartoonist, an architect, or a filmmaker.

rhetoric The arrangement of words, sentences, and ideas to achieve the writer's purpose in persuading an audience. Commonly called the art of written or spoken persuasion.

rhetorical act The act of communicating (speaking or writing), which includes a rhetor (a speaker or writer), an issue (found within a text), and an audience. For example, a writer might study a **rhetorical action**, such as web blogging or accident reporting, to consider the persuasive strategies and hidden agendas buried in the act of communicating.

rhetorical artifact The transcribed, printed, recorded, painted object of analysis or study. This might be a speech, a building, a sculpture, a recorded song, an essay, etc.

rhetorical context The requirements for persuasive writing. To be able to write persuasively, clearly, and convincingly, a writer needs to be aware of his or her audience, purpose, and occasion for writing. That includes both the overall situation or context (social, psychological, historical, etc.) and the form or organizing structure of the writing. An awareness of the rhetorical context helps writers establish clear communication with their readers and, in turn, helps readers fully relate to what they are reading.

rhetorical criticism A qualitative research method that studies how language is used in a particular rhetorical artifact to create meaning.

rhetorical tropes Figures of speech that change, twist, or turn the meaning of words from their standard or non-literal use. Examples include *metaphor* (something is something else: *life is a race you have to win*), *simile* (something is *like* something else: *life is like a race you have to win*), and *pun* (twists or plays with the meanings of words to create humour: Ernest (the attitude) /Earnest (the name)).

run-on sentence Also called a fused sentence; a grammatical error that joins two main clauses with no punctuation: *Two main clauses joined with a comma is a comma splice two main clauses joined with no punctuation is a run-on sentence.*

secondary sources Sources used to support your reading of a primary text. They can directly support your ideas, refute certain points or ideas, provide a context for, or add to the knowledge you are exploring.

semantics How language is used to make meaning.

semiotics The study of signs and how they produce meaning. A central concern is the way in which signs function socially to organize and disseminate meaning. *See* **signs.**

sentence A set of words that contains both a subject and a predicate (a verb and its modifiers). A **simple sentence** consists of a subject and a predicate, which can be a verb on its own: *John runs; John runs to the store.* A **compound sentence** contains two or more independent clauses: *John runs to the store, and he buys groceries.* A **complex sentence** contains one main clause and at least one subordinate clause: *John runs to the store because he needs groceries.* A **compound-complex sentence** contains at least two main clauses and at least one subordinate clause: *John runs to the store, and he buys groceries because he needs them.*

sentence fragment A grammatical error that punctuates a subordinate clause or a clause lacking a subject or verb as if it is a sentence:

An independent clause (fragment, missing verb/predicate);

Can stand alone (fragment, missing subject);

An independent clause can stand alone (revised);

An independent clause can stand alone. Because it contains a subject and a verb (subordinating conjunction fragment);

An independent clause can stand alone because it contains a subject and a verb (revised).

sign A term used in semiotics to refer to the arbitrary association between sound images (a *signifier*) and the concept they refer to (the *signified*). Saussure uses the example of the sound image or signifier *tree* (the word), and the concept of an actual tree. The relationship between the two (the word *tree* and our concept of a tree) is arbitrarily dictated by our common language and meaning that we all agree to live by.

signal phrases *See* **reporting expressions.**

situation The overall context (historical, social, cultural, psychological, or technical) to which writing refers and in which it is unavoidably embedded.

slippery slope A logical fallacy that portrays today's seemingly small concession as tomorrow's catastrophe, e.g., arguing that the legalization of assisted suicide could lead to the mass deaths of vulnerable peoples.

squinting modifier A modifier placed between two words that could modify either one: the word closest to it (*She wrote only the book.*—Should *only* modify the book or wrote?) or the wrong part of the sentence (*She served fries to the children on paper plates.*—What is *on paper plates*: the children or the fries?).

standard English Also known as formal English. A nation's formal, most widely accepted use of language (grammar, vocabulary, spelling, and conventions).

straw man A logical fallacy that occurs when someone twists or exaggerates an opponent's argument while pretending to respond to the opponent's actual position.

stacked evidence A logical fallacy that represents only one side of the issue.

structuralism A mid-twentieth century intellectual movement that argues that all human experience is constructed and driven by systematic conventions; the stories that are told, the kinship relationships that are formed, and even the way we organize our political systems all tell us about how we structure our experience according to divisive concepts of difference.

style The way in which something is expressed using language. Style can be entertaining, impressive, reflective, imposing, moral, understated, etc. Academic writing demands a clear, simple style.

subject The part of a sentence that names something or someone (noun) and asserts something in the predicate of the sentence. A **simple subject** consists of one noun; a **compound subject** consists of two or more nouns: a **complete subject** includes the subject and its modifiers.

substance An essay has substance when it logically and concisely expresses and provides sufficient evidence for the main argument and when it provides a logical structure to support the argument.

summary An accurate restatement of someone else's work put in your own words, usually around a quarter the length of the original. Summaries must always be cited.

syllogism *See* **categorical syllogism.**

synonyms Words or phrases that mean the same or almost the same as another word or phrase: for example, *examination* and *investigation* are synonyms, as is *to express* for the phrase *put into words.*

syntax The rule-bound grammatical relationship between words and the way words are used to form phrases and clauses.

tense The form of the verb that indicates the time of its action. The **simple tenses** are the present (*I write*), the past (*I wrote*), and the future (*I will write*). The **perfect tenses**, formed with the helping verbs *had* and *have*, indicate a completed action: *I have read the text.* The **progressive tenses**, which use forms of the helping verb *be*, indicate continuing action: *I was writing*; *I am writing.*

text Anything that can be read; while it might typically refer to a book, it might also include an essay, a short story, a film, a speech, a diary, an event, etc. These texts are often used as primary texts in an analysis.

thesis statement The main argument or controlling idea of a work; while they are usually associated with academic essays, it is important to realize that all texts make arguments. When writers draft their essays, they formulate **working thesis statements** that might change as the essay is developed.

tone Reflects the writer's attitude to the subject, context, and reader. It is revealed in the content, the use of words, and the choice of sentence structures.

valid An argument with a sound basis in logic or fact. *See* **reliable**.

variable A characteristic or condition that can change from one person or situation to another. A variable can be controlled (the variable or variables held constant in an experiment), dependent, or independent. An independent variable can be changed in an experiment. A measured dependent variable changes in direct relation to an independent variable.

verb In academic writing, the most important part of the sentence; The verb tells the reader what the subject of the sentence is doing, which might involve a specific action or state of being. The verb in *Nigel plays the guitar* describes what Nigel, the subject of the sentence, is doing: Nigel plays. The verb here might also describe how Nigel feels, as in *Nigel loves the guitar*.

verbal A verb form that functions as an adjective: *the running man*.

voice The form the verb takes: In **active voice** the subject of the sentence acts (*John wrote the book*). In **passive voice**, the subject is acted upon (*the book was written by John*). Academic writing primarily uses active voice.

well-triangulated An argument is well-triangulated when more than one point of view or perspective is measured and cross-referenced. By measuring and checking perspectives between and across three variables or aspects of a variable, a more accurate assessment can be made. This method is often used in quantitative studies in the social sciences and science disciplines.

working thesis statement A draft thesis statement that might change as an essay is developed. *See* **thesis statement**.

WORKS CITED

Alberta Curriculum. English. Grade 12. October, 2012. Web.

Alexie, Sherman. "How to Write the Great American Indian Novel." *The Poetry Foundation.* 1996. Web.

Anonymous. *Diary of a Mad Woman.* Circle of Moms. 25 January 2013. Web.

Aristotle. *Poetics.* Trans. Gerald F. Else. Ann Arbor: The University of Michigan Press, 1967. Print.

Arnold, Matthew. "Culture and Anarchy." *Cultural Theory and Popular Culture: A Reader.* Ed. John Storey. 3rd ed. London and New York: Pearson, 2006. 6–12. Print.

Avery, Oswald T., Colin M. MacLeod, and Maclyn McCarty. "Studies on the Chemical Nature of the Substance Inducing Transformations of Pneumococcal Types." *Journal of Experimental Medicine* 79 (1944): 137–58. Print.

Bartholomae, David. "Inventing the University." *Perspectives on Literacy.* Eds. Eugene R. Kintgen, Barry M. Kroll, and Mike Rose. Southern Illinois University Press, 1988. 273–85. Print.

——. "Writing with Teachers: A Conversation with Peter Elbow." *College Composition and Communication* 46.1 (Feb. 1995): 62–71. Print.

Barwashi, Anis. *Genre and the Invention of the Writer.* Utah: Utah State University Press, 2003. Print.

Becker, Carl. "Democracy." *The Norton Reader.* Eds. Arthur Eastman et al. 7th ed. New York and London: W.W. Norton, 1988. 832. Print.

Bhaba, Homi. *The Location of Culture.* Routledge, 1994. Print.

Blicq, Ronald, and Moretto, Lisa. *Technically Write.* 6th ed. Toronto: Pearson, 2004. Print.

Booth, Wayne. "The Rhetorical Stance." *College Composition and Communication* 14.3 (October 1963): 139–45. Print.

Bradley, Simon. "A/DA APP-1." *The Guitarist* (Sept. 2012): 125. Print.

Bronowski, Jacob. "The Creative Mind" *Science and Human Values.* London. Faber Finds, 2008. Web.

Brown, Ian. *The Boy in the Moon.* New York: St. Martin's Press, 2009. Print.

Bulwer-Lytton Fiction Contest. 2011 and 2012. 20 August 2013. Web.

Burke, Kenneth. *Language as Symbolic Action: Essays on Life, Literature, and Method.* Berkeley: University of California Press, 1966. Print.

Bush, George. "George Bush's Address on the Start of the War." *The Guardian.* 20 March 2004. Web.

Butler, Judith. "Further Reflections on the Conversations of Our Time." *Diacritics.* 1997. 13–15. Print.

Calmes, Jackie. "Partisanship Is a Worthy Foe in Debate on Stimulus." *New York Times.* 6 February 2009. Web.

Campbell, John Angus. "Charles Darwin: Rhetorician of Science." *Landmark Essays on Rhetoric of Science Case Studies.* Ed. Randy Allen Harris. Mahwah, NJ: Hermagoras, 1997. 3–17. Print.

Carver, Raymond. "Cathedral." 1981. Web.

Chew, M.K., and M.D. Laubichler. "Natural Enemies—Metaphor or Misconception?" *Science* 301.5629 (2003): 52–3. Print.

Childers, Joseph, and Hentzi, Gary. Eds. *The Columbia Dictionary of Modern Literary and Cultural Criticism.* New York: Columbia University Press, 1995. Print.

Coe, Richard M. *Process, Form, and Substance: A Rhetoric for Advanced Writers.* 2nd ed. Englewood Cliffs: Prentice Hall, 1990. Print.

Cohen, Carl. "The Case for the Use of Animals in Biomedical Research." *New England Journal of Medicine.* 315.14 (1986): 86570. Print.

Con Davis, Robert, and Schleifer, Ronald. *Contemporary Literary Criticism: Literary and Cultural Studies.* 3rd ed. New York and London: Longman. Print.

Concise Oxford English Dictionary. Eds. Angus Stevenson and Maurice Waite. 12th ed. Oxford and New York: Oxford University Press, 2011. Print.

Copi, Irving M., and Cohen, Carl. *Introduction to Logic.* 8th ed. New York and London: Collier Macmillan Publishers, 1990. Print.

Darwin, Charles. *On the Origin of Species by Means of Natural Selection.* 2nd ed. London: John Murray, 1860.

Darwin, Francis, ed. *The Life and Letters of Charles Darwin: Including an Autobiographical Chapter.* John Murray: London, 1887. Print.

Dasenbrock, Reed Way. "Intelligibility and Meaningfulness in Multicultural Literature in English." *PMLA* 102.1 (1997): 10–19. Print.

Davey, B. "Think-Aloud: Modelling the Cognitive Processes of Reading Comprehension." *Journal of Reading* 22 (1983): 44–7. Print.

Davis, Lennard J. *Enforcing Normalcy: Disability, Deafness, and the Body.* London and New York: Verso, 1995. xv. Print.

Day, Robert A. *How to Write and Publish a Scientific Paper.* 5th ed. Phoenix, AZ: Oryx, 1998. Print.

Didion, Joan. "On Self Respect." *Major Modern Essayists.* Eds. Gilbert H. Muller and Alan F. Crooks. 2nd ed. Englewood Cliffs, NJ: Prentice Hall, 1994. 215–19. Print.

Dutton, Denis. *The Bad Writing Contest.* 13 August 2013. Web.

Ekman, Paul, et al. "Buddhist and Psychological Perspectives on Emotions and Well-Being." *Current Directions in Psychological Science* 14.2 (2005): 59–63.

Elbow, Peter, and Belanoff, Patricia. *Community of Writers.* 3rd ed. New York: 1999. Print.

Elbow, Peter. "Exploring Problems with 'Personal Writing' and Expressivism." Amherst: University of Massachusetts, 2002. Web.

——. "Write First: Putting Writing before Reading is an Effective Approach to Teaching and Learning." *Educational Leadership* 62.2 (Jan. 2004): 8–14. Web.

——. *Writing with Power.* 2nd ed. New York and Oxford: Oxford University Press, 1998. Print.

Ennis, R.H. "Critical Thinking: A Streamlined Conception." *Teaching Philosophy* 14.1 (1991): 5–25. Web.

Ewert, Stephanie. "Fewer Diplomas for Men: The Influence of College Experiences on the Gender Gap in College Education." *The Journal of Higher Education* 83.6 (Nov.–Dec. 2012): 824–50. Print.

Fahnestock, Jeanne and Secor, Marie. *A Rhetoric of Argument.* New York: Random House, 1982. Print.

Father–son cartoon. Brainstuck.com. 10 January 2013. Web.

Fish, Stanley. *How to Write a Sentence.* New York: Harper Collins, 2011. Print.

Fiske, John. "Popular Culture." *Critical Terms for Literary Study.* Eds. Frank Lentricchia and Thomas McLaughlin. 2nd ed. Chicago and London: The University of Chicago Press, 1990. 321–35. Print.

Fitzgerald, F. Scott. *The Great Gatsby.* London: Wordsworth Editions, 1993. Print.

Flannery, Maura C. "Mirrors and Maps: Two Sides of Metaphor." *Biology Today* 71.6 (2009): 371–4. Print.

Foss, Sonja K. *Rhetorical Criticism: Explorations and Practice.* 2nd ed. Illinois: Waveland Press, 1996. 11–29. Print.

Foucault, Michel. "Body / Power." *Power Knowledge: Selected Interviews and Other Writings 1972–1977.* Eds. Colin Gordon. New York: Pantheon Books, 1980. 55–62. Print.

Frye, Northrop. "The Function of Criticism in Our Present Time." *Contemporary Literary Criticism: Literary and Cultural Studies.* 3rd ed. New York and London: Longman. 1994. 34–45. Print.

Garland-Thomson, Rosemarie. "Shape Structures Story: Fresh and Fiesty Stories about Disability." *Narrative* 15.1. (Jan. 2007): 113–23. Print.

Garneau, David. "Making It Like a Man!" *Making It Like a Man: Canadian Masculinities in Practice.* Ed. Christine Ramsay. Waterloo: Wilfred Laurier University Press, 2011. 55–77. Print.

Gillis, Charlie. "Robert Latimer's Angry Crusade." *MacLean's.* 6 March 2008. Web.

Giltrow, Janet, et al. *Academic Writing: An Introduction.* 2nd ed. Peterborough, Ontario: Broadview Press, 2009. Print.

Gramsci, Antonio. *The Antonio Gramsci Reader.* Ed. David Forgacs. New York: New York University Press, 2000. Print.

Greenaway, Kathryn. "Cruelty Dealt Out in the Name of Science: Profiles of Chimps Rescued from Research are Heart-Wrenching." *Edmonton Journal* 26 June 2011. Web.

Greenblatt, Stephen, J. "Invisible Bullets." *Contemporary Literary Criticism: Literary and Cultural Studies.* 3rd ed. New York and London: Longman. 472–506. Print.

Greening, D., and Gray, B. (1994). Testing a Model of Organizational Response to Social and Political Issues. *Academy of Management Journal* 37 (3): 467–98. Print.

Halloran, Michael S. "The Birth of Molecular Biology: An Essay in the Rhetorical Criticism of Scientific Discourse." *Rhetoric Review* 3 (1984): 70–83. Print.

Harris, Randy Allen, ed. *Landmark Essays in Rhetoric of Science Case Studies.* Mahwah, NJ: Hermagoras, 1997. Print.

Hardison, O.B. "Charles Darwin's Tree of Life." *Intersections: Readings in the Sciences and Humanities.* Ed. Steven D. Scott, Don Perkins, Erika Rothwell. Toronto: Pearson, 2005. 57–63. Print.

Harper, Stephen. "Statement of Apology on Behalf of Canadians for the Indian Residential School System." Ottawa, Ontario. 11 June 2008. Speech. 20 February 2014. http://www.pm.gc.ca/eng/news/2008/06/11/pm-offers -full-apology-behalf-canadians-indian-residential -schools-system. Web.

Hayward, Sally. "Dangerous Homosexualities and Disturbing Masculinities: The Disabling Rhetoric of Difference in Barbara Gowdy's *Mister Sandman*." *Making It Like a Man: Canadian Masculinities in Practice.* Ed. Christine Ramsay. Waterloo: Wilfred Laurier University Press, 2011. 215–32. Print.

Health Canada. "A Report of the Surgeon General: How Tobacco Smoke Causes Disease: What it Means to You." 2010. Web.

Heidegger, Martin. *On Time and Being.* Trans. Joan Stambaugh. Chicago and London: University of Chicago Press, 2002. Print.

Heisenberg, Werner. "What Is an Elementary Particle?" *Intersections: Readings in the Sciences and Humanities.* Ed. Steven D. Scott, Don Perkins, Erika Rothwell. Toronto: Pearson, 2005. 72–82. Print.

Hemingway, Ernest. *A Moveable Feast.* London: Vintage, 2000. Print.

——. "Hills Like White Elephants." *The Essential Hemingway.* London: Arrow Books, 2004. 402–6. Print.

Holland, Kathryn. "The Troubled Masculinities in Tsitsi Dangarambga's *Nervous Conditions.*" *African Masculinities.* Eds. Lahoucine Ouzgane and Robert Morrell. Palgrave Macmillan: New York. 121–36. Print.

hooks, bell. "Keeping Close to Home: Class and Education." *The Presence of Others: Voices that Call for Response.* Eds. Andrea A. Lunsford and John J. Ruszkiewicz. New York: St. Martin's Press, 85–96. Print.

House, Humphry. *Aristotle's Poetics.* London: Rupert Hart-Davis, 1958. Print.

Husky Oil Company. 13 December 2013. Web.

I am Sam. Dir. Jessie Nelson. Perf. Sean Penn, Michelle Pfeiffer, Dakota Fanning. New Line Cinema, 2001. Film.

Jacobs, Harriet. *Incidents in the Life of a Slave Girl.* Boston: Simon and Brown, 2012. Print.

Janz, Heidi. "Disabling Images and the Dangers of Public Perception: A Commentary on the Media's 'Coverage' of the Latimer Case. *Constitutional Forum.* 9.3 (1998): 66–70. Print.

Jenish, D. and T. Fennell. "What Would You Do: In Saskatchewan, a Wrenching Verdict of Murder Reignites a Long-simmering Debate about Mercy Killing," *Maclean's,* 28 November 1994.

Johnson, Chris. *A Handbook of Incident and Accident Reporting.* Glasgow: Publicity Services, 2003. Web.

Katila, R., and S. Shane. When Does Lack of Resources Make New Firms Innovative? *Academy of Management Journal 48.5* (2005): 814–29. Print.

Keel, P.K., and K.L. Klump. Are eating disorders culture-bound syndromes? Implications for conceptualizing their etiology. *Psychological Bulletin 129.5* (2003): 747–69. Print.

Kimmage, Paul. *Rough Ride: Behind the Wheel with a Pro Cyclist.* London: Random House, 2007. Print.

Kleege, Georgina. "Call It Blindness." *The Presence of Others.* Eds. Andrea A. Lunsford and John J. Ruszkiewicz. 2nd ed. New York: St. Martin's Press, 1997. 390–409. Print.

Klein, Carol. "The Promise of Spring." *Gardeners' World.* Jan. 2013. 32. Print.

Kuhn, Thomas. *The Revolution of Science.* Chicago: University of Chicago, 1970. Print.

——. "The Route to Normal Science." *Intersections: Readings in the Sciences and Humanities.* Eds. Steven D. Scott, Don Perkins, and Erika Rothwell. Toronto: Pearson, 2005. 106–15. Print.

Labrecque, Jeremy. "Neuroscience Finds Wisdom Centers in the Brain." *Discovery Magazine.* 6 July 2009. Web.

Lacy, Dan. "Reading in an Audiovisual and Electronic Era." *Daedalus.* Winter 1983. 117–28. Print.

Leavis, F.R. *English Literature in Our Present Time.* Cambridge: Cambridge University Press, 1979. Print.

Leavy, Patricia. *Method Meets Art: Arts-Based Research Practice.* New York and London: The Guilford Press, 2009. Print.

Lippmann, Walter. "Stereotypes." *Public Opinion.* New York: Free Press Paperbacks, 1997. 53–62. Print.

Livingston, S.A., and M.J. Zieky. "Passing Scores: A Manual for Setting Standards of Performance of Educational and Occupational Tests." Princeton, NJ: Educational Testing Service. 1982. Print.

Lofton, Kathryn. "Practicing Oprah or the Prescriptive Compulsion of a Spiritual Capitalism." *The Journal of Popular Culture 39.4* (Aug. 2006): 599–621. Print.

"Luckies Are Less Irritating." Advertisement. "The Doctors' Choice Is America's Choice: The Physician in US Cigarette Advertisements, 1930–1953." *American Journal of Public Health 92.2* (Feb. 2006): 222–32. Web. 5 February 2014.

Lunsford, Andrea, and John Ruszkiewicz. *Everything's an Argument.* 5th ed. Boston: Bedford St. Martin's, 2009. Print.

Manier, Edward. *The Young Darwin and His Cultural Circle.* Boston: D. Reidel, 1978. Print.

McArdle, Megan. "Worst Sentence Ever Written in Journalism?" *The Atlantic.* 7 Feb. 2009. Web.

McClelland, Susan. "The Lure of the Body Image." *Acting on Words.* Eds. David Brundage and Michael Lahey. Toronto: Pearson, 2003. 83–6. Print.

McDougall, Mary Lynn. "Protecting Infants: The French Campaign for Maternity Leaves, 1890s–1913." *French Historical Studies 13.1* (Spring 1983): 79–105. Print.

McEwan, Ian. *Saturday.* Toronto: Knopf Canada, 2009. Print.

McMichael, Tony. "Fine Battlefield Reporting, but It's Time to Stop the War Metaphor." *Science 295.5559* (2002): 1469. Print.

Mika, Marie. "Framing the Issue: Religion, Secular Ethics and the Case of Animal Rights Mobilization." *Social Forces 85.2* (Dec. 2006): 915–41. Print.

Miller, Carolyn. "Genre as Social Action." *Quarterly Journal of Speech 70* (1984): 151–67. Web.

Miller, Carolyn, Jamie Larsen, and Judi Gaitens. "What Can NCSU Students Expect?" *Center For Communication in Science, Technology, and Management.* North Carolina State University. No. 2. (October 1996): 1–40. Web.

Milton, John. *Paradise Lost.* Eds. Stephen Orgel and Jonathan Goldberg. Oxford and New York: Oxford University Press, 2008. Print.

Morris, David B. *Illness and Culture in a Postmodern Age.* Berkeley: University of California Press, 2000. Print.

Munro, Alice. "Voices." *The Telegraph.* 7 Nov. 2013. Web.

Murray, Donald M. "The Maker's Eye: Revising Your Own Manuscript." *Language Awareness: Readings for College Writers.* Ed. by Paul Eschholz, Alfred Rosa, and Virginia Clark. 8th ed. Boston: Bedford/St. Martin's, 2000: 161–165. Print.

Musgrave, Susan. "Arctic Poppies." *Things That Keep and Do Not Change.* Toronto: McClelland and Stewart, 1999. Print.

Nelkin, Dorothy. "Promotional Metaphors and Their Popular Appeal." *Public Understanding of Science* 3 (1994): 25–31. Print.

Nelson, J. Raleigh. *Writing the Technical Report.* New York: McGraw Hill, 1940. Print.

Nowak, David J. et al., "Effects of Urban Tree Management and Species Selection on Atmospheric Carbon Dioxide" in *Journal of Arboriculture* 28 (3): May 2002 pp. 113–122. Web.

Orwell, George. "Politics and the English Language." *20th Century Literary Criticism.* Ed. D. Lodge London: Longman. 1972. 361–69. Print.

Penguins and Logic cartoon. Glasbergen. Web. 3 November 2012.

Petrides, M.E. "Specialized Systems for the Processing of mnemonic Information Within the Primal Frontal Cortex." *Philosophical Transactions for the Royal Society.* 351 (1996): 1455–62. Print.

Plath, Sylvia. *The Bell Jar.* London: Faber and Faber, 2005. Print.

Plato. *The Republic.* New York and London: Oxford University Press, 1966. Print.

Raasch, S., and D. Etling. "Modeling Deep Ocean Convection: Large Eddy Simulation in Comparison with Laboratory Experiments." *American Meteorological Society* 21 (1998): 1786–802. Print.

Regan, Tom. "The Case for Animal Rights." *Defence of Animals.* Ed. Peter Singer. Oxford: Blackwell. 1985. 13–26. Print.

Roberts, Shannon. "An End to Downs Syndrome in New Zealand." Advertisment. Web. 6 March 2012.

Rybar, Susan. "Retreat to the Kootenay Rockies." *British Columbia Magazine.* 31 May 2013. Print.

Said, Edward. *Orientalism.* New York: Vintage, 1979. Print.

Salvatori, Mariolina. "Conversations with Texts: Reading in the Teaching of Composition." *College English* 58 (1996): 440–54. Print.

Schell, Jonathan. "The Roots of Nuclear Peril." *The Norton Reader.* Eds. Arthur M. Eastman, et al. 7th ed. New York: W.W. Norton, 1988. 848–55. Print.

Schryer, Catherine F. "The Lab vs. the Clinic: Sites of Competing Genres." *Genre and the New Rhetoric.* Eds. Aviva Freedman and Peter Medway. London: Taylor & Francis, 1994. 105–24. Print.

Sheridan, Joe. "Silence Before Drowning in Alphabet Soup." *Canadian Journal of Native Education* 18.1 (1991): 23–31. Print.

Soles, Derek. "What Is an Academic Essay?" *The Essentials of Academic Writing.* Boston: Houghton Mifflin Company, 2005. 6–16. Print.

Sommers, Nancy. "Revision Strategies of Student Writers and Experienced Adult Writers." *College Composition and Communication* 31.4 (1980): 378–88. Print.

——. "Between the Drafts." *The Writing Teacher's Sourcebook.* Eds. Edward P. J. Corbett, Nancy Myers, and Gary Tate. 4th ed. New York and Oxford: Oxford University Press, 2000. 279–85. Print.

Sontag, Susan. *Illness as Metaphor.* New York: Picador, 1989. Print.

Stake, Robert E. *Qualitative Research: Studying How Things Work.* New York and London: The Guilford Press, 2010. Print.

Stone, Michael. "Q and A on AIDS" *New York.* March 23 1987, 40. Web.

"Should Testing for the Aids Virus Be Mandatory?" *The Norton Reader.* Eds. Arthur M. Eastman, et al. 7th ed. New York: W. W. Norton, 1988. 646–9. Print.

Suleiman, Susan R. "Introduction: Varieties of Audience-Orientated Criticism." *The Reader in the Text: Essays on Audience and Interpretation.* Eds. Susan R. Suleiman and Inge Crosman. Princeton: Princeton University Press, 1980. 3–46. Print.

"Superman Returns." *Got Milk Campaign.* Brandon Routh. Web. 12 November 2011.

Sword, Helen. "Zombie Nouns." *New York Times* 23 July 2012. Web.

Tannen, Deborah. *The Argument Culture.* New York: Ballantine Books, 1999. Print.

Taylor, Drew Hayden. "Cry Me a River, White Boy." *Response, Responsibility, and Renewal: Canada's Truth and Reconcilliation Journey.* Eds. Gregory Younging, Jonathan Dewar, Mike DeGagne. Ottawa: Aboriginal Healing Foundation Research Series, 2009. 89–98. Print.

Vacca, Richard T. and Vacca, Jo Anne L. *Content Area Reading.* 4th ed. New York: Harper Collins, 1993. Print.

Van Hezewijk, Brian H., and R. Bourchier. "Is Two Company or a Crowd: How Does Conspecific Density Affect the

Small-Scale Dispersal of a Weed Biocontrol Agent?" *Biocontrol Science and Technology* 15.2 (2005): 191–205. Print.

Wagamese, Richard. "Returning to Harmony." *Response, Responsibility, and Renewal: Canada's Truth and Reconcilliation Journey.* Eds. Gregory Younging, Jonathan Dewar, Mike DeGagne. Ottawa: Aboriginal Healing Foundation Research Series, 2009. 127–34. Print.

Waterhouse, Keith. *Daily Mirror Stylebook.* London: Mirror, 1981. Print.

Watson, J.D., and F.H.C. Crick. "Molecular Structure of Nucleic Acids." *Nature* 171 (1953): 737–8. Print.

White, E. B. "Democracy." *The Norton Reader.* Eds. Arthur Eastman et al. 7th ed. New York and London: W.W. Norton, 1988. 833. Print.

"Why Trees?" International Tree Federation. Web. 28 October 2012.

Wolf, Naomi. *The Beauty Myth.* Toronto: Vintage Books, 1991, 143. Print.

Wright, Ronald. *A Short History of Progress.* Toronto: Anansi, 2004. Print.

X, Malcolm. *The Autobiography of Malcolm X.* London: Penguin, 1968. Print.

Yuan, David. "The Celebrity Freak: Michael Jackson's Grotesque Glory." *Freakery: Cultural Spectacles of the Extraordinary Body.* Ed. Rosemarie Garland-Thomson. New York: New York University Press, 1996. Print.

Zinsser, William. "Simplicity." *Landmarks: A Process Reader.* Eds. Roberta Birks, Tomi Eng, and Julie Walchli. Toronto: Prentice Hall, 2004. 45–9. Print.

INDEX

CLASSIFICATION OF READINGS BY ANALYTICAL PATTERNS